GW01465393

A SELECT ANALYTICAL
LIST OF BOOKS
CONCERNING
THE GREAT WAR.

By the late

Sir GEORGE W. PROTHERO, K.B.E.

INTRODUCTION

by

Dr. G.M. Bayless

The Keeper, Department of Printed Books, Imperial War Museum

THE IMPERIAL WAR MUSEUM
Department of Printed Books

In Association With
THE BATTERY PRESS, INC.
Nashville
and
ARTICLES OF WAR, LTD
Skokie

Originally released 1923
Published jointly by
The Imperial War Museum, London
Department of Printed Books
ISBN: 1-870423-54-2
and
The Battery Press, Inc.
P.O. Box 198885
Nashville, Tennessee 37219
Eighth in The Battery Press Reference Series
1995
ISBN: 0-89839-230-6
Printed in the United States of America

INTRODUCTION

by

Dr. G.M. Bayless

The Keeper, Department of Printed Books, Imperial War Museum

I am delighted that we are at last able to make Sir George Prothero's bibliography of the First World War available to students of that conflict. Back in the mid 1970's when compiling my own *Bibliographic Guide to the two World Wars* (New York: Bowker, 1977), I became acutely aware of the inadequate coverage of the Great War. Since then a former public librarian, A.G.S. Enser, has produced *A subject bibliography of the First World War: books in English, 1914-1978* (London: Andre Deutsch, 1979). Although a welcome aid, it was not well researched and was largely geared to the needs of the general public rather than the specialist. Significantly, it concentrated on more recently published works and included few contemporary wartime publications. The great value of Prothero's work is that it is a fairly comprehensive listing of publications that appeared between 1914 and 1922 in English and other European languages. It contains more entries than the slightly earlier *Subject index of the books relating to the European War, 1914-1918 acquired by the British Museum, 1914-1920* (London: British Museum, 1922). Prothero's subject listing is reinforced by an invaluable index of authors "a luxury of which circumstances" did "not permit" for the British Museum list.[1] It also covers more aspects of the war including sections on poetry, drama, humour, language, pacifism and conscientious objection.

The title of Prothero's compilation is well merited. He was uniquely qualified to produce a select analytical list of books concerning the Great War. A former lecturer in modern history and editor of the *Quarterly Review,* during the war he had been employed in the Intelligence Division at the Admiralty and subsequently became Director of the Historical Section of the Foreign Office.[2] Prothero himself had played a significant role in the production and dissemination of many of the propagandist publications listed in his bibliography. He had been a founder member of the Central Committee for the National Patriotic Organisations which was set up in the autumn of 1914. In *The Times* for the 21st November of that year, the Committee made a public appeal for funds to promote propaganda not only for domestic purposes but also for similar efforts to be made in neutral countries. The Prime Minister, H.H. Asquith, became Honorary President of the Committee, with the Earl of Rosebery and Arthur Balfour as its Honorary Vice-Presidents Harry Cust, former editor of the *Pall Mall Gazette* and George Prothero served as Chairman and Vice-Chairman respectively.

The Committee did stalwart work and in its first annual report it claimed to have funded "some 90,000 books and pamphlets and nearly a million leaflets bearing on the War." Prothero was a leading light in the group and contributed several titles himself, including *Our duty and our interest in the War* [1914] and *How goes the War* [May 1915]. The bibliographer was also emerging and he compiled the following three listings of contemporary propagandist publications:—

List of publications bearing on the War,
Second list of publications bearing on the War,
List of pamphlets bearing on the War.

The success of the voluntary efforts of people like Cust and Prothero eventually prompted the Government to establish its own official propaganda organisation at Wellington House and Prothero then turned his efforts to editing the multi-volume *Peace handbook series* for the British delegation at the Paris Peace Conference. Prothero's death at the age of 72 fortunately did not prevent the completion and publication of his bibliography by Sir Stephen Gaselee. The Librarian and Keeper of the Papers at the Foreign Office, in a worthy tribute to Sir George, only saw fit to add "about 20 or 30 titles" in the course of his revision.

---

[1]A. W. Pollard in his preface to the British Museum index.

[2]For more details of his career, see *Sir George Prothero, K.B.E., Litt.D.* by "A.C." in the Quarterly Review, vol. 238, October 1922; pp. 213-218 and, *Sir George Prothero and his circle* by C.W. Crawley in *Transactions of the Royal Historical Society,* fifth series, vol. 20, 1970.

PREFATORY NOTE.

The manuscript of the present work was ready for printing about three months before Sir George Prothero died and, after the necessary arrangements with the Stationery Office had been made, the work of printing was begun almost the same day as that of his death.

He had published three preliminary lists in 1915 and 1916, which are absorbed in the present list, the whole now containing about 8,000 items. Although the bibliography does not pretend to be exhaustive, it is certainly the most complete in existence as regards English books and it is rich in French. There are a good many entries of German books, probably nearly all that are of real importance, and not a few American, Italian and Russian. The list of British State Papers is practically exhaustive.

Owing to the necessity for brief entries, Prothero did not attempt to give more than the title, the names of the author (or editor) and publisher, the place and date of publication, and the price, when that could be ascertained. To go further would have largely increased the bulk of the list and the consequent cost of production.

Readers will naturally compare this list with that of Messrs. Lange and Berry, which only goes down to the end of 1916, and the Bibliographie der Kriegsliteratur, Berlin, 1920, in which German books naturally predominate. Other bibliographies will be found in section I of the present work and in the addenda on page 408.

After Prothero's death I undertook to see this, his last work, through the press, and I have not subsequently altered the shape in which he left it. I have made such few corrections as my own knowledge allowed, though I fear that there are still gaps which he would have filled if he had lived, and I may have occasionally introduced a confusion which he would have avoided. I have added about 20 or 30 titles in the course of my revision, but only of books which appeared to me to be of first-rate importance, without which the bibliography would be appreciably less useful. I have not considered myself justified in adding others of minor importance merely because of their interesting contents. The largest addition has been (as will be seen by the page of addenda) in the heading "Bibliographies," as these give the gist of war literature generally, and I have also not been able to resist the temptation of giving a reference to what I consider the best poem produced by the war.

The four most important collections of war literature existing to my knowledge in this country are those in the British Museum, the Imperial War Museum, the Cambridge University Library and the Library of the Athenæum. Anyone who may consult these with Prothero's "Bibliography" in his hand should find accessible practically everything literary that the war brought forth.

I do not think that this is the place to speak at any length of Prothero's life. I would refer readers to the first article, at once judicious and appreciative, in the issue of the *Quarterly Review* for October 1922. It may not, however, be out of place to state very briefly his connection with Government work during the war years, the stress of which probably hastened his end. In the very early days of the war, Prothero and the late Harry Cust formed on their own initiative a small committee for the purpose of sending out to people in neutral countries supplies of literature intended to support the British cause. They interested in their scheme many well known people in this country and were thus able to give a personal touch to what was in essence propaganda, by directing their literature from distinguished people in this country to their distinguished friends abroad. About the same time a more official propaganda organisation was arising under Government auspices and the two were soon working together. The official body supplied Prothero and Cust with any literature which they required for their purpose.

Prothero remained in this loose connection with propaganda institutions during the first half of the war. Early in 1917, when possibilities of peace were being much discussed, it was felt by the authorities in the Admiralty and Foreign Office (and probably in other Government departments as well) that some preparation should be made to equip the negotiators at the eventual peace conference with adequate information on the countries and questions with which they would have to deal. To meet this end a joint Admiralty and Foreign Office scheme was set on foot to issue a series of hand-books which should treat briefly the essential features, both of specific countries and of general questions likely to come up for discussion. A rough division of work was made by which a section of the Admiralty, working under the direction of Dr. H. N. Dickson, undertook the supply of geographical information, while Prothero was to provide the history, assisted by Sir H. Penson for economics.

The section of the Admiralty did the work of providing the geographical information and then took less part in the ultimate compilation of the hand-books. Some of their workers were nominally transferred to the Foreign Office and Prothero became more and more the head of the whole enterprise. In February 1918 the whole work was centred at a house in Great College Street, Westminster, and by the autumn of that year the staff had reached its full strength of 15 persons. By October 1918 the most important part of the materials, geographical, historical and economic, had been set up in type, but no book was absolutely finished. The printing presses, with depleted staffs, were flooded with urgent Government work, and it was clear that if the books were to be of use for the Paris Conference a general speeding-up would be necessary. A small committee was formed on the initiative of my predecessor, Mr. Alwyn Parker, which re-organised the work into a form that could be more quickly produced, and as a result most of the books were issued in time for the conference. When any given volume could not be completed, all the information collected was made available in Paris, in the form of page or slip proofs.

The worst stress was now over, and Prothero was summoned to Paris to advise in certain matters connected with the peace. He returned in the summer of 1919 and began the work of revising the hand-books for publication. It was felt a pity that the results of such assiduous and self-sacrificing labour should be confined to the few officials for whom they were originally intended, and it seemed clear that they would have a considerable sale if put on the market in an attractive form. Prothero accordingly (with the help of such of the original compilers as he could still reach) prepared them for public issue, cutting out a minimum of confidential information and numerical references to official papers. The task proceeded with regularity and despatch, and the little "Historical Section" of the Foreign Office was finally wound up at the end of November 1920, by which time the whole set was on sale. It is clear from reviews and other expressions of opinions that its issue has been widely appreciated both at home and abroad.

STEPHEN GASELEE,

Librarian and Keeper of the Papers at the Foreign Office.

[I think the abbreviations employed are familiar to British students generally. H.M.S.O. = His Majesty's Stationery Office; Cd. and Cmd. mean the "Command" numbers (two separate series) of parliamentary papers; O.P. = Oxford Pamphlet; see pp. 344 *seqq.*]

CONTENTS

PAGE

I.—BIBLIOGRAPHIES 1

II.—INTRODUCTORY WORKS:

A.—GENERAL:

(1) Historical 3
(2) Descriptive 6
(3) Geographical 7
(4) Collections of Treaties 7

B.—SPECIAL:

(1) Africa 9
(2) Albania 9
(3) Alsace-Lorraine 9
(4) Austria-Hungary... 11
(5) Balkan States (General) 14
(6) Belgium and Luxemburg 16
(7) British Empire 17
(8) Bulgaria 19
(9) China 19
(10) Eastern Question... 20
(11) France 21
(12) Germany:
(*a*) History 23
(*b*) Politics and Society 26
(*c*) Political Philosophy (Pangermanism) ... 31
(*d*) Commerce and Industry... 33
(*e*) Colonies 34
(13) Greece 35
(14) Holland 36
(15) Italy 36
(16) Japan 38
(17) Montenegro 39
(18) Morocco 39
(19) Ottoman Empire:
(*a*) General 39
(*b*) Arabia 41
(*c*) Armenia 41
(*d*) Cyprus 41
(*e*) Egypt 42
(*f*) Macedonia 42
(*g*) Mesopotamia 42
(*h*) Syria and Palestine 42
(20) Persia 42
(21) Poland 43
(22) Portugal 44
(23) Rumania 44
(24) Russia:
(*a*) Historical 45
(*b*) Descriptive, etc. 46

II.—INTRODUCTORY WORKS—*cont.* PAGE

B.—SPECIAL—*cont.*

(25) Scandinavian States 48
(26) Serbia 48
(27) Spain 49
(28) Switzerland 49
(29) United States 49
(30) Yugo-Slav Territories 50

III.—STATE PAPERS, ETC., ISSUED SINCE 1ST AUGUST, 1914:

A.—GENERAL 51

B.—SPECIAL:

(1) Austria-Hungary 54
(2) Belgium 54
(3) British Empire 55
(4) France 72
(5) Germany 73
(6) Greece 74
(7) Italy 74
(8) Japan 74
(9) Russia 74
(10) United States 74

C.—POST-WAR 74

IV.—SPEECHES, ETC., OF PUBLIC MEN:

A.—BRITISH 76

B.—FOREIGN 79

V.—SCIENCE AND METHODS OF WAR:

A.—GENERAL:

(1) Theory and Principles 81
(2) Transport 85
(3) Explosives 85
(4) Women's Work 85
(5) Miscellaneous 86

B.—NAVAL 88

C.—TERRITORIAL:

(1) Infantry 90
(2) Cavalry 99
(3) Artillery 99
(4) Machine Gunnery 100
(5) Map Reading, Scouting, etc. 101

D.—AVIATION 103

VI.—THE FIGHTING FORCES:

A.—GENERAL 105

B.—FLEETS 106

C.—ARMIES 110

D.—AIR FORCES 113

VII.—WAR MAPS 114

VIII.—CAUSES AND ISSUES OF THE WAR: PAGE

A.—COLLECTED DOCUMENTS:

(1) GENERAL ... 119

(2) SPECIAL:

(a) Austria-Hungary ... 119
(b) Belgium ... 120
(c) Brazil ... 120
(d) British Empire ... 120
(e) France ... 121
(f) Germany ... 122
(g) Greece ... 122
(h) Italy ... 123
(i) Russia ... 123
(j) Serbia ... 123

B.—VIEWS OF INDIVIDUALS:

(1) English and American ... 124
(2) French ... 132
(3) German ... 136
(4) Italian ... 139
(5) Other nation's ... 139

IX.—THE NATIONS AND THE WAR:

A.—BELLIGERENTS:

(1) Austria-Hungary ... 140
(2) Balkan States (General) ... 141
(3) Belgium and Luxemburg ... 141
(4) British Empire:
(a) General ... 147
(b) India and the Dominions ... 152
(c) Ireland ... 154
(d) Women's Work ... 154
(5) Bulgaria ... 155
(6) China ... 155
(7) France ... 155
(8) Germany:
(a) English and American ... 161
(b) French ... 165
(c) German ... 169
(d) Other Nations ... 174
(9) Greece ... 175
(10) Italy ... 176
(11) Japan ... 179
(12) Montenegro ... 180
(13) Ottoman Empire ... 180
(14) Poland ... 182
(15) Portugal ... 182
(16) Rumania ... 182
(17) Russia:
(a) General ... 183
(b) The Revolution ... 185
(18) Serbia ... 190
(19) United States ... 190
(20) Yugo-Slav Territories ... 194

IX.—THE NATIONS AND THE WAR—*cont.* PAGE

B.—NEUTRALS:
(1) Holland 194
(2) Scandinavia 194
(3) South American States 195
(4) Spain 195
(5) Switzerland 195
(6) The Vatican 196
(7) General 197

X.—RECORDS OF THE WAR:

A.—GENERAL:
(1) Chronologies 197
(2) Documents 198
(3) Histories 200
(4) Books for the Young 205
(5) Miscellaneous 205

B.—SPECIAL:
(1) Western Front:
(*a*) Despatches... 212
(*b*) Narratives:
(1) English 212
(2) French 219
(3) German 226
(4) Other Nations 227
(*c*) Apparitions, etc. 228
(2) Eastern Front and Rumania 228
(3) Italian Front 230
(4) The Balkans (Salonika, etc.) 232
(5) The Dardanelles:
(*a*) Despatches 234
(*b*) Narratives 234
(6) Asia Minor 236
(7) Egypt, Palestine, etc. 236
(8) Mesopotamia, Persia, etc.:
(*a*) Despatches... 237
(*b*) Narratives 237
(9) The Far East, Siberia, etc. 238
(10) Archangel... 238
(11) Africa 239

C.—NAVAL OPERATIONS:
(1) Despatches 240
(2) Narratives... 241
(3) Miscellaneous 245

D.—MEMOIRS, ETC:
(1) Memoirs of Distinguished Men 246
(2) Personal Experiences:
(*a*) English and American 247
(*b*) French 253
(*c*) German 256
(3) Diaries and Journals 256
(4) Letters 259
(5) Anecdotic 262

E.—WAR NEWSPAPERS 265

F.—ILLUSTRATIONS 266

XI.—BIOGRAPHIES: PAGE
A.—Collective 268
B.—Individual 269

XII.—BREACHES OF INTERNATIONAL LAW:
A.—Official 279
B.—Personal 283

XIII.—PRISONERS:
A.—Official... 286
B.—Personal 289

XIV.—LEGAL WORKS:
A.—Domestic Law 293
B.—Naval and Military Law 295
C.—International Law:
(1) Official 297
(2) Books 299

XV.—ECONOMICS AND FINANCE:
A.—Theoretical and Historical 303
B.—Practical 309

XVI.—TRADE, COMMERCE AND INDUSTRY:
A.—Trade and Commerce 310
B.—Industry... 311

XVII.—EDUCATION 312

XVIII.—SCIENCE AND PHILOSOPHY:
A.—Science 312
B.—Philosophy 313

XIX.—MEDICINE AND SURGERY:
A.—General 314
B.—Medicine and Hygiene 316
C.—Surgery, First Aid, Bandaging, etc. 317
D.—Hospitals, Ambulances, Nursing 320

XX.—RELIGION:
A.—Prayers and Devotions 324
B.—Sermons and Addresses 325
C.—Other Works 329

XXI.—ESSAYS AND REFLECTIONS:
A.—English and American 337
B.—French 352
C.—German 355
D.—Other Nations... 356

PAGE

XXII.—POETRY AND DRAMA:
A.—Anthologies and Reprints 357
B.—Poetry:
(a) English 359
(b) French 370
(c) Other Nations 371
C.—Drama 371

XXIII.—HUMOUR AND SATIRE:
A.—Literary... 371
B.—Pictorial 373

XXIV.—LANGUAGE:
A.—Grammars 376
B.—Dictionaries and Vocabularies 376
C.—Conversation Books, Manuals, etc. 378

XXV.—PEACE AND RECONSTRUCTION:
A.—The Peace:
(1) Anticipations 382
(2) The Paris Conference 387
(3) The Treaties of Peace 387
(4) Reflections on the Peace 390
B.—The League of Nations and other Schemes... ... 390
C.—Reconstruction and After-War Problems 396
D.—Pacifism; Conscientious Objectors; Union of Democratic Control 404

ADDENDA 408

INDEX 409

I.—BIBLIOGRAPHIES.

Athenæum Subject Index to Periodicals. List II: The European War: its Economic, Political and Military History, Jan.-June 1915. Published Aug. 14, 21, 28, 1915. Athenæum Office.

Bibliografia della Guerra delle Nazioni. Rivista di Roma. Began in the number for Feb.-March 1915.

Bibliographie, La, générale de la guerre de 1914-18. Catalogue du fonds de la guerre de la Bibliothèque de Lyon. Six fascicules par an, 36 fr. Fascicules 1-12 (2 vols.) published. Chiron 1917 . . .

Bulletin mensuel de la Librairie française. Numéro spécial sur la Guerre de 1914-15. Principaux ouvrages parus en France et en Suisse. Floury, July 1915.

Capek, Thomas, and Capek, Anna. Bohemian (Czech) Bibliography. A list of writings in English relating to Bohemia and the Czechs. Fleming H. Revell Co. 1918. $1.50.

Catalogue of the War Poetry Collection presented [to the Birmingham Free Libraries] in memory of Private W. J. Billington. Birmingham Printers 1921.

Catalogue of War Literature issued by H.M. Government 1914-19 (illustrated). H.M.S.O. 1921. *6d.*

Deutsche Kriegsliteratur, Die, vom Kriegsbeginn bis Anfang Dezember 1914. With continuations. . . Parts 1914- Leipzig: Hinrich.

Grande Guerre, La. Iconographie, bibliographie, documents divers. 6 vols. Vol. I: catalogue of engravings, stamps, medals, &c. Vol. II: catalogue of books, pamphlets, maps, &c. Bibliography, Vol. i (collection Henri Leblanc, destinée à l'Etat). Emile-Paul 1916-17. 22 fr. Vol. III (= vol. 2 of Bibliography). Vol. IV: Catalogue raisonné des ouvrages français et étrangers 1 Aug. 1914-31 March 1916. Vol. V (= vol. 2 of Iconography) 1918. Vol. VI: Repertoire méthodique de la presse quotidienne française. 1919.

Index to Periodicals ("Librarian"). Compiled by various authorities and arranged by A. Cecil Piper. Vol. I. 1914-15. Paul. *21s.*

Kerner, R. J. Slavic Europe: a selected Bibliography in the Western European languages (a guide to works on the history, language and literature of the Slavonic nations). Harvard Univ. Press 1918. $3.50.

Lange, F. W. T. and Berry, W. T. Books on the Great War. An annotated Bibliography of Literature issued during the European Conflict. Vols. I and II. Grafton 1915. *2s. 6d.* each.

—— —— An annotated Bibliography. Vol. III. Grafton 1915. *2s. 6d.*

—— —— An annotated Bibliography of Literature issued during the European conflict. In one vol. Preface by R. A. Peddie; with general indices. Grafton 1916. *7s. 6d.*

List of Publications issued by His Majesty's Stationery Office in connection with events arising from the state of War. (1) Acts of Parliament. (2) Statutory Rules and Orders. (3) London Gazettes, &c. (4) Parliamentary Papers. (5) Debates in Parliament. H.M.S.O. 1914-.

List, revised to 30th April 1918 of Military Publications issued by H.M. Stationery Office. H.M.S.O. 1918.

Mausset, Albert. Bibliographie des livres, brochures, &c. publiés en Espagne sur la guerre, de 1914 à 1918. Madrid: Tejo, and Paris: Collemant 1919.

Meyer, H. H. B. and others. A check list of the Literature and other material in the Library of Congress on the European War. Washington 1918.

Odavitch, R. J. Essai de Bibliographie française sur les Serbes, Croates et Slovenes depuis le commencement de la guerre actuelle. Chez l'auteur, 42 rue Denfert Rochereau, Paris. 1918. 5 fr.

Quarterly List of Official Publications (with prices) issued by H.M. Stationery Office from 1st Jan. to 31st Dec. 1914 [and subsequent years]. H.M.S.O. 1914-21.

Quarterly List of Parliamentary Publications (with prices) issued by H.M. Stationery Office from 1st Jan. to 31st Dec. 1914 [and subsequent years]. H.M.S.O. 1914-21.

Reiche, Paul. Deutsche Bücher über Polen. Ein Beitrag zu den Beziehungen zweier Nationen. Breslau; Priebatsch 1917. 5 m.

Subject Index of the books relating to the European War, 1914-18, acquired by the British Museum, 1914-20. London: British Museum 1922. *12s. 6d.*

Vic, Jean. La Littérature de guerre. Manuel méthodique et critique des publications de langue française (Aug. 1914-Aug. 1916). Avec préface de Prof. G. Lanson. 2 vols. Payot. 16 fr.

War and the Workers. A Study Guide for the use of Study Circles, Classes, &c., on questions arising out of the War. A useful Bibliography. Workers' Educational Association. *1d.*

II.—INTRODUCTORY WORKS.

A.—General.

(1) *Historical.*

Abbott, G. F. Turkey, Greece, and the Great Powers. A study in friendship and hate. Maps. Scott 1917. 7*s*. 6*d*.

Albin, Pierre. La Guerre allemande: d'Agadir à Sarajevo, 1911-14. Alcan. 3 fr. 50 c.

—— Le Coup d'Agadir. Origines et développement de la crise de 1911. Alcan. 3 fr. 50 c.

Andrews, Prof. C. M. Historical Development of Europe 1814-97. 2 vols. New York: Putnam. 12*s*. 6*d*.

Annual Register, The. A review of public events at home and abroad for the year 1914 . . . One vol. yearly. Longmans 1914 and 1915, 17*s*., 1916, 22*s*., 1917, 25*s*., 1918, 28*s*., 1919 . . . 30*s*.

Bullard, Arthur. The Diplomacy of the Great War (from 1878). New York: Macmillan 1916.

Cambridge Modern History, The. Vol. XII, 1871-1910. Camb. Univ. Press 1910. 16*s*.

Carrère, Jean. Pages d'Avant-Guerre: l'Impérialisme britannique et le Rapprochement Franco-anglais 1900-1905. Perrin 1917.

Chéradame, André. Le Monde et la guerre Russo-Japonaise. Plon-Nourrit 1906. 9 fr.

Coolidge, A. C. The origins of the Triple Alliance. New York: Scribner 1917. $1.25.

Debidour, A. Histoire diplomatique de l'Europe depuis le Congrès de Berlin jusqu'à nos jours. Pt. 1, La Paix Armée (1878-1904). Pt. 2, Vers la grande Guerre (1904-1916). Paris: Alcan 1917. 7 fr. each.

Driault, E. and Monod, G. Histoire générale: Le XIXe siècle 1789-1905. History for Écoles normales primaires. Alcan 1906. 3 fr. 50 c.

—— Histoire politique et sociale. Evolution du monde moderne 1815-1915. 6th edn. Alcan 1916. 5 fr.

Egelhaaf, G. Geschichte der neuesten Zeit, vom Frankfurter Frieden (1871) bis zur Gegenwart. Stuttgart: Krabbe 1913. 9 m.

Fraknoi, Bishop W. Kritische Studien zur Geschichte des Dreibundes 1882-1915. Budapest: Kilians Nachfolger 1917. 6 kr.

Friedjung, Heinrich. Das Zeitalter des Imperialismus, 1884-1914. Vol. I (to 1905). Berlin: Neufeld & Henius 1919

Fullerton, W. Morton. Problems of Power: a Study of International Politics from Sadowa (1866) to Kirk-Kilisse (1912). Fifth and definitive edn. Constable 1920. 7*s*. 6*d*.

Gauvain, Auguste. L'Europe au jour le jour. Recueil d'histoire contemporaine 1908-14 (Articles from the *Débats*). 6 vols. Paris: Bossard 1918-19. Vols. 1-4, 7 fr. 50 c. each; vols. 5, 6, 9 fr. each.

Gooch, G. P. Annals of Politics and Culture, 1492-1899; with Introductory Note by Lord Acton. Camb. Univ. Press 1901. 7*s*. 6*d*.

—— History of our Time (1885-1911). Williams & Norgate 1911. 1*s*.

—— and Masterman, J. H. B. A Century of British Foreign Policy (1814-1914). London: Council for study of International Relations 1917.

Haldane, Viscount. Before the War (His mission to Berlin in 1912, &c.). Cassell 1920. 7*s*. 6*d*.

Hanotaux, Gabriel. La Politique de l'équilibre 1907-11. Plon 1914. 3 fr. 50 c.

Hill, David Jayne. A History of Diplomacy in the International Development of Europe. Longmans 1914. 21*s*. each.

Hubert, Lucien. Politique extérieure (The Young Turks, France and Europe, France and Germany, &c.). Paris: Alcan. 3 fr. 50 c.

Introduction to the Study of International Relations. By A. J. Grant, A. Greenwood, J. D. Hughes, P. H. Kerr, F. F. Urquhart. Macmillan 1916. 2*s*.

Lavisse, E. and Rambaud, A. N. Histoire Générale, du IVe Siècle à nos jours. Vol. XII: Le Monde contemporaire, 1870-1900. Armand Colin 1901. 12 fr.

Lindbaek, Johannes. Le Prologue de la guerre mondiale (la politique des grandes puissances de 1870 à 1914). Copenhagen: Aschehoug 1917.

Maurras, Charles. Kiel et Tanger. Nouv. Libr. Nationale 1913. 4 fr.

Mévil, André. De la Paix de Francfort à la Conference d'Algésiras. Plon 1909. 3 fr. 50 c.

—— La Paix est malade (a prognostication of the war). Préface par le comte Albert de Mun. Plon-Nourrit 1914. 3 fr. 50 c.

Muir, Prof. Ramsay. The Expansion of Europe. Third enlarged edn. Constable 1922. 14*s*.

Ogg, Prof. F. Austin. Economic Development of Modern Europe (since the middle of the 18th century). New York: Macmillan 1917. $2.50.

Orsi, Count Pietro. From Waterloo to the Marne. Collins 1921. 15*s*.

Pflugk-Harttung, Prof. J. von. Die Mittelmächte und der Vierverband. Militärische, politische, und wirthschaftliche Betrachtungen. Berlin: Eisenschmidt 1916. 7 m. 50 p.

Phillimore, Lord. Three Centuries of Treaties of Peace and their teaching. Murray 1917. 7*s*. 6*d*.

Phillips, W. Alison. Modern Europe 1815-99. Rivingtons 1901. 6*s*.

Phillipson, Coleman. Termination of war, and treaties of peace. With appendix giving text of all peace treaties 1815-1913. Fisher Unwin 1916. 21*s*.

Pinon, René. L'Empire de la Méditerranée (1871-1910). Perrin 1912. 5 fr.

Ponsonby, Arthur. War and Treaties 1815-1914. Allen & Unwin 1918. 2*s*.

Reventlow, Graf Ernst von. Politische Vorgeschichte des grossen Krieges. 2nd edn. Berlin: Mittler 1919. 17 m. 60 p.

Rose, J. Holland. The Development of the European Nations 1870-1914. 5th edn. brought up to date. Maps. Constable 1915. 7*s*. 6*d*.

Sarolea, Dr. C. The Anglo-German Problem. Nelson 1912. 2*s*.

—— —— Popular edn. Jack 1915. 1*s*. 6*d*.

Schefer, C. D'une guerre à l'autre (1871-1914). Alcan 1920. 14 fr. 40 c.

Schulthess. Europäisches Geschichtskalender. Annual volumes, beginning 1861. Munich: Beck. 12 m. each.

Seignobos, Prof. C. Histoire Politique de l'Europe contemporaire. Evolutions des partis et des formes politiques 1814-96. Paris: Colin 1897. 12 fr. Heinemann. 10s.

—— English translation of the above. A Political History of Contemporary Europe since 1814. Popular edn. 1 vol. Heinemann. 6*s*.

Siebert, B. von (edr.). Diplomatische Aktenstücke zur Geschichte der Ententepolitik der Vorkriegsjahre (827 pp.). Berlin and Leipzig: W. de Gruyter 1921. 200 m.

Singer, A. Geschichte des Dreibundes. Mit einem Anhang: Der Inhalt des Dreibandes, von. H. F. Helmolt. Leipzig: Rabinowitz Verlag 1914.

Tardieu, André. Questions diplomatiques de 1904. Alcan 1905. 3 fr. 50 c.

—— La Conférence d'Algesiras. Histoire politique de la crise marocaine, Jan.-Avr. 1906. 3rd edn., with appendix on Le Maroc après la conférence 1906-9. Alcan. 10 fr.

Viallate, A. and Caudel, M. (edrs.). La Vie politique dans les deux mondes. Annual volumes, giving the political history of the world, under the different countries (1906-13). 7 vols. published. Alcan. 10 fr. each.

Weber, Georg. Allgemeine Weltgeschichte. Vol. XV, pt. 2, 1852-89. Leipzig 1889.

Webster, C. K. Study of Nineteenth Century Diplomacy. Bell 1915. 1*s.*

Welschinger, Henri. L'Alliance franco-russe. Les Origines et les résultats. Alcan 1919. 6 fr.

(2) *Descriptive.*

Baldwin, E. F. The World War. A sketch of the different nations now at war. Macmillan. 5*s.* 6*d.*

Dareste, F. R. Les constitutions modernes. 3rd edn. 2 vols. 1910.

Demombynes, G. Constitutions européennes. 2 vols. Paris 1881.

Dmowski, R. Problems of Central and Eastern Europe. (Privately printed.) London 1917.

Dominian, Leon. Linguistic Areas in Europe: their boundaries and political influence. Reprinted from the Bulletin of the American Geogr. Society. Vol. XLVII. June 1915. Nine maps.

Gibbons, Prof. H. A. The New Map of Europe. A study of contemporary European national movements and wars. Duckworth 1914. 6*s.*

Hannah, Ian C. Arms and the Map: a Study of Nationalities and Frontiers. Fisher Unwin. 3*s.* 6*d.*

Headlam, J. W. The Dead Lands of Europe. Hodder & Stoughton 1917. 3*d.*

Lowell, A. Lawrence. Government of France, Italy and Germany. Milford 1915. 5*s.* 6*d.*

Statesman's Year-book, The. Edited by Sir J. Scott Keltie and M. Epstein. Annual publication. Maps. Macmillan 1914 . . . 18*s.* . . . 20*s.*

Statistical Abstract for the Principal and other Foreign Countries in each year from 1901 to 1912. 39th number. Contains much valuable statistical matter. Wyman 1914. 2*s.* 2*d.* net.

Stoddard, T. Lothrop. Present-day Europe (European conditions before the war). New York: Century Co. 1917. $2.00.

Vizetelly, Ernest Alfred. In seven lands: Germany, Austria, Hungary, Bohemia, Spain, Portugal, Italy. Illustrated. Chatto & Windus 1916. 12*s.* 6*d.*

(3) *Geographical.*

Bowman, I. The new world, problems in political geography. Harrap 1922.

Cornish, Vaughan. The Strategic Geography of the Great Powers. Philip & Son 1918. 2*s.*

Dominian, Leon. The Frontiers of Language and Nationality in Europe. (By the Map Curator, Amer. Geogr. Society.) Twenty maps. New York: Holt 1917. $3.00. Constable 1917. 15*s.*

Droysen. Historischer Atlas. Leipzig and Bielefeld 1886.

Freeman, E. A. The Historical Geography of Europe. 3rd edn., edited by J. B. Bury. 2 vols. With maps. Longmans 1903. 18*s.* 6*d.*

Petermann, A. Mittheilungen aus Perthes' geographischer Anstalt 1855 . . . (and Ergänzungsheft 1860 . . .). Gotha: Perthes 1855 . . .

Poole, R. L. Historical Atlas of Modern Europe. Oxford Univ Press 1902.

Robertson, C. G. and Bartholomew, J. G. An Historical Atlas of Modern Europe, 1789-1914, with an historical and explanatory text. 43 maps. Oxford Univ. Press 1915. 3*s.* 6*d.*

Spruner-Menke. Hand-Atlas für Geschichte. 3rd edn. Gotha: Perthes 1880.

St. Martin and Rousselet. Nouveau Dictionnaire de Géographie universelle. 9 vols. Hachette 1900.

Salvioni, G. B. I numeri della Pace (statistics of the areas, populations and ethnology of Europe). Zanichelli 1918. l. 3.

(4) *Collections of Treaties.*

Aitchison, C. U. Treaties [&c.] relating to India and neighbouring countries. 4th edn. 13 vols. 1909.

Albin, Pierre. Les grands traités politiques. Recueil des principaux textes diplomatiques depuis 1815 jusqu'à nos jours, avec des commentaires et des notes. 2nd edn. Alcan 1912. 10 fr.

Clercq, de. M. Recueil des Traités de France. 22 vols. 1864 . . .

Hertslet, Sir Edward. China Treaties 1842-1907. 2 vols. H.M.S.O. 1908.

—— (edr.). Commercial Treaties. Treaties and Conventions between Great Britain and Foreign Powers, and Laws, Decrees, Orders in Council, etc., concerning the same, so far as they relate to Commerce and Navigation, Slavery, Extradition, Nationality, Copyright, Postal Matters, &c., and to the Privileges and Interests of the Subjects of the High Contracting Parties. Vol. XXVII. H.M.S.O. 1917. 15*s.* Vol. XXVIII. 1921. 32*s.* 6*d.*

Hertslet, Sir Edward. Map of Africa by Treaty 1778-1908. 3rd edn. 3 vols. and 1 vol. maps. H.M.S.O. 1909.

—— Map of Europe by Treaty, showing the various political and territorial changes 1814-91. 4 vols. (Vol. IV 1875-91.) H.M.S.O. 1875-91.

Holland, Prof. T. E. The European Concert and the Eastern Question: a Collection of Treaties and other public acts (1826-85). Oxford Univ. Press 1885. 12*s.* 6*d.*

Martens, G. F. and others. Nouveau Recueil des principaux Traités &c. Continuation (1839-74). 20 vols. Göttingen 1843-75.

—— Nouveau Recueil. 2me Série (1874-1907). 35 vols. Göttingen 1876-1908.

—— —— 3me Série (1907-14). 8 vols. Leipzig 1909-15.

Mowat, R. B. Select Treaties and Documents to illustrate the development of the Modern European States System. Oxford Univ. Press. 1*s.* 6*d.*

—— (edr.). Select Treaties and Documents to illustrate the development of the Modern European States System 1815-1916. With introduction by R.B.M. Enlarged edn. with 8 new documents. Oxford Univ. Press 1916. 2*s.*

Myers, Denys Peter. Manual of Collection of Treaties. Harvard Univ. Press 1922. $7.50.

Noradounghian, G. Recueil d'Actes internationaux de l'Empire Ottoman. 4 vols. Pichon 1897-1903.

Oakes, Sir A. and Mowat, R. B. The great European Treaties of the 19th century. With introduction by Prof. Sir Erle Richards. Oxford Univ. Press 1918. 7*s.* 6*d.*

O'Regan, J. R. H. (edr.). The German War of 1914 Illustrated by documents of European history 1815-1915 Milford 1915. 1*s.* 6*d.*

Ouroussow, A. M. Résumé historique des principaux Traités de Paix 1648-1878. Evreux: Leroux 1884. 16 fr. 2 c.

Pribram, A. F. (edr.). The Secret Treaties of Austria-Hungary 1879-1914. Vol. II. Negotiations leading to the treaties of the Triple Alliance. Engl. transl. by A. C. Coolidge. Harvard Univ. Press and Milford 1921. 12*s.* 6*d.*

Rockhill, W. W. Treaties [&c.] with or concerning China and Korea 1894-1904. Washington: Govt. Printing Office 1904.

Tétot. Repertoire des Traités de Paix (with supplements) 1866-99. 2 vols.

Treaty Series (British) 1892-1916. 7 vols. H.M.S.O. 1892-1921

Un Livre Noir. Diplomatie d'avant-guerre d'aprés les documents des Archives russes Nov. 1910-July 1914. Vol. I 1910-12. Préface par René Marchand. Paris : Librairie du Travail 1921. 10 fr.

Whittuck, E. A. International Documents : a collection of International Conventions, &c. 1856-1907. With Introduction, Notes and Appendices (includes the Hague Peace Conference 1907). New edn. Longmans 1909. 13*s*.

B.—SPECIAL.

(1) *Africa.*

Beyens, Baron. La Question Africaine. Brussels : Van Oest 1918. 2 fr. 50 c.

Gibbons, H. A. The new map of Africa (Colonial development of Africa). New York : Century Co. 1916. $2.00.

Kassner, Th. Die Zukunft Afrikas. Ratschläge für die Kolonisation. Leipzig : Stephan 1912. 50 pf.

Ronze, Raymond. La Question d'Afrique. Paris : Alcan 1918. 7 fr. 70 c.

Woolf, Leonard. Empire and Commerce in Africa. Allen & Unwin 1919. 20*s*.

(2) *Albania.*

Baldacci, Antonio. Itinerari albanesi (1892-1902), con uno sguardo generale all'Albania e alle sue comunicazione stradali Rome 1917. 12 l.

Gopčevic, Spiridion. Das Fürstentum Albanien, seine Vergangenheit, ethnographischen Verhältnisse, politische Lage, und Aussichten für die Zukunft. Illustrations and map. Berlin : Paetel 1914. 6 mk.

Peacock, Wadham. Albania, the foundling State of Europe. Illustrated. Chapman & Hall 1914. 7*s*. 6*d*.

Ratti, F. V. L'Adriatico degli altri (l'Albania nell'ora presente). Map and illustrations. Florence : Beltrami. 95 c.

Story, Sommerville (Edr.). The Memoirs of Ismail Kemal Bey. Preface by W. M. Fullerton. Constable 1920. 18*s*.

(3) *Alsace-Lorraine.*

Alsace-Lorraine ; la carte au lisère vert.

Batiffol, L. Les Anciennes Républiques Alsaciennes. Flammarion 1918. 1 fr. 25 c. and 3 fr. 50 c.

Blumenthal, Daniel. Alsace-Lorraine. A study of the relations of Alsace-Lorraine to France and Germany. (By an Alsatian.) Putnams 1918. 3*s.*

Church, Leslie F. Story of Alsace-Lorraine. Kelly 1915. 1*s.*

Duhem, Jules. La Question d'Alsace-Lorraine, de 1871 à 1914. Alcan 1917. 1 fr. 25.

—— Transl. under title, The Question of Alsace-Lorraine. Hodder & Stoughton 1918. 2*s.* 6*d.*

Eccles, F. Y. Alsace-Lorraine. (O.P.) Oxford University Press. 2*d.*

Florent-Matter. Les Alsaciens-Lorrains contre l'Allemagne. (Fidelity to France of the occupied provinces.) Berger-Levrault 1918. 5 fr.

Harrison, Marie. The Stolen Lands. A study in Alsace-Lorraine. With map of the French frontiers, 1792-1871. Kegan Paul 1918. 3*s.* 6*d.*

Hazen, C. Downer. Alsace-Lorraine under German rule. New York: Holt 1917. $1.25.

Helmer, Paul Albert. Alsace under German Rule. Unwin 1915. 6*d.*

—— France-Alsace. (Lectures and articles by an Alsatian barrister.) L'edition franç. illustrée 1916. 3 fr. 50 c.

—— The Case of Alsace-Lorraine. On the German treatment of the province. Fisher Unwin 1915. 6*d.*

Hinzelin, E. L'Alsace sous le joug. Paris 1915.

Holland, A. W. Alsace-Lorraine. (Peeps at Many Lands.) Black 1916. 1*s.* 6*d.*

Lavisse, Ernest, and Pfister, Christian. The Question of Alsace-Lorraine. Hodder & Stoughton 1918. 2*d.*

Lichtenberger, André et Henri. La Question d'Alsace. Chapelot 1915. 1 fr.

Phillipson, Coleman. Alsace-Lorraine: Past, Present and Future (Historical and Political; many documents). Fisher Unwin 1918. 25*s.*

Prignet, A. L'Alsace-Lorraine (Descriptive, with illustrations). Delagrave 1916. 4 fr.

Putnam, Ruth. Alsace and Lorraine: from Cæsar to Kaiser 58 B.C.—1871 A.D. Putnam 5*s.*

Reinach, J. L'Alsace-Lorraine devant l'histoire. Berger-Levrault 1917. 0 fr. 75 c.

Valloton, Benjamin. On changerait plutôt le cœur de place (Alsatian mentality). Payot 1917. 4 fr. 50 c.

Vidal de la Blache, P. La France de l'Est (Lorraine-Alsace). (Maps.) Armand Colin. 10 fr.

Vizetelly, E. A. The true story of Alsace-Lorraine. Chatto & Windus 1918. 10*s.* 6*d.*

Welschinger, Henri. La Protestation de l'Alsace-Lorraine. (A detailed study of the protests of 1871, with facsimiles.) Berger-Levrault 1918. 3 fr.

Wetterlé, l'abbé. Ce qu'était l'Alsace-Lorraine et ce qu'elle sera. With preface by Henri Welschinger. L'Edition franç, illustrée 1916. 3 fr. 50 c.

Wohin gehört Elsass-Lothringen. Zu Frankreich. Eine Erwiderung auf Lienhards Schrift, von einigen Elsassern. Lausanne : Payot. 1 fr.

(4) *Austria-Hungary.*

Auerbach, Bertrand. Les Nationalités en Autriche-Hongrie. 2nd edn. revised. (Maps.) Alcan 1918. 10 fr.

Austro-Magyar judicial crimes : political trials 1908-13. Preface by W. Joynson-Hicks, M.P. Howes 1917. 6*d.*

Barrault, H. E. Des Entreprises Austro-Allemandes constituées sous Forme de Sociétés Françaises et de l'Influence de la Présence d'Austro-Allemands dans les Sociétés. Tenin 1916.

Beneš, Edvard. Détruisez l'Autriche-Hongrie ! Delagrave 1916. 1 fr.

—— La Boemia contro l'Austria-Ungheria. Rome : Ansonia 1917.

—— Bohemian Case for Independence. With an Introduction by H. Wickham Steed. Allen & Unwin 1917. 2*s.* 6*d.*

Bertha, A. de. Magyars et Roumains devant l'histoire (in favour of the Magyars).

Bertrand, Adrien. La conquête de l'Autriche-Hongrie par l'Allemagne (une nouvelle forme du Pangermanisme le Zollverein). Berger-Levrault 1916. 60 c.

Capek, Thomas (Edr.). Bohemia under Hapsburg misrule. Ideals and aspirations of the Bohemian and Slovak peoples as affected by the European War. By various writers. New York : Revell. $1.00.

Charmatz, R. Œsterreichs innere Geschichte, 1848-1909. 2 vols. Teubner. 7 m. 50 pf.

Chéradame, André. L'Allemagne, la France, et la question d'Autriche. Plon-Nourrit. 3 fr. 50 c.

—— L'Europe et la question d'Autriche au seuil du XXme siècle. lon-Nourrit. 10 fr.

Chervin, Arthur. L'Autriche et la Hongrie de demain. Les différentes nationalités d'après les langues parlées. (Maps and tables.) Berger-Levrault 1915. 3 fr. 50 c.

Chlumecky, Leopold, Freiherr von. Œsterreich-Ungarn und Italien. Das west-balkanische Problem, &c. Vienna: Deuticke 1907. 4 m. 50 pf.
Chopin, Jules (J.-E. Pichon). L'Autriche-Hongrie 'brillant second.' Préface de Samuel Denis. Bossard 1917. 5 fr.
Chopin, Jules (Jules Pichon) and Osuzky, Stephen. Magyars et Pangermanistes. Préface de Louis Eisenmann. Paris: Bossard 1918. 3 fr. 50 c.
Conrad (von Hötzendorf), Feldmarschall. Aus meiner Dienstzeit 1906-18. Bd. I. Die Zeit des Annexionskrise 1906-09. Map. Vienna: Rikola 1921. 2950 kr.
Cvijitch, Dr. J. L'annexion de la Bosnie et la Question serbe. Hachette. 2 fr.
Denis, Prof. E. Les Slovaques. Delagrave 1917.
Diplomatische Aktenstücke betreffend die Ereignisse am Balkan, 13th Aug. 1912 bis 6th Nov. 1913 (Oesterr. Rotbuch). Vienna. 1914.
Drage, G. Austria-Hungary. Murray 1909. *21s.*
Eisenmann, Louis. Le Compromis Austro-Hongrois. Paris 1904.
Fournier, Aug. Oesterreich und Preussen im xiv-ten Jahsthundert, Ein Vortrag. Vienna and Leipzig: Braumüller 1907. 1 m.
Fournier, Dr. Wie wir zu Bosnien kamen. Vienna: Reisser 1909. 2 m.
Fournol, Étienne. De la Succession d'Autriche. Essai sur le régime des pays autrichiens avant, pendant et après la guerre. Berger-Levrault 1918. 3 fr. 50 c.
Gargas, Sigismond. La Question bosniaque. Paris: Giard et Brière. 1 fr.
Gayda, Virginio. Modern Austria: her racial and social problems. With a study of Italia Irredenta. Translated by Zoe M Gibson. Fisher Unwin. 10*s*. 6*d*.
Ghelli, S. Austria Nemica: i Ricotti degli Absburgo; gli Ultimi Anni della Triplice; l'Adriatico e l'Albania. Milan: Bonfiglio 1916.
Hinkovitch, M. H. Les Croates sous le joug magyar (brochure). Plon-Nourrit. 1915.
Jorga, N. Histoire des Roumains de Transylvanie et de Hongrie. 2 vols. Bucarest: Gutenberg 1916. 5 fr.
Kellner, L. Austria of the Austrians and Hungary of the Hungarians. Illustrated. Pitman 1914. 6*s*.
Knatchbull-Hugessen, Hon. C. M. Political Evolution of the Hungarian Nation. 2 vols. National Review Office. 15*s*.
Krek, Ivan. Les Slovènes. (Translated.) 2 maps. Alcan 1917. 1 fr.

Krunsky, M. L'Annexion de la Bosnie et de l'Herzegovine en 1908. Rousseau. 5 fr.
Larmeroux, Jean. La Politique extérieure de l'Autriche-Hongrie 1875-1914. 2 vols. Plon 1918-19. 20 fr.
Léger, Louis. Histoire de l'Autriche-Hongrie (to 1894). 4th edn. Hachette 1895. 5 fr.
—— English Transl. (to 1889) by Mrs. Birkbeck Hill, with preface by E. A. Freeman. Rivington 1889.
—— La liquidation de l'Autriche-Hongrie. Alcan 1915.
—— La renaissance tchéque au XIXe siècle. Alcan 1910.
Leutrum-Okoricsamzi, Countess. What I Know: Court and Diplomacy in Austria and Germany. Fisher Unwin 1917. 10*s*. 6*d*.
Masaryk, T. G. Vasič-Forgach-Aehrenthal. Prague: Tagblatt "Čas," E. Béaufort 1911.
Mitton, G. E. Austria-Hungary. Illustrated. Black 1914. 10*s*.
Namier, Lewis B. The Czecho-Slovaks: an oppressed nationality. Hodder & Stoughton 1917. 1*d*.
Popovici, Aurel C. Die vereinigten Staaten von Gross-Oesterreich (a scheme of federation).
Prezzolini, Giuseppe. La Dalmazia. Florence: Libreria della Voce 1915. 1 l.
—— La Dalmatie. Translated from the Italian by Ljubo Radic. Alcan 1918. 1 fr.
Pribram, Alfred F. (edr.). Die politischen Geheimverträge Oesterreich-Ungarns 1879-1914. Nach den Akten des Wiener Staatsarchivs. Vol. I. Vienna: Braumüller 1920. 28 kr.
—— English transl. Edited by A. C. Coolidge, under title Secret Treaties of Austria-Hungary. Oxford Univ. Press 1920. 8*s*. 6*d*.
Prochazka, J. (edr.). Bohemia's claim for Freedom. With introduction by G. K. Chesterton. Published for the London Czech Committee. Chatto & Windus 1915. 1*s*.
Radziwill, Princess Catherine. The Austrian Court from Within. A study of German politics as affecting Austria. Cassell 1916. 7*s*. 6*d*.
Ryan, Nellie. My Years at the Austrian Court. Lane 1915. 10*s*. 6*d*.
Seton-Watson, R. W. (Scotus Viator). Absolutism in Croatia. Constable 1912. 2*s*.
—— The Future of Austria-Hungary. Constable. 2*s*.
—— The Future of Bohemia. A lecture. Nisbet. 3*d*.
—— Racial Problems in Hungary. Map and illustrations. Constable 1908. 16*s*.
—— Corruption and Reform in Hungary. Constable 1911.

Seven Years in Vienna 1907-14. A record of intrigue (court and political life in Vienna). Constable 1916. 6*s.*

Sosnosky, T. von. Die Balkanpolitik Œsterreich-Ungarns seit 1866. 2 vols. Stuttgart 1913-14.

—— Die Politik im Habsburgerreiche. Randglossen zur Zeitgeschichte. 2 vols. Berlin: Paetel 1912-13.

Steed, H. W. The Hapsburg Monarchy. Constable. 7*s.* 6*d.*

Vosnjak, Dr. Bogumil. A bulwark against Germany; the fight of the Slovenes . . . for national existence. Translated by F. S. Copeland. Allen & Unwin 1917. 4*s.* 6*d.*

—— A Dying Empire (Sociological factors in the break-up of Austria). Allen & Unwin 1917. 4*s.* 6*d.*

Wertheimer, E. von. Graf Julius Andrassy: eein Leben und seine Zeit. 3 vols. Stuttgart: Deutsche Verlags-Anstalt 1900-13.

Yakchitch, Grégoire. Le Banat (republd. from the Revue Hebdomadaire). Brochure. Rev. Hebdom. 1915.

Yolland, Arthur B. Hungary. (The Nation's Histories series.) Jack 1917. 3*s.* 6*d.*

(5) *Balkan States.*

André, Louis. Les Etats Chrêtiens les Balkans (deals especially with their internal politics). Alcan 1918. 4 fr. 55 c.

Bailey, W. F. Slavs of the War Zone. Chapman & Hall 1916. 10*s.* 6*d.*

Bates, Jean Victor. Our Allies and Enemies in the Near East. With introduction by Sir Edward Carson. Chapman & Hall 1918. 10*s.* 6*d.*

Conway, A. E. A Ride through the Balkans. On classic ground with a camera. Map and illustrations. With introduction by Sir Martin Conway. Scott 1916. 5*s.*

Cvijić, Jovan. La Peninsula balkanique: Géographie humaine. Maps and illustrations. Armand Colin 1918. 17 fr.

—— Questions Balkaniques. Attinger 1916.

Durham, M. Edith. Twenty Years of Balkan Tangle. Allen & Unwin 1920. 16*s.*

Forbes, Nevill, and others. The Balkans; a history of Bulgaria, Serbia, Greece, Rumania, and Turkey. 3rd edn. Maps. Oxford Univ. Press 1918. 6*s.* 6*d.*

Fox, Frank. The Balkan Peninsula (Illustrated). Black 1916. 7*s.* 6*d.*

Garnett, Lucy M. J. Home Life in the Balkans. Methuen 1918. 10*s.* 6*d.*

Gordon, Mrs. W. A Woman in the Balkans (Descriptive of the different Balkan States before 1914). Hutchinson 1916. 12*s.* 6*d.*

Guéchoff, Ivan E. L'Alliance balkanique. An account of the formation and the results of the Balkan League 1911-13, by the late Bulgarian Premier. Hachette 1915. 3 fr. 50 c.

—— The Balkan League. Trans. by Constantin C. Mincoff. Murray 1915. 2*s*. 6*d*.

Hanotaux, Gabriel. La Guerre des Balkans. Paris: Plon-Nourrit 1914. 3 fr. 50 c.

Jorga, Prof. N. Histoire des États balcaniques à l'époque moderne. Bucarest: Sfetea 1914. 3 fr. 50 c.

Mijatovitch, Count Chedomille. The Memoirs of a Balkan diplomatist (formerly Foreign Minister of Serbia). Cassell 1917. 16*s*.

Miller, W. The Balkans (Servia, Montenegro, &c.). Fisher Unwin. 5*s*.

Murray, William S. The Making of the Balkan States (to 1903). Columbia Studies in History, &c. Bibliography. Longmans 1910.

Near East, The, from Within. By a diplomatist. Illustrated. Cassell. 10*s*. 6*d*.

Newbigin, Marion. Geographical Aspects of Balkan Problems in relation to the European War. Maps. Constable 1915. 7*s*. 6*d*.

Niox, le Général. Les Pays balkaniques. Ethnographical and geographical, with historical sketch to 1913. Delagrave 1915. 2 fr. 50 c.

Pernice, Angelo. Origine ed evoluzione storica delle Nazioni Balcaniche (to 1913). Milan: Hoepli.

Price, W. H. Craufurd. The Balkan Cockpit. Political and military history of the Balkan Wars 1912-13. 12*s*. 6*d*.

Rankin, Reginald. The Inner History of the Balkan War. Constable 1914. 15*s*.

Schurman, Jacob G. The Balkan Wars 1912-13. New edn., with continuation of Balkan history to Nov. 1914. Milford. 4*s* 6*d*.

Seton-Watson, R. W. The Balkans, Italy and the Adriatic. 2nd edn. Nisbet 1916. 1*s*.

—— The Rise of Nationality in the Balkans. Maps. Constable 1917. 10*s*. 6*d*.

Spalajkovic, Miroslav. La Bosnie et l'Herzégovine. Paris 1899.

Stoianovitch, Nikola. Bosnie-Herzégovine. Geneva: Knudig.

Tucić, Pl. Slav Nations. (Daily Telegraph War Books.) Hodder & Stoughton 1915. 1*s*.

Wace, A. J. B. and Thompson, M. S. The Nomads of the Balkans. A description of the Aroumanians or Kutzovlachs. Methuen 1914.

(6) *Belgium and Luxemburg.*

Belgische Aktenstücke. Berichte der belgischen Vertreter in Berlin, London and Paris an den Minister des Aeusseren in Brüssel 1905-14. Herausg. vom Auswärtigen Amt. (facsimiles). Berlin: Mittler 1915. 1 mk. 40.

Brangwyn, Frank, A.R.A. Belgium (Pictures). With text by Hugh Stokes. Kegan Paul 1916. 10*s*. 6*d*.

Bruckman, W. L. The Glory of Belgium. Illustrated in colour. Hodder & Stoughton 1914. 20*s*.

Delstanche, Albert. The little towns of Flanders. Woodcuts and descriptive notes. Preface by E. Verhaeren. Translated from the French. Chatto & Windus 1916. 3*s*. 6*d*.

Descamps, E. La Neutralité de la Belgique. Brussels: Larcier. Paris: Pedone 1902.

Destrée, Jules. Belgium and the principle of Nationality. (Translated from the French.) Council for Study of Internat. Relations 1916. 3*d*.

Documents belges (analysis in favour of Belgium). By the author of J'accuse [Richard Grelling]. French translation from the German original, published 1918. Payot 1919. 7 fr. 50.

Documents diplomatiques 1905-14. Lettres adressées par les Ministres et Chargés d'Affaires de Belgique à Berlin, Londres et Paris au Ministre des Affaires Etrangères à Bruxelles. (Transl. of Belgische Aktenstücke. Publ. by the German Government.) Berlin: Mittler 1915.

Dontenville, J. La Question Luxembourgeoise: la France et le Grand-Duché de Luxembourg. Jenin 1917.

Dumont-Wilden. La Belgique illustrée. With preface by Emile Verhaeren. 580 illustrations, 28 maps and plans. Larousse. In parts. 8*d*. each.

Ensor, R. C. K. Belgium. Historical and descriptive. (Home University Library.) Williams & Norgate. 1*s*.

Forestier, Amédée, and Omond, George W. T. Belgium. Painted by A. F., text by G. W. T. O. Cheaper re-issue. Black 1914. 7*s*. 6*d*.

Früs-Môller, Kai (edr.). Belgien (A collection of essays by Danish writers on the history, literature &c. of Belgium). Illustrated. Copenhagen: Pio 1916.

Hamélius, Paul, and Van der Linden, Herman. Une histoire des Relations Anglo-Belgiennes (points d'histoire politiques mal connus). 1918. English transl. under title Anglo-Belgian Relations. Constable 1918. 2*s*. 6*d*.

Hutchinson, W. (edr.). Belgium the Glorious: her Country and her People. Part 1. To be completed in 14 parts. Illustrations. Hutchinson 1915. 10*s*. each vol.

MacDonell, J. de C. Belgium, her Kings, Kingdom, and People. 4th edn. John Long. 15*s.*

Nothomb, Pierre. La Barrière Belge : essais d'histoire territoriale et diplomatique. Perrin 1916. 3 fr. 50.

Putnam, Ruth. Luxemburg and her Neighbours. Putnam 1918. $2.50.

Van der Essen, Prof. Léon. A short history of Belgium. Chicago : Univ. Press 1916. 4*s.*

Van der Linden, H. Belgium : the Making of a Nation (Histories of the Nations). Transl. by Sybil Jane. Maps. Oxford Univ. Press 1920. 7*s.* 6*d.*

—— Vue générale de l'histoire de Belgique. Payot 1918. 4 fr. 50.

Waële, G. de. Flamands et Wallons. Alcan 1917. 60 c.

Wampach, G. Le Luxembourg et les Luxembourgeois. Alcan 1917. 60 c.

Young, Alexander. A short History of Belgium and Holland. Popular edn. Fisher Unwin. 5*s.*

(7) *British Empire.*

Begbie, Harold. The Vindication of Great Britain. (Lord Haldane's visit to Berlin, and other British efforts to maintain peace.) Methuen 1916. 6*s.*

British and Foreign State Papers. 112 vols. (1812-1919) have so far been issued. H.M.S.O. 1825-1922.

Collier, Gerard. The Leading Ideas of British Policy. (O.P.) Oxford Univ. Press. 2*d.*

Cornish, V. Naval and Military Geography of the British Empire (considered in relation to the War with Germany). With Maps. (Lectures) 1916.

Cramb, J. A. Germany and England. Lectures delivered in 1913. Preface by A. C. Bradley. Murray. 2*s.* 6*d.*; cheap edn., 1*s.*

—— The Origins and Destiny of Imperial Britain and Nineteenth Century Europe. With biographical note and portrait. First published 1900. Murray 1915. 5*s.*

Egerton, H. E. British Foreign Policy in Europe to the end of the Nineteenth Century. A rough outline. Macmillan 1917. 6*s.*

—— A short history of British Colonial Policy. 2nd., revised. Methuen 1908. 12*s.* 6*d.*

Grice, J. Watson. The Resources of the Empire. (International Information Series.) Published for the International Information Committee. Athenæum Press 1917. 1*s.*

Haldane, Lord, and the Army: What he did to thwart Germany. An account of Lord Haldane's work at the War Office. Daily Chronicle Office. 1*d.*

Hayden, Mary, and Moonan, G. A. A Short History of Ireland, from the earliest times to 1920. Maps. Longmans 1921. 20*s.*

Hurd, Archibald. The Defences of the British Empire. (International Information Series.) Published for the International Information Committee. Athenæum Press 1917. 1*s.*

Innes, Arthur D. A History of England and the British Empire. Vol. IV. 1802-1914. Rivingtons. 6*s.*

Lanessan, J. L. de. Histoire de l'entente cordiale Franco-Anglaise. Les relations de la France et de l'Angleterre le XVIe siècle jusqu'à nos jours. Alcan 1916. 3 fr. 50.

Lemonon, E. L'Europe et la politique britannique (1882-1911). Alcan. 10 fr.

Lovett, Sir Verney. A History of the Indian Nationalist Movement. Murray 1920. 10*s.* 6*d.*

Low, S. J., and Sanders, L. C. The Political History of England 1837-1901. Longmans. 7*s.* 6*d.*

Lucas, Sir C. P. Historical Geography of the British Colonies. 13 vols. (Maps.) Oxford Univ. Press 1887-1915.

—— The British Empire. Six lectures on How this Empire came into being, and what it means. Macmillan. 2*s.*

McCarthy, Justin. A History of Our Own Times 1837-80. 4 vols. New edn. Chatto & Windus 1882. 24*s.*

—— A History of Our Own Times 1880-97. Chatto & Windus. 8*s.*

Marriott, J. A. R. England since Waterloo. Methuen. 10*s.* 6*d.*

Mills, J. Saxon. The Future of the Empire. An account of the growth and extent of the British Empire, and its possible future. Seeley 1917. 3*s.* 6*d.*

Muir, Prof. Ramsay. The Character of the British Empire. Constable 1917. 3*d.*

Murray, Prof. Gilbert. The Foreign Policy of Sir Edward Grey 1906-15. Oxford Univ. Press. 1*s.* 6*d.*

Newton, Arthur P. The Old Empire and the New. With Introduction by Sir Charles Lucas. Dent 1917. 2*s.* 6*d.*

Paladini, Carlo. Impero e libertà nelle colonie inglesi. Florence: Bemporad 1916. 2l. 50.

Pasley, Sir Charles W. The Military Policy and Institutions of the British Empire. An essay. 5th edn. Edited in the light of science of organization, by Col. B. R. Ward. Clowes 1914. 3*s.* 6*d.*

Paul, Herbert. A History of Modern England 1846-95. 5 vols. Macmillan 1904-6.

Peez, Alex. von. Englands Rolle im nahen Orient. 4th edn. Vienna and Leipzig: Fromme 1917. 2 kr. 20.

Reventlow, Count E. zu. The Vampire of the Continent. (British foreign policy as seen by a pan-German leader.) Translated from the German. New York: Jackson Press 1916. $1.35.

Schmitt, B. Everly. England and Germany 1740-1914 (by an American Rhodes Scholar). Milford 1916. 8*s*. 6*d*.

Schultze-Gävernitz, G. von. Britischer Imperialismus und englischer Freihandel, zum Beginn des 20ten Jahrhunderts. Leipzig: Duncker 1906. 10 mk.

Selected Speeches on British Foreign Policy 1738-1914. Edited by E. R. Jones. Oxford Univ. Press 1916. 1*s*.

Walpole, Sir Spencer. The History of 25 Years 1856-80. 4 vols. Longmans 1904-8.

Williamson, James A. The Foundation and Growth of the British Empire. With maps. Macmillan 1916. 2*s*. 6*d*.

(8) *Bulgaria.*

Andreas, Mui Sheeko. With Gypsies in Bulgaria. Young 1916. 2*s*. 6*d*.

Balkanicus. The Aspirations of Bulgaria. Translated from the Serbian. Simpkin 1915. 2*s*. 6*d*.

Dicey, Edward. The Peasant State. An account of Bulgaria. Murray 1894.

Fox, Frank. Bulgaria. Illustrated. Black 1915. 10*s*.

Monroe, Prof. W. S. Bulgaria and her people. Boston, U.S.: Page Co. $3.

O'Mahoney, The. Bulgaria and the Powers. A series of Letters on the Balkans, written from Sofia. Map. Dublin: Sealy. 1*s*.

(9) *China.*

Bland, J. O. P. and Backhouse. China under the Dowager Empress, being the History of the Life and Times of Tzu Hsi, compiled from State Papers, &c. (Illustrated.) Heinemann 1911. 20*s*.

Boulger, D. C. A Short History of the Chinese Empire. Allen 1893.

Chirol, Sir Valentine. The Far Eastern Question. Macmillan 1896. 8*s*. 6*d*.

Cordier, Henri. Histoire générale de la Chine et de ses relations avec les pays étrangers depuis les temps les plus anciens jusqu'à la chute de la dynastie mandchoue. 4 vols. Paris: Geuthner 1920-21. 100 fr.

Cordier, Henri. Histoire des relations de la Chine avec les puissances occidentales, 1860-1901. 3 vols. (Maps.) Paris: B. H. C. 1913.

Douglas, Sir R. K. China. 4th edn. revised by J. C. Hannah. 1912. 5*s.*

—— Europe and the Far East (to 1912). New edn. revised and brought up to date by J. H. Longford. Camb. Univ. Press 1913. 6*s.*

Gérard, A. (Ambassadeur de France). Ma Mission en Chine 1893-97. Plon-Nourrit 1918. 7 fr. 50.

Hornbeck, Prof. S. K. Contemporary Politics in the Far East. (The recent political history of China and Japan, and an account of their political institutions, &c.) Appleton 1917. $3.00.

Morse, H. B. The International Relations of the Chinese Empire 1834-1911. 3 vols. Longmans 1910.

Parker, Prof. E. H. China, Her History, Diplomacy and Commerce from the earliest times to the present day. Revised edn. with additional chapters. Murray 1916. 10*s.* 6*d.*

MacMurray, J. V. A. (edr.). Treaties and Agreements with and concerning China 1894-1919. 2 vols. Oxford Univ. Press 1921.

(10) *Eastern Questions.*

Abbott, G. F. Turkey, Greece and the Great Powers: A Study in Friendship and Hate. Scott 1916. 10*s.* 6*d.*

Cahuet, Albéric. La Question d'Orient dans l'histoire contemporaine 1821-1905. Preface by Frédéric Passy. Dujarric 1905. 6 fr.

Chéradame, André. La Question d'Orient. La Macédoine—Le chemin de fer de Bagdad. Plon-Nourrit 1903. 3 fr. 50.

Choublier, Max. La Question d'Orient depuis le traité de Berlin. Etude d'histoire diplomatique. Rousseau. 8 fr.

Driault, Edouard. La Question d'Orient depuis ses origines jusqu'à nos jours. Alcan 1898. 7 fr.

—— La reprise de Constantinople et l'alliance Franco-Russe. Recent history of the Near East and future prospects. Alcan 1915. 60 c.

Duboscq, André. L'Orient Méditerranéen. Perrin 1918 3 fr. 50

Ibero, C. Ibânez de D'Athènes à Constantinople (la situation politique en Orient). Attinger 1917. 3 fr. 50.

Ilitsch, Alex. Le Chemin de fer de Bagdad au point de vue politique, économique et financier: ou l'expansion d'Allemagne en Orient. Rivière 1913. 7 fr.

Marriott, J. A. R. The Eastern Question. An historical study in European diplomacy. Maps. Oxford Univ. Press 1917. 12*s.* 6*d.*

Nationalism and War in the Near East. By a diplomatist [George Young]. Edited by Lord Courtney of Penwith. Oxford Univ. Press 1915. 12*s.* 6*d.*

Rey, A. La question d'Orient devant Europe. Constantinople et des détroits. Vues historiques et diplomatiques. Two parts. Florence: 1917. l. 4.50.

Rohrbach, Paul. Die Baghdadbahn. Berlin: Wiegandt 1911. 1 m. 50 pf.

Savic, Vladislav R. The Reconstruction of South-Eastern Europe, Chapman & Hall.

Urquhart, F. F. The Eastern Question. (O.P.) Oxford Univ. Press. 3*d.*

Yovanowitch, Vladimir. The Near-Eastern Problem and Pan-German Peril. By a Serbian publicist (urges the formation of a Balkan Confederation). Watts. 6*d.*

(11) *France.*

Bainville, Jacques. Histoire de deux peuples. La France et l'Empire Allemand. Nour. Libr. nationale 1915. 3 fr. 50 c.

Baudin, Pierre. Anticipation (Essays and addresses dealing with the condition of France immediately before the war). Fasquelle 1916. 3 fr. 50.

Betham-Edwards, M. Twentieth-century France. Chapman & Hall 1917. 10*s.* 6*d.*

Bodley, J. E. C. France. First published 1898. 2 vols. Macmillan. 20*s.*

Bourgeois, Emile. History of France 1815-1913. 2 vols. Cambridge Univ. Press 1919.

—— Manuel historique de la Politique étrangère. 3 vols. (Vol. II 1830-78). Belin 1893-1905. 16 fr. 50.

Bracq, Jean C. The provocation of France. Fifty years of German aggression. Oxford Univ. Press (American Branch) 1916. $1.25.

Brunel, Georges. Les Incidents franco-allemands de 1871 à 1914. Avec un plan et 2 cartes. Pigeon 1917. 2 fr. 50.

Busson, H. and others. Notre empire colonial. Illustrations and maps. Alcan 1910. 5 fr.

Chéradame, André. La Crise française: faits, causes, solutions. An examination of contemporary conditions in France. Plon 1912.

Coubertin, Pierre de. L'Evolution française sous la Troisième République (1870-95). Plon-Nourrit 1898.

Davis, H. W. C. and Morgan, F. French Policy since 1871. (O.P.) Oxford Univ. Press. 2*d.*

Demi-siècle, un, de civilisation française 1870-1915. Preface by M. Lévy (essays by twenty French writers of high authority). Hachette 1916. 10 fr.

Dimnet, l'Abbé Ernest. The Evolution of Thought in Modern France. (O.P.) Oxford Univ. Press. *2d.*

Gaffarel, Paul. Notre expansion Coloniale en Afrique de 1870 à nos jours. Alcan 1918. 5 fr.

Hanotaux, Gabriel. Histoire de la France Contemporaire (1870-82). Transl. into English by J. C. Tarver. 4 vols. Constable 1903-9. 60*s.*

Headlam, C. France. A. & C. Black. 7*s.* 6*d.*

Henrique, L. Les Colonies françaises. Comp. Générale d'impression, etc. 1889.

L'Alliance franco-russe. Origines de l'Alliance 1890-93; Convention militaire, 1892-99; et Convention navale, 1912. Documents diplomatiques. Livre Jaune français. Berger-Levrault 1918. 2 fr. 50.

Lawton, Frederick. The Third French Republic (to 1908) Grant Richards. 12*s.* 6*d.*

Les Accords franco-italiens de 1900-1902. Documents diplomatique (Ministère des Affaires étrangères). Imprim. Nationale 1920. 4 fr.

Maurras, Charles. Quand les Français ne s'aimaient pas. Chronique d'une Renaissance 1895-1905. Nouv. Libr. Nationale 1916. 3 fr. 50.

Mirecourt. Paul de. Le Commerce français aux mains des Allemands. (The "peaceful penetration" of France before the war.) Editions & Libr. 1915. 1 fr. 50.

Nyrop, Prof. Christopher. France. (Transl. from the Danish). Heinemann 1917. 1*s.*

Péret, R. (late Minister of Commerce). La Population, le Budget, la Fortune et la Dette Publique de la France, de ses Alliés et de ses ennemis avant la guerre. Alcan 1917. 1 fr. English transl. same publishers and date. 2 fr.

Perrier, Edmond. France et Allemagne (mostly a criticism of Germany). Payot 1916. 3 fr. 50.

Pinon, René. France et Allemagne 1870-1913. Perrin 1913. 3 fr. 50.

Poincaré, Raymond. How France is governed. English transl. Popular edn. Fisher Unwin. 3*s.* 6*d.* & 7*s.* 6*d.*

Sembat, Marcel. Faites un Roi; sinon faites la Paix. 3rd edn. Figuière 1913. 3 fr. 50.

Stein, Henri. Notre Frontière de l'Est: la France et l'Empire à travers l'Histoire et les Origines du Pan-Germanisme. Alcan 1917. 1 fr. 25.

Tardieu, André. France and the Alliances: The Struggle for the Balance of Power. Alcan 1910. 3 fr. 50. Macmillan. 6*s*. 6*d*.
Vidal de la Blache, Prof. P. La France de l'est (European importance of the land on the eastern frontier of France). Armand Colin 1917. 12 fr.
Zévort, E. Histoire de la Troisième République (to 1894). 4 vols. Alcan. 30 fr.

(12) *Germany.*

(*a*) History.

Allen, J. W. Germany and Europe. Bell. 2*s*. 6*d*.
Andrillon, Henri. L'Expansion de l'Allemagne: ses causes, ses formes, ses conséquences. Marcel Rivière 1914 3 fr. 50.
Briefe Wilhelms II. an den Zaren 1894-1914 (mit einer historisch-politischen Einleitung von W. Goetz). English transl. under title Kaiser's Letters, The, to the Tsar, copied from the Government Archives in Petrograd. Edited by N. F. Grant. Hodder & Stoughton 1920. 12*s*. 6*d*.
Daudet, Léon. L'Avant-guerre. Études et documents sur l'espionage juif-allemand en France depuis l'affaire Dreyfus. Nouv. Libr. nationale 1914. 3 fr. 50.
Dawson, W. Harbutt. Modern Germany 1867-1914. 2 vols. Allen & Unwin 1919. 20*s*.
—— The Evolution of Modern Germany. Fisher Unwin. 5*s*.
Eckhardstein, Hermann Frhr. von. Lebenserinnerungen und politische Denkwürdigkeiten. 2 vols. Leipzig: List 1920.
—— Die Isolierung Deutschlands (Band III of Lebenserinnerungen &c.). Leipzig: List 1921.
Eppstein, Georg Frhr. von. Fürst Bismarcks Entlassung. Nach den hinterlassenen . . . Aufzeichnungen des Staatsecretärs . . . K. H. von Bötticher und des Chefs der Reichskanzlei . . . F. J. von Rottenburg, herausg. von Dr. G. Frhr. von Eppstein. Berlin: Scherl 1920.
Fife, R H. The German Empire between Two Wars. A study of development 1871-1914. Macmillan 1916. 6*s*. 6*d*.
Fisher, H. W. The Secret History of the Court of Berlin. From the papers and diaries of a German Lady-in-Waiting. 11th edn. Long 1*s*.
Germany in the Nineteenth Century. Two series of lectures by several scholars. Edited by Prof. C. H. Herford. Manchester Univ. Press 1912-15. 6*s*.
Haldane, Lord, and Germany (articles reprinted from the Manchester Guardian.) Guardian Office 1917. 3*d*.

Hammann, Otto. Erinnerungen: (1) der neue Kurs; (2) zur Vorgeschichte des Weltkriegs 1897-1906; (3) um den Kaiser 1906-1909. Berlin: Hobbing 1919. 24 mk.

Hartl, C. Preussen-Deutschlands diplomatische Niederlagen: eine historisch-politische Betrachtung zur Marokko-Affaire und zur deutsch-englischen Spannung. Leipzig: Xenien-Verlag 1912. 2 mk. 75.

Henderson, E. F. A short history of Germany. New edn. with additional chapters. 2 vols. Macmillan 1916. 15*s*.

Hohenlohe-Schillingfürst, Prince, Memoirs of. Edited by Fried. Curtius. Transl. from the first German edition by G. W. Chrystal. 2 vols. Heinemann 1906. 25*s*.

Innes, A. D. The Hohenzollerns: a Historical Study. Jack. 6*d*.

Jones, C. S. Story of the Hohenzollerns. Jarrold 1915. 5*s*.

Jones, J. P. and Hollister, P. M. The German Secret Service in America. Illustrated. Small, Maynard & Co. 1918. $2.00.

Keen, Edith. Seven Years at the Prussian Court. Nash 1916. 10*s*. 6*d*.

Laloz, Emile. La Diplomatie de Guillaume II, depuis son avènement jusqu'à la déclaration de guerre, 1888-1914. Bossard 1917. 6 fr.

Lamprecht, Prof. Karl. Deutsche Geschichte (11 vols.). Neueste Zeit (4 vols.). Berlin: Weidmann 1914. 6 mk. each.

—— Zur jüngsten deutschen Vergangenheit. 3 vols. Freiburg im B. 1904.

—— Deutscher Aufsteig 1750-1914: Einführung in das geschichtliche Verständniss der Gegenwart. 9th edn. Gotha: Perthes 1914. 60 pf.

Lanessan, J. L. de. L'Empire Germanique sous la direction de Bismarck et de Guillaume II. Paris: Alcan. 1 fr. 25.

Lavisse, Ernest. Essais sur l'Allemagne impériale. 4th edn. Hachette 1909. 3 fr. 50.

—— Études sur l'histoire de Prusse. 6th edn. Hachette 1912. 3 fr. 50.

Lichtenberger, Henri. The Evolution of Modern Germany. Transl. from the French by A. M. Ludovici. 2nd edn. 1913. Constable. 10*s*. 6*d*.

Lote, René. Germania. L'Allemagne et l'Autriche dans la Civilization et l'Histoire. Berger-Levrault 1917. 3 fr. 50.

Malleson, Col. G. B. The Refounding of the German Empire 1848-1914. With an additional chapter by N. J. Davidson. Seeley. 2*s*.

Manen, Charlotte A. van. L'épanouissement de l'Allemagne et l'hégémonie prussienne (transl. from the Dutch). The Hague: Nijhoff 1916. 1 fl.

Marriott, J. A. R. and Robertson, C. Grant. The evolution of Prussia: the making of an Empire. Oxford Univ. Press 1915. 5*s*.

Michaelis, Paul. Von Bismarck bis Bethmann: die Politik und Kultur Grosspreussens (including an Essay on Wilhelm II). Berlin: Schuster 1911. 6 mk.

Moltke, Gesammelte Schriften und Denkwürdigkeiten des Grafen Helmuth von. 5 vols. Abridged English transl. under title Essays, Speeches and Memoirs of Count Helmuth von Moltke. 2 vols. London 1883.

Nyström, Anton. Före, under, och efter 1914. An historical examination of Germanism down to the present day, concluding in favour of the Allies, by a Swedish writer. Stockholm: Svanbäck. 3 kr. 50.

—— Before, during, and after 1914. English transl. of Före, under. och efter 1914. With introduction by Edmund Gosse. Heinemann. 7*s*. 6*d*.

Oliphant, E. H. C. Germany and good faith: a study of the history of the Prussian Royal Family. Parker 1915. 3*s*. 6*d*.

Plehn, Hans. Bismarcks auswärtige Politik nach der Reichsgründung. Mit einem Vorwort von Otto Hötzch. Munich and Berlin: Oldenbourg 1920. 34 mk.

Prior, W. B. North Sleswig under Prussian Rule 1864-1914. Oxford Univ. Press. 2*d*.

Prothero, G. W. German Policy before the War. On the genesis of German opinion and policy, with a sketch of international politics 1890-1914. Murray 1916. 2*s*. 6*d*.

Rachfahl, Prof. Felix. Kaiser und Reich 1888-1913: 25 Jahre prussisch-deutscher Geschichte. Festschrift zum 25-jährigen Regierungsjubiläum Wilhelms II. Berlin: Voss 1913.

Radziwill, Princess Catherine. Germany under Three Emperors (Prussian diplomacy during the last 50 years). Cassell 1917. 16*s*.

Reventlow, Count von. Deutschlands auswärtige Politik 1888-1913. A presentation from the Pan-German point of view. First published 1914. New edn., revised and enlarged 1916. Berlin: Mittler. 10 mk.

Richard, Ernst. History of German Civilization. Macmillan 8*s*. 6*d*.

Roloff, Prof. G. Deutschland und Russland im Widerstreit seit 200 Jahren. (Series, Der deutsche Krieg.) Stuttgart: Deutsche Verlags-Anstalt. 50 pf.

Schiemann, Prof. Theod. Deutschland und die grosse Politik. A volume consisting mostly of articles contributed weekly to the Kreuz Zeitung, has appeared annually since 1901. Berlin : Reimer. 6 mk. each.

Schwering, Count Axel von (Pseudonym). The Berlin Court under William II. Illustrated. Cassell. 16*s.*

Sime, J. History of Germany. With a chapter on recent events by R. P. Mahaffy. Macmillan. 3*s.* 6*d.*

Situation dans le Slesvig du Nord, La, spécialement pendant les années de 1906 à 1914. Publié par Les Associations Slesvicoises Réunies du Danemark. Copenhagen 1915.

Smith, Prof. Munroe. Bismarck and German Unity. 2nd edn. Columbia Univ. Press 1910.

Soulange-Bodin, André. L'Avant-guerre allemande en Europe. Perrin 1917. 3 fr. 50.

Tardieu, André. Le Mystère d'Agadir. Calmann-Lévy 1912. 3 fr. 50.

Turquan, Joseph and Dauriac, Jules. Les Provocations allemandes de 1871 à 1914 (à l'égard de la France, de la Russie et de l'Angleterre). Tallandier 1917. 3 fr. 50.

Ward, Sir Adolphus W. Germany 1815-1890. With two supplementary chapters (on the reign of William II). 3 vols. Maps (Cambridge Historical Series). Cambridge Univ. Press 1916-18.

Wetterlé, L'Abbé E. Les Coulisses du Reichstag. Seize années de vie parlementaire en Allemagne. Préface de René Doumic. Bossard 1918. 5 fr.

—— Transl. under title Behind the Scenes in the Reichstag. Hodder & Stoughton 1918. 6*s.*

Zimmermann, Emil. The German Empire of Central Africa. Transl., with an Introduction, by Edwyn Bevan. Longmans 1918. 1*s.*

See also II B.7 : Begbie, Reventlow, Schmitt; II B.11 : Bainville, Bracq. Brunel, Perrier.

(*b*) Politics and Society.

Andler, Charles. Le socialisme impérialiste dans l'Allemagne contemporaine. 1912.

—— Dossier d'une polémique avec Jean Jaurès 1912-13 (on German socialism). Bossard 1918. fr.

Arnold, W. T. "Vigilans sed Æquus." German Ambitions as they affect Britain and the United States of America. (Reprinted, with Additions and Notes, from the Spectator.) First published 1903. New edn. 1914. Smith, Elder. 1*s.* 6*d.*

Bahr, Hermann. Schwarzgelb. Berlin : Fischer. 2 mk.

Barker, E. The Submerged Nationalities of the German Empire. Darling.

Barker, Ernest. Linguistic oppression in the German Empire. Longmans 1918. *6d.*

Barker, J. Ellis. Modern Germany. 5th edn., enlarged, brought up to January 1915. Murray. *7s. 6d.*

Barthélemy, Prof. Joseph. Les institutions politiques de l'Allemagne contemporaine. Alcan. 3 fr. 50.

Bérard, Victor. L'éternelle Allemagne. Colin 1916. 4 fr.

Bernhardi, General F. von. Deutschland und der nächste Krieg (1912). Transl. into English by Alan H. Powles, under the title Germany and the next War. Arnold. *2s.*

—— Unsere Zukunft: ein Mahnwort an das deutsche Volk. (1913.) Transl. into English by J. Ellis Barker, under the title Britain as Germany's vassal. Dawson. *2s.*

—— World Power or Downfall. Pearson 1915. *1s.*

Beyens, M. le Baron. L'Allemagne avant la Guerre. By the Belgian Minister at Berlin 1911-14. (Brussels and Paris: Van Oest 1915.) Transl. into English under title Germany before the War. Nelson. *3s. 6d.*

—— Germany before the War. Transl. from the French. Nelson 1915. *3s. 6d.*

Bleibtreu, Karl. Deutschland und England. Berlin: Curtius 1909. 2 mk. 30.

Bley, Fritz. Südafrika niederdeutsch! Munich: Lehmann 1898. 40 pf.

Borgese, G. A. La nuova Germania (a prophetic analysis). Turin: Bocca 1907.

Bourdon, Georges. The German Enigma: being an inquiry among Germans, as to what they think, what they want, what they can do. Transl. from the French by Beatrice Marshall. With Introduction by Dr. C. Sarolea. Dent. *2s. 6d.*

Brinville, M. J.-C. Hohenzollern et Démocratie. Attinger 1918. 1 fr.

Bülow, Prince von. Deutsche Politik (a revised edn. of his Imperial Germany). Berlin: Hobbing 1916.

—— Imperial Germany. Transl. by Marie A. Lewenz. Cassell 1914. *12s.*

—— Revised edn. of the above, with additions made since the war and preface by J. W. Headlam. Cassell 1916. *6s.*

Cambo, Julio. Alemania. (By a Spanish journalist. Impressions before the war). Madrid: Renacimiento 1916. 3 pes. 50.

Chuquet, A. L'Allemagne au dessus de tout. (Les dispositions intellectuelles et morales de l'Allemagne). Boccard 1916. 3 fr. 50.

Collier, Price. Germany and the Germans from an American point of view. Duckworth 1913. 7*s.* 6*d.*, cheap edn. 2*s.* 6*d.*

Dawson, W. H. Germany and the Germans. 2 vols. Chapman & Hall 1893. 26*s.*

—— Municipal Life and Government in Germany. Longmans 1914. 12*s.* 6*d.*

Delbrück, Prof. Hans. Bismarcks Erbe. Berlin: 1915.

Deutschland bei Beginn des 20 Jahrhunderts. Von einem Deutschen. Berlin: Felix 1900. 3 mk.

Deutschlands Ansprüche an das turkische Erbe. (Published by Pan-German League). Munich: Lehmann 1898. 40 pf.

Flandin, E. L'Allemagne en 1914. On the German constitution, German law, etc. Le Soudier. 3 fr. 50.

Fletcher, C. R. L. The Germans and What they Covet. (O.P.) Oxford Univ. Press. 2*d.*

—— The Germans, their Empire, and How they have made it. Oxford Univ. Press 2*d.*

François-Poncet, André. Ce que pense la Jeunesse allemande. Oudin 1913. 2 fr.

Frobenius, H. Des deutschen Reiches Schicksalsstunde. (Berlin 1914.) Transl. into English under title The German Empire's Hour of Destiny. Long. 2*s.*

Gautier, Paul. Un prophète, Edgar Quinet (whose writings. 1831-42, discussed the nationalism of Germany and predicted war). Plon 1917. 3 fr. 50.

German Culture. The contribution of the Germans to Knowledge, Literature, Art and Life. Edited by W. P. Paterson. Jack 2*s.* 6*d.*

Germans, The, by Themselves. Extracts from Bernhardi, Frobenius and other writers, arranged and analysed. Reprinted from The Field. Central Committee. 2*d.*

Germany's War Mania. The Teutonic Point of View as officially stated by her Leaders. A collection of speeches and writings by the German Emperor, and others. A. W. Shaw. 1*s.*

Grandvilliers, J. de. Essai sur le Libéralisme allemand. Historical, philosophical, and descriptive. Giard et Brière. 4 fr.

Grothe, Hugo. Die Bagdadbahn und das schwäbische Bauernelement in Transcaucasien und Palästina. Gedanken zur Kolonisation Mesopotamien. Munich: Lehmann 1902. 1 mk.

Gurlitt, Ludwig. Der Deutsche und sein Vaterland. An indictment of Prussian methods. 5th edn. 1906. Berlin: Wiegandt 1902. 1 mk. 50.

Harrison, Frederic. The German Peril: Forecasts, 1864-1914; Realities, 1915; Hopes. Fisher Unwin. 5*s*.

Hasse, E. Deutsche Weltpolitik. Munich: Lehmann 1898. 40 pf.

Hauser, Prof. Henri. Michelet et l'Allemagne de 1870. Review of M.'s book La France devant l'Europe, showing German methods as fully developed at that time. Libr. Recueil Sirey 1916. 50 c.

Henry, Marc. Beyond the Rhine. Transl. by M. T. H. Sadler. Constable 1917. 6*s*.

Holland, A. W. Germany. Illustrated. (The Making of the Nations.) Black 1914. 7*s*. 6*d*.

Holmes, Edmond. The Nemesis of docility. A study of German character. Constable 1916. 4*s*. 6*d*.

Howard, Burt Estes. The German Empire. Macmillan. 8*s*. 6*d*.

Howe, F. C. Socialised Germany. An account of German national organisation. New York: Scribner. $1.50.

Jäckh, E. Deutschland im Orient nach dem Balkankrieg. Munich 1913. 3 mk.

Kaiser's, The, Letters to the Tsar: Copied from Government Archives in Russia, and brought from Russia by Isaac D. Levine. Hodder & Stoughton 1920. 12*s*. 6*d*.

Lair, Maurice. L'Impérialisme allemand. Colin 1902. 3 fr. 50.

Lanessan, J. L. de. Comment l'éducation allemande a créé la barbarie germanique. Alcan. 60 c.

—— Les Empires germaniques et la politique de la force. Alcan. 3 fr. 50.

Learned, William Setchel. Oberlehrer. A study of the social and professional evolution of the German schoolmaster. (Harvard Studies in Education.) Milford 1915. 5*s*. 6*d*.

Lewin, P. Evans. The German road to the East. Heinemann 1917.

Lote, R. Le Péril allemande et l'Europe (revue des principaux événements historiques.) Alcan 1916. 1 fr. 25.

Martin, W. La Crise politique de l'Allemagne contemporaine. (By the editor of the Journal de Genève.) Alcan 1913. 3 fr. 50.

Moysset, Henri. L'esprit public en Allemagne vingt ans après Bismarck. Alcan 1913. 5 fr.

Naumann, Friedrich. Das blaue Buch von Vaterland und Freiheit. (Extracts from his works.) Leipzig: Langewiesche 1 mk. 80.

Pelissier, Jean. L'Europe sous la menace allemande en 1914. (Opinions of politicians and others before the outbreak of war.) Perrin 1916. 3 fr. 50.

Powys, John C. The Menance of German Culture. A reply to Prof. Münsterberg. Rider. 1*s*.

Prussian Officer, A. Our Future lies on the Water. A pre-war book. Transl. by M. Jebb Scott. Field Office. 1*s*.

Raymond, A. Intimate Prussia (experiences in a German family at Königsberg.) Black 1918. 5*s*.

Régamey, Jeanne and Frederick. The Daughters of Germany Transl. by Dr. A. S. Rappoport and C. A. Arfwedson. Holden & Hardingham, 1916. 5*s*.

Reich, Emil. Germany's Swelled Head. First published 1907. New edn., with additional chapter. Melrose 1914. 1*s*.

Rohrbach, Paul. Der deutsche Gedanke in der Welt. Leipzig: Langewiesche. 1 mk. 80.

—— Deutschland unter den Weltvölkern. Materialen zur auswärtigen Politik. Berlin: Hilfe 1908. 4 mk. 50.

Schlieben, M. H. (German consul at Belgrade in 1914.) Die deutsche Diplomatie, wie sie ist, wie sie sein sollte. Zurich: Füssli 1917. 1 fr. 25.

Schneider, Siegmund. Die deutsche Baghdad-Bahn und die projectirte Ueberbrückung des Bosporus, in ihren Bedeutung für Weltwirthschaft und Weltverkehr. (Maps and illustrations.) Leipzig and Vienna. Weiss 1900. 5 mk.

Seillière, E. The German Doctrine of Conquest. Transl. with an introduction by J. M. Hone. Maunsel. 2*s*.

Sidgwick, Mrs. A. Home Life in Germany. Methuen 1908. 10*s*. 6*d*.

Smith, T. F. A. The Soul of Germany: a twelve years' study of this people from within 1902-14. Hutchinson. 6*s*.

Tannenberg, Otto R. Le Rève allemand! La plus grande Allemagne. L'Œuvre du XXme siècle. (Transl. of Gross-Deutschland, one of the most important Pan-German works, published 1911.) Preface by M. Millioud. Payot 1916. 4 fr.

Tower, Charles. Changing Germany. Observations of a journalist who has lived in Germany. Fisher Unwin. 7*s*. 6*d*.

—— Germany of to-day. (Home Univ. Library.) Williams & Norgate. 1*s*.

Tudesq, A. et Dyssord, J. Les Allemands peints par eux-mêmes. Illustrations. Editions et Librarie 1916. 2 fr.

Verrier, Paul. La Folie Allemande. Documents allemands. (Pages d'Histoire.) Contains quotations from German writers. Berger-Levrault. 30 c.

Villard, O. G. Germany embattled: an American interpretation. The author is in sympathy with the older Germany, but strongly opposed to the new. Sampson Low 4*s*. 6*d*.

Walter, H. A. (Edr.) German Year-Book, The. (1914.) Anglo-German Publ. Co. 1914. 4*s*. 6*d*.

Wile, F. W. The Assault: Germany before the outbreak, and England in war-time. A personal narrative. Heinemann 1916. 6*s*.

—— Who's Who in Hunland: a Glossary of the persons, issues, places and things we read about in Germany. Simpkin, Marshall 1916. 1*s*.

Winterstein, Franz. Klein-Deutschland; ein Kehrbild. (Pan-German.) Munich: Lehmann 1903. 40 pf.

Ysiad (pseud.). L'Allemagne et son enfant terrible, Maximilian Harden. Berger-Levrault 1918. 3 fr.

(*c*) Political Philosophy (Pangermanism).

Andler, Charles. Collection de documents sur le Pangermanisme: I— Les origines (1801-88); II—Le Pangermanisme continental (1888-1914); III—Le Pangermanisme colonial; IV—Le Pangermanisme philosophique. 4 vols. Conard 1915-16. 20 fr.

—— Le Pangermanisme: ses plans d'expansion allemande dans le monde. (Études et documents sur la Guerre.) Colin 1915. 50 c.

Archer, W. Fighting a Philosophy. (O.P.) Clarendon Press 1915. 2*d*. net.

Baldwin, Prof. J. M. The Super-State and the Eternal Values; a Study in Pan-Germanism (The Herbert Spencer Lecture). Oxford Univ. Press 1916. 1*s*. 6*d*.

Barker, Ernest. Nietzsche and Treitschke: the Worship of Power in Modern Germany. (O.P.) Oxford Univ. Press. 2*d*.

Bevan, Edwyn (edr.). The Pan-German Programme· Petition of the Six Associations and the manifesto of the Intellectuals. Transl., with introduction, by E.B. Allen & Unwin 1918. 1*s*.

Blondel, Georges. La doctrine Pangermaniste. Chapelot. 1 fr.

Bonhard, O. Geschichte des Alldeutschen Verbandes. Leipzig and Berlin: Weicher 1920.

Brandes, Georg. Friedrich Nietzsche. A criticism and exposition of various points of Nietzsche's doctrine. Heinemann 1914. 6*s*.

Chamberlain, Houston Stewart. Die Grundlagen des XIXten Jahrhunderts. First published 1898. Popular edn. 2 vols. Munich: Bruckmann 1912. Transl. into English by John Lees, with preface by Lord Redesdale. 2 vols. John Lane. 25*s*.

Chéradame, André. Le Plan pangermaniste démasqué. With maps. Plon-Nourrit 1916. 4 fr.

—— English transl. by Lady Frazer under title The Pan-German Plot Unmasked. Murray 1916. *2s. 6d.*

Davis, H. W. C. The Political Thought of Heinrich von Treitschke. Constable 1914. *6s.*

Dewey, John. German Philosophy and Politics. Kant, not Nietzsche, the basis of German moral ideas. N.Y.: Holt. $1.50.

Eucken, Prof. Rudolf. Die weltgeschichtliche Bedeutung des deutschen Geistes. (Series, Der Deutsche Krieg). Stuttgart: Deutsche Verlags-Anstalt.

Froelich, Jules. Le Délire pangermanique. Avec dessins par Zislin (documents inédits). Berger-Levrault 1918. 3 fr. 50.

Gobineau, Count. On the Inequality of Human Races. Transl. from the French original, published about 1840. A source of German ideas. Heinemann 1915. *5s.*

Grell, Hugo. Der Alldeutsche Verband; seine Geschichte, seine Bestrebungen und Erfolge. Munich: Lehmann c.1898. 40 pf.

Guilland, Antoine. Modern Germany and her Historians. Transl. from the French. Jarrold 1915. *7s. 6d.*

Guillaume, James. Karl Marx pangermaniste. Written before the war. Colin. 1 fr. 50.

Harrison, Austin. The Pan-Germanic Doctrine. A study of German political aims and aspirations. Harper 1904. *10s. 6d.*

Hügel, Friedrich von. The German Soul in its attitude toward Ethics and Christianity, the State and War. Two studies. Dent 1916. *2s. 6d.*

Imbart de la Tour, P. Le Pangermanisme et la philosophie de l'Histoire. Reprinted from the Revue de Deux Mondes. Perrin 1916. 75 c.

Kennedy, J. M. The Quintessence of Nietzsche. Werner Laurie. 6s.

Kiersch, H. J. Het Pangermanisme en de oorlog (Pangermanism and the War). Amsterdam: Van Holkema 1916. 2 fr.

Laskine, Edmond. Les Socialistes du Kaiser: la fin d'un mensonge. Shows German social democracy to have always been Pangermanist. Floury. 75 c.

—— L'Internationale et le pangermanisme. Floury 1916. 6 fr.

Lasserre, Pierre. Le Germanisme et l'esprit humain. Champion 1915. 1 fr. 25.

McCabe, Joseph. Treitschke and the Great War. Fisher Unwin *2s.*

McClure, Canon E. Germany's War-Inspirers, Nietzsche and Treitschke. S.P.C.K. *3d.*

Nietzsche, Friedrich, The Complete Works of. (First complete and authorised translation, edited by Dr. Oscar Levy). 18 vols., with index. Foulis.

Pasquier, Félix. Théories pangermaniques au 17me siècle. Toulouse: Bonnet 1915. 1 fr.

Prussian, A. Why Germany will be Defeated. An examination of German character and philosophy, by a naturalised British subject. Letchworth: Garden City Press. 6*d*.

Rolland, Romain. The Idols. An essay on the Idols of German Kultur. Macmillan. 6*d*.

Seton-Watson, R. W. Pan-German aspirations in the Near East. (Journal of the Royal Society of Arts, No. 3306.) Bell 1916. 6*d*.

Stewart, Herbert Leslie. Nietzsche and the Ideals of Modern Germany. Arnold 1915. 7*s*. 6*d*.

Terry, Charles Sanford J. Treitschke, Bernhardi and some Theologians. Maclehose 1915. 3*d*.

Treitschke, Heinrich von. Politics. Transl. by Blanche Dugdale and Torben de Bille. With introduction by the Rt. Hon. A. J. Balfour, M. P. 2 vols. Constable 1915.

—— Politik. Vorlesungen gehalten an der Universität zu Berlin. Hrsg. von Max Cornicelius. Leipzig: Hirzel 1897.

—— Germany, France, Russia and Islam. Esays, transl. into English. Allen & Unwin. 7*s*. 6*d*.

—— Selections from Treitschke's Lectures on Politics. Transl. by Adam L. Gowans. Gowans & Gray. 2*s*.

—— Life and Works. Transl into English for the first time. Allen & Unwin. 7*s*. 6*d*.

Usher, Roland G. Pan-Germanism (first published 1913). The historical part should be read with caution. Constable 1914. 2*s*.

Vergnet, Paul. France in Danger. Describes the policy and work of the Pan-Germanists. Transl. by Beatrice Barstow. Murray. 2*s*. 6*d*.

Wagner, Klaus. Krieg.

Wirth, Albrecht. Volkstum und Weltmacht in der Geschichte. 1906.

Wolf, A. The Philosophy of Nietzsche. Three lectures delivered at University College, London. Constable. 3*s*. 6*d*.

Woltmann. Politische Anthropologie. 1903.

(*d*) Commerce and Industry.

Barker, J. Ellis. Foundations of Germany. A documentary account revealing the causes of her strength, wealth and efficiency. Smith, Elder 1916. 7*s*. 6*d*.

Blondel, Georges. L'essor industriel et commercial du peuple allemand. 3rd edn. Paris 1900.

—— Les embarras de l'Allemagne. On the German attempt at economic conquest, and its results. Paris 1912.

Claes, Jules. The German Mole. A study of German peaceful penetration. On the commercial methods of Germany, especially in Belgium, before the war. Bell 1915. *2s. 6d.*

Dawson, W. H. The German Workman: a Study in National Efficiency. King. *6s.*

Engerand, F. Les Frontières lorraines et les forces allemands. On German aims on coal and iron, and the necessity of recovering the lost provinces. Perrin 1916. 3fr. 50c.

German Economic Policy in Poland. Articles reprinted from The Times. Polish Information Comm. 1915. *3d.*

German Trade: Where it is, and What it is. A complete and detailed list of Germany's exports. Export World 1914. *1s.*

Gray, Ezio M. The Bloodless War. Translated from the Italian Guerra senza Sangue 1916. (Describes Germany's efforts to win economic supremacy in Italy.: Hodder & Stoughton 1917. *3s. 6d.*

Hauser, Prof. Henri. Les Méthodes allemandes d'expansion économique. Colin 1916. 3 fr. 50 c.

—— L'Allemagne économique: l'Industrie allemande considérée comme facteur de guerre. Reprinted from the Bulletin de la Société d'encouragement pour l'industre nationale. Renouard 1915.

Lichtenberger, H., and Petit, Paul. L'Imperialisme économique allemand. Flammarion 1918. 4 fr.

Schmoller, Gustav, and others. Handels-und Machpolitik. Reden und Aufsätze. 2 vols. Stuttgart: Cotta 1900. 10 m.

Wichter, R. Deutsche Wirtschaftspropaganda im Weltkrieg. Bibliography. Berlin: Mittler 1922.

(*e*) Colonies.

Africanus (pseud.). The Prussian Lash in Africa (Government of the German Colonies, with an argument against their return to Germany). Hodder & Stoughton 1918. *2s. 6d.*

Calvert, Albert F. The German African Empire. Illustrated. W. Laurie 1916. *6s.*

—— South-West Africa during the German Occupation (1884-1914). Laurie 1915. *5s.*

—— The German Cameroons: German East Africa: Togoland. Werner Laurie 1918. *5s.* each vol.

Cana, Frank R. German East Africa (reprinted from the Journal of the African Society). The African Society 1918.

Chéradame, André. La Colonisation et les colonies allemandes. 8 maps. Plon. 12 fr.

Clifford, Sir Hugh. German Colonies: A Plea for the Native Races (by the Governor of the Gold Coast). Murray 1918. 2*s*. 6*d*.

Eveleigh, William. British South-West Africa (formerly German S.W.A.). Geographical and descriptive. Fisher Unwin. 5*s*.

Giordani, Paolo. The German Colonial Empire: Its Beginning and Ending. Translated from the Italian by Gustavus W. Hamilton. Bell 1916. 2*s*. 6*d*.

Hauser, Prof. Henri. Colonies allemandes, impériales et spontanées. Nouy 1900.

Le Sueur, G. Germany's Vanishing Colonies. A History of German Colonisation. Everett. 2*s*.

Lewin, P. Evans. The Germans and Africa: their aims on the Dark Continent, and how they acquired their African Colonies. Cassell. 10*s*. 6*d*.

——— The Germans in Africa. (O.P.) Oxford Univ. Press.

——— German Rule in Africa. Fisher Unwin 1918. 3*d*.

Maclean, Frank. Towards extermination. Germany's treatment of the African native. St. Albans: Campfield Press 1918.

Phillips, W. A., Headlam, J. W., Holland, A. W. Germany and her Colonies. Encycl. Brit. Co. 2*s*. 6*d*.

Rohrbach, Paul. Das deutsche Kolonialwesen 1906-9. Berlin: Gloeckner, 1911. 3 m. 20 pf.

Roscher, W., and Jannasch, R. Kolonieen, Kolonialpolitik. Leipzig: Winter 1885. 9 m.

Schützgebiete, Die Deutschen, in Afrika und der Südsee. 2 vols. Berlin: Mittler 1909-11.

Tymms, T. Vincent. The Cameroons (West Africa): a Historical Review. Carey Press 1915. 3*d*.

Weston, Rt. Rev. F., Bishop of Zanzibar. The Black Slaves of Prussia. An open letter addressed to General Smuts (on the treatment of African natives by Germans). Univ. Mission to Central Africa 1918.

Zimmermann, Alfred. Geschichte der deutschen Kolonialpolitik. Berlin: Mittler 1914. 9*s*. 6*d*.

(13) *Greece*.

Cassavetti, D. J. Hellas and the Balkan Wars. Illustrated. Unwin 1914. 10*s*. 6*d*. net.

Polybius (pseud.). Greece before the Conference. With preface by T. P. O'Connor, M.P., and an ethnological map. Methuen 1920. 5*s*.

Sergeant, L. Greece 1821-97. Unwin 1897. 10*s*. 6*d*.
Toynbee, A. J. Greek Policy since 1882. (O.P.) Oxford Univ. Press. 4*d*.

(14) *Holland.*

Edmondson, G. History of Holland (Bibliography and maps). Camb. Univ. Press 1921. 10*s*.

(15) *Italy.*

Battisti, Cesare. Il Trentino: cenni geografici, storici, economici, con un' appendice per l'Alto Abige. Edn. 2. Illustrated. Novara: Instituto geografico de Agostini 1917. 3 l.
Bagot, Richard. The Italians of To-day. Revised and popular edn. of a book published in 1912. Mills and Boon. 1*s*.
Caburi, F. Italiani e Jugoslavi nell'Adriatico. Milan: 1917. 2.00 l.
Cassi, Gellio. Il Mare Adriatico; sua funzione attraverso i tempi. Milan: Hoepli 1915. 5 f. 50 c.
Castellini, Gualtiero. Trento e Trieste; l'irredentismo e il problema Adriatico (quaderni della guerra). Milan: Trèves 1 l.
Crispolti, Crispolto and Aureli, Guido. La Politica di Leone XIII, da Luigi Galimberti a Mariano Rampolla, su documenti inediti Rome: Bontempelli 1912. 15 l.
Feiling, Keith. Italian Policy since 1870. (O.P.) Oxford Univ. Press. 2*d*.
Illyricus. Dalmazia e Italia. Rome, 1914.
Gayda, Dr. Virginio. L'Italia d'oltre confine: le provincie Italiane d'Austria. Italia irredenta. Turin: Bocca. 5 l.
Gray, Ezio. L'Invasione tedesca in Italia: professori, commercianti, &c. Florence: Bemporad. 1 l. 90 c.
Italy and the Jugoslav Peoples. By Civis Italicus. Translated by G. F. Hill. Council for study of International Relations 1916. 3*d*.
King, Bolton, and Okey, Thomas. Italy of To-day. 1901. King 1912. 6*s*.
L'Adriatico. Studio geografico, storico e politico. By * * * . Milan: Trèves. 5 l.
Lemonon, Ernest. L'Italie Économique et Sociale (1861-1912). Alcan 1913. 7 fr.
Mantegazza, Vico. Il Mediterraneo e il suo equilibrio. With preface by Giovanni Bettolo; and illustrations. Milan: Trèves. 5 l.
Maranelli, C. and Salvemini, G. La questione dell'Adriatico. Florence: 1918. 6 l.

Mastery of the Adriatic, The, and the Jugo-Slav Question. Italy in Asia Minor. Contributions and criticism. Compiled by Salvatore Raineri. Syren and Shipping, Ltd., 91, Leadenhall Street 1916. n.p.

Palamenghi-Crispi, Thomas. The Memoirs of Francesco Crispi. Compiled from Crispi's Diary and other documents. Translated by Mary Prichard-Agnetti. 3 vols. Hodder & Stoughton. 16*s.* each.

Panzini, Alfredo. La Madonna di Mama (On the conditions in Italy before her intervention in the War). Milan : Trèves 1916. 3 l. 50 c.

Paribeni, R. L'Italia e il Mediterraneo Orientale. (No. 3 of the series Problemi Nazionali.) Roma : Società L'Italiana 1916. 2 l.

Pattini, Giovanni. L'Italia irredenta. Illustrated Soc Editoriale Milanese 1916. 2 fr. 50 c.

Pingaud, Albert. L'Italie depuis 1870. Préface de E. Denis. Delagrave 1915. 3 f. 50 c.

Politica, estera italiana, La, 1875-1916. Bitonto : Comm. N. Garofalo 1916. 18 l.

Preziosi, Giovanni. La Germania alla conquista dell'Italia. Introduction by Prof. M. Pantaleoni. 2nd edn. revised. Florence : Libr. della Voce 1916. 2 l. 50 c.

Probyn, J. W. Italy, 1815-90. Cassell 1891. 7*s.* 6*d.*

Revelli, Paolo. L'Italia e il Mar di Levante. Maps. Milan : 1917. 6 l. 50 c.

Salvemini, Gaetano. La Politica estera di Francesco Crispi. (Quaderni de la Voce.) Rome : La Voce 1919. 3 l.

—— Da Algesiras a Tripoli. (Quaderni de la Voce.) Rome : La Voce 1920.

Stillman, W. J. The Union of Italy, 1815-95. New edn., with Epilogue by G. M. Trevelyan. Camb. Univ. Press 1909. 4*s.* 6*d.*

Tamaro, Attilio. L'Adriatico—Golfo d'Italia : L'Italianità di Trieste. (Quaderni della Guerra.) Milan : Trèves. 2 l.

—— Italiani e Slavi nell'Adriatico. Rome : Athenæum 1915. 4 fr.

Tittoni, Tommaso (Italian Foreign Minister). Italy's Foreign and Colonial Policy. Speeches delivered, 1903-9. Translated by the Baron di San Severino. Smith, Elder 1914 7*s.* 6*d.*

Vellay, Charles. La Question de l'Adriatique. Chapelot. 1 f.

Vivante, Angelo. Irredentismo Adriatico. Florence 1912.

Zimmern, Helen and Agresti, Antonio. New Italy (since 1866). Constable 1918. 6*s.*

(16) *Japan.*

Ballard, Adm. G. A. The Influence of the Sea on the Political History of Japan. Murray 1921. 18*s.*

Brinkley, Capt. F. Japan, its History, Arts and Literature. 8 vols. Jack 1903-4.

—— and Kikuchi, Baron. A History of the Japanese People to the end of the Meiji Era. Encycl. Brit. Co. 1915. 11*s.*

Chamberlain, Basil Hall. Things Japanese; being notes on subjects connected with Japan. 5th edn. Murray 1905. 10*s.* 6*d.*

Douglas, Sir R. K. Europe and the Far East 1506-1912. Revised and corrected, with an additional chapter (1904-12) by Joseph H. Longford. Camb. Univ. Press 1913. 7*s.* 6*d.*

Gérard, A. (Ambassadeur de France). Ma Mission au Japon 1907-14; avec un epilogue de 1914 à 1919. Plon-Nourrit 1919. 12 fr.

Harrison, E. J. The Fighting Spirit of Japan. Fisher Unwin. 5*s.*

Hearn, Lafcadio. Japan: an Interpretation. Macmillan 1909. 8*s.* 6*d.*

Kawakami, K. K. Japan in World Politics. New York. Macmillan 1917. $1.50.

Loti, Pierre. Japan. Translated by Laura Ensor. Illustrated by Rossi and Myrbach. Laurie 1915. 7*s.* 6*d.*

McGovern, W. M. Modern Japan. Fisher Unwin 1920. 15*s.*

McLaren, Prof. W. W. The Political History of Japan in the Meiji Era (since 1868). Allen & Unwin 1916. 12*s.* 6*d.*

Murray, David. Japan. 6th edn. revised, with supplementary chapters by J. H. Longford (Story of the Nations). Fisher Unwin 1920. 7*s.* 6*d.*

Naoichi Masaoka (edr.). Japan to America. A series of Essays by prominent Japanese on Japanese life and the relations between Japan and the U.S. Putnam. 5*s.*

Okakura, Kakuzo. Les Idéaux de l'Orient. Le Reveil du Japon. Transl. by Jenny Serruys. Preface by Auguste Gérard. Payot 19 . 5 fr.

Pooley, A. M. Japan's Foreign Policies. Allen & Unwin 1920. 10*s.* 6*d.*

Porter, Hon. R. P. Japan: the New World Power. . . . . Progress and Rise of the Japanese Empire. Originally published 1911. Oxford Univ. Press 1915. 6*s.*

—— Japan: the Rise of a Modern Power. Oxford Univ. Press 1918. 6*s.* 6*d.*

Terry's Japanese Empire: including Korea and Formosa. A guide-book for travellers. Constable 1914. 21*s.*

(17) *Montenegro.*

Devine, Alex. Montenegro: In History, Politics and War. Fisher Unwin 1918. *2s. 6d.*
Gopcević, S. Geschichte von Montenegro und Albanien. Maps. Gotha: Perthes. 8 m.
Stevenson, Francis S. History of Montenegro. Jarrold 1915. *2s. 6d.*

(18) *Morocco.*

Bernard, Augustin. Le Maroc (Bibl. d'histoire contemporaine). Maps. 4th edn. Alcan 1916. 5 fr.
La Revelière, le Comte de. Les énergies françaises au Maroc. Plon-Nourrit 1917. 12 fr. 50 c.
Maurice, L. La Politique Marocaine de l'Allemagne (1905-1914). Plon-Nourrit 1916. 3 fr. 50 c.
Morel, E. D. Morocco in Diplomacy. Smith Elder 1912. *6s.*
Piquet, Victor. Le Maroc. Géographie; Histoire; Mise en valeur. Maps. Colin 1917. 6 fr.

(19) *Ottoman Empire.*

(*a*) General.

Bareilles, Bertrand. Les Turcs: ce que fut leur empire: leurs comédies politiques. Perrin 1917. 3 fr. 50 c.
Benson, E. F. Crescent and Iron Cross. Hodder & Stoughton.
Childs, W. J. Across Asia Minor on Foot. Blackwood 1917. *15s.*
Coolidge, A. C. Claimants to Constantinople. Harvard Univ. Press 1917. *3s. 6d.*
Cuinet, V. La Turquie d'Asie. Géographie administrative, statistique, descriptive et raisonnée. Leroux.
—— Syrie, Liban et Paléstine. Géographie administrative, statistique, descriptive et raisonnée 1896-1901. Leroux.
Czaplicka, Miss M. A. The Turks of Central Asia in History and at the Present Day. An ethnological enquiry into the Pan-Turanian Problem [&c.]. Bibliography. Oxford Univ. Press 1918. *13s.*
Dardanelles, The: Their story and their significance in the Great War. By the author of The Real Kaiser. Melrose. *2s.*
Dascovici, N. La Question du Bosphore et des Dardanelles (an historical sketch). Geneva: Georg 1916.
Dieterich, K. Hellenism in Asia Minor. New York: Oxford Univ. Press 1918.

Dwight, H. G. Constantinople: Old and New. Longmans 1915. *21s.*

Eversley, Lord. The Turkish Empire, from 1288 to 1914. (Maps.) New edn., with 3 fresh chapters on the War down to the Peace of Sèvres (1914-1920), by Sir V. Chirol. Fisher Unwin 1921. *21s.*

Fowle, T. C. Travels in the Middle East: Impressions by the way in Turkish Arabia, Syria and Persia. Smith Elder 1916. *7s. 6d.*

Hawley, Walter A. Asia Minor (its people, antiquities, and future). Lane 1918. *12s. 6d.*

Holdich Col. Sir T. H. Boundaries in Europe and the Near East. Macmillan 1910. *8s. 6d.*

Jonquière, Vicomte de la. Histoire de l'Empire Ottoman. New edn. 2 vols. (Vol. II 1878-1913). Paris: Hachette. 12 fr. 50 c.

Lane-Poole, Stanley. Turkey. Fisher Unwin. *5s.*

Le Strange, G. The Lands of the Eastern Caliphate. Camb. Univ. Press 1917. *15s.*

Miller, W. The Ottoman Empire 1801-1913. Camb. Univ. Press 1913. *6s.*

Montier, Edouard. La Route des Dardanelles. Visions d'Orient. Soc. Franç. d'Imprimerie et Librairie.

Müller, Karl H. Die Bedeutung der Bagdadbahn. Hamburg: 1916.

Odysseus [Sir Charles Eliot]. Turkey in Europe. Arnold 1900. *7s. 6d.*

Parfit, Canon J. T. Twenty Years in Baghdad and Syria, showing Germany's bid for the mastery of the East. By the present Chaplain of Jerusalem. Simpkin, Marshall 1916. *1s.*

Pears, Sir Edwin. Forty Years in Constantinople. Illustrated. Jenkins 1915. *16s.*

—— Turkey and its People. Methuen 1911. *12s. 6d.*

Phillipson, Coleman, and Buxton, Noel. The Question of the Bosphorus and Dardanelles. Stevens & Haynes 1917. *12s. 6d.*

Pinon, René. L'Europe et l'Empire Ottoman. Aspects actuels de la Question d'Orient. Perrin 1909. 5 fr.

—— L'Europe et la jeune Turquie. Les aspects nouveaux de la Question d'Orient. Perrin 1911. 5 fr.

Ramsay, Sir W. M. Impressions of Turkey during Twelve Years' Wanderings. Cheaper edn. Hodder & Stoughton 1916. *2s.*

—— The Revolution [of 1908] in Constantinople and Turkey. A Diary. With episodes and photographs by Lady Ramsay. Cheaper edn. Hodder & Stoughton 1916. *5s.*

Ramsay, Sir W. M. The Intermixture of races in Asia Minor. Published for the Brit. Academy. Milford 1907. 3*s.* 6*d.*

Sykes, Lieut. Col. Sir Mark, M.P. The Caliph's Last Heritage: a short history of the Turkish Empire. Illustrations and maps. Macmillan 1915. 20*s.*

Toynbee, Arnold J. The Murderous Tyranny of the Turks. With Preface by Viscount Bryce. Hodder & Stoughton 1917. 2*d.*

Turkey: A Past and a Future. With maps. Reprinted from the Round Table. Hodder & Stoughton 1917. 6*d.*

Turkey in Asia. With a map. (O.P.) Oxford Univ. Press. 2*d.*

Van Dyck, E. A. Capitulations of the Ottoman Empire 1881-82.

Warfield, Wm. The Gate of Asia. Putnam 1917.

(*b*) Arabia.

Bury, G. Wymans. Arabia Infelix; or, The Turks in Yamen. Macmillan.

Doughty, C. M. Travels in Arabia Deserta. 2 vols. Camb. Univ. Press 1888. New edn. Cope 1920.

—— Wanderings in Arabia. Abridged edn. by Edmund Garnett. 2 vols. Duckworth 1912. 30*s.*

(*c*) Armenia.

Buxton, Noel, and Buxton, Harold. Travel and Politics in Armenia. Illustrated. Smith, Elder 1914. 5*s.*

Ciobanian, Arsciag. L'Armenia sotto il giogo turco. (A lecture delivered in Paris, May 1915.) Introduction by Paul Doumer. Illustrated. Turin: 1917. 1 l.

—— (Tchobanian). The people of Armenia: their past, their culture, the future. Dent 1914. 1*s.* 6*d.*

Williams, W. Llewellyn. Armenia, Past and Present. P. S King & Son.

(*d*) Cyprus.

Cromer, Earl of. Modern Egypt. 2 vols. Macmillan 1908. 30*s.*

—— Abbas II [1892-95]. Macmillan 1915 7*s.* 6*d.*

—— Speeches and Miscellaneous Writings 1882-1911. (Privately printed.) 1912.

Green, A. O. Cyprus: A Short Account of its History and Present State. Collart 1915. 2*s.* 6*d.*

Milner, Lord. England in Egypt. Tenth edn. Arnold 1903. 7*s.* 6*d.*

Orr, C. W. Cyprus under British Rule. R. Scott 1918.

(*e*) Egypt.

Weigall, A. E. History of Events in Egypt 1798-1914. Blackwood 1915. 10*s*. 6*d*.

(*f*) Macedonia.

Brailsford, H. N. Macedonia: its races and their future. Methuen 1906. 12*s*. 6*d*.

(*g*) Mesopotamia.

Bevan, Edwyn. The Land of the Two Rivers. An Historical Account of Mesopotamia. Arnold 1918. 3*s*.

Brooks, Charles S. Journeys to Bagdad. Yale Univ. Press: Milford 1916. 6*s*. 6*d*.

Parfit, Rev. Canon. Mesopotamia, the Key to the Future. Map. Hodder & Stoughton 1917. 6*d*.

(*h*) Syria and Palestine.

Bentwich, Norman. Palestine of the Jews: Past, Present and Future. Broadway House 1918. 6*s*.

Hyamson, A. M. Palestine: The Re-birth of an Ancient People. Sidgwick & Jackson.

Jannaway, F. G. Palestine and the Powers. Elliot Stock.

Montran, Nadra. Le Syrie de demain. French interests in Syria, railways, &c. Plon-Nourrit 1916. 6 fr.

Roederer, Dr. C. et Paul. La Syrie et la France. Berger-Levrault 1917. 4 fr.

Ruppin, A. Syrien als Wirthschaftsgebiet. 1917. 11 mk. 50.

Smith, Very Rev. Sir G. Adam. Syria and the Holy Land. Maps. Hodder & Stoughton 1918. 1*s*.

Tyan, Prince Ferdinand. The Entente Cordiale in Lebanon. T. Fisher Unwin.

(20) *Persia.*

Chirol, Sir Valentine. The Middle Eastern Question. Murray 1903. 18*s*.

Curzon of Kedleston, Lord. Persia and the Persian Question. 2 vols. 1892.

Hamilton, A. Problems of the Middle East. Eveleigh Nash 1909 12*s*. 6*d*.

Sykes, Lieut.-Colonel P. M. A History of Persia. With maps and illustrations. 2 vols. 2nd edn. Macmillan 1921 40*s*.

(21) *Poland*.

Askenazy, Prof. Simon. Dantzig and Poland. Transl. from the Polish by W. J. Rose. Allen & Unwin 1921. 10*s*.

Boswell, A. Bruce. Poland and the Poles. Plates and maps. 1919. 12*s*. 6*d*.

Brandes, Georg. Poland: a Study of the Land, People, and Literature. Constable. 12*s*.

D'Acandia, Giorgio. La Questione Polacca. Catania: Battiati 1916. 5 l.

Dmowski, R. La Question Polonaise. Translated from the Polish, with preface by Anatole Leroy-Beaulieu. Colin. 4 fr.

Drogoslaw (pseud). Poland and the Polish Nation. (Translation.) With Preface by Percy Alden, M.P. St. Catherine Press 1917. 1*s*

Ehrlich, Ludwik. Poland, Prussia and Culture. (Oxford Pamphlets.) Milford 1916. 3*d*.

Eversley, Lord. The Partitions of Poland. An historical sketch dealing specially with Prussia's share in the partitions. Fisher Unwin. 7*s*. 6*d*.

Feldman, W. Geschichte der politischen Ideen in Polen seit dessen Teilungen (1795-1914). Münich and Berlin: Oldenbourg 1917. 30 mk.

Gardner, Monica M. Poland: a Study in National Idealism. Burns & Oates 1915. 3*s*. 6*d*.

Gurney, A. E. The Population of the Polish Commonwealth. With preface by Ludwig Janowski. Published for the Polish Information Committee. Allen & Unwin 1916. 6*d*.

Harley, J. H. Poland, Past and Present. With introduction by Ladiolas Mickiewicz. Allen & Unwin 1917. 4*s*. 6*d*.

Hill, Ninian. Poland and the Polish Question. Impressions and Afterthoughts. Illustrated. Allen & Unwin 1916. 10*s*. 6*d*.

Holewinski, Jan de. An Outline of the History of Polish Literature. Preface by G. P. Gooch. Allen & Unwin 1916. 6*d*.

Kowalczyk, Jan. J. Prussian Poland: A Stronghold of German Militarism. Copenhagen: Petersen 1917. n.p.

Kozicki, S. La Pologne depuis le Congrès de Vienne (1815-1915). Agence Polonaise de Presse 1917. n.p.

Kucharski, Rajmund. Poland's Struggle for Independence. Allen & Unwin 1916. 6*d*.

Ledochowska, Countess Julie. Poland, Ravaged and Bereaved. A lecture. With preface by H. Sienkiewicz. St. Catherine Press 1916. 6*d*.
Lipkowski, Joseph. La Question polonaise et les Slaves de l'Europe centrale. Edition anglo-française. Preface by Prof. Séailles. Maps. Polonia (10 rue N.D. de Lorette) 1915. 3 fr. 50 c.
Little, Frances Delanoy. Sketches in Poland. Melrose 1915. 9*s*.
Litwinski, Léon. Intellectual Poland. A lecture. With preface by Viscount Bryce. Published for the Polish Information Committee Allen & Unwin 1916. 6*d*.
Natkowski, Waclaw. Poland as a Geographical Entity. With preface by J. Fairgrieve. Published for the Polish Information Committee. First published 1912. Allen & Unwin 1917. 6*d*.
Phillips, Prof. W. A. Poland (a history of the Polish Question). Home Univ. Library. Williams & Norgate 1916.
Polish Question, The, as an International Problem. Published for the Polish Information Committee. Allen & Unwin 1916. 6*d*.
Posner, Stanislaw. La Pologne d'hier et de demain. Introduction par M. G. Renard. Alcan 1916. 1 fr. 25 c.
—— Poland as an Independent Economic Unit. Introduction by Sidney Webb. Allen & Unwin 1916. 6*d*.
Slocombe, G. E. Poland. Jack 1917. 2*s*. 6*d*.
Waliszewski, K. Poland the Unknown. Translation from the French. Heinemann 1919. 10*s*. 6*d*.
Whitton, Lieut.-Colonel. F. E. A History of Poland; from the earliest times to the present day. Maps. Constable 1917. 8*s*. 6*d*.
Woroniecki, E., Zaleski, S. S. and Perlowski, J. Poland: her People, History, Industries, Finance, &c. Edited by Erasmus Piltz. Jenkins 1918. 6*s*.
Zaleski, August. Landsmarks of Polish History. With introduction by R. W. Seton-Watson. Published for the Polish Information Committee. Allen & Unwin 1916. 6*d*.

(22) *Portugal.*

Young, G. History of Portugal. Clarendon Press 1917. 5*s*.

(23) *Rumania.*

Comnéne, N. P. La Dobrogea (Dobrudja). Essai historique, économique, ethnographique et politique. Maps. Payot. 3 fr.
Damé, Fr. Histoire de la Roumanie contemporaine. Alcan. 7 fr.

Gordon, Mrs. Will. Rumania Yesterday and To-day, with introduction and two chapters by the Queen of Rumania. Illustrated. John Lane 1918. 10*s*. 6*d*.
Hunfalvy. Die Rumänen und ihre Ansprüche (antagonistic to Rumania). 1883.
Hurst, A. Hersecovici. Rumania and Great Britain, with Preface by Sir Thomas Dunlop. Hodder & Stoughton 1917. 1*s*.
Jorga, Prof. N. Histoire des relations anglo-roumaines. Jassy: Neâmul Romanesc 1917. 3 fr.
—— Histoire des Roumains de Transylvanie et de Hongrie. 2 vols. Bucarest: Göbl 1916.
—— Histoire des relations entre la France et les Roumains. Préface de M. Charles Bemont. Payot 1918. 4 fr. 50 c.
Kirke, Dorothea. Domestic Life in Rumania. Lane 1916. 5*s*.
Lebrun, Francis. La Dobroudja, esquisse historique, géographique et statistique. Avec carte (terre roumain qui les Bulgares prétendent leur appartenir ethnographiquement). Alcan 1918. n.p.
Magnus, Leonard A. Rumania's Cause and Ideals. Kegan Paul 1917. 3*s*. 6*d*.
Marie, Queen of Rumania. My Country (published for the Times). Hodder & Stoughton 1916. 5*s*.
Mavrodin, Const. D. La Roumanie contemporaine. Son importance dans le Concert balkanique, et pour la Guerre présente. Preface by G. Lacour-Gayet. Plon. 3 fr.
Mitrany, D. Rumania: her History and Politics. (O.P.) Clarendon Press 1915. 4*d*.
Montesquiou, Comte Léon de. Notes sur la Roumanie. Illustrated. Nouv. Libr. Nationale. 2 fr.
Pittard, Eugène. La Roumanie (Valachie-Moldavie, Dobroudja). Illustrations. Paris: Bossard 1918. 9 fr.
Sirianu, M. R. La Question de Transylvanie et l'unité politique roumaine. Jouve 1916. 7 fr. 50 c.

(24) *Russia.*

(*a*) Historical.

Beazley, R., Forbes, N., and Birkett, G. A. Russia from the Varangians to the Bolsheviks. With introduction by Ernest Barker. Oxford Univ. Press 1918. 8*s*. 6*d*.
Cazalet, Lucy. A Short History of Russia. With illustrations and a map. Oxford Univ. Press 1915. 2*s*.
Gilliard, Pierre. Thirteen Years at the Russian Court. A personal record of the last years and death of Nicholas II and his family. Transl. from the French. Hutchinson 1921. 24*s*.

Iswolsky, Alexander, Memoirs of, formerly Minister of Foreign Affairs and Ambassador to France. Hutchinson 1920. 12*s.* 6*d.*

Kluchevsky, V. O. A History of Russia. Translated from the Russian by C. J. Hogarth. 3 vols. Dent 1913. 42*s.*

La Chesnais, P. G. La Révolution Russe et ses résultats, 1904-1908. Mercure de France 1917. 75 c.

Mavor, Prof. J. An Economic History of Russia. 2 vols. Dent. 31*s.* 6*d.*

Milioukov, Paul. La Crise russe; ses origines, son évolution, ses conséquences. Translated from the Russian. Paris: Libr. Universelle 1907. 15 fr.

Nekludoff, A. Diplomatic Reminiscences before and during the World War, 1911-17 (by the former Russian Minister at Sofia and Stockholm and Ambassador at Madrid). Transl. from the French. Murray 1920. 15*s.*

Rambaud, Alfred. Histoire de la Russie depuis les origines jusqu'à nos jours. 6th edn. Hachette 1914. 6 fr.

Shearwood, J. A. Russia's Story; being a short history from the earliest times. Illustrated. Jarrolds 1918. 5*s.*

Skrine, F. H. Expansion of Russia, 1815-1900. 2nd edn. Camb. Univ. Press 1904. 6*s.*

Yarmolinsky, A. (Edr.) Memoirs of Count Witte. Transl. from the Russian. Heinemann 1921. 18*s.*

(*b*) Descriptive, etc.

Alexinsky, Gregor. Russia and Europe (by an ex-Deputy to the Duma). Translated by B. Miall. Fisher Unwin 1917. 10*s.* 6*d.*

—— Modern Russia. Translated by Bernard Miall. Fisher Unwin. 15*s.*

Baring, Hon. Maurice. An Outline of Russian Literature. Williams & Norgate 1914. 1*s.*

—— A Year in Russia (the year of revolt, 1906). Revised edn. Methuen 1917. 6*s.*

—— The Mainsprings of Russia. Nelson. 2*s.*

—— The Russian People. Methuen. 15*s.*

Bishop, Rev. G. B. H. The Religion of Russia. A study of the Orthodox Church in Russia. Society of SS. Peter & Paul. 5*s.*

Briantchaninoff, A. N. Ideological Foundations of Russian Slavonism. Translated from the Russian. King 1916. 1*s.*

Byford, Charles S. The Soul of Russia. Being an account of the religious forces at work in the modern Russian Empire. Kingsgate Press 1914. 5*s.*

Drage, Geoffrey. Russian Affairs. Murray 1904. *21s.*

Elchanninov, Major-General A. The Tsar and his People. Translated by A. P. W. Hodder & Stoughton. *2s.*

Gettlich, Wlad. The German Grip on Russia. Translated from the French. Williams, Lea & Co. 1918. n.p.

Heyking, Baron A. (edr.). Practical Guide for Russian Consular Officers and all Persons having Relations with Russia. 2nd edn., revised and amplified. King 1916. *12s.*

Howe, Sonia E. Some Russian Heroes, Saints and Sinners. Illustrated. Lippincott 1917. $2.50.

Jarintzoff, Mme. M. Russia; the Country of Extremes. Illustrated. Sidgwick & Jackson 1914. *18s.*

Kennard, H. P., and Peacock, Neata (Edrs.). Russian Year Book 1914. Eyre & Spottiswoode. *10s. 6d.*

Leger, Louis. Le Panslavisme et l'intérêt francais. Flammarion 1917. 3 fr. 50 c.

Leroy-Beaulieu, Anatole. L'Empire des Tsars, et les Russes. 3 vols. English transl. 1896. Hachette. 7 fr. 50 c. per vol.

Lethbridge, Alan. The New Russia: from the White Sea to the Siberian Steppe. Mills & Boon. *16s.*

Lethbridge, Marjorie and Alan. The Soul of the Russian. Lane 1916. *3s. 6d.*

Mackail, J. W. Russia's Gift to the World. Hodder. *2d.*

Masaryk, Prof. T. G. Russland und Europa. Studien über die geistigen Strömungen in Russland. Transl. under title The Spirit of Russia. Allen & Unwin 1919.

Morfill, W. R. Russia. Fisher Unwin. *5s.*

Novikoff, Olga ("O.K"). Russian Memories. With introduction by Stephen Graham. Jenkins 1916. *10s. 6d.*

Pokrowski, M. Aus den Geheim-Archiven des Zaren. Berlin: Scherl 1919. 2 m.

Rudwitsky, S. The Ukraine and the Ukrainians. By a lecturer at the University of Lemberg. Translated from the German by J. W. Hartman. Ukrainian Nat. Council.

Russian Church, The. Lectures on its history, constitution, doctrine and ceremonial. Preface by the Lord Bishop of London. S.P.C.K. 1916. *1s. 6d.*

Sarolea, Charles. Europe's Debt to Russia. Heinemann 1915. *3s. 6d.*

Sherwell, A. The Russian Vodka Monopoly. King. *4d.*

Siefert, B. von. (Edr.). Diplomatische Aktenstücke (Russian) zur Ententepolitik der Vorkriegsjahre (first published in the Hearst Press). Verein wissenschaftl. Verleger, Berlin 1921.

Steveni, William B. Petrograd Past and Present. Richards 1915. *12s. 6d.*

Times Book of Russia : Finance, Commerce and Industries. With introduction by Sir Donald Mackenzie Wallace. Maps. Times Office 1916. *2s.*

Vinogradoff, Prof. Paul. Russia : the Psychology of a Nation. (O.P.) Oxford Univ. Press. *1d.*

—— The Russian Problem. Constable. *1s.*

—— Self-Government in Russia. Constable 1915. *2s. 6d.*

Wallace, Sir D. Mackenzie. Russia. Revised edn. 2 vols. Cassell 1905. *12s. 6d.*

—— Russia and the Balkan States. Encycl. Brit. Co. *2s. 6d.*

Wesselitsky, G. de. Russia and Democracy : the German Canker in Russia. Influence of Germany on Russian Government and Administration. With Preface by Henry Cust. Heinemann, for the Central Committee. *1s.*

Wiener, Prof. Leo. An Interpretation of the Russian People (from the Liberal point of view). With introduction by Sir D. Mackenzie Wallace. McBride. $1.25.

Windt, Capt. Harry de. Russia as I Know It. Chapman & Hall 1917. *10s. 6d.*

(25) *Scandinavian States.*

Brown, R. N. Rudmore. Spitsbergen. An account of exploration, mineral riches, and future potentialities 1919. *25s.*

Buyse, T. C. Le régime prussien en pays conquis. Le Slesvig danois de 1864 à 1916. Payot 1917. 75 c.

Hansen, M. H. P. and Mœller, J. C. La Question du Slesvig, traduction Jacques de Coussange. (Comment ce duché, tout danois pendant tant de siècles est-il devenu tout allemand au sud, incertain dans sa partie centrale.) Chapelot 1918.

Jessen, F. de. Manuel historique de la question du Slesvig. Copenhagen 1906.

Rosendal, H. The problem of Danish Slesvig. A question for the British Empire. (Translated from the Danish.) Oxford Univ. Press 1916. *8d.*

Spitsbergen, Conférence internationale de. Actes et documents. Christiania, Gröndahl 1914.

(26) *Serbia.*

Bérard, Victor. La Serbie et son histoire. A lecture. Colin 1915. 50 c.

Chirol, Sir Valentine. Serbia and the Serbs. (O.P.) Oxford Univ. Press. *2d.*

Denis, Prof. E. La Grande Serbie. Geographical and historical, including Bosnia and Herzegovina, 1804-1915. Delagrave 1915. 3 fr. 50 c.

Gordon, Jan. A Balkan Freebooter: being the exploits of the Serbian outlaw and comitaj, Petko Moritch. Translated by J. G. Smith, Elder 1916. 7*s.* 6*d.*

Laffan, R. G. D. The Guardians of the Gate. Historical lectures on the Serbs. Preface by Admiral Troubridge. Oxford Univ. Press 1918. 5*s.*

Lazarovich-Hrebelelianovich, Prince and Princess. The Servian People: their Past Glory and their Destiny. 2 vols. Illustrated. Werner Laurie. 24*s.*

Mijatovich, Chedo. Servia of the Servians. Pitman. 6*s.*

Petrovitch, Woislav M. Hero Tales and Legends of the Serbians. With preface by Chedo Mijatovitch, and 32 illustrations by W. Sewell and Gilb. James. Harrap 1914.

—— Serbia: her History and Customs. Harrap. 3*s.* 6*d.*

—— Serbia: her People, History and Aspirations. Harrap 1915. 3*s.* 6*d.*

Price, Crawfurd. The Dawn of Armageddon, or The Provocation by Serbia. An account of the Pre-War relations of Serbia and Austria-Hungary. Simpkin Marshall 1917. 6*d.*

Temperley, H. W. V. A History of Serbia. Maps. Macmillan 1917. 10*s.* 6*d.*

Waring, Miss L. F. Serbia (Home Univ. Library). Williams & Norgate 1917. 1*s.*

Yakchitch, Grégoire. L'Europe et la Résurrection de la Serbie, 1804-54. Preface by Emile Haumant. 2nd edn. Hachette 1917. 10 fr.

Zupanić, Dr. Niko. The Strategical Significance of Serbia. Reprinted from the *Nineteenth Century*. 1916.

See also II. B. (30) *Yugo-Slavs.*

(27) *Spain.*

Clarke, H. Butler. Modern Spain 1815-98. Camb. Univ. Press 1906. 7*s.* 6*d.*

Hume, Martin A. S. The Spanish People. 1901.

—— Modern Spain 1788-1898. 1899.

(28) *Switzerland.*

Oechsli, Prof, W. Switzerland 1492-1911. Camb. Univ. Press 1921. 10*s.* 6*d.*

(29) *United States.*

America's Foreign Relations. 2 vols. Nash 1916. 24*s.*

Bishop, J. B. Life of Theodore Roosevelt. 2 vols. Hodder & Stoughton 1920. 42*s.*

Channing, E. Students' History of the United States. 1898.

Hart, A. B. American History 1492-1900. 4 vols. 1897-1901.

Roosevelt, Theodore. Addresses &c. 1902-4. 1904.

Root, Elihu. Military and Colonial Policy of the United States. Harvard and Oxford Univ. Presses 1917. 8*s.* 6*d.*

(30) *Yugo-Slavs.*

Bailey, W. F. The Slavs of the War Zone. Chapman & Hall 1916. 10*s.* 6*d.*

Evans, Sir Arthur. A diagrammatic Map of Slav Territories east of the Adriatic, showing the ethnological divisions of Bosnia, Herzegovina, Croatia, Dalmatia, &c. also Montenegro and part of Serbia. Published for the Balkan Committee. Sifton, Praed 1915. 2*s.* 6*d.*

Forbes, Nevill. The Southern Slavs. (O.P.) Oxford Univ. Press. 2*d.*

Hinkovitch, M. H. Les Yougoslaves. Leur passé, leur avenir. Republished from Revue Anthropologique. Alcan 1916.

Histoire Yougoslave. Bibliothèque Yougoslave, No. 3.) Plon-Nourrit 1916. 50 c.

Illyricus (pseud.). La Question de Trieste. Essai sur le problème jougoslave dans les pays "irredente." Par Illyricus. Geneva: Renaud 1915. 50 c.

Krek, Ivan. Les Slovènes. Traduit par A. U. Maps. Félix: Paris 1917. 1 fr.

Lanux, Pierre de. La Yougoslavie. La France et les Serbes. Aves une préface de M. Paul Adam. Payot 1916. 3 fr. 50 c.

Léger, Louis. Serbes, Bulgares, et Croates. Paris 1915.

Le pays et le peuple yougoslaves. (Bibliothèque yougoslave, No. 2.) Plon-Nourrit 1916. 50 c.

Les lettres, les sciences, et les arts yougoslaves. (Bibliothèque yougoslave, No. 4.) Plon-Nourrit 1916. 50 c.

Les persécutions des Yougoslaves. Preface by Victor Bérard. Plon-Nourrit 1916. 50 c.

L'unité yougoslave. Manifeste de la jeunesse serbe, croate et slovène réunies. Avec préface du professeur Masaryk. Map. Plon-Nourrit 1915. 1 fr.

Primorac, Von K. La Question Yougo-Slave. En de historique, économique et sociale. Paris: Société Yougoslavia 1918.

Seton-Watson, R. W. The Southern Slav Question and the Hapsburg Monarchy. Constable. 12*s.* 6*d.*

Southern Slav Programme. The Southern Slavs: Land and People. A sketch of Southern Slav history and culture. (The Southern Slav Library.) Nisbet 1915-16. 2*d.* each.

Taylor, A. H. E. The Future of the Southern Slavs. T. Fisher Unwin.

See also II. B. (26) *Serbia.*

III.—STATE PAPERS &c. ISSUED SINCE 1st AUGUST, 1914.

A.—General.

Agreement between France, Russia, Great Britain and Italy, signed at London, April 25, 1915. Miscellaneous, No. 7 (1920). [Cmd. 671.] H.M.S.O. 1920. 1*d.*

Allied Note, The, of January 10, 1917—Despatch to H.M. Ambassador at Washington respecting. Miscellaneous, No. 3 (1917). [Cd. 8439.] H.M.S.O. 1917. 1*d.*

Allied War Aims. Note from the Russian Provisional Government and the British Reply respecting the. Miscellaneous, No. 10 (1917). [Cd. 8587.] H.M.S.O. 1917. 1*d.*

Armistices concluded between the Allied Governments and the Governments of Germany, Austria-Hungary and Turkey. Terms of the. [Cmd. 53.] H.M.S.O. 1919. 2*d.*

Conditions of an Armistice with Germany, signed Nov. 11, 1918. With map. Miscellaneous, No. 25, 1918 [Cd. 9212]. H.M.S.O. 1918. 4*d.*

Declaration between the United Kingdom, France and Russia, engaging not to conclude peace separately during the present European War; signed Sept. 5, 1914. Treaty Series 1915. No. 1 [Cd. 7737.] H.M.S.O. ½*d.*

Declaration between the United Kingdom, France, Italy, Japan and Russia engaging not to conclude Peace separately during the present War. Signed at London Nov. 30, 1915. Treaty Series, 1915. No. 14. [Cd. 8107.] H.M.S.O. 1915. ½*d.*

Economic Conference of the Allies. Recommendations of the Economic Conference held at Paris on June 14, 15, 16, and 17, 1916. [Cd. 8271.] H.M.S.O. 1916. 1*d.*

Examination of Parcels and Letter Mails. Memorandum presented by H. M. Government and the French Government to Neutral Governments regarding the. Miscellaneous, No. 9 (1916). [Cd. 8223.] H.M.S.O. 1916. 1*d.*

Examination of Parcels and Letter Mails. Memorandum addressed by the French and British Governments to the United States Government respecting the. Miscellaneous, No. 2 (1917). [Cd. 8438.] H.M.S.O. 1917. 1*d.*

Exchange of Notes respecting the Accession of Japan to the Declaration of Sept. 5, 1914, between the United Kingdom, France, and Russia, engaging not to conclude Peace separately during the present European War. London, Oct. 19, 1915. Treaty Series, 1915. No. 9. [Cd. 8014.] H.M.S.O. 1915. ½*d.*

German Note, The (Dec. 19, 1916), and the reply of the Allies (Dec. 30, 1916). Texts. Fisher Unwin. 1917. 1*d.*

German Peace Note. Reply to the, communicated by the French Government, on behalf of the Allied Powers, to the United States Ambassador in Paris, Dec. 30, 1916. Miscellaneous, No. 4 (1917). [Cd. 8467.] H.M.S.O. 1917. 1*d.*

Greek Government. Collective Note addressed to the Greek Government by the French, British, and Russian Ministers, and the Reply thereto. Miscellaneous, No. 27 (1916). [Cd. 8298.] H.M.S.O. 1916. 1*d.*

Guerre de 1914. Documents officiels. Textes législatifs et réglementaires. (Vol. XIII, to Sept. 15, 1916.) Dalloz 1916

Guerre de 1914, La. Recueil de Documents intéressant le Droit International. With introduction by P. Fauchille. Vol. I. Paris. Pedone 1916.

Imperial War Conference, 1917. Extracts from the Minutes of Proceedings; and Papers laid before the Conference. [Cd. 8566.] H.M.S.O. 1917. 1*s.* 6*d.*

Imperial War Conference, 1918. Resolutions agreed to by the Conference. Extracts from Minutes of Proceedings; and Papers laid before the Conference. [Cd. 9177.] H.M.S.O. 1918, 2*s.*

Imports into Scandinavia and Holland during 1916 and 1917. Statistics of. Miscellaneous, No. 8 (1918). [Cd. 8989.] H.M.S.O. 1918. 1*d.*

Inter-Allied Conference on the After-care of Disabled Men, May 20-25, 1918. Supplement to volume of Reports. H.M.S.O. 1918. 2*s.*

Intoxicating Liquors. Restriction in Foreign Countries during the War. Correspondence relative to the measures taken. H.M.S.O. 1915. 2½*d.*

Merchant Tonnage and the Submarine. Supplementary Statement, showing for the United Kingdom and for the World, for the period Aug. 1914-Oct. 1918. (1) Merchant Tonnage losses, (2) Merchant Shipbuilding output, (3) enemy vessels captured (&c.). [Cd. 9221.] H.M.S.O. 1918. 2*d.*

Note addressed, Sept. 1918, by the Austro-Hungarian Government to the Governments of all the Belligerent States, proposing conversations respecting the fundamental principles for the conclusion of Peace. Miscellaneous, No. 21 (1918). [Cd. 9148.] H.M.S.O. 1918. 1*d.*

Note communicated by the United States Ambassador, Dec. 12, 1916. Proposal by Germany and her Allies to enter into Peace Negotiations. Miscellaneous, No. 38 (1916). [Cd. 8406.] H.M.S.O. 1916. ½*d.*

Note communicated by the United States Ambassador, Dec. 20, 1916. Suggestion that the Belligerents in the present European War may state terms. Miscellaneous, No. 39 (1916). [Cd. 8431.] H.M.S.O. 1916. ½*d.*

Peace imposed upon Roumania by the Central Powers. Observations by the Allied Ministers at Jassy with regard to the conditions of. Miscellaneous, No. 15 (1918). [Cd. 9102.] H.M.S.O. 1918. 1*d.*

Peace Proposals made by His Holiness the Pope to the Belligerent Powers on Aug. 1, 1917, and correspondence relative thereto. Miscellaneous, No. 7 (1919). [Cmd. 261.] H.M.S.O. 1919. 2*d.*

Prizes Captured During the Present War. Exchange of Notes between the United Kingdom and France and Russia modifying Article 2 of the Convention of Nov. 9, 1914, relating to Treaty Series, 1916, No. 5 (8vo.). [Cd. 8401.] H.M.S.O. 1916. ½*d.*

—— Accession of Italy to the Convention of Nov. 9, 1914, between the United Kingdom and France. London, Jan. 15, 1917. Treaty Series, 1917, No. 6 (8vo.). [Cd. 8475.] H.M.S.O. 1917. 1*d.*

Recueil des Documents relatifs à la Guerre. (1) Aug. 3-Nov. 30; (2) Dec. 1-31; published in the Journal Officiel by the Ministère des Finances, Egypt. Cairo: Imprimerie Nationale. 3*s.*

Reply of the Allied Governments to the Note communicated by the United States Ambassador on Dec. 20, 1916, containing the suggestion by the President of the United States of America that the Belligerents . . . may state terms. . . Miscellaneous, No. 5 (1917). [Cd. 8468.] H.M.S.O. 1917. 1*d.*

Secret Agreements, The. Texts, with preface by C. R. Buxton. National Labour Press, Manchester, 1918. 6*d.*

Secret Treaties, The, and understandings. Text of the available documents, with comments and notes by F. S. Cocks; and a preface by Charles Trevelyan, M.P. 2nd edn. Union of Democrative Control, 1918. *2s.*

Treatment of Belligerent Submarines in Neutral Waters. Memorandum communicated by the Allied Governments to the Governments of certain Neutral Maritime States respecting the. Miscellaneous, No. 33 (1916). [Cd. 8349.] H.M.S.O. 1916. *½d.*

B.—Special (Separate Countries.)

(1) *Austria-Hungary.*

Diplomatische Aktenstücke betreffend die Beziehungen Oesterreich-Ungarns zu Italien in der Zeit vom 20 Juli 1914 bis 23 Mai 1915. (Austrian Red Book.) Vienna: Manzsche Hofverlag 1915. 1 mk. 20.

Diplomatische Aktenstücke betreffend die Beziehungen Oesterreich-Ungarns zu Rumänien in der Zeit vom 22 Juli 914 bis 27 August 1916. (Austrian Red Book.) Vienna: Manzsche Hofverlag 1916. 1 mk.

Manteyer, C. E. (edr.). The Austrian Peace Offer (documents). Constable 1920.

Note addressed by the Austro-Hungarian Government to the Governments of all the Belligerent States (Sept. 1918). Miscellaneous, No. 21 (1918). [Cd. 9148.] H.M.S.O. 1918. *1d.*

(2) *Belgium.*

Aktenstücke, Belgische. Berichte d. belgischen Vertreter in Berlin, London u. Paris an d. Minist. d. Aeusseren in Brüssel 1905-14. Hrsg. v. Auswärt. Amt. Neue Ausg. 1 mk. 40.

Arrêtés et proclamations de guerre allemandes du 20 Août, 1914, au 25 Janvier 1915. Documents historiques affichés à Bruxelles pendant l'occupation. The Hague: Van Stockum 1915.

Belgian Government, Protest by the, against the German allegation that Belgium had forfeited her Neutrality before the outbreak of War. H.M.S.O. *1d.*

Belgique, La, et l'Allemagne. Textes et documents, précédés d'un avertissement au lecteur par Henri Davignon. Harrison 1915.

Belgium and Germany. Texts and documents. With foreword by Henri Davignon. Translated from the French. Nelson. *6d.*

Belgium, The Case of, in the light of Official Reports found in the Secret Archives of the Belgian Government after the occupation of Brussels; with facsimiles of the Documents. Introduction by Dr. Bernhard Dernburg (on the German side). The Internat. Monthly, 1123 Broadway, New York.

German Calumnies: The Anglo-Belgian Conventions. With introduction by Emile Brunet, Member of the Brussels Bar. (Facsimiles of the Documents.) Hicks & Wilkinson. *2d.*

Réponse au Livre Blanc allemand du 10 Mai 1915, Die völkerrechswidrige Führung des belgischen Volkskriegs. (Official reply to the German charges against the Belgians.) Berger-Levrault 1916. English translation: Reply to the German White Book of May 10, 1915, Die völkerrechtswidrige Führung des belgischen Volkskriegs, by the Belgian Ministry of Justice and Ministry of Foreign Affairs. (Belgium Grey Book, III.) H.M.S.O. 1918. *5s. 5d.*

Reports of the Commission for Relief in Belgium. (1) Belgian Section for period of eight months to June 30, 1915; (2) Northern France Section for period of three months to June 30, 1915. 3 London Wall Buildings, E.C.

Violation, The, of the Neutrality of Belgium. With preface (9 pp.) by M. Paul Hymans, Belgian Minister in London. (Documents.) Darling.

(3) *British Empire.*

Agriculture. Report (Part I) of the Agricultural Policy Sub-Committee appointed in August 1916, to consider and report upon the methods of effecting an increase in the home-grown food supplies. [Cd. 8506.] H.M.S.O. 1917. *3d.*

Aliens. Alien Enemies Repatriated from India on the S.S. 'Golconda.' Correspondence with the United States Ambassador respecting the safety of. Miscellaneous, No. 4, 1916. [Cd. 8163.] H.M.S.O. 1916. *½d.*

—— —— Further correspondence with the United States Ambassador respecting the safety of. Miscellaneous, No. 8 (1916). [Cd. 8178.] H.M.S.O. 1916. *1d.*

—— Draft of an Order in Council to regulate the admission of Aliens to the United Kingdom, and the Supervision of Aliens in the United Kingdom after the War. [Cmd. 172.] H.M.S.O. 1919. *2d.*

Allied Territories in the Occupation of the Enemy, Relief of. Correspondence with the United States Ambassador regarding the. Miscellaneous, No. 24 (1916). [Cd. 8295.] H.M.S.O. 1916. *½d.*

Allied Territories in the Occupation of the Enemy, Relief of. Further Correspondence respecting the. Miscellaneous, No. 32 (1916). [Cd. 8348.] H.M.S.O. 1916. 3*d.*

Archibald, J. F. Austrian and German Papers found in possession of. Falmouth, Aug. 30, 1915. [Cd. 8012.] H.M.S.O. 1915 (Sept.). 2½*d.*

Armenians. Treatment of, in the Ottoman Empire 1915-16. Documents presented to Viscount Grey of Fallodon, Secretary of State for Foreign Affairs, by Viscount Bryce. Miscellaneous, No. 31 (1916). (8vo.) (With map.) [Cd. 8325.] H.M.S.O. 1916. 2*s.*

Army. Papers relating to Scales of Pensions and Allowances of Officers and Men of the Oversea Contingents and their Dependants. [Cd. 7793.] H.M.S.O. 1915. 1½*d.*

—— Shops' Committee. Report of the Committee appointed to consider the Conditions of Retail Trade which can best secure that further Enlistment of Men or their Employment in other National Services may not interfere with the Operations of that Trade. [Cd. 8113.] H.M.S.O. 1915. 1½*d.*

—— Regulations made by the Military Service (Civil Liabilities) Committee, with the concurrence of . . . H.M. Treasury. [Cd. 8249.] Wyman, May, 1916. 1½*d.*

—— List of Certified Occupations (for military exemption). R. 136 (revised). H.M.S.O. 1918. 1*d.*

Bad Time. Report and Statistics kept in Shipbuilding, Munitions and Transport Areas. H.M.S.O. 1915. 3*d.*

Belgian Refugees. First Report of the Departmental Committee appointed . . . to consider and report on questions arising in connection with the reception and employment of the Belgian Refugees in this country. [Cd. 7750.] H.M.S.O. 1914. 6½*d.*

—— Minutes of Evidence taken before the Departmental Committee [concerning] [etc., as above]. [Cd. 7779.] H.M.S.O. 1915. 1*s.* 10*d.*

—— Report on the work undertaken by the British Government in the reception and care of. H.M.S.O. 1920. 1*s.* 8*d.*

Belgium. Agreement between the United Kingdom and, respecting boundaries in East Africa, signed at London, Feb. 3, 1915. Maps. [Cmd. 517] H.M.S.O. 1920. 4*s.*

Censorship, Memorandum on the. [Cd. 7679.] 1915. 1*d.*

Ceylon. Correspondence relating to Disturbances in. [Cd. 8167.] H.M.S.O. 1916. 6*d.*

Clerical and Commercial Employments Committee. Report of the, with a view to advising what steps should be taken by the employment of women, or otherwise, to replace men withdrawn for service in the Military Forces. [Cd. 8110.] H.M.S.O. 1915. 1½*d.*

Coal. Conditions prevailing in the coal-mining industry due to the War. Departmental Committee on. Report. With Appendices, Part I. [Cd. 7939.] H.M.S.O. 1915. 5½*d.*

—— Part II. Minutes of Evidence and Index. [Cd. 8009.] H.M.S.O. 1915. 2*s.*

—— Second General Report. [Cd. 8147.] H.M.S.O. 1916. 3½*d.*

—— Third General Report. With Appendices. [Cd. 8345.] H.M.S.O. 1916. 2½*d.*

Coal. Report of the Departmental Committee appointed . . . to consider the position of the Coal Trade after the War. [Cd. 9093.] H.M.S.O. 1918. 4*d.*

Commercial and Industrial Policy, Committee on. (1) Interim Report on certain essential industries. [Cd. 9032.] (2) Interim Report on importation of goods from the present enemy countries after the War. [Cd. 9033.] (3) Interim Report on the treatment of exports from the United Kingdom and Overseas Possessions, and the conservation of the resources of the Empire during the transitional period after the War. [Cd. 9034.] H.M.S.O. 1918. 3*d.* each.

—— Final Report on commercial and industrial policy after the War. [Cd. 9035.] H.M.S.O. 1918. 10*d.*

Commissions and Committees, List of, set up to deal with Public Questions arising out of the War (1915.) [Cd. 7855.] H.M.S.O. ½*d.*

—— [Cd. 8256.] H.M.S.O. 1916. 1*d.*

—— [Cd. 8741.] H.M.S.O. 1917. 2*d.*

Defence of the Realm Losses Royal Commission, 1st Report. [Cd. 8359.] H.M.S.O. 1916. 1*d.*

—— 2nd Report. [Cd. 8751.] H.M.S.O. 1917. 6*d.*

—— 3rd Report. With Appendices. [Cd. 9181.] H.M.S.O. 1918. 6*d.*

—— 4th Report of the Commissioners (Dec. 1919). [Cmd. 404.] H.M.S.O. 1919. 6*d.*

Defence of the Realm Regulations (Manuals of Emergency Legislation). Consolidated and revised to Jan. 31, 1918. H.M.S.O. 1918. 7*d.*

Disabled Sailors and Soldiers, Committee on the Provision of Employment for. Report. [Cd. 7915.] H.M.S.O. 1915. 1½*d.*

Disabled Sailors and Soldiers, Report of the Departmental Committee on Compensation for, under the Workmen's Compensation Act 1906. H.M.S.O. 1918. 2*d.*

Distress. Prevention and Relief of Distress due to the War, Memorandum on the steps taken for the. [Cd. 7603.] H.M.S.O. 1914. 5½*d.*

Dominions. Correspondence relating to the Representation of the Self-governing Dominions on the Committee of Imperial Defence, and to a proposed Naval Conference (1914). H.M.S.O. 2*d.*

—— Correspondence regarding the Naval and Military Assistance afforded to H.M. Government by H.M. Overseas Dominions (Sept 1914). [Cd. 7607.] H.M.S.O. 2*d.*

—— Advances to H.M. Self-governing Dominions to meet the Naval and Military Expenditure, etc. Treasury Minute, dated Nov. 17, 1914. H.C. 47/1914-15. H.M.S.O. 1914-15. ½*d.*

—— Correspondence relating to Gifts of Foodstuffs and other Supplies to H.M. Government from the Oversea Dominions and Colonies. [Cd. 7608.] H.M.S.O. 1914. 2½*d.*

—— Further Correspondence regarding Gifts from the Oversea Dominions and Colonies. [Cd. 7646.] H.M.S.O. 1914. 5½*d.*

—— —— [Cd. 7875.] H.M.S.O. 1915. 1*s.* 2*d.*

East India. Papers relating to the support offered by the Princes and Peoples of India to His Majesty in connection with the War 1914). [Cd. 7624.] H.M.S.O. 2*d.*

East India (Constitutional Reforms). Addresses presented in India to His Excellency the Viceroy and the Right Honourable the Secretary of State for India. With Index. [Cd. 9178.] H.M.S.O. 1918. 1*s.*

—— Letter from the Government of India, 5th March 1919, and Enclosures, on the Questions raised in the Report on Indian Constitutional Reforms. (With map.) [Cmd. 123.] H.M.S.O. 1919. 3*s.* 6*d.*

East India (Government of India Bill). Memorandum by the Secretary of State for India regarding the Bill to make further Provision with respect to the Government of India. [Cmd. 175.] H.M.S.O. 1919. 2*d.*

East India (Constitutional Reforms: Lord Southborough's Committees). Vol. III. Views of the Government of India upon the Reports of Lord Southborough's Committees. [Cmd. 176.] H.M.S.O. 1919. 9*d.*

East India (Government of India Bill). Copy of the Government of India Act, 1915-16, showing Amendments proposed to be made by the Government of India Bill 1919. [Cmd. 187.] H.M.S.O. 1919. 6*d.*

East India (Sedition Committee 1918). Report of Committee appointed to investigate Revolutionary Conspiracies in India; with two Resolutions by the Government of India. [Cd. 9190.] H.M.S.O. 1918. 9*d.*

Electricity. Report of the Committee appointed to consider the question of Electric Power Supply. [Cd. 9062.] H.M.S.O. 1918. 3*d.*

—— Report of the Departmental Committee appointed to consider the position of the Electrical Trades after the War. [Cd. 9072.] H.M.S.O. 1918. 2*d.*

Emergency Legislation, 1st and 2nd Reports from the Select Committee on, together with the Proceedings of the Committee and Minutes of Evidence. H.M.S.O. 1919. 7½*d.*

Emergency Legislation, Manual of, comprising all the Acts of Parliament, Proclamations, Orders, etc., passed and made in consequence of the War, to Sept. 30, 1914. (Edited by Alexr. Pulling.) Darling 1914. 3*s.* 6*d.*

Emergency Legislation: Manual of, to Sept. 30, 1914. 3*s.* 6*d.* Supplement No. 2, to Dec. 5, 1914. 1*s.* 6*d.* Supplement No. 3, to April 30, 1915. 2*s.* 6*d.* Supplement No. 4, to Aug. 31, 1915. 2*s.* 6*d.* Financial edn., to June 4, 1915. 1*s.* Defence of the Realm Manual, 8th edn. 5*s.* Food Supply Manual, to Nov. 30, 1919. 6*s.* War Material Supplies Manual, 5th edn. 7s. 6d. H.M.S.O. 1914-19.

Emergency Legislation, Manuals of. Defence of the Realm Regulations. Consolidated and revised to March 31, 1918. H.M.S.O. 1918. 7*d.*

Emergency Legislation. Report (1st) from the Select Committee (on the meaning of the phrase "the end of the war.") H.M.S.O. 1918. 1*d.*

Employment, State of, in the United Kingdom in Oct. 1914. Report of the Board of Trade on the. [Cd. 7703.] H.M.S.O. 1914-15. 4½*d.*

—— [Cd. 7755.] H.M.S.O. 1915. 1½*d.*

Employment, State of, in the United Kingdom during February, 1915. With Appendices. [Cd. 7850.] H.M.S.O. 1915. 2½*d.*

Enemy Banks (London Agencies). Report of Sir W. Plender to the Chancellor of the Exchequer, dated Dec. 16, 1916. [Cd. 8430.] H.M.S.O. 1917. 3*d.*

—— Second Report of Sir William Plender, dated Dec. 13, 1917, covering the operations of the London Branches of these Banks for the period Oct. 1, 1916, to Sept. 30, 1917. With Appendices. [Cd. 8889.] H.M.S.O. 1918. 3*d.*

Engineering. Report of the Departmental Committee appointed . . . to consider the position of the Engineering Trades after the War. [Cd. 9073.] H.M.S.O. 1918. 6*d.*

Financial Facilities [after the War], Report of the Committee on. [Cd. 9227.] H.M.S.O. 1918. 2*d.*

Food. Reports (Interim and Final) of the Departmental Committee appointed . . . to consider the Production of Food in England and Wales. [Cd. 8048, 8095.] H.M.S.O. 1915. 2½*d.*

Food. Report of Scottish Departmental Committee on Food Production. H.M.S.O. 1915. 2*d.*

—— Report of Departmental Committee on Food Production in Ireland. H.M.S.O. 1915. 3*d.*

—— Defence of the Realm. Ministry of Food. Orders made by the Food Controller. [Cd. 8524-8540.] (Jan. 26 to April 3, 1917.) H.M.S.O. 1917. 1*d.* each No.

Food Supply of the United Kingdom. Report drawn up by a Committee of the Royal Society at the request of the President of the Board of Trade. [Cd. 8421.] H.M.S.O. 1916. 4*d.*

Food (Supply and Production) Manual, revised to Oct. 21, 1917; comprising all the Food Supply and Production Legislation, with Orders thereunder of the Food Controller [&c.]. Introductory Note and Index, and Addenda to Jan. 31, 1918. Edited by Alex. Pulling. (Manuals of Emergency Legislation.) H.M.S.O. 1918. 5*s.*

German Propaganda. Despatches from H.M. Ambassador at Berlin respecting an official German organization for influencing the Press of other countries. (1914.) [Cd. 7595.] H.M.S.O. ½*d.*

German Colonies. Correspondence relating to the wishes of the Natives of the German Colonies as to their future government. [Cd. 9210.] H.M.S.O. 1918. 6*d.*

Germany, Sea-borne Commerce of, Statement of Measures adopted to intercept the. [Cd. 8145.] H.M.S.O. 1916. 1d.

Germany. Reports of British Officers on the Economic Conditions prevailing in Germany, Dec. 1918-March 1919. [Cmd. 52.] H.M.S.O. 1919. 9*d.*

German Government. Further Correspondence with the German Government respecting the incidents alleged to have attended the Sinking of a German Submarine . . . on Aug. 19, 1915. Miscellaneous, No. 7 (1916); in continuation of Miscellaneous No. 1 (1916). [Cd. 8176.] H.M.S.O. 1916. 1*d.*

Goltz, Horst Von Der, *alias* Bridgeman Taylor. Sworn Statement by. Miscellaneous No. 13 (1916). [Cd. 8232.] H.M.S.O. 1916. 1½*d.*

Holland. Transit Traffic across Holland of Materials Susceptible of Employment as Military Supplies. Further Correspondence respecting the. (With map.) Miscellaneous No. 2 (1918). [Cd. 8915.] H.M.S.O. 1918. 1*s.* 9*d.*

—— Correspondence respecting the Internment of Seaplanes, &c., salved on the High Seas and brought into Netherlands jurisdiction. Miscellaneous No. 4 (1918). [Cd. 8985.] H.M.S.O. 1918. 3*d.*

—— Report on the export of cement from the United Kingdom to Holland. Miscellaneous No. 9 (1918). [Cd. 9023.] H.M.S.O. 1918 (April). 2*d.*

—— Correspondence between H.M. Government and the Netherlands Government respecting the treatment by the latter of Belligerent Merchant Vessels whose status has been changed as the result of an act of war. Part I, Cases of Steamships Maria and Huntstrick. Part II, German Ships at Antwerp at the Outbreak of War. Miscellaneous No. 12 (1918). [Cd. 9026.] H.M.S.O. 1918. 4*d.*

—— Despatch of a Dutch Convoy to the East Indies. Correspondence respecting the. Miscellaneous No. 13 (1918). [Cd. 9028.] H.M.S.O. 1918. 2*d.*

Horses, Supply of, for Military Purposes (England and Wales). Committee on. Report. With Appendices. [Cd. 8134.] H.M.S.O. 1915. 3*d.*

Insurance (War Risks): Government Scheme. Report of the Aircraft Insurance Committee. H.M.S.O. 1915. 1½*d.*

—— Text of the agreements made between H.M. Government and the War Risks Insurance Associations. H.M.S.O. 1915. 3*d.*

Ireland, Men of Military Age in. Statement giving Particulars regarding. [Cd. 8390.] H.M.S.O. 1916. ½*d.*

Ireland. Report of the Royal Commission on the Rebellion in Ireland, June 26, 1916. [Cd. 8279.] H.M.S.O. 1916. 2*d.*

Ireland, Government of. Heading of a Settlement as to the. [Cd. 8310.] H.M.S.O. 1916. ½*d.*

Ireland, Rebellion in. Royal Commission on. Minutes of Evidence and Appendix of Documents. [Cd. 8311.] H.M.S.O. 1916. 1*s.* 0*d.*

Ireland. Mr. Francis Sheehy Skeffington, Mr. Thomas Dickson and Mr. Patrick James McIntyre. Royal Commission on the Arrest and subsequent Treatment of. Report. [Cd. 8376.] H.M.S.O. 1916. 1½*d.*

Ireland. Army (Courts of Inquiry) Act, 1916. Reports of the Court of Inquiry (on the cases of Lieut. P. Barrett and Lieut.-Colonel Owen-Thomas) Jan. 2, 1917. [Cd. 8435.] H.M.S.O. 1917. 2*d.*

—— Letter from the Prime Minister regarding. [Cd. 8573.] H.M.S.O. 1917. 1*d.*

—— Irish Convention, Report of the Proceedings of the [Cd. 9019.] H.M.S.O. 1918. 1*s.* 6*d.*

Iron, &c. Report of the Departmental Committee appointed . . . to consider the position of the Iron and Steel Trades after the War. [Cd. 9071.] H.M.S.O. 1918. 6*d.*

Kogrund Passage, Mining of the. Correspondence with the Swedish Government respecting the. Miscellaneous No. 8 (1917). [Cd. 8478.] H.M.S.O. 1917. 2*d.*

Labour. Commission of Enquiry into Industrial Unrest. Reports of the Commissioners in England (six divisions), Wales and Scotland. [Cd. 8662-8669.] July 1917. H.M.S.O. 1917. 1*s.* 6*d.*

—— Works Committees. Report of an Enquiry made by the Ministry of Labour (Industrial Reports, No. 2) 8vo. H.M.S.O. 1918. 6*d.*

—— Industrial Reports (8vo.). (1) Industrial Councils (the Whitley Report). 1*d.* (2) Works Committees. Report of Enquiry by the Ministry of Labour. H.M.S.O. 1918. 6*d.*

—— Industrial Councils and Trade Boards. Memorandum by the Minister of Reconstruction and the Minister of Labour. [Cd. 9085.] H.M.S.O. 1918 (June 7). 1*d.*

Liability to Military Service of British Subjects in France and French Citizens in Great Britain. Agreement between the United Kingdom and France. Signed at Paris, Oct. 4, 1917. Miscellaneous, No. 15 (1917). [Cd. 8691.] H.M.S.O. 1917. 1*d.*

Liability to Military Service of British Subjects in Greece and of Greek Subjects in Great Britain. Agreement between the United Kingdom and Greece respecting the. Miscellaneous No. 16 (1918). [Cd. 9103.] H.M.S.O. 1918. 1*d.*

Liability to Military Service of British Subjects in Italy and Italian Subjects in Great Britain. Agreement between the United Kingdom and Italy. Miscellaneous No. 17 (1917). [Cd. 8694.] H.M.S.O. 1917. 1*d.*

Liability to Military Service of British Subjects resident in Russia and Russian Subjects resident in Great Britain, Agreement concluded between H.M. Government and the Provisional Government of Russia relative to the. Miscellaneous No. 11 (1917). [Cd. 8588.] H.M.S.O. 1917. 1*d.*

Liability to Military Service of British Subjects in the United States and of United States Citizens in Great Britain, Convention between the United Kingdom and the United States of America respecting the. Miscellaneous No. 4 (1918). [Cd. 9101.] H.M.S.O. 1918. 1*d.*

Local Government. Report on the Special Work of the Local Government Board arising out of the War, to Dec. 31, 1914. With appendix. [Cd. 7763.] H.M.S.O. 1915. 4½*d.*

Local Government Board. Annual Report (44th). For 1914-15. Part I, including Report on Special Work arising out of the War. Prevention and Relief of Distress; Reception and Accommodation of War Refugees; Distribution of Gifts from the Dominions and Colonies, &c. [Cd. 8195.] H.M.S.O. 1916. 5*d.*

Liquor Control. Intoxicating Liquors (Restriction in Foreign Countries during the War). Correspondence relative to the Measures taken in certain Foreign Countries. [Cd. 7965.] H.M.S.O. 1915. 2½*d.*

—— Defence of the Realm Regulations 1915. Second Report of the Central Control Board (Liquor Traffic). With Appendix. [Cd. 8243.] H.M.S.O. 1916. 3½*d.*

—— —— Third Report of the Central Control Board (Liquor Traffic). [Cd. 8558.] H.M.S.O. 1917. 3*d.*

—— Liquor Traffic. Memorandum submitted to the Government in Dec. 1916 by the Central Control Board (Liquor Traffic). [Cd. 8613.] H.M.S.O. 1917. 1*d.*

—— Defence of the Realm Regulations 1915. Fourth Report of the Central Control Board (Liquor Traffic). (With Charts and a Sketch Map of Carlisle). [Cd. 9055]. H.M.S.O. 1918. 3*d.*

—— Reports of English, Scotch and Irish Committees on the State Purchase and Control of Liquor Trade. [Cd. 9042.] H.M.S.O. 1918. 9*d.*

Luxury Duty, Report from the Select Committee on, together with the proceedings of the Committee, and Appendices. H.M.S.O. 1918. 6*d.*

Mails. Correspondence with the Swedish Minister on the detention by the Swedish Government of the British Transit Mail to Russia as a reprisal for the search of Parcels Mail by H.M. Government. Miscellaneous No. 8 (1916). [Cd. 8322.] H.M.S.O. 1916. 3*d.*

—— Examination of Parcels and Letter Mails. Note from the United States Government regarding the. Miscellaneous No. 20 (1916.) [Cd. 8261.] H.M.S.O. 1916. 1*d.*

Mercantile Marine. Statement by the Board of Trade as to Compensation for Death or Injury caused by War Risks, and as to other arrangements made for the Benefit of Officers and Seamen of British Merchant Ships during the War. [Cd. 8706.] H.M.S.O. 1917. 1*d.*

—— Merchant Tonnage and the Submarine. Statement issued by War Cabinet showing Losses, Shipbuilding Output, and Enemy Vessels captured and brought into Service for the period Aug. 1914 to Dec. 1917. [Cd. 9009.] H.M.S.O. 1918. 1*d.*

—— Supplementary statement, showing for the United Kingdom and for the world, for the period Aug. 1914 to Oct. 1918, (1) Merchant Tonnage Losses by Enemy Action and Marine Risk; (2) Merchant Shipbuilding Output; (3) Enemy Vessels captured and brought into service; together with diagrams, &c. [Cd. 9221.] H.M.S.O. 1918. 2*d.*

Munitions: Limitation of Profits of a Controlled Establishment. Provisional Rules with respect to the. H.C. 353/1914-15. H.M.S.O. 1914-15. 1*d.*

Munition Workers Committee, Health of. Report on Sunday Labour. [Cd. 8132.] H.M.S.O. 1915. 1*d.*

—— Report on Industrial Canteens. [Cd. 8133.] H.M.S.O. 1915. 1*d.*

Munitions, Ministry of. Health of Munition Workers' Committee. Memorandum No. 2. Welfare supervision. [Cd 8151.] H.M.S.O. 1916. 1*d.*

—— —— Memorandum No. 4. Employment of Women. [Cd. 8185.] H.M.S.O. 1916. 1½*d.*

—— —— Memorandum No. 5. Hours of Work. [Cd. 8186.] H.M.S.O. 1916. 1½*d.*

—— —— Memorandum No. 6. [Appendix to Memorandum No. 3. (Industrial Canteens).] Canteen Construction and Equipment. [Cd. 8199.] H.M.S.O. 1916. 4*d.*

—— —— Memorandum No. 7. Industrial Fatigue and its Causes. [Cd. 8213.] H.M.S.O. 1916. 1½*d.*

—— —— Memorandum No. 8. Special Industrial Diseases. [Cd. 8214.] H.M.S.O. 1916. 1*d.*

—— —— Memorandum No. 9. Ventilation and Lighting of Munition Factories and Workshops. [Cd. 8215.] H.M.S.O. 1916. 1½*d.*

—— —— Memorandum No. 10. Sickness and Injury. [Cd. 8216] H.M.S.O. 1916. 1½*d.*

Munitions, Ministry of. Health of Munition Workers' Committee. Memorandum No. 11. [2nd Appendix to Memorandum No. 3 (Industrial Canteens).] Investigation of Workers' Food and Suggestions as to Dietary. [Cd. 8370.] H.M.S.O. 1916. 1½*d.*

—— —— Memorandum No. 12. [Appendix to Memorandum No. 5 (Hours of Work).] Statistical Information concerning Output in relation to Hours of Work. [Cd. 8344.] H.M.S.O. 1916. 1½*d.*

—— —— Memorandum No. 13. Juvenile Employment [Cd. 8362.] H.M.S.O. 1916. 1*d.*

—— —— Memorandum No. 14. Washing Facilities and Baths. [Cd. 8387.] H.M.S.O. 1916. 1*d.*

—— —— Memorandum No. 15. The Effects of Industrial Conditions upon Eyesight. [Cd. 8409.] H.M.S.O. 1916. 1*d.*

—— —— Interim Report. Industrial Efficiency and Fatigue. [Cd. 8511.] H.M.S.O. 1917. 1*s.* 3*d.*

—— —— Memorandum No. 16. Medical Certificates for Munition Workers. [Cd. 8522.] H.M.S.O. 1917. 1*d.*

—— —— Memorandum No. 18, being an Appendix to Memo. No. 5 (Hours of Work.) Further Statistical Information concerning Output in Relation to Hours of Work. [Cd. 8628.] H.M.S.O. 1917. 3*d.*

—— —— Memorandum No. 19. A second Appendix to Memo. No. 3 (Industrial Canteens.) Investigation of Workers' Food and Suggestions as to Dietary. Revised edn. [Cd. 8798.] H.M.S.O. 1917. 2*d.*

—— —— Memorandum No. 20. Supplementary to Memorandum No. 5 (Hours of Work.) Weekly Hours of Employment. [Cd. 8801.] H.M.S.O. 1917. 1*d.*

—— —— Final Report. Industrial Health and Efficiency. (With Text Illustrations, Plans, and Plates.) [Cd. 9065.] H.M.S.O. 1918. 2*s.* 0*d.*

—— Mr. Justice McCardie's Committee of Enquiry. Interim Report on Labour Embargoes. H.M.S.O. 1918. 1*d.*

Munition Workers' Committee, Health of. Health of the Munition Worker. A Handbook for Directors, Managers, Foremen and others in authority in Munition Works of all kinds. Illustrated. H.M.S.O. 1918. 1*s.* 6*d.*

National Expenditure. Report, First (of Session 1918) from the Select Committee on National Expenditure (23). H.M.S.O. 1918. 2*d*

—— Fourth Report (of Session 1919) from the Select Committee. H.C. Paper 238. H.M.S.O. 1920. 2*d.*

National Expenditure. Fifth Report (of Session 1919) from the Select Committee. H.C. Paper 245. H.M.S.O. 1920. 2*d.*

—— Reports (First, Second, Third, Fourth, and Fifth) from the Select Committee on. 113, 142, 168, 238, 245. H.M.S.O. 1919. 1*d.*, 1*d.*, 2*d.*, 2*d.*, 2*d.*

—— Reports (Sixth and Seventh) from the Select Committee on (on the Ministry of Information and the Form of Public Accounts). 97, 98. H.M.S.O. 1918. 1*d.*, 6*d.*

—— Ninth Report (Procedure of the House) from the Select Committee on, together with an Appendix. Oct. 22, 1918. (121.) H.M.S.O. 1918. 3*d.*

—— Reports from the Select Committee on, together with the Proceedings of the Committee and the Minutes of Evidence [&c.]. Printed at various dates from March to Nov., 1918. H.M.S.O. 1918. 2*s.* 6*d.*

—— Report and Reports (Special) from the Select Committee on, together with the proceedings of the Committee (Aug. 1, Oct. 24, Dec. 13, 1917, and Feb. 5, 1918). [125, 151, 167, 188.] H.M.S.O. 1918. 9*d.*

—— Report (Tenth) from the Select Committee on (132). Nov. 13, 1918. H.M.S.O. 1918. 1*d.*

National Relief Fund. Report on the Administration of the Fund up to March 31, 1915. With Appendices. [Cd. 7756.] H.M.S.O. 1916. 2½*d.*

—— Report on the Administration of, up to March 31, 1916. With Appendices. [Cd. 8286.] H.M.S.O. 1916. 5½*d.*

—— Report on the Administration of the, up to Sept. 30, 1917. With Appendices. [Cd. 8920.] H.M.S.O. 1918. 2*d.*

—— Report on the Administration of the, up to March 31, 1918. [Cd. 9111.] H.M.S.O. 1918. 2*d.*

—— Report on the Administration of the, up to June 30, 1919. [Cmd. 356.] H.M.S.O. 1919. 2*d.*

National War Savings Committee. First Annual Report, March 1, 1917. [Cd. 8516.] H.M.S.O. 1917. 3*d.*

—— 2nd Annual Report, for 1917. [Cd. 9112.] H.M.S.O. 1918. 2*d.*

—— 3rd Annual Report, for 1918. [Cmd. 194.] H.M.S.O. 1919. 1*d.*

Naval and Army Services, Warlike Operations and other Expenditure arising out of the War. Vote of Credit, 1915-16. [H.C. 135/1914-16.] H.M.S.O. ½*d.*

—— Four Papers, Supplementary Vote of Credit, 1915-16. [H.C. 378, ½*d.*; H.C. 329, ½*d.*; H.C. 297, ½*d.*: H.C. 258, ½*d.*] H.M.S.O. 1914-16.

Naval and Military Services (Pensions and Grants). Select Committee on. Special Report, with Proceedings. H.C. 53/1914-15. H.M.S.O. 1914-15. 1½*d*.

—— Select Committee on Special Report and Second Special Report, with Proceedings, Minutes of Evidence, and Appendices. H.C. 196/1914-15. H.M.S.O. 1914-15. 2*s*. 3*d*.

—— Select Committee on Third Special Report with Proceedings. H.C. 328/1914-15. H.M.S.O. 1914-15. 1*d*.

Navy and Army Allowances and Pensions in respect of Seamen, Marines, and Soldiers and their Wives, Widows and Dependants. [Cd 7662.] H.M.S.O. 1914-15. 2*d*.

Navy. Separation Allowances to Wives and Children of Seamen, Marines and Reservists borne on the books of H.M. Ships. [Cd. 7619.] H.M.S.O. 1914. ½*d*.

Navy (Rescues). Return showing number of Rescues effected from German Warships by H.M. Vessels and from H.M. Vessels by German Warships respectively. [Cd. 7921.] H.M.S.O. 1915. ½*d*.

Navy. Return showing the losses of ships of the Royal Navy. . . . and the losses of Auxiliary Ships, during the period Aug. 4, 1914—Nov. 11, 1918. H.M.S.O. 1919. 4*d*.

Offices. Return of the various new Departments or new Sub-Departments of Permanent Offices that have been created since the outbreak of the War and are now in existence, &c. Oct. 23, 1918. H.M.S.O. 1918. 3*d*.

Papen, Captain von. Selection from papers found in the possession of. Falmouth, Jan. 2 and 3, 1916. Miscellaneous, No. 6. 1916. [Cd. 8174.] H.M.S.O. 1916. 6*d*.

Press Bureau, Memorandum on the Official. [Cd. 7680.] H.M.S.O. 1915. ½*d*.

Prices. Retail Coal Prices. Departmental Committee on Causes of the present rise in the retail price of Coal sold for Domestic Use. Report. [Cd. 7866.] H.M.S.O. 1915. 1½*d*.

—— —— Minutes of Evidence. With Appendices. (With Charts). [Cd. 7923.] H.M.S.O. 1915. 2*s*. 3*d*.

—— Reports (Interim, Second, Third and Final) of the Departmental Committee Appointed . . . . to investigate the principal Causes which have led to the increase of Prices and Commodities since the beginning of the War. [Cd. 8358, 8483.] H.M.S.O. 1916-17. 5½*d*.

—— Report of the Committee appointed to enquire into and report on (1) the actual increase, since June 1914, in the cost of living; (2) any counterbalancing factors, &c. [Cd. 8980.] H.M.S.O. 1918. 3*d*.

Prices. Special Report from the Select Committee on High Prices and Profits, together with the Minutes of Evidence. 166. H.M.S.O. 1919 (Aug.). 4*d.*

Railway Working during the War. Statement showing the Cost of running the Railways in Great Britain during the Period of Government Control (1914-18). [Cmd. 147.] H.M.S.O. 1919. 1*d.*

Railway Working. Statement showing the results of working the Railways during the period of Government Control of the Railways in Great Britain (Aug. 5, 1914—Aug. 31, 1919) and Ireland (Jan. 1, 1917—Aug. 31, 1919). [Cmd. 402.] H.M.S.O. 1919. 2*d.*

Reconstruction, Ministry of. Coal Conservation Sub-Committee. Interim Report on Electric Power Supply in Great Britain. [Cd. 8880.] H.M.S.O. 1918. 3*d.*

—— Committee on relations between Employers and Employed. Supplementary Report on Works Committees. [Cmd. 9001.] Second Report on Joint Standing Industrial Councils. [Cd. 9002]. H.M.S.O. 1918. 2*d.*

—— —— Report on Conciliation and Arbitration. [Cd. 9099.] (In substitution for [Cd. 9081.]). H.M.S.O. 1918. 1*d.*

—— —— Final Report. [Cd. 9153.] H.M.S.O. 1918. 1*d.*

—— A list of Commissions and Committees set up to deal with questions which will arise at the close of the war. [Cd. 8916.] H.M.S.O. 1918. 5*d.*

—— Report of the Agricultural Policy Sub-Committee appointed in Aug. 1916, to consider and report upon the methods of effecting an increase in the home-grown Food Supplies . . . together with Reports by Sir M. G. Wallace. [Cd. 9079.] Summaries of evidence taken before the same. [Cd. 9080.] H.M.S.O. 1918. 1*s.* 3*d.* each.

—— Housing in England and Wales. Memorandum by the Advisory Housing Panel on the emergency problem. [Cd. 9087.] H.M.S.O. 1918. 2*d.*

—— Reports of the Committee appointed . . . to consider the legal interpretation of the term "period of the war." [Cd. 9100.] H.M.S.O. 1918. 7*d.*

—— First (Interim) Report of the Civil War-Workers Committee. [Cd. 9117.] H.M.S.O. 1918. 2*d.*

—— Final Report of the Civil War-Workers Committee. Substitute Labour. [Cd. 9228.] H.M.S.O. 1918. 1*d.*

—— Second Report of the Committee dealing with the law and practice relating to the Acquisition and Valuation of Land for public purposes. [Cd. 9229.] H.M.S.O. 1918. 4*d.*

Reconstruction, Ministry of. Report of the Machinery of Government Committee. [Cd. 9230.] H.M.S.O. 1918. *6d.*

—— Reconstruction Problems. (1) The Aims of Reconstruction. (2) Housing in England and Wales. (3) Demobilisation and Resettlement of the Army. (4) Housing in Scotland. (5) New fields for British Engineering. (6) Raw Materials and Employment. (7) Guide to work and benefits for soldiers, &c. (8) Resettlement of Civil War Workers. (9) Naval Demobilisation. H.M.S.O. 1918. *2d.* each.

—— Statement with regard to Advisory Bodies (other than Reporting Committees) appointed by the Minister. [Cd. 9195.] H.M.S.O. 1918. *2d.*

—— Women's Advisory Committee. Interim Report . . . on the Co-ordination of the Vocational Training of Women. H.M.S.O. 1918. *3d.*

Requisitioning by H.M. Government of British-owned or chiefly British-owned Ships under Neutral Flags. Correspondence with the Netherlands Government. Miscellaneous No. 5 (1918). [Cd. 8986.] H.M.S.O. 1918. *1d.*

Requisitioning of Dutch Ships by the Associated Governments. Correspondence with the Netherlands Government respecting the. Miscellaneous No. 11 (1918). [Cd. 9025.] H.M.S.O. 1918. *2d.*

Retrenchment, Public. Committee on. What Savings in Public Expenditure can be effected in the Civil Departments. First Report. [Cd. 8068.] H.M.S.O. 1915. *1d.*

—— —— Second Report. [Cd. 8139.] H.M.S.O. 1915. *½d.*

Retrenchment in the Public Expenditure. Third Report of the Committee on. [Cd. 8180.] H.M.S.O. 1916. *½d.*

—— Final Report of Committee on. [Cd. 8200.] H.M.S.O. 1916. *3d.*

Royal Flying Corps, Final Report of the Committee on the administration and command of the, &c. Nov. 1916. [Cd. 8194.] H.M.S.O. 1916. *3d.*

Royal Patriotic Fund Corporation, Report (Eleventh) of the, 1914. H.M.S.O. 1915. *8½d.*

Russia. Recent Events in Moscow, and more especially the Unexampled Treatment by the Bolsheviks of the British Colony and the British Consulate-General. Despatches from H.M. Consul-General at Moscow, Aug. 5 to 9, 1918. Miscellaneous No. 30 (1918). H.M.S.O. 1918. *2d.*

Shipping. Methods hitherto adopted for dealing with Ships and Cargoes brought into British Ports under the Order in Council of March 11 1915. Report of the Committee appointed to enquire whether any avoidable delay is caused by the. Miscellaneous No. 6 (1917). [Cd. 8469.] H.M.S.O. 1917. 1*d.*

—— Reports of the Departmental Committee appointed . . . to consider the position of the Shipping and Shipbuilding Industries after the War. [Cd. 9092.] H.M.S.O. 1918. 1*s.* 3*d.*

Staffs, Committee on. First, Second and Third Interim Reports of the Committee appointed to enquire into the organisation and staffing of Government Offices. [Cd. 9074, 9219, 9220.] H.M.S.O. 1918. 1*d.*, 1*d.*, 3*d.*

Staffs of Government Departments. Statement showing the Staffs employed in Government Departments on Aug. 1 1919. [Cmd. 343.] H.M.S.O. 1919. 1*d.* (Followed periodically by similar returns.)

Sugar. Report (First) of the Royal Commission on the Sugar Supply, showing the operations of the Commission . . . to beginning of Dec. 1916. [Cd. 8728.] H.M.S.O. 1917. 1*d.*

Textiles. Report of the Departmental Committee appointed by the Board of Trade to consider the position of the Textile Trades after the War. [Cd. 9070.]

Trade. Agreement between the United Kingdom and Russia for the reciprocal waiver of Consular fees on certificates of origin relating to exports. Signed at Petrograd, July 3 (16) 1915. Treaty series, 1915, No. 8. H.M.S.O. ½*d.*

—— Government Assistance to Credit and Business. Further Papers relating to the Measures taken by H.M. Government for sustaining Credit and facilitating Business. [Cd. 7684.] H.M.S.O. 1914-15. 1½*d.*

Trade of the United Kingdom with Foreign Countries and British Possessions. Annual Statement for 1915, compared with four preceding years. Vols. I, II. [Cd. 8284, 8357.] H.M.S.O. 1916. 5*s.* 10*d.*, 4*s.* 3*d.*

—— Annual Statement for 1916, compared with the four preceding years. Vols. I, II. [Cd. 8632, 8714.] H.M.S.O. 1917. 6*s.*, 4*s.* 6*d.*

—— Annual Statement for 1917, compared with the four preceding years. Vols. I, II. [Cd. 9127, 9136.] H.M.S.O. 1918. 6*s.*, 4*s.* 6*d.*

—— Annual Statement for 1918, compared with the four preceding years. Vols. I and II. [Cmd. 342, 366.] H.M.S.O. 1919. 7*s.*, 4*s.* 6*d.*

Trade. Report to the President of the Board of Trade by the Committee appointed to advise the Board of Trade on matters arising under the Trading with the Enemy Act, 1916. [Cd. 9059.] H.M.S.O. 1918 (May). 1*d.*

—— British Trade after the War. Measures for securing the position of certain Branches of British Industry. Sub-Committee of the Advisory Committee to the Board of Trade on Commercial Intelligence with respect to. Report. [Cd. 8181.] H.M.S.O. 1916. 2½*d.*

—— —— Summaries of Evidence. [Cd. 8275.] H.M.S.O. 1916. 4*d.*

—— Trading with the Enemy (Extension of Powers Act 1915). Correspondence with the United States Ambassador respecting the. Miscellaneous No. 11 (1916). [Cd. 8225.] H.M.S.O. 1916. ½*d.*

—— —— Further Correspondence with the United States Ambassador respecting the. Miscellaneous No. 36 (1916). [Cd. 8353.] H.M.S.O. 1916. 1*d.*

—— Trading with the Enemy (Statutory List). Proclamation, together with the Consolidated Statutory List of Persons and Firms in Countries, other than Enemy Countries, with whom Persons and Firms in the United Kingdom are prohibited from trading. With Notes for British Merchants engaged in Foreign Trade. Complete to Nov. 15, 1918. No. 68a. H.M.S.O. 1918. 6*d.*

—— —— —— —— Complete to Feb. 21, 1919. No. 76a. H.M.S.O. 1919. 6*d.*

Transport. First and Second Reports from the Select Committee on, with Appendices (130, 136). Nov. 1918. H.M.S.O. 1918. 1*d.* and 3*d.*

Treasury Assistance to Banks, &c. Papers relating to Treasury Assistance to Banks and Discount Houses since the outbreak of War on 4th Aug. 1914, and to the questions of the advisability of continuing or ending the Moratorium, and of the nature of the banking facilities now available. H.C. 457/1914. H.M.S.O. 1914. 1*d.*

Treaties, &c., between the United Kingdom and Foreign States, Accessions, Withdrawals, &c. Treaty Series 1915. No. 10. [Cd. 8015.] H.M.S.O. 1915. ½*d.*

—— Treaty Series 1916. No. 4 (8vo.). [Cd. 8350.] H.M.S.O. 1916. ½*d.*

—— In continuation of Treaty Series No. 4 (1916). [Cmd. 302.] H.M.S.O. 1919. 1*d.*

Vatican. Despatch to Sir H. Howard containing instructions respecting his Mission to the Vatican. Miscellaneous No. 1 (1915). [Cd. 7736.] H.M.S.O. ½*d.*

Venereal Diseases, Prevention and Treatment of. Recommendation of the Royal Commission; Action taken by the Local Government Board; Progress made with Schemes of Treatment; Particulars of certain Schemes. [Cd. 8509.] H.M.S.O. 1917. 1*d.*

War Cabinet. Report for 1917. With Appendices, Chart, and Maps. (8vo.) [Cd. 9005.] H.M.S.O. 1918. 1*s.*

—— Report for 1918. With Appendices and Maps. [Cmd. 325.] H.M.S.O. 1919. 3*s.* 6*d.*

War Charities, Committee on. Report. [Cd. 8287.] H.M.S.O. 1916. 1*d.*

War Graves. How the cemeteries abroad will be designed. Report to the Imperial War Graves Commission by Lieut.-Col. Sir Frederick Kenyon. H.M.S.O. 1918. 3*d.*

W.A.A.C. Report of the Commission of enquiry appointed . . . to enquire into the Women's Army Auxiliary Corps in France. (M.40/56.) H.M.S.O. 1918. 1*d.*

Women, Employment of, Interim Report of the Central Committee on. With Appendices. [Cd. 7478.] H.M.S.O. 1915. 4½*d.*

Women and Girls, Industrial Employment of. Being Section IV and Appendix B extracted from the Final Report of the Committee (which was published as Parliamentary Paper [Cd. 9065] of Session 1918, price 2*s.*). H.M.S.O. 1918. 3*d.*

Women, Employment of. Report of the Board of Trade on the Increased Employment of Women during the War in the United Kingdom. With statistics up to April, 1918. [Cd. 9164.] H.M.S.O. 1918. 2*d.*

(4) *France.*

Documents officiels relatifs à la guerre 1914-'16. Les Allemands à Lille et dans le Nord de France. (Deportations in April, 1916). Hachette 1916.

Deportation, The, of women and girls from Lille. Transl. from the Note addressed by the French Government to the Governments of Neutral Powers. Hodder & Stoughton 1916. 6*d.*

German War Proclamations. Arrêtés et Proclamations de Guerre allemandes du 20 Août, 1914, au 25 Janvier, 1915. Allen & Unwin. 2*s.*

Guerre de 1914. Documents officiels, textes législatifs et régle mentaires. 3 vols., with 2 supplements. Dalloz. 8 fr.

Législation française depuis la Guerre. Récueil des lois, décrets, arrêtés [etc.], parus au Journal Officiel depuis la mobilisation; classés méthodiquement. Vol. I, July 31—Oct. 15, 1914. Tenin. 3 fr.

—— Les Baux à ferme, les Métayages, et le Moratorium. Textes officiels, avec notice (Législation de Guerre.) Collection edited by A. Saillard. Berger-Levrault. 40 c.

—— Les Dommages de Guerre : constatation et évaluation. Textes officiels, avec commentaire pratique (Législation de Guerre. Collection edited by A. Saillard). Berger-Levrault. 1 fr. 25.

—— Les Finances publiques et la Guerre. Textes officiels, précédés d'une étude générale. (Législation de Guerre. Collection edited by A. Saillard). Berger-Levrault. 1 fr. 25.

(5) *Germany.*

German White Book II. (Civilian Warfare in Belgium). Published by the Auswärtiger Amt.

Germany and Finland—Treaty of Peace between, signed at Berlin, March 7, 1918, with the Commercial and Shipping Agreement. Miscellaneous No. 29 (1918). H.M.S.O. 1918. 2*d*.

Huberich, C. H., and Nicol-Speyer, A. (edrs.). German Legislation for the occupied territories of Belgium. 2nd series, Jan.-March 1915. The Hague: Nijhoff. 3*s*.

—— Législation allemande en Belgique. Bulletin officiel des lois et arrêtes pour la territoire belge occupé, Sept. 5—Dec. 26, 1914. Réimpression textuelle. The Hague: Nijhoff. 3 fr.

Lepsius, J. Deutschland und Armenien, 1914-18. Sammlung diplomatischer Aktenstücke. 1919. 15 mk.

Memorandum of the German Government in regard to incidents alleged to have attended the destruction of a German Submarine and its crew by H.M. Aux. Cruiser Baralong on Aug. 19, 1915; and reply of H.M. Government thereto (Jan. 1916). Miscellaneous No. 1 (1916). [Cd. 8144.] H.M.S.O. 2½*d*.

Stenographische Bericht über die öffentlichen Verhandlangen des Untersuchungsansschusses, ii. Beilagen: Aktenstücke zur Friedensaktion Wilsons, 1916-17. Berlin: Norddeutsche Buchdrückerei 1920.

Vorgeschichte des Waffenstillstandes. 110 Dokumente aus d. Archiven d. auswärt. Amtes u. d. Reichskanzlei. Amtliche Ausg. 1919. 4 mk.

Treaty of Peace signed at Brest-Litovsk between the Central Powers and the Ukrainian People's Republic, together with the Supplementary Treaty thereto. Miscellaneous No. 18 (1918). [Cd. 9105.] (8vo.). H.M.S.O. 1918. 2*d*.

(6) *Greece.*

Documents diplomatiques, 1913-17. Min. des affaires étrangères, Athens 1917.

(7) *Italy.*

Italian Decrees relative to Enemy Merchant Vessels, together with Italian Naval Prize Regulations. Miscellaneous No. 18 (1915). [Cd. 8104.] H.M.S.O. 1915. 1*d.*

(8) *Japan.*

Exchange of Notes respecting Accession of Japan to the Declaration of Sept. 5, 1914, between the United Kingdom, France and Russia . . . Treaty series, No. 1 (1915). London, Oct. 19, 1915. [Cd. 8014.] H.M.S.O. ½*d.*

(9) *Russia.*

Accession of Russia to the Convention of Nov. 9, 1914, between the United Kingdom and France, relating to prizes captured during the present European War. Signed: London, March 5, 1915. Treaty series 1915, No. 4; amended version. H.M.S.O. ½*d.*

Despatch from H.M. Ambassador at Petrograd, enclosing a Memorandum on the subject of the Temperance Measures adopted in Russia since the outbreak of the European War. Miscellaneous No. 2 (1915). [Cd. 7738.] H.M.S.O. ½*d.*

(10) *United States.*

China. No. 1 (1918). Text of Notes exchanged between the United States and Japanese Governments regarding their Policy in China, and Declaration of China on the subject. [Cd. 8895.] H.M.S.O. 1918. 1*d.*

C.—Post-War.

Adriatic Question. Correspondence relating to the. Miscellaneous No. 2 (1920). [Cmd. 586.] H.M.S.O. 1920. 3*d.*

Afghanistan, Papers regarding hostilities with, 1919. [Cmd. 324.] H.M.S.O. 1919. 4*d.*

Agreement between H.M. Government and the Soviet Government of Russia for Exchange of Prisoners (Russia, No. 1, 1920). [Cmd. 537.] H.M.S.O. 1920. 1*d.*

Agreement between MM. Loucheur and Rathenau, made at Wiesbaden, Oct. 6, 1921. [Cmd. 1547.] H.M.S.O. 1921.

Aliens Repatriation. Report of Committee appointed to consider Applications for Exemption from Compulsory Repatriation submitted by Interned Enemy Aliens. [Cmd. 383.] H.M.S.O. 1919. 1*d.*

Angora. Despatch from H.M. Ambassador in Paris, enclosing the Franco-Turkish Agreement signed at Angora on Oct. 20, 1921. (Turkey, No. 2, 1921.) [Cmd. 1556.] H.M.S.O. 1921. 4*d.*

Army. Operations in Russia. Cost of the Naval and Military Operations from the date of the Armistice to July 31, 1919. [Cmd. 307.] H.M.S.O. 1919. 1*d.*

—— Cost of Naval and Military Operations in Russia from the date of the Armistice to Oct. 31, 1919. [Cmd. 395.] H.M.S.O. 1919. 1*d.*

—— Revised Statement of Army Expenditure 1919-20, by the Secretary of State for War. [Cmd. 378.] H.M.S.O. 1919. 1*d.*

—— Report of the Committee constituted by the Army Council to enquire into the Law and Rules of Procedure regulating Military Courts Martial. [Cmd. 428.] H.M.S.O. 1919. 2*d.*

British War Graves in Belgian Territory. Agreement between the United Kingdom and Belgium respecting. Signed at Brussels, June 13, 1919. Treaty Series, 1919, No. 9. [Cmd. 301.] H.M.S.O. 1919. 1*d.*

British War Graves in France. Agreement between the United Kingdom and France respecting. Signed at Paris, Nov. 26, 1918. Treaty Series, 1919, No. 1. [Cmd. 7.] H.M.S.O. 1919. 1*d.*

Coal Industry Commission Act 1919. Reports, March 20 1919: Interim Report by the Honourable Mr. Justice Sankey, G.B.E. (Chairman), Mr. Arthur Balfour, Sir Arthur Duckham, K.C.B., M.I.C.E., and Sir Thomas Royden, Bart., M.P. With Appendix. [Cmd. 84.] H.M.S.O. 1919. 1*d.*

—— —— Report by Messrs. R. Smillie, Frank Hodges, Herbert Smith, R. H. Tawney, and Sidney Webb, and Sir Leo Chiozza Money. [Cmd. 85.] H.M.S.O. 1919. 2*d.*

—— —— Interim Report by Messrs. R. W. Cooper, J. T. Forgie, and Evan Williams. [Cmd. 86.] H.M.S.O. 1919. 1*d.*

Currency and Foreign Exchanges. First Interim Report of the Committee on Currency and Foreign Exchanges after the War. [Cd. 9182.] H.M.S.O. 1918. 2*d.*

—— Final Report of the Committee on Currency and Foreign Exchanges after the War. [Cmd. 464.] H.M.S.O. 1919. 1*d.*

Economic Conditions in Central Europe (I). Miscellaneous No. 1 (1920). [Cmd. 521.] H.M.S.O. 1920. 2*d.*

Economic Conditions Prevailing in Germany. Further Reports by British Army Officers. April 1919. [Cmd. 54.] H.M.S.O. 1919. *3d.*

—— —— March and April 1919. [Cmd. 208.] H.M.S.O. 1919. *8d.*

Ex-Service Men in Government Offices. Statement relating to the Employment of on July 1, 1919, and Dec. 1, 1921. [Cmd. 1568.] H.M.S.O. 1921. *3d.*

Food Conditions in Germany, Report on, by E. H. Starling, C.M.G.; with Memoranda on Agricultural conditions in Germany, by A. P. McDougall; and on Agricultural Statistics, by C. W. Guillebaud, and statistical tables and charts. [Cmd. 280.] H.M.S.O. 1919. *6d.*

Mesopotamia, Review of the Civil Administration of. [Cmd. 1061.] H.M.S.O. 1921. *2s. 6d.*

National Debt. Return showing the aggregate gross Liabilities of the State as represented by the Nominal Funded Debt, etc., the estimated Assets, and the Exchequer Balances at the close of each financial year, from 1875-6 to 1918-19, both inclusive; also the Gross and Net Expenditure charged annually during that period against the Public Revenue on account of the National Debt, etc. [Cmd. 429.] H.M.S.O. 1920. *6d.*

Occupation of the Rhine Provinces, Declaration by the Governments of the United States of America, Great Britain and France in regard to the. [Cmd. 240.] H.M.S.O. 1919. *1d.*

Profiteering Act, 1919. Findings by Committees appointed to enquire into: The existence of a combine in the Farriery Trade. [Cmd. 540.] Costs of Production, Prices, etc., of Clogs. [Cmd. 541.] H.M.S.O. 1920. *1d.* each.

—— —— The Effect of Road Transport Rates caused by the alleged Existence of a Combine. [Cmd. 549.] Worsted Yarns. [Cmd. 550.] H.M.S.O. 1920. *1d.* each.

—— Findings by a Committee appointed to enquire into the existence of a Trade Combination in the Tobacco Industry, and into the Effect which its Operation has on Prices and on the Trade generally. [Cmd. 558.] H.M.S.O. 1920. *1d.*

Statements of Production, Price Movements, and Currency Expansion in certain countries. [Cmd. 434.] H.M.S.O. 1919. *1d.*

IV.—SPEECHES, Etc., of Public Men.

A.—British.

Asquith, The Rt. Hon. H. H. A Call to Arms. A speech at the Guildhall, Sept. 4, 1914. Authorised edn., revised by Mr. Asquith. Methuen. *1d.*

Asquith, The Right Hon. H. H. How do we stand To-day? A speech delivered on Nov. 2, 1915. Fisher Unwin. 1*d.*

—— A United Empire. A speech in Dublin, Sept. 25, 1914. Authorised edn., revised by Mr. Asquith. Methuen. 1*d.*

—— The War, its Causes, and its Message. Speeches in the House of Commons on Aug. 6 and 27; at the Guildhall on Sept. 4; in Edinburgh on Sept. 18; in Dublin on Sept. 25; in Cardiff on Oct. 2, 1914. Methuen. 3*d.*

—— The War of Civilisations. A speech in Edinburgh, Sept. 18, 1914. Authorised edn., revised by Mr. Asquith. Methuen. 1*d.*

—— and Bonar Law, The Rt. Hon. A.; Balfour, The Rt. Hon. A. J.; Churchill, The Rt. Hon. W. S. To a Victorious Conclusion. The Prime Minister's Appeal to the Nation. Speeches delivered at the Guildhall, London, on Sept. 4, 1914. Parliamentary Recruiting Committee.

—— A free future for the world. Speech delivered at the Guildhall, Nov. 9, 1916. Published by authority. Fisher Unwin 1916. 1*d.*

—— and others. Companionship in Arms. Speeches delivered on April 12, 1917, to celebrate America's adhesion to the Allies' cause. Hodder & Stoughton 1917. 1*d.*

Balfour, Rt. Hon. A. J., First Lord of the Admiralty. Speech at the London Opera House, Aug. 4, 1915 (reviewing the first year of war and especially the work of the Navy. Darling & Son.

Balfour, Viviani, and Joffre. Speeches in America, April-July 1917.. Edited by Francis Halsey. Funk & Wagnalls 1917. $1.50.

Balfour, Rt. Hon. A. J. and others. England's Welcome to Venizelos. Speeches at the Mansion House, Nov. 1917. Anglo-Hellenic League 1918. 3*d.*

Bikanir, H.H. the Maharaja of. India's Imperial Partnership. Speeches delivered by the Maharaja of Bikanir as one of the Indian Delegates to the Imperial Conference, March-May 1917. The Times Office 1917.

Borden, Sir Robert. Speech to the Canadian People, delivered at Toronto, Dec. 5, 1914. Ottawa: Federal Press.

—— Canada at War. Speeches delivered before the Canadian Club.

Carson, Sir Edward. The War on German Submarines. A summary, with quotations, of the speech delivered on Feb. 21, 1917. Fisher Unwin 1917. 1*d.*

Cecil, Lord R., and Lloyd George, Rt. Hon. D. Censorship and Trade. Letter of Lord Robert Cecil (June 23, 1916); speech of Mr. Lloyd George (Aug. 8, 1916) and his explanation (Sept. 15, 1916); and other utterances. Eyre & Spottiswoode 1916.

Cecil, Lord Robert. Black List and Blockade. An interview with Lord R. Cecil in reply to the Swedish Prime Minister, Oct. 5, 1916. Eyre & Spottiswoode 1916.

Churchill, Rt. Hon. Winston S. The Fighting Line. Two speeches delivered in the House of Commons, May 23 and 31, 1916. Macmillan 1916. 1*d.*

Empire, The, and the War. What the Statesmen of the Empire have said. A collection of extracts from speeches. Edited by Howard d'Egville. Empire Parliamentary Association, 6a, Victoria Street, S.W.

Falconer, R. A. The German Tragedy, and its meaning for Canada. Addresses delivered in Canada during the War. Toronto: Univ. Press. 50 c.

French, Lord. The Germans and the small nations. An interview. Keliher 1917. n.p.

George, Rt. Hon. D. Lloyd. Honour and Dishonour. A speech at the Queen's Hall, London, Sept. 19, 1914. Methuen. 1*d.*

—— The Task before us. Speech delivered at Bangor, Feb. 28, 1915. Jarrold. 1*d.*

—— Through Terror to Triumph: an Appeal to the Nation. A speech delivered at the Queen's Hall, London, on Sept. 19, 1914. Authorised edn. Parliamentary Recruiting Committee.

—— Through Terror to Triumph: Speeches and Pronouncements since the beginning of the War. Collective edn. Hodder & Stoughton 1915 (Sept.). 1*s.*

—— Peace Proposals and the attitude of the Allies. Speech delivered in the House of Commons on Dec. 19, 1916. Hay man, Christy & Lilly 1916.

—— Fact and Fiction. A Statement on Shipping and Food Supplies. Hodder & Stoughton 1917. 1*d.*

—— The Great Crusade. (Extracts from Speeches delivered during the War, arranged by F. L. Stevenson.) Hodder & Stoughton 1918. 1*s.* 6*d.*

Grey, Rt. Hon. Viscount. Why Britain is in the war, and what she hopes from the future. A speech delivered to the representatives of the Foreign Press in London, Oct. 23, 1916. Published by authority. Fisher Unwin 1916. 1*d.*

Harcourt. Rt. Hon. Lewis. A Free Empire in War Time. A speech delivered on Jan. 26, 1915. Victoria League 1*d.*

Hughes, Rt. Hon. W. M. The Day—and After. War Speeches, arranged by K. A. Murdoch. With Introduction by the Rt. Hon. D. Lloyd George. Cassell 1916. 1*s.*

—— —— New edn., with additional speeches. Cassell 1917. 5*s.*

Law, Rt. Hon. A. Bonar. The War Loan. A speech delivered by the Chancellor of the Exchequer at the Guildhall on Jan. 11, 1917. Reprinted from the Times. Hollebone & Trench, 18, Birchin Lane, E.C. 1917. n.p.

Lee, Col. Arthur, M.P. The need of National Service. Lessons of the War. Address at Fareham, Aug. 17, 1915. National Service League.

Montagu, Rt. Hon. Edwin. The means of victory. Speech delivered by the Minister of Munitions on Aug. 15, 1916. Fisher Unwin 1916. 6*d.*

Pankhurst, Christabel. America and the War. A speech delivered at the Carnegie Hall, New York. W.S.P.U. 1*d.*

—— The War. A speech delivered at the London Opera House on Sept. 8, 1914. W.S.P.U. 1*d.*

Redmond, J. E., M.P. Ireland and the War. Extracts from speeches made since the outbreak of war. Dublin: Sealy. 1*d.*

Rosebery, Lord. War! A Fight to the Finish. Stirling: Mackay. 1*d.*

Smuts, Lieut.-General J. C. The British Commonwealth of Nations. Hodder & Stoughton 1917. 1*d.*

—— The Coming Victory. A Speech. Hodder & Stoughton 1917. 1*d.*

—— War Time Speeches (delivered in Great Britain). Hodder & Stoughton 1917. 1*s.*

—— East Africa. An address given on Jan. 28. Royal Geographical Society 1918. 1*s.*

War by Sea, The Conduct of the. Speeches by the Rt. Hon. Winston Churchill, Feb. 15, 1915, and the Rt. Hon. H. H. Asquith, March 1, 1915, in the House of Commons; with the reply of the Foreign Office to the American Note of Feb. 16, 1915. Darling & Son.

War Speeches by British Ministers 1914-16. Fisher Unwin 1917. 1*s.*

War Speeches, 1914-17. Edited, with preface, by Benedict Ginsburg. Oxford Univ. Press 1917. 2*s.* 6*d.*

B.—FOREIGN.

Bethmann Hollweg, Th. v. Kriegsreden. Hrsg. v. Fr. Thimme (Polit. Bücherei). 1918. 10 mk.

Cammaerts, Emile. To the men behind the Armies. An address given on behalf of the Fight-for-Right movement. Fisher Unwin 1917. 1*d.*

D'Annunzio, Gabriele. Per la piu grande Italia: Orazioni e Messaggi. Milan: Treves. 2 l. 50.

Helfferich, K. Reden u. Aufsätze aus d. Kriege Mit 1 Bildn. 1917. 6 mk. 50.

Huysmans, Camille. Policy of the International [Socialist Bureau]. A speech. Allen & Unwin 1916. 6*d.*

Jonesco, Take. La Politique de l'instinct national. Speech delivered in the Roumanian Chamber of Deputies on Dec. 16 and 17, 1915. Bucharest: Le Roumanie 1915.

Lodge, Senator H. Cabot. War Addresses, 1915-17. Houghton Mifflin 1917. $2.50.

Mercier, Cardinal. The Voice of Belgium; being the war utterances of Card. M. With a preface by Cardinal Bourne. Burns & Oates 1917. 2*s.* 6*d.*

Poincaré, Raymond. Messages, Discours, Allocutions, [&c.], de M. Raymond Poincaré, President de la République, 31 Juillet 1914-17 Nov. 1918. 2 vols. Bloud et Gay 1919.

Root, Hon. Elihu. Speech delivered in New York, Feb. 15, 1916, on American Neutrality and the Policy of President Wilson. Waterlow.

—— The United States and the War. The Mission to Russia. Political addresses by E. R. Ed. by R. Bacon and J. B. Scott. Harvard Univ. Press & Milford 1918. 10*s.* 6*d.*

Salandra, Antonio. (Prime Minister of Italy). Notre guerre est une guerre sainte. Discours prononcé le 2 Juin, 1915. Payot 1915. 50 c.

—— Speech delivered on June 2, 1915, in vindication of Italian policy. Transl. by Thomas Okey. Fisher Unwin. 6*d.*

—— and others. I'Italie et la guerre, d'après les témoignages de ses hommes d'état. (Speeches by Salandra, Tittoni, Barzilai, Orlando, and Sonnino, delivered in 1915-16). Armand Colin 1917.

Venizelos, E. La Politique de la Grèce (six speeches delivered in the Greek Chamber, Oct.-Nov., 1915.) With preface by Jos. Reinach. Paris: Imprimerie de l'est 1916. 3 fr.

—— and others. Cinq ans d'Histoire grecque, 1912-1917. Discours prononcés . . . en août 1917 par Venizélos, Politis, Repoulis et Cafandaris. Traduction de Léon Maccas. Berger Levrault 1917. 4 fr.

Viviani, René. La Mission française en Amerique. Préface de M. Henri Bergson. (Discours prononcés sur le sol des États Unis, 24 avril-13 mai 1917.) Hammarion 1917. 3fr. 50.

Wildgrube, M. Zwei Reden gegen England. Dresden 1915. 1 m. 50.

Wilhelm II, and others. Der Kriegsausbruch, 1914. Thron- und Kanzlerrede; Denkschrift und Actenstücke. Speeches of the Emperor, the Chancellor and others; historical sketch and documents. Berlin: Heymann. 1 m.

Wilson, President Woodrow. The new freedom. (Collection of the more suggestive portion of speeches delivered by the President. Jan.-Feb., 1916). Dent 1916. 1*s.*

—— America and Freedom. Being the statements of President Wilson on the War. Preface by Viscount Grey. Allen & Unwin 1917. 1*s.*

—— Why we are at war. (Messages to Congress, Proclamations, &c., Jan.-April, 1917). Harper 1917. 50 c.

—— The Challenge accepted. Address to Congress. April 2, 1917. Fisher Unwin 1917. 1*s.*

—— In our first year of war (Presidential war-messages). Portrait. New York: Harper 1918. $1.00.

—— Foreign Policy: Messages, Addresses and Papers. Edited by J. B. Scott. Oxford Univ. Press 1918. 15*s.*

—— La guerre et la paix. Recueil des déclarations du Président. Berger-Levrault 1918. 2 fr.

V.—SCIENCE AND METHODS OF WAR.

A.—General.

(1) *Theory and Principles.*

Altham, E. A. Principles of War historically illustrated. 1914. Macmillan. 10*s.* 6*d.*

Anderson, Lieut.-Col. C. C. The War Manual. A comprehensive work of reference. 2 vols. Fisher Unwin 1915-16. 5*s.* each vol.

Andrews, Lincoln C. Fundamentals of Military Service. Lippincott 1916. 6*s.*

Aston, Major-Gen. Sir George. Sea, Land and Air Strategy. Second edn. Diagrams. Murray 1916. 10*s.* 6*d.*

—— War lessons, new and old. Murray 1918. 7*s.* 6*d.*

Atteridge, A. Hilliard. Famous Land Fights. Developments of armaments and tactics in warfare on land. Illustrated by typical battles in each period. Methuen 1914. 6*s.*

Azan, Col. P. The warfare of to-day. Translated by J. L. Coolidge. Boston: Houghton Mifflin 1918. $2.50.

Bailey, L. H. Universal Service. N.Y.: Spurgis & Walton 1918. $1.25.

Barzini, L. La guerre moderne sur terre, dans les airs, et sous les eaux. Translated from the Italian by J. Mesnil. Payot 1917.

Bellet, Dan., & Darvillé, Will. La guerre moderne et ses nouveaux procédés. (Illustrated.) Hachette 1916. 4 fr.

Belloc, Hilaire. Essays on War. With maps and plans. Constable 1915. 6*s*.

Bernhardi, Gen. F. von. How Germany makes War. Hodder & Stoughton. 2*s*.

—— On War of To-day. Authorised translation by Karl von Donat. Two vols. Hugh Rees. 18*s*.

Blanchon, G. La guerre nouvelle (progress of the military art). Colin 1916. 3 fr. 50.

—— English translation under title The New Warfare. Harrap 1917. 3*s*. 6*d*.

Bonnal, Général. Les conditions de la guerre moderne. Fontemoing 1916. 3 fr. 50.

Bourdaire. L'Alimentation des armées dans les guerres modernes. Berger-Levrault 1914. 2 fr. 50.

Clausewitz, Gen. Karl von. On War. Translated by Col. J. J. Graham. New and revised edn. With introduction and notes by Col. F. N. Maude. 3 vols. Kegan Paul & Co. 21*s*.

—— —— Translated by Miss Maguire. Clowes. 7*s*. 6*d*.

—— War according to Clausewitz. (An abridgment of vol. I of the treatise On War). Edited, with Commentary, by Major-General T. B. Pilcher, C.B. Cassell 1918. 7*s*. 6*d*.

Coulton, G. G. The case for Compulsory Military Service. Macmillan 1918. 7*s*. 6*d*.

Fischer, Wilh. Spionage, Spione und Spioninnen. 1916. 3 m.

Fletcher-Vane, Major Sir F. The Principles of Military Art for Officers of all ranks. Dent 1916. 2*s*. 6*d*.

Foch, Marshal. The Principles of War. Translated by Hilaire Belloc, with maps and diagrams. Chapman & Hall 1918. 16*s*.

Foster, Colonel H., R.E. War and the Empire : the Principles of Imperial Defence. Williams & Norgate. 2*s*. 6*d*.

Franklin, T. Bedford. Tactics and the Landscape. Gale & Polden 1914. 3*s*.

Freytag-Loringhoven, General Baron von. Geschultes Volksheer oder Miliz? Kriegslehren aus Vergangenheit und Gegenwart. 9th edn. 1918. 3 mk. 95.

—— English translation under title A Nation Trained in Arms, or a Militia. Constable 1918. 4*s*.

—— Folgerungen aus dem Weltkriege. 19th edn. 1918 3 mk. 60.

Freytag-Loringhoven, General Baron von. English translation under title Deductions from the World-War. Constable 1917. 2*s*. 6*d*.

George, Eric. National Service and National Training. King 1913. 1*s*.

Gizycki, H. V. Exercises in Strategy and Tactics. Translated by H. L. Rocca and Spenser Wilkinson. New edn. Milford 1915. 3*s*. 6*d*.

Goltz, Baron Colmar von der. The Conduct of War. A short treatise on its most important branches and guiding rules. Translated by Major G. F. Leverson. Kegan Paul. 10*s*. 6*d*.

—— The Nation in Arms. Translated by P. A. Ashworth. New edn., revised in accordance with the fifth German edn. Hugh Rees. 7*s*. 6*d*. Popular edn. Hodder & Stoughton. 2*s*.

Grande, Julian. Citizens' Army : the Swiss System. With introduction by Col. Feyler. Chatto & Windus 1916. 3*s*. 6*d*.

Grant, Hamilton. Spies and Secret Service. Historical and contemporary, with a bibliography. Grant Richards. 7*s*. 6*d*.

Hamley, Gen. Sir E. B. The Operations of War : explained and illustrated. New edn., brought up to date by Brig.-Gen. Kiggell. Blackwood. 30*s*.

Hearnshaw, Prof. F. J. C. Freedom in Service. On the combination of political liberty with national military service. Murray 1916. 2*s*. 6*d*.

Hartmann, Gen. Julius von. Militärische Notwendigkeit und Humanität. Deutsche Rundschau, Vols. XIII, XIV, 1877-78.

James, Lieut.-Col. W. H. Modern Strategy. Blackwood 1903. 16*s*.

Jaurès, Jean. Democracy and Military Service. An abbreviated translation of L'Armée nouvelle. Edited by G. G. Coulton. Simpkin, Marshall 1916. 1*s*.

Johnson, Prof. D. W. Topography and Strategy in the War. Constable 1918. 10*s*. 6*d*.

Johnstone, Capt. H. M., R.E. The Foundations of Strategy. Allen & Unwin 1914. 5*s*.

Kent, John. Conscription : National Service, Industrial and Military. Newspaper Publ. Co. 1915. 6*d*.

Kernshaw, Coulson, and Moulton, Prof. J. H. The Black Hour : Armaments and War. C. H. Kelly. 3*d*.

Levey, Capt. J. H. Five Instructional Lectures to Regimental Officers on the Western Campaign. Foster Groom 1915. 2*s*. 6*d*.

Ludlow, W. R. National Military Service. A lecture. Birmingham : Journal Office 1915. 2*d*.

Macfall, Haldane. Battle : showing how Battles are Fought, and the Why and the Wherefore. Simpkin 1915. *6d.*

Marcosson, J. S. The Business of War. Lane 1918. *5s.*

Maude, Col. F. N. Evolution of Modern Strategy from the 18th century to the present time. Clowes 1905. *5s.*

—— War and the World's Life. With diagrams and maps. Smith, Elder 1914. *12s. 6d.*; reduced to *5s.*

Meakin, A. M. B. Enlistment or Conscription? A study. Routledge. *1s.*

Murray, Major Stewart L. The Reality of War. A companion to Clausewitz. Popular edn., edited by A. H. Atteridge. Hodder & Stoughton. *2s.*

Nash's War Manual. Nash. *2s.*

Oliver, F. S. Democracy and National Service. The concluding part of Ordeal by Battle, with an abridgement of the earlier chapters. Macmillan 1916. *1s.*

Pearce, C. E. War up to Date. A handbook of various information. Stanley Paul 1915. *1s.*

Practical Warfare. Chapters on armies and navies in action. Eveleigh Nash 1915. *3s. 6d.*

Radiguet, René, Général de Division. The Making of a Modern Army, and its Operations in the Field. Translated from the French. Putnam 1918. *6s.*

Roscoe, J. E. The Ethics of War Spying and Compulsory Training. Nutt 1914. *1s.*

Shirley, Lieut.-Col. W. Moral : the Most Important Factor in War. An address. Sefton, Praed 1916. *6d.*

Skrine, Francis H. Wanted : a Citizen Army and Navy. Longmans 1914. *3d.*

Treitschke, H. von. The Organization of the Army. Gowans & Gray 1914. *6d.*

"Ubique" (pseud.). How Armies Fight. With maps, diagrams and illustrations. Nelson 1914. 1s.

Universal Service, The Case for. Sydney : Univ. Service League. *1d.*

Voluntary Service, the Case for. Handbook of the Voluntary Service Committee. King. *1s.*

Wilkinson, Spenser. First Lessons in War. Methuen. *1s.*

—— The Nation's Servants. Three essays on the education of officers. Constable 1916. *6d.*

—— The Study of War. Oxford Univ. Press. *1s.*

—— The Brain of an Army. An essay on the German General Staff, with Letters from Count Moltke and Lord Roberts. Constable. *2s. 6d.*

(2) *Transport.*

Iiedell, Major J. S., A.S.C. Transport and Commissariat. A Manual of the organization and work of the Army Service Corps. Murray 1916. 1*s.*

Kirkaldy, Adam W., and Evans, Alfred D. History and Economics of Transport. Pitman 1915. 7*s.* 6*d.*

Motor Transport Year-Book and Directory. Electrical Press 1916. 10*s.* 6*d.*

Wyatt, Horace. Motor Transports in War. (Daily Telegraph War Books.) Hodder & Stoughton 1914. 1*s.*

(3) *Explosives.*

D'Arman, R. Turpin et ses poudres. Editions et Librairie. 50*c.*

Hall, C., and Howell, S. P. Tests of Permissible Explosives. (U.S. Bureau of Mines.) Illustrated. Wesley 1914. 2*s.* 6*d.*

Koppe, S. W. Glycerine: its Production, Uses, and Examination. Translated from the German. 2nd edn. Ed. by William H. Simmons. Scott Greenwood 1915. 7*s.* 6*d.*

List of Authorized Explosives. H.M.S.O. 1915. 2*d.*

Marshall, A. Explosives: their Manufacture, Properties, Tests and History. By the Chemical Inspector, Indian Ordnance Dept. Illustrated. Churchill 1915. 24*s.*

—— A short account of Explosives. (By the Chemical Inspector, Indian Ordnance Dept.) Churchill 1917. 5*s.*

—— Explosives. 2 vols. Churchill 1917. £3 3*s.*

Martin, Geoffrey, and Barbour, William. Industrial Nitrogen Compounds and Explosives. A practical treatise on the manufacture, properties and industrial uses of nitric acid, nitrates, nitrites, ammonia, ammonia salts, cyanides, etc., including the most recent modern explosives. Crosby Lockwood 1915. 7*s.* 6*d.*

Ramsey, A. R. J., and Weston, H. C. A Manual on Explosives. Routledge 1916. 1*s.*

Schopin, H., and Driver, J. F. Shell-turning for Munition Workers. Blackie 1916. 1*s.*

(4) *Women's Work.*

Call to Women: or Woman's Part in the Great World Conflict. Garden City Press 1915. 2*d.*

Churchill, Lady Randolph (edr.). Women's War Work. Chapters by ten contributors. Pearson 1916. 2*s.* 6*d.*

Ellis, T. Mullett. What can a Woman Do for the Empire? Holden & Hardingham 1915. 1*s.*

Paget, Mrs. Luke. The Women's Part. Oxford Univ. Press. *2d.*

Webster, Nesta H. Britain's Call to Arms: an Appeal to our Women. H. Rees 1914. *1d.*

(5) *Miscellaneous.*

Baden-Powell, Lieut.-General. Quick Training for War. A few practical suggestions, illustrated by diagrams. Jenkins. *1s.*

Barlow, Sir Montague, and Williams, Gordon. War Pensions, Gratuities, Allowances, Treatment and Training for Officers, N.C.O.'s and Men. Davy & Sons 1918. *1s.*

Beatson, Lieutenant A. M. The Motor-Bus in War. Impressions of an A.S.C. Officer during two and a half years at the Front. Fisher Unwin 1918. *5s.*

Beaumont, Roberts. Standard Cloths, Structure and Manufacture: General, Military and Naval. G. Scott 1916. *12s. 6d.*

Beddington, Major F. M. How to become a Useful and Efficient Officer. Forster, Groom 1916. *6d.*

Beggs, Captain S. T., R.A.M.C. The selection of the Recruit. Detailed guide to physical requirements. Baillière 1915. *2s. 6d.*

Bonnett, Frank. Revolvers and Pistols and how to use them. Aldine Publishing Co. 1915. *1s.*

Brockington, W. A. Elements of Military Education. By the Director of Education, Leicestershire Regiment. Longmans 1916. *4s. 6d.*

Brown's Signalling: How to Learn the Commercial Code and all other Forms of Signalling. 17th edn. J. Brown 1915. *2s. 6d.*

Burns, John. Extinction of Casualties. 2nd edn. Green 1916. *15s.*

Dawson, A. J. How to help Lord Kitchener. Hodder & Stoughton. *7d.*

Festing, Gabrielle. The Civilian in War Time. National Service League. *1d.*

Frost, J. Albert. Shire Horse in Peace and War. Vinton 1915. *2s.*

General's, A, Letters to his son on Minor Tactics. Hugh Rees 1918. *2s.*

Guide to Official Letter-Writing, Orders, etc. By an Adjutant. 3rd edn., revised. Gale & Polden. *1s.*

Hale, Colonel Sir Lonsdale. What to Observe and How to Report it. 8th edn., revised by E. W. Sheppard. Hugh Rees 1915. *9d.*

Hall, Cyril. Modern Weapons of War: by Land, Sea and Air. Illustrated. Blackie 1914. *2s. 6d.*

Hardwicke, W. Wright. Sight-Testing made easy. 3rd edn. Churchill 1916. *2s. 6d.*

Hogge, J. M., M.P. Pensions, allowances, and civil disabilities. (Information useful to applicants.) Daily Mail 1916. *3d.*

—— and Garside, T. H. War Pensions and Allowances. Hodder & Stoughton 1918. *6s.*

Jones, Bernard E. Workshop Hints for Munition Workers. (Work Handbooks.) Cassell 1916. *1s.*

Macartney, Douglas H. Naval and Military Cadet Training. King. *6d.*

Mallory, George. War Work for Boys and Girls. Allen & Unwin 1916. *3d.*

Maltby, W. R. Active Service: the Share of the Non-combatant. (Papers for War Time.) Milford 1914. *2d.*

Museums and the War. Articles containing suggestions as to the help that Museums may render. By various writers. The Museums Journal.

Newbold, J. T. W. How Europe Armed for War. A study of vested interests in the manufacture of war-material. Blackfriars Press 1916. *1s.*

New War Encyclopædia and Dictionary. Jarrold. *6d.*

On the March. A Companion for Soldiers and Sailors on Active Service. Simpkin 1915. *2d.*

Parry, Judge E. A., and Codrington, Lieut.-General Sir A. E. War Pensions, past and present. Nisbet 1918. *5s.*

Pratt, Edwin A. The Rise of Rail-power in War and Conquest, 1833-1914. King 1916. *7s. 6d.*

Provisional Regulations, Rules, etc. (Munitions.) Wyman 1915. *½d.* and *1d.*

Pull, Ernest. The Munition Worker's Handbook. A guide for persons taking up Munition work. Illustrated. C. Lockwood 1916. *2s. 6d.*

Spurgeon, Caroline F. E. The Training of the Combatant. An address delivered for the Fight for Right movement. Dent 1916. *2d.*

Steers, H. D. Officers' Training Corps Year-Book and Diary, 1916. Groom 1916. *1s.*

Tips for the Front: What to Do and What to Avoid on Active Service. Gale & Polden. *6d.*

Tweney, C. F. Dictionary of Naval and Military Terms, with Names and Description of the Principal Ships in the British Navy, etc., from Official Sources. Fisher Unwin. *2s. 6d.*

Waite, Surgeon-Major E. How to keep Fit: the Soldier's Guide to Health. *3d.*

B.—Naval.

Anderson, R. C. (edr.). The Naval Pocket-Book. 20th year of issue. Thacker 1915. *7s. 6d.*

Attwood, Edward L. The Modern Warship. Camb. Univ. Press 1913. *1s.* and *2s. 6d.*

—— War ships. A textbook of theoretical naval architecture. 6th edn., revised and enlarged. Illustrated. Longmans. *7s. 6d.*

Baden-Powell, Lieut.-General. Sea Scouting and Seamanship for Boys. New edn. Brown 1916. *1s. 6d.*

"Barfleur" (pseud.). Naval Policy: a Plea for the Study of War. Blackwood. *2s. 6d.*

Baudry, A. The Naval Battle. Studies of the tactical factors. H. Rees 1914. *8s. 6d.*

Blanchon, G. The new [Naval] Warfare. (Transl. from the French.) Harrap 1918. *3s. 6d.*

Bridge, Admiral Sir Cyprian. Sea Power and other Studies. Smith, Elder. *5s.*

Clarke, Colonel Sir G. S. and Thursfield, J. R. The Navy and the Nation; or, Naval Warfare and Naval Defence. Maps. Murray. *14s.*

Currey, E. Hamilton. The Man-of-War: What she has done and What she is doing. Jack 1914. *3s. 6d.*

Custance, Admiral Sir R. The Ship of the Line in Battle. Blackwood 1913. *5s.*

Dommett, W. E. Submarines, Torpedoes, and Mines. Illustrated. Whittaker 1915. *1s.*

Domville-Fife, C. W. The Submarine in War. Hodder & Stoughton 1914. *1s.*

—— Submarines, Mines and Torpedoes in the War. (Daily Telegraph War Books.) 1915. *1s.*

Edelsheim, Freiherr von. Germany's Naval Plan of Campaign against Great Britain and the United States. Transl. by A. Gray. Hodder & Stoughton. *1s.*

Eley, Charles V. How to Save a Big Ship from Sinking, even though Torpedoed. Simpkin 1915. *3s. 6d.* New edn. 1916. *2s. 6d.*

Ferraby, H. C. The Grand Fleet. What the Navy does and how it does it. Illustrated. Jenkins 1916. *2s. 6d.*

Field, Cyril. The Story of the Submarine, from the earliest ages to the present day. Illustrated. Sampson Low 1915. *6s.*

Five Minutes to One Bell. A few hints to junior watch-keepers, together with some remarks on the duties of a destroyer First Lieutenant. By a Watch-keeper. Hogg 1915. *2s. 6d.*

Fowler, G. H. Charts: Their Use and Meaning. (Prepared for the Challenger Society for the Promotion of the Study of Oceanography.) With 8 charts. J. D. Potter 1916. 4*s*.

Fyfe, H. C. Submarine Warfare, Past and Present, and its allied subjects, Submarine Navigation, Torpedo Construction, etc. Revised by John Leyland, with introduction by Admiral Freemantle. Grant Richards. 7*s*. 6*d*.

Hannay, David. The Navy and Sea Power. Williams & Norgate 1913. 1*s*.

Hay, Marley F. Secrets of the Submarine. Skeffington 1918. 2*s*. 6*d*.

Hovgaard, William. Structural Design of Warships. Many illustrations. Spon 1915. 21*s*.

Hurd, Archibald. The Command of the Sea: Some Problems of Imperial Defence. Chapman & Hall. 5*s*.

Joly, J. Synchronous Signalling in Navigation. Unwin 1916. 3*s*. 6*d*.

Kipling, Rudyard. Sea Warfare. Macmillan 1916. 5*s*.

Mahan, Admiral A. T. Naval Administrations and Warfare: some General Principles. Sampson Low. 7*s*. 6*d*.

Margerison, John S. The Navy's Way. (Chapters reprinted from periodicals.) Duckworth 1916. 1*s*.

Mason, Frank H. Book of British Ships. New and revised edn. Frowde & Hodder, 1915. 3*s*. 6*d*.

Mess Accounts and Messing. By an "A.P." (R.N. Gieve 1916. 3*s*. 6*d*.

Naval Officer, A. Break! How the British Seamen prepare for War. The Fleet Office. 1*s*.

Newbolt, Sir Henry. A Note on the History of Submarine War. Longmans 1918. 2*d*.

—— Submarine and Anti-Submarine. Longmans 1918. 7*s*. 6*d*.

Noyes, Alfred. Mystery Ships: Trapping the U-Boats. Hodder & Stoughton 1916. 2*s*.

P., R. Notes on Torpedo Work in H.M. Ships. F. Hogg 1914. 1*s*.

Pollen, A. The Navy in Battle. Illustrated. Chatto & Windus 1916. 7*s*. 6*d*.

Rousseau, A. Sous-marins et blocus avec 1 carte et 2 diagrammes. Alcan 1917. 2 fr.

Simpson, George. Naval Constructor. 3rd edn., revised and enlarged. Kegan Paul 1915. 21*s*.

Stirling, Commander Yates. Fundamentals of Naval Service. (An American manual.) Lippincott 1917. 8*s*. 6*d*.

Talbot, F. A. Submarines. Illustrated. Heinemann 1915. 3*s*. 6*d*.

Thursfield, James R. Naval Warfare. Camb. Univ. Press 1913. 1*s.*

—— Sea Power and the War. Oxford Univ. Press. 2*d.*

Thursfield, J. K. The Navy and the War. (O.P.) Oxford Univ. Press. 3*d.*

Troeltsch, Rudolf. Deutschlands Flotte im Entscheidungskampf. Berlin: Mittler 1914. 2 mk. 50.

Walker, Sydney F. Submarine Engineering. Illustrated. (How Does it Work series.) Pearson 1914. 1*s.*

C.—Territorial.

(1) *Infantry.*

Active Service Hints: a Campaigner's Tips for the Bivouac Camp; and Trenches. Written and illustrated by the staff of *The Regiment.* Temple Press. 6*d.*

Agate, Captain James E. (A.S.C.). L. of C. (Lines of Communication). Constable 1917. 6*s.*

Army Drill Made Easy. A handbook on dismounted drill for everyone, with an A.B.C. of the Army. Written and illustrated by the staff of *The Regiment.* Temple Press 1914. 6*d.*

Administrative Staff Work. Forster Groom 1917. 3*s.* 6*d.*

Audebert, Capitaine. Resolution des Problèmes tactiques. (New and enlarged edn., first published 1910.) Berger-Levrault 1917. 3 fr. 50.

Azan, Lieut.-Colonel Paul. The War of Positions (on modern tactics, by the Chief of the French Military Mission in the United States). Harvard Univ. Press 1917. $1.25.

Bacon, E. V. A Chart of the New Company Drill. With diagrams and notes. Hugh Rees 1915. 6*d.*

Banbury, Captain H. Wood. Aiming and Firing. The Hythe method of instructing recruits. With a note on Fire Discipline. Forster Groom 1916. 6*d.*

Banning, Lieut.-Colonel S. T. Tactics Made Easy. 3*s.* 6*d.*

Battalion Movements in the Attack, at a Glance. By an Adjutant. Forster Groom 1916. 6*d.*

Beca, Colonel. A Study of the Development of Infantry Tactics. Translated by Captain A. F. Custance. With preface by Colonel Hacket Pain. New edn. Allen & Unwin 1915. 1*s.*

Bent, James. From Training Camp to Fighting Line. Kelly 1915. 6*d.*

Bertrand, G., & Solbert, O. N. Tactics and Duties for Trench Fighting. New York: Putnam 1918. $1.50.

Bostock, J. N.C.O.'s Musketry Small Book. 5th edn. W. H. Smith 1914. 1*s*. 6*d*.

—— Soldier's Standard Test Pocket Book. 3rd edn. W. H. Smith 1914. 2*d*.

Broad, Captain W. J. Instruction and Training for Miniature Rifle Range Practices. Gale & Polden. 3*d*.

Broman, Allan. A Short Course of Physical Training for the Recruits of the New Armies. Illustrated. Bale 1915. 1*s*. 6*d*.

Caillet, sous-lieut. Le nouvel officier d'infanterie en guerre : ce qu'il doit savoir. Berger-Levrault 1916. 1 fr.

Captain (pseud.). Platoon Drill at a Glance. Field Office 1915. 6*d*.

Cartwright, J. C. The Musketry Instructor. L. U. Gill 1915. 6*d*.

Casserly, Major Gordon. Manual of Company Training: for the New Armies and Volunteers. Hodder & Stoughton 1915. 1*s*.

—— Tactics for Beginners: for the Use of Officers of the New Armies and Volunteers. Hodder & Stoughton 1915, 1916. 1*s*.

—— Training of the Volunteers for War. Hodder & Stoughton 1915. 1*s*.

—— Training for Trench Warfare: for the Armies and Volunteers. Sefton Praed 1917. 6*d*.

Cawston, E. P. Practical Notes on Field Entrenchments: for Use in the Cambridge University Cadet Battalions. Hall & Son 1916. 1*s*.

Choosing Kit. A guide to active service requirements. By the author of Choosing Kit in *Land and Water*. McBride 1915 1*s*.

Coffey, Lieutenant G. E. Notes on Method of Giving Fire Orders. Paine 1915. 6*d*.

Cold Steel: How to Use the Bayonet, Sword and Lance. With a chapter on the pistol at close quarters. Written and illustrated by the staff of The Regiment. Temple Press 1915. 6*d*.

Collins, Major G. R. N. Military Organization and Administration. (Lectures given in the Canadian Military School.) Hugh Rees 1918. 8*s*. 6*d*.

Commander (*pseud.*). Hints and Tips for Members of the O.T.C. Groom 1915. 6*d*.

Company Commander (pseud.). From the Front. Notes for the New Armies. Harrison 1915. 6*d*.

Company Drill Illustrated. Harrison 1914. 6*d*.

Company Drill in Close Order. For the use of training corps. W. H. Smith & Son 1915. 2*d*.

D'André, le commandant. Guerre de 1914-15: Le Tir pour vaincre. A treatise on shooting. Illustrated. Berger-Levrault 1915. 3 fr.

Dane, Edmund. Trench Warfare: the Effects of Spade-Power in Modern Battles. United Newspapers 1915. *6d.*

—— (edr.). Secrets of Success in War: how Modern Armies Organize, Train and Fight. Hodder & Stoughton 1914. *2s.*

Davies, O. St. Leger. The Discipline of Musketry. A sequel to The Theory of Musketry. Forster Groom 1916. *6d.*

Davson, Major Ivan B. Elementary Principles of Musketry and Fire Tactics. Sifton 1915. *1s.*

Dixhuit (pseud.). Safety in Trench Warfare for Yourself and your Men. Gale & Polden 1918. *2s.*

Douglas, H. Automatic Pistols and Revolvers. Harrison 1915. *6d.*

—— Fire Orders, Direction and Control. Supplement to Rifle Shooting for War. Harrison 1915. *6d.*

—— Machine-Gun Manual. Illustrated. Harrison 1916. *1s.*

—— Rifle Shooting for War. Harrison 1915. *6d.*

Duval-Arnauld, P. Crapouillots (trench-mortars, etc.). Plon-Nourrit 1916. 3 fr. 50.

Entrenching Made Easy. By the Staff of *The Regiment.* Temple Press 1915. *6d.*

Esson, Captain C. C. Battalion Drill Illustrated. With many diagrams. Harrison 1915. *1s.*

—— Company Drill Illustrated. 6th edn. Harrison 1915. *6d.*

—— Squad Drill Illustrated: including Platoon Drill. 6th edn. Harrison 1915. *6d.*

—— Platoon Drill Illustrated. Philip & Son 1916. *6d.*

F., J. I. Cardinal Points in the Attack. Edinburgh: Grant 1915. *6d.*

Foley, F. W. Trench Reliefs and Duties. Practical Press 1916. *6d.*

For Foreign Service: Hints on Soldiering in the Shiny East. By the Staff of *The Regiment.* Temple Press 1915. *6d.*

Forsyth-Major, Captain O. A. Elements of Tactics. Substance of a series of lectures. Gale & Polden 1916. *4s.*

Friend, B. J. Aids to Musketry for Officers and N.C.O.s. Harrison 1916. *6d.*

Fuller, J. F. C. Mobilization of a Territorial Infantry Battalion. Reprinted from The Army Review. Edinburgh: A. Brown 1914. *6d.*

—— Training Soldiers for War. H. Rees 1914. *2s.*

Fusilier (pseud.). Every Officer's Note-Book of Movements and Words of Command on Infantry Drill. Milford 1915. 1*s.*

Gaucher, André. Les principes du combat à la baionette à l'usage du combattant. Berger-Levrault 1916. 1 fr. 25.

Gompert, M. L. A. The Indian Army Quarter-Master's Manual. Thacker 1914. 4*s.* 6*d.*

Goodwin, J. C. Practical Musketry Instruction. Melrose 1916. 2*s.* 6*d.*

Greener, W. W. Sharpshooting for War and Defence. Illustrated. Emergency edn. Simpkin 1914. 1*s.*

Grenadier (pseud.). Notes on Elementary Field Training. Parts I and II. Rees 1915. 1*s.* each.

—— Notes on Outposts. Rees 1915. 3*d.*

Hall, Middleton. Hints on Rifle Shooting. Hodges 1914. 6*d.*

—— Practical Rifle Shooting for Soldiers and Civilians. 1*s.*

Hamilton, W. H. Rapid Training for Young Officers. Groom 1915. 1*s.*

Hanbury, H. Wood. Aiming and Firing: the Hythe Method of Instructing Recruits, with a Note on Fire Discipline Training. Groom 1915. 6*d.*

Handbook for Company Officers. Harrison 1915. 1*s.* 6*d.*

Hay, Lieut.-Col. A. W., and Horan, Capt. H. J. Syllabus of Infantry Training, as suggested by notes on Company Training issued by the General Staff and adopted by 52nd Overseas Battalion, Canadian Expeditionary Force. Rees 1916. 4*s.*

Holbrook. Drill Diagrams: Extensions. Cooke & Vowles 1915. 6*d.*

—— Drill Diagrams: Section, and Platoon and Company Drill. Twelve diagrams illustrating at a glance the commands, execution and formation. Cooke & Vowles 1915. 1*s.*

—— Drill Diagrams: Squad, Section, Platoon and Company Drill. Cooke & Vowles 1915. 1*s.*

—— Squad Drill Diagrams. Cooke & Vowles 1914 [1915]. 6*d.*

Hood, Basil. Duties for All Ranks: specially compiled for the new Armies and Volunteer Training Corps. Harrison 1915. 6*d.*

Hornby, Col. M. L., D.S.O. How to March. Hugh Rees 1915. 9*d.*

—— Regent Section of Platoon Roll Book. Rees 1915. 1*s.*

How to Use a Rifle or Pistol. With a chapter on map-reading. Temple Press 1914. 6*d.*

Howard, C. Main points for Musketry Instructors. 4th edn. Deighton Bell 1915. 6*d.*

Imperial Army Series. Based on official documents, and written by Officers of the Regular Army. Edited by E. John Solano:
1. Drill and Field Training.
2. Field Entrenchments.
3. Signalling.
4. Musketry.
5. Ceremonial (Billets, Camps, Cooking, etc.).
6. Physical Training (Senior).
7. ,, ,, (Junior). John Murray 1914. 1*s.* each.

Infantry Recruit Training. By Two Officers of the Dorsetshire Regiment. 3rd edn. Harrison 1915. 6*d.*

Invicta (pseud.). Hints for Volunteers. Gale & Polden 1913. 1*s.* 6*d.*

Kinsman, Lieut.-Col. H. J. Tactical Notes. H. Rees 1914. 5*s.*

Laffargne, le capitaine André. Étude sur l'attaque dans la période actuelle de la guerre. Impressions et réflexions d'un commandant de compagnie. 1916.

Lake, Capt. B. C. Knowledge for War: Every Officer's Handbook for the front. Harrison 1916. 2*s.* 6*d.*

Legge, R. F. Guide to Promotion for Officers in Subject (*a*) 1: Regimental Duties. 5th edn., revised to date. Gale & Polden 1914. 4*s.*

—— Mainly about Discipline. Gale & Polden 1914. 6*d.*

Levey, J. H. What to Teach on Landscape Targets. Groom 1915. 3*d.*

Lings, Harold C. Musketry Lectures for Non-Commissioned Officers of the Territorial Force. Gale & Polden 1914. 2*s.*

—— Musketry Lectures for Officers and N.C.O.s. With introduction by Major-Gen. Douglas. 2nd edn. Gale & Polden 1915. 1*s.* 6*d.*

Lynch, George. War Wire. On wire entanglements, by a war correspondent. Bird 1916. 1*s.*

McClean, W. N., C.E. Some Notes on Trench Construction. Illustrated. Vacher 1916. 1*s.*

McLaglen, Leopold. Bayonet Fighting for War. Illustrated. Harrison 1916. 9*d.*

—— Infantry Pocket-Book: a Concise Guide for Infantry Officers and N.C.O.s. Harrison 1916. 1*s.*

MacGuarrie, Hector. How to Live at the Front: Tips for American Soldiers. Lippincott 1918. 5*s.*

Making of an Officer, The. By C. N. (five articles published in The Times). Hodder & Stoughton 1916. 1*s.*

Mann, W. Mortlake. Physical Drill for Home Defence Corps. Harrison 1916. 6*d.*

Martian (pseud.). Lectures and Lessons on Musketry Instruction for Officers and N.C.O.s. Hugh Rees 1916. *2s.*

Meath, The Earl of (edr.). The Soldier's Pocket Companion. Crosby Lockwood 1915. *1s.*

Mechanism, The, of the Rifle at a Glance. (Short Rifle Magazine Lee-Enfield, Mark III). Gale & Polden 1916. *6d.*

Merriman, P., and Coney, H. R. H. Canvas and Camaraderie: the Compleat Territorial. Illustrated. Harrison & Sons 1914. *6d.*

Milton, Major (pseud.). Drill Blocks. Designed by a Field Officer Instructor to facilitate the private study of squad drill and platoon and double company manœuvres. G. Philip 1915. Blocks *2s. 6d.*; Handbook *6d.*

Moffitt, F. W. Infantry Field Work: Lectures to Non Commissioned Officers. H. Rees 1914. *6d.*

Monk, M. G. The New Company Drill at a Glance. L. U. Gill 1914. *6d.*

Morris, A. Musketry Teacher. A complete Guide for Instructors of Musketry. Gale & Polden 1915. *1s.*

Musketry. (1) Aiming Instruction and Firing Instruction. (2) Visual Training and Judging Distance. (3) Theory of Rifle Fire, Elementary and Advanced. (Whitehall Series.) Forster, Groom 1916. *6d.* each.

Naylor, H. E. Marching Terms and Evolutions. Gale & Polden. *1s. 6d.*

O'Donnell, H. Ammunition Supply and Fire Direction and Control.

—— Attack and Defence. A Lecture to Company Officers.

—— Attack from the Company Officer's Point of View.

—— Defence.

—— Deportment.

—— Fighting in Close Country.

—— Fire and Formations.

—— Hints on Preparing Short Company Lectures and Addresses to Young Officers on Joining.

—— Protection when at Rest.

—— Reconnoitring and Scouting.

—— Training of the Soldier: Intercommunication and Passing Orders and Messages.

—— Twelve Lectures on the Military Art.

—— Use of Ground and Advancing Under Fire. Gale & Polden 1915. *6d.* each.

Officers' Training Corps Year-Book and Diary. Groom 1915. *1s.*

Ommundsen, H., and Robinson, E. H. Rifles and Ammunition, and Rifle Shooting. Cassell 1915. *21s.*

Out There! or The Platoon Commander in Warfare. Sifton, Praed 1915. *9d.*

Plant, H. L. Maze Drill Illustrated. For the army and navy, volunteer corps, schools, displays, scouts, boys' brigades, etc. Harrison 1916. *1s.*

Platoon and Company Drill. Compiled by the Commandant and Officers on the Staff of the London District School of Instruction. Illustrated. Harrison 1916. *1s.*

Platoon Commander (pseud.). Guard and Sentry Duty Simplified. Practical Press 1915. *2d.*

Pollard, Capt. Hugh. The Book of the Pistol and Revolver (partly historical). McBride Nast 1917. *10s. 6d.*

Pollock, H. W. A. Elementary Military Training. 3rd edn., revised and enlarged. Clowes 1915. *4s.*

Power of the Company Commander: with Specimen of Conduct Sheet. Gale & Polden 1915. *6d.*

Practical Bayonet Fighting. By an Officer. Bazaar, Exchange & Mart. *6d.*

Raker, Sergt.-Major. Notes on Musketry Training. Paine 1915. *6d.*

Rapid Training of Recruits. A practical scheme. By Instructor. Gale & Polden 1916. *1s. 6d.*

Recruit's Handbook. Hodder & Stoughton 1915. *6d.*

Recruit's Problems Solved. A manual for recruits undergoing military training. Dawson 1915. *3½d.*

Recruit Training: Infantry 1914. An aid to all instructors. By two Officers of the Dorsetshire Regiment. Harrison 1914. *6d.*

Richardson, Major A. R. Trench Warfare. Westminster Press 1916. *4d.*

Riggs, Charles. Practical Points in Musketry and the Care of a Rifle. Practical Press 1915. *3d.*

Robinson, Ernest H. How to Drill. Aldine Publishing Co. 1915. *2d.*

—— Rifle and Carton: Training with the Rifle for Sport and War. 3rd edn. E. Seale 1914. *1s.*

—— Rifle Training for War. Illustrated. Cassell 1914. *1s.*

Roudil, Capitaine. Petit Questionnaire à l'usage des gradés et soldats des sections de mitrailleuses. Berger-Levrault 1916.

Searchlight (pseud.). Kit and Equipment for Active Service. Groom 1915. *6d.*

Second in Command (pseud.). Notes on Trench Routine and Discipline. Forster, Groom 1916. *6d.*

Senior Major (pseud.). The Young Officer's Guide to Knowledge. 3rd edn. Harrison 1915. 1*s.*

Shaw, Fred G. Drilling Made Easy. T. G. Shaw 1915. 3*d.*

Simplex (pseud.). Musketry: consisting of Introductory, and Mechanism and Care of Arms. (Whitehall Series.) Forster, Groom 1916. 6*d.*

—— One-man Range Finders, and how to use them. Barr & Stroud, Marindin, etc. (Whitehall Series.) Forster, Groom 1916. 6*d.*

Sleeman, J. L. First Principles of Tactics and Organization. For Officers and N.C.O.s of the regular, special reserve and territorial forces. Gale & Polden 1914. 2*s.* 6*d.*

Smith, Lieut. J. S. Trench Warfare. By an American serving with the British army. New York: Dutton 1917. $1.50.

Smyth, E. J. B.S.A. Musketry Score Book, for use in the General Musketry Course. Forster, Groom 1918. 3*d.*

Solano, Capt. E. J. (edr.). Hand and Rifle Grenades. (Imperial Army Series.) Illustrated. Murray 1916. 1*s.*

Soldier's Pocket Companion. A little book with a wide range for the man on active service. Crosby Lockwood 1915. 1*s.*

Spivey, J. H. and Hendrie, H. A. Miniature Rifle Range. Illustrated. Harrison 1916. 6*d.*

Squad Drill Illustrated: including Platoon Drill, Rifle Exercises, and Extended Order. Harrison 1915. 6*d.*

Squad Military Drill, Rifle Exercises, and Extended Order. Illustrated. Harrison 1915. 6*d.*

Squad, Section, Platoon and Company Drill Made Easy For four-company organization in accordance with Infantry Training. Revised and brought up to date by an Adjutant. Gale & Polden 1914. 1*s.* 6*d.*

Standing Orders of an Infantry Battalion. Hugh Rees 1917. 3*s.* 6*d.*

Stewart, Capt. Bertrand. Active Service Pocket Book. 6th edn. Wyman 1915. 5*s.*

Stone, E. H. Quick Rifle Training for National Defence. Diagrams. Fisher Unwin 1915. 1*s.*

Subaltern's Handbook of Useful Information. By the author of Rapid Training of Recruits. Gale & Polden 1916. 2*s.* 6*d.*

Tactician (pseud.). The Battalion in Attack. Groom 1916. 1*s.*

—— Tactics for Field Officers and Company Commanders of the New Armies. Groom 1916. 2*s.* 6*d.*

Taylor, Brig.-Gen. A. W. Duties of Adjutants. Hugh Rees 1915-16. 6*d.*

Taylor, Brig.-Gen. A. W. How to Organize and Administer a Battalion. Hugh Rees 1915. 1*s*.

Todd, Col. Campbell. Guide to Keeping Company Accounts in the New Armies. Gale & Polden 1916. 1*s*.

Trapman, Capt. A. H. Straight Tips for Subs. 2nd edn. Groom. 6*d*.

Tracy, Capt. C. D. Revolver Shooting in War. A practical handbook. Sifton, Praed 1916. 1*s*.

—— —— 3rd edn., revised and enlarged. Sifton, Praed 1917 1*s*. 6*d*.

Trench Construction. The theories of a subaltern. Forster, Groom 1916. 1*s*.

Trydell, Major W. F. Tactical Notes for Scheme Problems or Outdoor Exercises. Clowes 1916. 5*s*.

Volunteer Training Corps Guide to Squad Drill and Rifle Exercises. By an Adjutant. Gale & Polden 1915. 1*s*

Volunteer Training Corps, Official Regulations for. Central Assn. V.T. Corps 1915. 6*d*.

Volunteer Training Corps, Regulations for. (Official Notices issued by the War Office, etc.). Clerkenwell Press. 6*d*.

Wakefield, Major H. G. R., and Harington, Capt. H. D., D.S.O. The Platoon Commander's Vade-mecum. Hugh Rees 1916. 1*s*. 6*d*.

Watts, Col. C. N. Notes on Street Fighting. In amplification of Sect. 145 of Infantry Training, 1914. Forster, Groom 1916. 6*d*.

Weaver, Major-Gen. Erasmus M. Notes on Military Explosives. 4th edn. Chapman & Hall 1918. 13*s*. 6*d*.

Webb-Johnson, Cecil. Soldiers' Feet and Footgear. Thacker 1915. 1*s*. 6*d*.

Webster, F. A. M. Duties for Officers, Non-Coms., and Men. Dawson 1915. 6*d*.

—— From Recruit to Firing-line. Sidgwick & Jackson 1914. 2*s*.

—— Volunteer Training Corps Handbook. Sidgwick & Jackson 1915. 6*d*. & 1*s*.

What Every Soldier Ought to Know. Compiled from the Official Manuals. Oxford Univ. Press. 2*d*.

When I Join the Ranks: What to Do and How to Do it. By the Major. A practical vade-mecum for recruits. Gale & Polden 1916. 1*s*.

Williams, Capt. Basil. Raising and Training the New Armies. Constable 1918. 5*s*.

Winans, Walter. Automatic Pistol Shooting, together with information on handling the duelling pistol and revolver. Illustrated. Putnam 1915. 3*s*. 6*d*.
Wyndham, Capt. H., B.S.F. Soldiers on Service. A Manual of practical information for members of the Expeditionary Force. Nash. 6*d*.
X.Y.Z. (pseud.). N.C.O.'s Pocket Book. Groom 1915. 1*s*.
—— Notes on Quick Training for Active Service Groom 1915. 1*s*.

(2) *Cavalry.*

Bernhardi, General F. von. Cavalry. A popular edn. of Cavalry in War and Peace. Hodder & Stoughton. 2*s*.
Galtrey, Capt. Sidney. The Horse and the War. Illustrated, with a note by Sir Douglas Haig. Country Life 1918. 6*s*.
Monsenergue, Colonel. Cavalry Tactical Schemes: a series of Practical Exercises for Cavalry. Transl. by E. Louis Spiers. (Pall Mall Military series.) H. Rees 1914. 6*s*.
Notes on Modern Cavalry Training. By a Cavalry Officer. Hugh Rees. 4*d*.
Wingfield, W. J. R. Lectures to Cavalry Subalterns of the New Armies. Groom 1915. 2*s*. 6*d*.

(3) *Artillery.*

Artillery Map-Reading, and Elementary Gunnery made easy. By "Gunlayer" and "Contour." Gale & Polden 1916. 3*s*. 6*d*.
Dixhuit (pseud.). Artillery Experience of Shooting and Observation in Trench Warfare. Gale & Polden 1918. 2*s*.
Grenadier (pseud.). Some Notes on Artillery: Considered from an Infantry standpoint. Rees. 1*s*.
Hill, H. W. Conditions necessary to produce Shrapnel Effect and report on Grouping Trials. Rees 1915. 6*d*.
Hunt, Lieut. A. L. Artillery Lines of Fire. With Map and Compass. Groom 1915. 1*s*.
Jackson, L. E. S. Why and the Wherefore of Indirect Laying. A simple explanation for officers, n.c.o.s and men. Groom 1915. 1*s*.
MacAlister, Lieut. D. A. Field Gunnery. A practical manual. with special reference to the heavies. 2nd edn. Murray 1916. 1*s*. 6*d*.
Making of a Gunner, The. By F.O.O. (author of With the Guns). Nash 1916. 3*s*. 6*d*.
Marre, Francis. Notre 75. On the famous French cannon. Bloud et Gay 1915. 60 c.

Mason, R. C. Handbook on Battery Drill: for a Four-Gun Battery, R.F.A. Revised by Lieut. A. L. Hunt, R.F.A. Forster Groom 1915. 1*s.*

O'Donnell, H. Ammunition Supply and Fire Direction and Control. Gale & Polden 1915. 6*d.*

Rawes, Lieut. J. N. Gunnery formulæ simplified (Whitehall series of Artillery Books). Forster Groom 1916. 1*s.*

Verner, R. H. C. Guns and Projectiles. Hogg 1914. 2*s.* 6*d.*

(4) *Machine Gunnery.*

Applin, Major. Machine-Gun Tactics. New and cheaper edn. Hugh Rees 1915. 3*s.* 6*d.*

Bostock, Lieut. J. The Machine Gunner's Handbook; including the Vickers' light gun. 3rd edn. W. H. Smith & Son 1914. 2*s.* 6*d.*

Charteris, Capt. N. K. Some Lectures and Notes on Machine Guns. W. H. Smith 1915. 1*s.*

Guide for the .303 Vickers' Machine Gun, Magazine Rifle Chamber: Mounted on Tripod mounting. Mark IV. Gale & Polden, 1915. 6*d.*

Hicks, P. M., and others. Instructional Handbook of the .303 Lewis Automatic Machine-Gun. Paine 1915. 1*s.*

Ironside, H. A. Machine-Gun: its Drill, Signals and Control. H. Rees 1914. 1*s.*

James, Lieut. D. McG. Instruction in the Machine-Gun. Groom 1915. 2*s.*

—— Notes on Musketry Instruction and Miniature Range-Shooting. 3rd edn., revised. Groom 1915. 1*s.*

Johnston, H. J. Handbook of the Colt Gun. Paine 1915. 2nd edn. 1916. 1*s.* 6*d.*

Longstaff, Major F. V., and Atteridge, A. H. The Book of the Machine-Gun. Illustrations. Hugh Rees 1917. 8*s.* 6*d.*

Machine-Gun Training. (Imperial Army series.) Edited by E. J. Solano. Murray 1915. 1*s.*

Rouse, Seymour. Practical Notes for Machine-Gun Drill and Training. To be read in conjunction with official handbooks. Groom 1916. 6*d.*

Simplex (pseud.). Instruction on the Lewis Automatic Machine-Gun. Groom 1916. 2*s.* 6*d.*

—— Musketry. Groom 1916. 6*d.*

—— Musketry, consisting of instructions in Machine-Guns and their uses. Forster Groom 1917. 1*s.*

Singleton, J. E. Hotchkiss Machine-Gun and Instructional Course. Author: Wolverhampton 1918. 2*s.* 6*d.*

(5) *Map-Reading, Scouting, etc.*

Adams, Morley. Camping and Pioneering. Illustrated. Frowde. 1*s.*

—— (edr.). The Scout's Active Service Book. Frowde, and Hodder & Stoughton 1915. 1*s.*

Axe, E. C. Military Panorama Sketching. A handbook on the preparation of panorama sketches [etc.] from a military standpoint. Forster, Groom 1916. 6*d.*

Brown's Signal Reminder: all Methods. J. Brown 1915. 9*d.*

Cameron, Lieut. L. C. Infantry Scouting. A practical manual for the use of Scouts at home and at the front. Illustrated. Murray 1916. 1*s.*

Carter, L. Bellin. Landscapes for Army Class Drawing. E. Arnold 1916. 2*s.*

Cooke, F. G. Scouting by Night. A sequel to the following. Gale & Polden 1916. 1*s.*

—— The Value of Observation in War. Gale & Polden 1916. 1*s.*

Craigen, W. G. Umty iddy:- the Quickest and Simplest Method of Learning the Morse Alphabet. Murray 1915. 6*d.*

Drew, T. Aids to the use of Maps employed by the English, French, Belgian, and German Armies. Jarrold 1916. 1*s.*

Eggar, H. C. Alphabetical Key to Message Form Signals, as used in Semaphore and Morse, with up-to-date instructions in Semaphore. F. Groom 1915. 4*d.*

—— How to Learn the Morse Alphabet in Rhymes about Dots and Dashes. F. Groom 1915. 3*d.*

Foot, P. B. Training of a Territorial Scout. Gale & Polden 1914. 1*s.* 6*d.*

Grinling, A. G. The Use of Field Telephones in the Field. Rees 1916. 1*s.*

Griffith, W. J. (edr.). Précis Writing and Reproduction for Army Classes. Arnold 1916. 2*s.* 6*d.*

Henderson, Major-Gen. Sir David. The Art of Reconnaissance. 3rd and enlarged edn. Murray 1916. 5*s.*

Henriques, R. L. Q. Guide to Army Signalling. 3rd edn. Gale & Polden 1908. 1*s.*

How to Become a Perfect Scout. By a B.P. Scout. Revised edn. Gale & Polden 1915. 6*d.*

Lake, Charles Sidney. Motor Cyclist's Handbook. 4th edn., revised and enlarged. Marshall 1915. 2*s.*

Lectures on Map Reading and Field Sketching. By Instructor. Edinburgh: Grant 1915. 6*d.*

Maclear, H. Night Marching by the Stars. With diagrams and maps. Rees 1915. 1*s.*

Map Reading and Panorama Sketching. By an instructor. 2nd edn., revised and enlarged. Sifton, Praed 1917. 4*s*. 6*d*.

Maunder, E. Walter. The Stars as Guides for Night Marching in North Latitude 50°. Kelly 1916. 2*s*.

Military Map: Elements of Modern Topography. (French School of War.) Macmillan 1916. 2*s*. 6*d*.

Military Map, The. (Additional chapters.) Elements of Modern Topography. (French School of War.) 8vo. Macmillan 1917. 3*s*.

Military Map Reading: Complete Guide. Specially compiled for candidates for first-class Army School certificates. Gale & Polden 1914. 1*s*.

Montague-Bates, F. S. Infantry Scout: an Outline of his Training. 2nd edn., revised and enlarged. Rees 1915. 1*s*. 6*d*.

Newton, W. G. Military Landscape Sketching and Target Indication. With introduction by Lieut.-Col. May. Hugh Rees 1916. 1*s*. 6*d*.

Norcock, Capt. L., and Wilson, Capt. F. S. Map Reading: a Self-instructional Manual. Sifton, Praed 1915. 4*s*. 6*d*.

Palmer, L. S. Guide to Pioneering with Instruments. Gale & Polden 1917. 1*s*. 6*d*.

Pathfinder (pseud.). Soldier's Night-Guide for Egypt, Arabia and India. Gale & Polden 1916. 3*d*.

Ryle, Arthur L. Morse Made Easy. Jordan & Gaskell 1916. 3*d*.

Signalling and Map Reading Made Easy. By the Staff of *The Regiment*. Temple Press 1914. 6*d*.

Soldier's Night-Guide for Egypt, Arabia and India. Gale & Polden 1916. 3*d*.

Terrell, Courtney. Notes of Lectures on Map Reading and Sketching. 2nd edn. Gale & Polden 1916. 1*s*.

Tilney, W. A. Marching or Flying by Night without a Compass. With tables of direction stars for use in the British Isles. New edn. H. Rees 1914. 2*s*.

Walsh, Capt. H. P. On Taking Bearings. 2nd edn. Murray 1916. 1*s*.

Weatherhead, R. Star Pocket-book; or, How to find your way at Night by the Stars. With foreword by Sir Robert Ball. 2nd impression, with appendix. Longmans 1915. 1*s*. and 1*s*. 6*d*.

Widner, Emil J. Military Observation Balloons (Captive and Free). Crosby, Lockwood 1918. $3.00.

Wyatt, Major G. N. Finding the way by the sun, moon and stars in the Northern Hemisphere without the aid of plans or tables (with charts). Woolwich: R.A. Institute Printing House 1916.

D.—AVIATION.

(1) Air Force Law, Provisional Manual of 1918.
(2) —— King's Regulations and Orders 1918. H.M.S.O. 1918. each 1*s*. 6*d*.

Berget, A. The Conquest of the Air. Illustrated. Revised edn. Heinemann 1911. 6*s*.

Berriman, A. E. Aviation: an Introduction to the Elements of Flight. Revised edn., illustrated. Methuen. 10*s*. 6*d*.

Brewer, R. W. A. The Art of Aviation. Lockwood 1913. 5*s*.

Bruce, Eric Stuart. Aircraft in War. (Daily Telegraph War Books.) Hodder & Stoughton 1914. 1*s*.

Buist, H. M. Aircraft in the German War. Methuen. 1*s*.

Claxton, William J. The Mastery of the Air. Illustrated. Blackie 1914. 2*s*. 6*d*.

Corbin, Thomas W. Aircraft, Aeroplanes, Airships, etc. Illustrated. (How Does it Work series.) Pearson 1914. 1*s*. 6*d*.

Crouvezier, Gust. L'Aviation pendant la Guerre. Illustrated. Preface by M. Barrès. Paris: Berger-Levrault 1915. 3 fr. 50.

—— La guerre aérienne. Le Rôle de la cinquième arme. Illustrated. (Pages d'histoire.) Berger-Levrault 1916. 90 c.

Dixie, Lieut.-Commander A. E. Air Navigation for Flight Officers. Gieve 1917. 10*s*. 6*d*.

Dommett, W. E. Aeroplanes and Airships: including steering, propelling and navigating apparatus, bombs, flechettes, anti-aircraft guns and searchlights . . . and exploits in the present war. Whittaker 1915. 1*s*. & 2*s*.

Duchene, Commandant. Flight without Formulæ: Simple Discussions on the Mechanics of the Aeroplane. Longmans 1914. 7*s*. 6*d*.

Fage, A. The Aeroplane: a Concise Scientific Study. By a Research Scholar in Aeronautics. Griffin. 6*s*.

Flight Lieutenant (pseud.). Hints for Flight Sub-Lieutenants. (Royal Naval Air Service.) F. Groom 1916. 1*s*.

Gill, N. J. The Flyer's Guide: an Elementary Handbook for Aviators. Rees 1916. 3*s*. 6*d*.

Grahame-White, Claude, and Harper, Harry. The Aeroplane. Illustrated. Jack 1914. 3*s*. 6*d*.

—— The Aeroplane in War. Illustrated. Cheaper edn. Laurie 1914. 5*s*.

—— Learning to Fly. A practical Manual for beginners. Laurie 1916. 2*s*. 6*d*.

—— With the Airmen. New edn. Frowde 1914. 3*s*. 6*d*

Grahame-White, Claude. Heroes of the Flying Corps. A description of the work of the airmen during the early stages of the war. Frowde & Hodder 1915. 5*s.*

—— Air Power; Naval, Military and Commercial. Chapman & Hall 1917. 7*s.* 6*d.*

Hamel, Gustav, and Turner, Charles C. Flying: Some Practical Experiences. Illustrated. Longmans 1914. 12*s.* 6*d.*

Harper, E. H., and Ferguson, Allan. Aerial Locomotion. Camb. Univ. Press 1911. 1*s.*

Hearne, R. P. Airships in Peace and War. (2nd edn. of Aerial Warfare.) With introduction by Sir Hiram Maxim.

—— Zeppelins and Super-Zeppelins. Lane 1916. 2*s.* 6*d.*

Lanchester, F. W. Aircraft in Warfare. Articles contributed to *Engineering*, in Sept.-Dec. 1914, with two new chapters on aerial strategy and raids. Preface by Gen. Sir David Henderson. Constable 1915. 12*s.* 6*d.*

—— The Flying Machine from an Engineering Standpoint. Constable 1916. 4*s.* 6*d.*

L'Armée de l'air, sa prédominance et sa tactique. Par * * * Illustrated. Berger-Levrault 1915. 2 fr.

McMinnies, Flight-Commander W. J. Practical Flying: complete course of instruction. With introduction by Major-General W. S. Brancker, and chapter on medical aspects of aviation. Illustrated by E. L. Ford. Temple Press 1918. 3*s.* 9*d.*

Matthews, R. Borlase. Aviation Pocket-Book 1914-15-16. Crosby Lockwood. 3*s.* 6*d.*

Middleton, Edgar. Airfare of To-day. Illustrated. Constable 1917. 3*s.* 6*d.*

Pemberton-Billing, N. Air War: How to Wage it. Gale & Polden 1916. 1s.

Robson, W. A. Aircraft in War and Peace. Illustrated. Macmillan 1916. 2*s.* 6*d.*

Royal Flying Corps, Work and Training of the. With illustrations and introduction by Lord Hugh Cecil. Illustrated London News 1917. 2*s.* 6*d.*

Saundby, Capt. R. H., R.A.F. Flying Colours. (Coloured plates of aeroplanes in action.) With a preparatory note by General Ashmore. The Aeroplane 1918. 15*s.*

Simmonds, Ralph. All about Aircraft: a Book for Boys. Cassell 1915. 6*s.*

Spaight, J. M. Aircraft in War. (Gives special attention to legal questions). Macmillan 1914. 6*s.*

Talbot, F. A. Aeroplanes and Dirigibles of War. Heinemann 1915. 3*s.* 6*d.*

Wade, W. L. (edr.). The Flying Book. (First published 1914; new edn. brought up to date.) Longmans 1917. 3*s*. 6*d*.

War Flying. Murray 1917. 1*s*.

Way of the Air, The. By an Air Pilot. Heinemann 1917. 3*s*. 6*d*.

Woodhouse, Henry. Text-Book of Military Aeronautics. Copiously illustrated. Werner Laurie 1918. 35*s*.

VI.—THE FIGHTING FORCES.

A.—General.

Dorling, Lieut.-Commander S. Ribbons and Medals: Naval, Military and Civil. G. Philip 1916. 2*s*.

Johnson, Stanley C. The Medals of Our Fighting Men (Illustrated). Black 1916. 3*s*. 6*d*.

Navy and Army Illustrated. New series. Newnes 1914. 6*s*. & 7*s*. 6*d*. each vol.

Officers and Men Mentioned in Despatches and Lists of Honours and Rewards. In parts. Army & Navy Gazette Office. 1*s*. each.

Our Army and Navy. Sixty-four large plates illustrating the British forces by land and sea, with explanatory letterpress. Nelson 1915. 1*s*.

Our Navy, our Army, in Peace and War. Gale & Polden 1914. 1*s*.

Our Sailors and Soldiers. Gale & Polden 1915. 2*s*. 6*d*.

Our Soldiers and Sailors: the Empire's Defenders in War and Peace. Illustrated. Ward, Lock 1914. 6*s*.

Rank at a Glance. Illustrations. Philip 1915. 1*s*.

Sellers, William E. With our Fighting Men: the story of their faith, courage and endurance in the Great War. Religious Tract Society. 2*s*. 6*d*.

Service Medals, Ribbons, Badges, and Flags (a collection of the smaller books on Ribbons and Medals, &c., previously issued by same publishers). Philip 1916. 5*s*.

Spurr, Frederick C. Some Chaplains in Khaki. An account of the work of chaplains of the United Navy and Army Board. Allenson 1915. 2*s*.

Stewart, Major Rupert. The Book of the Victoria Cross (Record of the deeds which won the V.C. from its institution in 1856 to the present day). Hugh Rees 1916. 6*s*.

War List, The, of the University of Cambridge, 1914-18. Camb. Univ. Press 1921. 20*s*.

Wood, Field-Marshall Sir Evelyn. Our Fighting Services and how they made the Empire. With 10 photogravures and many plans. Cassell 1916. *21s.*

B.—Fleets.

Abbot, Willis J. Soldiers of the Sea: the story of the United States Marines in the War. Illustrated. Dodd, Mead & Co. 1918. $1.50.

Archer, William. The Pirate's Progress. A short history of the U-boat. Chatto & Windus 1918. *6d.*

Attwood, Edwin L. A text book on the construction, protection, stability, turning, &c., of war vessels. 6th and revised edn. Longmans 1917. *12s. 6d.*

Balincourt, Commandant de. Les Flottes de combat en 1917: avec croquis et plans. Challamel 1917. 6 fr. 50.

Bartimeus (pseud.). The Navy Eternal. Illustrated. Hodder & Stoughton 1918. *6s.*

Bell, J. J. Little Grey Ships. Murray 1916. *2s. 6d.*

Brassey, Earl. Naval Annual, 1915-16. Edited by John Leyland. (War edn.). Clowes. *10s.*

British Navy from Within. By Ex-Royal Navy. Hodder & Stoughton 1915. *2s.*

Burgoyne, Alan. What of the Navy? Cassell. *5s.*

Clowes, Sir W. Laird. The Royal Navy: a History from the earliest times to the present. Illustrated. 7 vols. Sampson Low. £8 *10s.*

Corelli, Marie. Eyes of the Sea: A tribute to the Grand Fleet and the Grand Fleet's Commander. Marshall Bros. 1917. *1s.*

Cornford, L. Cope. Merchant Seaman, The, in War. Preface by Admiral Sir J. Jellicoe. Hodder & Stoughton 1917. *6s.*

Dixon, W. MacNeile. The British Navy at War. Heinemann 1917. *1s.*

—— The Fleets behind the Fleet. The work of the Merchant Seamen and Fishermen in the War. Hodder & Stoughton 1917. *2s. 6d.*

Favre, Louis E. Les forces navales en présence. Illustrations. Payot 1916. 1 fr. 25.

Field, Cyril. British Navy Book. Blackie 1915. *3s. 6d.*

Fiennes, Gerard. Our Navy at War. Newnes 1916. *1s.*

Fleet Annual and Naval Year Book, The (1914). Fleet, Ltd. 1914. *1s.*

Fleets of the World, 1915. Compiled from official sources and classified according to types. Illustrated. Nash 1915. *7s. 6d.*

Fleets of the World, 1916. Classified according to types. Nash 1916. 6*s.*

Fleets (Great Britain and Foreign Countries). Return, showing the Fleets of Great Britain, France, Russia, Germany, Italy, Austria-Hungary, United States of America, and Japan. [Jan. 1, 1914.] [H.C. Paper No. 113.] H.M.S.O. 1914. 7½*d.*

Golding, Harry (edited). Wonder-book, The, of the Navy (by various contributors. For the young). Ward, Lock 1917. 3*s.* 6*d.*

Grand-Fleet Days. By the Author of In the Northern Mists. Hodder & Stoughton 1917. 5*s.*

Hislam, P. A. The Navy of To-day. Jack. 6*d.*

—— Navy shown to the Children. (Shown to the Children series.) Jack 1915. 2*s.* 6*d.*

Hoar, A. The Submarine Torpedo-Boat: Its Characteristics and Modern Development. Crosby, Lockwood 1917. 9*s.*

Horton-Smith, L. G., and Wyatt, H. F. The Passing of the Great Fleet. 1909. 8*s.* 6*d.*

Hurd, Archibald, and Castle, Henry. German Sea Power: Its Rise, Progress and Economic Basis. With maps and appendices giving the Fleet Laws, etc. Murray 1913. 10*s.* 6*d.*

Hurd, Archibald. The Fleets at War. (Daily Telegraph War Books.) Hodder & Stoughton 1914. 1*s.*

—— German Fleet. (Daily Telegraph War Books.) Hodder & Stoughton 1915. 1*s.*

—— Our Navy. (Imperial Library.) Warne 1914. 1*s.*

—— A Merchant Fleet at War. (War record of the British Mercantile Marine.) Cassell 1920. 12*s.* 6*d.*

Hutter, J. Les Sous-Marins. Berger-Levrault 1917. 90 c.

In the Northern Mists. A Grand-Fleet Chaplain's notebook (describes the daily life of the Navy). Hodder & Stoughton 1916. 5*s.*

Jane, F. T. The British Battle Fleet: Its Inception and Growth throughout the Centuries. Partridge. 10*s.* 6*d.*

—— Fighting Ships. (Annual.) Sampson Low. 21*s.*

—— Naval Recognition Book. German ships. Sampson Low 1915. 1*s.*

—— Naval Recognition Book: or, How to identify British Warships at Sea. Sampson Low 1914. 1*s.*

—— Recognition Book of German Torpedo-craft. A supplement to All the World's Fighting Ships. Sampson Low 1915. 1*s.* 6*d.*

—— Warships at a Glance. Silhouettes of the world's fighting ships. Sampson Low 1914. 2*s.* 6*d.*

Jane, F. T. World's Warships. Sampson Low 1915. 2*s.* 6*d.*

—— Your Navy as a Fighting Machine. F. & C. Palmer 1914. 1*s.*

—— All about the German Navy. With maps and illustrations. Sampson Low 1915. 1*s.* New and revised edn. 1916. 1*s.*

—— —— Illustrations of German fighting ships. (New and revised edn.) Sampson Low 1916. 1*s.*

Jane's Fighting Ships 1918. With supplement, British Navy: War Construction. Edited by M. Prendergast. 21st year of issue. Sampson Low 1918. 30*s.*

Jefferey, E. Jefferey. Servants of the Guns. Smith, Elder 1917. 5*s.*

Kipling, Rudyard. The Fringes of the Fleet. Macmillan 1915. 6*d.*

Klaxon (pseud.). H.M.S. ———. Sketches of life in the Navy. Reprinted from *Blackwood.* Blackwood 1918. 6*s.*

Lake, Simon. The Submarine in War and Peace: Its Developments and Possibilities. Lippincott 1918. $3.00.

Latymer, Lord. Royal Marines. Humphreys 1915. 1*s.*

Laughton, L. G. Carr. The British Navy in War. Methuen. 1*s.*

Lecky, Halton Stirling. The King's Ships. In 6 vols. Illustrated. Muirhead 1914. 42*s.*

Leyland, J. The German Navy: Its Significance and its Development. Kegan Paul. 1*d.*

—— The Royal Navy: Its Influence in English History and in the Growth of Empire. Camb. Univ. Press. 1*s.*

Liddell, Kenneth. British and German Navies. With chart showing all the ships in these Navies in 1915. Compared ship by ship. Simpkin 1915. 1*s.*

—— Charts of Ships in the British and German Navies in 1915. Simpkin 1915. 6*d.*

McDermaid, Neil T. Shipyard Practice, as Applied to Warship Construction. With diagrams. Longmans 1917. 12*s.* 6*d.*

Margerison, John S. The Sure Shield (Everyday Life in the Navy). Duckworth 1917. 6*s.*

—— Action! Stories of the modern Navy. Hodder & Stoughton 1917. 5*s.*

—— The Sea Services. A complete guide to the Royal Navy and the Mercantile Marine. Hodder & Stoughton 1917. 1*s.* 3*d.*

Naval Intelligence. By the author of "In the Northern Mists." (Sketches and stories by a Naval Chaplain.) Hodder & Stoughton 1918. 6*s.*

Naval Pocket-Book. Founded by Sir W. Laird Clowes. Thacker 1914. 7*s.* 6*d.*

Navies at War. Complete naval handbook, and register for gains and losses. Victoria House Printing Co. 1915. 1*s.*

Navies of the World, The. Ben Johnson & Co. 6*d.*

Navy League Annual, The (1915-16). Edited by Robert Yerburgh and others. Murray 1916. 5*s.*

Noble, Edward. Outposts of the Fleet. (Stories of the Merchant Service in Peace and War.) Heinemann 1917. 1*s.*

Our Boys' Book of the Navy. Newnes 1915. 3*s.* 6*d.*

Our Navy. A descriptive handbook of the Navy. Illustrated. Empire Publishing Co. 1914. 1*s.*

Our Sailors at Work and at Play. A picture book for boys and girls. Ward, Lock 1914. 1*s.*

Our Warships. (G. and P. series for children.) Gale & Polden 1915. 6*d.*; enlarged, 1*s.*

Patterson, J. E. A War-time Voyage; being the itinerary of an ocean-tramp from port to port 1916-17. Dent 1918. 6*s.*

Protheroe, Ernest. The British Navy: Its Making and its Meaning. Illustrations. Routledge 1915. 7*s.* 6*d.*

Reeve's Chart of the Navies of Great Britain and Germany. St. Catherine Press 1915. 6*d.*

Rousseau, M. A. Notre Marine et la leur. (Exposant la situation réciproque des marines ennemies au cours des trois premières années de guerre.) Alcan 1917.

Royal Navy List: or, Who's Who in the Navy. Special War supplement. New edn. Witherby 1916. 7*s.* 6*d.*

Ships of the British, French, Russian and German Navies. Their names, class, tonnage, and date of completion. Hornden 1915. 6*d.*

Taffrail (pseud.). Pincher Martin, O.D. (The inner life of the Royal Navy.) Chambers 1916. 3*s.* 6*d.*

Terry, Prof. C. S. German Sea Power. (O.P.) Oxford Univ. Press. 3*d.*

Times' Book of the Navy. With a preface by Admiral Lord Charles Beresford. The Times Publishing Co. 1*s.*

Vaux, Patrick. Gadgets (the work of the Navy). Hodder & Stoughton 1917. 5*s.*

Weekly Dispatch Naval War Guide, The. Weekly Dispatch Office 1914. 6*d.*

White, A. Our Sure Shield: The Navy. Illustrated. Macdonald & Evans 1917. 1*s.* 6*d.*

Wood, Walter. Fisherman, The, in War-time. (Seamen who work behind the front Naval line.) Sampson Low 1918. 7*s.* 6*d.*

World's Warships, The. Compiled from Jane's Fighting Ships. 6th edn. Sampson Low 1917. 3*s.* 6*d.*

Yexley, Lionel. Fleet Annual and Naval Year Book 1915. The Fleet, 11, Henrietta Street, W.C. 1*s.* 3*d.* and 2*s.* 9*d.*

—— The Fleet Annual and Naval Year Book 1918. Fourth War number. Chapman & Hall 1918. 4*s.* 6*d.*

C.—Armies.

Angell, Col. Le Soldat Serbe. Traduction de J. de Coussange. Préface de M. R. Vesnitch. Illustrated. Delagrave 1916. 2 fr. 50.

Army Recruiting, Report on. By the Earl of Derby, K.G. [Cd. 8149.] H.M.S.O. 1916. 1*d.*

Army, Report on, Recruiting in Ireland. [Cd. 8168.] H.M.S.O. 1916. ½*d.*

Atteridge, A. H. Army Shown to the Children. Jack 1915. 2*s.* 6*d.*

—— The British Army of To-day. Jack 6*d.*

—— The German Army in War. Methuen 1*s.*

Barrés, Maurice. Une visite à l'armée anglaise. Berger-Levrault 1916. 1 fr. 25.

Bellegarde, Sophie de. The Russian Soldier—peasant. War sketches and incidents. Illustrations. Edited by Rev. E. H. Day, D.D. Mowbray 1917. 1*s.* 6*d.*

Benjamin, René. Les soldats de la guerre: Gaspard, Paris: Fayard 1915. 3 fr. 50.

—— —— English translation under title Gaspard, the Poilu. Heinemann 1916.

Bibikoff, Massia. Our Indians at Marseilles. Transl. by L. Huxley. With introduction by Maurice Barrés. Illustrated. Smith, Elder 1915. 5*s.*

Bilse, Lieut. Life in a [German] Garrison Town. Lane 1914 1*s.*

British Officer. The Germany Army from Within. By a British Officer who has served in it. Hodder & Stoughton. 2*s.*

Cavalry Standards, Guidons, and Drum Banners of the British Army Gale & Polden 1916. 1*s*

Chambran, Lieut.-Col. de, and Marenches, Cap. de. L'Armée américaine dans le conflit Européen. Payot 1919. 10 fr.

Clifford, W. G. British Army. Illustrated (Peeps series.) Black 1915. 1*s.* 6*d.*

Coxhead, G. E. S. The Younger Branch. Sketches of a cadet camp. Melrose 1918. 3*s.* 6*d.*

Crests and Badges of the Regiments of Yeomanry in daily use Re-issue. Gale & Polden 1915. 1*s.*

Crests of our Imperial Forces. Gale & Polden 1916. 1*s.*

D'Almeida, P. C. L'Armée allemande avant et pendant la guerre de 1914-18. Berger-Levrault 1920. 14 fr. 50.

Danby, Paul. The British Army Book. Illustrated. Blackie 1914. 3*s.* 6*d.*

Dawbarn, Charles. Joffre and his Army. Mills & Boon 1916. 2*s.* 6*d.*

Dekobra, M. Messieurs les Tommies. Illustré. Notes, tableaux, anecdotes, croquis. Renaissance des lettres. 1917. 3 fr. 50.

Elliott, Ivo d'O. The Historical Precedent for the New Army. (O.P.) Oxford Univ. Press. 3*d.*

Ex-Trooper. The French Army from Within. Hodder & Stoughton. 2*s.*

French Army from Within. Froude & Hodder 1915. 1*s.*

Gaëll, René. Priests in the Firing Line. Transl. from the French. Longmans 1916. 3*s.* 6*d.*

Gemelli, Padre Agostino. Il Nostro Soldato. Studies by a Modernist priest. Milan: Vita e Pensiero 1918. n.p.

Graham, Stephen. A Private in the Guards. Macmillan 1919. 10*s.*

Grande, Julian. Grossbrittanien und sein Heer. An account of the formation and character of our Army, by a sympathetic Swiss writer. Zürich: Füssli 1917. 4 fr.

Haig-Brown, Capt. A. R. The O.T.C. and the Great War. With preface by Col. Sir E. Ward. Newnes 1915. 7*s.* 6*d.*

Hardy, E. J. The British Soldier: his Courage and Humour. Unwin 1915. 3*s.* 6*d.*

Hodder, Reginald. British Regiments at the Front: the Story of their Battle Honours. (Daily Telegraph War books.) Hodder & Stoughton 1914. 1*s.*

Holmes, Robert. My Police Court Friends with the Colours Blackwood 1915. 2*s.*

Infantry Privates: Comparison between Pay, Allowances, and Regular Compulsory Deductions at Home and in India. Wyman 1915. ½*d.*

Inner Life of the Prussian Cadet. Transl. from the German by W. D. Lowe. Routledge 1914. 6*d.*

Kilpatrick, James A. Atkins at War: as told in his own letters. Jenkins 1914. 1*s.*

Kipling, Rudyard. The New Army in Training. Macmillan 1915. 6*d.*

—— —— Harrap 1916. 3*s.* 6*d.*

Lamb, Lieut. Charles. A Pocket History of the Regiments. Oliver & Boyd 1916. 1*s.*

Lethbridge, M. C. Russian Chaps. Tales of the Russian soldier, by one who has seen him in war. Lane 1916. 1*s.*

Lyons, A. Neil. Kitchener Chaps. Lane 1915. 1*s.*

Mille, Pierre. Joffre Chaps and Others. Transl. by Bérengère Drillien. Lane 1915. 1*s.*

Milne, James. Epistles of Atkins. (Wayfarer's Library.) Dent 1914. 1*s.*

Newbolt, Sir Henry. Book of the Thin Red Line. Longmans 1915. 5*s.*

Our Foot Soldiers. (G. and P. series for Children.) Gale & Polden 1915. 6*d.* net; enlarged 1*s.*

Our Gallant Guards. Gale & Polden 1916. 1*s.*

Our Guns and Men. Gale & Polden 1915. 6*d.* net; enlarged 1*s.*

Our Horse Soldiers. Gale & Polden 1915. 6*d.* net; enlarged 1*s.*

Peeps at Our Soldiers. Illustrated. Gale & Polden 1915. 1*s.*

Rally of the Empire, The: our Fighting Forces—Australia, Canada, India, South Africa. Newnes 1914. 2*s.* 6*d.*

Regimental Nicknames and Traditions of the British Army. 4th edn., enlarged and revised. Gale & Polden 1915. 2*s.*

Regimental Pets of the British Army. Gale & Polden 1915. 1*s.*

Regimental Ribbons and Buttons of the British Army. Gale & Polden 1915. 1*s.*

Raffin, Henry, and Tudesq, André. Notre Camerade Tommy. Préface de M. Arthur Balfour. Hachette 1917. 3 fr. 50.

—— The Square Jaw. Transl. from the French. Nelson 1917. 1*s.*

Schlicht, Baron von. Life in a German Crack Regiment. (Circulation forbidden in Germany.) Fisher Unwin. 1*s.*

Scotland for Ever! A gift-book of the Scottish Regiments. With preface by the Earl of Rosebery. Hodder & Stoughton 1915. 3*s.*

Singh, Saint Nihal. India's Fighters: their Mettle, History and Services to Britain. Illustrated. Low 1914. 3*s.* 6*d.*

Sommers, Cecil. Temporary Heroes. Pictures of the life of the modern soldier. Lane 1917. 3*s.* 6*d.*

Steveni, Barnes W. The Russian Army from Within. Hodder & Stoughton. 2*s.*

Stirling, Major John. The Territorial Divisions, 1914-18. Dent 1921. 6*s.*

Times Book of the Army. Times Office 1914. 1*s.*

Vial, F. Territoriaux de France. Berger-Levrault 1918. 90 c.

Vivian, E. Charles. The British Army from Within. Hodder & Stoughton. 2*s.*

Wallace, Edgar. Kitchener's Army and the Territorial Forces: the Full Story of a Great Achievement. Illustrated. Newnes 1915. 6*s.*

Ward, Herbert. Mr. Poilu. Notes and sketches with the fighting French. Illustrated. Hodder & Stoughton 1916. 7*s.* 6*d.*

Webster, F. A. M. Britain in Arms. Sidgwick & Jackson. 1*s.*

—— Britain's Territorials in Peace and War. Sidgwick & Jackson 1915. 1*s.*

White, C. Our Regiments and their Glorious Records. Detailed list of the Regular Regiments, with an account of the Territorials. Pearson 1915. 1*s.*

World's Soldiers, The. Nister 1914. 3*s.* 6*d.*

Wylie, Alex. The Future of the British Army. A scheme for a post-war Army. Hugh Rees 1917. 1*s.*

Wyndham, Horace. Following the Drum. Reissue. A. Melrose 1914. 2*s.* 6*d.;* popular edn. 1*s.*

Z., Capitaine. L'Armée de la Guerre (The French Army). Payot 1916. 3 fr. 50.

—— L'Armée de 1917. Payot 1917. 4 fr.

—— L'Officier et le Soldat Français. Nouv. Libr. Nationale 1918. 4 fr.

D.—Air Forces.

Abbott, W. J. Aircraft and Submarines. Development and present day uses. Illustrated. New York: Putnam 1918. $3.50.

All the World's Aircraft, 1918. War flying annual. Founded by F. T. Jane. Edited by C. G. Gray. Sampson Low 1918. 25*s.*

Barber, H. The Aeroplane Speaks. Handbook of instruction about aeroplanes. Illustrated. 7th edn. McBride 1918. 8*s.* 6*d.*

Berry, W. H. Aircraft in War and Commerce. With introduction by Gen. Lord Montagu of Beaulieu. Barrow & Co. 1918. 1*s.* 6*d.*

Air Ministry. Synopsis of British Air Effort during the War. With Appendix. [Cmd. 100.] H.M.S.O. 1919. 3*d.*

Campbell, Capt. G. L. and Blinkhorn, R. H. Royal Flying Corps (Military Wing). Casualties and honours during the war, 1914-17. Picture Advertising Co. 1917. 3*s.*

Dommett, W. E. A Dictionary of Aircraft. Electrical Press. 2*s.*

Driggs, Laurence La T. Heroes of Aviation. Authentic stories of the great aviators in the war. Little, Brown & Co. 1918. $1.50.

Grahame-White, C. and Harper, H. Aircraft in the Great War. A record and a study. Fisher Unwin 1915. 7*s.* 6*d.*

Imperial Aircraft Flotilla, The. Recording gifts of aircraft presented by British subjects overseas, &c. Overseas Club 1916. n.p.

L'Armée de l'air. Par * * * (By a professional military aviator.) Berger-Levrault 1916. 2 fr.

McCudden, J. V.C. Five Years in the Royal Flying Corps. Illustrated. Aeroplane Publishing Co. 1919. 7*s*. 6*d*.

Neumann, Major G. P. (edr.). Die deutschen Luftstreitkräfte im Weltkriege. Unter mitwirkung von 29 Offizieren und Beamten der Heeres- und Marine-Luftfahrt. From official sources. Illustrated. Berlin: Mittler 1921. 70 mk.

Rosher, H. In the Royal Naval Air Service. With introduction by Arnold Bennett. Chatto & Windus 1916. 3*s*. 6*d*.

Royal Air Force, Permanent Organisation of the. Note by the Secretary of State for Air on a scheme outlined by the Chief of the Air Staff. [Cmd. 467.] H.M.S.O. 1919. 1*d*.

Turner, C. C. Aircraft of To-day. Seeley 1916. 5*s*.

Walker, Frederick. All about the Zeppelins and other Enemy Aircraft. Illustrated. Kegan Paul. 6*d*.

Wing Adjutant (pseud). The Royal Flying Corps in the War. Cassell 1918. 2*s*.

See also X.D. (4): Walcott, Stuart.

VII.—WAR MAPS.

African War Atlas. Nine maps to illustrate the fighting in the German Colonies in Africa. *South Africa* Office. 6*d*.

Atlas de la guerre. (Cartes Larousse.) Published in parts, 6 maps (13 in. by 10 in.) in each part. 18 parts issued (Sept. 1916). Larousse 1916. 75 c. a part.

Atlas-Index de tous les Théâtres de la Guerre. 3 vols. published, each with about 40 maps and index of names. Berger-Levrault 1915-16. 3 fr. per vol.

Atlas of the War. Maps, Plans, Diagrams and Pictures, illustrating the Great European War. Nelson 1914. 1*s*.

Bacon's New War Map of South Central Europe. Scale 43 miles to the inch. Bacon. 1*s*.

—— New War Map: Paris to Berlin. Bacon 1914. 1*s*. and 2*s*.

—— War Map of Europe: embracing all the countries involved. Bacon 1914. 1*s*.

—— War Map of the Dardanelles, Sea of Marmora, and Bosphorus. Bacon. 6*d*.

—— War Map of the Italian and Austrian Frontiers. 23 miles to the inch. Bacon 1915. 6*d*.; on cloth, 1*s*.

Bacon's Large-Scale Map of the British Battle Front in France and Belgium. 4 miles to inch. Size, 20 by 30 inches. Bacon 1916. Paper, *6d.*; cloth, *1s.*

—— Large-Scale Map of the French Battle Front (Peronne to Verdun). 4 miles to inch. Size, 35 by 22 inches. Bacon 1916. Paper, *1s.*; cloth, *1s. 6d.*

—— Large-Scale Map of the Salonika Battle Front (Uskub and Monastir to Salonika and Kavalla). 6 miles to inch. Size, 30 by 20 inches. Bacon 1916. Paper, *1s.*; cloth, *1s. 6d.*

—— War Map of South Central Europe (Warsaw and Budapest to Greece and Sebastopol). 43 miles to inch. Size, 20 by 28 inches. Bacon 1916. Paper, *6d.*; cloth, *1s.*

Bartholomew's Large-Scale Map of Central Europe 1914; No. 2. Bartholomew 1914. *2s.*

—— Reduced Survey Map of N.E. France, Belgium and the Rhine. Bartholomew 1914. *2s.*

—— War Map of Central Europe. Bartholomew 1914. *1s.*

—— War Map of Europe and the Mediterranean. With insets of the Dardanelles, etc. Edinburgh: Geogr. Institute. *1s.*

—— War Map of Italy and the Balkan States. Bartholomew 1915. *1s.*

Belgium and the North-East of France. Issued by the Geograph. Section of the General Staff, at the Ordnance Survey Office, Southampton. Scale; 6 inches to the mile. *2s. 6d.*

Carte du Front de Salonique (Grèce, Albanie, Monténégro, Serbie, Bulgarie). En quatre couleurs. Berger-Levrault 1916. 1 fr.

Clauss, P. R. Sketch Maps: illustrating Important Phases in the Great War. With historical notes, August 1914-May 1916. Blackie **1917. *1s.***

Daily Chronicle New Sectional War Map of Europe. Daily Chronicle Office. *6d.*

—— War Atlas. 72 maps. Daily Chronicle Office 1915. *6d.*

Daily Express Large Print War Map. C. Smith 1914. Cloth, *2s. 6d.*; *1s.*

Daily Mail Bird's-eye Map of the British Front. Daily Mail Office. *6d.*

—— Bird's-eye Map of the Front. Section 2. Daily Mail Office 1915. *6d.*

—— Large-Scale Military Maps: (1) Franco-Belgian and German Frontiers; (2) Western Frontiers of Russia, Germany and Austria. Daily Mail Office. *3d.* each.

—— War Panorama. Twenty bird's-eye views and maps of the World-Wide War. Daily Mail Office 1915. *6d.*

—— World Map of War and Commerce. G. Philip 1914. *1s.*

Daily Telegraph Gazetteer War Map of Western Europe. No. 4. Geographia 1914. 1*s*.

—— War Map (The). No. 2. Large scale map of the fighting areas. Geographia 1914. Paper, 1*s*.; cloth, 2*s*. 6*d*.; varnished and mounted on roller, 5*s*. 6*d*.

—— War Map (The). No. 3. The Naval Fighting Areas. Geographia 1914. Linen, 2*s*. 6*d*.

—— War Map of Eastern Europe. No. 5. Geographia 1914. 1*s*.; cloth, 2*s*. 6*d*.

—— War Map of Egypt and the Near East. No. 6. Geographia 1914. 1*s*.; linen, 2*s*. 6*d*.; varnished and mounted on roller, 5*s*.

—— War Map. No. 8. Italian and Austro-German Fighting Areas. Geographia 1915. 1*s*. and 2*s*. 6*d*.

—— War Map of Europe. Daily Telegraph Office. 1s. *See also* Gross, Alexander.

Darbishire, B. V. War Atlas. Milford 1915. 8*d*.

Gross, Alexander. Daily Telegraph War Map of the Belgian and British Fronts, in contour colouring. No. 21. Geographia 1916. 1*s*., 2*s*. 6*d*., and 5*s*. 6*d*.

—— —— War Map of the Gallipoli Peninsula. No. 12. Geographia 1915. 1*s*.

—— —— War Map of the new British Front, in contour colouring. Geographia 1915. 1*s*.

—— —— War Map of the Russian War Areas. Geographia 1915. 1*s*. and 2*s*. 6*d*.

—— —— War Map of the Western Balkans, including Serbia, Albania, N. Greece and Western Bulgaria. Geographia 1915. 1*s*.

—— ——Picture Map of the Dardanelles and Bosphorus, including the whole of Turkey in Europe. Geographia 1915. 1*s*.

—— —— War Map: Balkans and Eastern Europe. Geographia 1915. 1*s*.

—— —— War Map of the Eastern Balkans, including Bulgaria, Rumania, Turkey, etc. Geographia 1915. 1*s*., 2*s*. 6*d*., & 5*s*. 6*d*.

—— —— War Map of the French Fighting Line: Arras to Verdun. Geographia 1915. 1*s*.

—— —— War Map of the French Fighting Line: Verdun to Belfort. Geographia 1915. 1s. *See also* Daily Telegraph.

—— The Daily Telegraph Special War Map of the British Front. 56 in. by 30 in. Geographia 1916. 6*s*.

—— Races of Eastern Europe (Daily Telegraph Map, No. 25). Daily Telegraph Office 1918. 4*s*. 6*d*.

Johnston's (W. and A. K.) European War Map. Johnston. 2*s*. 6*d*.

—— Paris to Berlin. Orographically coloured. Johnston 1914. 1*s*. 6*d*.

—— War Map: Middle East. Johnston 1916. Cloth 1*s*. 6*d*.; unmounted, 6*d*.

—— Map of the Eastern Theatre of War. Mounted. Johnston. 4*s*.

—— War Map of the Balkan States. Printed in colour. Johnston 1915. 6*d*., 1*s*. 3*d*., and 2*s*.

—— War Map of Europe 1914-15. Full coloured, showing the whole of the War Areas. Johnston 1915. 6*d*. and 2*s*.

—— Map of the Frontiers of Central Europe, present and future (25 by 20 inches). Macmillan 1918. 1*s*. 6*d*.

—— Balkan States, The. Macmillan 1918. Cloth, 1*s*. 3*d*.; sheet, 6*d*.

—— War Map of Palestine. Macmillan 1917. 6*d*., 1*s*. 3*d*., and 2*s*.

—— Middle East, The: Campaigns in Mesopotamia, Persia and the Caucasus. Macmillan 1918. Cloth, 1*s*. 6*d*.; sheet, 6*d*.

Land and Water Map of the War, drawn under the direction of Hilaire Belloc, with explanatory article by H. B. Mounted. Land and Water Office. 2*s*. 6*d*.

Large Scale War Map, showing scene of operations by the Allied Armies in Flanders. Simpkin 1915. 6*d*.

Map-Book of the World-Wide War. 56 maps and a diary of the War. Nelson 1915. 7*d*.

Nelson's Map-Book of the World-Wide War. (New and enlarged edn. Nelson 1917. 1*s*. 6*d*.

Offensives, Les, de 1917. (8 sheets of maps, etc.) Berger-Levrault 1917. 50 c. each.

—— Les, de 1918. 3 bis: Calais (Nieuport, Dunkerque, Boulogne-sur-Mer, Furnes, Hazebrouck, Béthune). 5 bis: Abbeville (Montreuil-sur-Mer, Berck-sur-Mer, Hesdin, Saint-Pol, Saint-Valery-sur-Somme, Doullens). 7 bis: Amiens (Albert, Bray-sur-Somme, Corbie, Rosières-en-Santerre, Moreuil, Montdidier). Berger-Levrault 1918. 50 c.

Oxford Large Scale War Map. Oxford Univ. Press. 15*s*. and 10*s*. 6*d*.

Oxford Wall Maps: The Western War Area from the Seine to the Rhine and from the Swiss Frontier to the Rhine Delta. With contour lines and layered colouring. Milford 1915. Various prices: with names, 12*s*. 6*d*. to 17*s*. 6*d*.; without names, 10*s*. 6*d*. to 15*s*.

Philip's Large Scale strategical War Map of Europe, with complete index. Edited by George Philip, assisted by a military expert. Philip 1915. 2*s*. 6*d*.

—— Photo-Relief Model War Map of Central Europe. G. Philip 1914. 1*s*.

—— Large Scale Strategical War Map of Europe, Western Area. With index and plans. Inset of the British Battle Front (5 miles to the inch). Philip & Son 1916. 2*s*. 6*d*.

—— Large Scale Battle Front Map of Europe. Philip 1916. 2*s*. 6*d*.

—— Western Front, The, at a Glance. Large Scale Atlas of Allies' fighting line in the West. Philip & Son 1917. 1*s*. 3*d*.

—— World's Battle Fronts, The, at a Glance. (32 reference maps.) G. Philip 1918. 1*s*. 3*d*.

—— Strategical Record Map, The, of the Western Front (36 by 30 inches). Philip & Son 1918. 2*s*.

—— Contoured Map of the European Battle Fronts (14 by 35 inches). Philip & Son 1918. 1*s*. 6*d*.

—— Large Scale Strategical War Map of Europe: The Balkans. Philip 1916. 2*s*. 6*d*.

—— Strategical Map of Palestine, Syria and the Sinai Peninsula. G. Philip 1918. 2*s*. 6*d*. and 6*s*.

—— Strategical Map of Mesopotamia and Asia Minor. G. Philip 1918. 2*s*. 6*d*. and 6*s*.

Pope-Hennessy, Mrs. Map of the Main Prison Camps in Germany and Austria. 2nd edn. Nisbet 1918. 2*s*.

Stanford's Seat of War in the Dardanelles and the Bosphorus. Stanford. 5*s*.

—— Shilling Map of the Austro-Italian Frontier. Stanford 1915. 1*s*.

—— Central and Eastern Europe. Stanford. 5*s*. and 8*s*. 6*d*.

Star War Map, The. Star Office 1914. 3*d*.

Strand Coloured Detail Map of Mesopotamia. Newnes 1916. 6*d*.

—— Coloured Detail Map of the Dardanelles, Constantinople, etc. Newnes 1915. 6*d*.

—— Coloured Map of the Balkan States. Newnes 1916. 6*d*.

Theatre of War in Western Asia Minor. Stanford. 3*s*.

Times, The, War Atlas and Gazetteer, with reference index of 14,000 place-names. Times Office 1917. 2*s*. 6*d*.

Times War Atlas. Times Office. 1*s*. 6*d*. and 9*d*.

War Map of Central Europe. After Darbishire's wall map. Milford 1915. 3*d*.

Zupanic, Dr. N. Map of Southern Slav Territory. Published by the Jugoslav Committee. Christophers 1916. 6*d*.

VIII.—CAUSES AND ISSUES OF THE WAR.

A.—Collected Documents.

(1) General.

Beer, Max (transl. and edr.). Regenbogenbuch, Das. Die Europäischen Kriegsverhandlungen, Die Massgebenden Doumente chronologisch und sinngemäss zusammengestellt, übersetzt und erläutert. 1915. 8 mk.

Bourgeois, E. and Pagés, G. La Responsibilité de la guerre. Hachette 1921. 25 fr.

Collected Diplomatic Documents Relating to the Outbreak of the European War. Includes the British White Book, French Yellow Book, Russian Orange Book, Belgian Grey Book, Serbian Blue Book, German White Book, Austro-Hungarian Red Book, with documents published subsequently. Miscell. No. 10 (1915). [Cd. 7860.] In octavo. H.M.S.O. 1*s.*

Diplomatic Documents Relating to the Outbreak of the European War. Edited with an Introduction by James Brown Scott. Parts I and II (Carnegie Endowment for International Peace). Milford 1917. 25*s.*

Foreign State Papers, French translations of. Including the Belgian Grey Book, Russian Orange Book (I and II), Serbian Blue Book, German White Book, Austrian Red Book. (90 c.) (Pages d'Histoire, 1914-15.) Berger-Levrault. 60 c. each.

Guirand, Félix. Les Livres diplomatiques des nations belligérantes analysés et commentés. Portraits. Larousse 1915. 90 c.

Headlam, J. W. The History of Twelve Days: a study of the Diplomatic Origins of the War. Fisher Unwin. 10*s.* 6*d.*

Mach, E. von (edr.). Official Diplomatic Documents Relating to the Outbreak of the European War. (The documents are here arranged in chronological order.) New York: Macmillan 1916. $6.00.

Stowell, Prof. Ellery C. The Diplomacy of the War. Vol. I: The Beginning of the War. Aims at giving, in other vols., an entire diplomatic history of the War. Boston: Houghton Mifflin. Constable 1915. 21*s.* each vol.

(2) Special.

(a) *Austria-Hungary.*

Diplomatische Aktenstücke zur Vorgeschichte des Krieges 1914. Abdruck der offiziellen Ausgabe mit einer Einleitung. Austrian Red Book. Vienna: Manzsche Universitäts-Buchhandlung 1915. 80 pf.

Diplomatische Aktenstücke. Ergänzungen und Nachträge zum österreichisch-ungarischen Rotbuch (Issued by the Government of the Austrian Republic). Three parts: June 28-Aug. 27, 1914. Vienna: Staatsdruckerei 1919. 8 kr.

Dokumente zur Geschichte des Europäischen Krieges, 1914, mit besonderer Berücksichtigung von Oesterreich-Ungarn und Deutschland. Gesammelt und chronologisch herausg. von Carl Junker. 20 Parts. Vienna: Perles 1914-18. 1 kr. each part

Gooss, Roderich. Das Wiener Kabinett und die Entstehung des Weltkrieges. Mit Ermächtigung des Leiters des deutsch-österreichischen Staatsamtes für Aeusseres auf Grund aktenmässiger Forschung dargestellt. Wien. Seidel 1919. 10 kr.

Fraknoi, Wilhelm. Die ungarische Regierung und die Entstehung des Weltkrieges auf Grund aktenmässiger Forschung dargestellt. Wien: Seidel 1919. 5 kr.

(b) *Belgium.*

Belgique, Royaume de: Correspondance diplomatique, relative à la Guerre de 1914, July 24-Aug. 29. Belgian Grey Book. Hachette. 25*c.*

Belgian Grey Book. English transl. Diplomatic Correspondence respecting the War, published by the Belgian Government. Miscell. No. 12 (1914). [Cd. 7627.] H.M.S.O. 4½*d.*

Belgium. Correspondance diplomatique rélative à la Guerre de 1914-15. Second Belgian Grey Book. Hachette 1915. 75 c.

Belgian Grey Book, Second. Parts I and II (Section 10). H.M.S.O. 1915. 3*d.*

Belgische Neutralität. Dokumente und Mitteilungen. Berlin: Stilke 1915. 40 pf.

Langenhove, Fernand van. Le Dossier diplomatique de la Question belge (full collection of official documents bearing on the question of Belgian neutrality). Van Oest 1917. 4 fr.

(c) *Brazil.*

Brazilian Green Book, The. Diplomatic Documents, 1914-1917. Allen & Unwin 1918. 7*s.* 6*d.*

(d) *British Empire.*

Correspondence respecting the European Crisis. The British White Paper. Miscell. No. 6 (1914). [Cd. 7467.] H.M.S.O. 9*d.*

Despatch from H.M. Ambassador at Berlin respecting the Rupture of Diplomatic Relations with the German Government. [Cd. 7445.] H.M.S.O. 1*d.*

Despatch from H.M. Ambassador at Vienna respecting the Rupture of. Diplomatic Relations with the Austro-Hungarian Government. [Cd. 7596.] H.M.S.O. 1*d.*

Correspondence respecting events leading to the Rupture of Relations with Turkey. [Cd. 7628.] H.M.S.O. 9*d.*

Despatch from H.M. Ambassador at Constantinople summarising events leading up to Rupture of Relations with Turkey, and reply thereto. [Cd. 7716.] H.M.S.O. 1½*d.*

Great Britain and the European Crisis. Correspondence and Statements in Parliament, together with an Introductory Narrative of Events. H.M.S.O. 1*d.*

Grey's, Sir Edward, Reply to Dr. von Bethmann-Hollweg. A letter addressed to the British Press on Aug. 25, 1915; together with a statement issued by the Foreign Office on Sept. 1, 1915. Fisher Unwin. 1*d.*

President of the French Republic, Letter of July 31, 1914, from the, to the King, respecting the European Crisis; and His Majesty's reply of Aug. 1, 1914. Miscell. No. 3 (1915). [Cd. 7812.] H.M.S.O. ½*d.*

(e) *France.*

Documents diplomatiques, 1914. La Guerre Européenne. Pièces relatives aux Négociations qui ont précédé les Déclarations de Guerre de l'Allemagne à la Russie et à la France. French Yellow Book. Imp. Nat.; Hachette. 50 c.

Deuxième livre jaune francais. Lille, 1916. Preface par M. Henri Welschinger. (Pages d'histoire, 1914-1916, No. 117.) (Extracts de la Note . . . sur la conduite des autorités allemandes à l'égard des populations des départements français commerciales.) Berger-Levrault 1917. 75 c.

Diplomatic Correspondence respecting the War, published by the French Government, March, 1913, to August, 1914. Miscell. No. 15 (1914). [Cd. 7717.] H.M.S.O. 1914-15. 1*d.*

France and the European War. Full text of diplomatic documents. Authorized translation by the Paris correspondent of The Times for the French Government. The Times 1914. 2*s.*

Mensonge, le, du 3 Août, 1914 (D'après des documents secrets des Archives du Ministère de la Guerre et de temoignages inédits, français et allemands). Maps and facsimiles. Payot 1917. 5 fr.

Mensonge. Transl. under title, The Lie of the 3rd of August, 1914. Hodder 1917. 6*s*.

Reinach, J. Histoire de Douze jours: origines diplomatiques de la guerre (l'ensemble de toutes les pièces (647) que les gouvernements belligérants ont échangées durant la période décisive du 23 juillet au 3 août 1914). Alcan 1917. 12 fr.

(f) *Germany.*

Aktenstücke zum Kriegesausbruch. Hrsg. v. Auswärt. Amt (Das neue Weissbuch). 4°. 1 mk.

Dokumente, Die deutschen, zum Kriegesausbruch. Vollständ. Sammlung der von K. Kautsky zusammengest. amtlichen Aktenstücke. Hrsg. v. M. Montgelas u. W. Schücking. 4 Bde. 1919. 34 mk.

England's Complicity in the Great War. An examination of Official Publications and of English Documents in particular. Berlin: Liebheit (printer).

Englische Weissbuch, Das, in deutscher Uebersetzung. With introduction alleging errors and falsifications. Berlin: Zillessen. 1 mk. 50.

German White Book (only authorized transl.). How Russia and her Ruler betrayed German confidence and thereby caused the European War; with the original telegrams and notes Berlin: Liebheit, 40 pf.; Oxford Univ. Press. 6*d*.

Hat der deutsche Generalstab zum Kriege getrieben? (Urkunden des deutschen Generalstabs). Nebst Anlage: Aeusserungen der belgischen Gesandten. Berlin: Mittler 1919.

Helmolt, H. F. Die geheime Vorgeschichte des Weltkrieges; auf Grund urkundlichen Stoffes übersichtlich dargestellt. 1914. 4 mk.

Höniger, R. Russlands Vorbereitung zum Weltkrieg. Auf Grund unveröffentl. amtl. russisch. Urkunden. 1919. 6 mk.

Kautsky, K. Wie der Weltkrieg entstand, Dargest. nach d. Aktenmaterial d. auswärt. Amtes. 1919. 6 mk.

—— English transl. under title, The Guilt of William Hohenzollern. Skeffington 1920. 16*s*.

Sauerbeck, E. Der Kriegsausbruch. Eine Darstellung von neutraler Seite an Hand d. gesamten Aktenmaterials. (Polit. Bücherei.) 1919. 16 mk.

(g) *Greece.*

Διπλωματικὰ 'Εγγ*ραφά* (Diplomatic Documents); the Greek White Book. Athens 1917.

Les Pourparlers diplomatiques (1913-1917). Le Livre blanc grec. (Pages d'histoire.) Berger-Levrault 1917. 1 fr. 50.

(h) *Italy.*

Documenti diplomatici presentati al Parlamento Italiano. Austria-Ungheria. Italian Green Book. Rome: Tipografia della Camera dei Deputati. May 1915.

Diplomatic Documents submitted to the Italian Parliament by the Minister for Foreign Affairs, Austria-Hungary: Sessions, 1913-15. Italian Green Book. Hodder & Stoughton 1915. 6*d*.

Documenti della Grande Guerra. Raccolti da Gius. A. Andriulli, con una prefazione di Guglielmo Ferrero. Milan: Ravà. 2 fr.

Documents of the Great War. Collected by G. A. Andriulli; with preface by Gugl. Ferrero. Transl. by Thomas Okey. Fisher Unwin. 1*s*.

Documents diplomatiques entre l'Italie et l'Autriche-Hongrie, présentés au Parlement Italien, Mai 20, 1915. The Italian Green Book, in French. 1 fr.

(i) *Russia.*

Russian Orange Book, I. Recueil de Documents diplomatiques: Négociations ayant précédé la guerre. July 23-Aug. 6, 1914. Petrograd: Imprimerie de l'Etat. (Russian Orange Book). English translation published also as a Government Paper [Cd. 7626]. H.M.S.O. 3*d*.

Russian Orange Book, II. Recueil de Documents diplomatiques. Négociations ayant précédé la guerre avec la Turquie, Oct. 19-Nov. 1, 1914. Petrograd: Imprim. de l'Etat 1915. 2*s*. 6*d*.: also published (Pages d'Histoire, 1914-15) by Berger-Levrault. 60 c.: also English translation, published by H.M.S.O.

(j) *Serbia.*

Serbian Blue Book I. Note to Governments Signatory of the Hague Convention. Berger-Levrault 1916.

Serbian Blue Book, II. Diplomatic Documents antecedent to the War.

Deuxième Livre bleu serbe, 1916. Pages d'histoire, 1914-1916. No. 120. Berger-Levrault 1917. 75 c.

—— German translation. Heymann, Berlin, 1916.

B. Views of Individuals.

(1) *English and American.*

Adams, W. G. S. Responsibility for the War. (O.P.). Milford. *2d.*

Adkins, F. J. The War: its Origins and Warnings. Allen. *2s. 6d.*

Angell, Norman. Prussianism and its Destruction. (A reprint of Part 2 of Norman Angell's book, The Great Illusion, with a new introduction dealing with the causes which led up to the present War.) Heinemann 1915. *1s.*

Archer, William. Six of One and Half a Dozen of the Other. A letter in reply to Mr. L. Simons, of the Hague. Fisher Unwin 1917. *2d.*

—— The Thirteen Days (July 23-Aug. 4, 1914). A chronicle and an interpretation. Oxford Univ. Press. *3s. 6d.*

—— The Villain of the World-Tragedy. A letter to Prof. Ulrich von Wilamowitz-Möllendorf. Fisher Unwin 1917. *2d.*

Armstrong, George G. Our Ultimate Aim in the War. Allen & Unwin 1916. *2s. 6d.*

Ashton, H. A. One Clear Call: an Explanation and a Reminder. Voluntary Recruiting League. *1d.*

Austro-Servian Dispute, The. Reprinted from the Special War Number of The Round Table, Sept. 1914. Macmillan. *6d.*

Ballard, Frank. Britain Justified: the War from the Christian Standpoint. Methodist Publ. Co. 1914. *1s.*

Barker, E. Great Britain's Reasons for going to War. Darling.

Barron, Clarence W. The Audacious War. An examination of the causes, especially financial and economic, of the War, by the edr. of the Boston News Bureau. Boston: Houghton Mifflin. $1.00. Constable. *4s.* 6d.

Barry, Rev. Canon W. The World's Debate. An historical defence of the Allies. Hodder & Stoughton 1917. *5s.*

Barton, A. The War—How it was made? Who shall profit by it? (Anti-capitalist.) Keighley: Rydal Press 1915. *2d.*

Beck, James M. (late Assistant Attorney-General, U.S.). The Evidence in the Case in the Supreme Court of Civilization as to the Moral Responsibility for the War. Putnam. *2s. 6d.*

—— —— Revised edn., with introduction by Jos. H. Choate. Putnam. *2s. 6d.*

—— The Case of the Dual Alliance *v.* the Triple Entente. Reprinted by The Times from the New York Times under title, An American on the War. The Times. *1d.*

—— The Double Alliance *v.* The Triple Entente. (O.P.). Oxford Univ. Press. *3d.*

Beck, James M., and Eliot, Charles W. (late President of Harvard). America's View of Germany's Case (includes The Case of the Dual Alliance v. The Triple Entente, and An Address to the Business Women of Boston). Central Committee. *2d.*

Belloc, Hilaire. The Two Maps of Europe: Germany's ideas and ours. Pearson. *1s.*

Bennett, Arnold. Liberty: a Statement of the British Case. Hodder & Stoughton. *1s.*

Benson, B. G. The Future Peace and Prosperity of the United States, with special reference to the Great War. An outspoken defence of the Allies and of England in particular. Minneapolis: Heywood Mfg. Co. n.p.

Brereton, Cloudesley. Who is responsible? Armageddon and after? Harrap. *7d.*

Bevan, Edwyn. The Method in the Madness. A fresh consideration of the case between Germany and ourselves. Arnold 1917. *5s.*

—— German War Aims (a review of the ruling principles). Longmans 1918. *3d.*

Bullard, Arthur. The Diplomacy of the Great War. New York: Macmillan 1916. $1.50.

Burgess, Prof. J. W. The European War of 1914: its Causes, Purposes, and Probable Results. A defence of Germany by an American Exchange Professor. New York: McClure. $1.

Burroughs, E. A. The Fight for the Future. Nisbet 1916. *1s.*

Casement, Sir Roger. The Crime against Ireland, and how the War may right it. Berlin: Liebheit.

Chitwood, Prof. O. P. The Immediate Causes of the Great War. A digest of the published correspondence of the Powers. New York: Crowell 1917. $1.20.

Church, S. H. (President, Carnegie Institute, Pittsburg). The American Verdict on the War. Reply to the Manifesto of 93 German professors. Times Office. *1d.*

Clifford, Dr. John. Our Fight for Belgium, and what it means. Hodder & Stoughton 1918. *4d.*

Conybeare, Dr. F. C. The Awakening of Public Opinion in England. A letter (anti-British). New York: Vital Issue Co. 1915. 5 c.

Cook, Sir Edward. Britain and Turkey: the Causes of the Rupture, set out, in brief form, from the Diplomatic Correspondence. Macmillan. *2d.*

—— Britain and the Small Nations: Her Principles and Her Policy. Victoria League. *½d.*

Cook, Sir Edward. How Britain Strove for Peace. A record of Anglo-German negotiations 1898-1914. Told from authoritative sources. Macmillan. 2*d.*

—— Why Britain is at War: the Causes and the Issues. Set out in brief form, from the Diplomatic Correspondence and Speeches of Ministers. Macmillan. 2*d.*

Costa, Gabriel. Jews and the War. On the issues of the war in relation to Jewish ideas and principles. With preface by Leopold de Rothschild. Also transl. into Yiddish. Central Committee. 1*d.*

Cowan, A. R. Britain's Best War: its Causes and Consequences. Bell & Bradfute 1915. 3*d.*

Dark, Sidney. Thou art the Man: the Story of a Great Crime. Daily Express War Books 1915. 1*s.*

Davenport, Briggs. The Genesis of the Great War. Putnam 1916. 9*s.*

Davis, Muriel O. The Great War, and what it means for Europe. For use in the lower and middle forms of secondary schools. Maps. Oxford Univ. Press. 1*s.* 6*d.*

Davis, Prof. W. Stearns. The Roots of the War (written in collaboration with Prof. W. Anderson and Prof. Mason W. Tyler of Minnesota University). 7th edn., with maps. Century Co. 1918. $1.50.

Dawson, W. H. What is Wrong with Germany. Longmans. 2*s.* and 2*s.* 6*d.*

Dillon, E. J. Ourselves and Germany. With introduction by Hon. W. M. Hughes. Chapman & Hall 1916. 7*s.* 6*d.*

—— From the Triple to the Quadruple Alliance: Why Italy went to War. Hodder & Stoughton 1915. 5*s.*

Doyle, Sir A. Conan. The German War: some Sidelights and Reflections. Hodder & Stoughton. 1*s.*

Duchesne, A. E. Asia and the War. (O.P.) Oxford Univ. Press. 2*d.*

England on the Witness Stand: the Anglo-German Case tried by a Jury of Englishmen. A collection of articles, letters, etc., by Ramsay Macdonald, Philip Snowden, F. C. Conybeare, E. D. Morel, and others, against the British cause. New York: Fatherland Corporation. 50 c.

Fisher, H. A. L. The War: its Causes and Issues. Addresses given in Sheffield, Aug. 31, Sept. 1 and 2, 1914. Longmans. 6*d.*

Fitzpatrick, Percy. Origin, Causes and Object of the War. Simpkin 1915. 2*s.* 6*d.*

Foreign Opinion. A collection of the utterances of foreign publicists. Vol. I, No. 1. Jarrold. 3*d.*

Geddes, Patrick and Slater, Gilbert. Ideas at War. Williams and Norgate 1917. 5*s*.

Germany's Just Cause: as viewed by eminent American writers and thinkers. (Profs. Burgess, Sloane, Sanborn, Jastrow, and others.) New York: Fatherland Corporation. 10 c.

Gorham, C. T. The World War: Who is to Blame? A reply to Prof. Haeckel and Dr. P. Carus. Watts 1915. 3*d*.

Grant, Prof. W. L., and Colquhoun, Mr. and Mrs. Our Just Cause: Facts about the War, for ready reference. Abbreviated and revised edn., prepared under the auspices of the Royal Colonial Institute. Heinemann. 6*d*.

Grigg, E. W. G. Why the Dominions came in: the Power of Liberty and Law. Victoria League. ½*d*.

Guezoni, Ch. The Causes of the International European War. Twentieth Century Press. 1*s*.

Gwatkin, Prof. H. M. England's Case against Germany. A letter to a neutral. Reprinted from the *Nation*, Oct. 14, 1916. Fisher Unwin 1916. 1*d*.

Harrison, Austin. England and Germany. Macmillan. 2*s*. 6*d*.

—— The Kaiser's War. With an introduction by Frederic Harrison. Allen & Unwin. 2*s*. 6*d*.

Hart, Albert Bushnell. The War in Europe: its Causes and Results. Appleton 1915. 2*s*.

Hassall, Arthur. Just for a Scrap of Paper. (O.P.) Oxford Univ. Press. 1*d*.

Hayens, H. Teuton versus Slav. Collins. 1*s*.

Headlam, J. W. The German Chancellor and the Outbreak of War. Fisher Unwin 1917. 3*s*. 6*d*.

Hearnshaw, Prof. F. G. C. The Historical Antecedents of the War. Reprinted from The School World, Oct. 1914. Macmillan. 6*d*.

Hillis, Newell Dwight. Studies of the Great War: What each Nation has at Stake. Revell 1915. 3*s*. 6*d*.

Hobhouse, L. T. The World in Conflict. The psychological causes of the War. Fisher Unwin. 2*s*.

How the Great War Arose. Parliamentary Recruiting Committee. Gratis.

International Crisis, The, in its Ethical and Psychological Aspects. Lectures delivered at Bedford College (Feb.-March 1915) by Mrs. Sidgwick, Gilbert Murray, A. C. Bradley, L. P. Jacks, G. F. Stout, and Bernard Bosanquet. Oxford Univ. Press. 3*s*. 6*d*.

Irish-American, An. The Catechism of Balaam, Jr. (Sarcastically anti-British.) New York: Masterson, 170, Chambers Street. 1 c.

Is this War Justifiable? The point of view of an English anti-militarist. A defence of Great Britain as waging War against War. Miss Fry, 21, Gayton Road, Hampstead.

Jastrow, Prof. Morris. The War and the Bagdad Railway. The story of Asia Minor and its relation to the present conflict. Illustrations and map. Lippincott 1918. 6*s.*

Kahn, Otto H. Right above Race. (By a German-American.) Hodder & Stoughton 1918. 3*s.*

Kennedy, J. M. How the War began. With an introduction by W. L. Courtney, LL.D. Hodder & Stoughton. 1*s.*

Kirkpatrick, Prof. John. Origin of the Great War: or the British case. A. & C. Black. 1*d.*

Kylie, Prof. E. (of Toronto). Who Caused the War? A study of the Diplomatic Negotiations leading to the War. Mitford. 6*d.*

Law, H. A., M.P. Why is Ireland at War? A statement of the case for the Allies. Maunsel. 6*d.*

Legge, Edward. King Edward, the Kaiser, and the War. Grant Richards 1917. 16*s.*

Letter from an American in London to an Englishman in New York. (Anti-British.) New York: Vital Issue Co. 1915. 5 c.

Loreburn, Earl. How the War came. Methuen 1919. 7*s.* 6*d.*

Lyttelton, Rev. and Hon. E. What are we Fighting for? A sermon, preached on August 9, 1914, in St. Martin's Church, Overstrand. Longmans. 6*d.*

McCurdy, C. A., M.P. Guilty! Prince Lichnowsky's disclosures. Published for the National War Aims Committee. W. H. Smith & Sons 1918.

McClure, S. S. Obstacles to Peace. Attitude of the chief countries engaged, with introduction on the causes of the war. Houghton Mifflin 1917. $2.00.

Mach, Edmund von (former President of the Bostoner Deutsche Gesellschaft). What Germany Wants. Little, Brown & Co. $1.00.

Magnus, L. A. Pros and Cons in the Great War. A record of foreign opinion with a register of fact. Cheap edn. Kegan Paul 1917. 1*s.* 3*d.*

Marten, J. Currie. Force or Faith? Being a study of the ideas behind the present war. The Fircroft Central Council. 1*d.*

Marti, O. A. Anglo-German rivalry as a cause of the Great War. Boston: Stratford 1918. $1.00.

Massingham, H. W. Why we came to help Belgium. Reprinted from The Nation, Oct. 3, 1914. Harrison & Sons.

Medley, D. J. Why Britain Fights: a popular account. Maclehose & Sons. 1*d.*

Morris, Charles, and Dawson, L. H. Why the Nations are at War: the Causes and Issues of the Great Conflict. Maps and illustrations. Harrap 5*s.*

Muir, Prof. Ramsay. Britain's Case against Germany. An examination of the historical background of the German action in 1914. Sherratt & Hughes. 2*s.* and 2*s.* 6*d.*

Munro, Robert. From Darwinism to Kaiserism. Origin, effects and collapse of Germany's attempt at world-dominion. Maclehose 1918. 4*s.*

Münsterberg, Prof. Hugo. The War and America. A presentation of the German case. Appleton 1914. $1.00.

Murray, H. Robertson. Krupps and the International Armaments Ring. Holden & Hardingham. 2*s.* 6*d.*

Namier, Lewis B. Germany and Eastern Europe. With introduction by H. A. L. Fisher. Duckworth. 1*s.*

New German Empire, The. A study of German War Aims from German sources. (Reprinted from the Round Table.) Hodder & Stoughton 1917. 3*d.*

Okie, H. P. Causes and Consequences of the War of 1914. Maps and documents. In favour of the Entente Powers. Washington: Washington Publ. Co. 75 c.

Oman, John. The War and its Issues: an Attempt at a Christian Judgment. Cambridge Univ. Press 1915. 3*s.*

Our Just Cause. Facts about the War for ready reference. Prepared under the auspices of The Royal Colonial Institute. Heinemann. 1*s.*

Oxford Scholars. To the Christian Scholars of Europe and America. A reply from Oxford to the German Address to Evangelical Christians. (O.P.) Oxford Univ. Press. 2*d.*

Paganism or Christ? By the author of Why Germany will be Defeated. Garden City Press 1915. 6*d.*

Parker, Sir Gilbert. The World in the Crucible. An account of the origins and conduct of the Great War. Murray 1915. 6*s.*

Payne-Gallwey, Sir R. W. F. The War: a criticism. Spottiswoode 1915. 6*d.*

Petre, F. L. Why are we Fighting? A Plain Account of the War and its Causes. Oswestry: Woodall & Co. 1914. 2*d.*

Pollard, Prof. A. F. The War: its History and its Moral. A lecture delivered Oct. 5, 1914. Longmans. 6*d.*

Pollock, Sir Frederick. German Truth and European Facts about the War. An answer to Truth about Germany. Central Committee. 2*d.*

Powers, H. H. The things men fight for (the case of the different belligerents, by an American publicist). Macmillan 1916. 6*s*. 6*d*.

Prince, Morton. The American versus the German view of the War. Fisher Unwin. 1*s*.

Problems of the War. Papers read before the Grotius Society in 1917. Sweet & Maxwell 1918. 5*s*.

Prothero, G. W. A Lasting Peace (the Allies' terms): a conversation. Hodder & Stoughton 1917. 3*d*.

Prüm, Emile. Pan-Germanism versus Christendom: The Conversion of a neutral. An open letter. Edited, with comments, by René Johannet. Hodder & Stoughton 1916. 3*s*. 6*d*.

Rait, Prof. R. S. Why we are Fighting Germany. 1*d*.

Raleigh, Sir Walter. Might is Right. (O.P.) Oxford Univ. Press. 2*d*.

—— The War of Ideas. Oxford Univ. Press 1917. 6*d*.

—— Some Gains of the War. Oxford Univ. Press 1918. 6*d*.

Randolph, Carman F. The great Alliance against the Prussian: with papers on International State Commerce. Nat. Marine League of U.S.A.: Washington D.C. 1917. n.p.

Rawnsley, Canon. What the War is all about; some Lessons from the War. Addresses. Carlisle: Thurnam. 6*d*.

Reasons Why We are at War: an Address to the Rural Population showing the Case against Germany. The Rural League. 1*d*.

Rees, J. Aubrey. Fall In! An Appeal to the Youth of Britain. Includes contributions by F. D. Acland, M.P., John Galsworthy and others. Daily Chronicle Office. 1*d*.

—— The Duties of To-day—the Aims for To-morrow. War maxims. L. B. Hill 1914. 2*d*., on cards.

Repplier, Agnes, and White, J. W. Germany and Democracy: the Real Issue. A reply to Dr. Dernburg. Philadelphia: Winston 1915. 10 c.

Robertson, Rt. Hon. J. M., M.P. Britain versus Germany. An open letter to Prof. Edward Meyer, of Berlin. Fisher Unwin 1917. 6*d*.

—— German Truth and a Matter of Fact. (Disproving German report that French aeroplanes had dropped bombs before War proclaimed.) Fisher Unwin 1917. 1*d*.

—— War and Civilization. An open letter to a Swedish Professor. 2nd edn. With a postscript. (First published in 1915.) Allen & Unwin 1917. 2*s*. 6*d*.

Rogers, Lindsay. America's Case against Germany. (Statements of the points at issue, mainly legal). New York: Dutton 1917. $1.50.

Rose, J. Holland. How the War came about. Explained for young people. 2 maps. Patriotic Publ. Co. 4*d.*

—— The Origin of the War. Cambridge Univ. Press. 2*s.*

—— —— Popular edn. Cambridge Univ. Press. 1*s.*

—— Why Are We at War? Cambridge: Heffer. 1*d.*

—— Why We Carry On. (The Allied and the British case, and necessity of the overthrow of the German-Austrian-Turkish system.) Fisher Unwin 1918. 1*s.* 6*d.*

R. S. R. Why We are Fighting Germany. A village lecture, by R. S. R. Hazell, Watson & Viney. 4*d.*

Samuel, Rt. Hon. Herbert. The War and Liberty, and an address on Reconstruction. Hodder & Stoughton 1917. 1*s.* 6*d.*

Sanday, Rev. Dr. The meaning of the War for Germany and Great Britain: an attempt at synthesis. Oxford Univ. Press. 1*s.* 6*d.*

—— The Deeper Causes of the War. (O.P.) Oxford Univ. Press. 3*d.*

Sanger, C. P., and Norton, H. T. J. England's Guarantee to Belgium and Luxemburg, with the full text of the treaties. Allen & Unwin 1915. 4*s.* 6*d.*

Seton-Watson, R. W. German, Slav and Magyar. A study in the origins of the Great War. Williams & Norgate 1916. 2*s.* 6*d.*

—— What is at Stake in the War? Milford 1915. 2*d.*

Seymour, Charles. The Diplomatic Background of the War 1870-1914. Yale Univ. Press 1916. $2.00

Simms, J. J. The War of 1914: a Conflict of Ideals. Intended for simple folk. Walter Scott Publ. Co. 3*d.*

Sladen, Douglas. Germany's Great Lie: the Official German Justification of the War, exposed and criticised. Hutchinson. 1*s.*

Slater, Gilbert. Peace and War in Europe. Six lectures dealing with the meaning of the War, and its lessons for the future. Constable. 2*s.* 6*d.*

Supreme Issue: Law *versus* Anarchy in International Affairs. London: Internat. Union of Ethical Societies. n.p.

Thayer, W. Roscoe. Germany *versus* Civilization: notes on the atrocious war. Boston: Houghton Mifflin 1916. $1.00.

Tillett, A. W. Militancy *versus* Civilisation. Based on Herbert Spencer. King. 6*d.*

Vedette (pseud.). Britain and Armageddon: what we are fighting for. Hugh Rees. 6*d.*

Villard, Oswald G. Germany Embattled: an American interpretation. Strongly in favour of the Allies. New York: Scribner. $1.00.

War of Democracy, The. Statements by Allied leaders of their aims and ideals. Doubleday 1917. $2.00

War in Europe, The. Reprinted from The Round Table. Macmillan. 3*d*.

Ward, Wilfrid. England and the present War. Eyre & Spottiswoode.

Watchman (pseud.). Rome and Germany: the plot for the downfall of Britain. 2nd edn., revised. Drane 1916. 1*s*.

—— Rome and the War and coming events in Britain. Written to show that Rome and the Jesuits are the real authors of the War. McBride 1916. 3*s*. 6*d*.

Weston, Jessie L. Germany's Crime against France. Nutt. 3*d*.

Whitbridge, F. W. One American's Opinion of the European War: an answer to Germany's appeals. New York: Dutton. 2*s*. Darling & Son.

White, Dr. J. William. America and Germany: a text-book of the War. Revised and enlarged. Unwin 1915. 5*s*.

—— America's Arraignment of Germany. Fisher Unwin. Harrap. 1*s*.

—— —— Cheap edn., revised. Central Committee. 3*d*.

—— A Primer of the War for Americans. Written and compiled by an American. Philadelphia: Winston Co. 25 c.

—— A Text-Book of the War for Americans. An amplification of America's Arraignment, with much corroborative evidence. Philadelphia: Winston Co. $1.00.

Wile, Frederick W. The German-American Plot. Pearson. 1*s*.

Willmore, J. S. The great crime and its moral. Diplomatic events and German methods, leading to the War. Hodder & Stoughton 1917. 6*s*.

Wolf, Lucien. Jewish Ideals and the War. An address to the Jewish Historical Society. Central Committee. 1*d*.

Woods, H. Charles. The Cradle of the War. The Near-East and Pan-Germanism. With preface by A. Laurence Lowell. Murray 1918. 12*s*.

Why Europe is at War. A collection of addresses by representatives of the leading countries engaged. Putnam. 3*s*. 6*d*.

Yoxall, Sir James, M.P. Why Britain went to War. Cassell. 1*d*.

(2) *French*.

Adam, Madame. The Schemes of the Kaiser. Translated by J. O. P. Bland. Heinemann 1917. 5*s*.

Allemand, Un (Kurt Gutmann). La Vérité est en marche! (contre l'auteur de *J'accuse* et du *Crime*). Zurich: Orell Fussli 1918. 3 fr. 50.

Ambitions, Les, de l'Allemagne en Europe (recueil des conférences faits au cours de la guerre par divers publicistes). Alcan 1918. 3 fr. 50.

Baillod, C. Pourquoi l'Allemagne devait faire la Guerre. Perrin 1915. 2 fr.

Bainville, Jacques. Histoire de deux peuples: la France et l'Empire allemand. (Explains the historical reasons of the war.) Nouv. Libr. Nationale. 3 fr. 50.

Batiffol, Mgr. P. À un neutre catholique. Bloud et Gay 1916. 60 c.

Beck, G. La responsabilité de la Hongrie. Etude . . . suivie de revélations sur la conjuration de Serajevo. Payot 1917. 4 fr. 50.

Bellet, Daniel. Chiffons de Papier. Ce qu'il faut savoir des origines de la guerre de 1914. Plon-Nourrit. 1 fr. 50.

Bertrand, Pierre. L'Autriche a voulu la Grande Guerre. Editions Bossard 1916. 7 fr. 50.

Bourgeois, E., and Pagès, G. Les origines et les responsabilités de la grande guerre. Preuves et aveux. Hachette 1921. 25 fr.

Chéradame, André. Les Bénéfices de guerre de l'Allemagne et la Formule boche—Ni annexions, ni indemnités. Avec 4 cartes. Plon 1918. 50 c. Transl. under title, German War Profits, &c. Hodder 1918. 2*s*.

Chopin, Jules (J. E. Pichon). L'Autriche-Hongrie, brillant second. (La préméditation austro-hongrorie, le mystère de Serajevo, &c.) Rossard 1917. 5 fr.

—— Le Complot de Sarajevo. Bossard 1918. n.p.

Clemenceau, G. La France devant l'Allemagne. Payot 1916. 5 fr.

Daniélou, Charles. Responsabilités et Buts de Guerre. . . . Documents recueillis de 1914 . . . au Nov. 11, 1918, pour servir à l'étude de la question de la paix, et précédés d'un avantpropos et d'une préface. 3 vols. Figuière 1918. 18 fr.

Daudet, Ernest. Les auteurs de la guerre de 1914. Vol. I, Bismarck. II, William II and Franz Josef. Attinger 1916-17. 3 fr. 50 each.

Debrit, Jean. Et ce fut la guerre! (Examines the Austrian charge that Serbia was guilty of the crime of Serajevo.) Geneva: Atar 1917.

Denis, Prof. Ernest. Qui a la responsabilité de la guerre? le dernier plaidoyer de M. Bethmann-Hollweg. Bureaux de Foi et Vie 1917. 1 fr. 50.

—— La Guerre: causes immédiates et lointaines. L'intoxication d'un peuple. Le Traité. Delagrave. 3 fr. 50.

Dimier, Louis. La Guerre de 1914. L'Appel des intellectuels allemands. A reply to the 93 Professors. Nouv. Libr. Nationale. 2 fr.

Dontenville, J. L'Angleterre n'a pas voulu la Guerre. Floury 1914. 60 c.

Durkheim, E., and Denis, E. Qui a voulu la Guerre? Les origines de la guerre d'après les documents diplomatiques. (Études et Documents sur la Guerre.) Colin. 50 c.

—— Who Wanted War? English transl. of Qui a voulu la Guerre? Colin. 50 c.

Etudes et Documents sur la Guerre:

Bédier. German Atrocities.
—— How Germany seeks to justify, etc.
Durkheim and Denis. Who wanted War?
Lavisse and Andler. German theory, etc., of War.
Reiss. How Austria-Hungary waged War, etc.
Weiss. Violation by Germany of Neutrality of Belgium, etc.
Colin 1914.

Férasson, Louis. La Question du fer. Le Problème franco-allemand du fer. Pagot. 3 fr.

Gauvain, Auguste. Les Origines de la Guerre Européenne. European politics since the annexation of Bosnia and Herzegovina. 6th edn. Colin. 3 fr. 50.

Giraud, P. Devant l'Histoire. Causes connues et ignorées de la guerre. Berger-Levrault 1917. 3 fr. 50.

Guyot, Yves. Les causes et les conséquences de la Guerre. Alcan. 3 fr. 50.

—— English transl. under title, The causes and consequences of the war. Hutchinson 1916. 10*s.* 6*d.*

Hauser, Prof. Henri. Le Problème colonial. German colonial aims and methods, and their connection with the war. Chapelot 1915. 1 fr.

Hovelaque, Emile. Les causes profondes de la Guerre. Alcan 1915. 1 fr. 25.

—— Translated under title, The deeper causes of the War. With introduction by Sir Walter Raleigh. Allen & Unwin 1916. 2*s.* 6*d.*

Jaulmes, Th. Ignorance? Inconscience? ou Hypocrisie? Étude méthodique de l'appel des intellectuels allemands . . . avec documents. Attinger. 1 fr.

L'Allemagne et les Alliés devant la conscience Chrétienne. With preface by Mgr. Baudrillart. (Published by the Comité Catholique de Propagande française à l'étranger.) Bloud et Gay 1916. 3 fr. 50.

Lanesson, J. L. de. Introduction à le guerre de 1914; les empires germaniques et la politique de la force. Alcan 1915. 3 fr. 50.

Larnaude, F., and Lapradelle, A. de. Examen de la responsabilité pénale de l'Empereur Guillaume II. Imprimerie Nationale 1918.

Leurs Buts de guerre: choix de documents sur la paix allemande. (Selected by G. Pariset.) Pages d'histoire, 1914-1917, No. 137. Berger-Levrault 1917. 1 fr. 50.

Lévy-Bruhl, Prof. L. La conflagration européenne: ses causes économiques et politiques. Alcan 1915. 60 c.

Lichtenberger, Henri and André. La guerre européenne et la question d'Alsace. Chapelot. 1 fr.

Louis, Paul. La guerre d'Orient et la crise européenne (the Eastern Question explains the great war). Alcan 1916. 1 fr. 25.

Loyson, Paul Hyacinthe. Etes-vous neutres devant le Crime? Avec une lettre de Emile Verhaeren. Berger-Levrault 1916. 3 fr. 50.

—— Translated under title, The Gods in the Battle. With preface by H. G. Wells. Hodder & Stoughton 1917. 3*s*. 6*d*.

Margerie, E. de. Lettres échangées au sujet de la guerre européenne entre M. le prof. Albert Heim, correspondant de l'Institut de France à Zurich, et M. Emmanuel de Margerie. Hemmerlé 1917.

Millioud, Maurice. La Caste dominante allemande. An examination of the economic causes of the War. Lausanne: Payot 1915.

—— English translation under title, The Ruling Caste, and frenzied trade in Germany. With preface by Sir F. Pollock. Constable 4*s*. 6*d*.

Nicot, Alphonse. La Grande Guerre. Les Prétextes. L'Invasion avec 6 grav. Collection Pour tous. 1 fr. 50.

Orlet, Paul. Les Problèmes internationaux de la guerre. Rousseau 1916. 8 fr.

Pélissier, Jean. L'Europe sous la menace allemande en 1914: Le Pacifisme anglais; l'Impérialisme allemand; l'Enigme russe; l'Agonie de l'Autriche. Perrin 1915. 3 fr 50.

Pétain, Gen., Lavisse, E., and Ribot, A. Pourquoi nous nous battons. Pages d'histoire, No. 140. Berger-Levrault 1917. 60 c.

Poincaré, R. Les origines de la guerre. Conférences prononcées à la Societé des Conférences en 1921. Plon-Nourrit 1921. 10 fr.

—— English transl. under title, The Origins of the War. Cassell 1921. 12*s*.

Puaux, René. Études de la Guerre (la crise de juillet 1914 révélée par le procès Soukhomlinof, &c.). Payot 1917. 1 fr. 50.

Ruyssen, Th. La responsabilité de l'Autriche. La Paix par le Droit 1917. 60 c.

Saintyves, P. La responsabilité de l'Allemagne dans la guerre de 1914. Nourrit. 4 fr.

Toutey, E. Pourquoi la Guerre. Comment elle se fait. (Illustrated.) Hachette 1916. 4 fr.

Wampach, Gaspard. Le Dossier de la Guerre. Le prétexte; la crise diplomatique; pièces justificatives. 3 vols. Fischbacher 1915. 12 fr.

—— Ce qu'ils pensaient. Deux témoins: Daniel Frymann; Hermann Fernau. Fischbacher 1916. 3 fr. 50.

—— Ce qu'ils disent (les écrivains germaniques). Fischbacher 1917. 3 fr. 50.

(3) *German.*

Andrassy, Graf Julius (former Hungarian Minister). Wer hat den Krieg verbrochen? Leipzig: Hirzel 1915.

—— Considerations sur les origines de la Guerre. Lausanne: Rev. polit. internationale. 1 fr.

Below, Georg von. Kriegs- und Friedensfragen. Dresden: Globus 1918. 2 mk. 50.

Bergelvasser, Ludwig. Die diplomatischen Kämpfe vor Kriegsausbruch. Eine kritische Studie auf Grund der offiziellen Veröffentlichungen aller beteiligten Staaten. Munich and Berlin: Oldenbourg 1915. 6 mk. 50.

Bissing, Frhr. von. Die Kriegeziele unserer Feinde. Dresden: Globus 1917. 2 mk.

Bley, Fritz. Wie kam es doch? 1918. 3 mk. 20.

Bitterauf, T. Die deutsche Politik und die entstehung des Krieges. Munich: Beck 1915.

Carrière, L. Die Kriegsziele der kämpfenden Völker. 1917. 4 mk.

Chamberlain, H. S. Who is to blame for the War? In English. Leipzig: Bruckmann 1915.

Class, H. Zum deutschen Kriegsziel. Eine Flugschrift. 1917. 1 mk. 40.

Das Verbrechen. By the author of "J'accuse" (Dr. Richard Grelling). Payot 1917. 6 fr.

—— Engl. transl. by Alex. Gray, under title The Crime. Hodder & Stoughton 1918. 10*s.* 6*d.*

Dernburg, Dr. B. Germany and the War: not a Defence but an Explanation. N.Y.: Fatherland Corporation. 10 c.

Dernburg, Dr. B. Search-Lights on the War. Germany and England—the real issue: England's share of guilt—critical analysis of the English White Book: Germany and the Powers: When Germany wins, &c. N.Y.: Fatherland Corporation 1915.

Deutsche Schuld am Kriege: ein Mahnwort an das deutsche Volk, ein Versuch zum Frieden zu helfen. (By "un capitaine prussien.") Zurich: Füssli 1917. 1 fr. 25.

Eckhardstein, Hermann Frhr. von. Diplomatische Enthüllungen zum Ursprung des Weltkrieges. Bruchstücke aus meinen politischen Deutwürdigkeiten. Berlin: Curtius 1920.

Federn, K. Die Politik des Dreiverbandes u.d. Krieg. Legenden u. Tatsachen. 1915. 3 mk. 50.

Fernau, Hermann. Gerade weil ich Deutscher bin. Written in support of the author of J'accuse. Zürich: Füssli 1916. 1 mk. 50.

—— English transl. under title Because I am a German. With introduction by T. W. Rolleston. Constable 1916. 2*s*.

German designs on French Lorraine (Secret memorandum of the German Iron and Steel Manufacturers). Allen & Unwin 1918. 6*d*.

Grumbach, S. Der Irrtum von Zimmerwald-Kienthal Vortrag gehalten 3 Juni 1916. (German aims of conquest.) Bern: Benteli 1916. 90 c.

Helfferich, Karl. Die Entstehung des Weltkrieges, im Lichte der Veröffentlichungen der Dreiverbandmächte. Berlin: Stilke 1915. 30 pf.

—— Die Vorgeschichte des Weltkriegs (Band I of Der Weltkrieg). Berlin: Ullstein 1919.

Hofer, K. Die Keime des grossen Kriegs. Zürich: Schulthess 1917.

Hünerwadel, Prof. W. Die geschichtliche Vorbedingungen des europäischen Krieges. Zürich: Füssli 1916. 80 pf.

J'accuse. Von einem Deutschen. Hrsg. von Dr. Anton Suter. Lausanne: Payot 1915. 6 fr.

J'accuse! By a German. Transl. into English from the German original by Alex. Gray. Hodder & Stoughton 1915. 5*s*.

Jagow, G. von. Ursachen und Ausbruch des Weltkrieges. Berlin: Reimar Hobbing 1919. 3 mk.

Kammerer, I. Die deutsche Mission im Weltkriege. 1 mk. 20.

Lammasch, H. Europas elfte Stunde. 1918. 9 mk. 80.

Mantel, H. Englands Kriegsziele. Stuttgart 1917. 1 mk. 50.

Meinecke, F. Probleme des Weltkrieges. Munich: Oldenbourg 1917. 1 mk. 80.

Meyer, Prof. A. O. Worin liegt Englands Schuld. Series, Der deutsche Krieg. Stuttgart: Deutsche Verlags-Anstalt.

Morel-Fatio, A. Les versions allemande et française du Manifeste des Intellectuels allemands, dit des Quatre-vingt-trieze, publiées d'après les originaux et avec un avant-propos. Picard 1915. 60 c.

Mühlon, Dr. W. Revelations by an ex-director of Krupp's. Text of Dr. M.'s memorandum and of his letter to Herr von Bethmann-Hollweg. Hodder & Stoughton 1918. *3d.*

Müller-Meiningen, E. Diplomatie und Weltkrieg. Ein Führer durch die Entstehung und Ausbreitung der Weltkrisis auf Grund amtlicher Materialien. 2 vols. 1917. 50 mk.

Nielsen, H. L'empereur Guillaume et le tsar Nicolas. (Télégrammes échangés de 1904 à 1907, révélés par Bourtsev). Copenhagen: Aschehoug 1918.

Niemann, Hans. Unser Kriegsziel. Berlin: 1916. 50 pf.

Nowak, K. F. Der Weg zur Katastrophe. Durchgesehen und autorisiert von Conrad von Hötzendorf (chef des österr-ungar. Generalstabs).

Révai, Mauras. Das Endziel des Krieges: Englands Ausschaltung aus Europa. Berlin: Puttkamer & Muehlbrecht 1916

Ritter, Prof. Moriz. Der Ausbrach des Weltkrieges nach den Behauptung Lichnauskys und nach dem Zeugnis der Akten. Murich and Berlin: Oldenbourg 1918. 4 mk.

Rohrbach, P. Chauvinismus u. Weltkrieg. I. Die Brandstifter der Entente: v. P. Rohrbach u. J. Kühn. 2nd edn. 1919. 15 mk.

—— Woher es kam. 15th Impr. 1919. 1 mk. 80.

—— Woher kam der Krieg? Wohin führt er? 1917. 1 mk. 50.

Sänger, A. Die Schuld der deutschen Regierung am Kriege. 1 mk. 20.

Salomon, F. Wie England unser Feind wurde. 1914. 50 pf.

Schäfer, D. Die Schuld am Kriege. 1919. 2 mk. 25.

Schiemann, Prof. Theod. Die letzten Etappen zum Weltkrieg (Last vol. of Deutschland und die grosse Politik, for 1914). Berlin: Reimer. 4 mk. 50.

Schiemann, Th. Ein Verleumder. Glossen zur Vorgeschichte des Weltkrieges. Berlin: Reimer 1915. 1 mk.

Schulte, A. Frankreich und das linke Rheinufer. 4 maps. 2nd edn. 1918. 12 mk.

Vernichtung der Englischen Weltmacht und des russischen Zarismus durch den Dreibund und das Islam. 2 mk. 50.

Warum war der Weltkrieg eine Notwendigkeit? 1915. 60 pf.

What Caused the War: German Policy explained by a German. Extracts from Bernhardi. Central Committee. *1d.*

Wichtl, Fr. Weltfreimauerei, Weltrevolution, Weltrepublik. Eine Untersuchung über Ursprung u. Endziele des Weltkrieges. 15th Impr. 1919. 7 mk.

Zurlinden, S. Der Weltkrieg: vorläufige Orientirung von einem schweizerischen Standpunkt aus. Vol. 1: Die Würzeln des Weltkrieges (A condemnation of German militarism). Zürich: Füssli 1917. 12 fr.

(4) *Italian.*

Colajanni, Prof. Napoleone. Le Responsibilità e le cause della Guerra. Rome: Rivista Popolare 1917. 3 l.

Ferrero, G. La guerre européenne (Philosophical and other causes and issues). Payot 1916. 3 fr. 50.

—— Who willed the European War? Translated from the Italian by P. E. Matheson, and supervised by the author. Oxford Univ. Press. 8*d*.

Mariani, Mario. Il ritorno di Machiavelli. Studi sulla catastrofe europea. Milan: Soc. editr. italiana 1916. 4 l.

Piazza, Giuseppe. I Dardanelli: l'Oriente e la Guerra Europea. (Quaderni della guerra.) Milan: Treves 1915. 2 l.

Rignano, Eugenio. Les facteurs de la guerre et le problème de la paix. Preface by Ad. Landry. (Result of an international enquiry in *Scientia*.) Alcan 1915.

Salvemini, Gaetano. Delenda Austria. Paris: Bossard 1918. 1 fr. 20.

Tittoni, Tommaso. Le Jugement de l'histoire sur la responsabilité de la guerre. Preface par M. Hanotaux. (Pages actuelles, 1914-1916, Nos. 96-97.) Bloud et Gay 1916. 1 fr. 20.

(5) *Other Nations.*

Fredenheim, L. S. [Lotten Scholander]. Skulden (who is guilty of the war). Stockholm: Svenska Andelsförlaget 1918.

Galiano, Alvaro Alcalá. The Truth about the War. Translated from the Spanish. Fisher Unwin 1915. 1*s*.

Jonesco, Take. (Rumanian statesman.) Les origines de la Guerre: déposition d'un témoin. Didier 1915. 75 c.

Jörgensen, Johannes. False Witness (translated from the Danish Klokke Roland). Hodder & Stoughton 1916. 3*s*. 6*d*.

Kjellén, R. Die politischen Probleme des Weltkriegs. Maps. 8th edn. 1918. 3 mk. 55.

Mendonça, Henrique Lopes de. Moral aspects of the European War. A lecture delivered on May 13, 1917. (Translated from the Spanish.) Fisher Unwin 1917. 2*d*.

Ossianilsson, K. G. Vem har Rett i Varldskriget? Stockholm: Lundberg 1916. 80 öre.

—— Translated under the title, Who is right in the World-War? Fisher Unwin 1917. 3*s*. 6*d*.

Palacio-Valdés, Armando. La Guerre injuste: Traduction de A. Glorget. Bloud et Gay 1917.

Snouck-Hurgronje, Dr. C. The Holy War, made in Germany. With introduction by R. J. Gottheil. Putnam. 3*s*.

Wesselitsky, G. de. The German Peril and the Grand Alliance: how to crush Prussian Militarism (a lecture delivered on behalf of the Russia Society). Fisher Unwin 1916. 1*s*.

Wigforss, Ernst. Världskriget och Världsfreden. Dokumenter och Reflexioner. A strong defence of British policy by a Swedish writer. Stockholm: Tidens Förlag. 3 kr.

IX. THE NATIONS AND THE WAR.

A.—Belligerents.

(1) *Austria-Hungary*.

Andrassy, Count Julius. Diplomatie und Weltkrieg. Berlin & Vienna: Ullstein 1921.

—— Transl. under title Diplomacy and the War. Bale & Danielson 1921. 17*s*. 6*d*.

Cramon, A. von. Unser Oesterreich. Ungarisches Bundesgenosse im Weltkriege: Erinnerungen aus meiner vierjährigen Tätigkeit als bevollmächtigter deutscher General beim k.u.k. Armeeoberkommando. 1920. 20 mk.

Demblin, August. Czernin und die Sixtus-Affaire. Munich, Drei-Marken Verlag 1920. 2 mk. 50.

Fels, Comte de. L'Entente et le Problème Autrichien. Grasset 1918. 4 fr.

Hildebrand, K. Die Donaumonarchie im Kriege. Studien u. Eindr. in Osterreich. Ungarn. Juni-Juli, 1915. Mit 12 Taf. 1916. 3 mk. 65.

Kanner, H. Kaiserliche Katastrophen-politik. Ein Stück zeitgenössischer Geschichte. Vienna: Tal. 1921.

Léger, Louis. La liquidation de l'Autriche-Hongrie. Alcan 1915. 1 fr. 25.

Leutrum, Countess. Court and Diplomacy in Austria and Germany: What I know. Illustrated. Fisher Unwin 1918. 10*s*. 6*d*.

Macdonald, Mina. Some experiences in Hungary: Aug. 1914 to Jan. 1915. Illustrated. Longmans 1916. 3*s*. 6*d*.

Müller-Guttenbrunn, A. Kriegstagebuch eines Daheimgebliebenen. Eindrücke und Stimmungen aus Osterreich-Ungarn. 1916. 3 mk. 50.
Munin. Oesterreich nach dem Kriege. Jena 1915. 60 pf.
Nosek, Vladimir. Austrian Socialism and the Present War. Twentieth Century Press 1918. *2d.*
Szillassy, Baron J. von. Der Untergang der Donau-Monarchie Berlin: Berger 1921.
Vosvjak, Bogumil. A Dying Empire. G. Allen & Unwin.

(2) *Balkan States (general).*

Buxton, Noel, and Buxton, Charles R. The War and the Balkans. Information gathered during a recent visit, as to the attitude of Rumania, Bulgaria and Greece. Allen & Unwin. *2s. 6d.*
Buxton, Noel, & Leese, C. L. Balkan Problems and European Peace. Allen & Unwin 1919. *4s. 6d.*
Colonna di Cesarò, G. A. (Duke of Cesarò). Quadruple Diplomacy in the Balkans; its errors and its remedies (pamphlet). The Utopia Press, 44, Worship St., E.C. 1916.
Gordon, Mrs. Will. A Woman in the Balkans. Hutchinson 1916. *12s. 6d.*
Price, C. Light on the Balkan Darkness. Simpkin 1915. *1s.*
Woods, H. C. War and Diplomacy in the Balkans. Cox. *6d.*
—— The Cradle of the War: the Near-East and Pan-Germanism. (Illustr.) 1918. *12s.*

(3) *Belgium, with Luxemburg.*

Ablay, M. De la gloire et du sang (Belgian heroism in the early part of the war). Libr. Moderne 1918. 4 fr.
Administrative Separation. Letters by leading Belgians, March to Nov. 1917, with a preface by M. H. Carton de Wiart. Fisher Unwin 1918. *6d.*
Anthonis, H. Les Réfugiés belges taxés par les allemands. Blackwell 1915. *3d.*
Bassompierre, Albert de. La Nuit du 2 au 3 Août au Ministère des Affaires Etrangères de Belgique. Perrin 1916. 1 fr.
Belgian Workmen, Appeal of the, to the workmen of all nations. Speaight & Sons 1916.
Belgian Workmen now Refugees in England, Condition of the. (Reply to false statements in the *Volksrecht*). Fisher Unwin 1917. *1d.*
Belgique, La, sous la griffe allemande. By X., a barrister of Brussels. Fontemoing. 3 fr. 50.

Berden, Louis. Pictures of ruined Belgium. 72 pen and ink sketches drawn on the spot. Lane 1917. *7s. 6d.*

Bloeher, Eduard. Belgische Neutralität. (By a German-Swiss, hostile to Belgium.) Zurich 1915.

Book of Belgium's Gratitude, A. Comprising literary articles by representative Belgians, with translations. Illustrated by Belgian artists. Special limited edn. Lane 1915. *21s.*

Boubée, l'Abbé J. La Belgique loyale, héroique, et malheureuse. (By a French eye-witness of the invasion.) Preface by M. H. Carton de Wiart. Plon-Nourrit 1916, 3 fr.

Cammaerts, Emile. Through the iron bars. Two years of German occupation. N.Y.: John Lane 1918. 75 c.

Campbell, H. Belgian soldiers at home in the United Kingdom. (By the Transport Superintendent of the War Refugees Committee.) Saunders & Cullingham 1918. *2s.*

Chesterton, G. K. The Martyrdom of Belgium: an Appeal. Belgian Relief and Reconstruction Committee.

Clairens, Florimond. A plain Tale from Malines. The authentic story of a refugee. Transl. by R. W. Pugh. Illustrated. Oxford: Blackwell. *1s.*

Clapham, Margaret, and Clarke, Ethel B. Le Ménage belge en Angleterre. Prepared for the Belgian Hospitality Committees in Cambridge. Introduction by Prof. de Jace (of Liège). *6d.*

Dans la geôle bruxelloise: deux années sous le joug allemand. Préface de Paul Deschanel. Van Oest 1918. 3 fr. 50.

Davignon, H. Les Procédés allemands de guerre en Belgique.

—— Un Peuple en exil. La Belgique en Angleterre. (Pages actuelles.) Bloud et Gay 1916. 60 c.

Davis, H. W. C. What Europe owes to Belgium. (O.P.) Oxford Univ. Press. *2d.*

De Flemalle, Captain G. de L. Fighting with King Albert. Belgium before and since the outbreak of war. Hodder & Stoughton. *6s.*

De Marès, Roland. La Belgique envahie. (Illustrated.) Crès 1915. 3 fr. 50.

Deportations, The. Statement of the American Minister to Belgium. Fisher Unwin 1917. *1d.*

Des Ombiaux, Maurice. Un Royaume en exil. La Belgique du dehors. Berger-Levrault 1917. 3 fr.

Destrée, Jules. Deportations, The, of Belgian Workmen. By a deputy to the Belgian Parliament. Translated from the French. Fisher Unwin 1917. *2d.*

Fox, Frank. The Agony of Belgium: being Phase 1 of the Great War. By the War Correspondent of the Morning Post. Hutchinson. *6s.*

Frank, Prof. Reinhard. Die belgische Neutralität. Tubingen 1915.

Fuehr, Alexander. The Neutrality of Belgium. From the German point of view. N.Y.: Funk & Wagnall 1915. $1.50.

Gerlache de Gomery, le commandant de. La Belgique et les Belges pendant la guerre. Avec illustrations et cartes. Berger-Levrault 1916. 6 fr. Transl. under title Belgium in War-time. Hodder & Stoughton 1917. 5*s.*

Gibson, Hugh. A diplomatic diary. Publd. with permission of the U. S. State Dept. (By the Secretary of the American Legation in Brussels.) Illustrated. Hodder & Stoughton 1917. 7*s.* 6*d.*

Giran, Étienne. Sous le joug. Placards et avis de l'armée allemande dans les régions envahies. Hachette 1918. 1 fr.

Grasshoff, Richard. Belgiens Schuld. Berlin: Elsner 1915.

Gray, Ezio M. Il Belgio sotto la Spada Tedesca. Describes the peace penetration of Belgium by German commerce, etc., before the war, with some account of the military operations. Florence: Libr. Internazionale. 95 c.

Gribble, Francis. In Luxemburg in war-time (Aug.-Sept. 1914). Headley 1916. 5*s.*

Halasi, Odön. Belgium under the German Heel. Cassell 1917. 6*s.*

Hampe, Prof. Karl. Belgiens Vergangenheit und Gegenwart. Berlin: Teubner 1915.

Havard de la Montagne, Madeleine. La Vie agonisante des pays occupés. Lille et la Belgique: notes d'un tèmoin (octobre 1914-juillet 1916). Perrin 1918. 3 fr. 50.

Hawkin, R. C. The Belgian Proposal to neutralize Central Africa during the European War. Sweet & Maxwell. 1*s.*

Headlam, J. W. Belgium and Greece. Hodder & Stoughton 1917. 1*d.*

How Belgium is Fed. An account of the distribution of American relief. Illustrated. National Committee for Relief in Belgium.

Kellogg, Paul V. The Fourth Year in Belgium. How help is reaching the Lowlands through the American Red Cross. Paris: 4 Pl. de la Concorde 1918. n.p.

Kervyn de Lettenhove, Baron H. La Guerre et les œuvres d'art en Belgique. Illustrated. Brussels: Van Oest 1917. 4 fr. 50.

King Albert's Book: a Tribute to the Belgian King and People from representative men and women throughout the World. Illustrated. Hodder & Stoughton 1914. 3*s.*

Langenhove, Fernand van. Comment naît un cycle de légendes. Francs-tireurs et atrocités en Belgique. Reply to German charges, based on German documents. Payot 1916. 3 fr.

—— Transl. under title: The Growth of a Legend. Putnam 1917. 5*s*.

Lecomte, Maxime, and Lévi, Lieut.-Col. Camille. La Neutralité Belge et l'Invasion Allemande. Lavauzelle. 10 fr.

Lichtervelde, Louis de. Le 4 août 1914 au Parlement belge (Heures d'histoire). Van Oest 1914. 1 fr. 25.

Little Nun, The. Diary of one of Belgium's unhappy victims from her original MS.) Cassell 1916. 1*s*.

Loti, Pierre. La Grande Barbarie. Short papers on Ypres; interviews with the King and Queen of the Belgians, etc. Calmann-Lévy. 50 c.

Mack, Louise (Mrs. Creed). A woman's experiences in the Great War. Especially in Antwerp and Brussels during the German occupation. Fisher Unwin. 10*s*. 6*d*.

Malo, Henri. En Belgique: la Zone de l'Avant (tableaux, portraits, paysages). (Région de l'Yser.) Perrin 1918. 3 fr. 50.

Markland, Russell. Glory of Belgium: a tribute and a chronicle. With a preface by Emile Cammaerts. Macdonald 1915. 2*s*. 6*d*.

Massart, Jean. Comment les Belges résistent à la domination allemande. Contribution au livre des douleurs de la Belgique. (Illustrated.) Payot 1916. 5 fr.

—— Belgians under the German Eagle. Transl. by Bernard Miall (new and independent evidence of German atrocities in Belgium). Fisher Unwin 1916. 10*s*. 6*d*.

—— La Presse Clandestine dans la Belgique occupée. Berger-Levrault 1917. 6 fr.

—— —— Transl. under title, The Secret Press in Belgium. Fisher Unwin 1918. 2*s*. 6*d*.

Mercier, Cardinal. An Appeal to Truth. A letter addressed by Cardinal Mercier and the Bishops of Belgium to the Cardinals [etc.] of Germany, Bavaria and Austria-Hungary. Hodder & Stoughton 1916. 2*d*.

Mokveld, L. The German fury in Belgium. (By the war correspondent of De Tijd. Preface by John Buchan. Hodder & Stoughton 1917. 3*s*. 6*d*.

Narsy, Raoul. Le supplice de Louvain. Bloud et Gay 1915. 1 fr. 80.

Norden, Dr. Fritz. Das neutrale Belgien and Deutschland, im Urteil belgischer Staatsmänner und Juristen. Munich: Bruckman 1916. 4 mk.

Nothomb, Pierre. Les Barbares en Belgique. Avec une lettre-préface de M. H. Carton de Wiart, Ministre de la Justice. Perrin. 3 fr. 50.

—— —— Tranls. by Jean E. H. Findley, under title, The Barbarians in Belgium. Jarrold. 2*s*. 6*d*.

—— La Belgique Martyre. Summarises the results of the Belgian Commission of Inquiry. Perrin. 50 c.

Nyrop, Prof. Christ. L'arrestation des professeurs belges et l'université de Gand. Un conflit entre la force et le droit. (Transl. from the Danish.) Illustrations. Payot. 1 fr. 50.

—— The imprisonment of the Ghent Professors. A question of might and right. My reply to the German Legation in Stockholm. (The Professors are P. Frédericq and H. Pirenne). Hodder & Stoughton 1917. 2*s*.

Olijff, F. La Belgique sous le joug (un recueil de témoignages). Perrin 1917. 3 fr. 50.

Ossiannilsson, K. G. Militarism at work in Belgium and Germany (Deportations, Preventive Arrest Law, &c.) Fisher Unwin 1917. 2*s*. 6*d*.

Passelecq, Fernand. L'altération officielle des documents Belges. Le second Livre Blanc allemand (Pages d'historie). Berger-Levrault 1916. 1 fr.

—— Pour teutoniser la Belgique: l'effort allemand pour exploiter la querelle des races et des langues. Bloud et Gay 1916. 1 fr. 30 c.

—— La Question Flamande et L'Allemagne. Berger-Levrault 1917. 4 fr.

—— Les Déportations Belges à la lumière des Documents Allemands. Berger-Levrault 1917. 7 fr. 50.

—— Y-a-t-il une nation belge? Van Oest 1917.

—— La Magistrature belge contre le despotisme allemand (histoire psychologique). Berger-Levrault 1918. 2 fr. 50.

—— Unemployment in Belgium during the German occupation, and its general causes. Hodder & Stoughton 1918. 1*s*.

Piérard, L. La Belgique sous les armes, sous la botte, en exil. Perrin 1917. 3 fr. 50.

Prussiens, Les, en Belgique. Par X . . ., avocat près la Cour d'appel de Bruxelles. Fontemoing 1916. 3 fr. 50.

Radelet, Lieut. Le Livre d'or du peuple belge, août 1914-mai 1915. 1er vol. (Le recueil de tous les Belges qui ont obtenu une décoration.) Rouen: Laîne 1916. 4 fr.

Randolph, J. A. Call of Belgium, and other War Area articles. Illustrated. Architect Office 1915. 1*s*.

Sarolea, Dr. C. The Martyrdom of Belgium. An Appeal Belgian Relief and Reconstruction Committee.

Schönborn, Prof. Walter. Die Neutralität Belgiens. Leipzig: Teubner 1915.

Scraps of Paper. Reduced photographic facsimiles of German proclamations in Belgium and France. Preface by Ian Malcolm, M.P. Hodder & Stoughton 1917. 1*s.*

Somville, Gustave. Vers Liège: le chemin du crime, Août 1914. A minute inquiry into the doings of the Germans in the Province of Liège. Perrin 1915. 3 fr. 50.

Standaert, Eugène. A Belgian Mission to the Boers (sent by the Belgian Government, Oct. 1914, to counteract German intrigues in S. Africa). Hodder & Stoughton 1917. 3*s.* 6*d.*

Strupp. Die Neutralisation und die Neutralität Belgiens. Gotha 1917. 5 mk.

Torn, Paul. Huit mois avec les Boches dans le Luxembourg. Perrin 1916. 3 fr. 50.

Toynbee, Arnold J. The German Terror in Belgium (documentary evidence). Hodder & Stoughton 1917. 1*s.*

Van den Heuvel, J. De la Déportation des Belges en Allemagne. Pedone 1917. 1 fr.

—— Slave Raids in Belgium. Facts about the deportations (documents). Fisher Unwin 1917. 2*d.*

Vandervelde, E. La Belgique envahie et le socialisme internationale. Préface par Marcel Sembat. Berger-Levrault 1917. 3 fr. 50.

Varlez, Armand. Les Belges en exil. Illustrated. Simpkin 1917. 7*s.* 6*d.*

Verhaeren, Emilie. La Belgique sanglante. Nouv. Revue Française. 3 fr. 50.

—— Transl. under the title: Belgium's Agony. Includes several poems. Constable. 3*s.* 6*d.*

—— Parmi les cendres: la Belgique devastée (with frontispiece). Crès 1916. 1 fr. 50.

Visscher, Ch. de. La Belgique et les juristes allemands (la neutralité permanente du royaume de Belgique). Payot 1917. 2 fr. 50.

—— Belgium's Case: A Juridical Enquiry. Transl. from the French by E. F. Jourdain. With a Preface by J. Van den Heuvel. Hodder & Stoughton 1916. 3*s.* 6*d.*

Vossaert, Emmanuel. Les Emigrés de l'an XV. A study of life in Brussels under German domination. Libraire Moderne 1917. 1*s.* 3*d.*

Wallez, N. La Belgique de demain et la politique. Van Oest 1918. 2 fr.

Warr, Charles L. Echoes of Flanders. Simpkin, Marshall 1916. 5*s*.

Waxweiler, Emile. La Belgique neutre et loyale. (A defence of Belgium against the German charges.) Lausanne: Payot. 2 fr. 50.

—— English transl. under title: Belgium Neutral and Loyal. Putnam. 5*s*.

—— Le Procès de la neutralité belge. Réplique aux accusations. Payot 1916. 2 fr.

—— Transl. under title: Belgium and the Great Powers. Her neutrality explained and vindicated. Putnam 1916. 3*s*. 6*d*.

Whitaker, J. P. Under the Heel of the Hun. (Experience in Belgium from Sept. 1914.) Hodder & Stoughton 1917. 2*s*.

Whitehouse, J. H., M.P. Belgium in War. Illustrated. Camb. Univ. Press. 1*s*.

Whitlock, Brand. Belgium under German occupation 1914-17. (By the U.S. Minister to Brussels.) 2 vols. Heinemann 1919. 24*s*.

Wiart, H. Carton de. La Politique de l'honneur. (Conséquence de la conduite de la Belgiques au mois d'août 1914.) Bloud et Gay 1917. 3 fr.

Zimmermann, K. Das Problem Belgiens. (Map.) 1915. 2 mk. 20.

(4) *British Empire.*

(*a*) General.

Adcock, A. St. J. Seeing it through: how Britain answered the Call. Hodder & Stoughton 1915. 1*s*.

Barker, J. Ellis. The great problems of British statesmanship. Murray 1917. 10*s*. 6*d*.

Basu, Bhupendranath. Why India is Heart and Soul with Great Britain. Macmillan. 1*d*.

Benians, E. A. The British Empire and the War. Fisher Unwin. 6*d*.

Bennett, W. England's Mission. (O.P.) Oxford Univ. Press. 2*d*.

Binyon, Laurence. For Dauntless France. An account of Britain's aid to the French wounded and victims of the War. Preface by M. Paul Cambon. Hodder & Stoughton 1918. 10*s*.

British Finance and Prussian Militarism. Interviews with the Rt. Hon. T. McKinnon Wood and the Rt. Hon. Arthur Henderson. Hodder 1917. 1*d*.

British Labour Movement and the War. Manifestos, etc. Harrison & Sons.

British Universities and the War. A record and its meaning (compiled at the request of United States correspondents). The Field and Queen 1917. 1*s*.

Broughton, U. H., M.P. The British Empire at War. Edinburgh: Morrison & Gibb 1916.

Brownrigg, Rear-Admiral Sir Douglas. Indiscretions of the Naval Censor. Illustrations. Cassell 1920. 12*s*. 6*d*.

Bryce, Viscount. The Attitude of Great Britain in the present War. Originally written for a Swiss journal. Macmillan 1916. 1*d*.

Buckrose, J. E. War time in our Street. Hodder & Stoughton 1917. 2*s*. 6*d*.

Bull, Rev. P. B. Our Duty at Home. Mowbray. 2*d*.

Bourne, C. S. Papers for the People: (1) Playing the Game. (2) Might or Right? (3) King George or Kaiser Wilhelm? (4) A Scrap of Paper. Central Committee, 62, Charing Cross. 1*d*. each; 5*s*. per 100.

C. M. The War Cabinet as an Imperial Council. St. Catherine Press 1917. 1*d*.

Cable, Boyd. Doing their bit. War work at home. With preface by the Right Hon. D. Lloyd George. Hodder & Stoughton 1916. 1*s*.

Catholics of the British Empire and the War (collected from various books and periodicals). Burns & Oates 1916. 6*d*.

Cazamian, Louis. La Grande Bretagne et la Guerre. Flammarion 1917. 3 fr. 50.

Cestre, Ch. L'Angleterre et la Guerre. Didier 1916. 3 fr. 50.

—— France, England, and European democracy, 1215-1915. Translated from the French (democratic ideals of the two nations in connexion with the war). Putnam 1918. 12*s*. 6*d*.

Chevrillon, André. L'Angleterre et la Guerre. Hachette 1916. 3 fr. 50.

—— Translated under title, England in War time. With preface by Rudyard Kipling. Hodder & Stoughton 1916. 5*s*.

Cohn, August. Some aspects of the War as viewed by naturalized British subjects (a defence of Great Britain). Issued by the Council of Loyal British Subjects of German, Austrian and Hungarian birth. 13, Clifford's Inn, E.C., 1916.

Cook, Sir Edward. The Press in War-time; with some account of the Official Press Bureau. Macmillan 1920. 7*s*. 6*d*.

Corbett, Julian. The Spectre of Navalism. Darling 1915.

Cravath, Paul D. Great Britain's part. An answer to the question, What has Britain done? Appleton 1917. $1.00.

Crazannes, J. M. L'Empire britannique et la guerre européenne. Lettres d'Angleterre. Belin 1916. 3 fr. 50.

Davenport, Briggs. What the British Empire is doing in the War. With introduction by Joseph Reinach. Fisher Unwin 1916. 6*d*.

Davray, Henry D. Through French eyes. Britain's effort. Constable 1916. 6*s*.

Desjardins, Lieut.-Colonel. L'Angleterre, le Canada, et la Grande Guerre. (An appeal to French-Canadians by a compatriot.) Quebec 1917.

Destrée, Jules. L'Effort britannique : contribution de l'Angleterre à la guerre européenne, Août 1914-Févr. 1916. With preface by M. Clemenceau. Van Oest 1916. 3 fr. 50.

—— Translated under title, Britain in Arms. Lane 1917. 5*s*.

Dewar, G. A. B. The great munition feat. Constable 1921. 21*s*.

Doyle, Sir A. Conan. To Arms ! Hodder & Stoughton. 1*d*.

Draper, W. H. (Edr.). Courage ! or the Days of our Fathers. A record and remembrance of the spirit of Great Britain a hundred years ago, from the works of Sydney Smith and others. Leeds : Jackson 1915. 1*s*.

Duchesne, A. E. Democracy and the Empire. Maps and diagrams. Oxford Univ. Press 1916. 2*s*. 6*d*.

English Spirit, The. Extract from a letter to a Neutral. By an Englishman. Darling 1916. n.p.

Fisher, H. A. L. The British Share in the War. Nelson, Aug. 1915. 2*d*.

Fletcher, C. Brunedon. The new Pacific : British policy and German aims. With preface by Lord Bryce, and foreword by Rt. Hon. W. M. Hughes. Macmillan 1917.

Formby, Rev. C. W. The Soul of England, or a Great Empire at the Cross Roads. Wells, Gardner, Darton, 1916. 2*s*. 6*d*.

Furse, Michael (Bishop of Pretoria). The Nation under Orders. Reprint of letter to The Times. Times Office. ½*d*.

Gleason, Arthur. Inside the British Isles (on the social and political results of the war). New York : Century Co. 1917. $2.00.

Gopčevič, Graf Spiridion. Aus dem Lande der unbegrenzten Heuchelei. Englische Zustände. 1915. 2 mk. 90.

Hale, Col. Sir Lonsdale. Awake, you Britishers, to your Peril from Over-the-Way, and hasten to face it. Love & Malcolmson. 2*d*.

Hard, William. How the English take the War (reprinted from The Metropolitan, New York). Hodder & Stoughton 1917. 2*d*.

Harrison, Frederic. The Meaning of the War : for Labour—Freedom—Country. Macmillan. 1*d*.

Headlam, J. W. England, Germany and Europe. Reprinted from the Church Quarterly Review. Macmillan. 2*d*.

Headlam, J. W. The Truth about England (exposed in a letter to a Neutral): her attitude and services in the War. Nelson 1916. *2d.*

Hettner, A. Englands Weltherrschaft und ihre Krisis. 3rd edn. 1917. 6 mk.

Imelmann, Paul. Der deutsche Kreig und die englische Literatur. Bonn 1916.

Imperialism and Patriotism and the European Crisis, 1914. Sydney edn., 1915. Black. *5s.*

Jacques, N. London und Paris im Krieg. Erlebnisse auf Reisen durch England u. Frankreich in Kriegszeit. 1915. 3 mk. 50.

James, Henry, and Clutton-Brock, A. England at War. Two essays, with contrasted excerpts from various German writers. Central Committee. *1d.*

Jersey, Countess of, and Cook, Sir Edward. Britain's part in the War. Victoria League 1917. *3d.*

Jones, C. Sheridan. London in War time. Grafton 1917. *2s. 6d.*

Knight, W. S. M. A History of Britain during the Great War. To be issued in fortnightly parts. Ridd Masson Co. *7d.* each.

Lambert, Richard C. The Parliamentary History of Conscription in Great Britain. Debates, with text of the Military Service Acts, &c. Allen & Unwin 1917. *5s.*

Lash, Z. A. Defence and foreign affairs. A suggestion for the Empire. Macmillan Co. of Canada 1917.

Le Queux, William. Britain's Deadly Peril: Are We Told the Truth? Stanley Paul 1915. *1s.* and *2s.*

—— German Spy. Newnes 1915. *6d.*

—— German Spies in England: an Exposure. Stanley Paul 1915. *1s.* and *2s.*

—— Spies of the Kaiser. Hurst & Blackett 1914. *6d.*

Luke, C. H. The War and the Parting of the Ways: a short study of the British Empire in relation to the Great War. Sampson Low. *1s.*

Lyttelton, Rev. and Hon. E. Britain's Duty To-day. Patriotic Publishing Co. *4d.*

Madariaga, Salvador de. La Guerra desde Londres. Tortosa: Monchis 1918. 3 p. 50.

Maguire, T. Miller. The Gates of Our Empire. Australasia: H. Rees 1914. *1s.*

Meyer, Eduard. England: seine staatliche und politische Entwicklung und der Krieg gegen Deutschland. 1916. 5 mk. Popular edn. 1 m. 80.

Michael, W. Englands Politik und der Krieg. Berlin 1915. 80 pf.

Miller, Frederick. Under German Shell Fire: the Hartlepools, Scarborough and Whitby. 1915. 1*s*.

Morgan, Rev. J. Vyrnwy. The War and Wales. With preface by H. Stuart Jones. Chapman & Hall 1916. 10*s*. 6*d*.

Murray, Gilbert. Great Britain's Sea Policy: a reply to an American critic. (Reprinted from the Atlantic Monthly.) Fisher Unwin 1917. 2*d*.

—— The way forward. Three articles on Liberal policy. Preface by Viscount Grey of Fallodon. Allan & Unwin 1917. 1*s*.

North Britain (pseud.). British Freedom, 1914-1917; with Foreword by John Clifford. National Council for Civil Liberties 1917. 1*s*.

O'Connor, J. K. The Afrikander Rebellion: South Africa To-Day. An exposure of German intrigue in South Africa. Allen & Unwin. 1*s*.

Page, E. Judson. The War and the Welsh Church Act. Exeter: Trinity Press 1915. 6*d*.

Paget, Rt. Rev. H. L. (edr.). Records of the Raids. With introduction by Sir F. Lloyd, and conclusion by the Bishop of London. S.P.C.K. 1918. 6*d*.

Palmer, Mrs. J. Purdry. Dates and Days in Europe. By an American Resident in London, 1914-15. Routledge 1915. 2*s*. 6*d*.

Paul-Dubois, Louis. L'effort Économique et Financier de l'Angleterre. Perrin 1918. 4 fr.

Prothero, G. W. Our Duty and our Interest in the War. Issued by the Central Committee. Murray 1914. 2*d*.

—— How Goes the War? An estimate of the present situation, and the need for further effort. Maps. Central Committee 1915. 2*d*.

Raleigh, Prof. Sir Walter. England and the War. Speeches and Addresses. Oxford Univ. Press 1918. 4*s*. 6*d*.

Reventlow, Graf Ernst zu. England, der Feind. (Series, Der deutsche Kreig.) Stuttgart: Deutsche Verlags-Anstalt. 50 pf.

—— Die Vampir des Festlandes: eine Darstellung der englischen Politik [etc.]. Berlin: Mittler 1915. 6 mk.

—— Heucheleien englischen Minister in ihren Kriegsreden. 1915. 2 mk.

Rifat, Dr. M. M. Die Knechtung Aegyptens. Belastende Dokumente für Englische Heuchelei. Berlin: Curtius 1915. 1 mk.

Roberts, Field-Marshal Earl. The Supreme Duty of the Citizen at the present crisis. The last message to his fellow-countrymen. Reprinted from the Hibbert Journal. Williams & Norgate. 3*d*.

Roberts, Richard. Are we worth Fighting for? Papers for War time, No. 2. Oxford Univ. Press. 2*d.*

Russell, Rt. Hon. G. W. E. The Spirit of England. Papers written in 1914 and 1915. Smith, Elder. 5*s.*

Sidler, Brunner E. Englische Politik in neutraler Beleuchtung. Bern 1915.

Siebold, H. Im südwest unter englischer Herrschaft. 1916. 40 pf.

Sloss, Robert. An American's view of the British Mail Censorship. (A description, explanation, and defence.) Spraight 1916.

Stead, Francis Herbert. Our Duty in the War. Reprinted with additions from Fellowship for Aug. 1914. F. H. Stead, 29, Grosvenor Park, S.E. 1*d.*

Steed, H. Wickham. L'Angleterre et la Guerre. Colin. 50 c.

Steinmann-Bucher, A. Englands Niedergang. 1917. 7 mk.

Stuart, Sir Campbell. Secrets of Crewe House. The story of a famous campaign. Hodder & Stoughton 1920. 7*s.* 6*d.*

Unus, Walter. England als Henker Frankreichs. Brunswick 1915.

War Distress and War Help. Catalogue of the leading War Help Societies, showing their scope and objects, and the addresses of their offices. Edited by Helen Donald Smith. Murray 1915. 6*d.*

Ward, Mrs. Humphry. (1) England's effort: with preface by Lord Rosebery. Smith Elder 1916. 2*s.* 6*d.* (2) Towards the Goal: with introduction by Theodore Roosevelt. Murray 1917. 2*s.* 6*d.* (3) Fields of Victory. Hutchinson 1919. 7*s.* 6*d.*

Webster, R. G. The awakening of an Empire (the British). Murray 1917. 6*s.*

Wile, Frederic W. Explaining the Britishers. The story of the British Empire's mighty effort in liberty's cause. Written by an American for American soldiers and sailors. Heinemann 1918. 2*s.* 6*d.*

Wilkinson, Spenser. Britain at Bay. Constable. 6*s.*

—— Great Britain and Germany. (O.P.) Oxford Univ. Press. 2*d.*

Wrong, George M. Growth of Nationalism in the British Empire. Reprinted from the American Historical Review 1916.

(*b*) India and the Dominions.

Bell, Captain Ralph W. Canada in War Paint. Dent 1917. 2*s.* 6*d.*

Chirol, Sir V. The Egyptian Problem. 1920. 7*s*. 6*d*.

Egerton, Prof. H. E. The War and the British Dominions. (O.P.) Oxford Univ. Press. 2*d*.

Haydon, W. Canada and the War. Arrowsmith. 6*d*.

Jairazbhoy, Cassamally (Vice-President of the Moslem League, Bombay Branch). India and the War: an examination of the German Policy and of India's duty. The first of a series of pamphlets to be issued in English and the Indian vernaculars for free circulation in India. Bombay: Times Press 1915.

Keith, A. B. Imperial Unity and the Dominions. Milford 1916. 12*s*. 6*d*.

—— War government of the British Dominions. Economic and social history of the Great War (British Series). Publ. for the Carnegie Endowment. Oxford Univ. Press 1921. 15*s*.

Lucas, Sir Charles (edr.). The Empire at War. Being a history of Imperial co-operation up to and including the Great War. Publ. on behalf of the Royal Colonial Institute. 6 vols. Oxford Univ. Press 1916. 63*s*.

McLennan, J. S. The Canadian Current 1850-1914: per angusta ad augusta. Effingham Wilson 1915. 1*s*.

Matthai, John. India and the War. (Papers for War time.) Milford, 1915. 2*d*.

Mills, J. Saxon. The Gathering of the Clans. How the British Dominions have helped in the War. Fisher Unwin 1916. 2*d*.

Peterson, W. War through Canadian Eyes. (O.P.) Milford 1915. 2*d*.

Pollard, Prof. A. F. The Commonwealth at War. Longman 1917. 6*s*. 6*d*.

Schuler, Phillip F. E. Australia in Arms. Illustrated. Fisher Unwin 1916. 12*s*. 6*d*.

Singh, Saint Nihal. The King's Indian Allies: the Rajas and their India. Low 1916. 7*s*. 6*d*.

Sloss, Robert. Some Facts about India. Interviews with Lord Islington (Parliamentary Under-Secretary for India) in November 1916. (German intrigues.) Burrup & Sprague 1917. n.p.

Strong, A. T. Australia and the War. Articles contributed to the Melbourne Herald. Melbourne: Robertson 1915. 1*s*.

Sydenham, Lord. India and the War. New York: Doran. $1.00.

Trevelyan, Sir E. J. India and the War. Oxford Univ. Press. 1*d*.

Tucker, A. B. Canada and the War. (O.P.) Oxford Univ. Press. 3*d*.

(*c*) Ireland.

Boyle, J. F. The Irish Rebellion of 1916. Constable 1916. 4*s*. 6*d*.

England, Germany and the Irish Question. By an English Catholic. Hodder & Stoughton 1917. 2*d*.

Escouflaire, R. C L'Irlande ennemie. Payot, 1918.

—— English transln. Murray 1919. 6*s*.

Hamilton, E. W. The Soul of Ulster. Hurst & Blackett 1917. 2*s*. 6*d*.

Knott, George H. (edr.). Trial, The, of Sir Roger Casement. Hodge 1917. 7*s*. 6*d*.

Lynch, Arthur. Ireland: the Vital Hour. (Maps.) Stanley Paul

McKenzie, F. A. The Irish Rebellion. What happened, and why. Pearson 1916. 1*s*.

McLaren, Mrs. Women of the War. With preface by the Rt. Hon. H. H. Asquith. Portraits. Hodder & Stoughton 1917. 3*s*. 6*d*.

Norway, Mrs. Hamilton. The Sinn Fein Rebellion as I saw it. Smith, Elder 1916. 2*s*.

Pim, F. W. The Sinn Fein Rising. A narrative and some reflections. Dublin: Hedges & Figgis 1916. 3*d*.

Redmond-Howard, L. G. Six Days of the Irish Republic. Maunsel 1916. 1*s*.

Russell, G. W., and Plunkett, Sir H. The Irish Home Rule Convention. With introduction by John Quinn. New York: Macmillan 1917. 50 c.

Stephens, James. The Insurrection in Dublin. A diary. Maunsel 1916. 2*s*. 6*d*.

Wells, Warre B. An Irish Apologia. Some thoughts on Anglo-Irish relations and the War. Maunsel 1917. 1*s*.

—— and Marlowe, N. A History of the Irish Rebellion of 1916. Maunsel. 7*s*. 6*d*. Cheaper edn. 1917. 1*s*. 6*d*.

—— The Irish Convention and Sinn Fein. Maunsel 1918. 5*s*.

(*d*) Women's Work.

Beck, A. M. de. Women of the Empire in War Time. In honour of their devotion and self-sacrifice. Dom. of Canada News Co. 1916. 1*s*. 6*d*.

Billington, Mary F. The Roll-Call of Serving Women: a Record of Woman's Work for Combatants and Sufferers in the Great War. Religious Tract Society. 3*s*. 6*d*.

Caine, Hall. Our Girls: Their Work for the War. With photographs. Hutchinson 1916. 1*s*.

Foxwell, A. K. Munition Lasses. (Six months as principal overlooker in danger buildings.) Hodder & Stoughton 1917. 1s. 3*d.*

Liverpool Women's War Service Bureau Report. August 7, 1915-August 7, 1916. Liverpool: Northern Publ. Co. 1916.

Martin, H. The Girl he left behind him. A description of women's munition work and the efforts of the Y.W.C.A. Witherby 1916. 1*d.*

Stone, Gilbert (edr.). Women War Workers. Foreword by Lady Jellicoe. Harrap 1917. 3*s.* 6*d.*

Usborne, H. M. Women's Work in War Time. A handbook of employments. With Preface by Lord Northcliffe. Werner Laurie 1918. 1*s.*

Women Helpers of their Nation. By the author of The Six Maries, etc. Skeffington 1916. 2*s.*

Yates, L. K. The Woman's Part. A record of munitions work. Illustrated. Hodder & Stoughton 1918. 1*s.* 3*d.*

(5) *Bulgaria.*

Duncan, Marcel. L'Été Bulgare. Juillet-Octobre, 1915. The story of the entry of Bulgaria into the War. Chapelot 1917. 4 fr. 50.

Kuhne, Victor. Les Bulgares peints par eux-mêmes. Préface d'Auguste Gauvain. Recueil de coupures de journaux et publications bulgares. Payot 1918. 5 fr.

Naumann, F. Bulgarien und Mitteleuropa. Berlin: Reimer 1916. 1 mk. 50.

O'Mahoney, The. Bulgaria and the Powers. Sealy, Bryern & Walker.

Price, C. Intervention of Bulgaria and the Central Macedonian Question. Lecture Agency. 3*d.*

Rizoff, D. Bulgarien und Russland. Berlin: Kronen-Verlag 1917. 1 mk.

Savodjian, Léon. La Bulgarie en Guerre. Geneva: Georg.

(6) *China.*

Weale, Putnam. The Truth about China and Japan. Appendix of documents. New York: Dodd, Mead & Co. 1919. $2.50.

(7) *France.*

Abensour, Léon. Les Vaillantes (French Women in the War). Chapelot 1917. 4 fr.

Achievement of France, The. A series of articles reprinted from The Times. Methuen 1915. 1*s.*

Adam, Madame Juliette. L'Heure vengeresse des crimes bismarckiens. Nouv. Libr. Nationale 1915.

Aicard, Jean. Des cris dans la mêlée (1914-1916). Libres propos de Jean d'Auriol. Flammarion 1916. 3 fr. 50.

Albert-Petit, M. La France de la Guerre. Articles from the Journal des Débats. 2 vols. De août 1914 à septembre 1917. Bossard 1918. 9 fr. each.

Alexandre, Arsène. Les Monuments Français détruits par l'Allemagne. Berger-Levrault 1918. 20 fr.

Alphaud, G. La France pendant la guerre. Hachette 1917. 3 fr. 50.

Ardant, Abbé, and others. L'éveil de l'âme française devant l'appel aux armes. Bloud et Gay 1915.

Barnard, C. I. Paris War Days. A War-Time Diary of a Journalist in Paris. Illustrated. Werner Laurie. 10*s*.

Barrès, Maurice. L'Ame française et la Guerre : l'Union sacrée. Articles contributed to the Echo de Paris since the outbreak of war. Emile-Paul 1915.

—— The Soul of France. Fisher Unwin 1916. 2*d*.

—— Le Blason de la France, ou ses traits éternels dans cette guerre et dans les vieilles épopées. A lecture given before the British Academy. Milford 1916. 1*s*.

Barthou, Louis. L'Heure du droit : France, Belgique, Serbie. Crès 1916. 1 fr. 75.

Basly, Emile. Le Martyre de Lens : trois années de captivité. Plon 1918. 4 fr. 50.

Baudrillart, Mgr. Alfred. La France, les Catholiques, et la Guerre (Pages actuelles). Bloud et Gay 1917.

Bazin, René. La Campagne Française et la Guerre. Eggimann 1916.

—— Récits du temps de la Guerre. Calmann-Lévy. 3 fr. 50.

Beauregard, Paul. La vie économique en France pendant la guerre actuelle (Pages d'histoire). A lecture given Feb. 15, 1915. Berger-Levrault. 4c.

Bermejo de la Rica, Antonio. Sur quoi le Kaiser ne comptait pas. Traduit de l'espagnol par Christian de l'Isle. (The attitude of France.) Lethielleux 1915. 1 fr. 50.

Blanche, Jacques-Emile. Cahiers d'un artiste. Quatrième série. (Débute le 15 novembre 1915. Deuxième retour à Paris pendant la guerre.) Emile-Paul 1918. 3 fr. 50.

Book of France, The. A collection of articles, &c., by leading French writers, including M. Barrès, R. Boylesve, P. Loti, Anatole France, &c., transl. by T. Hardy, H. James, E. Gosse, Mrs. Woods, &c., and illustrated by well-known French artists. Ed. by Miss W. Stephens. Macmillan. 5*s*.

Calthrop, Dion Clayton. The Wounded French Soldier. St. Catherine Press 1916. 1*s.* 6*d.*

Clarke, M. E. Paris Waits: 1914. Inside view of Paris, Aug.-Dec., 1914. Smith, Elder. 5*s.*

Clermont, Mme Camille. Souvenirs de Parisiennes en temps de Guerre. Berger-Levrault 1918. 4 fr.

Combarieu, Jules. Les jeunes filles françaises et la Guerre. Avec introduction de Jacques Flach. Colin 1916. 3 fr. 50.

Coubé, l'Abbé Stéphen. Le Patriotisme de la femme française. Lethielleux 1916. 3 fr. 50.

Courson, la Comtesse de. La femme française pendant la Guerre. Lethielleux 1916. 1 fr. 25.

Dark, Sidney. The Glory that is France. Nash 1916. 3*s.* 6*d.*

Dauzet, P. L'Effort militaire de la France (Pages d'histoire 1914-1916). Berger-Levrault 1916. 60c.

Dawbarn, C. France at Bay. Mills & Boon 1915. 5*s.*

Delécraz, Antoine. Paris pendant la mobilisation. Payot 1916. 3 fr. 50.

De Pratz, Claire. A Frenchwoman's Notes on the War. Record of life in a Breton village during the first weeks of hostilities. Constable 1916. 6*s.*

—— France from Within. 2nd edn. Hodder & Stoughton 1914. 2*s.* & 2*s.* 6*d.*

Dugard, M. Ames françaises: pages vécues. Illustrations. Fischbacher 1917. 5 fr.

Espionnage allemand en France (1914-1916). Téqui 1916. 50 c.

Fage, André. Lille sous la griffe allemande. Perrin 1918. 3 fr. 50.

Finot, Jean. The Anglo-French Nation. A study. Constable 1916. 1*s.*

Fortescue, G. France bears the burden. New York: Macmillan 1917. $1.50.

France, Anatole. The Path of Glory. French text and English transl. Lane. 6*s.*

Geoffrey, J. L'Ame héroïque de la France. Douze estampes (50/65) par J.G. Delagrave 1916. En feuilles, 18 fr. Montées, 30 fr.

Giachetti, Cipriano. Civiltà francese e civiltà germanica. Rome: Athenæum 1915. 3l. 50.

Giraud, Victor. La Troisième France. Hachette 1917. 3 fr. 50.

Gohier, Urbain. La Grande Guerre. Gardons la France au Français. Propagande au sujet des étrangers et des naturalisés. Fleury 1915. 75c.

Gosse, l'Abbé M. M. Echos de Guerre: France et Kultur. Tequi 1915. 3 fr. 50.

Grant, Marjorie. Verdun Days in Paris. Collins 1918. 6*s*.

Hélys, Marc (Mme). Les Provinces françaises pendant la Guerre. Résultat de l'enquête faite pour le Correspondant. Perrin 1918. 3 fr. 50.

Hervé, G. La Patrie en danger. Articles publiés dans la Guerre sociale du 1er juillet au 1er novembre 1914. Bibliothèque des ouvrages documentaires 1918. 2 fr. 25.

Hollebecque, Mad. La Jeunesse scolaire de France et la Guerre. Lessons and work for children in the War. Didier 1916. 1 fr. 25.

Hoog, Georges. Lettres aux neutres sur l'union sacrée. Préface de M. le baron d'Anthouard. Publication du Comité catholique de propagande française à l'étranger. Bloud et Gay 1918. 3 fr. 50.

Huard, Frances W. My Home in the Field of Honour. France in War-time. By an American. Illustrated. New York: Doran 1917. $1.35.

Hueffer, Ford Madox. Between St. Denis and St. George. A study of three civilizations (chiefly a vindication of France). Hodder & Stoughton. 2*s*. 6*d*.

Jerrold, Laurence. France To-day. Murray 1916. 7*s*. 6*d*.

Johnson, Owen. The Spirit of France. Boston: Little, Brown 1916. $1.35.

Jörgensen, Johannes. The War Pilgrim. Impressions in France and Belgium (transl. from the Danish). Burns & Oates 1917. 2*s*. 6*d*.

Jourdan, Prof. Sauvaire. La vitalité économique de la France avant et après la Guerre. Alcan 1918. 4 fr. 55.

Kipling, Rudyard. France at War. Reprint of articles from the Daily Telegraph. Macmillan 6*d*. Harrap 1916. 3*s*. 6*d*.

Labbé, Paul. L'Effort de la France et de ses Alliés. "L'Hommage français" series. Bloud et Gay. 50c. each.

Lagardère, le Chanoine. Haut les cœurs! Téqui 1916. 2 fr.

Lauder, Fernand. Paris pendant la Guerre: impressions. Perrin 1915.

Launay, L. de. France-Allemagne: Problèmes miniers; Munitions; Blocus; Après Guerre. Colin 1917. 3 fr. 50.

Lavedan, H. Les Grandes Heures, 1914-1915. France during the War. First series, Aug., 1914-Jan., 1915. Second series, Feb.-Aug., 1915. Paris: Perrin 1915. 3 fr. 50 each.

Leger, Prof. Louis. Le Panslavisme et l'intérêt français. Flammarion 1917. 3 fr. 50.

Le Goffic, Charles. Bourguignottes et pompons rouges. (Brittany in War-Time, Breton sketches, &c.) Crès 1916. 3 fr. 50

Leroux, Ernest. France et Allemagne : les deux cultures. 28 rue Bonaparte 1915. 50 c.

Le Roux, Hugues. La France et le Monde. I. Angleterre. Etats Unis. Plon-Nourrit 1917. 3 fr. 50.

Lettres à tous les Français : patience, effort, confiance. By E. Durkheim, E. Lavine, E. Denis and others. Colin 1916. 1 fr.

Lévy, A. 1914 (août, septembre et octobre) à Paris. Physionomie de Paris aux premiers mois de la Guerre. Plon 1917. 3 fr. 50.

Lévy-Bruhl, L. L'Effort industriel de la France (Pages d'historie 1914-1916). Berger-Levrault 1916. 60 c.

Loyson, Paul Hyacinthe. France the Apostle, and the Ethics of the War. (Lectures delivered before the Royal Institution.) Univ. of London Press 1918. 3*s*.

Lucatelli, Luigi. Francia sanguinante. Florence : Bemporad 1915. 95 c.

Malherbe, Henry. The Flaming Sword of France. Translated from the French. Dent 1918. 6*s*.

Martin, W. Sur les Routes de la Victoire. (Impressions gained on a mission to France.) Alcan 1916. 3 fr. 50.

Maurras, Ch. Devant l'ennemi. Les conditions de la Victoire. I. La France se sauve elle-même (de juillet à mi-novembre 1914). II. Le Parlement se réunit (de mi-novembre 1914 à fin août 1915). III. Ministère et Parlement (de septembre à fin decembre 1915). Nouv. Libr. Nationale 1916. 3 fr. 50 each.

—— La Blessure intérieure : de janvier à fin mai 1916. (The wound inflicted by conscious or unconsious friends of Germany.) Nouv. Libr. Nationale 1918. 4 fr.

Michaux, la baronne J. Journal d'une Parisienne pendant la Guerre, 1915-1916 (2e serie). Perrin 1918. 3 fr. 50.

Morant, Comte Georges de. La Noblesse Française au Champ d'Honneur 1914, 1915, 1916, avec la Liste Alphabetique des Morts au Champ d'Honneur [&c.]. Le Nobiliare 1916.

Müller, Dr. Max. Frankreich im Kriege, 1914-1916, avec planches. Fischbacher 1917.

Nothomb, P. La Belgique en France. Préface par Emile Verhaeren (the part, civic and charitable, France has played with regard to her Belgian refugees). Berger-Levrault 1916. 3 fr.

Ohnet, Georges. Journal d'un bourgeois de Paris pendant la Guerre de 1914. Fascicules 1, 2. Société d'Editions Littéraires. 1 fr.

Perrier, Edmond. France et Allemagne. Payot. 4 fr. 50.

Pons, Mgr. A. La Guerre et l'âme française : vers une double victoire ! Bloud et Gay 1915 3 fr.

Potez, Henri. Arras (an account of the town and of its destruction). Illustrated. Van Oest 1918. 2 fr.

"Probus." La plus grande France. La tâche prochaine. Colin 1916. 3 fr.

Randolph, W. French Churches in the War Zone. Illustrated. Kegan Paul ; Routledge 1916. 2*s*. 6*d*.

Renard, Prof. Georges. Les Répercussions économiques de la Guerre actuelle sur la France, 1914-1917. Alcan 1918. 11 fr.

Rey, A. La France et l'Italie ; hier, aujourd'hui, et demain. Florence 1917. 1 l. 50.

Roux, Marquis de. Le Défaitisme et les manœuvres pro-allemandes, 1914-1917 (The Bolo, Caillaux, and other *affaires*). Nouv. Libr. Nationale 1918. 1 fr. 80.

Sabatier, Paul. A Frenchman's thoughts on the War. Fisher Unwin 1915. 4*s*. 6*d*.

—— The Ideals of France : a letter on the Great War. Fisher Unwin. 1*s*.

—— The Soul of Fighting France. By the author of the Life of St. Francis. English transl. Fisher Unwin. 5*s*.

Saillens, Dr. Reuben. The Soul of France. Morgan & Scott 1917. 5*s*.

Sarolea, Charles. Le Reveil de la France. Crès 1916. 1 fr. 50.

Séailles, Prof. and others. L'Effort de la France (l'effort moral, l'effort industriel, l'effort militaire). Berger-Levrault 1917. 40 c.

Séris, Raymond, and Aubrey, Jean. Les Parisiens pendant l'état de siège. Berger-Levrault 1915. 3 fr. 50.

Sheehan, P. Poore, and Davis, Robert H. We are French ! With introduction by Sir Gilbert Parker. Simpkin 1915. 1*s*.

Strong, Rowland. The Diary of an English Resident in France during twenty-two weeks of War. Nash. 6*s*.

Suarès, André. Nous et Eux. A comparison between France and Germany. Emile Paul. 3 fr. 50.

Sutton-Pickard, Maud F. France in War-Time, 1914-1915. Methuen 1915. 5*s*.

Talmeyr, Maurice. Portraits de la belle France (de l'héroïsme pendant la Guerre). Perrin 1918. 3 fr. 50.

Thamin, R. L'Université et la Guerre. Hachette 1917. 3 fr. 50.

Thande, Pierre. Le prix du sang. An epitome of the religious spirit of France. Beauchesne 1916. 1 fr. 50.

Tonelli, Luigi. Lo spirito francese contemporaneo. Milan: Treves 1917. 5 l.

Vachon, Marius. Les villes martyres de France et de Belgique. Statistique des villes et villages détruits par les Allemands. Avec vue de villes et de monuments &c. Payot. 2 fr. 50.

Vaillat, L. La Maison des Pays de France: Les Provinces dévastées. Orné de 80 dessins de André Ventre. Flammarion 1917. 8 fr.

Vallotton, Benjamin. Au Pays de la Mort (The ravaged country in Northern France). Attinger 1917. 80 c.

Wolff, Jetta S. Les Français en Guerre. Arnold 1915. 1*s*. 6*d*.

Wram, H. Paris, 1914-1918. 2 mk. 50.

Wray, W. F. (Kuklos). Across France in War Time (Wayfarers' Library). Dent 1916. 1*s*.

(8) *Germany.*

(*a*) English.

Ackerman, Carl W. Germany—the next Republic? (By the late representative of the United Press in Germany.) Illustrated. Hodder & Stoughton 1917. 7*s*. 6*d*.

Archer, William. 501 Gems of German Thought. (Collection of extracts illustrating German ambitions, &c.) Fisher Unwin 1917. 1*s*.

Ashley, Prof. W. J. The Economic Position of Germany. A paper read at a meeting of the Royal Society of Arts, Feb. 24, 1915. Journal of the Society, No. 3249. Bell. 6*d*.

Australian Girl, An, in Germany. (Experiences just before and during the War. Melbourne: Specialty Press 1916.

Beaufort, J. M. de. Behind the German Veil. A record of a journalistic war pilgrimage. Hutchinson 1917. 6*s*.

Bevan, Edwyn. German Social Democracy during the War. Allen & Unwin 1918. 5*s*.

—— The Method in the Madness. (A study of German opinion.) Arnold 1917. 5*s*.

Blatchford, Robert. General von Sneak. A little study of the war. (Methods and policy of Germany, &c.) Hodder & Stoughton. 1918. 2*s*. 6*d*.

Blücher, Evelyn, Princess. An English Wife in Berlin. A private memoir of events, politics, and daily life in Germany during the war and the social revolution of 1918. 1920. 19*s*.

Bonn, Prof. M. J. German War Finance. New York: Huebsch 1917. $1.00.

Bullitt, Mrs. E. D. An Uncensored Diary from the Central Empires (1916). Stanley Paul 1918. 6*s*.

Burne, C. S. Might gives Right: the new Gospel of Germany. Central Committee. *1d.*

Bury, Prof. J. B. Germany and Slavonic Civilisation. Eyre & Spottiswoode. n.p.

Butler, T. Boche-Land: Before and During the War. Heinemann, 1916. *3s. 6d.*

Chapman, John Jay. Deutschland über Alles; or, Germany Speaks. A collection of the utterances of representative Germans. New York: Putnam. 75 c.

Chesterton, Cecil. The Prussian hath said in his heart. Chapman & Hall. *2s.*

Chesterton, G. K. The Barbarism of Berlin. Cassell 1914. *6d.*

—— The Crimes of England. On the inner causes of Prussian barbarism and on German military philosophy. Arnold 1915. *1s.*

—— Letters to an old Garibaldian. A discussion of the German character. Methuen. *3d.*

Chirol, Sir Valentine. Germany and The Fear of Russia. (O.P.) Oxford Univ. Press. *2d.*

Cook, Sir T. A. Kaiser, Krupp, and Kultur. Reflections on the war, reprinted from The Field. Murray. *1s.*

—— Kultur and Catastrophe. A continuation of the foregoing. Reprinted from The Field. Murray. *1s.*

—— The Mark of the Beast. (A further collection of war essays by the editor of The Field.) Murray 1916. *5s.*

Cromer, The Earl of. Germania contra mundum. Letters and articles on Germany, reprinted from The Spectator. Macmillan 1915. *3d.*

Curtin, D. Thomas. The Land of Deepening Shadow: Germany, 1916. Hodder 1916. *6s.*

Damning Revelations of Germany's Turpitude. (Contains the attack made on the Kaiser by Herr August Thyssen.) Baltimore: Manufacturers Record 1918. 5 c.

Darwin, M. D. My German Professor. A true story of yesterday and to-day. (Notes the change in German character.) Allenson 1917.

Edgeworth, Edward. The Human German. Methuen. *10s. 6d.*

Elwell-Sutton, A. S. Humanity versus Un-Humanity. A criticism of the German idea in its political and philosophical development. Unwin 1916. *4s. 6d.*

Ex-Intelligence Officer. The German Spy System from Within. Hodder & Stoughton. *2s.*

Fox, Edward Lyell. William Hohenzollern & Co. (An account of visits to the German war zone and to Berlin by an American journalist.) Hurst & Blackett 1918. *6s.*

Gardiner, J. B. W. German Plans for the Next War. New York: Doubleday 1918. $1.00.

German Business and German Aggression. (Showing the political effects of Germany's economic expansion.) Fisher Unwin 1917. 2*d.*

Germany and the Prussian Spirit. Reprinted from the Special War Number of The Round Table, Sept. 1914. Macmillan. 6*d.*

Germany's Two Gospels. Being an answer to the appeal of the German Evangelicals. Central Committee. 1*d.*

Gray, A. The New Leviathan. Some illustrations of current German political theories. Methuen. 6*d.*

—— The True Pastime. Some observations on the German attitude towards war. Copious quotations from German writers. Methuen. 6*d.*

Gray, Alex. The Upright Sheaf: Germany's Intentions after the War. An examination of German War Literature, with copious quotations. Methuen. 6*d.*

Hall, Oscar S. Germany: A Shattered Ideal. Sherratt & Hughes. 6*d.*

Harris, John H. Germany's Lost Colonial Empire and the Essentials of Reconstruction. Simpkin Marshall. 1*s.*

Hill, G. F. The Commemorative Medal in the Service of Germany. Illustrated. (By the Keeper of Coins and Medals at the British Museum.) Longmans 1918. 6*d.*

Hope, Anthony. The New (German) Testament: some texts and a commentary. Criticisms on Bernhardi, &c. Methuen. 3*d.*

Houghton, Mary. In the Enemy's Country. Being the diary of a little tour in Germany and elsewhere during the early days of the War. Chatto 1915. 5*s.*

Hueffer, Ford M. When Blood is their Argument. An analysis of the Prussian spirit. Hodder & Stoughton. 2*s.* 6*d.*

Jephson, Lady. A War Time Journal: Germany, 1914. A picture of the German mind, Aug.-Sept. 1914. Elkin Mathews.

Jones, John Price. The German Spy in America. (The misdeeds of Von Papen, Boy-Ed and others.) With preface by Col. Roosevelt. Hutchinson 1917. 5*s.*

Legge, J. G. Rhyme and Revolution in Germany. (Analysis of the German mind.) Constable 1918. 15*s.*

Lewin, Evans. The German Road to the East. (Germany's Balkan policy.) Heinemann 1916. 7*s.* 6*d.*

Lux Animæ (pseud.). Ancient Babylon and Modern Germany versus the New Jerusalem—the Holy City—both in this World and the World to come. Stockwell 1916. 2*s.* 6*d.*

McAuley, M. E. Germany in War Time. (An apology for Germany.) Chicago: Open Court Publishing Co. 1918. $1.50.

McCurdy, C. A. The Truth about the Secret Treaties. (The Treaties contracted by Germany during the last four years.) W. H. Smith 1918. *3d.*

Macfall, Major H. Germany at Bay. Introduction by Lord French. (On the importance of the German Mitteleuropa scheme.) Cassell 1917. *6s.*

McLaren, A. D. Germanism from Within. Constable 1916. *7s. 6d.*

—— Peaceful Penetration. (German commercial and financial methods in foreign countries.) Constable 1916. *3s. 6d.*

MacLeod, G. Hamilton. The Blight of Kultur. Sampson Low 1918. *5s.*

Markham, Violet. A Woman's Watch on the Rhine. Sketches of the occupation. Hodder & Stoughton 1921. *15s.*

Muirhead, J. H. German Philosophy and the War. (O.P.) Oxford Univ. Press. *2d.*

—— German Philosophy in Relation to the War. An examination of Kultur as a reaction against Kant, Fichte, Hegel, &c. Murray. *2s. 6d.*

Piermarini. What I saw in Berlin and other European Capitals during War-time. (The other capitals are Vienna, Brussels, Constantinople, &c.) Nash. *5s.*

Pyke, Ernest Lionel. Desperate Germany. (The author was Kitchen Inspector at Ruhleben, and often visited Berlin.) Hodder & Stoughton 1918. *6s.*

Osborne, Sidney. The Upper Silesia Question and Germany's Coal Problem. (Pro-German.)

—— (edr.). The Problem of Upper Silesia. (Papers by various writers, mostly pro-German.)

Robertson, C. G. Germany and the Economic Problem. (O.P.) Oxford Univ. Press. *2d.*

Robertson, Rt. Hon. J. M., M.P. The Germans. Controversial and polemical. Williams & Norgate 1916. *7s. 6d.*

Rose, J. Holland. German Misrepresentations. Reprint of three articles in the Saturday Review. Saturday Review Office.

Royer, Emile. German Socialists and Belgium. Allen & Unwin 1915. *6d.*

Santayana, Prof. G. Egotism in German Philosophy. Dent 1916. *5s.*

Sarolea, Charles. German Problems and Personalities. Chatto & Windus 1917. *5s.*

—— The Curse of the Hohenzollern. With appendix by Albert Sorel. Allen & Unwin 1916. *1s.*

Schreiner, George A. The Iron Ration. (The economic and social effects of the Allied blockade on Germany and the German people.) Murray 1918. 10*s.* 6*d.*

Sefton-Jones, H. German Crimes and our Civil Remedy. (Advocates strong economic pressure by the Allies.) Lane 1916. 6*d.*

Smith, Sir Swire, M.P. The Real German Rivalry: Yesterday, To-day and To-morrow. Unwin 1916. 1*s.*

Smith, T. F. A. What Germany Thinks: or, The War as Germans see it. Numerous extracts. Hutchinson 1915. 6*s.*

—— The Soul of Germany. (Cheap edn.; the 10th.) Hutchinson 1916. 2*s.* 6*d.*

Taylor, Rev. R. O. P. Germanism and its Great Assize. F. Griffith. 1*s.*

Thorburn, J. Hay. Débacle of Kultur, 1914-15. Drane. 6*d.*

Through German Spectacles. Reprinted from the Daily Express, with appendix of German newspapers and public men. Nisbet 1917. 1*s.*

To Make Men Traitors. Germany's attempts to seduce her prisoners of war. (Based on German documents published in the Swiss *Volksrecht.*) Hodder & Stoughton 1918. 2*d.*

Veblen, T. B. Imperial Germany and the Industrial Revolution. New York: Macmillan 1915. $1.50.

Victory or Free Trade. By a British Resident in Germany. (On the possibility of negotiating with Germany.) With preface by L. J. Maxse. National Review Office 1917. 2*s.* 6*d.*

Waldstein, Sir Charles. What Germany is Fighting For. Longmans 1917. 1*s.* 6*d.*

Weerdt, Raymond Collége de. Spider's Web: an Exposition of the Origin, Growth, and Methods of German World-Power madness, with special reference to Belgium. Iris Publishing Co. 1915. 1*s.*

Wrong, Prof. G. M. The War Spirit of Germany. Milford. 6*d.*

(*b*) French.

Ackerman, Carl W. L'Allemagne de l'Arrière. (Experiences et désillusions de l'auteur concernant . . . conditions en Allemagne.) Payot 1918. 4 fr. 50.

Ambitions, Les, de l'Allemagne en Europe. Conférences de la Société de Géographie. With Preface by M. Paul Deschanel. (Vol. 1 of the series, Les Appétits allemands.) Alcan 1918. 4 fr. 55.

Andler, Charles. Ce qui devra changer en Allemagne. Foi et Vie 1918. 1 fr.

Andler, Charles. La Décomposition politique du socialisme allemand. Bossard 1919. 6 fr.

Balmer, P. Les Allemands chez eux pendant la guerre. De Cologne à Vienne. Impressions d'un neutre. (By a Swiss Barrister.) Perrin. 2 fr. 50.

Bédier, Prof. Joseph. Comment l'Allemagne essaye de justifier ses crimes. (Essais et Documents sur la Guerre.) Colin. 50 c.

Bourgin, H. Le Militarisme allemand : Ce qu'il est, pourquoi il faut le détruire. Alcan 1915. 1 fr. 25.

Boutroux, Emile. Germany and the War. Nutt 1915. 6*d.*

Cadoux, Gaston. The Economical Prosperity of Germany. Her place in the sun and the War (in English). (Pages d'Histoire.) Berger-Levrault 1916.

Celarié, Henriette. Slaves of the Huns. The experiences of two girls of Lille. (Transl. from the French.) Cassell 1918. 2*s.* 6*d.*

Ce que pensent les Allemands (Pages actuelles; No. 121-122). (L'influence pernicieuse des philosophes allemands.) Bloud et Gay 1918. 60 c.

Cerfberr, Gaston. L'Allemagne en détresse—d'après ses propres documents : Les hommes : Les approvisionnements : L'argent. Boccard 1916. 3 fr. 50.

Chéradame, André. La Paix que voudrait l'Allemagne. A study of Pan-Germanism and its results. Chapelot. 1 fr.

Chevrillon, André. L'Allemagne et la Guerre. Three articles from the Revue de Paris, March-May 1915. Paris : Pochy.

Civilisation et Kultur. Préface par Lieut.-Col. Bernard. (Un recueil des diverses conférnces faites par des intellectuels.) Berger-Levrault 1916. 75 c.

Clouard, Henri. Les Allemands par eux-mêmes. (Extracts from German authors on the doctrine of war, etc.) Larousse 1916. 75 c.

Cochin, D. Le Dieu allemand. (Ils n'ont de culte que pour le Dieu-État.) Bloud 1917. 60 c.

D'Arc, P. L. Pour l'Après-Guerre. (German education before and during the war.) Grasset 1918. 3 fr. 50.

Denis, Prof. Ernest. La Guerre : l'intoxication d'un peuple. An essay on German psychology and German unity. Delagrave. 3 fr. 50.

Deribespray, F. G. Deux études sur l'Allemagne. L'évolution nécessaire. Payot 1916. 2 fr. 50.

Descamps, Paul. La formation sociale du Prussien moderne. Colin 1916. 4 fr.

Durkheim, E. L'Allemagne au-dessus de tout. La mentalité allemande de la Guerre. Paris : Colin.

Dyssord, Jacques. L'Espionnage allemand à l'œuvre. Editions et Libr. 1915. 3 fr. 50.

Fonsegrive, G. Kultur et Civilisation. (Pages actuelles.) Bloud et Gay 1916. 60 c.

François, B. Condamnés par eux-mêmes. (A series of quotations, from German sources, illustrating German character, etc.) Nilsson. 2 fr. 50.

Froelich, Jules. Le délire Pangermanique. Illustrations by Zislin. Berger-Levrault 1918. 4 fr.

Gandeau, le chanoine B. L'Allemagne ennemie de Dieu et de toute religion. Paris: La Foi catholique 1916. 2 fr. 15.

Gaultier, Paul. La mentalité allemande et la Guerre. Alcan 1916. 1 fr. 25.

Gorse, l'Abbé M. Echos de Guerre. France et Kultur. (On German espionage, German duplicity at the opening of war, etc.) Téqui 1917. 3 fr. 50.

Hallays, André. L'Opinion allemande pendant la Guerre. 1918.

Hubert, Lucien (Sénateur). L'effort brisé: la situation économique de l'Allemagne à la veille de la Guerre. Alcan 1915. 1 fr. 25.

Huillard, Alph. Les Buts de l'Allemagne annoncés par les auteurs allemands. Payot 1917. 15 c.

La Chesnais, P. G. Le groupe socialiste du Reichstag et la déclaration de guerre. Shows how the German Socialists were won over. (Colin 1915. 1 fr. 50.) Transl. under title, The Socialist Party in the Reichstag, etc. Fisher Unwin. 1*s*.

Langlois, G. L'Allemagne barbare. Walter 1915. 3 fr. 50.

Lanoir, Paul. The German Spy System in France. Transl. from the French by an English Officer. Mills & Boon. 6*d*.

Lasserre, Pierre. Le Germanisne et l'esprit humain. Paris: Champion 1916. 1 fr. 25.

Lavisse, Ernest. La Paix que les Allemands voudraient faire. A résumé of the secret memorandum addressed by the great industrial and agricultural associations to the Imperial Chancellor. Ligue française 1916. 10 c.

—— and Andler, C. Pratique et doctrine allemandes de la Guerre. (Études et documents sur la guerre.) Colin. 50 c.

Lavressan. Pourquoi les Germains seront vaincus. Paris: Alcan. 1 fr. 25.

Le Berquier, Edmond. Les Allemands; la Guerre; pensées des autres. Quatrième série. Hachette 1916. 3 fr. 50.

Lenotre, G. La Petite Histoire (2e série). Prussiens d'hier et de toujours. Perrin 1917. 3 fr. 50.

Lichtenberger, H., and Petit, P. L'Impérialisme économique allemand. Flammarion 1918. 4 fr.

Liesse, A. Les Emprunts de guerre de l'Allemagne. (Pages d'histoire 1914-1916.) Berger-Levrault 1916. 60 c.

Louis, P. Les Crises intérieures allemandes pendant la guerre (crises politiques, économiques et financières). Alcan 1917. 1 fr. 25.

Mackenna, A. Le Triomphe du Droit (articles à démasquer les funestes desseins allemands) Santiago du Chili : "Barcelona" 1917.

Madelin, Lieut. L. L'Aveu. La Bataille de Verdun et l'opinion allemande. Documents inédits et facsimiles. Plon 1916. 1 fr. 50.

Manen, Charlotte van. L'Épanouissement de l'Allemagne et l'hégémonie prussienne (traduit du hollandais par Pierre Waelbroeck). La Haye : Nijhoff 1916.

Martin, W. La crise politique de l'Allemagne contemporaine. Alcan 1913. 3 fr. 50.

Matter, Florent. L'Alsace-Lorraine pendant la Guerre. Berger-Levrault 1918. 6 fr.

Mélot, M. J. La Propagande allemande et la question belge. Van Oest 1917. 60 c.

Muret, Maurice. L'Orgueil allemand : psychologie d'une crise. Payot 1915. 3 fr. 50.

—— Pas d'illusions sur l'Allemagne (revue des éléments constitutifs du néo-germanisme). Payot 1918. 5 fr.

Péladan, le maître. L'Allemagne devant l'humanité et le devoir des civilisés. Fontemoing 1916. 3 fr. 50.

Pierre-Alype. L'Éthiopie et les convoitises allemandes. (The designs of Germany in Egypt and Central Africa.) Berger Levrault 1917. 7 fr. 50.

Pingaud, A. Le Développement économique de l'Allemagne contemporaine (1871-1914). (Pages d'histoire 1914-1916.) Berger Levrault 1916. 75 c.

Pour avoir la paix. La manœuvre allemande (la séance historique du Reichstag). (Pages d'histoire 1914-1917.) Préface par G. Reynald. Berger-Levrault 1917. 1 fr.

Raphaël, Paul. Antisémitisme et pangermanisme. Alcan 1916. 40 c.

Ruplinger, Jean. Also sprach Germania (ainsi parlait l'Allemagne). Préface de M. Edouard Herriot. Illustrated. Editions de la Sirène 1918. 3 fr. 50

Santo, M. J. Les Crimes allemands et leur châtiment. Avec illustration de René Santo fils. Chez l'auteur, 131 rue de Vaugirard 1917. 3 fr. 50.

Sayous, André E. Les effets du blocus économique de l'Allemagne. L'organisation du commerce et de l'industrie allemande pendant la guerre. Payot 1916. 2 fr. 50.

Soulange-Bodin, A. L'Avant-Guerre allemande en Europe. Perrin 1918. 3 fr. 50.

Tissot, Victor. L'Allemagne casquée. Voyage au pays des milliards. Perrin 1916. 3 fr. 50.

Visscher, M. F. de. La Liberté politique en Allemagne et la Dynastie de Hohenzollern. Tenin 1917. 2 fr. 50.

Vorst, F. Van de. La Nation criminelle. Etude historique de la Déformation morale allemande. Paris: Van Oest 1916.

Wagner, Emile R. L'Allemagne et l'Amérique Latine. Alcan 1918. 3 fr. 50.

Wetterlé, l'Abbé. L'Allemagne qu'on voyait, et celle qu'on ne voyait pas. Edn. francaise illustrée 1916. 3 fr. 50.

Wyzewa, T. de. La nouvelle Allemagne (1e et 2e série). Derrière le front boche. Perrin 1914-16. 3 fr. 50 each.

(c) German.

Bahr, Hermann. Kriegssegen. (The Blessings of War.) Munich 1915.

Becker, Prof. Deutschland und Islam. (Series Der deutsche Krieg.) Stuttgart: Deutsche Verlag-Anstalt.

Bernhardi, The New. His latest views on the War. Transl. of his apologetical articles contributed to certain American newspapers; with a refutation. Pearson. 1*s.*

Braun, von. Kann Deutschland durch Hunger besiegt werden? October, 1914.

Bülow, H. von. Deutschlands Aushungerung. Dresden: Globus 1920. 1 mk. 50.

Chamberlain, Houston S. Un Catéchisme pangermaniste à l'usage du soldat allemand. Lethielleux 1916. 50 c.

—— Kriegsaufsätze. Essays on German liberty, &c. Munich: Bruckmann 1915.

—— The same, transl. by C. H. Clarke, under title Ravings of a Renegade. Jarrold 1916. 2*s.* 6*d.*

—— Hammer oder Ambon? Munich: Bruckmann 1916 70 pf

—— Politische Ideale. Munich: Bruckmann 1915

—— Rasse und Nation. Munich, Lehmann 1918. 1 mk.

Class H. Zum deutschen Kriegsziel. Munich: Lehmann 1917. 1 mk.

Clockener, Hans. Warum und wie muss Deutschland annektieren? Berlin: Curtius 1917. 80 pf.

Crime, The (Das Verbrechen). By the author of J'accuse. Transl. by Alexander Gray. Vol. I, Vol. II. Hodder & Stoughton 1918. 10*s*. 6*d*. each.

Delbrück, Hans. Krieg und Politik 1914-16, 1916-17. 2 Bde. 1918, 1919. Bd. 1, 10 mk. Bd. 2, 18 mk.

Deutschland über Alles: ou la folie pangermaniste. Traduit sur le manuscrit inédit du Prof. X. par Maurice Lanzel. Floury 1914. 60 c.

Diary of a German Agent, The. German Intrigues in Persia. The Niedermeyer Expedition through Persia to Afghanistan and India. Transl. from the German. Hodder & Stoughton 1918. 4½*d*.

Dix, Arthur. Wirthschaftskrieg und Kriegswirthschaft. Zur Geschichte des deutschen Zusammenbruchs. Berlin: Mittler 1921. 20 mk. 50.

Domelier, Henri. Behind the scenes at the German headquarters. Introduction by Maurice Barrés. Transl. from the French. 1920. 16*s*.

Dunkmann, Karl. La Grande Guerre à la lumière de la Bible. Transl. from the German. (Interprets the Bible in favour of Pangermanism.) Lethielleux 1917. 1 fr. 25.

Ehrhardt, Paul. Disclosures of a German Staff Officer. The letters of P. E., merchant, soldier and spy. With facsimiles in his own handwriting. The Field & Queen 1918. 6*d*.

Engelbrecht, Kurt. Das grosse Friedensziel. Halle, Mühlmann 1917. 1 mk. 50.

Foss, Adm. Was erwartet das deutsche Volk von einem Frieden für seine militärische Sicherheit? Halle: Mühlmann 1918. 1 mk. 50.

Frobenius, H. Kriegsziele und Friedensziele. Berlin: Curtius 1916. 1 mk. 50.

Geiger, Ludwig. Los von Italien? Dresden: Globus 1917. 1 mk. 50.

German [Republican] Constitution, The. (Edition without notes.) H.M.S.O. 1919. 6*d*.

German legislation for the occupied territories of Belgium. Official texts. Edited by C. H. Huberich and A. Nicol-Speyer. The Hague: Nijhoff 1915.

German War Proclamations. Allen & Unwin. 2*s*.

Goltz, Capt. Horst von der. My Adventures as a German Secret Service Agent. Cassell 1918. 6*s*.

Gowans, Adam L. A month's German newspapers. Selections from eight leading German papers published during December, 1914. Gowans & Gray. 2*s*. 6*d*.

Grumbach, S. Das annexionistische Deutschland. A collection of documents in favour of annexations publicly or secretly distributed in Germany since Aug. 4, 1914. With an appendix of anti-annexation utterances. Lausanne: Payot 1917. 7 fr. 50.

—— L'Allemagne annexionniste. Traduction (les documents publiés en Allemagne depuis le 4 août 1914). Payot 1917. 7 fr. 50.

—— Germany's Annexionist Aims. Translated and introduced by J. Ellis Barker. (Abbreviated edn.) Murray 1917. 3*s*. 6*d*.

—— L'Allemagne et l'Alsace-Lorraine (German views and intentions). Lausanne & Paris: Payot. 3 fr. 50.

—— La Social-démocratie allemande pendant la guerre. Lausanne & Paris: Payot 1917. 4 fr.

Hänsch. An der Schwelle des grösseren Reichs. Munich: Lehmann 1916. 7 mk.

Harbou, Th. v. Deutsche Frauen. Bilder stillen Heldentums. 1915. 3 mk. 50.

Harden, Maximilien. Krieg und Frieden (articles published in the Zukunft). Berlin: Reiss 1918. 20 mk.

Harnack, Prof., Meinecke, Prof., and others. Die deutsche Freiheit. Fünf Vorträge. Gotha: Pesther 1917. 5 mk.

Hedin, Sven. Nach Osten! Leipzig: Brockhaus 1916. 10 mk.

—— A selection (Auszug) with same title, same publishers and date. 1 mk. 50.

Hettner, Alfred. Englands Weltherrschaft und der Krieg. Leipzig & Berlin: Trubner 1915. 5 mk.

Hindenburg's March into London. Being a transl. from the German. Edited with preface by L. G. Redmond-Howard. Long 1916. 2*s*. 6*d*.; swd. 1*s*. 3*d*.

Hobohm, Martin. Wir brauchen Kolonieen. Berlin: Engelmann 1918. 50 pf.

Höffner, Joh. Der deutsche Friede (four pamphlets on the peace to be expected from Russia, Italy, France and England respectively). Halle: Mühlmann 1918. 1 mk. 80 each.

Jäckh, Ernst. Das grössere Mitteleuropa. Weimar: Kiessenheuer 1916. 60 pf.

Kautsky. Die Internationalität und der Krieg (Socialist view of war and military service). Berlin: Vorwärts Bücherverlag 1915.

Kerlen, Kurt. Flandern und Deutschland: die Flamen und wir. Arneberg i. W.: Stahl 1915. 1 mk. 50.

Kluck, Gen. von, and others. Das deutsche Volk und der Friede. Berlin: Curtius 1918. 1 mk.

Labberton, J. H. Die sittliche Berechtigung der Verletzung der belgischen Neutralität (Transl. from the Dutch). Berlin: Curtius 1916. 2 mk.

Lensch, Paul. Die deutsche Sozialdemokratie und der Weltkrieg. Berlin: Vorwärts Bücherverlag 1915.

Leutwein, Paul. Mitteleuropa-Mittelafrika. Dresden & Leipzig: Globus 1917. 2 mk.

Liebig, H. V. Die Politik von Bethmann Hollweg. Das B-System vor und im Kriege. Third edn. 1919. 9 mk.

Liebknecht, Dr. Karl. Militarism and Anti-Militarism. Glasgow: Socialist Labour Press 1917. 1*s*.

Losch, Hermann J. Der mitteleuropäische Wirthschaftsblock und das Schicksal Belgiens (Zwischen Krieg und Frieden). Leipzig: Hirzel 1914. 1 mk. 50.

Mann, Thomas. Betrachtungen eines Unpolitischen. Berlin: Fischer 1918. 15 mk.

Meinecke, Prof. F. Probleme des Weltkrieges. Munich: Oldenbourg 1917. 3 mk.

Meyer, A. O. Deutsche Freiheit und Englischer Parlamentarismus. Munich: Bruckmann 1915. 50 pf.

Muehlon, Wilhelm. Die Verheerung Europas. Aufzeichnungen aus den ersten Kriegsmonaten (Aug.-Nov. 1914). Zürich: Füssli 1918. 2 mk. 50.

—— Transl. under title, Dr. Muehlon's Diary. Cassell 1918. 5*s*.

Müller-Holm, E. Der Englische Gedanke in Deutschland. Zur Abwehr des Imperialismus. Munich: Reinhardt 1915. 3 mk.

Müller-Meiningen, Dr. E. Der Reichstag und der Friedenschluss. Munich: Duncker & Hamblot 1918. 1 mk.

Naumann, Friedr. Deutschland und Frankreich. (Series, Der deutsche Krieg.) Stuttgart: Deutsche Verlags-Anstalt.

—— Mitteleuropa. Berlin: Reimer 1915.

—— Transl. by C. M. Meredith, with introduction by W. J. Ashley, under title Central Europe. King 1916. 7*s*. 6*d*.

—— Wie wir uns im Kriege verändern. Vienna 1916. 1 mk. 20.

Nicolai, Col. W. Nachrichtendienst, Presse, und Volksstimmung im Weltkrieg. Berlin: Mittler 1921. 15 mk. 50.

Niemann, Hans. Unser Kriegsziel. Berlin: Mittler 1916. 1 mk.

Nippold, Prof. Otfried. Dangerous Optimism (on the illusion that the Germans are at heart democratic). Allen & Unwin 1918. 2*d*.

Nippold, Prof. Otfried. The Awakening of the German People. Translated by A. Gray. (The German people have not awakened to the dangers of militarism.) Allen & Unwin. 1*s*.

Ober Ost, Das Land. Deutsche Arbeit in den Verwaltungsgebieten Kurland, Litauen, und Bialystok-Grodno. Stuttgart & Berlin: Deutsche Verlag 1917.

Oncken, H. Das alte und das neue Mitteleuropa. Historisch-politische Betrachtungen über deutsche Bündnispolitik im Zeitalter Bismarcks und im Zeitalter des Welt. Kriege 1917. 3 mk. 20.

Osten-Sacken-Rhein, Frhr. v.d. Deutschlands nächster Krieg. Berlin: Bath 1915. 3 mk.

Reventlow, Graf. E. zu. Brauchen wir die flandrische Küste? Berlin: Mittler 1918. 3 mk.

Rohrbach, Paul. Der Krieg und die deutsche Politik. Translated by Prof. von. Mach, under title Germany's World-Policies. New York: Macmillan 1915. $1.25.

—— Zum Weltvolk hindurch! On the events leading to the war, and the German aims. Stuttgart: Engelhorn 1914. 1 mk. 50.

—— Warum es der deutsche Kreig ist. (Series, Der deutsche Krieg.) Stuttgart: Deutsche Verlags-Anstalt. 50 pf.

—— Unsere koloniale Zukunftsarbeit. Stuttgart: Die Lese 1915. 80 pf.

—— Die alldeutsche Gefahr. Berlin: Engelmann 1918. 1 mk. 50.

Rösemeier, Dr. H. A German to Germans. An open letter (of remonstrance). Hodder & Stoughton 1917. 2*d*.

Schanz, F. Frauenwerk im Kriege. 3 mk.

Schuchardt, Ottomar. Der mitteleuropäische Staatenbund. Dresden: Globus 1918. 1 mk.

Solf, W. Weltpolitik und Kolonialpolitik. 1918. 2 mk. 40.

Sommerfeld, A. How Germany crushed France. An anticipation, 1914. Translated from the German by L. G. Redmond-Howard. Everett. 1*s*.

—— Le partage de la France. Ce qu'on verra un jour. Translated from the German. Librairie 40 rue de Seine. 1 fr. 50.

Stier-Somlo, Fr. Grund und Zukunftsfragen deutscher Politik. 1917. 8 mk. 65.

Suter-Lerch, H. J. Deutschland sein eigener Richter! Antwort eines kosmopoliten Schweizers auf die deutsche Propaganda zum Weltkrieg 1914. Zurich: Orell Füssli 1917. 2 fr. 50.

—— Transl. under title Germany Her Own Judge. Allen & Unwin 1918. 1*s*.

Truth about Germany: Facts about the War. The German case, stated by a committee of prominent men—Ballin, Bülow, Gwinner, Harnack, &c.—with appendix containing nine telegrams. New York: Trow Press.

Wertheimer, Fritz. Deutschland und Ostasien. (Series, Der deutsche Krieg.) Stuttgart: Deutsche Verlags-Anstalt. 50 pf.

Winterstetten, Konrad von (Dr. Ritter). Der organische Aufbau Europas. 1916.

Wolff, Julius. And der Wiege Mitteleuropas. Leipzig: Deschert 1917. 2 mk. 20.

Zimmermann, E. Kann uns Mesopotamien eigene Kolonieen ersetzen? Berlin 1917. 40 pf.

(*d*) Other Nations.

Bang, Prof. J. P. Hurrah and Hallelujah! The spirit of new Germanism. (Transl. from the Danish.) Hodder & Stoughton 1916. 3*s*. 6*d*.

Barroetavena, M. F. C. L'Allemagne contre le Monde. (Commentaires parus dans El Diario de Buenos-Aires.) Buenos Ayres: Otero 1917.

Can Germany Win? The Resources and Aspirations of its People. By an American. Pearson. 1*s*.

Doty, Madeleine Z. Short Rations. An American woman in Germany, 1915-16. Illustrated. Century Co. 1917. $1.50. Methuen 5*s*.

Eastman, Max. Understanding Germany. (An impartial discussion of patriotism, militarism, war a delirium, &c.) New York: Mitchell Kennerley 1916. $1.25.

Francke, Prof. Kuno. A German-American's Confession of Faith Temperately pro-German. New York: Huebsch 1915. 50 c

Gerard, James W. (late Ambassador to Germany). Face to Face with Kaiserism. Illustrated. Hodder & Stoughton 1918 7*s*. 6*d*.

In Germany To-day. Letters by a Neutral; reprinted from The Times. Methuen. 1*s*.

Johnson, Prof. Douglas W. The Perils of Prussianism. (An address delivered at Des Moines, June, 1917.) Pitmans 1917 3*s*. 6*d*.

Lewisohn, Ludwig. The Spirit of Modern German Literature New York: Huebsch 1917. $1.00

Lugaro, Ernesto. An Emperor's Madness; or, National Aberration? Translated by W. N. Robinson. (By a Professor of Psychiatry at Modena.) Routledge 1916. 2*s*. 6*d*.

Maccas, Léon. German Barbarism. A neutral's indictment. (A systematic arraignment, by a Greek lawyer). Hodder & Stoughton 1916. *2s. 6d.*

Mariani, Mario. La Germania nelle sue condizioni militari ed economiche dopo nove mesi di guerra. Milan: Trèves 1915. 2 fr.

Olszewski. The economic value of Upper Silesia for Poland and Germany respectively.

Out of their own Mouths. Utterances of German rulers, statesmen and soldiers, &c. Appleton 1917. $1.00.

Packer, Stanley. Prussia's bid for World-Power. An examination of Prussian ambitions with the aid of documents. Fisher Unwin 1915. *1s.*

Pan-Germanism versus Christendom. A Catholic neutral's challenge to the German Centre Party. Hodder & Stoughton 1916. *3s. 6d.*

Passelecq, Fernand. The "Sincere Chancellor." (Bethmann-Hollweg's utterances compared.) Reprinted from the Nineteenth Century. Fisher Unwin 1917. *1d.*

—— Le Testament politique du Général von Bissing. G. van Oest 1917. 70 c.

Smith, Prof. Munroe. German Land-hunger. (Based on Grumbach's Das annexionistische Deutschland.) Reprinted from the Political Science Quarterly. New York: Acad. of Polit. Science 1917.

—— Militarism and Statecraft. (The German militarist mind in Bismarck's time and in the present War.) Putnam 1918. *6s.*

Sprague, Franklin M. Made in Germany. With introduction by Theodore Roosevelt. Boston: Pilgrim Press 1916. $1.00.

Swope, H. B. Inside the German Empire. With foreword by J. W. Gerard, American Ambassador to Berlin. Illustrated. New York: Century Co. 1916. $2.00.

Wellman, Walter. The German Republic (a forecast). New York: Dutton 1916. $1.00.

Wierzlicki. The truth about Upper Silesia (pro-Polish).

Willoughby, Westel W. Prussian Political Philosophy. Appleton 1918. $1.50.

Wister, Owen. The Pentecost of Calamity. On German character and the War. Macmillan. *2s.*

(9) *Greece.*

Alaux, Louis-Paul et Puaux, Réne. Le Déclin de l'Hellénisme. Payot 1917. 2 fr. 50.

Gauvain, Auguste. L'Affaire grecque (depuis l'adhésion . . . de la Grèce à la politique de guerre de la Triple Entente, jusqu'à l'abdication du roi Constantin). Bossard 1918. 3 fr.

Greece and the War. Anglo-Hellenic League 1916. 3*d.*

Guet-apens, Le, du 1er Décembre 1916 à Athènes. Documents (Royalist). Geneva : L'Union Hellénique de Suisse 1917. 50 c.

Maccas, Léon. Ainsi parla Venizelos. Plon 1916. 3 fr. 50.

—— Cinq ans d'Histoire Grecque (1912-17) : Discours prononcés à la chambre grecque en août 1917. Berger-Levrault 1918. 4 fr.

Passaris, Michael. L'Entente et la Grèce. Part I. Aperçu général de la politique grecque. Part II. La révolte de Venizélos (Royalist). Geneva : Pfeffer 1917. 1 fr.

Recouly, Raymond. M. Jonnart en Grèce et l'Abdication de Constantin. Plon-Nourrit 1918. 3 fr.

Vaucher, R. Constantin détroné : les événements de Grèce, Février-Août 1917. Perrin 1918. 4 fr.

Willmore, J. Selden. The Story of King Constantine, as revealed in the Greek White Book. Longmans 1919.

(10) *Italy.*

Ajalbert, J. L'Heure d'Italie : Voyage de Guerre, 1916. Illustré. Bossard 1917. 3 fr.

Alazard, Jean. L'Italie et le conflit européen, 1914-1916. (An account of the motives which led Italy to join the Allies, and of the obstacles.) Alcan 1917. 3 fr. 50.

Amendola, G., Borgese, G. A., and others. Il Patto di Roma [1918]. (Quaderni de la Voce.) Rome : La Voce 1919. 3 l. 50.

Bainville, Jacques. Le Guerre et l'Italie. Fayard 1916. 3 fr. 50

—— Translated under title, Italy and the War. Hodder & Stoughton 1916. 3*s.* 6*d.*

Barzilai, Salvatore. L'Italia in armi. Scritti e discorsi. Milan 1917. 3 l. 50.

Basset, Serge. L'Italie en armes. Paris & Milan : 1916.

Borgese, G. A. Italia e Germania. La Guerra delle idee. (Articles from the Corriere della Sera.) 2 vols. Milan : Trèves 1915-16.

—— French transl. under title L'Italie contre l'Allemagne. Payot 1917. 3 fr. 50.

—— L'Italia e la nuova alleanza. Milan 1917. 1 l.

Branialti, Attilio. Trento e Trieste. Turin : Unione Tipo graphica 1917. n.p.

Bruccoleri, Giuseppe. Dal conflitto europeo alle guerra nostra. Diario di un Giornalista, Agosto 1914-Giugno 1915. (Political psychology of Italy during the period of neutrality.) Rome: Società Italia 1915. 3 l. 50.

Bucaille, Victor. Les Catholiques italiens et la guerre européenne. Lethielleux 1915.

Caburi, Franco. L'Austria e l'Italia: note e appunti di un giornalista italiano a Vienna (Quaderni della guerra). Milan: Trèves 1915. 1 l. 50.

Caprin, Giulio. L'Ora di Trieste. Rome 1915.

—— Trieste e l'Italia. (Problemi Italiani.) Milan: Ravà. 10 c.

Carnovale, Luigi. Why Italy entered into the Great War. Chicago: Italian-American Pub. Co. 1917.

Castellini, Gualt. Trento e Trieste: l'Irredentismo e il problema adriatico. (Quaderni della Guerra.) Milan: Treves. 1 l.

Catellani, Enrico. Italy and Austria at War. English Version by Helen Zimmern and Agnes McCaskill. Florence: Barbèra 1918. 3 fr.

Charriaut, H. & Amici-Grossi, M. L. L'Italie en guerre. Flammarion 1916. 3 fr. 50.

Civis Italicus. L'Italia e i popoli jugoslavi. Rome 1915.

Colonna Di Césaro, G. A. Germania imperiale e il suo programma in Italia. Florence: Libr. della Voce 1916. 1 fr. 50

—— The Adriatic Question. Utopia Press 1917.

Coppola, Francesco. La Crisi italiana 1914-15. (Collection of articles published in L'Idea Nazionale.) Rome: L'Italiana 1916. 3 fr. 50.

De Filippi, Sir F. Italy's Protection of Art Treasures and Monuments during the War. (A Lecture.) Milford 1918. 6*d*.

Del Vecchio, Prof. Giorgio. The moral basis of Italy's War. Fisher Unwin 1917. 1*d*.

Destrée, Jules. En Italie pendant la guerre. Van Œst 1917. 3 fr. 50.

De Viti de Marco, Marchese. La guerra Europea; scritti e discorsi (on Italian problems). Rome: L'Unità 1918. 5 l.

Doerkes, W. N. Das Ende des Dreibunds, nach diplomatischen Aktenstücken und Quellen. Berlin: Mittler 1916.

Edleston, R. H. Italian Neutrality. Cambridge: Heffer. 2*s*.

Fedele, Prof. Pietro. Why Italy is at War. (Series, Italy and the War, No. 1; in English.) Rome: Soc. Ital. per il progresso delle Scienze. n.p.

Gruner. Der Treubruch Italiens, mit Benützung amtlicher Urkunden. Munich: Lehmann 1916. 1 mk. 20.

Italia e Jugoslavia. By a group of Italian and Yugo-Slav writers (with Sir A. Evans' map of the Yugo-Slav State). Florence: Libreria della Voce 1918. 8 l.

Italy and the War. Ten essays by an Italian Professor. Transl. from the Italian by Mrs. G. W. Hamilton. Bell 1917. *2s. 6d.*

J. T. Le problème italo-slave. 2nd edn. (Concludes that Italy has no rights over Dalmatia.) Brochure. Plon-Nourrit 1915.

L'Adriatico. (Problemi Italiani.) Reasons why Trieste and Fiume should be annexed to Italy. Milan: Ravà 1915.

Lanino, P. La Nuova Italia Industriale. 4 vols. Rome: Società Editrice L'Italiana 1917. 53 l.

Libro, Il, della patria. Edizione del Giornale d'Italia, a cura di Fernando Gentili. Illustrated. Rome: Giorn. d'Italia 1917. 8 l.

L'Italie et la guerre. (A collection of utterances by well-known Italians, bearing especially on Italian difficulties.) Edited by Prof. Hauvette. Colin 1916. 1 fr. 50.

Low, Sidney. Italy in the War. Illustrated. (Results of a visit to the Italian front.) Longmans 1916. *6s.*

Macdonald, J. N. A Political Escapade: the Story of Fiume and D'Annunzio. Murray 1921. *6s.*

Marini, Giuseppe. Le rivendicazioni italiane nella grande guerra di liberazione. Milan 1918. 2 l. 50.

Mario, Alberti, and others. Italy's great War, and her national aspirations. With introduction by H. Nelson Gay. (Illustrated.) Milan 1918. 5 l.

Maugain, Gabriel. L'opinion italienne et l'intervention de l'Italie dans la guerre actuelle. Champion 1916. 2 fr.

Maurel, André. La Jeune Italie: l'effort économique et financier de l'Italie pendant la guerre. Emile-Paul 1918. 3 fr. 50.

Mayer, A. Das geistige Italien gegen den krieg. Munich 1916. 2 mk.

Ojetti, Ugo. I Monumenti Italiani e la Guerra. Milan: Alfieri e La Croix 1918.

Pace, Biagio. L'Italia e l'Asia Minore: appunti. Palermo 1917. 2.30 l.

Pantaleoni, Maffeo. Note in margine della guerra. (L'auteur revient à la charge contre les socialistes.) Bari: Laterza 1917. 5 fr. 50.

—— Tra le incognite: problemi suggeriti della guerra. Bari: Laterza 1917. 5 fr. 50.

Piccoli, Dr. Raffaello. Italy and the War. A lecture delivered in the University of Cambridge. Fisher Unwin 1915. *3d.*

Politica, La, italiana di guerra e la manovra tedesca per la pace. (1915-17.) 2 vols. Milan: Treves 1917. 7.50 l.

Preziozi, Giovanni. La Germania alla conquista d'Italia. Introduction by Prof. Pantaleoni. Second edn. entirely re-written. Florence: Libr. della voce 1916. 2 fr. 50. French transl. under title L'Allemagne à la conquête de l'Italie. Delagrave 1916. 3 fr. 50.

Re-Bartlett (Mrs.), Lucy. Internationalism; essays on Anglo-Italian relationships. Ward 1916. 1*s*.

Rosso, G. A. I Diritti d'Italia oltremare (Enciclopedia nazionale, serie politica, 3). 8 cartes. Roma: l'Italiana 1916. 2 fr. 50.

Sacerdote, Cesare. La guerra e la crisi del carbone in Italia (Tesi di laurea). Turin 1917. 3 l.

Saint-Cyr, C. de. Pourguoi l'Italie est notre alliée. Mignot 1916. 3 fr. 50.

Salvemini, G. Guerra o Neutralità. (Problemi Italiani.) Milan: Ravà 1914.

Scialoja, Vittorio. I problemi dello Stato Italiano dopo la Guerra. Bologna: Zanichelli 1918. 6.50 l.

Serao, Matilde. Parla una donna. Diario feminile di Guerra. (Italy during the War, &c.) Milan: Treves 1916. 4 l.

"Severus." Zehn Monate italienischer Neutralität. 1915. 1 mk. 80.

Vivian, Herbert. Italy at War. Dent 1917. 5*s*.

Voix italiennes sur la guerre de 1914-15. (Pages d'histoire.) By various authors. Berger-Levrault 1915. 60 c.

Wallace, W. K. Greater Italy. Maps. Constable 1917. 10*s*. 6*d*.

(11) *Japan*.

Akiyama, Rear-Admiral. A Japanese View of the War. Fisher Unwin 1917. 1*d*.

Engelhardt, Emil. Japans Weltpolitik um den stillen Ozean. Dresden: Globus, c. 1917. 1 mk.

Gèrard, A. Nos Alliés d'Extrême-Orient. (By the former French Ambassador at Tokio.) Payot 1918. 4 fr. 50.

McCormick, F. The Menace of Japan (to America). Little, Brown 1917. $2.00.

Pooley, A. M. Japan at the Cross Roads. Allen & Unwin 1917 10*s*. 6*d*.

Robertson-Scott, R. W. Japan, Great Britain, and the World. A letter to my Japanese friends (in English and Japanese). Tokyo: Japan Advertiser 1916.

Spagnolo, E. Il Giappone, nel presente e nell' avvenire. Milan: Treves 1919.

Sunderland, Jabez T. Rising Japan. Is she a menace or a comrade? Putnam 1918. 5*s*.

(12) *Montenegro.*

Popovitch, V. G. Le Monténégro pendant la Grande Guerre (l'auteur réfute les imputations que le Monténégro devenait le client de l'Autriche). Lang, Blanchonz 1918.

(13) *Ottoman Empire.*

Aramais. Les Massacres et la lutte de Mousch-Sassoun (Arménie) 1915. Genève: Revue Dvorak 1917.

Aulneau, J. La Turquie et la guerre (historical, down to Oct. 1914.) Alcan 1915. 3 fr. 50.

Barby, Henry. Au pays de l'épouvante. L'Arménie martyre. Albin Michel 1918. 3 fr. 50.

Benson, E. F. Crescent and Iron Cross (the means by which Germany secured domination over Turkey). Hodder & Stoughton 1917. 5*s*.

Czaplicka, Miss M. A. The Turks of Central Asia. An ethno logical enquiry into the Pan-Turanian Problem [&c.]. Milford 1918. 15*s*.

Duboscq, A. L'Orient méditerranéen: impressions et essais sur quelques éléments du problème actuel (especially Syria and Palestine). Perrin 1917. 2 fr. 50.

Edwards, E. Journal d'un habitant de Constantinople, 1914-15. By a French Mahomedan. Plon, Nourrit, 1916. 3 fr. 50.

Einstein, Lewis. Inside Constantinople. (A diary from April to September, 1915.) Murray 1917. 6*s*.

Faiz El-Ghusein. Martyred Armenia (story of the massacres). Pearson 1918. 3*d*.

Georgevitch, T. R. Macedonia (written to show that it is Serbian). Allen & Unwin 1918. 7*s*. 6*d*.

Gibbons, H. A. The blackest page of modern history. Events in Armenia, 1915. Putnam 1916. 3*s*. 6*d*.

Griselle, l'Abbé. Une victime du pangermanisme; l'Arménie martyre. Bloud et Gay 1916. 1 fr.

Grothe, Hugo. Die Türken und ihre Gegner. (Maps.) Frankfurt a/M: Hendschel 1915. 1 mk. 50.

Hacobian, A. P. Armenia and the War. An Armenian's point of view, with an appeal to Great Britain. With a preface by the Rt. Hon. Viscount Bryce. Hodder & Stoughton 191- 2*s*. 6*d*.

Jabotinsky, Vladimir. Turkey and the War. (By the war correspondent of the Russkia Vedomosti.) Fisher Unwin 1917. 6*s.*

Jairazbhoy, Cassamally. The Suicide of Turkey. A paper addressed primarily to Mahomedans, by a Vice-President of the Moslem League, Bombay Branch. Central Committee. 2*d.*

Liman von Sanders, General. Fünf Jahre Türkei. Berlin: Scherl 1920. 60 mk.

Mandelstam, André. Le sort de l'Empire ottoman. Payot 1917.

Mehrmann-Coblenz, Karl. Der diplomatische Krieg in Vorderasien, unter besonderer Berücksichtigung der Geschichte der Bagdadbahn. Dresden: Das Grössere Deutschland 1916. 4 mk.

Mohr, A. La Lutte pour la Turquie d'Asie. Kristiania: Cammermeyer 1917.

Morgenthau, Henry. The Secrets of the Bosphorus. By the American Ambassador at Constantinople, 1913-16. Hutchinson 1918. 8*s.* 6*d.*

—— The Tragedy of Armenia. By the late American Ambassador at Constantinople. Spottiswoode 1918. 3*d.*

Mugerditchian, Mrs. Esther. From Turkish Toils. The narrative of an Armenian Family's escape. Transl. from the Armenian. Pearson 1918. 3*d.*

Ostrorog, Count Leon. The Turkish Problem. Things seen and a few deductions. Transl. from the French. Chatto & Windus 1918. 6*s.*

Palestine during the War, being a record of the preservation of the Jewish Settlements in Palestine. Zionist Organisation, London, 1921. 1*s.*

Pinon, René. La suppression des Arméniens; méthode allemande, travail turc. Perrin 1916. 1 fr.

—— (edr.). Le Rapport secret du Dr. Johannes Lepsius . . . sur les Massacres d'Arménie. Payot 1919. 5 fr.

Richard, H. La Syrie et la guerre (deals especially with French interests in Syria). Chapelot 1916.

Roederer, C. and P. La Syrie et la France. Berger-Levrault 1917. 3 fr.

Schweder, P. Im türkischen Hauptquartier. 1916. 4 mk. 80.

Snouck-Hurgronje, Prof. C. The revolt in Arabia. With preface by R. J. H. Gottheil. Putnam 1917. 4*s.*

Stuermer, Dr. Harry. Deux ans de guerre à Constantinople: Etudes de morale et politique allemandes et jeunes-turques. Payot 1917. 3 fr. 50.

—— Transl. under title, Two War Years in Constantinople. Hodder 1917. 6*s.*

Swaine, Martin. In Mesopotamia. Hodder & Stoughton 1917. 5s

Toynbee, Arnold J. Armenian Atrocities: the murder of a nation. With speech by Lord Bryce. Hodder & Stoughton 1915. 1*d.*

Willmore, J. S. The Welfare of Egypt. Hodder 1917. 2*d.*

Woolf, Leonard S. The Future of Constantinople. Allen & Unwin 1917. 2*s.* 6*d.*

(14) *Poland.*

Benson, E. F. The White Eagle of Poland (the German occupation and problem of reconstruction). Hodder & Stoughton 1918. 6*s.*

Drogoslav, S. Pologne, La: son passé et son présent. Lausanne: l'Aigle blanc 1917. 2 fr.

France, La, pour la Pologne (les résultats d'une enquête. Recueil de l'opinion française). La Revue Polonia 1917. 4 fr.

Gasztowit, Metz, and Kozakcwicz. Le Comité de la Pologne libre au gouvernement polonais de Varsovie (la lettre du Comité du 14 juillet 1918). 1918.

Naumann, Friedrich. Was wird aus Polen? (By the author of Mitteleuropa.) Berlin: Reimer 1917. 1 mk.

Olozwski, Witold. L' ora presente in Polonia. Bologna. 1916.

Poland for the Poles. (Short essays by M. Maeterlinck, C. Richet, &c.) Published for the Polish Information Committee. Allen & Unwin 1916. 3*d.*

Poland's Case for Independence. Being a series of essays illustrating the continuance of her national life. By several writers. Allen & Unwin 1916. 7*s.* 6*d.*

Posner, S. La Pologne d' Hier et de Demain. Introduction de Georges Renard. Alcan 1917. 1 fr. 50.

Privat, Edmond. La Pologne sous la rafale. Pagot 1916. 1 fr.

Roth, P. Die politische Entwicklung in Kongresspolen während der deutschen Okkupation. Unter Mitwirkung v. W. Stein. 1919. 14 mk. 50.

Toynbee, A. J. Destruction of Poland: A Study of German Efficiency. Fisher Unwin 1916. 2*d.*

(15) *Portugal.*

Le Portugal et la guerre: Un peuple qui a voulu et qui se battra contre l'Allemagne. Payot 1918. 1 fr.

(16) *Rumania.*

Bujac, Colonel. La Roumanie (première contribution à l'histoire de la Grande Guerre). Fournier 1916. 1 fr. 50.

Kennard, Lady. A Rumanian Diary. 1915-17. Heinemann 1917. 5*s*.

Lacroix, M. le général. L'Effort de la Roumanie. Alcan 1917. 60 cts.

Leeper, A. W. A. The Justice of Rumania's Cause. Hodder 1917. 2*d*.

Matarollo, G. Letters from Roumania and Constantinople. Translated by A. Evans. Stockwell 1916. 1*s*.

Mavrodin, Const. D. La Roumanie contemporaine; son importance dans le concert balkanique et pour la guerre présente. (Maps and illustrations.) Plon 1915.

Mitrany, David. Greater Rumania: A Study in National Ideals. (Map.) Hodder & Stoughton 1917. 2*d*.

Serbesco, Sébastien. La Roumanie et la guerre. (Why and how Rumania entered the war, &c.) Colin 1918. 5 fr. 25.

Seton-Watson, R. W. Roumania and the Great War. Constable 1915. 2*s*.

(17) *Russia.*

(*a*) General.

Alexinsky, Gregor. La Russie et la Guerre. Russian policy before the War; economical conditions; Polish and other questions. Colin. 3 fr. 50.

Andréieff, Léonid. Le joug de la guerre (transl. from the Russian). An essay in Russian psychology. Didier 1917. 3 fr. 50.

Bechhofer, C. E. Russia at the Cross Roads. With introduction by A. H. Murray. Kegan Paul 1916. 5*s*.

Belevsky, A., and Voronoff, B. Les Organisations publiques russes et leur Rôle pendant la Guerre. Avec une Préface de Prof. E. Denis. Hachette 1917. 3 fr. 50.

Brennan, Hugh. Sidelights on Russia. (By the Lecturer in Russian at Glasgow University.) Nutt 1918. 2*s*. 6*d*.

Bury, Bishop. Russian Life To-day. Mowbray 1915. 3*s*. 6*d*.

Child, R. W. Potential Russia. (A guide to Russia's possibilities after the war.) Fisher Unwin 1917. 4*s* 6*d*.

Coxwell, C. F. Through Russia in War Time. Fisher Unwin 1917. 12*s*. 6*d*.

Dearmer, Percy. Russia and Britain. (O.P.) Oxford Univ. Press. 2*d*.

Delbrück, Hans (edr.). Die Motive und Ziele der russischen Politik. Nach zwei Russen (Prof. von Mitrosanoff und Fürst Kotschubey). Berlin: Stitke 1915.

Doroshevitch, V. The Way of the Cross. A picture of the Russian fugitives after the German invasion of Aug.-Sept. 1915. With introduction by Stephen Graham. Constable 1916. 2*s*. 6*d*.

Drew, A. N. Russia: a study. Simpkin, Marshall 1918. 3*s*. 6*d*.

Fraser, John Foster. Russia of To-day. Cassell 1915. 6*s*.

Friedlaender, Israel. Jews of Russia and Poland: a bird's-eye view of their history and culture. Putnam 1915. 5*s*.

Game of Diplomacy, The. (Deals throughout with Russia.) By A European Diplomat. Hutchinson 1918. 3*s*. 6*d*.

Garstin, Denis. Friendly Russia. Introduction by H. G. Wells. Unwin 1915. 3*s*. 6*d*.

—— Our Friends the Russians. With introduction by H. G. Wells. Includes a description of Russia since the outbreak of war. Fisher Unwin. 3*s*. 6*d*.

Gourko, General Basil. Russia in 1914-17. Memories and Recollections of war and revolution. (Portraits, maps and illustrations.) Murray 1918.

Graham, Stephen. The Way of Martha and the Way of Mary. Impressions of the Russian people. Macmillan 1915. 7*s*. 6*d*.

—— Russia and the World. A study of Russia since the outbreak of war. Cassell 1915. 10*s*. 6*d*.

—— Russia and the World: a study of the war and a statement of the world-problems that now confront Russia and Great Britain. New edn. Cassell 1916. 3*s*.

Herriot, E. L'Effort russe. (Published by the Committee L'Effort de la France et du ses Alliés.) Bloud 1917. 60 c.

Hoeniger, Prof. R. Russlands Vorbereitung zum Weltkrieg. Berlin: Mittler. 6 mk. 60.

Hubback, John. Russian Realities; being impressions gathered during recent journeys to Russia. Illustrated. Lane 1915. 5*s*.

Kucharzewski, J. L'Europe et le problème russo-polonais. Lausanne: l'Aigle blanc 1916. 2 fr.

Liddell, R. Scotland. Actions and Reactions in Russia. Chapman & Hall 1917. 10*s*. 6*d*.

Merry, Rev. W. M. Two months in Russia, July-Sept. 1914. (By the Vicar of St. Michael's, Oxford.) Blackwell 1916. 2*s*. 6*d*.

Milyukov, P. Le mouvement intellectuel Russe. Traduit du Russe par J. W. Bienstock. Portraits. Bossard 1918. 12 fr.

—— and others. Russian realities and problems. Lectures delivered at the Cambridge Summer meeting in Aug. 1918. Edited by J. D. Duff. Cambridge Univ. Press 1917. 5*s*.

Novikoff, Madame More Searchlights on Russia. East and West 1917. 3*d*.
Ossip-Lourié. La Russie en 1914-1917. (Studies, chiefly psychological.) Alcan 1918. 4 fr. 55.
Raffalovitch, Arthur. La Russie et la Guerre. Especially on the Finances of Russia. Alcan 1915.
Rohrbach, Paul. Russische Selbstzeugnisse. Stuttgart: Engelhorn 1916. 2 mk. 50.
Russian Court Memoirs, 1914-16. With some account of court, social and political life in Petrograd before and since the war. By a Russian. Illustrated. Jenkins 1917. 12*s*. 6*d*.
Russian diary of an Englishman. Petrograd 1915-17. 1919. 12*s*. 6*d*.
Russian Union of Zemstvos. A brief report of the Union's activities during the war. With introduction by Prince G. E. Lvov. Published by the General Committee. King 1916. 1*s*.
Russlands Mobilmachung für den Weltkrieg. Neue Uskunden. (Maps and plans.) Berlin: Mittler. 2 mk. 80.
Sarolea, Charles. Europe's Debt to Russia. Author, 20, Royal Terrace, Edinburgh. 1917. 3*s*. 6*d*.
Savtchenko, Th. L'Ukraine et la question ukrainienne. Préface du Cercle d'études franco-ukrainiennes. Edition du Cercle d'études franco-ukrainiennes 1918.
Sering, M. (edr.). Westrussland in seiner Bedeutung für die Entwicklung Mitteleuropas. Berlin: Teubner 1917. 7 mk. 50.
Shield, The. (Articles on the treatment of Jews in Russia, by Seventeen Russian Writers.) Edited by Maxim Gorky, L. Andreyev, and F. Solegub; and translated by A. Yarmolinsky. New York: Knopt 1917. $1,25.
Simpson, J. Y. The Self-Discovery of Russia. (Illustrated.) Constable 1916. 6*s*.
Stephens, Winifred (editor). The Soul of Russia. (Articles by various writers, on the lines of "The Book of France.") Macmillan 1916. 10*s*. 6*d*.
Suchomlinov. Die russische Mobilmachung im Lichte amtlicher Urkunden und der Enthüllungen des Prozesses. Bern: Wyss 1917. 30 pf.
Thurstan, Violetta. The People who run: the tragedy of the Refugees in Russia. Putnam 1916. 2*s*. 6*d*.
Vinogradoff, Prof. Paul. Self-Government in Russia. Constable 1916. 2*s*. 6*d*.

(*b*) The Revolution.

Anet, Claude (pseud. of J. Schopfer). La Révolution Russe. 4 vols. Payot 1918.

Anet, Claude (pseud. of J. Schopfer). Through the Russian Revolution. (Illustrated.) Hutchinson 1917. 6*s.*

Archives, Les, de la revolution russe. Vols. I. and II. Berlin 1921.

Bainville, Jacques. Comment est née la Révolution russe. Nouv. Libr. Nationale 1917. 1 fr. 50.

Bolshevism in Russia, A collection of reports on. Russia, No. 1 (1919). [Cmd. 8.] H.M.S.O. 1919. 9*d.*

—— Abridged edition. H.M.S.O. 1919. 6*d.*

Brailsford, H. N. The Russian Workers' Republic. Allen & Unwin 1921. 6*s.*

Buchanan, Meriel. The City of Trouble. Petrograd since the Revolution (from the death of Rasputin to the departure of the British Ambassador). Scribner 1918. $1.35.

Buisson, Etienne. Les Bolchéviki (1917-19); Faits, Documents, Commentaires. Fischacher 1919. 5 fr.

Cantacuzene, Princess (Countess Speransky). Revolutionary Days: Recollections of Romanoffs and Bolsheviki. (Illustrated.) 1920. 12*s.* 6*d.*

Chasles, P. La Révolution russe et la guerre européenne. Alcan 1918. 60 c.

Denikin, Gen. A. T. Ocheski Russkoy Smutz (outlines of the Russian Turmoil). Part I, Vol. I. Paris: Povolozky 1921.

—— English transl., under title The Russian Turmoil. Hutchinson 1922. 24*s.*

Dillon, E. J. The Eclipse of Russia. Dent 1918.

Domergue, Gabriel. La Russie rouge. Perrin 1918. 3 fr. 50.

Dorr, Rheta C. Inside the Russian Revolution (first-hand evidence). New York: Macmillan 1917. $1.50.

Farbman, Michael. The Russian Revolution and the War. National Council for Civil Liberties 1917. 6*d.*

—— Russia and the Struggle for Peace. Allen & Unwin 1918. 5*s.*

Fall of the Romanoffs, The. By the Author of Russian Court Memoirs. (How the Ex-Empress and Rasputin caused the Russian Revolution.) Illustrations. Jenkins 1917. 12*s.* 6*d.*

Freytag-Loringhoven, Dr. A. Freiherr v. Die Geschichte der russischen Revolution. 10 mk. 80.

From a Russian Diary 1917-20. By an Englishwoman. 1921. 15*s.*

Gilbreath. Olive. Russia in Travail. (A record of experiences in Russia.) Murray 1918. 7*s.* 6*d.*

Goode, W. T. Bolshevism at work. Allen & Unwin 1920. 2*s.* 6*d.*

Graevenitz, Baron P. From Autocracy to Bolshevism. Allen & Unwin 1918. 5*s.*

Herval, René. Huit mois de révolution russe. Hachette 1918. 3 fr. 50.

Hessen, I. V. (edr.). Arhiv Russkoy Revoliutziy (Archives of the Russian Revolution). Vols. I and II. Berlin: Slovo 1921. 15 fr. each vol.

Heyking, Baron A. Problems confronting Russia. King 1918. 10*s.* 6*d.*

Hirschberg, M. Bolschevismus. Eine Kritische Untersuchung über die amtlichen Veröffentlichungen der russischen Sowjet-Republik. 1919. 2 mk. 80.

Jones, Stinton. Russia in Revolution: being the experiences of an Englishman in Petrograd during the upheaval. Jenkins 1917. 5*s.*

Kadomtzeff, Boris. The Russian collapse. A politico-economic essay. Roworth 1918. 2*s.*

Kerensky, A. F. The Prelude to Bolshevism: the Kornilov Rebellion. Unwin 1919. 16*s.*

La Chesnais, P. G. Les Soviet et a paix. L'Action Nationale 1918.

—— Sans annexions. Que signifie la formule? (Politique du Soviet). L'Action Nationale 1918.

Lange, Dr. Christian L. Russia, the Revolution and the War. Account of a visit to Petrograd and Helsingfors, March 1917. Washington: Carnegie Endowment 1917.

Lansbury, George. What I saw in Russia. Parsons 1920. 4*s.* 8*d.*

Lenin, Nicholas. Lessons of the Russian Revolution. British Socialist Party 1918. 3*d.*

Les dangers mortels de la révolution russe. By * * * Payot 1918. 3 fr. 50.

Levine, Isaac Don. The Russian Revolution (with the forces that caused it and the events leading up to it). Lane 1917. 3*s.* 6*d.*

Litvinoff, Maxim. The Bolshevik Revolution: Its Rise and Meaning. British Socialist Party 1918. 1*s.* 3*d.*

Marcosson, Isaac F. The Rebirth of Russia. (Interviews with Kerensky, Miliukoff, etc.). Lane 1917. 3*s.* 6*d.*

Markovitch, Marylie (Mme. Amélie de Néry). La Révolution Russe, vue par une Française. Préface par Henri Bidou. Perrin 1918. 4 fr.

Maxe, Jean. De Zimmerwald au Bolchevisme, ou le Triomphe du Marxisme pangermaniste. Bossard 1919. 7 fr. 50.

Merejkowsky, D., Hippius, Z., and Philosophoff, D. M. Le Tsar et la Révolution. Editions du Mercure de France 1917. 3 fr. 50.

Milyukov, P. Istoriya Vtoroy Russkoy Revoliutzii (History of the second Russian Revolution). Vol. I, part I. London: Jaeshke 1921. 6*s*. 6*d*.

—— Williams, Harold, and others. Russian Realities and Problems. Edited by J. D. Duff. Camb. Univ. Press 1917. 7*s*. 6*d*.

Miliukov, Paul. Bolshevism: an international danger. Allen & Unwin 1919. 12*s*. 6*d*.

Murat, la Princesse Lucien. Raspoutine et l'Aube sanglante. Préface de M. Vandervelde. De Boccard 1917. 3 fr. 50.

Nolde, Prof. Baron B. Lenins Räterepublik. Ein Beitrag zur Geschichte der politischen und wirthschaftlichen Entwicklung im neuen Russland. (Transl. from the French.) Berlin: Mittler 1921. 6 mk 50.

Olgin, M. J. The Soul of the Russian Revolution. N.Y.: Holt 1917. $ 2.50.

Omessa, Charles. Rasputin and the Russian Court. Transl. from the French by Frances Keyzer. Newnes 1918. 2*s*. 6*d*.

Ossip-Lourié. La Révolution russe. Rieder 1921. 3 fr.

Paléologue, Maurice. La Russie des Tsars pendant la grande guerre. (Illustrated.) By the French Ambassador at Petrograd. Plon 1921. 33 fr.

Pollock, John. War and Revolution in Russia. Sketches and Studies. Constable 1918. 6*s*.

—— The Bolshevik Adventure. 1919. 7*s*. 6*d*.

Poole, Ernest. The Pillage: Russian impressions (personal experiences during the Revolution). Illustrated. N.Y: Macmillan 1918. $1.50.

Postgate, R. W. Bolshevik theory. Richards 1920. 7*s*. 6*d*.

Price, M. Philips. War and Revolution in Asiatic Russia. (Experiences in N. Persia, Armenia and the Caucasus.) Allen & Unwin 1918. 8*s*. 6*d*.

—— My reminiscences of the Russian Revolution. Allen & Unwin 1921. 18*s*.

Radziwill, Princess Catherin. Rasputin and the Russian Revolution. N.Y.: Lane 1918. $3.00.

—— Russia's Decline and Fall. The Secret history of a great debâcle. Cassell 1918. 7*s*. 6*d*.

Ransome, Arthur. The Revolution in Russia. Methuen 1917. 6*s*.

—— Adventures in Russia (during the Revolution; by the Daily News correspondent). Methuen 1918. 6*s*.

—— The Crisis in Russia. Allen & Unwin 1921. 5*s*.

Rappoport, Dr. Angelo S. Pioneers of the Russian Revolution. Stanley Paul 1918. 6*s.*

Réau, Louis. La République indépendante de l'Ukraine. Collection de l'Association France-Russie 1918. 1 fr.

Rey, A. La Russie et la Révolution. Le grand courant des idées libérales et démocratiques en Russie depuis de debut de la guerre. Florence 1917. 1 l. 50.

Rivet, Charles. The last of the Romanofs. Transl. from the French (Russia before and during the Revolution). Constable 1918. 7*s.* 6*d.*

Rohrbach, P., und Axel Schmidt. Die russische Revolution. 1 mk. 80.

Ross, Edward A. Russia in upheaval (experiences in the latter half of 1917, by an American Professor). Fisher Unwin 1918. 12*s.* 6*d.*

Russell, Bertrand. The Practice and Theory of Bolshevism. Allen & Unwin 1920. 6*s.*

Russell, Charles E. Unchained Russia (by a member of the Root Mission). Appleton 1918. $1.50.

S. R. (Serge Raffalovitch). L'Histoire de la Revolution russe (1905-1917). (Pages d'histoire, No. 135). Berger-Levrault 1917. 1 fr. 25.

Sarolea, Charles. The Russian Revolution and the War. Allen and Unwin 1917. 1*s.*

Stebbing, E. P. From Czar to Bolshevik. Lane 1918. 12*s.* 6*d.*

Tagebuch der Fürstin Maria Bolkonskaya während der Petersburger Revolution. Berlin 1917. 1 mk. 80.

Trotzky, Leon. The Bolsheviki and World Peace. With introduction by Lincoln Steffens. N.Y.: Boni & Livewright 1918. $1.50.

Trotsky, L. The Defence of Terrorism. Allen & Unwin 1921. 3*s.* 6*d.*

Vandervelde, Emile. Trois aspects de la Révolution Russe, 7 Mai-25 Juin, 1917. Berger-Levrault 1917. 2 fr. 50.

—— Transl. under title, Three aspects of the Russian Revolution. Allen & Unwin 1918. 5*s.*

Verow, N. E. Die grosse russische Revolution. 1917. 2 mk. 50.

Wells, H. G. Russia in the shadows. Hodder & Stoughton 1920. 6*s.*

Williams, Mrs. Harold. From Liberty to Brest-Litovsk. The first year of the Russian Revolution. Macmillan 1919. 16*s.*

Wilton, Robert. Russia's Agony. (By the Times correspondent in Petrograd). Arnold 1918. 15*s.*

—— Last days of the Romanovs. 1920. 15*s.*

Zagorsky, Prof. S. La République des Soviets.

Zagorsky, Prof. S. L'Evolution actuelle du Bolchévisme russe. Preface by M. Emile Vandervelde. Paris: Povolozky 1921. 6 fr. 50.

(18) *Serbia.*

Boppé, Auguste. A la suite du gouvernement serbe. De Nich à Corfou, 20 octobre 1915—19 janvier 1916. Bossard 1917. 3 fr.

Checchia, N. Un regno distrutto. Lettere dalla Serbia insanguinata (settembre-dicembre, 1915). Milan 1917. 1 l. 75.

Doumic, René. L'héroique Serbie. Bloud et Gay 1915. 60 c.

Hauser, Henri. La Serbie dans la crise européenne. A lecture. Dijon: Imprim. Darantière.

Karageorgevitch, Princess Alexis. For the better hour (Pictures of Serbia in war-time). Illustrated. Constable 1918. 2*s.* 6*d.*

L'Unité yougoslave. Manifeste de la Jeunesse serbe, croate et slovène réunie. With preface by Prof. Masaryk (of Prag). Plon-Nourrit 1915. 1 fr.

Novakovitch. L'occupation Austro-Bulgare en Serbie (the systematic destruction of Serbia). Berger-Levrault 1918. 3 fr.

Perrier, Edmond, Reinach, Joseph, and Vesnitch, R. L'Effort Serbe. Alcan 1917. 60 c.

Seton-Watson, R. W. The Spirit of the Serb. A lecture. Nisbet. 3*d.*

Velimirovic, Father Nicholas. Religion and Nationality in Serbia. With preface by R. W. Seton-Watson. Nisbet 1915. 3*d.*

—— Religious Spirit of the Slavs. Three lectures. 3rd series. Macmillan 1916. 1*s.*

—— Serbia in Light in Darkness. With Preface by the Archbishop of Canterbury. Longmans 1916. 3*s.* 6*d.*

—— Serbia's Place in Human History. (Foreign Series, No. 1.) Council for Study of Internat. Relations. 3*d.*

—— Serbia's Tragedy. A lecture. Morgan & Scott 1915. n.p.

—— Soul of Serbia. Faith Press 1916. 1*s.*

(19) *United States.*

Alphaud, Gabriel. L'action allemande aux États-Unis. Observations made on an official mission to the United States. Payot 1915.

—— L'Action allemande aux États-Unis pendant la guerre, 1914-15. Avec une préface de M. Ernest Lavisse. Payot 1916. 5 fr.

—— Les États-Unis contre l'Allemagne: du Rappel de Dumba à la déclaration de guerre (25 sep^{t}. 1915—4 avril 1917). Payot 1917. 6 fr.

America's Opinion on the War. A collection of utterances by prominent American citizens in favour of the Allies' cause. Fisher Unwin. 1*s*.

Angell, Norman. America and the cause of the Allies. (In defence of the President's policy.) Union of Dem. Control. 1916. 1*d*.

Baldwin, Prof. J. M. American Neutrality: its Cause and Cure. Putnam 1916. 2*s*.

Beck, James M. The War and Humanity. (Deals especially with the policy of the United States and its duties.) Putnam 1916. $1.50.

Beck, James M., and Bryce, Viscount. The United States and the War. Addresses delivered in London and Philadelphia, with other remarks. Edited by Barr Ferree. New York: Pennsylvanian Society 1916.

Bernstorff, Graf. Deutschland und America. 1920 (?). 30 mk.

Bernstorff, Count. My three years in America (transl. from the German). Skeffington 1920.

Bullard, Arthur. Mobilising America (How to profit by our mistakes). New York: Macmillan 1917. $0.50.

Burgess, Prof. J. W. America's relations to the great war. Chicago: McClurg 1916. $1.00.

Chéradame, André. The United States and Pan-Germania. Maps. Scribner 1918. $1.00.

Clarke, Prof. G. H. Why the United States of America entered the War. Hodder & Stoughton 1917. 2*d*.

Clarke, Ida C. American women and the World-War. New York: Appleton 1918. $2.00.

Coar, John F. Democracy and the War. (Based on lectures delivered in the United States by an American professor.) Putnam 1918. 5*s*.

Dawson, Coningsby. Out to Win. (The preparation and activities of the United States forces.) Lane 1918. 4*s*.

Eliot, C. W. America and the Issues of the European War. Reprinted from the New York Times of Oct. 2, 1914. New York: Bonbright & Co. n.p.

Eliot, Dr. C. W. (late President of Harvard). The American People and the War. The Lindsey Press. 1*d*.

Ferri-Pisani. L'Intérèt et l'Idéal des Etats-unis dans la guerre mondiale. Perrin 1918. 3 fr. 50.

Fish, Carl Russell. American Diplomacy. (American Historical series.) Bell 1916. 10*s*. 6*d*.

Fulda, Ludwig. Amerika und Deutschland während des Weltkrieges. Dresden: Globus 1919. 1 mk. 20.

Fullerton, W. Morton. The American Crisis and the War. (A criticism of President Wilson's policy.) Constable 1916. 2*s*. 6*d*.

Gauss, Christian. Why we went to war (the United States *versus* Germany). Appendix of documents. Scribner 1918. $1.50.

German spy, The, in America. The secret plotting of German spies in the United States, and the inside story of the sinking of the Lusitania. Preface by Th. Roosevelt. Hutchinson 1917. 5*s*.

Gould, Benj. A. The War-thoughts of an Optimist. Articles by an American citizen, long resident in Canada, on Canada's point of view, the policy of the U.S., etc. Dent. 2*s*. 6*d*.

Greene, Francis Vinton. Our first year in the Great War. (American doings.) Putnam 1918. 3*s*.

Hanotaux, Gabriel. Les États-Unis et la France. English text by Morton Fullerton. Alcan 1918. 1 fr.

Hervier, Paul-Louis. Les Volontaires Américains dans les rangs alliés. La Nouvelle Revue 1918. 5 fr.

Johnson, Prof. Douglas W. Plain Words from America. A letter to a German Professor. Hodder & Stoughton 1917. 3*d*.

Johnson, Willis. America and the great war for Humanity and Freedom. Philadelphia: Winston Co. 1917. $1.50.

Lechartier, G. Intrigues et diplomaties à Washington (1914-17). Plon-Nourrit 1919.

Lichtenbeger, Henri. L'opinion Américaine et la Guerre. Bloud et Gay 1916. 60 c.

McMaster, Prof. John B. The United States in the World-War. 2 vols. Appleton 1919-20. 30*s*.

Münsterberg, Hugo. The Peace and America. New York: Appleton 1915. $1.00.

Ohlinger, Gustavus. Their true faith and allegiance. (German immigrants to America, and the German propaganda in the U.S.) With preface by Owen Wister. New York: Macmillan 1916. 2*s*.

Palmer, Frederick. With our faces in the light. By an American, to explain to Britons America's spirit in the war. Murray 1917. 2*s*. 6*d*.

Nicholson, Prof. J. S. The Neutrality of the United States in relation to the British and German Empires. Macmillan 1915. 6*d*.

Okie, H. P. America and the German Peril. Heinemann 2*s*. 6*d*.

Oncken, Prof. H. Deutschlands Weltkrieg und die Deutsch-Amerikaner. (Series, Der deutsche Krieg.) Stuttgart: Deutsche Verlags-Anstalt.

Robinson, E. E., and West, V. J. The foreign policy of President Wilson (since 1913). New York: Macmillan 1917. $1.75.

Roosevelt, Theodore. America and the World War. Strongly in favour of a more active policy. Murray 1915. 5*s.*

—— Why America should join the Allies. Pearson 1915. 6*d.*

—— Fear God and take your own part: the United States and the War. Hodder & Stoughton 1916. 7*s.* 6*d.*

Rouquette, Louis. Allemagne et Amérique: La Propagande germanique aux États-Unis. Chapelot 1916. 2 fr. 50.

Royce, Prof. Josiah. The Duties of Americans in the present War. Speech delivered at Boston on Jan. 30, 1916. W. D. Austin, Boston, Mass. 5 c.

Scott, James B. A survey of International relations between the United States and Germany, Aug. 1, 1914, to April 6, 1917 (based on official documents). Oxford Univ. Press 1918. 21*s.*

Seldes, Gilbert V. The United States and the War. Allen & Unwin 1917. 2*s.* 6*d.*

Sixty American Opinions on the War. Unwin 1915. 1*s.*

Skaggs, W. H. German conspiracies in America. With an introduction by T. A. Cook. Fisher Unwin 1915. 5*s.*

—— (edr.). America and the War in Europe. A compilation by various authors. Chicago: Kenfield Leach Co. 25 c.

Sumichrast, Frederick C. de. Americans and Britons. Duckworth 1915. 7*s.* 6*d.*

Taft, William H. The United States and Peace. Murray 1914. 5*s.*

Usher, Roland G. Pan-Americanism: a Forecast of the inevitable clash between the United States and Europe's victor. Constable 1915. 8*s.* 6*d.*

—— The Challenge of the Future. A study in American Foreign Policy (in the light of the War). Constable 1916. 7*s.* 6*d.*

Viallate, Achille. Les États-Unis d'Amérique et le conflit européen 4 août 1914—6 avril 1917. Alcan 1918. 3 fr. 50.

Villeneuve-Tram, R. de. L'Ambassade de Washington, Oct. 1917—Apr. 1919. Boesard 1921. 9 fr.

Voix Américaines sur la Guerre de 1914-16. By S. R. Berger-Levrault 1916. 60 c.

Weston, Dr. W. M. America and the War. A lecture. Croydon: Glaisher. 3*d.*

Weyl, W. E. American World Policies. New York: Macmillan 1917. $2.25.

World Peril, The. America's Interest in the War. By members of the Faculty of Princeton University. Milford 1918. 4*s.* 6*d.*

(20) *Yugo-Slavs.*

Cviéticha, Frano. Les Yougoslaves (Problèmes nationaux d'Autriche-Hongrie). Paris: Bossard 1918. 3 fr.

Idea of Southern-Slav unity (The Southern-Slav Library, V). The Near East 1916. *3d.*

Mastery of the Adriatic, The, and the Jugo-Slav Question. Italy in Asia Minor. Contributions and criticism. Compiled by Salvatore Raineri. Syren & Shipping, Ltd., 91, Leadenhall St., 1916. n.p.

Primorać, Vouk (pseud.). La Question yougo-slave (différents groupes qui se rattachent à la race). Société Yougo Slavia, rue Cujas, 1918. n.p.

Taylor, A. H. E. The Future of the Southern Slavs. Fisher Unwin 1917. *12s. 6d.*

Vosnjak, Dr. Bogumil. A Bulwark against Germany (advocates the establishment of an independent Jugo-Slav state). Transl. from the Slavonic. Allen & Unwin 1917. *4s. 6d.*

B.—Neutrals.

(1) *Holland.*

Piérard, Louis. La Hollande et la Guerre. (Pages d'histoire, No. 124.) Berger-Levrault. 75 c.

Rocheblave, Samuel. Chez les neutres du Nord: Hollande et Scandinavie. (Impressions recueilles pendant un voyage.) Bloud et Gay 1918. 2 fr. 50.

Scott, T. W. R. War time and peace in Holland. Heinemann 1915.

Treub, Van M. W. F. Oorlogstijd Herinneringen en Indrukken. (War Time in Holland). Amsterdam: Scheltema & Holkema 1916.

Van Dyke, Henry. Fighting for peace. (The Germans in Holland.) By the late U.S. Minister at The Hague. Hodder & Stoughton 1917. *5s.*

(2) *Scandinavia.*

Aall, H. H. Le Sort du Nord. (Sur les origines de la guerre; favorables aux empires du centre). Kristiania: Parmann 1917.

Berggrav-Jensen, E., and others. Au croisement des chemins (la situation de la Norvège discutée par quatre auteurs). Kristiania: Steen 1918.

Bjorkman, E. Scandinavia and the War. (O.P.) Oxford Univ. Press. *2d.*

Maury, Lucien. Les Problèmes scandinaves. Le Nationalisme suédois et la guerre 1914-18. Perrin 1918. 5 fr.

Murray, Prof. Gilbert. Impressions of Scandinavia in War time. Fisher Unwin 1916. *2d.*

Stieve, F. Schwedische Stimmen zum Weltkrieg. Übersetzt. 1916. 4 mk. 80.

Thommessen, Rolf. La politique extérieure de la Norvège pendant la guerre mondiale. Aschehoug 1917.

(3) *South American States.*

Gaillard, Gaston. Amérique latine et Europe occidentale. (L'attitude des peuples dans la grande guerre.) Berger-Levrault 1918. 3 fr. 50.

Kirkpatrick, F. A. South America in the War. Map. Cambridge Univ. Press 1918. 4*s.* 6*d.*

Silva-Vildósola, C. Le Chili et la Guerre. Transl. from the Spanish. Alcan 1918. 2 fr.

Voix de l'Amérique latine. (Collection of pro-Ally opinions by prominent South Americans). Berger-Levrault 1916. 75 c.

Wagner, E. R. L'Allemagne et l'Amérique latine. Préfable de M. Edmond Perrier (d'outre-Rhin dans l'Amérique du Sud). Alcan 1918. 3 fr. 50.

(4) *Spain.*

Ballesteros, Lazaro. La Guerra europea y la neutralidad espanola : observaciones y consideraciones. Madrid : Ratés 1917. 1 fr.

Coust, J. Félicien. Chez les neutres. En Espagne. Illustrated. Giard et Brière 1916. 3 fr. 50.

Deploige, Simon, Mgr. La voix des Neutres (l'impression produite en Espagne par la violation de la neutralité belge). Plon 1918. 2 fr.

Espagne, l', et la Guerre : L'Esprit public, la situation politique. Bloud et Gay 1916. 3 fr. 50.

Galiano, A. A. L'Espagne en face du conflit européen. Bloud et Gay 1917. 3 fr. 50.

Sorgnes, Maurice de. Les Catholiques espagnols et la Guerre. Bloud et Gay 1916. 60 c.

Voix espagnols sur la guerre de 1914-15. (Pages d'histoire). By various authors. Berger-Levrault. 60 c.

(5) *Switzerland.*

Dumur, Louis. Les Deux Suisse. (French and German Switzerland : their attitude in the war). Bossard 1918. 6 fr.

Earll, M. R. A Backwater of War: being letters from Switzerland, Sept. to Dec., 1914. With introductory note by E. S. Woods. Headley 1915. 1*s.* 6*d.*

Feyler, Colonel F. La crise politique suisse pendant la guerre. Payot. 2 fr. 50.

Secrétan, Colonel. Articles et Discours (1er août 1914-1er août 1917). (Attitude generale de la Suisse aux belligérants). Payot 1918. 4 fr.

Turmann, Max. La Suisse pendant la Guerre. Paris: Perrin 1917. 3 fr. 50.

Zurlinden, S. von. Der Weltkrieg und die Schweizer. Zurich: Orell Füssli 1917. 2 fr. 50.

(6) *The Vatican.*

Brennan, Anthony. Pope Benedict XV and the War (in favour of the Vatican). King 1917. 1*s.*

Canelini, M. Il Papa nella guerra e per la pace. Civello (Como): Author 1916. 1 fr. 50.

D'Agnel, l'Abbé G. Arnaud. Benoît XV et la Conflit européen. 1re série. 2 vols. I, À la lumière de l'Evangile. II, À la lumière de l'histoire. Lethielleux 1916. 7 fr.

Diplomaticus (pseud.). No Small Stir. What the Pope really said about the Great War. (By a layman of the Church of England.) Soc. of SS. Peter & Paul. 6*d.*

Ford, Hugh Edmund. Pope Benedict's Note to the Belligerents, with some explanations (to show that the Note is not pro-German). Arrowsmith 1917. 2*d.*

Martyn, Gabriel (Edr.). His Holiness Pope Benedict XV on the Great War. A collection of his utterances in the cause of peace. Burns & Oates 1916. 1*s.*

Maurras, Ch. Le Pape, la guerre et la paix (articles publiés dans l'Action francaise). Nouv. Libr. Nationale 1917. 3 fr. 50.

Pape, Le, et la Guerre: simples réflexions d'un catholique français sur la situation religieuse (1915-16) (trois mémoires confidentiels). Alcan 1916. 60 c.

Papst, Kurie, und Weltkrieg. Historisch-kritische Studie von einem Deutschen. Berlin: Säemann 1918.

Pinchard, Arnold. The Pope and the Conscience of Christendom. A lecture. Midland Educational Co. 1915. 2*d.*

Porcelli, Baron. The Pope and the War. Protestant Truth Society 1918. 3*d.*

Quadrotta, Guglielmo. Il Papa, l'Italia, e la guerra. Milan: Ravà 1915. 2 l.

Rome and Germany: the Plot for the Downfall of Britain. By Watchman. 2nd (revised) edn. Drane 1916. 1*s*.

Rumeau, M. Pape, Le, et la Paix (sa note sur la paix). Bonne Presse 1918.

Spahn, Martin. Die päpstliche Friedensvermittlung. Berlin: Scherl 1919. 3 mk.

Touchet, M. La Paix pontificale (n'est pas une paix allemande). Letheilleux 1918. 1 fr.

Tyrrell, Francis. Pope and the Great War: the Silence of Benedict XV: Can it be Defended? Hampden Press 1915. 6*d*.

Vanneufville, G. Le Pape Benoît XV et la Guerre (articles destinés à justifier le Pape). Limoges: Guillemot 1917. 1 fr.

Wehberg, H. Papstum und Weltfriede. 1915. 1 mk. 80.

Welschinger, Henri. La mission du prince de Bülow à Rome (Dec. 1914—May 1915). (Pages actuelles.) Bloud et Gay. 60 c.

"Y. de la B." (le Père de la Brière). Médiation pontificale et relations avec le Vatican. Tequi 1917. 50 c.

—— Les Puissances belligerants et la Médiation pontificale (extraits des Études, 5 octobre et 20 novembre 1917) (les réponses qui ont été faites par les divers États). Téqui 1918. 50 c.

(7) *General.*

Barbosa, Ruy. Le devoir des Neutres. (By a Brazilian Senator and Jurist.) Alcan 1917. 2 fr.

Lémonon, E. Les Alliès et les Neutres (Allied relations with the Powers at first or still neutral). Delagsane 1918. 3 fr. 50.

Moulin, R. La Guerre et les Neutres (Articles from the Revue Hebdomadaire, 1915-16). Plon-Nourrit 1916. 3 fr. 50.

X. RECORDS OF THE WAR.

A.—General.

(1) *Chronologies.*

Baer, C. H. Völkerkrieg, Der. Eine Chronik der Ereignisse seit Juli 1914. Mit Abb. Vols. I-XVI, 8 mk. per vol. Vols. XVII-XIX, 6 mk. 50 per vol.

Chronik des deutschen Krieges nach amtl. Berichten und zeitgenöss. Kundgebungen. Bd. I-X. 1914-18. 4 mk. 40 per vol.

Chronologie de la Guerre. Vol. I, July 31-Dec. 31, 1914; Vol. II, Jan. 1-June 30, 1915, and later volumes. (Pages d'histoire.) Berger-Levrault. 60 c. each.

Chronology of the War : issued under the auspices of the Ministry of Information. 3 vols. With separate vol. of War Maps. [by Lord Edward Gleichen.] Constable 1918-1920. Vol. I 5*s.*; Vol. II 7*s.* 6*d.*; Atlas 36.

Gretton, M. Sturge. Kalendar of the War. Nisbet 1916. 2*s.* 6*d.*

Jollivet, Gaston. Six mois de guerre (Aug. 1, 1914—Feb. 1, 1915); Trois mois de guerre (Feb. 1-May 1, 1915). Résumés et documents reliés et classés dans l'ordre chronologique. 2 vols. Hachette 1915-16. 3 fr. 50 each.

Notre Epopée 1914-15. Récits officiels des combats (down to Sept. 1915). Soc. franç. d'Imprimerie 1916. 3 fr. 50.

Principal Events 1914-1918. Compiled by the Historical Section of the Committee of Imperial Defence. H.M.S.O. 1922. 10*s.* 6*d.*

Schultess' Europäischer Geschichtskalender Kreigsjahrgänge 1914-18. 5 vols. Münich : Beck 1915-21. 600 mk.

Tablettes chronologiques de la guerre. Larousse. 1-2 fr. each.

(2) *Documents.*

Archives, Les, de la grande guerre. Revue mensuelle (Des faits racontés par leurs lémoins.). Annual subscription, 36 fr. Chiron.

Buchner, E. Kriegsdokumente. Der Weltkrieg in d. Darstell. d. zeitgenöss. Presse. Bd. I-IX. 1914-18. 7 mk. per vol.

Communiqués officiels, Les, depuis la déclaration de guerre. (Pages d'histoire.) Suité chronologique des dépêches du gouvernement français. 16 parts, to Oct. 31, 1915; then published monthly. Berger-Levrault. 60 c. each.

Communiqués officiels, Recueil des, des Gouvernements et Etat-Major de tous les belligérants. Séries I-X (July 24-Dec. 31, 1914), 1 fr. 25 each. Séries XI-XXVI (Jan. 1, 1915-March 22, 1916), 2 fr. each. Berger-Levrault. Payot.

Documentary History of the War. Military, Naval, Diplomatic. The Times 1917-20. 11 vols. 21*s.* each.

Documente zur Geschichte des Krieges 1914-16. Bd. 1-4. Hrsg. von W. v. Massow. 1 mk. 20 per vol.

Documents, Recueil des, insérés au Bulletin officiel du Ministère de la guerre, et concernant spécialement la période des hostilités du 2 août 1914 (to July 31, 1916). Lavanzelle 1916.

French Official Review, The, of the First Six Months of the War. English transl. Constable 1*s.*

German War (The) of 1914. Illustrated by Documents of European History 1914-15. Edited by J. R. H. O'Regan. Oxford Univ. Press. 1*s.* 6*d.*

Guerre, la, de 1914; Documents Officiels. 23 vols. Dalloz 1916-18

Helmolt, Hans F. Der Weltkrieg in Bildern and Dokumenten, nebst einem Kriegstagebuch. Leipzig : Meulenhoff 1914. 5 mk.

Histoire de la Guerre, par Le Bulletin des Armées. Vol. I, Aug. 1914-Jan. 1915 ; Vol. II, Feb.-Aug. 1915, &c. Hachette 1915. 3 fr. each.

Junker, C. Documente zur Geschichte d. europäischen Krieges 1914-16, gesammelt u. in chronolog. Folge herausgegeben. 1915, 6 mk. Vol. I ; 1915, 11 mk. Vol. II. 2 Abteilung. Der Krieg mit Italien 1915-16. 1916. 6 mk. 50.

Kriegs-Depeschen 1914-18 Nach den amtlichen, vom W.T.B., den österreich. u. türk. amtl. Stellen verbreiteten Berichten. Bd. I-VI. 1915-18. 9 mk. 15 per vol.

Kriegsverlauf, Der. Sammlung der amtlichen Nachrichten von den Kriegsschauplätzen. Die Depeschen des Grossen Hauptquartiers, des österr. Generalstabes, des türk. Grossen Hauptquartiers, des bulgar. Generalstabes u. des W.T.B. Bd. I, Aug. 1914 bis Jul. 1915 ; Bd. II, Aug. 1915 bis Jul. 1916 ; Bd. III, Aug. 1916 bis Jul. 1917. Berlin : Heymann 1915-17. 12 mk. per vol.

La Défense nationale. Un an de Guerre. (1) Discours, circulaires, documents officiels. Ed. by L. Lumet. Fontemoing 1915. 3 fr. 50.

L'Aveu de la Défaite allemande : les origines de l'Armistice. Documents officiels allemands, publiés par ordre du Cabinet (transl. from the German). Renaissance du Livre 1919. 5 fr.

London Gazette. Wyman. 1*s*. each.

London Gazette Supplements. Contains lists of war awards, etc. Wyman. 4*d* each.

Ludendorff, Gèneral (edr.). Urkunden der Obersten Heeresleitung über ihre Tätigkeit, 1916-18. 2nd edn. Berlin : Mittler 1921. 95 mk.

Mermeix (pseud.). Les négociations decrètes et les quatre Armistices, avec pièces justificatives. Paris : Ollendorff 1921.

Musée, Le, et l'Encyclopédie de la Guerre. Recueil mensuel, illustré de documents [&c.], publié sous la direction de M. John Grand-Carteret No. 1, Feb. 1917. Paris : F. Pigeon, 57 rue Richelieu. 75 c. the number.

Naval and Military Despatches relating to Operations in the War, Sept.-Nov. 1914. With Map. H.M.S.O. 1915. 2*d*.

—— Part 2, Nov. 1914—June 1915, with names of Officers and Men mentioned ; and Awards of the Victoria Cross. With Map. H.M.S.O. 1915. 6*d*.

—— Part III, July to Oct. 1915. With names of Officers and Men mentioned, and Awards of the Victoria Cross. H.M.S.O. 1916. 3*d*.

Naval and Military Despatches relating to Operations in the War, Part V, Jan.-April 1916. With names of Officers and Men mentioned, and Awards of the Victoria Cross. H.M.S.O. 1917. 6*d.*

—— Part VI, May-Dec. 1916. With names of Officers and Men awarded the Victoria Cross. H.M.S.O. 1917. 1*s.*

—— Part VII, Dec. 1916—July 1917. With names of Officers and Men awarded the Victoria Cross. H.M.S.O. 1918. 9*d.*

—— Part VIII, July 1917 to June 1918. With names of Officers and Men awarded the Victoria Cross. H.M.S.O. 1919. 1*s.* 6*d.*

—— Part IX, July 1918 to Dec. 1918. With names of Officers and men awarded the Victoria Cross. H.M.S.O. 1919. 1*s.*

—— Nos. I-IX (Sept. 1914—Dec. 1918). H.M.S.O. 1917. 3*s.* 4*d.*

(3) *Histories.*

Adam, Paul. La Terre qui tonne : France-Italie. (The war in France and Italy.) Chapelot 1918. 3 fr. 50.

Adcock, A. St. John. Australasia Triumphant. With the Australians and New Zealanders in the Great War. Simpkin, Marshall, 1916. 2*s.* 6*d.*

Aguilar, A. Pagés Y. La Guerra de 1914-1915 : antecedentes y cronica de las operaciones. Madrid : Renacimiento 1916. 3 fr. 50.

Allen, G. H., and others. The Great War. Philadelphia : Barrie 1916.

Anzacs, The Story of the. An historical account of the part taken by Australia and New Zealand in the Great War, Aug. 1914—Dec. 1915. Melbourne : Ingram 1918. 5*s.* 6*d.*

Atteridge, A. Hilliard. First phase of the Great War. Illustrated. (Graphic extras.) Hodder & Stoughton 1914. 5*s.*

—— Second phase of the Great War. Illustrated. (Graphic extras.) Hodder & Stoughton 1915. 5*s.*

Aulard, Prof. A. La guerre actuelle commentée par l'histoire. Vues et impressions au jour le jour (1914....). Payot. 4 fr. 50.

Aus den Tagen des grossen Krieges 1915-17. A series of 17 monographs, ranging in price from 1 mk. 30 to 3 mk. 90. 1915-18.

Ayres, Col. Leonard. The War with Germany. A statistical summary (from the American point of view), by the Chief of the Statistical Branch of the General Staff. 1921.

Barzini, Luigi. Scènes de la Grande Guerre. Traduction de Jacques Mesnil. Payot 1915. 3 fr. 50.

Battine, Cecil. A Military History of the War. Vol. I. Hodder & Stoughton 1916. 5*s.*

Belloc, Hilaire. A General Sketch of the European War: the First Phase. Nelson. 6*s.*

—— A General Sketch of the European War: the Second Phase. Nelson 1916. 6*s.*

Bernard, Jean. Histoire générale et anecdotique de la Guerre de 1914. Monthly parts; five parts published, March 1916. Berger-Levrault. Part 1, 50 c.; subsequent parts, 75 c. each.

Brandstaedter, O. Der Weltkrieg 1914-18. Eine ausführliche Darstellung sämtl. Vorgänge im Kriege. Bd. I—VI. Mit Abb. 1915-19. 7 mk. per vol.

Buchan, John. History of the Great War. 25 vols. Nelson 1916. 1*s.* 3*d.* per vol.

—— —— 4 vols. Nelson 1921. 15*s.* each.

Cana, F. R. The Great War in Europe. Vols. II and III. Virtue 1915. 7*s.* 6*d.*

Canonge, le général. La Grande Guerre de 1914-19. Récit succinct. Maps and drawings. Fournier 1919. 5 fr.

Charmes, Francis. L'Allemagne contre l'Europe. La Guerre (1e série, Aug. 1914—May 1915; et 2e série, May 1915—Jan. 1916). With memoir by Emile Faguet. Perrin 1916. 3 fr. 50 each.

Chenu, Charles. De l'arrière à l'avant: Chronique de la Guerre, Oct. 1914—Dec. 1915. Plon-Nourrit 1915. 3 fr. 50.

Cobb, Irvin S. The Red Glutton. An account of the earlier phases of the War, by an American Journalist with the German Army. Hodder & Stoughton. 6*s.*

Cornet, Lucien. Histoire de la Guerre 1914-1915. 2 vols. Charles-Lavauzelle 1917. 10 fr.

Current History of the War. New York Times. Useful for the Documents, Speeches, etc., which it contains. Monthly parts (Dec. 1914—June 1916) issued. New York Times Office. 25c. each no.

Daudet, Ernest. Mes Chroniques de 1915 et 1916. Altinger 1917. 3 fr. 50.

Davenport, Briggs. A History of the Great War, 1914. Putnam 1916. 9*s.*

Debrit, Jean. La Guerre de 1914: notes au jour le jour. 4 vols. Illustrated. Crès 1917. 2 fr. 50 each.

De Civrieux, le commandant. Les étapes vers la victoire, 1914-15. Edn. et Librairie 1915. 3 fr. 50.

Doyle, Sir A. Conan. British Campaigns in France and Flanders. Hodder & Stoughton 1916. 6*s.*

Egli, K. Zwei Jahre Weltkrieg. Ein Uberblick üb. d. kriegerischen Ereignisse v. Aug. 1914 bis Aug. 1916.. Mit 22 Kartenskiggen. 1918. 9 mk.

—— Das dritte Jahr Weltkrieg. Vom August 1916 bis Aug. 1917. Mit 21 Kartenskiggen. 1918. 7 mk.

Falkenhayn, Er. v. Die Oberste Heeresleitung 1914 bis 1916 in ihren wichtigsten Entschliessungen. Mit 12 Karten. 1920. 35 mk.

Franc-Nohain, and Deloy, Paul. Histoire anecdotique de la guerre, 1914-15. 8 parts. Berger-Levrault & Lethielleux 1915. 4 vols. 75 c. per fasc.

Freytag-Loringhoven, Frhr. von. Heeresführung im Weltkriege. Vergleichende Studien. 2 vols. Berlin, Mittler, 1920-21.

Frobenius, H. Deutsche Schwertschrift, Erläut. Chronik d. ersten Weltkrieges auf Grund v. Urkunden u. amtl. Berichten. Bd. I, II, III. 1915-18. 8 mk. 80 per vol.

—— Der erste Weltkrieg. Mit 34 Kartenskiggen, 85 photogr. Abb., 101 Federgeichn. u. Kopfleisten v. Hammel u.a. 2 Bde. 1917. 28 mk.

Gauvain, Auguste. L'Europe au jour le jour. Vols. IX-XI. La Guerre européenne, Nov. 1915—Dec. 1917.. Bossard 1921. 15-18 fr. each.

Geschichte, Illustrierte, des Weltkrieges 1914-18. Mit Abb. Karten u. Plänen. Bd. I-VIII. Vols. I-VII, 12 mk. 50 per vol. Vol. VIII, 15 mk.

Grande Guerre, la, du XXe siècle. 1914.... Maison de la Bonne Presse 1917.

Guerra, La, delle nazioni (1915-...) storia illustrata. (Many documents.) Milan : Treves 1915.

Hanotaux, Gabriel. Histoire illustrée de la Guerre de 1914. Vols. I-IX. Gounouilhou 1914-19.

—— Études diplomatiques et historiques. Pendant la Grande Guerre (août-decembre 1914). (Articles publd. by the author in the Figaro et la Revue hebdomadaire). Plon-Nourrit 1916. 3 fr. 50.

Helfferich, K. Der Weltkrieg. I, Die Vorgeschichte des Weltkrieges. II, Vom Kriegsausbrach bis zum uneingeschr. U-Bootkrieg. 2 vols. Berlin : Ulletrin 1919. 22 mk. 50.

Helmolt, H. F. Der Weltkrieg in Bildern u. Dokumenten nebst e. Kriegstagebuch. Bd. I-IV. 1915-17. 4 mk. 50 per vol.

Hemberger, A. Der europäische Krieg u. der Weltkrieg. Histor. Darstellung d. Kriegsereignisse v. 1914-17. Mit vielen Abb., Karten u. Plänen. Bd. I-IV. 12 mk. per vol.

History of the War (Manchester Guardian), 1914-15. Heywood 1915. 10*s*. 6*d*. and 12*s*. 6*d*. each vol.

Hölscher, G. Kurzgef. Geschichte d. Weltkriegs. Mit Abb. u. Karten. Bd. I, Vorgeschichte, Belgien, Nordfrankreich bis 1914. Bd. II, Elsass-Lothr., Ostpreussen, Galizien, Polen, Seekrieg, Luftkrieg bis Ende 1914. Bd. III, Das Jahr 1915 auf allen Kriegsschauplätzen. 1915. Vol. I, 3 mk. 50; Vol. II, 4 mk. 50. 1916. Vol. III, 4 mk. 50.

Hoetzsch, O. Der Krieg und die grosse Politik. 3 Bde. I, Bis z., Anschluss Bulgariens an d. Mittelmächte 1917. 18 mk. 20. II, Bis z., Eintritt Rumäniens in d. Weltkrieg 1917. 18 mk. 20. III, Bis z., deutsch-russ. Waffenstillstand 1918. 25 mk. 20.

Ibañez, V. Blasco. Historia de la guerra Europea de 1914. Many illustrations. 3 vols. published. Also in weekly parts at 50 cents. Valencia: Prometeo 1915. 17 pes. 50.

Immanuel, Col. F. Der Weltkrieg 1914-18. Volkstümliche Darstellung des Krieges zu Lande, zur See in den Schutzgebieten (maps). Berlin: Mittler 1920. 30 mk.

Jollivet, Gaston. Six mois de guerre, Août 1914-Janvier 1915 (followed by other vols. under title Trois mois de guerre &c. to June 1916). Illustrations. Hachette 1915-17. 3 fr. 50 each.

Knight, W. S. M. The History of the Great European War: its Causes and Effects. (In progress.) Caxton Publishing Co. 8*s.* 6*d.* each vol.

Krieg, Der grosse, in Einzeldarstellungen. Unter Benutzung amtlichen Materials hrsg. im Auftrag des Generalstabes des Feldheeres. Issued in 11 parts ranging in price from 2 mk. 40 to 3 mk. 30 per part.

Kuhl, Gen. H. von. Der deutsche Generalstab in Vorbereitung und Durchführung des Weltkrieges. 2nd edn. Berlin: Mittler 1921. 38 mk.

Le Queux, William. The War of the Nations: a history of the great European conflict. Illustrated. Newnes 1914. 5*s.* each.

Leroy-Beaulieu, Paul. La guerre de 1914 vue en son cours chaque semaine. Articles contributed weekly to L'Économiste française. Delagrave 1915. 3 fr. 50.

Metchim, D. B. Our own history of the War: from a South London view. Stockwell 1918. 2*s.* 6*d.*

Moraht, E. Tage des Krieges. Militär. u. polit. Betrachtungen 1914-16. Mit Karten u. Kartenskiggen. Bd. I, II. 1914-16. 17 mk. 60.

Mumby. F. A. The Great World-War. A History. Edited by F. A. M. Parts. Gresham Publishing Co. 2*s.* 6*d.* each.

Murray, Col. A. M. The Fortnightly History of the War [to July 1916]. With a Foreword by Field-Marshal Sir Evelyn Wood. Chapman & Hall 1916. 10*s.* 6*d.*

Penny History of the War. Fortnightly parts. Geographia. 1*d.* each.

Pollard, Prof. A. F. A short history of the Great War. Methuen 1920. 10*s.* 6*d.*

Price, M. P. The Diplomatic History of the War. Revised and enlarged edn. Allen & Unwin. 7*s.* 6*d.*

Purlitz, F. Krieg'Der europäische, in aktenmässiger Darstellung. 10 vols., averaging 27 mk.

Schäfer, D., u.a. Der Krieg 1914-17. Werden u. Wesen des Weltkrieges, dargestellt in umfassenderen Abhandlungen und kleineren Sonderartikeln. Mit Karten u. Abb. 3 Bde. Bd. I, II. 16 mk. per vol.

Schaffstein, H. Die Geschichte des Völkerkrieges 1914-18. Illustrated. Bd. I-III. 21 mk. 60 per vol.

Schlachten des Weltkrieges 1914-18. Herausg. unter Mitwirkung des Reichsarchives. (1) Antwerpen 1914. (2) Baranowitschi 1916. (Continuation of series published by the German Gen. Staff down to 1920.)

Simonds, F. H. The Great War: the First Phase (to the Fal of Antwerp). Rider. 6*s.*

Souza, Count Charles de, and McFall, Major H. Germany in defeat: a strategic history of the War. Kegan Paul 1915 6*s.*

—— Germany in Defeat: Phase II (with plans of battles) Kegan Paul & Routledge 1916. 6*s.*

Sparrow, Geoffrey, and Ross, J. N. MacBean. On Four Front with the Royal Navy Division. (By two Surgeons, R.N. Illustrated. Hodder & Stoughton 1918. 12*s.*

Swinton, E. D., and the Earl Percy. A Year Ago: Eye-Witness' Narrative of the War from March 30 to July 18, 1915. Arnold 1916. 2*s.* & 2*s.* 6*d.*

Times History of the War. Illustrated. Weekly pts., 8*d.* 21 vols. published, at from 10*s.* 6*d.* to 21*s.* per vol. Time Office 1914...

Van Vorst, B. A popular history of the War from 1914 to 1918 Larousse 1918. 2 fr.

Viallare, A., and Caudel, M. La Vie politique. Vol. IX. L grande Guerre, 2 août 1914—11 nov. 1918 (Le Monde et l Guerre: La diplomatie: guerre militaire et navale: vi économique: finances). Alcan 1921. 25 fr.

Wallace, Edgar. Standard History of the War. (In progress Newnes 1914. 1*s.* each vol.

—— War of the Nations: a History of the Great Europea Conflict. Newnes 1914. 5*s.* each vol.

War Magazine, The. A record of the events of the month. Published monthly. Alex. Thomson, 50, Parliament Street 1917... 3*d*. monthly.

Watson, H. W. History of the War. 7*d*: weekly.

Weltkrieg, Der, 1914-18, politisch, militärisch und wirthschaftlich dargestellt vom Reichsarchiv. Zehn Bände, mit vielen Karten. Berlin: Mittler 1922.

Wilson, P. W. The Unmaking of Europe. The first phase of the Hohenzollern War (Aug.-Dec. 1914). Nisbet. 3*s*. 6*d*.

Wilson, H. W., and Hammerton, J. A. (Edrs.). The Great War: the Standard History of the All-Europe Conflict. Amalgamated Press. 12*s*. and 14*s*. each vol.

Wyrall, E. Europe in Arms: a concise history of the Great European War. (In progress.) Glasgow: Wright 1915. 10*s*. each vol.

(4) *For the Young.*

Lowndes, Mrs. Belloc. Told in Gallant Deeds: a Child's History of the War. Nisbet 5*s*.

MacKenzie, D. A. Great Deeds of the Great War. (Book for Boys.) Blackie 1916. 2*s*. 6*d*.

O'Neill, Elizabeth. The War 1914-15: a History and Explanation for Boys and Girls. Illustrated. (In progress.) Jack. 1*s*. 6*d*. each.

—— The War 1915: a History and Explanation for Boys and Girls. A continuation of The War of 1914 and The War 1914-15. Jack. 1*s*. 6*d*.

—— The War 1914-16: a History and an Explanation for Boys and Girls. Jack 1916. 5*s*.

—— Battles for Peace. The story of the Great War told for children. With Maps. Hodder & Stoughton 1918. 3*s*. 6*d*.

Parrott, Sir Edward. Children's Story of the War. Illustrated. Nelson. 3*s*. 6*d*. each vol.

Whitworth, Geoffrey, and North, Stanley. The Child's A.B.C. of the War. Allen 1914. 1*s*.

Wilson, Richard. First Year of the Great War: the story of the first phase, told for boys and girls of the British Empire. Chambers 1916. 1*s*. 6*d*.

(5) *Miscellaneous.*

Agate, Capt. James E. L. of C. (Lines of Communication). Constable 1917. 6*s*.

Aghion, Max. A travers l'Europe sanglante. Flammarion 1916. 3 fr. 50.

Altrock, General C. von. Vom Sterben des deutschen offizierkorps. 2nd edn. Berlin: Mittler 1921. 12 mk.

Begbie, Harold. Behind the Firing Line. A picture of the workshops of destruction at the front. Newnes 1915. 1*s.*

Benoist, Charles. L'Europe en feu. Perrin 1918. 3 fr. 50.

Bethmann Hollweg, Th. von. Betrachtungen zum Weltkriege. Part I, Vor dem Kriege. Berlin: Hobbing 1919. Transl. into English under title Reflections on the World War. Butterworth 1919. 25*s.*

Blanchon, G. La Guerre nouvelle. Colin 1917. 3 fr. 50.

Borden, Rt. Hon. Sir R. L. The War and the Future. (A narrative compiled by P. Hurd from speeches delivered by Sir R. L. B. in Canada and elsewhere.) Hodder & Stoughton 1917. 2*s.*

Brandès, G. La guerre mondiale. (Articles publiés au cours de la guerre.)

Brownrigg, Rear-Admiral Sir D. Indiscretions of the Naval Censor: recollections of four and a half years' strenuous service. Cassell 1920. 12*s.* 6*d.*

Bruchmüller, Colonel. Die deutsche Artillerie in den Durchbruchschlachten des Weltkrieges. (Many plans.) Berlin: Mittler 1921. 28 mk. 50.

Cable, Boyd. Action Front. (A sequel to Between the Lines.) Smith, Elder 1916. 5*s.*

—— Between the Lines (cheap edn.). Murray 1917. 2*s.* 6*d.*

—— Grapes of Wrath (Describes a great Advance). Cassell 1917. 5*s.*

—— Airmen o' War. Murray 1918. 6*s.*

—— Front Lines. Lines from the Front, about the Front, and dedicated to the Front. Murray 1918. 6*s.*

Caine, Hall. The Drama of Three Hundred and Sixty-five Days. Short essays on the salient features and leading personalities of the war. Heinemann. 1*s.*

Calvo, G., and Brilla, J. La Guerra europea, 1914-...... Reconstitucion informativa de la Campaña y ens Derivaciones politicas y Sociales. Barcelona: Maucci.

Cammaerts, Emile. The Adoration of the Soldiers (Christmas in the Trenches). Illustrated by Louis Raemaekers. Longmans 1916. 21*s.*

Campbell, R. W. The Mixed Division. Hutchinson 1916. 6*s.*

Camps' Library (connected with the Supply of Literature to the Troops during the War), Report on the Work of the. [Cmd 174] H.M.S.O. 1919. 2*d.*

Canada in Khaki. A tribute to the officers and men now serving in the Canadian Expeditionary Force. Illustrated. Contributions by several writers. Pict. Newspaper Co. 1917. 12*s.* 6*d.*

Carrillo, E. Gomez. En el corazon de la tragedia. Madrid: sucesores de Hernado 1916. 3 fr. 50.

—— French transl. under title Au Cœur de la Tragédie. Berger-Levrault 1917. 3 fr. 50.

—— English transl. under title In the heart of the tragedy (War notes by a Spanish journalist). Hodder & Stoughton 1918. 2*s.* 6*d.*

Darde, Fernand. La bataille de l'air (Collection France). Berger-Levrault 1918. 90 c.

Dawson, Coningsby. The Glory of the Trenches (By the author of Khaki Courage). Lane 1918. 3*s.* 6*d.*

Dixon, Agnes M. The Canteeners (experiences in a French Red Cross Canteen). Murray 1917. 3*s.* 6*d.*

Doyle, Sir A. Conan. A visit to three Fronts, June 1916. Hodder & Stoughton 1916. 6*d.*

Erlande, Albert. En Campagne avec la Légion étrangère. Payot 1917. 3 fr. 50.

Everitt, N. British Secret Service during the Great War. Hutchinson 1920. 16*s.*

Falkenhayn, Gen. Erich von. Die oberste Heercsleitung 1914-16, in ihren wichtigsten Entschliessungen. Berlin: Mittler 1919. 21 mk. Transl. into English under title General Headquarters 1914-16, &c. Hutchinson 1919.

Faure, G. Passages de Guerre. The battlefields of France, Flanders and Italy. Perrin 1915. 2 fr. 50.

Felstead, S. T. German spies at bay, and record of the German espionage in Great Britain, 1914-18, compiled from official sources. (Illustrated.) 1920. 8*s.* 6*d.*

Ferrero, G. La Guerre européenne. Payot. 4 fr. 50.

Feyler, Colonel F. Le problème de la Guerre. (Problèmes de stratégie tirés de la guerre européenne.) Payot 1920. 12 fr.

Foerster, Wolfgang. Graf Schlieffen und der Weltkreig 1914-18 (by the Chief of the General Staff of the General Command). Three parts in one vol. (Maps.) Berlin, Mittler 1921. 60 mk.

Freeman, Lewis R. Many Fronts (experiences in France, Italy, Macedonia &c.). Murray 1918. 6*s.*

Freytag-Loringhoven, General Frhr. von. Heerführung im Weltkriege. Vergleichende Studien. 2 vols. (Maps and plans.) Berlin: Mittler 1920. 47 mk. 25.

The Last Lap. (Reviews of the Military position.) Reprinted from the Morning Post and other journals. Melrose 1917. 2*s.* 6*d.*

Gatti, A. La Guerre des Nations. Transl. of articles from the Corriere della Sera, giving a review of the War to the end of 1914. Berger-Levrault 1916. 3 fr. 50.

Gleichen, Major-General Lord E. The doings of the Fifteenth Infantry Brigade Aug. 1914 to Mar. 1915. Blackwood 1917. 5*s*.

Graham, Stephen. The Challenge of the dead: a vision of the war and the life of the common soldier in France, seen two years afterwards. Cassell 1921. 7*s*. 6*d*.

Graux, Lucien (Dr.). Les Fausses nouvelles de la Grande Guerre. (La déclaration de guerre; trente premiers jours du conflit—et de toute leur série de fausses nouvelles propagées surtout en Allemagne.) l'Edition française 1918. 6 fr.

Hamon, Agustin. Las lecciones de la guerra mundial. (Lectures given in London, on the conduct and character of the war, and its probable consequences). Valencia: Prometeo 1916. 2 pes.

Hay, Ian. Carrying on—After the first Hundred Thousand. Blackwood 1917. 6*s*.

Hervé, Gustav. Après la Marne. 2 fr. 50. La Muraille. 3 fr. 50. Jusqu'à la Victoire. 3 fr. 50. (Articles publiés dans la Guerre Sociale.) Bibliothèque des ouvrages documentaires' rue Alphonse-de-Neuville. 1918.

Hervier, Paul-Louis. Les Volontaires Américains dans les rangs Alliés. Nouvelle Revue 1918. 5 fr.

Hilditch, A. Neville. Battle sketches, 1914-15 (Cameroon, Liège, the Aisne, Ypres, Coronel, &c.). Oxford Univ. Press 1917. 2*s*. 6*d*.

Hoetzch, O. Der Krieg und die grosse Politik (to Nov. 1917). 3 vols. 1917-18. 52 mk. 80.

Howe, M. A. de Wolfe. The Harvard Volunteers in Europe. (Personal records of their experiences.) Harvard Univ. Press 1916. $1.00.

Hudson, Stephen. War-time Silhouettes. Allen & Unwin 1916. 3*s*. 6*d*.

Irwin, Will. Men, Women and War. Includes the Splendid Story of Ypres. By an American War Correspondent. Constable 1916. 1*s*.

Johnson, D. W. Battlefields of the World War. Western and Southern Fronts. Oxford Univ. Press 1921.

Johnston, Sir Harry. The Truth about the War: Lest we Forget. (A series of articles contributed to the Review of Reviews.) Review of Reviews 1916. 1*s*.

—— The Black Man's part in the War. Simpkin 1917. 1*s*. 6*d*.

Keating, Joseph, & Lavery, Felix. Irish Heroes in the War. Story of the Tyneside Irish Brigade. Everett 1917. 7*s*. 6*d*.

Knyvett, Captain R. H. Over there with the Australians (deals especially with the Scouts, in Egypt, Gallipoli and France). Hodder and Stoughton 1918. 6*s*.

Kennedy, J. M. How the Nations Waged War. A companion volume to How the War Began. (Daily Telegraph War Books.) Hodder & Stoughton 1914. 1*s.*

Kerr, S. Parnell. What the Irish Regiments have done. With a diary of a visit to the Front by J. E. Redmond, M.P. Fisher Unwin 1916. 1*s.* 6*d.*

Kuhl, General H. von. Der deutsche Generalstab in Vorbereitung und Durchführung des Weltkrieges. Berlin: Mittler 1920. 27 mk.

—— Französisch-englische Kritik des Weltkrieges. 2nd edn. Berlin: Mittler 1921. 12 mk. 50.

L'Almanach Hachette. By various Writers. 1916. Contains an illustrated Encyclopédie de la Guerre, and a summary history of the War, with maps, etc. Hachette 1916. 2 fr.

Langevin, le Capitaine. Cavaliers de France. Avec une Préface de Theodore Chège. (Premiers mois de la guerre.) L'Edition française 1917. 3 fr. 50.

Lavedan, Henri. Les grandes heures. 6 series (Aug. 1914- . . .) Perrin 1915-21. 3 fr. 50.

Lensch, Paul. Drei Jahre Weltrevolution. Berlin: Fischer 1918. 4 mk. English transl. under title Three years of World Revolution. 1918. 5*s.*

Loti, Pierre. L'Horreur allemande. (Articles, impressions et notes sur les à côtés de la guerre.) Calmann Levy 1918. 3 fr. 50.

—— The Trail of the Barbarians. Translated by F. Maddox Hueffer from L'Outrage des Barbares. Longmans 1918. 3*d.*

Louis, Paul. La Guerre d'Orient et la Crise Européenne. Alcan 1916. 1 fr. 25.

Ludendorff, Gen. Erich. Kriegführung und Politik. Berlin: Mittler 1921. 54 mk.

Lytton, Neville. The Press and the General Staff. Collins 1921. 15*s.*

MacDonagh, Michael. The Irish at the Front. With introduction by John Redmond, M.P. Hodder & Stoughton 1916.

Maclean, J. Kennedy, and Reddle, T. Wilkinson. The Y.M.C.A. with the Colours. Marshall Bros. 1915. 1*s.*

Malleterre, le Général. Études et impressions de guerre. (Monthly causeries on the war, by a wounded officer.) Tallandier 1917. 3 fr. 50.

Mentioned in Despatches. Parts. A record of officers and men so mentioned, and a list of honours and rewards conferred. Army & Navy Gazette. 1*s.* each

Military Correspondent of The Times, The. Essays and Criticisms. Constable. 4*s.* 6*d.*

Millerand, A. La Guerre libératrice. Colin 1918. 2 fr.

Millet, Philippe. En liaison avec les Anglais. (On the co-operation of the two armies and their characteristics.) Perrin 1916. 3 fr. 50.

—— Translated under title Comrades in Arms. Hodder & Stoughton 1916. 3*s*. 6*d*.

Milne, James. News from "Somewhere." Chapman & Hall 1915. 5*s*.

Moraht, E. Unser gemeinsamer Krieg. Frankfurt a M 1915. 1 mk.

Moser, Gen. Otto von. Feldzugsaufzeichungen (Campaign Notes), 1914-18 (on campaigns in France, Galicia, and Serbia, and behind the lines). Stuttgart: Belser 1920. 12 mk.

—— Kurzer strategischer Ueberblick über den Weltkreig, 1914-18. (Maps.) Berlin: Mittler 1920. 24 mk.

Nasmith, Col. G. G. On the Fringe of the Great Fight. Toronto: McClelland 1918. $1.50.

New Zealand at the Front. Written and illustrated by men of the New Zealand Division. Cassell 1917. 2*s*. 6*d*.

Northcliffe, Lord. At the War. (Reprint of letters in the Times.) Hodder & Stoughton 1916. Enlarged edn. 1917. 5*s*.

Puaux, René. Etudes de la guerre. First series. (12 "cahiers.") Payot 1917-18.

Record of the 5th Batt. Connaught Rangers, Aug. 19, 1914-Jan. 17, 1916. With maps. Printed for private circulation. Clarendon Press 1916.

Reinach, Joseph. Commentaires de Polybe. . . . . Series. Charpentier, Fasquelle 1915-19. 3 fr. 50-4 fr. 90.

Reports of the Joint War Committee and the Joint War Finance Committee of the British Red Cross Society and the Order of St. John of Jerusalem in England, on voluntary aid rendered to the Sick and Wounded at home and abroad and to the British Prisoners of War, 1914-19, with appendices. H.M.S.O. 1921. 12*s*. 6*d*.

Rothschild, Dr. H. de, and Gourraigne, L. G. (Edrs.). La Grande Guerre d'après la Presse Parisienne. Hachette 1915. 5 fr.

Ruffin, Henry. La Ruée: l'histoire d'une déception (événements de 1917 et 1918). 1918.

Schian, Prof. Martin. Die evangelische Kirche im Weltkriege. I. Die Arbeit der evangel. Kirche im Felde. Berlin: Mittler 1921. 48 mk.

Schwarte, Gen. M. (edr.) Die militärischen Lehren des grossen Krieges (unter Mitwirkung von 19 Fachmännern). Berlin: Mittler 1920. 38 mk.

Schwarte, Gen. M. (edr.). Die Technik im Weltkriege. Unter Mitwirkung von 45 technischen und militärischen Mitarbeitern. (Plates and Sketches.) Berlin: Mittler 1921. 38 mk.

Sugden, C. K. War Facts and Fgures. An Encyclopædia of useful information. L. B. Hill, 2, Langham Place. 6*d*.

Supplement to the London Gazette of April 1, 1915. List of awards of the Distinguished Service Medal to N.C.O.'s and Men, with accounts of the gallant deeds for which they were awarded. H.M.S.O. 4*d*.

Synton, Edward. Tunnellers All (doings of the Royal Engineers). Grant Richards 1918. 6*s*.

Trefusis, Arthur. The War in a New Light. Rider 1915. 6*d*.

Tuohy, Capt. F. The secret corps: a tale of Intelligence on all fronts. Murray 1920. 7*s*. 6*d*.

Turner, Major C. C. The struggle in the air, 1914-18. 1919. 16*s*.

War A.B.C. Froude & Hodder 1915. 1*s*.

War Book of Facts, The. A. W. Shaw. 2*s*. 6*d*.

War Chronicle. Soldiers' letters; Diary; Pictures of the War. (German publication, in English, giving facsimiles of the supposed Conventions between Belgium and Great Britain, with other documents, articles, etc.) November 1914. No publisher or price.

War, The, from this Side. (Editorials from the North American.) Philadelphia: Lippincott 1916.

Wells, H. G. The War of the Future: Italy, France and Britain at war. (Impressions of the Italian and western fronts, with papers on How people think about the war.) Cassell 1917. 6*s*.

Weston, Lt.-Col., D.S.O. Three years with the New Zealanders. Maps and illustrations. Skeffington 1918. 6*s*. 9*d*.

Wilkinson, Spenser. August, 1914. Milford. 1*s*.

Wright, Capt. Peter. At the Supreme War Council. Eveleigh Nash. 1921. 7*s*. 6*d*.

Yapp, Sir Arthur K. The Romance of the Red Triangle: the story of . . . the service rendered by the Y.M.C.A. to the soldiers and sailors of the British Empire. Hodder & Stoughton 1918. 6*s*.

Year, 1914, The, illustrated. A record of notable achievements and events. (Annual publication, for 1908, and later years.) Headley 1914-19. 5*s*. annually.

Zurlinden, S. Der Weltkrieg. Vorläufige Orientirung von einem schweizerischen Standpunkt aus. Zürich: Füssli 1917.

B.—Special.

(1) *Western Front.*

(*a*) Despatches.

French, Sir John. Despatches: official records of the great battles of Mons, the Marne, and the Aisne, as told in his despatches by Field-Marshal Sir John French to Field-Marshal Lord Kitchener. Illustrated by maps. The Graphic 1914. 6*d*.

—— Despatches: Mons, the Marne, the Aisne, Flanders. With a map. Chapman & Hall 1914. 1*s*.

—— Sir John French's despatches (second series): Official story of the battle around Ypres, Armentières, etc., and the defence of Antwerp. (Graphic Special, No. 2.) The Graphic 1914. 6*d*.

French, Lord. Complete Despatches of Lord French, from Mons to Loos), including the names of all those officially mentioned. (Maps and portraits.) Chapman & Hall 1917. 21*s*.

Haig, Sir Douglas. Despatches, Dec. 1915—April 1919. Edited by Lieut.-Col. J. H. Goraston. 2 vols. (one of maps). Dent 1919. 42*s*.

L'Action de l'armée belge pour la défense du pays et le respect de sa neutralité. Rapport du Commandement de l'Armée (period, July 31—Dec. 31, 1914). Official publication, with maps. Collingridge 1915. 1*s*.

(*b*) Narratives.

(1) *English.*

Adam, G. Behind the Scenes at the Front. By the Paris Correspondent of the Times. Chatto. 6*s*.

Adams, Bernard. Nothing of Importance. A Record of 8 months at the front with a Welsh Battalion, Oct. 1915—June 1916. Methuen 1917. 6*s*.

Aitken, Sir Max, M.P. [Beaverbrook, Lord.] Canada in Flanders. First volume of the official history of the Canadian Force. Hodder & Stoughton 1916. 1*s*. Vol. II, 1917, 1*s*. 3*d*. *See also* Roberts, Major C. G. D.

Aldrich, Mildred. On the edge of the war-zone. (By the author of A hilltop on the Marne.) Sept. 1914—April 1917. Boston: Small, Maynard, 1917. $1.25. Constable 1918. 5*s*.

Alexander, Major H. M. On Two Fronts. Adventures of an Indian Mule Corps in France and Gallipoli. Heinemann 1917. 3*s*. 6*d*.

Allen, H. Warner. The Unbroken Line: Along the French Trenches from Switzerland to the North Sea. Smith, Elder, 1916. 6*s*.

Ashmead Bartlett, E. From the Somme to the Rhine. (Last Phase of the War.) Lane 1921. 7*s*. 6*d*.

Ashton, H., War Correspondent of the Daily News. First from the Front. Pearson. 2*s*. 6*d*.

Aston, Major-Gen. Sir G. The Triangle of Terror in Belgium. (Germany's strategical plan and the atrocities connected with it.) Murray 1918. 2*s*. 6*d*.

Ayscough, Rev. John. French Windows. Experiences of a chaplain at the front. (Papers contributed to The Month.) Arnold 1917. 5*s*.

Bartlett, Vernon. Mud and Khaki. Sketches from Flanders and France. Simpkin, Marshall, 1917. 3*s*. 6*d*.

Beadnell, Fleet Surgeon C. Marsh, R.N. A Naval Medical Officer's impressions of a visit to the Trenches. Bale & Danielssohn 1917.

Beaverbrook, Lord. *See* Aitken, Sir Max.

Bennett, Arnold. Over there: War scenes on the Western Front. Methuen 1915. 1*s*.

Bevan, Tom. With Haig at the Front. Collins' Clear-Type Press 1916. 5*s*.

Bolwell, F. A. With a Reservist in France. Maps. (Engagements in which the 1st Div. 1st Corps took part.) Routledge 1917. 2*s*. 6*d*.

Brittain, H. E. To Verdun from the Somme: an Anglo-American Glympse of the Great Advance. With an Introduction by the Hon. James M. Beck. Lane 1916. 2*s*. 6*d*.

Brown, Heywood. The A.E.F. With Pershing's Army in France. Appleton 1918. $1.50.

Brownlow, Capt. C. A. L. The breaking of the storm. (Impressions of an artillery officer in the early months of the war.) Methuen 1918. 6*s*.

Buchan, John. The Battle of the Somme: First Phase. Illustrated. Nelson 1916. 1*s*.

Burke, Kathleen. The White Road to Verdun. (Illustrated.) Hodder & Stoughton 1916. 1*s*. 3*d*.

Campbell, Gerald. From Verdun to the Vosges. (By a Special Correspondent of the Times.) 2nd edn. Arnold 1916. 10*s*. 6*d*.

Casualty (pseud.). Contemptible. (The early actions of the Expeditionary Force.) Heinemann 1916. 3*s*. 6*d*.

"Chaplain, A." Vermelles: Notes of the Western Front, with Introductory Chapter by the Bishop of Glasgow. The Scottish Chronicle 1918. 2*s*.

Coleman, Frederic. With Cavalry in 1915. The British Trooper in the Trench Line, through the Second Battle of Ypres. Illustrated. Sampson Low 1916. 6*s*.

Coleman, Frederic. With Cavalry. Illustrated. Sampson Low Marston 1917. 3*s.* 6*d.*

—— From Mons to Ypres with French: a personal narrative. By an American correspondent. Illustrated. Sampson Low 1916. 6*s.*

Corbett-Smith, Major A. The Retreat from Mons. Cassell 1916. 3*s.* 6*d.*

—— The Marne—and after. (The British Army in the early months of the war.) Cassell 1917. 5*s.*

Curry, F. C. From the St. Lawrence to the Yser: with the 1st Canadian Brigade. With photographs. Smith, Elder, 1916. 3*s.* 6*d.*

Dane, Edmund. Battle of the Rivers. (Daily Telegraph War Books.) 1915. 1*s.*

—— Hacking through Belgium. (Daily Telegraph War Books.) Hodder & Stoughton 1914. 1*s.*

—— Battle in Flanders: from Ypres to Neuve Chapelle. (Daily Telegraph War Books.) 1915. 1*s.*

Davis, H. W. C. The Battle of Ypres—Armentières. (O.P.) Oxford Univ. Press. 6*d.*

—— The Battles of the Marne and Aisne. (O.P.) Oxford Univ. Press. 4*d.*

—— The Retreat from Mons. (O.P.) Oxford Univ. Press. 3*d.*

Davis, R. H. With the French in France and Salonika. (Illustrated.) Duckworth 1916. 3*s.* 6*d.*

Dawson, Capt. A. J. Somme battle stories. Illustrated by Capt. Bairnsfather. Hodder & Stoughton 1916. 2*s.* 6*d.*

—— For France (C'est pour la France). English impressions of the French front. Illustrated by Capt. Bairnsfather. Hodder 1917. 5*s.*

Day, Susanne R. Round about Bar-le-Duc (an account of a woman's twenty months in the war zone). Skeffington 1918. 6*s.*

De Flemalle, Capt. G. de L. Fighting with King Albert. Includes an account of Belgium and its forces before the war Hodder & Stoughton. 1*s.*

Doyle, Sir A. Conan. The British Campaigns in France and Flanders. 6 vols. Hodder & Stoughton. 1916-20. 7*s.* 6*d.* each.

Duncan, Rev. J., C.F. With the C.L.B. Battalion in France (the doings of the Churchman's Battn.—the men enlisted from the Church Lads' Brigade). Skeffington 1916. 2*s.* 6*d.*

Durell, Rev. J. C. V. Whizzbangs and Woodbines. Tales from the Western Front. Hodder & Stoughton 1918. 3*s.* 6*d.*

Eye-Witness's Narrative of the War. Collection of accounts, compiled by Eye-Witness, of the operations in France and Flanders, Sept. 1914—March 1915. Arnold. 1*s*.

Fox, Frank. The Battles of the Ridges. Arras-Messines. March-June 1917. Illustrated. Pearson 1918. 1*s*.

French, Field-Marshal Lord. 1914. With preface by Marshal Foch. Constable 1919. 21*s*.

Frightfulness in retreat. Hodder 1917. 3*d*.

Germans, The, at Louvain. (By a member of the University.) Hodder & Stoughton 1916. 3*d*.

Gibbs, Philip. The Soul of the War. Descriptive of events in France and Flanders. Heinemann. 7*s*. 6*d*.

—— The Battles of the Somme. Heinemann 1916. 6*s*.

—— From Bapaume to Passchendaele (by the author of The Soul of the War). Heinemann 1918. 6*s*.

—— Open Warfare. From Cambrai to the Marne. Heinemann 1918. 7*s*. 6*d*.

Gordon, Capt. G. S. Mons and the Retreat. Preface by Field-Marshal Lord French. Constable 1918. 1*s*. 6*d*.

Graves, Arnold T. The Turn of the Tide. Continuation of the Long Retreat. Murray 1916. 1*s*.

Great Advance, The. Tales from the Somme battlefield told by wounded officers and men on their arrival from the Front, and published by permission. Cassell 1916. 1*s*.

Grey, W. E. With the French Eastern Army. Hodder & Stoughton. 1*s*.

Hamelius, Prof. Paul. The Siege of Liège. T. Werner Laurie. 1*s*.

Hamilton, Cicely. Senlis (an account of the German occupation and ravage of the town). Illustrated. Collins 1917. 3*s*. 6*d*.

Hamilton, Lord Ernest. The First Seven Divisions. A detailed account of the fighting from Mons to Ypres. Hurst & Blackett 1916. 6*s*.

Hammerton, J. A. Wrack of War (battlefields of France and Flanders). With 8 drawings by C. M. Sheldon. Murray 1918. 7*s*. 6*d*.

Hay, Ian. The First Hundred Thousand. By "The Junior Sub." Blackwood 1915. 6*s*.

Hayens, Herbert. Midst Shot and Shell in Flanders (the tale of a young Canadian). Collins' Press 1916. 3*s*. 6*d*.

Hilditch, A. N. The Stand of Liège. Maps. (O.P.) Oxford Univ. Press. 4*d*.

—— Troyon. An Engagement in the Battle of the Aisne. (O.P.) Oxford Univ. Press. 2*d*.

Huard, Frances Wilson. My Home in the Field of Honour (Experiences of an American lady in a chateau on the Marne). Hodder & Stoughton 1916.

Hurd, Percy. The Fighting Territorials. The London Territorials on the Western Front. Vol. I, 1915; Vol. II, 1916. Country Life Office 1915. 1*s*.

Ingpen, Roger. The Fighting Retreat to Paris. (Daily Telegraph War Books.) Hodder & Stoughton 1914. 1s.

Kennedy, J. M. The Campaign round Liège. Hodder & Stoughton. 1*s*.

Kennedy, Rev. L. J. With the Immortal Seventh Division. The doings of the Division from it's landing at Zeebrugge to Oct. 31, 1914, by an Army Chaplain. Hodder & Stoughton 1915. 2*s*. 6*d*.

Liddell, R. Scotland. The Track of the War. Relates the story of the German invasion of Belgium from personal observation. Maps and illustrations. Simpkin, Marshall. 6*s*.

Macdonagh, Michael. The Irish on the Somme. With an Introduction by John Redmond, M.P. Hodder & Stoughton 1917. 2*s*.

MacDonald, M. Under the French Flag. A Britisher in the French Army. Scott 1916. 3*s*. 6*d*.

MacGill, Patrick. The Great Push (on the Battle of Loos, by a stretcher-bearer). Jenkins 1916. 2*s*. 6*d*.

—— The Red Horizon. Experiences of the London Irish on the Western Front in 1915. Jenkins 1916. 5*s*.

—— The Diggers. The Australians in France. With introduction by the Rt. Hon. W. M. Hughes. Jenkins 1919. 2*s*. 6*d*.

Macintosh, J. C. Men and Tanks. Lane 1920. 5*s*.

McKenzie, F. A. Americans at the Front. Illustrated. Hodder & Stoughton 1917. 2*d*.

—— Through the Hindenburg Line. Crowning days on the Western Front. (By a Canadian War Correspondent.) Hodder & Stoughton 1918. 7*s*.

Maclean, Rev. A. M., C.M.G. With the Gordons at Ypres. Paisley: Gardner 1916. 1*s*.

McNair, Wilson. Blood and Iron. Connected view of the first nine months of the Western campaign. Seeley 1916. 6*s*.

Malcolm, Ian, M.P. War Pictures behind the Lines. With illustrations. Smith, Elder 1915. 6*s*.

Marcosson, I. S. America's Miracle in France (illustrated). Lane 1919. 7*s*. 6*d*.

Masefield, John. The Old Front Line, or The Beginning of the Battle of the Somme. Heinemann 1917. 2*s*. 6*d*.

Maurice, Major-General Sir F. Forty Days in 1914 (a study of German strategy during the retreat from Mons). Constable 1919. 9*s*.

—— The Last Four Months: the End of the War in the West. Two maps. Cassell 1919. 10*s*. 6*d*.

Merewether, Lieut.-Col. J. W. B., and Smith, Sir Frederick E. The Indian Corps in France. Murray 1917. 10*s*. 6*d*.

Middleton, Edgar C. The Way of the Air. Incidents in the Air Service in the North of France. Heinemann 1917. 2*s*. 6*d*.

Monash, Lieut.-General Sir J. Australian Victories in France, 1918 (illustrated). Hutchinson 1920. 24*s*.

Newton, W. Douglas. Undying Story: the work of the British Expeditionary Force on the Continent, from Mons, Aug. 23, 1914, to Ypres, Nov. 15, 1914. Jarrold 1915. 6*s*.

On the Road from Mons with an Army Service Corps Train. By its Commander. Hurst & Blackett 1916. 2*s*. 6*d*.

Operations of the II American Corps in the Somme Offensive, Aug. 8-Nov. 11, 1918. Prepared by the Historical Branch, War Plans Division, General Staff. 1921. 15 c.

Oxenham, John. High Altars. Reminiscences of the battle-fields of France and Flanders. Methuen 1918. 1*s*. 3*d*.

Palmer, Frederick. With the New Army on the Somme. My second year of the war. Murray 1917. 6*s*.

—— America in France (history of the A.E.F., May 1917-Sept. 1918). Dodd, Mead & Co. 1918. $1.75.

Perkins, Rev. A. M. Between Battles, at a base in France. Fisher Unwin 1918. 2*s*. 6*d*.

Perris, G. H. The Campaign of 1914 in France and Belgium. Maps and illustrations. Hodder & Stoughton. 10*s*. 6*d*.

Pollard, Capt. Hugh. The Story of Ypres. Macbride 1917. 1*s*.

Powell, E. A. Fighting in Flanders. Illustrated. Heinemann 1915. 3*s*. 6*d*.

—— Vive la France. The Western Front, 1915-16. Illustrated. Heinemann 1916. 3*s*. 6*d*.

Pym, Rev. T. W., and Gordon, Rev. Geoffrey. Papers from Picardy. Constable 1917. 4*s*. 6*d*.

Rae, Herbert. Maple Leaves in Flanders fields (experiences of the first Canadian contingent). Martin Secker 1916. 5*s*.

Rhys, Ernest (edr.). The Roar of Battle: scenes and episodes of war. With a special chapter on the siege of Liège, 1914. Jarrold 1914. 1*s*.

Rickard, Mrs. Victor. The Story of the Munsters at Etreux, Festubert, Rue du Bois, and Hulluch. With introduction by Lord Dunraven. Hodder & Stoughton 1918. 2*s*. 6*d*.

Roberts, Major C. G. D. Canada in Flanders. Official story of the Canadian Expeditionary Force. Vol. III. With introduction by Lord Beaverbrook. Maps. Hodder & Stoughton 1918. 2*s*.

Robinson, H. Perry. The Turning-point (Despatches on the Battle of the Somme). By the Special Correspondent of The Times. Illustrated. Heinemann 1917. 6*s*.

Ross, Capt. R. B. The Fifty-first in France. Illustrated. Hodder & Stoughton 1918. 10*s*. 6*d*.

Ruffin, Henry, & Tudesq, André. Brother Tommy. The British Offensive on the Western Front, Jan. to June, 1917. Fisher Unwin 1918. 1*s*. 3*d*.

Sapper (pseud.). No Man's Land. Hodder & Stoughton 1917. 5*s*.

Sarolea, Dr. Charles. How Belgium Saved Europe. Heinemann. 2*s*.

Silver Lining, A: The Glasgow Highlanders in France. By D.R.M. Simpkin, Marshall 1916.

Sparrow, W. S. The Fifth Army in March, 1918. With introduction by Gen. Sir H. Gough. Maps. Lane 1920. 21*s*.

Stewart, Col. H. The New Zealand Division, 1916-19. A popular history based on official records. Auckland: Whitcombe 1921. 6*s*.

Thomas, W. Beach. With the British on the Somme. By an authorised correspondent. Methuen 1917. 6*s*.

Toynbee, Arnold J. The German Terror in France. With maps and illustrations. Hodder & Stoughton 1917. 1*s*.

Tucker, A. B. The Battle Glory of Canada: being the story of the Canadians at the Front, including the Battle of Ypres. Cassell. 1*s*.

Vallotton, Benjamin. In the Land of Death. Impressions of the French front, and the destruction wrought by the Germans. Cassell 1917. 3*d*.

Warr, C. L. Echoes of Flanders. Stories of the Scottish regiments in the War. Simpkin, Marshall 1916. 5*s*.

Whitton, Major F. E. The Marne Campaign. Constable 1917. 10*s*. 6*d*.

Wilson, Beckles. In the Ypres Salient. The story of a fortnight's Canadian fighting. June 2-16, 1916. Simpkin, Marshall 1916.

Young, Geoffrey W. Winthrop. From the Trenches: Louvain to the Aisne. Fisher Unwin 1914. 2*s*.

Zerta, Gabrielle & Marguerite. Six Women and the Invasion. Preface by Mrs. Humphry Ward. What the French suffered in the occupied territories. Macmillan 1917. 6*s*.

(2) *French.*

Allier, Raoul. Les Allemands à Saint-Dié (27 août-10 septembre 1914). Avec 15 cartes, plans et fac-similés. Payot 1918. 4 fr. 50.

Angle, B. Petits aspects sentimentaux du front anglais. Avec une gravure au burin. Dorbon 1918. 6 fr.

Au Front de France. Preface by Capt. A. J. Dawson. Armand Colin 1916. 3 fr. 50.

Babin, Gustave. La Bataille de la Marne (6-12 Sept. 1914). Maps. Plon-Nourrit. 3 fr. 50.

Barbusse, Henri. Le Feu. Journal d'un escouade. Flammarion 1916. 3 fr. 50. Transl. under title Under Fire. Dalton 1917. $1.50.

Barzini, L. En Belgique, et en France (1915). Suite des Scènes de la Grande Guerre. Traduction de Jacques Mesnil. Payot 1916. 3 fr. 50.

Basly, Emile. Le Martyre de Lens (a record of the German occupation of the town). Plon-Nourrit 1918. 4 fr. 50.

Baulu, Marguerite (Mme). La Bataille de l'Yser. Perrin 1918. 3 fr. 50.

Benjamin, René. Sous le Ciel de France. Fayard 1917. 3 fr. 50.

Berger, Marcel. The Ordeal by Fire, by a Sergeant in the French Army. Translated by Mrs. C. Curtis. Putnam 1917.

Bertrand, Capt. A. La Victoire de Lorraine (Aug. 24—Sept. 12, 1914). Maps and plans. Berger-Levrault 1917. 2 fr. 50.

Bidon, Henry. Verdun (nombreuses cartes). Bossard 1917. 6 fr.

Bocquet, Léon, and Hosten, Ernest. L'Agonie de Dixmude. Episodes de la bataille de l'Yser. Preface by Chas. le Goffic. Illustrated. Tallandier 1916. 3 fr. 50.

—— Un fragment de l'Epopée Sénégalaise. Van Oest 1918. 2 fr.

Bordeaux, Henri. Les derniers jours du fort de Vaux, et l'héroïque résistance de Verdun. Plon 1916. 3 fr. 50.

—— English transl. under title The Last Days of Fort Vaux. Nelson 1917. 3*s.* 6*d.*

—— Les Captifs Délivrés (Douaumont-Vaux). The recapture of the forts of Verdun. Plon-Nourrit 1917. 4 fr.

Boubée, l'Abbé Joseph. Parmi les blessés allemands. (Among the wounded in Belgium in the first five months of war.) Plon-Nourrit 1916. 3 fr. 50.

Breton, Comm. Willy. Un régiment belge en campagne (The 2nd Chasseurs à pied, Aug. 1914-Jan. 1915). Berger-Levrault 1916. 1 fr. 50.

Brinon, Ferd. de. En guerre. (A succinct account of the Battle of the Marne and its immediate consequences, by the Editor of the Débats.) Blond et Gay 1916. 60 c.

Buffin, le Baron C. La Belgique héroïque et vaillante. Récits de combattants. Plon-Nourrit. 3 fr. 50.

Caix de Saint-Aymour, le Comte de. Guerre de 1914. La marche sur Paris de l'aile droite allemande. Ses derniers combats, 26 août-sept. 4, 1914. (3 maps.) Lavauzelle 1916. 2 fr.

—— Autour de Noyon: Sur les traces des Barbares. Illustré et accompagné de 2 cartes. Boyvin 1917. 15 fr.

Calippe, Chas. La guerre en Picardie (during Aug.-Oct. 1914). Illustrated. Paris: Téqui 1916. 3 fr. 50.

—— La Somme sous l'occupation allemande (27 août 1914-19 mars 1917). 2nd vol. Téqui 1918. 3 fr. 50.

Canonge, le général F. Guerre de 1914. La Bataille de la Marne, avec 2 cartes (étude des deux armées opposées et des hommes). Fournier 1918. 3 fr.

Carrillo, Gomez. Parmi les ruines. Observations from visits to Reims, Senlis and other French towns damaged or destroyed by the Germans. Translated from the Spanish. Berger-Levrault. 3 fr. 50.

—— —— English transl. under title Among the Ruins. Heinemann. 3*s*. 6*d*.

Chambrun, Lieut.-Col. de, and Marenches, Cne de. L Armée américaine dans le conflit européen. Payot 1921. 10 fr.

Christian-Frogé, R. Morhange et les Marsouins en Lorraine. With a Preface by J. H. Rosny. Illustrations and maps. Berger-Levrault 1916. 3 fr. 50.

Colin, Alice. The Ransacking of Dinant, Aug. 1914. Translated from the French. Brussels: Imprimerie Financière 1918. 2*s*.

Courrière, P. H. Comment fut sauvé Paris. With preface by General Maunoury. Perrin 1918. 4 fr. 50.

—— Histoire héroïque de la Grande Guerre. Avant les hostilités. En Alsace (août 1914). Fasc. I, avec grav. et cartes. Editions et Librairie 1917. 2 fr.

Dauzet, Pierre. (1) De Liège à la Marne. (2) La Bataille de Flandres, Oct. 16-Nov. 15, 1914. Lavanzelle 1917. 2 fr. 50.

Deguise, Lieut.-Gen. La défense de la position fortifiée d'Anvers en 1914 (20 août-10 oct.). Berger-Levrault 1921. 25 fr.

Delvert, Capitaine. Histoire d'une Campagne. (Diary Nov. 1915-April 21, 1916, giving the story of Verdun, by a defender of the Fort de Vaux.) Berger-Levrault 1918. 4 fr. 50.

Demblon, C. La Guerre à Liège. The siege and afterwards, during August, 1914. Libr. anglo-française. 2 fr. 50.

Des Ombiaux, Maurice. La résistance de la Belgique envahie. Bloud et Gay 1916. 3 fr. 50.

Des Touches, René. Pages de gloire et de misère (la mobilisation, la Marne, les villages mutilés, etc.). de Boccard 1917. 3 fr. 50.

D'Estre, C. H. L'Enigme de Verdun. Essai sur les causes et la genèse de la bataille. Chapelot 1917. 1 fr.

—— D'Oran à Arras (1914-15). Impressions de guerre d'un officier d'Afrique. Plon-Nourrit 1916. 3 fr. 50.

Dévastations allemandes dans les départements envahis, mars-avril 1917 (documents réunis par M. Henri Welschenger). Illustrations. Pages d'histoire 1914-1917, No. 132. Berger-Levrault 1917. 1 fr. 25.

D'Hartoy, Maurice. Au Front. Préface par le Marquis de Ségur. Perrin 1916. 3 fr. 50.

Dieterlen, J. Le Bois le Prêtre. (The fighting there, Oct. 1914-April 1915.) Hachette 1917. 3 fr. 50.

Dubail, Général. Quatre années de Commandement 1914-18. Journal de Campagne. Vol. III, Aug. 1915-March 1918. (Vols. I and II, 1920-21.) Fournier, 1920-21. 24 fr. each.

Dubrelle, Paul. Mon Régiment, dans la fournaise de Verdun, dans la bataille de la Somme: impressions de guerre d'un prêtre soldat. Plon-Nourrit 1917. 4 fr.

Dugard, H. La Bataille de Verdun, 21 février-7 mai 1916. Perrin 1916.

—— —— Translated under title The Battle of Verdun. Illustrated. Hutchinson 1916. 6*s*.

Dupont, Marcel. En Campagne. L'Attente; impressions d'un officier de légère (1914-15-16). Plon-Nourrit 1918. 4 fr. 50.

Duwez, M. Jusqu'à l'Yser (août 1914-novembre 1915). Deauville 1917.

Engerand, Fernand. Le Secret de la Frontière Charleroi. (Maps.) Bossard 1918. 15 fr.

Fabrequettes, P. Les batailles de la Marne (1914). Reprinted from the Grande Revue. With map. Didier 1915. 1 fr. 50.

Fage, André. Lille sous la griffe allemande. Avec 8 gravures (du 24 août 1914 jusqu'au 1er decembre 1915). Perrin 1917. 3 fr. 50.

Fiolle, P. La Marsouille. (A regiment of marines in the early days of the war.) Payot 1917. 3 fr. 50.

Fleury-Lamure. Charleroi: Notes et impressions. An eye-witness's account of the Battle of the Sambre, Aug. 1914. By a war correspondent of The Times. Maps. Berger-Levrault 1916. 1 fr. 50.

Fribourg, André. Les martyrs d'Alsace et de Lorraine d'après les débats des conseils de guerre allemands. (German atrocities in Alsace-Lorraine; an account based on their own reports.) Plon 1916. 2 fr.

Galopin, F.-A. Guerre de 1914: une Trésorerie en campagne: de la mobilisation à la victoire de la Marne. Libràiries Imprimeries 1916.

Gattier-Boissière, Jean. En rase campagne 1914. Un hiver à Souchez 1915-16. Illustrated. Berger-Levrault 1917. 3 fr. 60.

Genevoix, Maurice. Nuits de Guerre. (Narrative of personal experiences early in the war.) Flammarion 1917. 3 fr. 50.

—— Sous Verdun, août-octobre 1914. (By a young French lieutenant.) Hachette 1916. 3 fr. 50.

—— —— Translated under title 'Neath Verdun. With introduction by Ernest Lavisse. Hutchinson 1916.

Ginisty, P., and Alexandre, A. Le Livre du Souvenir: Guide du Voyageur dans la France envahie en 1914. Vol I, La Bataille de la Marne (histoire détaillée et topographique). Flammarion 1917. 5 fr.

Giraudoux, Jean. Retour d'Alsace. (The early days of the war.) Emile Paul 1916. 2 fr.

Gobart, Alb. de. La Campagne de 1914. Paris Télégrammes, 156 rue Montmartre. 2 fr.

Gouvieux, M. Notes d'un officier observateur en avion (premiers jours de la lutte aux batailles de l'Yser et en Artois, Nov. 1914). Lafette 1917. 3 fr. 50.

Guerre, La, en Artois. Paroles épiscopales, documents, récits. Publié sous la direction de Mgr. Lobbedey, évêque d'Arras. Téqui 1916. 3 fr. 50.

Guerre, La, en Champagne, au diocèse de Châlons (a collection of signed statements). Publié sous la direction de Mgr. Tissier, évêque de Châlons. Téqui 1916. 3 fr. 50.

Guides Michelin pour la visite des champs de bataille. Tome I, L'Ourcq. Tome II, Marais de Saint-Gond, Coulommiers, Provins, Sézanne. Illustré et avec des cartes et des plans. Berger-Levrault 1918. 3 fr. 50.

Hanotaux, G. l'Enigme de Charleroi. Edition française illustré 1917. 1 fr. 50.

Hardie, Capt. Martin. Boulogne; a Base in France. 32 drawings. Black 1918. 5*s*.

Henriot, Emile. La bataille de la Marne. I. Les combats de l'Ourcq. Notice historique. (Maps and plans.) Editions d'art et histoire 1916.

Herscher, Lieut. E. Quelques images de la Guerre. (Battles of the Woëvrez (1915) and the later operations round Verdun). Berger-Levrault 1917. 3 fr. 50.

Hourticq, Louis. Récits et réflexions d'un combattant. Aisne, Champagne, Verdun 1915-1917. Hachette 1918. 3 fr. 50.

Jollivet, Gaston. L'Epopeé de Verdun, 1916. Préface du Lieutenant-Colonel Rousset. Hachette 1917. 3 fr. 50.

Jubert, Raymond. Verdun; mars-avril-mai, 1916. Preface by Paul Bourget. Payot. 4 fr. 50.

Kadoré, P. de. Mon groupe d'autos-canons (la bataille de la Marne). Hachette 1917. 3 fr. 50.

Laflotte, D. Bertrand de. Dans Les Flandres. Preface par M. Henri Robert. (Narrative of Red Cross Service in Flanders.) Bloud et Gay 1916.

Lafont, Bernard. Au Ciel de Verdun. Berger-Levrault 1918. 4 fr. 50.

Lanrézac, le Général. Le plan de campagne français et le premier mois de guerre. Payot 1920. 7 fr. 50.

Le Bail, G. (Député). La Brigade des Jean-le-Gouin; histoire documentaire et anecdotique des fusiliers marins de Dixmude. Avec deux cartes et neuf hors-texte. Perrin 1917. 3 fr. 50.

Le Goffic, Charles. Dixmude. Describes the resistance of the Belgian troops and the French Fusiliers Marins. Plon. 3 fr.

—— —— Translated under title Dixmude. The epic of the French Marines (Oct. 17-Nov. 10, 1914). Heinemann 1916. 3*s*. 6*d*.

—— Les Marais de Saint-Gond (dealing with some of the conflicts grouped under the general term of The Battle of the Marne). Plon-Nourrit 1917. 3 fr. 50.

—— —— English transl. under title General Foch at the Marne. Dent 1918. 4*s*. 6*d*.

—— Steenstraete. Un deuxième chapitre de l'histoire des Fusiliers Marins (10 novembre 1914-20 janvier 1915). Cartes et gravures. Plon-Nourrit 1918. 4 fr.

Léry, Jean. La Bataille dans la forêt (Argonne, sept. 1915): impressions d'un téncoin. Hachette 1916. 2 fr.

Libermann, Henri. l'Infanterie héroïque et douloureuse. Thiaumont (juillet-août 1916), Moronvilliers (mars-avril 1917). Perrin 1918. 3 fr. 50.

L'Offensive du 16 avril 1917. Ligue des Droits de l'homme 1918. 50 *c*.

MacOrlan, Pierre. Les Bourreurs de Crâne. Renaissance du Libre 1917. 3 fr. 50.

—— Les Poissons Morts. Illustrations de Gus Bofa. Payot 1917. 3 fr. 50.

Madelin, L. La Victoire de la Marne. Maps. Plon 1917. 2 fr.

—— La Mêlée des Flandres. (Early battles of Ypres and on the Yser.) Plon-Nourrit 1918. 3 fr. 50.

Malleterre, le Général. De la Marne à l'Yser: la victoire des forces morales. Chapelot 1915. 2 fr.

—— Les Campagnes de 1915. Berger-Levrault 1918. 4 fr.

Malo, Henri. Le drame de Flandres. Un an de guerre: Aug. 1914-Aug. 1915. Illustrated. Perrin 1915. 3 fr. 50.

Marabini, Capitaine. Les Garibaldiens de l'Argonne. Payot 1917. 3 fr. 50.

Marbeau, Emmanuel (Bishop of Meaux). Avant, pendant, et après la Bataille de la Marne. Extracts from the Bishop's diary. Illustrated. La Revue Hebdomadaire. 50 c.

Masson, A. L'Invasion des Barbares 1914-1916. 3 vols. Fontemoing 1916. 3 fr. 50 each vol.

Masson, F. A l'arrière, août 1914-août 1915. Ollendorff 1916.

Mazé, Jules. Les Champs de bataille de l'Épopée. Première partie. La Marne. De Nanteuil-le-Haudouin à Sommesous. Vermot 1917. 3 fr. 50.

Mercier, René. Nancy sauvée (les heures d'angoisse de 1914). Berger-Levrault 1918. 3 fr. 50.

Mieille, Paul. Le Rôle du Général Foch à la Marne. Tarbes: Croharé 1917. 1 fr.

Mokveld, L. L'Invasion de la Belgique: témoignage d'un neutre. trad. du hollandais. Avec 1 grav. Bloud et Gay 1916. 3 fr. 50.

Mourey, Gabriel. La Guerre devant le Palais. (M. Mourey was in charge of the Palace of Compiègne during the German occupation.) Ollendorff. 2 fr.

Mugnier, G. Aux Paysans du Front! Avec une Lettre-Préface de M. François Veuillot. Bloud et Gay 1918. 2 fr. 50.

Nicot, A. La Grande Guerre. Vol III, Des Flandres à Verdun. Tours: Marne 1916.

Nohain, Fr., and Delay, Paul. Paris menacé, Paris sauvé. Extraits de l'Histoire anecdotique de la guerre. Selected and edited by G. H. Clarke. Edn. autorisée. Oxford Univ. Press 1917. 6*d*.

Nothomb, Pierre. L'Yser: Les villes saintes: La victoire: La bataille d'été. Perrin 1915. 3 fr. 50.

Palat, Gen. (Pierre Lehautcourt). La Grande Guerre sur le Front Occidental. 7 vols. (to Oct. 15, 1914). Chapelot 1917-21. Various prices.

Pastre, J.-L. Gaston. Trois ans de Front. Belgique, Aisne et Champagne, Verdun, Argonne, Lorraine. Berger-Levrault 1918. 3 fr. 50.

Péchenard, Mgr. P.-L. La Grande Guerre. Le Martyre de Soissons, août 1914-juillet 1918. Beauchesne 1918. 7 fr. 50.

Péricard, Lieut. Ceux de Verdun. Payot 1917. 3 fr. 50.

Pic, Eugène. Dans la tranchée: Des Vosges en Picardie. Tableaux du Front. Préface par Georges Blondel. Perrin 1917. 2 fr. 50.

Pierrefeu, Jean de. G.Q.G. Secteur I. Trois ans au Grand Quartier Général, par le rédacteur du communiqué. 2 vols. L'Edition française illustrée. 1920. 10 fr.

Pirenne, J. Les Vainqueurs de l'Yser. Avec desseins de James Thiriar. Payot 1917. 3 fr. 50.

Poirier, J. Reims, 1er août-31 décembre 1914. Payot 1917. 3 fr. 50.

Prévost, Marcel. D'un poste de commandement (bataille de l'Ailette ou du Chemin des Dames [23 Oct.-2 Nov., 1917]). Flammarion 1918. 3 fr. 50.

Reinach, Joseph. La Guerre sur le Front Occidental; étude stratégique 1914-15. Paris: Fasquelle 1916.

—— L'Armée de Verdun. Fasquelle 1918. 3 fr. 50.

René, Henri. Lorette; une bataille de douze mois, Oct. 1914-Oct. 1915. Perrin 1916. 3 fr. 50.

—— Jours de gloire, jours de misère . . . Histoire d'un bataillon. Alsace, Lorraine, Marne, Ypres, Artois, Verdun, 1914-1916. Perrin 1917. 3 fr. 50.

Revol, Lieut.-Col. L'effort militaire des Alliés sur le front de France. (Based on the archives of the Ministry of War.) Payot 1921. 5 fr.

Ruffin, Henry, and Tudesq, André. La mâchoire Carree. (English troops in the Campaign of the Ancre.) Nelson 1917.

Schewaebel, J. La Pentecôte à Arras 22-25 mai 1915. Crès 1916. 1 fr. 75.

Sibille, J., and Mauveaux, J. Le Premier Sang versé par l'Allemagne. L'Affaire de Joncherey du 2 août 1914. Besançon, Millot.

Somville, Gustave. The Road to Liège: the Path of Crime, August, 1914. With preface by M. H. Carton de Wiart, Minister of Justice. Translated from the French. Hodder & Stoughton 1916. 3*s*. 6*d*.

Tesson, F. de. Quand on se bat (les aspects différents que revêt la bataille). Verdun. Plon 1917. 3 fr. 50.

Vachon, Marius. Les villes martyres de France et de Belgique (Statistiques des villes et villages détruits par les Allemands . . . avec 37 vues). Payot 1915. 2 fr. 50.

Variot, Jean. La Croix des Carmes. (Sketches of the fighting at Bois le Pietre; illustrated.) Berger-Levrault 1916. 2 fr.

Vignes-Rouges, Jean des. Bourru : Soldat de Vauguois. (A study of the Poilu, and of operations in the Argonne.) Perrin 1918. 3 fr. 50.

Wharton, Edith. Voyage au front, de Dunkerque à Belfort. Plon-Nourrit 1916. 3 fr. 50.

X., Le Commandant. La Campagne de 1914-15. Les Fastes de l'Armée belge. Première Serie : de la Gette à l'Yser. A technical account of the fighting of the Belgian army. Berger-Levrault 1915.

(3) *German.*

Aus den Kämpfen vor Arras. Arrasschlacht 1917. Hrsg. v.d. Feldpressestelle beim Generalstab des Feldheeres. Mit 4 Taf. u. Karten. 1918. 1 mk. 75.

Aus der Flandernschlacht 1917. Kriegsaufsätze. Hrsg. v. der Feldpressestelle beim Generalstab des Feldheeres. Mit 4 Abb. u. 1 Karte. 1918. 2 mk. 75.

Baumgarten-Crusius, Gen. Die Marneschlacht. 1919.

Fehr, Major Otto. Die Märzoffensive 1918. Strategik oder Taktik? Leipzig : Köhler 1921. 10 mk.

Heubner, H. Unter Emmich vor Lüttich. Unter Kluck vor Paris. Selbsterlebtes a. d. Herbstfeldzug 1914. 6th edn. 1915. 2 mk. 40.

Kluck, Generaloberst v. Der Marsch auf Paris und die Marneschlacht 1914. 1920. 20 mk.

—— English transl. under title, The March on Paris, &c. 1920. 10*s.* 6*d.*

Kuhl, Gen. H. von. Der Marnefeldzug, 1914. Maps and plans. Berlin : Mittler 1921. 40 mk.

Marne, Les Batailles de la : par un officier d'état-Major Allemand. With a preface by Joseph Reinach. Van Oest 1917. 3 fr.

Müller, K. Von der deutschen Westfront. Bielefeld 1916. 1 mk. 60.

Müller-Loebnitz, Capt. W. Der Wendepunkt des Weltkrieges. Beiträge zur Marneschlacht au 5-9 Sept. 1914. Maps and sketches. Berlin : Mittler 1921. 12 mk.

—— Die Sendung der Oberstleutnant Hentsch. (German retreat at the Battle of the Marne.) Berlin : Mittler 1921. 15 mk.

Pflugk-Harttung, J. v. Die Weltgeschichte ist das Weltgericht. Ereignisse u. Stimmungsbilder 1914. Der Westliche Kriegsschauplatz. 1915. 4 mk. 30.

Poseck, Gen. M. von. Die deutsche Kavallerie in Belgien und Frankreich 1914. 2nd edn. Maps. Berlin: Mittler 1921. 70 mk.

Tappen, Gen. Bis zur Marne 1914. Beiträge zur Beurtheilung der Kriegführung bis zum Abschluss der Marneschlacht. 2nd edn. Oldenburg & Berlin: Stalling 1920.

Vaux. Die Kämpfe um die Feste Vaux. 1916. 4 mk.

Wetzell, Capt. G. Von Falkenhayn zu Hindenburg, Ludendorff. Der Wechsel in der deutschen Obersten Heeresleistung im Herbst 1916 und der rumänische Feldzug. Map. Berlin: Mittler 1921. 5 mk.

Ypres, 1914: An official account published by the German General Staff. With introduction and notes by the Historical Section (Military Branch) of the Committee of Imperial Defence. Constable 1919.

Zwehl, Gen. von. H. von. Die Schlachten im Sommer 1918, an der Westfront. Berlin: Mittler 1921. 8 mk.

(4) *Other Nations.*

Crokaert, Paul. La Surprise: Les jours épiques de Liége (Cahiers belges). Van Oest 1917. 60 c.

Diaz-Retg, E. Verdun: diario de las batallas del Mosa desde 21 de febrero hasta fin de marzo de 1916. (Avec cartes portraits et illustrations.) Barcelona: Granada 1916. 4 fr.

—— —— French translation by Gabriel Ledos. Preface by Maurice Barrés. Colin 1918. 5 fr.

Feyler, Col. F. La Guerre européenne. Avant-propos stratégiques. La manœuvre morale. Front d'occident, août 1914-mai 1915. Maps and plans. Payot 1916. 7 fr. 50.

Galiano, A. A. Junto al volcàn . . . impresiones del fronte occidental. Madrid: Fortanet 1917. 2 fr.

Gezelle, Cæsar. De Dood van Yper (The Death of Ypres). Amsterdam: Veen 1918.

Hedin, Dr. Sven. With the German Armies in the West. (Written with a strong pro-German bias.) Lane. 10*s.* 6*d.*

Horrors of Louvain, The. By an eye-witness (a Belgian professor). With introduction by Lord Halifax. Sunday Times 1916. 3*d.*

Jörgensen, J. Dans l'extrême Belgique. Traduit du danois par Jacques de Coussange. Bloud et Gay 1918.

Lupold, Jean. Sur le Front britannique: impressions d'un neutre. Ypres, Arras, Albert, Bapaume, Peronne, &c. (accompagnés du rapport de Sir Douglas Haig du 31 mai 1917). Illustrated. Neuchâtel: Delachaux et Niestlé 1918. 2 fr.

Sette, Mario. Ao Clarão das Obuzes. Short stories of the War in France. Ed. da Liga Pernambucana & Alliados: Recife 1917.

Van der Essen, Prof. Léon. L'Invasion allemande en Belgique . . . avec une esquisse des négociations diplomatiques précédant le conflit. Payot 1917. 7 fr. 50.

—— English transl. under title, The Invasion and the War in Belgium, &c. Unwin 1917. 15*s.*

—— Petite histoire de l'Invasion et de l'occupation Allemande en Belgique. Brussels & Paris: C. van Oert 1918.

(*c*) Apparitions, etc.

Altsheler, Joseph A. The Hosts of the Air: the Story of a Quest in the Great War. Appleton 1915. 3*s.* 6*d.*

Begbie, Harold. On the side of the Angels. A reply to Arthur Machen. Hodder & Stoughton 1915. 1*s.*

Crosland, T. W. H. The Showmen: a Legend of the War. Laurie 1915. 1*s.*

Garnier, Col. The Visions of Mons and Ypres: their Meaning and Purpose. R. Banks 1916. 3*d.*

Machen, Arthur. Bowmen and other Legends of the War. (Angels of Mons.) 2nd edn. Simpkin 1915. 2*s.* 6*d.*

Pearson, John J. The Rationale of the Angel Warriors at Mons during the Retreat and the Apparitions at the Battles of the Marne and the Aisne. Christian Globe 1915. 2*d.*

Shirley, Ralph. Angel Warriors at Mons: an Authentic Record. Newspaper Publishing Co. 1915. 1*d.*

Taylor, I. E. Angels, Saints, and Bowmen at Mons. Theosoph. Publ. Society 1916. 1*s.*

Warr, Charles L. Unseen Hosts: Stories of the Great War. Gardner 1916. 3*s.* 6*d.*

(2) *Eastern Front and Rumania.*

Befreiung Siebenbürgens, Die. Herausg. ùn Auftrage der Generalstabs des Feldheers. Oldenburg: Stalling 1918. 4 mk. 80.

Bracht, R. Unter Hindenburg von Tannenburg bis Warschau. Mit 4 Bildertaf. u. 3 Kart. 1917. 2 mk. 60.

Brandt, R. Fünf Monate au der Ostfront. Kriegsberichte. 1915. 4 mk.

—— Grosse Vormarsch, Der, 1915. 1915. 4 mk.

Falkenhayn, E. von. Der Feldzug der 9ten Armee gegen die Rumänen und Russen 1916-17. Erster Theil: der Siegeszug durch Siebenbürgen. Zweiter Theil: Die Kämpfe und Siege in Rumänien. Berlin: Mittler 1920-21. 15 mk.

Finnemore, John. A Boy Scout with the Russians. Chambers 1915. 5*s*.

Floericke, K. Gegen die Moskowiter. Vol. I. Die Masurenschlachten. Das Ringen um Galizien 1916. 3 mk. 20.

—— —— Vol. II. Gegen Lodz u. Warschau. Der Siegeszug in Polen 1916. 3 mk. 20.

—— —— Vol. III. Der Siegeszug in Polen Sommer 1915. Die Schlacht um San usw. 1918. 3 mk. 20.

Gozdawa-Turczynowicz, Laura de. When the Prussians came to Poland. The Experiences of an American Woman during the German Invasion. Patnam 1917. 6*s*.

Knox, Maj.-Gen. Sir A. With the Russian Army, 1914-17. 2 vols. Hutchinson 1921. 36*s*.

Köster, A. Die Sturmschar Falkenhayns, Kriegsberichte aus Siebenbürgen und Rumänien. 1917. 4 mk.

Liddell, R. S. On the Russian Front (the Great Retreat of 1915). Illustrated. Simpkin 1916. 8*s*. 6*d*.

Lindenberg, P. Gegen d. Russen mit der Armee Hindenburgs. 2nd edn. 1915. 3 mk. 60.

Long, R. E. C. A Book of the Russian Campaign. Methuen.

McCormick, Major R. With the Russian Army. Macmillan 1915. 6*s*.

Miessner, W. Am Feinde. Der Augustfeldzug in Ostpreussen. Heilbronn 1915. 1 mk. 50.

Monkévitz, Gen. N. de. La décomposition de l'Armée russe. Transl., with preface, by S. Persky. Payot 1921. 5 fr.

Morse, John. An Englishman in the Russian Ranks: Ten months' fighting in Poland. Duckworth 1915. 6*s*.

—— —— Cheap edn. Duckworth 1916. 2*s*. 6*d*.

Murray, Marr. The Russian Advance. (Daily Telegraph War Books.) Hodder & Stoughton 1914. 1*s*.

Niederwerfung Rumäniens, Die. Dargestellt auf Grund der amtl. Veröffentlichungen. Mit 8 Zeichnungen. 1917. 2 mk. 90.

Niemann, Hans. Hindenburgs Siege bei Tannenberg und Angerburg. Berlin 1916. 60 pf.

—— Hindenburgs Winterschlacht in Masurien. Berlin 1916. 60 mk.

Olberg, A. von. Der Siegeszug durch Rumänien. Berlin 1918. 3 mk.

Osborn, M. Gegen die Rumänen. Mit d. Falkenhayn-Armee bis zum Sereth. Mit 2 Uebersichtskarten. 1917. 3 mk.

Pares, Bernard. Day by Day with the Russian Army. By the official British observer in Russia. Maps. Constable 1915. 7*s*. 6*d*.

Pflugk-Harttung, J. v. Die Weltgeschichte ist d. Weltgericht. Ereignisse u. Stimmungsbilder 1914-15. Der östliche Kriegsschauplatz. 1915. 4 mk. 30.

Reed, John. The War in Eastern Europe (Illustrated by Boardman Robinson). Nash 1916. 10*s.* 6*d.*

Rohrbach, P. Der Kampf um Livland. Munich: Brockmann 1917. 2 mk. 50.

Standing, Percy Cross. Campaign in Russian Poland. (Daily Telegraph War Books.) Hodder & Stoughton 1915. 1*s.*

Stiénon, Charles. Le mystère roumain et la défection russe. Avec cartes. Plon 1918. 4 fr. 50.

Sturdza, Lieut. M. Avec l'armée roumaine. With preface by M. G. Lacour-Gayet. Hachette 1918. 3 fr. 50.

Taslauanu, Octavian. Trois Mois de Campagne et Galicie (carnet de route d'un officier transylvain de l'armée austro-hongroise). Attinger 1916. 3 fr. 50.

—— Transl. under title, With the Austrian Army in Galicia. Skeffington 1918. 65*s.*

Tolstoi, Comte Alexis. Le Lieutenant Demianoff. Récits de Guerre 1914-15. (On the Russian War, transl. from the Russian.) Payot 1916. 3 fr. 50.

Washburn, Stanley (Times Correspondent). Field Notes from the Russian Front. (To Jan., 1915.) Melrose. 6*s.*

—— The Russian Campaign. April-Aug., 1915. Melrose. 10*s.* 6*d.*

—— Victory in Defeat: the agony of Warsaw and the Russian retreat (1915). Constable 1916. 4*s.* 6*d.*

—— The Russian Offensive. Vol. III. (June 5-Sept. 1, 1916.) Constable 1917. 7*s.* 6*d.*

Wertheimer, Fr. Von der Weichsel bis zur Dnjestr (illust.). 1915. 3 mk.

—— Im polnischen Winterfeldzug mit der Armee Mackensens (illust.). 1915. 3 mk.

—— Hindenburgs Mauer im Osten. 1916. 2 mk.

—— Kurland und die Dunafront (illust.). 1916. 5 mk.

(3) *Italian Front.*

Allatini, Eric. Savoia: la Guerre des Cimes (faits et tableaux des trois premières années du conflit). l'Edn. Française 1918. 2 fr.

Barrès, Maurice. Dix Jours en Italie. Crès 1916. 1 fr. 75.

Barzini, Luigi. Al fronte (May-Oct. 1915). Milan: Treves 1915. 5 fr.

—— La Guerra d'Italia. 2 vols. Milan: Treves 1916-17.

Battisti, C. Gli Alpini. Milan: Treves 1916. 1 fr.

Benedetti, Achille. La Conquista di Gorizia (I libri d'oggi). Avec 11 illustr. photogr. Firenze: Bemporad 1917. 1 fr. 90.

Cadorna, Gen. L. La Guerra alla fronte italiana. 2 vols. Milan: Treves 1921.

Capello, Gen. Note di Guerra. 2 vols. Milan: Treves 1921.

Dalton, Hugh. With British Guns in Italy: a tribute to Italian achievement. (Illustrated.) 1919. Methuen 8s. 6d.

Destrée, Jules, & Dupierreux, Richard. Aux armées d'Italie. Bloud et Gay 1916. 1 fr. 50.

Diario della guerra d'Italia: raccolta dei bulletini ufficialise altri documenti. (Quaderni della guerra.) Parts I . . . . Milan: Treves 1915. 1 fr. each.

Diario della nostra guerra (a collection of bulletins, &c., with maps). No. 12, June 1916. Milan: Ravà 1915.

Faure, G. De l'Autre Côté des Alpes: sur le Front Italien. Perrin 1916. 2 fr. 50.

Fraccaroli, A. L'Invasione respinta (aprile-luglio 1916). Milan: Treves 1916. 4 fr.

Guerra, La, d'Italia, 1915-18. Storia illustrata. Milan 1915, etc. l. 9.

Guerra, La, italiana nel 1916. Riassunto dai documenti ufficiali. Rome: 1917. l. 0.50.

Guerre, La, en Italie. Vol. I. En haute montagne. Illustrated. Published by the Photographical Section of the Italian Army. Milan: Treves 1916. 3 fr. 50.

Guerra, La. Vols. 1-17. Dalla raccolta del reparto fotograf. del Commando Supremo del R. Esercito. Milan: 1916-1919. l. 16.

Hales, A. G. Where Angels fear to tread (fighting on the Italian Front). Hodder & Stoughton 1918. 6*s.*

Hardie, M., and Allen, Warner. Our Italian Front (Illustrated) Black 1920. 25*s.*

Lindenberg, P. Unter Habsburgs Fahnen gegen Italien. Stuttgart 1915. 3 mk.

Morretta, Rocco. A tu per tu (la vita vissuta in trincea) (impressions du Front). Parma: tip. Silvio Orsatti 1917. 3 fr.

Powell, E. Alex. With the Italians. (Illustrated.) Heinemann 1917. 5s.

Prezzolini, G. Caporetto (written in 1918). Rome: La Voce 1920. l. 2.50

Price, Julius M. Six months on the Italian Front. Chapman & Hall 1917. 10*s.* 6*d.*

Rovito, Teodoro. Oltre gli antichi confini. Impressioni di un giornalista nel teatro della guerra italo-austriaca. Napoli: Jovene 1916. 2 l.

Trevelyan, G. M. Scenes from the Italian War. Nelson 1919. 7*s.* 6*d.*

Türr, Stefania. Alle Trincee d'Italia. (By the edrs. of La Madre Italiana.) Milan: Cordani 1918. 10 l.

Vaucher, Robert. Avec les armées de Cadorna (Opérations italiennes depuis la déclaration de guerre jusqu'à la prise de Gorizia). Payot 1916. 3 fr. 50.

Villetti, Roberto. La nostra guerra vista da vicino, dalle Alpi Retiche alle Alpi Giulie, agosto-sett. 1915. Illustrated. Milan: Albrighi 1916. 4 fr.

(4) *The Balkans.*

Aldridge, Olive M. The Retreat from Serbia: Through Montenegro and Albania. With Map. Minerva Publishing Co. 1916. 2*s.* 6*d.*

Askew, Alice & Claude. The Stricken Land (the Serbian retreat from Prishtina to Alessio). Nash 1916. 10*s.* 6*d.*

Barby, Henry. Avec l'armée serbe (La guerre mondiale). De l'ultimatum autrichien à l'invasion de la Serbie. Albin Michel 1918. 4 fr.

—— L'épopée serbe. Story of the Serbian retreat, by an eye-witness. Illustrated. Berger-Levrault 1916. 3 fr. 50.

Boppe, Auguste. À la suite du Gouvernement serbe de Nich à Corfou (an account of the Serbian retreat). By the French Minister in Serbia. Paris: Bossard 1917. 3 fr.

Comnène, N. P. Notes sur la guerre roumaine. With letter by M. Albert Thomas, and preface by M. Maurice Muret. Payot 1918. 4 fr.

Dammert, R. Serbische Feldzug, Der. Erlebnisse deutscher Truppen. Mit 67 Abb. u. 2 Karten. 1916. 3 mk.

Dane, Edmund. British Campaigns in the Nearer East 1914-18 (Maps and Plans). 2 vols. Hodder 1919. 15*s.*

Ferri-Pisani. Le Drame Serbe: Octobre 1915-mars 1916. Perrin 1916. 3 fr. 50.

France, La, en Macédoine: Études publiés par les Officiers [&c.], de l'Armée d'Orient dans la Revue Franco-Macédoine, avril-mai-juin 1916. Preface by Edouard Herriot. Crès 1917.

Gordon, Jan, and Mrs. The Luck of Thirteen. Adventures in the Balkans, especially in the flight from Serbia to the Adriatic. Illustrated. Smith, Elder 1916. 7*s.* 6*d.*

Gordon-Smith, G. Through the Serbian Campaign. The great retreat of the Serbian Army. (By an American correspondent.) Hutchinson 1916. 12*s.* 6*d.*

Immanuel, Fr. Serbiens und Montenegros Untergang. Beitr. zu Gesch. d. Weltkrieges. Mit 9 Kart. 3rd edn. 1917. 2 mk. 90.

Jones, Fortier. With Serbia into exile (Story of the retreat). Illustrated. New York: Century Co. 1916. $1.60.

Köster, A. Mit den Bulgaren. Kriegsberichte aus Serbien und Mazedonien. 1916. 4 mk.

Labry, Raoul. Avec l'armée serbe en retraite à travers l'Albanie et le Monténegro. (By an officer of the French Medical Mission in Serbia.) Perrin 1916.

Lake, Harold. In Salonika with our Army. Melrose 1917. 3*s.* 6*d.*

—— Campaigning in the Balkans. McBride 1918. $1.50.

Libermann, H. Face aux Bulgares (in Macedonia). (Récits des temoins series). Berger-Levrault 1918. 3 fr. 50.

Lipton, Sir Thomas. The Terrible Truth about Serbia. British Red Cross Society 1915. 1*d.*

Ludwig, E. Der Kampf auf dem Balkan. Berichte aus der Turkei, Serbien u. Griechenland 1915-16. 1916. 5 mk. 50.

Mann, Capt. A. J. The Salonika Front. Illustrated. 1920. 25*s.*

Price, Crawfurd. Serbia's part in the War. The political and military story of the Austro-Serbian campaign. Vol. I. Simpkin, Marshall 1918. 7*s.* 6*d.*

Price, Ward. The Story of the Salonica Army. Hodder & Stoughton 1917. 6*s.*

Reiss, R. A. Lettres du front macédono-serbe 1916-18. (By a Swiss military attaché.) Geneva: Boissonas 1921.

Saison, Jean. D'Alsace à la Cerna. Notes et Impressions d'un Officer de l'Armeé d'Orient (octobre 1915-août 1916). Plon-Nourrit 1918. 4 fr. 50.

Sandes, Flora. An Englishwoman-Sergeant in the Serbian Army (first a nurse, then a soldier in the Serbian ranks). Hodder & Stoughton 1916. 2*s.* 6*d.*

Sarrail, le Général. Mon Commandement en Orient (1916-18). Flammarion 1920. 7 fr. 75.

Schmidtbonn, W. Krieg in Serbien. Mit einem deutschen Korps zum Ibar. 1916. 5 mk.

Seligman, V. J. Macedonian Musings (events on the Balkan front, and character sketches from Greece). Allen & Unwin 1918. 5*s.*

—— The Salonica Side-show. Illustrated. 1919. 5*s.*

Stanley, Monica M. My Diary in Serbia, April 1-Nov. 1, 1915. Simpkin, Marshall 1916. 2*s.*

Stebbing, E. P. At the Serbian Front in Macedonia. Illustrations. John Lane 1917. 6*s.*

Stobart, Mrs. St. Clair. The Flaming Sword in Serbia and Elsewhere. Illustrated. Hodder & Stoughton 1916. 6*s.*

Sturzenegger, Madame. La Serbie en guerre 1914-16. Episodes vécus (by a Swiss lady). Fischbacher 1916.

Thomson, L. L. La Retraite de Serbie. (By a surgeon in the French Army.) Hachette 1916. 3 fr. 50.

Wynne, May. An English Girl in Serbia. Collins 1916. 5*s.*

(5) *Dardanelles.*

(*a*) Despatches.

Dardanelles Commission—First Report [Cd. 8490]. H.M.S.O. 1917. 6*d.*

Dardanelles Commission—Supplement to First Report [Cd. 8502]. H.M.S.O. 1917. 1*d.*

Dardanelles Commission—Final Report (Part II—Conduct of Operations, &c.), with an Appendix of Documents and Maps [Cmd. 371]. H.M.S.O. 1919. 2*s.*

Hamilton's Sir Ian, Despatches from the Dardanelles, &c. Introduction by Field-Marshal Sir Evelyn Wood. Newnes 1915. 1*s.*

Hamilton's, Sir Ian, Final Despatch. Five maps. Newnes 1916. 1*s.*

Naval and Military Despatches Relating to Operations in the War. Part IV. Despatch, dated Dec. 11, 1915, from General Sir Ian Hamilton, G.C.B., describing the operations in the Gallipoli Peninsula, including the landing at Suvla Bay. H.M.S.O. 1916. 2*d.*

(*b*) Narratives.

Anzac Book. Written and illustrated in Gallopoli by the men of Anzac. Cassell 1916. 2*s.* 6*d.*

Anzac Memorial. With illustrations and portraits Soldiers' stories of Gallipoli; memorial verses and tributes; General Hamilton's three despatches, &c. Fisher Unwin 1916. 10*s.* 6*d.*

Ashmead-Bartlett, E. Despatches from the Dardanelles. April-July 1915. Newnes. 1*s.*

Bigwood, George. The Lancashire Fighting Territorials (in Egypt and Gallipoli). Country Life 1916. 1*s.*

Bridges, Roy. The Immortal Dawn (The Australians at Gallipoli). Hodder 917. 5*s.*

Bridges, T. C. On Land and Sea at the Dardanelles. Collins 1915. 2*s.* 6*d.*

Buley, E. C. A Child's History of Anzac. Hodder & Stoughton 1916. *2s. 6d.*

Canudo, Capitaine. Combats d'Orient (Dardanelles, Salonique 1915-16). Hachette 1917. 3 fr. 50.

Cooper, Major Bryan. The 10th (Irish) Division. Story of the Irish in Gallipoli. With introduction by Major-Gen. Sir Bryan Mahon. Appreciations by Mr. Asquith and others. Jenkins 1917. 6*s.*

Creighton, Rev. O. With the 29th Division in Gallipoli. Longmans 1916. 3*s.* 6*d.*

Dardanelles: their story and their significance in the Great War. By the author of The Real Kaiser. Illustrated. Melrose 1915. 2*s.*

Le Loghe, Sydney. The Straits Impregnable. Murray 1917. 5*s.*

Fallon, Capt. David. The big fight (Australians at Gallipoli and elsewhere). Cassell 1918. 5*s.*

Fortescue, Granville. What of the Dardanelles? An analysis. Hodder & Stoughton 1915. 1*s.*

Gallishaw, John, Trenching at Gallipoli (by a Harvard man). Illustrated. New York: Century Co. 1916. $1.30.

Gillam, Major J. Graham. Gallipoli Diary (March 1915-Jan. 1916). Allen & Unwin 1918. 12*s.* 6*d.*

Green, James. News from No-Man's Land. With introduction by Lieut.-Gen. Sir W. R. Birdwood. Kelly 1917. 1*s.* 6*d.*

Hanna, Henry. The Pals at Suvla Bay (Dublin Fusiliers). Foreword by Lieut.-Gen. Sir Bryan T. Mabon. Ponsonby 1917. 12*s.* 6*d.*

Hargrave, J. At Suvla Bay: Being Notes and Sketches of the Dardanelles Campaign. Illustrated. Constable 1916. 5*s.*

Hogue, Oliver. Trooper Bluegum at the Dardanelles. Narratives of the more desperate engagements on the Gallipoli Peninsula. Melrose 1916. 3*s.* 6*d.*

Hurst, Gerald B. With the Manchesters in the East (especially at Gallipoli). Longmans 1918. 2*s.* 6d.

Juvenis (pseud.). Suvla Bay and after. (The Soldier Books.) Hodder & Stoughton 1916. 1*s.*

McCartney, R. H. Gallipoli. New York: Cook.

McCustra, Trooper L. Gallipoli Days and Nights (The Soldier Books). Hodder 1916. 1*s.*

Masefield, John. Gallipoli: a short history of the campaign. Heinemann 1916. 2*s.* 6*d.*

Moseley, Sydney A. The truth about the Dardanelles. (By an eyewitness. Condemns the evacuation.) With maps. Cassell 1916. 5*s.*

Patterson, Col. J. H. With the Zionists in Gallipoli (Maps). 2nd edn. Hutchinson 1916. 6*s.*

Prigge, E. R. Der Kampf um die Dardanellen. Weimar 1916. 4 mk.

Priestman, E. T. (late Scoutmaster). With a B.P. Scout in Gallipoli. Foreword by Sir Robert Baden-Powell. Illustrated. Routledge 1916. 6*s.*

Sartiaux, F. Troie : la Guerre de Troie. Historical and descriptive. Maps and illustrations. Paris : Hachette 1915. 5 fr.

Silas, Ellis (Signaller). Crusading at Anzac, Anno Domini 1915. The British Australasian 1916. 2*s.* 6*d.*

—— —— Cheap edn. 1917. 1*s.*

Stiénon, Charles. L'Expédition des Dardanelles. Sur le chemin de Constantinople. Chapelot 1916. 2 fr.

Testis (pseud.). L'Expédition des Dardanelles, d'après les documents officiels anglais. Payot 1917. 3 fr. 50.

Tudesq, André. Les compagnons dee l'aventure (Dardanelles, Egée, Adriatique, Mediterranée). Attinger 1916. 3 fr. 50.

Vassal, J. Dardanelles, Serbie, Salonique : impressions et souvenirs de la guerre (avril 1915-février 1916). Preface par le General d'Amade. Maps and illustrations. De Boccard 1916. 3 fr. 50.

(6) *Asia Minor.*

Gibbins, Herbert Adams. The Blackest Page of Modern History : Events in Armenia in 1915. Putnam 1916. 3*s.* 6*d.*

Levison, Leon. How the Turk makes War. (Includes the Armenian massacres and the attack on Egypt.) Marshall 1915. 6*d.*

Stiénon, Charles. Les Campagnes d'Orient et les Intérêts de l'Entente (Armenia and Mesopotamia). Avec 15 cartes. Payot 1918. 7 fr. 50.

(7) *Egypt, Palestine, etc.*

Aaronsohn, Alexander. With the Turks in Palestine. (by a young man pressed into the Turkish army). Illustrated Houghton Mifflin 1916. $1.25.

Brief record, A, of the advance of the Egyptian Expeditionary Force under General Allenby, July 1917-Oct. 1918. Compiled from official sources. H.M.S.O. 1919. 6*s.*

Australia in Palestine. Edited by H. S. Gullett and Charles Barrett ; David Barker, art editor. (Copious illustrations. Sydney : Angus & Robertson 1919.

Douin, Georges. L'attaque du Canal de Suez (3 févr. 1915). Delagrave 1921. 15 fr.

Gwatkin-Williams, Mrs. In the Hands of the Senussi. Pearson 1916. 2*s.*

Kressenstein, Gen. Frhr. Kress von. Egypt and Palestine, 1915-18; in Zwischen Kaukasus and Sinaï (Jahrbuch des Bundes der Asienkämpfer). Berlin: Mutzer 1921. 20 mk

Massey, W. T. The Desert Campaigns. With illustrations from drawings by James McBey. Constable 1918. 6*s.*

Masterman, E. W. G. The Deliverance of Jerusalem. Hodder & Stoughton 1918. 1*s.*

Murray's, Sir Archibald, Despatches (June 1916-June 1917). Dent 1920. 35*s.*

Thornton, Captain Guy (Chaplain N.Z.E.F.). With the Anzacs in Cairo. Allenson 1917. 2*s.* 6*d.*

With the Springboks in Egypt. By "Captain." (Soldier Books.) Hodder & Stoughton 1916. 1*s.*

(8) *Mesopotamia, Persia, etc.*

(*a*) Despatches.

East India (Military). Despatches regarding Operations in the Persian Gulf and Mesopotamia. [Cd. 8074.] H.M.S.O. 1915. 5½*d.*

—— Papers relating to Major-General C. V. F. Townshend's appreciation of the position after the Battle of Kut-el-Amara. [Cd. 8253.] H.M.S.O. 1916. 1*d.*

Mesopotamia Commission. Report of the Commission appointed to inquire into the Origin, Inception and Operations of War in Mesoptamia, etc. With a separate report by Commander J. J. Wedgwood. Appendices, Sketch map and diagram. [Cd. 8610.] H.M.S.O. 1917. 2*s.*

East India (Afghanistan). Papers regarding hostilities with Afghanistan, 1919. [Cmd. 324.] H.M.S.O. 1919. 4*d.*

East India (North-West Frontier Campaign, 1919), No. 2. Further correspondence regarding the medical arrangements and comforts for the troops on the North-West Frontier (in continuation of Cmd. 310). [Cmd. 398.] H.M.S.O. 1919. 3*d.*

(*b*) Narratives.

Barber, Major Charles. Besieged in Kut and After. Blackwood 1917. 5*s.*

Black Tab (pseud.) On the Road to Kut. An officer's story of the Mesopotamia Campaign. Illustrated. Hutchinson 1917. 10*s.* 6*d.*

Candler, Edmund. The Long Road to Baghdad. 2 vols. Cassell 1919. 35*s*.

Clark, A. T. To Baghdad with the British. Illustrated. New York: Appleton 1918. $1.50.

Donohoe, Major M. H. With the Persian Expedition. 1921 (?) 16*s*.

Dunsterville, Major-Gen. L. C. The Adventures of Dunsterforce. 1921. 18*s*.

Egan, Eleanor. The War in the Cradle of the World: Mesopotamia. Hodder & Stoughton 1918. 12*s*.

Ewing, Rev. William. From Gallipoli to Baghdad. (By an Army Chaplain.) Hodder & Stoughton 1917. 5*s*.

Lawley, Hon. Sir Arthur. A Message from Mesopotamia. (A failure repaired.) Hodder & Stoughton 1917. 2*s*. 6*d*.

Parfit, J. T. Serbia to Kut: an account of the War in the Bible Lands. Illustrated. Hunter & Longhurst 117. 1*s*.

Sandes, Major E. W. C. In Kut and Captivity with the Sixth Indian Division. Plates and maps. 1919. 24*s*.

Swayne, Martin. In Mesopotamia. Hodder & Stoughton 1917. 5*s*.

Tennant, Lieut.-Col. J. E. In the Clouds above Baghdad: being the records of an Air Commander. Illustrated. Palmer 1920. 15*s*.

(9) *The Far East.*

Burnell, F. S. Australia *versus* Germany: the story of the taking of New Guinea. Allen & Unwin. 3*s*. 6*d*.

Jones, Jefferson. The Fall of Tsingtau. Illustrated. Constable. 7*s*. 6*d*.

Leary, L. P. New Zealanders in Samoa. (The story of the capture of that island by New Zealand forces.) Heinemann 1918. 6*s*.

Millard, T. F. The Great War in the Far East. Shanghai: Mercantile Printing Co. 50 c.

Samoa. Correspondence relating to the occupation of German Samoa by an Expeditionary Force from New Zealand. [Cd 7972.] H.M.S.O. 1915. 2½*d*.

Walter, R. Tsingtau unterm Feuer. 1915. 3 mk.

Western Pacific. Correspondence respecting Military Operations against German Possessions in the Western Pacific. [Cd 7975.] H.M.S.O. 1915. 3*d*.

(10) *Archangel.*

Despatches on the North Russian Operations, May 1918-Oct 1919. Supplement to the London Gazette, April 7, 1920.

Evacuation, The, of North Russia 1919. [Cmd. 818.] H.M.S.O. 1920. 1*s.* 6*d.*

(11) *Africa.*

Buchanan, Capt. A. Three Years of War in East Africa. Murray 1919. 12*s.*

Crowe, Brigadier-General J. H. General Smuts' Campaign in East Africa. With introduction by Right Hon. J. C. Smuts. Murray 1918. 10*s.* 6*d.*

Daye, Pierre. Avec les vainqueurs de Tabora: Notes d'un colonial belge en Afrique orientale allemande (série de notes). Perrin 1918. 3 fr. 50.

—— Les Conquêtes africaines belges (óperations des Belges au Congo belge). Berger-Levrault 1918. 2 fr.

Dolbey, Major R. Sketches of the East African Campaign Murray 1918. 6*s.*

Fendall, Brig.-Gen. C. P. The East African Force 1914-19. Witherby 1921. 16*s.*

Frennsen, Gustav. Peter Moor: a narrative of the German campaign in South-West Africa. New edn. Constable 1914. 2*s.* and 1*s.*

Hennig, Rittmeister R. Deutsch-Südwest im Weltkriege. Berlin: Süsserott 1920. 24 mk.

How Botha and Smuts Conquered German S.W. Africa. By Reuter's War Correspondents with the Forces. Simpkin, Marshall 1916. 2*s.*

Kennedy, Joan. Sun, Sand and Sin. (Botha's force in German S.W. Africa.) Hodder & Stoughton 1916. 1*s.*

Morris, K. Louis Botha: or, Through the Great Thirst Land. Botha's campaign in German South-West Africa. Stevens 1915. 1*s.*

O'Neill, H. C. The War in Africa, 1914-17, and in the Far East, 1914. With maps. Longmans 1918. 2*s.*

Rayner, W. S., and O'Shaughnessy, W. W. How Botha and Smuts conquered German South-West Africa. A full record of the campaign, from official information, by Reuter's special War Correspondents. Illustrated. Maps. Simpkin 1916. 2*s.*

Ritchie, Moore. With Botha in the Field. Illustrated. Longmans 1915. 2*s.* 6*d.*

Robinson, J. P. Kay. With Botha's Army. Introductory letter by General Botha. Allen & Unwin 1916. 3*s.* 6*d.*

Röhl, K. Ostafrikas Heldenkampf. Nach eigenen Erlebnissen dargestellt. Mit 12 Taf. u. Karte. 1918. 2 mk.

Sampson, Philip J. Capture of De Wet. An account of the South African Rebellion 1914, by the late editor of the Transvaal Chronicle. Arnold 1915. 10*s.* 6*d.*

Schnee, Gouverneur Dr. Heinrich. Deutsch Ost-Afrika im Weltkrieg. Leipzig: Quelle 1921. 100 mk.

South-West Africa. Correspondence respecting the Proposed Naval and Military Expedition against German South-West Africa. [Cd. 7873.] H.M.S.O. 1915. ½*d.*

—— Report on the Natives of, and their Treatment by Germany. Prepared in the Administrator's Office, Windhuk, South-West Africa, Jan. 1918. (With plates.) [Cd. 9146.] H.M.S.O. 1918. 2*s.* 6*d.*

Stiénon, Charles. La Campagne anglo-belge de l'Afrique orientale allemande. Avec 46 illus. et 2 cartes. Bérger-Levrault 1917. 6 fr.

Suchier, W. Deutsch-Südwest im Weltkrieg: Kriegseindrücke a.d. Jahren 1914-15. Mit Karte. 2nd edn. 1918. 3 mk. 45.

Togoland, Correspondence relating to Military Operations in (April 1915). [Cd. 7872.] H.M.S.O. 5½*d.*

Union of South Africa. Report on the outbreak of the Rebellion and the Policy of the Government with regard to its suppression (April 1915). [Cd. 7874.] H.M.S.O. 8*d.*

—— Papers relating to certain trials in German South-West Africa. [Cd. 8371.] H.M.S.O. 1918 (Oct.). 5½*d.*

—— Proposed Naval and Military Expedition against German South-West Africa, Correspondence respecting. [Cd. 7873.] H.M.S.O. 1915. 1½*d.*

Walker, Dr. H. F. B. A Doctor in Damaraland. (By a doctor who served under General Botha.) Illustrated. Arnold 1917. 7*s.* 6*d.*

Whittall, Lieut.-Commander W., R.N. With Botha and Smuts in Africa. Cassell 1917. 6*s.*

Willich, C. Kriegstage im Südwest 1914-15. 1 mk.

Young, Capt. F. B. Marching on Tanga. (Impressions of the East African Campaign.) Illustrated. Collins 1917. 6*s.*

C. Naval Operations.

(*a*) Despatches.

Admiralty Reports of the Battle of the Bight; destruction of the German East Asiatic Squadron; sinking of the Emden, and other work of the Navy in the War. (Graphic Special.) Graphic Office 1915. 6*d.*

Naval and Military despatches relating to operations in the War. 10 parts. H.M.S.O. 1914-20. Prices vary from 2*d.* to 2*s.*

Terry, C. Sanford (edr.). The Battle of Jutland Bank, May 31-June 1, 1916. The Despatches of Admiral Sir J. Jellicoe and Vice-Admiral Sir D. Beatty. 2nd edn. With lists of officers, &c. Oxf. Univ. Press 1916. 1*s*. 6*d*.

—— Ostend and Zeebrugge, April 23, May 10, 1918. The Despatches of Vice-Admiral Sir Roger Keyes, and other narratives of the operations. Maps, plans, and illustrations. Oxf. Univ. Press 1919. 6*s*. 6*d*.

(*b*) Narratives.

Bartimaeus (pseud.). Naval occasions and some traits of the sailor man. Popular edn. W. Blackwood 1914. 1*s*.

—— Tall ship and other naval occasions. Cassell 1915. 1*s*.

Battle of the Bight, The: Heligoland, Friday, Aug. 28, 1914. With drawings by Frank Mason and Arthur Briscoe, and Rudyard Kipling's poem, The Destroyers. Yachting Monthly 1914. 7*d*.

Buchan, John. The Battle of Jutland. Map and illustrations. Nelson 1916. 3*d*.

Buchan, W. The Log of H.M.S. Bristol: May 13, 1914-Dec. 17, 1915, in American waters and the Mediterranean. (The Log series.) Westminster Press 116. 4*s*.

Carpenter, Capt. A. F. B., R.N. The Blocking of Zeebrugge. By the Commander of the Vindictive. Introduction by Lord Beatty and appreciations by Marshal Foch and Admiral Sims. From official papers. Jenkins 1921.

Cornford, L. Cope. Echoes from the Fleet. Williams & Norgate 1914. 2*s*. 6*d*.; bds., 2*s*.

—— Lord High Admiral and others. Williams & Norgate 1915. 2*s*. 6*d*. & 2*s*.

—— With the Grand Fleet: and a Message from Admiral Lord Charles Beresford. Williams & Norgate 1915. 6*d*.

Coxon, Lieut.-Commander. Dover during the dark days. Lane 1919. 7*s*.

Carry On! Naval sketches and stories. By "Taffrail." Pearson 1916. 1*s*.

Cato, Conrad. The Navy in Mesopotamia. Constable 1918. 3*s*. 6*d*.

Copplestone, Bennet. The Secret of the Navy. Naval exploits during the War. Murray 1918. 7*s*. 6*d*.

Corbett, Sir Julian. History of the Great War, based on official documents. Naval operations. Vol. I, to the Battle of the Falkland Islands, Dec. 1914. With maps and charts in separate case. Vol. II, The Dardanelles. Longmans 1920-21. Vol. I, 17*s*. 6*d*. Vol. II, 21*s*.

Currey, Commander E. H. How we kept the sea. A popular naval history of the War. Nelson 1917. *3s. 6d.*

Curtain of Steel, The. By the author of In the Northern Mists (description and tales of the Grand Fleet). Hodder & Stoughton 1918. 6*s*.

Darde, Fernand. Vingt mois de Guerre à bord du Croiseur Jeanne d'Arc (9 août 1914-12 avril 1915): en manche—aux Dardanelles—en Syrie. Perrin 1918. 4 fr. 55.

Degouy, Le contre-amiral. Guerre navale, La, et l'offensive (articles parus depuis juin 1914 jusqu'en août 1916). Chapelot 1917. 4 fr.

Diary of a U-boat Commander. Introduction and explanatory notes by Etienne. Illustrated. Hutchinson 1920. 8*s*. 6*d*.

Dick, C. Das Kreuzergeschwader. Sein Werden, Sieg u. Untergang. Mit zahlr. Abb. u. Gefechtsplänen. Berlin 1917. 7 mk. 60.

East Coast Raids by the German Navy and Airships. Illustrated memorial. Hood 1915. 9*d*.

F., Hubert. La guerre navale. Mer du Nord; mers lointaines. Illustrated. Payot 1916. 3 fr. 50.

Fawcett, H. W., R.N., and Hooper, G. W., R.N. (edrs.). The Fighting at Jutland (abridged edn.). A collection of separate experiences. Macmillan 1921. 21*s*.

Fayle, C. E. Seaborne Trade: Vol. I, The Cruiser Period. Maps in separate vol. History of the Great War, based on official documents. Murray 1920. 21*s*.

Fierre, Jacques. 80,000 milles en torpilleur: récits de chasse aux sous-marins (1914-16). Perrin 1918. 3 fr. 50.

Fleming, Rev. J. A. The last voyage of H.M.S. Britannic. Marshall Brothers 1917. 7*d*.

From Dartmouth to the Dardanelles: a Midshipman's Log. Ed. by his mother. Heinemann 1916. 1*s*.

Frost, Wesley. German submarine warfare (by the former U.S. Consul at Queenstown). Illustrated. Appleton 1918. $1.50.

G.F. A Naval Digression. Blackwood 1916. 1*s*.

Gayer, Capt. A. Die deutschen U-Boote in ihrer Kreigsführung 1914-18 (in five parts). Berlin: Mittler 1921. Parts I-III, 8 mk.

German Raid on Scarborough, Dec. 16, 1914. Dennis 1915. 6*d*.

Gibson, R. H. Three years of Naval Warfare. Heinemann 1918. 12*s*. 6*d*.

Gill, C. C. What happened at Jutland. The tactics of the battle. Doran 1921. 15*s*.

Goodchild, G. The last cruise of the Majestic. From the log book of Ex-Petty-Officer J. G. Corvie. Simpkin, Marshal 1917. 1*s*. 6*d*.

Gottberg, Otto von. Kreuzerfahrten und U-Bootsfahrten (voyages on cruisers and submarines). Berlin: Ullstein 1918 1 mk.

Guihéneuc, O. La Bataille navale du Jutland 31 mai 1916. Perrin 1917. 3 fr. 50.

Hilditch, A. N. Coronel and the Falkland Islands. (O.P.) Oxford Univ. Press. 4*d.*

Howard, Keble. The Glory of Zeebrugge and the Vindictive. (With the official narratives.) Chatto & Windus 1918. 1*s.*

Hurd, Archibald. Ordeal by Sea. (The doings of the Merchant Service in the War.) Jarrolds 1918. 5*s.*

—— The British Fleet in the Great War. Constable 1918. 7*s.* 6*d.*

—— Italian Sea-power in the Great War. Constable 1918. 2*s.*

—— The Merchant Navy. Vol. I, History of the Great War, based on official documents. Maps. Murray 1921. 21*s.*

—— and Bywater, H. C. From Heligoland to Keeling Island: 100 days of Naval War. (Daily Telegraph War Books.) Hodder & Stoughton. 1*s.*

Hutter, J. Les Sous-Marins (Pages d'histoire 1914-17. No. 130.) Berger-Levrault 1917. 90 c.

Jellicoe, Admiral Viscount. The Grand Fleet 1914-16. Cassell 1919. 31*s.* 6*d.*

—— The crisis of the Naval War Cassell 1920. 31*s.* 6*d.*

Kalau vom Hofe. Unsere Flotte im Weltkriege. Die Ereignisse zur See 1914-16 dem deutschen Volke geschildert. Mit 17 Kartenzeichnungen. 2nd edn. Berlin: Mittler 1917. 5 mk. 65.

Kann der uneingeschränkte U-Bootkrieg den Frieden erzwingen? By ***.

Kirchner, J. Das U-Boot bei der Arbeit. Seine Technik und Wirkungsweise in Wort u. Bild. Mit Abb. 8th edn. 1918. 2 mk. 60.

Klaxon (pseud.). The Story of our Submarines. Blackwood 1919. 7*s.* 6*d.*

König, Paul. The Voyage of the Deutschland. Transl. from the German. Pearson 1917. 1*s.*

Le Bruyère, René. Deux années de Guerre navale (résumé des opérations maritimes jusqu' au 1er janvier 1917; articles parus dans la Revue politique et parlementaire). Chapelot 1917. 6 fr.

Leyland, John. The Achievement of the British Navy in the World War. Illustrated. Hodder & Stoughton 1918. 1*s.*

Mantey, Vice-Adm. von (edr.). Das Admiralstabswerk über der Krieg zur See. 1914-18 (official). In three sections: A. I. Der Krieg in der Nordsee, Aug.-Sept. 1914. B. I. Der Krieg in der Ostsee, Aug. 1914-March 1915. C. I. Der Kreuzerkrieg in der auslandischen Gewässern. (Maps and plans throughout.) Berlin: Mittler 1921. Vols I and II, 38 mk. 50 each.

Milan, René. Les vagabonds de la gloire: Campagne d'un Croisseur, août 1914-mai 1915. Plon-Nourrit 1916. 3 fr. 50.

—— Trois Étapes. (Exploits by the French Navy in the War.) Plon-Nourrit 1917. 3 fr. 50.

Milne, Adm. Sir A. B. The flight of the Goeben and the Breslau. Nash 1921. 6*s*.

Moore, Henry Charles. Under Jellicoe's Command. Illustrated. Collins 1916. 5*s*.

Naval War Services of Officers. With a diary of events of the War connected with the Royal Navy. The Royal Navy List 1917. 1*s*. 6*d*.

Newbolt, Henry. A Naval History of the War 1914-18. Hodder & Stoughton 1920. 15*s*.

Noble, Edward. The Naval Side. Decorations by Frank Brangwyn. Palmer & Hayward 1918. 7*s*. 6*d*.

Noyes, Alfred. Open Boats. (Articles on the action of German submarines contributed to the Times.) Blackwood 1917. 2*s*.

Otto, F. Das Unter-seeboot im Kampfe. Illustrated. 4 mk.

Outis (pseud.). The Truth about the Blockade. Preface by D. G. Pinkney. (Reprinted with additions from the English Review.) Kealey 1916. 2*d*.

Pochhammer, H. Graf Spees letzte Fahrt. Erinnerungen an d. Kreuzergeschwader. Mit 13 Bildern u. 1 Karte. 1918. 6 mk. 50.

Pohl, H. von. Aus Aufzeichnungen u. Briefen während d. Kriegszeit. 1920. 10 mk.

Pollen, Arthur H. The Navy in Battle (Battle of Jutland, &c.). Chatto & Windus 1918. 12*s*. 6*d*.

Price, William H. With the Fleet in the Dardanelles. Some impressions of naval men and incidents during the campaign in the Spring of 1915. With preface by Sir Ernest Fraser. Melrose 1915. 1*s*. 6*d*.

Reuter, Adm. von. Scapa Flow: der Grab der deutschen Flotte (The Sinking of the German Fleet, by the Commander-in-Chief.) Leipzig 1921.

Rousseau, A. L'Action des Alliés sur les mers. By the Naval editor of the Temps. Alcan 1916. 1 fr.

—— Trois ans de guerre: Notre marine et la leur. Alcan 1918 1 fr.

Saint Pierre, Adm. E. B. di. Gli avvenimenti navali importanti accaduti durante la guerra (Estratto dalla Rivista Nautica). Rome: Rivista Nautica 1921.

Scheer, Admiral. Deutschlands Hochseeflotte im Weltkriege. 1920. 25 mk.

—— English transl. under title Germany's High Sea Fleet in the World War. With maps and plans. Cassell 1920. 25*s*.

Sims, Rear-Adm. W. S. Victory at Sea (plans and illustrations). 1920. 21*s*.

Steinwäger, L. U-Boot Englands Tod (illustrated). 1917. 1 mk.

Stewart, Comm. A. T., and Peshall, Rev. C. J. The Immortal Gamble, and the part played in it by H.M.S. Cornwallis. Illustrated. Black 1917. 6*s*.

Taffrail (pseud.). A little ship (life on a destroyer, with an account of the bottling of Zeebrugge). Chambers 1918. 6*s*.

Toeche-Mittler, S. Die deutsche Kriegsflotte und ihre Verbündeten: ein Jahr im Kampfe. 6th edn. 1915. Br. 1 mk. 45.

Vedel, Commandant Emile. Nos Marins à la guerre, sur mer et sur terre. Payot 1916. 3 fr. 50.

—— Sur nos Fronts de Mer (work of the French Navy). Plon-Nourrit 1918. 4 fr. 50.

Vaux, Patrick. Sea Salt and Cordite. Hodder & Stoughton 1914. 2*s*. & 1*s*.

War, The, on Hospital Ships (Narratives of Eye-witnesses). Fisher Unwin 1917. 2*d*.

Wheeler, Harold F. B. Stirring deeds of Britain's Sea-dogs (in the present war). Illustrated.

—— Daring Deeds of Merchant Seamen in the Great War. Harrap 1918. 5*s*.

—— War in the Under-seas (illustrated). Harrap 1919. 6*s*.

Wieting. Der Ostseekrieg 1914-18. Mit 52 Abb. u. 2 Kart. 1918. 3 mk. 50.

Wood, Walter. Fishermen in Wartime (Work of Naval Auxiliaries illustrated). Sampson Low 1918. 7*s*. 6*d*.

Wyllie, W. L., and Wren, M. F. Sea Fights of the Great War during the first nine months. Cassell 1918. 12*s*. 6*d*.

"Y." L'Odyssée d'un transport torpille. Payot 1917. 4 fr.

Young, Filson. With the Battle-Cruisers (illustrated). Cassell 1921. 25*s*.

Young, Lieut.-Comm. Hilton. By Sea and Land: Some Naval Doings. Jack 1920. 12*s*. 6*d*.

See also XII. C. (2) Pflugk-Harttung.

(*c*) Miscellaneous.

Balfour, Rt. Hon. A. J. The Navy and the War, 1914-15. A Letter to the New York World, July 31, 1915. Darling.

Reventlow, E. zu. Der Einfluss der Seemacht im grossen Kriege. 5th edn. Berlin: Mittler 1917. 10 mk. 65.

[D.] Memoirs &c.

(1) *Memoirs of Distinguished Men.*

Bethmann Hollweg. Betrachtungen. Vols. I and II. Reimar Hobbing, 1919-21.

Czernin, Graf Ottokar. Im Weltkriege. Berlin: Ullstein 1919. 20 mk.

—— Transl. into English under title In the World War. Cassell 1919. 25*s.*

Eckardstein, Frhr. von. Lebenserinnerungen und politische Denkwurdigkeiten. 3 vols. Leipzig; List 1919-21.

Erzberger, M. Erlebnisse im Weltkrieg. Stuttgart; Deutsche Verlagsanstalt 1920.

Galliéni, le Général. Mémoires. Payot 1920. 16 fr.

Gerard, James W. My Four Years in Germany. (By the late American Ambassador to Berlin.) Hodder & Stoughton 1917. 7*s.* 6*d.*

Hayashi, Count. Secret Memoirs. Ed. by A. M. Pooley. Nash 1915. 10*s.* 6*d.*

Hindenburg, Generalfeldmarschall von. Aus meinem Leben 1919. Allgemeine Ausgabe. 30 mk.

—— Vorzugsausgabe. 120 mk.

—— Transl. under title Out of my Life. Cassell 1920. 25*s.*

Lettow-Vorbeck. Meine Erinnerungen a. Ostafrika. Mit Abb. 1919. 25 mk.

Lichnowsky, Prince. Mémoire du prince Lichnowski. Avant-propos de M. Albert Thomas. Grasset 1918. 0 fr. 75.

—— Engl. transl. under title My Mission to London 1912-14 With preface by Prof. Gilbert Murray. Cassell 1918. 6*d.*

—— —— Édition nouvelle. Ed. by R. Puaux. (Avec une introduction tout à fait differente de la première.) Payot 1918

Ludendorff, Gen. Erich. Meine Kriegserinnerungen 1914-18 Berlin; Mittler 1919. 95 mk.

—— —— Pop. edn. 22 mk.

—— —— Transl. into English under title My War Memorie 1914-18. 2 vols. Maps and plans. Hutchinson 1919. 34*s.*

Mercier, Cardinal. Cardinal Mercier's Own Story. Preface b Cardinal Gibbons. Hodder & Stoughton 1920. 25*s.*

Nekludoff, A. Diplomatic reminiscences before and during th War 1911-17 Murray 1920. 21*s.*

Nabokoff, C. Ordeal of a Diplomatist. Four years' personal recollections at the Russian Embassy in London. Duckworth 1921. 15*s*.

Pourtalès, Graf. Am Scheidewege zwischen Krieg u. Frieden Meine letzten Verhandlungen in St. Petersburg, Ende Juli 1914. 1919. 3 mk.

Scheer (Admiral). Deutschlands Hochseeflotte im Weltkriege. Persönl. Erinnerungen. 1919. 25 mk.

Schoen, Frhr. von. Erlebtes: Beiträge zur politischen geschichte der neuesten Zeit. Stuttgart; Deutsche Verlags. Anstalt 1921. 30 mk.

—— The Memoirs of an Ambassador. Transl. by Constance Vesey. Allen & Unwin 1921. 10*s*. 6*d*.

Stein, Gen. von. Erlebnisse u. Betrachtungen aus der Zeit des Welt-krieges. 1919. 14 mk. 50.

—— —— Transl. under title A War Minister and His Work. Reminiscences of 1914-18. Skeffington 1920. 16*s*.

Tirpitz, Adm. Alfred von. Erinnerungen. Leipzig: Köhler 1919. 60 mk.

—— —— Transl. into English under title My Memories. 2 vols. Hurst & Blackett 1919. 34*s*.

Windischgraetz, Prinz Ludwig. Vom roten zum schwarzen Prinzen. Mein Kampf gegen das U.K. system. Berlin: Ullstein 1920. 20 mk.

—— My Memoirs. Transl. by Constance Vesey. Allen & Unwin 1921. 16*s*.

(2) *Personal Experiences and Impressions*.

(*a*) English and American.

Ashmead Bartlett, E. Some of my experiences in the Great War. Newnes 1918. 3*s*. 6*d*.

Baggs, T. A. Back from the Front: an Eye-witness's Narrative of the Beginnings of the Great War of 1914. Palmer. 1*s*.

Birmingham, The Bishop of. A fortnight at the Front. Longmans. 6*d*.

Bishop, Major W. A., V.C. Winged Warfare (his own experiences). Illustrated. Hodder & Stoughton 1918. 6*s*.

Black, James. Around the guns: Sundays in camp. Clarke. 1*s*.

Boullier, John A. Jottings by a Gunner and Chaplain. Kelly 1917. 1*s*.

Bradley, Shelland. More Adventures of an A.D.C. Lane 1915. 3*s*. 6*d*.

Bury, Rt. Rev. Bishop Herbert. Here and there in the War Area. (Illustrated.) Mowbray 1916. 3*s*. 6*d*.

Cadenhead, J. F. The Canadian Scottish: Stray Papers by a Private. With introduction by Brig.-Gen. R. G. E. Leckie, C.M.G. Aberdeen: Rosemount Press 1915. 1*s.*

Campbell, Rev. R. J. With our Troops in France. Articles contributed to various papers. Chapman & Hall 1916. 1*s.*

Cappuyns, Englebert. Louvain: a Personal Experience. Kingston-on-Thames: Knapp. 3*d.*

Carnbee, Rev. G. T. War Memories and Sketches. By a Scottish Chaplain (mostly reprinted from The Scotsman). Paisley: Gardner 1916. 1*s.* 3*d.*

Centurion (pseud.). Gentlemen at Arms. (Experiences of the writer and his friends, reprinted from Land and Water). Heinemann 1918. 6*s.*

Clarke, Basil. My round of the War (experiences on various fronts). Heinemann 1918. 6*s.*

Contact (pseud.). An Airman's Outings. With Introduction by Major-Gen. W. S. Brancker (Deputy Director-General of Military Aeronautics). Blackwood 1917. 5*s.*

Crawshay-Williams, Eliot. Leaves from an Officer's note book. (Impressions of two years of war: Ypres, Egypt, the Mediterranean). Arnold 1917. 10*s.* 6*d.*

Creighton, Rev. Oswin. With the 29th Division in Gallipoli. A Chaplain's experiences. Illustrated. Longmans 1916. 3*s.* 6*d.*

Cuttriss, G. P. Over the Top. With the 3rd Australian Division. With Introduction by Major-Gen. Sir John Monash. Kelly 1918. 3*s.*

Davis, Richard Harding. Somewhere in France. Duckworth 1916. 3*s.* 6*d.*

—— With the Allies. Illustrated. Duckworth. 3*s.* 6*d.*

Dunn, Lieut. E. A. Three Anzacs in the War. (Training in Australia, Fighting in France, Sojourn in England.) Skeffington 1918. 6*s.*

Empey, Arthur Guy. From the Fire Step. Experiences of an American Soldier in the British Army. Putnam 1917. 5*s.*

—— Over the Top. (By an American soldier with the Allied forces.) Putnam 1917. $1.50.

Erichsen, Eric. Forced to Fight (Soldiers' Tales Series). (The narrative of a Schleswig Dane.) Heinemann 1917.

Farnol, Jeffery. Some War Impressions. (Visits to France, Flanders, and Munition Centres.) Sampson Low 1918. 1*s.* 6*d.*

Fetterless, Arthur. Battle days. Blackwood 1918. 6*s.*

Finzi, Kate John. Eighteen Months in the War Zone. Cassell 1916. 6*s.*

Fortescue, Granville. At the Front with three Armies. (The three armies are the French, the Belgian and the German.) Melrose. 6*s*.

—— Russia, the Balkans, and the Dardanelles. Experiences of a War Correspondent. Melrose 1915. 6*s*.

—— Campaigning from Warsaw to Constantinople. Melrose 1915. 6*s*.

Foster, Rev. H. C. At Antwerp and the Dardanelles. (An account of life with the 2nd Naval Brigade.) Mills & Boon 1918. 5*s*.

From Snotty to Sub. By the authors of From Dartmouth to the Dardanelles. (Life in the Fleet, including experiences in the Battle of Jutland.) Heinemann 1918. 1*s*. 6*d*.

Fryer, E. R. M. Reminiscences of a Grenadier, 1914-19. Digby Long 1921. 6*s*.

German Deserter's, A, War experiences. (By a Socialist, who served during the first 14 months of the war.) New York: Huebsch. $1.00.

Hall, Lieut. Bert. In the Air. Three years on and above Three Fronts. Hurst & Blackett 1918. 2*s*. 6*d*.

Hall, J. N. Kitchener's Mob. The adventures of an American in the British Army (from Aug. 1914). Constable 1916. 4*s*. 6*d*.

Hall, Sapper Robert. Somewhere (The Soldier Books). Experiences in France. Hodder 1916. 1*s*.

Hall, J. Norman. High adventure. (Records of two American Volunteers in the Lafayette Flying Corps.) Constable 1918. 6*s*.

Heilgers, Louise. Somewhere in France. Dryden Publ. Co. 1915. 1*s*. and 3*s*. 6*d*.

Herringham, Major-Gen. Sir W A Physician in France. Illustrations. 1919. 15*s*.

Holmes, Corporal R. Derby. A Yankee in the Trenches. (By an American volunteer in the British Army.) 1918. $1.35.

Humphrey, Rev. Frederick. The Experiences of a Temporary C.F. Hunter & Longhurst 1916. 2*s*.

Irwin, Will. The Latin at War. (Adventures and Impressions with the Italian and French armies.) Constable 1917. 6*s*.

Kettle, Prof. T. M. The ways of War. With a memoir by his wife, and portrait. Constable 1917. 7*s*. 6*d*.

Légionnaire 17889 (pseud.). In the Foreign Legion. New edn. Duckworth 1915. 2*s*.

Liveing, Lieut. Edward G. D. Attack. An infantry subaltern's impressions of July 1, 1916. Introduction by John Marefield. Heinemann 1918. 1*s*. 6*d*.

Livingston, St. Clair, and Steen-Hansen, Ingeborg. Under Three Flags: with the Red Cross in Belgium, France, and Serbia. Macmillan. 3*s*. 6*d*.

Lloyd, Gladys. An Englishwoman's Adventures in the German Lines. Pearson. 1*s*.

McConnell, Serjeant. Flying for France. (Experiences of an air-pilot, who was killed in March 1917.) Doubleday 1917. $1.00.

McCudden, Major J. T. B., V.C., D.S.O. Five years in the Royal Flying Corps. (The author was killed in returning from England to France.) The Aeroplane 1918. 7*s*. 6*d*.

Martin, A. A. A Surgeon in Khaki. Pictures of the battle-fields from the Battle of the Marne onwards. Arnold 1915. 10*s*. 6*d*.

—— Poplar edn. Arnold 1917. 2*s*. 6*d*.

Martin, Hugo. Life among the sand-bags. Hodder 1916. 1*s*.

Mitton, Miss G. E. The Cellar-House of Pervyse: A Tale of Uncommon Things from the Journals and Letters of the Baroness T'Serclaes de Rattendael and Miss Mairi Chisholm. Illustrated. Black 1916. 6*s*.

Morgan, J. H. Leaves from a Field Note-Book. By the late Home Office Commissioner with the Forces in France. Macmillan 1916. 5*s*.

Musgrave, Capt. G. C. Under four flags for France. (Experiences on the western front since 1914.) Illustrated. New York: Appleton 1918. $2.00.

My Secret Service. By the man who dined with the Kaiser. Jenkins 1916. 2*s*.

Nagpur, Bishop of. Ten days with the Indian Army Corps at the Front. S.P.C.K. 1915. 4*d*.

Nobbs, Capt. Gilbert, L.R.B. On the right of the British line. (The author was blinded on the Somme, and three months a prisoner in Germany.) Scribner 1917. $1.25.

—— Englishman, Kamerad! (description of the author's sensations during action). Heinemann 1918. 3*s*. 6*d*.

Observer. Oxford and Flanders. Blackwell 1916. 1*s*.

Odysseus (pseud.). The Scene of War. (Reprinted from Blackwood. Experiences in France, Italy, Egypt, Macedonia, &c.) Blackwood 1917. 5*s*.

O.F.O. (a gunner). With the Guns. Eveleigh Nash 1916. 3*s*. 6*d*.

Ogston, Sir A. Reminiscences of three campaigns. Hodder and Stoughton 1919. 16*s*.

On leave and very cold. A book of rememberings. By a Highland Minister. (Work among Highland soldiers in East and West.) Ajmer (India): Scottish Mission Industries Company 1917.

One of the Jocks. Odd Shots. Hodder & Stoughton 1916. 1*s.*

Page-Croft, Brigadier-Gen. H., M.P. Twenty-one months under Fire. Murray 1917. 5*s.*

Palmer, Frederick. My Year of the War. Murray 1915. 6*s.*

Platoon-Commander (pseud.). From the Aisne to La Bassée. Heinemann 1915. 3*s.* 6*d.*

—— With my Regiment. Experiences at the Front. Heinemann 1916. 3*s.* 6*d.*

Plummer, Lieut. Mary (edr.). With the first Canadian Contingent. Hodder & Stoughton 1915. 2*s.* 6*d.*

Ponsonby, Rev. Maurice, M.C. Visions and Vignettes of War. Longman 1918. 2*s.* 6*d.*

Private No. 940 (pseud.). On the Remainder of our Front. (From after the Battle of Loos till the following March.) Harrison 1917. 2*s.* 6*d.*

Pulitzer, R. Over the Front in an Aeroplane: and Scenes inside the French and Flemish trenches. Illustrated. Harper 1916. 3*s.* 6*d.*

Red Cross and Iron Cross. By a Doctor in France [Axel Munthe]. (Experiences on the French front; German officers and wounded, etc.) Murray 1916. 2*s.* 6*d.*

Renwick, G. War Wanderings: A Record of War and War Travel. Chapman & Hall 1916. 7*s.* 6*d.*

Rineheart, Mary R. Kings, Queens and Pawns. Personal experiences on the Western Front, by a member of the American Red Cross Association. New York: Doran 1915. $1.50.

Robinson, W. J. My fourteen months at the Front. By an American Volunteer. Boston: Little, Brown, 1916. $1.00.

Ruhl, Arthur. Antwerp to Gallipoli. A year of war on many fronts—and behind them. (By an American journalist.) Illustrated. Allen & Unwin 1916. 7*s.* 6*d.*

Scott, J. Cuthbert. A Thousand Strong. Cornish. 1*s.* 6*d.*

Shaw, Rev. Kenneth E. Jottings from the Front. Allen & Unwin 1918. 2*s.* 6*d.*

Sheahan, Henry. A Volunteer Poilu. (By an American in the French service.) Illustrated. Houghton Mifflin 1916. $1.25.

Sheppard, J. J. (edr.). Territorials in India. Illustrated. 1917.

Sinclair, May. A journal of impressions in Belgium. Record of experiences with a field ambulance in the autumn of 1914. Hutchinson. 6*s.*

Smith, Rev. G. Vernon. The Bishop of London's Visit to the Front. Longmans. 1*s.*

Spin (pseud.). With the Cloud Cavalry. By an officer in the R.F.C. Hodder & Stoughton 1918. 5*s.*

Spin (pseud.). Short Flights. (Sketches of life in a flying squadron.) Hodder & Stoughton 1918. 5*s*.

Sutherland, Millicent, Duchess of. Six Weeks at the War. Times Office. 1*s*.

Sweeter, Arthur. Roadside Glimpses of the Great War. Illustrated. Macmillan 1916. 5*s*. 6*d*.

Tales of a Dug-out. By an officer of the Die-Hards. E. George 1915. 1*s*.

Temporary gentleman, A, in France. Preface by Capt. A. J. Dawson. Cassell 1916. 1*s*.

Thompson, Rev. G. War Memories and Sketches. By a Scottish Chaplain. Paisley: Gardner 1918. 2*s*.

Toland, E. D. The Aftermath of battle. With the Red Cross in France. (Diary of a young American.) With preface by Owen Wister. Macmillan 1916. 3*s*. 6*d*.

Twelve Months with the Australian Expeditionary Force. By an Anzac. Newnes 1916. 1*s*.

Vedette (pseud.). The Adventures of an ensign. Personal experiences with the Guards on the Somme. Blackwood 1917. 5*s*.

Vivian, E. Charlès. With the Scottish Regiments at the Front. Hodder & Stoughton 1915. 1*s*.

Wagger (pseud.). Battery Flashes. Murray 1916. 2*s*. 6*d*.

Watkins, Owen Spencer. With French in France and Flanders: being the experiences of a Chaplain attached to a Field Ambulance. Kelly 1915. 1*s*.

Watson, Capt. W. H. L. Adventures of a Despatch-Rider. Blackwood 1915. 6*s*.

—— —— Cheap edn. Blackwood 1917. 1*s*.

Watt, Rev. L. Maclean. In the Land of War: a Padre with the Bagpipes. Turnbull & Spears 1915. 1*s*.

—— In France and Flanders with the fighting men. (Experiences of a roving missioner.) 1914-1915. Hodder & Stoughton 1917. 3*s*. 6*d*.

Wharton, Edith. Fighting France: from Dunkerque to Belfort. (Mrs. Wharton's own experiences.) Illustrated. New York: Scribner 1915. $1.00.

Williams, G. Valentine. With our Army in Flanders. Arnold 1915. 12*s*. 6*d*.

Williams, Wythe. Passed by the Censor. Dutton 1917. $1.50.

Wing Adjutant (pseud.). Over There. (The doings of the R.A.F. by land and sea.) Cassell 1918. 7*s*.

—— Plane tales from the skies. (Sketches of actual experiences of pilots and observers.) Cassell 1918. 2*s*. 6*d*.

Wings (pseud.). Over the German lines, and other sketches, illustrating the work of the R.A.F. in France. With introduction by Apteryx. Hodder & Stoughton 1918. 6*s*.

Winnifrith, Rev. D. P. The Church in the Fighting Line. Experiences of an Army Chaplain. With preface by the Bishop of London. Hodder & Stoughton 1915. 2*s*. 6*d*.

Winslow, C. D. With the French Flying Corps. Illustrated. Constable 1917. 3*s*. 6*d*.

Wood, Eric Fisher. The Notebook of an Attaché: Seven Months in the War Zone. The author was an Attaché in the American Embassy in Paris. Grant Richards 1915. 6*s*.

Yeo (pseud.). Soldier Men. (Sketches of soldier life, mostly in Egypt and Gallipoli.) John Lane 1917. 3*s*. 6*d*.

(*b*) French.

Berger, Marcel. In the Fire of the Furnace. By a serjeant in the French Army. Translated by Mr. Cecil Curtis. Smith, Elder 1916. 6*s*.

Binet, Valmer. Mémoires d'un engagé volontaire. (By a Swiss of Huguenot stock.) Flammarion 1918. 3 fr. 50.

Boucher, J. F. Souvenirs de la Grande Guerre, 1914-15. Mignot 1916.

Bréant, Commandant. De l'Alsace à la Somme: souvenirs du Front. Août, 1914-Janvier, 1917. (Mémoires et récits de la guerre.) Hachette 1917. 3 fr. 50.

Breton, Jean. A l'arrière. (Recollections of scenes behind the lines, 1914-15.) Delegrave 1916. 2 fr.

Buteau, Max. Tenir. (Holding-on: military life behind the lines.) Plon-Nourrit 1918. 4 fr.

Coutras, Pierre. Les Tribulations d'un auxiliaire. Lethielleux 1916. 1 fr. 50.

Dauzat, Albert. Impressions et choses vues, Juillet-Décembre, 1914. Attinger 1916. 3 fr. 50.

D'Estre, Henri. D'Oran à Arras. Impressions de guerre d'un officier d'Afrique. Plon, Nourrit 1916. 3 fr. 50.

Dollé, André. Pages de gloire, d'amour et de mort. Guerre de 1914-16. Impressions, récits et nouvelles. Berger-Levrault 1916. 3 fr.

—— La Côte 30A. Souvenirs d'un officier de Zouaves. (Illustrated.) Berger-Levrault 1917. 3 fr. 50.

Dupont, Marcel. En campagne (1914-15): impressions d'un officier de cavalerie légère (40th edn.). Plon-Nourrit 1916. 3 fr. 50.

Dupont, Marcel. L'Attente. Impressions d'un Officier de Légère, 1915-17. Plon-Nourrit 1918. 4 fr.

Forge, Henry de (Caporal au —e Territorial). Ah! la belle France! Impressions du Front. Flammarion 1916. 3 fr. 50.

Gaëll, René. Dans la bataille. Scènes de la guerre. Niort: Boulord 1916. 1 fr. 50.

Galopin, A. Sur la ligne de feu. Faits de la guerre entre septembre, 1914, et août, 1916.) Allin, Michel 1917. 3 fr. 50.

Ginisty, P., & Gagneur, Capit. M. Histoire de la guerre par les Combattants. (Selected personal narratives in chronological order.) Garnier 1917.

Grandmaison, L. de (edr.). Impressions de guerre de Prêtres soldats. Deux Séries. Plon-Nourrit 1917. 3 fr. 50 each.

Grimautz, Fernand H. Six mois de guerre en Belgique. Personal experiences of a Belgian soldier, Aug. 1914-Feb. 1915. Perrin. 3 fr. 50.

Hassler, Capitaine. Ma Campaigne. Au Jour le Jour. Preface by Maurice Barrès. Perrin 1916. 3 fr. 50.

Hourticq, L. Récits et Reflexions d'un Combattant. (Mémoires et Récits de guerre.) Hachette 1918. 4 fr. 50.

Julia, E. F. La Fatalité de la guerre: scènes et propos du Front. Perrin 1917. 3 fr. 50.

Klein, L'Abbé Felix. La Guerre vue d'une Ambulance. By a Roman Catholic Chaplain attached to the American War Hospital in Paris. Armand Colin. 3 fr. 50.

—— —— English translation of the above, under title The Diary of a French Army Chaplain. Melrose. 3*s*. 6*d*.

Lacroix, Francy. En plein cïel: impressions d'aviateur. Sensations de vol. La Guerre en Avion. Plon-Nourrit 1918. 4 fr. 50.

Larguier, Leo. Les Heures déchirées. Notes du front. Illus. L'Edition Française 1918. 3 fr. 50.

Lauzanne, Stéphane. Feuilles de route d'un mobilisé. Payot 1916. 3 fr. 50.

Libermann, H. Ce qu'a vu un officier de Chasseur à Pied. Aug. 2-Sept. 28, 1914. Plon 1916.

Limosin, Jean. De Verdun à l'Yser; notes d'un aumônier militaire. Avec 68 illus. Bonne Presse 1918. 2 fr.

Lintier, Paul. Avec une batterie de 75. Ma pièce. Souvenir d'un canonnier, 1914. Plon-Nourrit 1916. 3 fr. 50.

—— —— Translated under title My 75. Heinemann 1917. 3*s*. 6*d*.

Magne, Vital. Heures de guerre. D'Afrique en Flandre et en Champagne. (Une série d'impressions.) Perrin 1918. 3 fr. 50.

Mallet, Christian. The experiences and impressions of a French Trooper. Constable 1916. 3*s*. 6*d*.

Maurie, J. Impressions d' un simple, 1913-1916. Préface de M. Welschinger. Editions et Librairie, 1917. 3 fr. 50.

Meunier, G. Jusqu 'au bout ! Images de Guerre d'un jeune Poilu. Illustré par l'auteur. Delagrave 1917. 5 fr. 50.

Nadaud, M. En Plein Vol. : souvenirs de Guerre Aérienne. Nachette 1916. 3 fr. 50.

Nordmann, C. À Coups de Canon : notes d'un combattant. Perrin 1917. 3 fr. 50.

Paris, l'Abbé J. L. Notes d'un prêtre mobilisé (qui soigne les blessés). Daragon 1916. 3 fr. 50.

Pastre, J. L. Gaston. Trois Ans de Front. (Account by a gunner of experiences in the first three years.) Berger-Levrault. 4 fr. 50.

Péricard, Lieut. Face à face. Souvenirs et impressions d'un soldat de la Grande Guerre. Préface de Maurice Barrés. Illustrated. Payot 1917. 3 fr. 50.

Péricard, Lieut. Jacques. Debout les Morts ! Souvenirs and impressions d'un soldat de la grande guerre. Preface by Maurice Barrés. 2 vols. Illustrated. Payot 1918. 4 fr. 50 each.

Perrin, Jules. Un Parisien sur l'Yser : Le Fusilier marin Luc Platt, d'après son Journal et sa correspondance. Préface par Charles Le Goffic. Larousse 1917. 75 ct.

Pilon, G. Pélérinages de Guerre. (Experiences and descriptions.) Perrin 1917. 3 fr. 50.

Pratz, Claire de. A Frenchwoman's notes on the war. Dutton 1917. $1.50.

Renaud, Capt. Jean. La Tranchée rouge : Feuilles de route, Sept., 1914-Mars., 1916. (In Champagne, the Woëvre, &c) Hachette 1916. 3 fr. 50.

Rimbaud, Isabelle. Dans les Remons de la Bataille. (July 28-Sept. 23, 1914.) Chapelot. 3 fr. 50.

Rolin, Jeanne. Ce que j'ai vu de la guerre. Constable 1915. 1*s*. 6*d*.

Schmitz, André. Sous la rafale. Bloud et Gay 1918. 3 fr. 50.

Simonin, M. J. De Verdun à Mannheim. (Souvenirs sur les combats des débuts de la guerre et de la capbirté en Allemagne d'auteur.) Vitet 1918. 4 fr.

Souvenirs de Guerre d'un sous-officier Allemand. (The doings of a German battalion during the first two years of war.) Payot 1918. 4 fr. 50.

Thomas, L. Avec les Chasseurs. Crès 1916. 3 fr. 50.

Wastelier du Pare, Léon. Souvenirs d'un réfugeé : Douai, Lille, Paris, Boulogne-sur. Mar., 1914-15. Perrin 1916. 3 fr. 50.

(*c*) German.

Bloem, W. Vormarsch. Persönl. Kriegserlebnisse. 9 mk.
Eberlein, G. W. Deutschland im Kriege. Erschautes u. Erlebtes. Mit zahlr. Abb. 1916. 14 mk.
Geijerstam, Gösta af. Finska Bataljonen. (Experiences of a member of the Finnish battalion in the German Army.) Stockholm : Svenska Andelsförlaget 1918. Kr.3.75.
Hagemann, C. Mit. d. fliegenden Division. Eindrücke eines Batterieführers auf drei Kriegsschauplätzen. 4th edn. 1915. 3 mk.
Heuled, J. (edr.). In den Gluten des Weltbrandes. Berichte und Erzähl. aus d. grossen heil. Kriege. Mit Abb. 7 vols. 1915-18. 3.60-6 mk.
Im Feuer. 1. Heldentaten. 2. Feldbriefe. 3. Soldatenhumor. 4. Aus Schützengräben. 5. Heisse Kämpfe. 1914-15. 2 mk. 40 per vol.
Pingaud, Albert. La guerre vue par les combattants allemands. Perrin 1918. 4 fr. 75.

(3) *Diaries and Journals.*

Ansac (pseud.). On the Anzac Trail. Extracts from the diary of a New Zealand Sapper. Heinemann 1916. 3*s.* 6*d.*
Beaume, Georges. Le Carnet d'un chasseur à pied. (Letters from the front, Feb.-Dec. 1915). Illustrated. Larousse 1916. 75 c.
Black Hole, The, of the Desert. The diary of a Yeoman-Signaller, one of the survivors of H.M.S. Tara. (Soldier Books). Hodder & Stoughton 1916. 1*s.*
Blanche, Jacques-Emile. Cahiers d'un Artiste (deuxième série) Novembre, 1914-Mai, 1915. Emile Paul 1916. 3 fr. 50.
Carnet de route d'un officier d'Alpins. Berger-Levrault 1916. 1 fr. 50.
Civray, Jacques (capitaine Pliaux de Diusse). Journal d'un officier de liaison. La Marne, La Somme, L'Yser, 1 Sept.-28 Oct. 1914). Jouve 1917. 3 fr. 50.
Dacquois, G. Dans un Port du Détroit. Diary kept at Boulogne, July-Dec., 1914. Landing of the British Force, etc. Ollendorff 1915. 3 fr. 50.
Dampierre, Jacques de (edr.). Carnets de route de combattants allemands. Traduction intégrale, avec introduction et notes. (Autorisé par le Ministère de la guerre.) Facsmiles. Berger-Levrault 1916. 3 fr. 50.

D'Arguibert, Mlle. Märten. Journal d'une famille française pendant la guerre. Perrin 1916. 3 fr. 50.

Diary of a Nursing Sister on the Western Front, 1914-15. Blackwood. 5*s*.

Delvert, le capitaine. L'histoire d'une compagnie. (Journal de Marche). Berger-Levrault 1918. 3 fr. 50.

Deville, Lt. Robert. Carnet de route d'un artilleur. Virton; la Marne. (The first six weeks of the War). Chapelot 1916. 2 fr.

Drumont, Mad. E. Le journal d'une mère pendant la guerre. Attinger 1916. 3 fr. 50.

—— Transl. under title A French mother in War-time. Arnold. 3*s*. 6*d*.

Dupont, M. En campagne. Extracts from the diary of a French cavalry officer, from Aug. 28 to Dec 24, 1914. Plon-Nouritt. 3 fr. 50.

—— Transl. under title, In the Field 1914-15. Heinemann 1916. 3*s*. 6*d*.

E. R., Lieutenant (Capitaine Tuffrau). Carnet d'un Combatant. Illustré par Carlègle. Payot 1917. 3 fr. 50.

Gaunt, F. The Immortal First. A private Soldier's Diary of his Experiences with the original B.E.F. in France (down to the first battle of Ypres). Erskine Macdonald 1917. 1*s*.

Genty, R. La Flamme Victorieuse. (War diary from August to November 1914). Berger-Levrault 1917. 3 fr. 50.

Hamilton, Gen. Sir Ian. A Gallipoli Diary. 2 vols. Arnold 1920. 35*s*.

Henriot, Emile. Carnet d'un Dragon dans les tranchées 1915-1916. Hachette 1918. 3 fr. 50.

Joubaire, Alfred. Pour la France. Carnet de route d'un fantassin. Preface by Prof. F. Strowski. Perrin 1917. 3fr. 50.

Jones, Denis. The Diary of a Padre at Suvla Bay. Faith Press 1916. 1*s*. 6*d*.

Kühn, J. Aus französischen Kriegstagebüchern. I, Stimmen aus der deutschen Gefangenschaft. Mit 16 Faks.-Beilagen. 1918. 3 mk. 70. II, Der Poilu im eigenen Urteil. Mit 16 Faks.-Beilagen. 1918. 3 mk. 20.

Kutscher, A. Kriegstagebuch. I, Namur, St. Quentin, Morin, Reims, Winterschlacht in der Champagne. 1915. 3 mk. 75. II, Vogesenkämpfe. 1916. 2 mk. 75.

La Frégeolière, R. de. À tire d'ailes. Carnet de vol d'un aviateur, et souvenirs d'un prisonnier de guerre. Plon-Nourrit 1916. 3 fr. 50.

Leleux, C. Feuilles de route d'un ambulancier. Berger-Levrault 1915. 1 fr. 50.

McFall, D., and Bellasis, B. My diary of the great War. Buyers & Sellers 1914. 1*s.* & 1*s.* 6*d.*

Macnaughtan, Miss S. A Woman's Diary of the War. Experiences in Belgium. Nelson 1915. 1*s.*

Mallet, Christian. Étapes et combats: souvenirs d'un Cavalier devenu Fantassin. Passages from the diary of a French officer from the outset of the war to May 1915. Plon 1916. 3 fr. 50.

—— Transl. under title Impression and experiences of a French Trooper, 1914-15. Constable 1916. 3*s.* 6*d.*

Marc, Lieut. Notes d'un Pilote disparu. (Notes from the diary of an unnamed aviator.) Hachette 1918. 4 fr. 55.

Mercier, René. Nancy Sauvée. Journal d'un bourgeois de Nancy. Préface de M. L. Mirman. Berger-Levrault 1917. 3 fr. 50.

—— Journal d'un bourgeois de Nancy. Nancy bombardée. Berger-Levrault 1918. 3 fr. 50.

Michaux, la Baronne J. En marge du drame. Journal d'une Parisienne pendant la guerre, 1914-15. Deuxième Série: 1915-16. Perrin 1916-18. 3 fr. 50 & 4 fr. 55.

Mons, Anzac, and Kut. Diary of an Intelligence Officer (a M.P.) on different fronts. Arnold 1919. 14*s.*

Nicolas, Lieut. René. Campaign Diary of a French Officer. Transl. from the French. Houghton Mifflin 1917. $1.25.

Ouy-Vernazobres, C. Journal d'un officier de cavalerie. Illustrated. (Du début des opérations à la première bataille de l'Yser). Berger-Levrault 1917. 3 fr. 50.

Peckelsheim, Freiherr Spiegel von und zu. U. 202 Kriegstagebuch. (War Diary of the Submarine, U. 202). Berlin: Scherl 1918. 3 mk.

Quercy, Jean. Journal d'un curé de campagne pendant la guerre.

Repington, Col. à Court. The First World War. (A Diary). 2 vols. Constable 1920. 42*s.*

Rimbault, Capitaine. Journal de campagne d'un officier de ligne: Sarrebourg. La Mortagne. Forêt d' Apremont. Illustrations et cartes. Berger-Levrault 1916. 3 fr. 50.

Rion, Gaston. Journal d'un simple soldat. Hachette 1916. 3 fr. 50.

—— Transl. under title The Diary of a French Private 1914-16. Allen & Unwin 1917. 5*s.*

Roger, Mad. Noëlle. Les Carnets d'une Infirmière (a series of six pamphlets, Soldats blessés, &c.). Attinger 1916. 75 c. each.

Roujon, Jacques. Carnet de route, Aug. 1914-Jan. 1915. (By a journalist on the staff of the Figaro.) Plon-Nourrit 1916. 3 fr. 50.

Roujon, Jacques. Transl. under title Battles and Bivouac: a French Soldier's Notebook. Allen & Unwin 1916. 5*s*.

Stewart, Major H. A., D.S.O. From Mons to Loos: being the diary of a Supply Officer. Blackwood 1916. 5*s*.

Strong, Rowland. The diary of an English resident in France during War-time (second series, 1915). Simpkin, Marshall 1916. 6*s*.

Tardieu, C. Sous la pluie de fer. (A war diary of the earlier part of the war). Calmann-Lévy 1917. 3 fr. 50.

Waddington, Madame. My War Diary (impressions of France during the War). Scribner 1917. $1.50.

West, Arthur Graeme. The Diary of a dead officer. Being the posthumous papers of A. G. W. Allen & Unwin 1918. 5*s*.

Wilde, Robert de. De Liège à l'Yser. Mon journal du campagne. Plon 1918. 3 fr. 50.

(4) *Letters.*

Barker, Elsa. War letters from the living dead man. With an introduction. Rider 1915. 3*s*. 6*d*.

Bean, C. E. W. Letters from France (By the War Correspondent for the Commonwealth of Australia). From the landing in France to the attack on Pozières (1916). Cassell 1917. 5*s*.

Belmont, F. Lettres d'un officier de Chasseurs Alpins. Preface par M. Henri Bordeaux. Plon-Nourrit 1916. 3 fr. 50.

—— Transl. under title A Crusader of France. Melrose 1917. 5*s*.

Bentinck, Major Henry. Letters of Major H. B., Coldstream Guards. Rob. Scott 1918. 6*s*.

Bourguet, Lieut.-Col. L'Aube Sanglante (Family letters by a distinguished French officer, killed in Sept. 1915). Berger-Levrault 1917. 3 fr.

Bucaille, Victor (edr.). Lettres de prêtres aux armées. With preface by Denys Cochin. Payot 1916. 3 fr. 50 c.

Canadian Subaltern, A. Billy's letters to his mother (the voyage, England, war in France). Constable 1917. 2*s*.

Casalis, A. E. A young soldier of France and of Jesus Christ. Letters of Alf. Eugène Casalis 1915. Transl. by C. W. Mackintosh. Eastbourne: Strange 1916. 1*s*.

Chapin, Harold. Soldier and Dramatist: being the letters of H.C. Edited, with a biography, by Sidney Dark. Lane 1916. 5*s*.

Cochin, Jean. Quelques Lettres d'Augustin Cochin a sa famille et à ses amis (tiré à part). Paris: imp. de Soye 1916.

Daudet, Ernest (edr.). L'Ame française et l'Ame allemande. Lettres de soldats, avec une introduction. Paris: Attinger. 1 fr.

Dawson, Coningsby. Khaki Courage. Letters in War Time. With introduction by W. J. Dawson. Lane 1917. 3*s.* 6*d.*

Devenish, George Weston. A Subaltern's Share in the War. Letters of G. W. D., with introduction by Mrs. H. Porter. Constable 1918. 3*s.* 6*d.*

Doc. (pseud.). Letters from Somewhere (by a captain in the R.A.M.C., from France and Egypt). Heath Cranton 1918. 3*s.* 6*d.*

Dubarle, le capitaine Robert. Lettres de guerre d'un capitaine au 68e bataillon de chasseurs alpins, mort au champ d'honneur. Avec 4 grav. Perrin 1918. 3 fr. 50.

Farrer, Reginald. The Void of War. Letters from three fronts. Constable 1918.

Foley, Charles. 1914-15: La vie de guerre contée par les soldats. (Letters from soldiers at the Front.) Berger-Levrault 1915. 3 fr. 50.

From Dug-out and Billet: an officer's letters to his mother. Hurst & Blackett 1916. 2*s.* 6*d.*

Geare, Rev. W. D. Letters of an Army Chaplain. Wells Gardner 1918. 2*s.* 6*d.*

Gillespie, Lieut. A. D. Letters from Flanders, written to his home people (An In Memoriam of two brothers, both educated at Winchester and New College, with biographical introduction by the Bishop of Southwark). Smith, Elder 1916. 5*s.*

Heath, Lieut. A. G. Letters. With memoir by Gilbert Murray. Blackwell 1917. 3*s.* 6*d.*

Henches, Commandant J. E. À L'École de la Guerre. Letters of an Artillery Officer. Hachette 1918. 4 fr. 55.

Henderson, Keith. Letters to Helen. Impressions of an Artist on the Western Front. Chatto & Windus 1917. 6*s.*

Hewett, Lieut. Stephen H. A scholar's letters from the front. With introduction by F. F. Urquhart, and portrait. Longmans 1918.

Johnston, Alec. At the Front. (Letters contributed to Punch.) With preface by Sir Owen Seaman and an appreciation by Captain Ingram. Constable 1917. 3*s.* 6*d.*

Jones, Lieut. Paul. War letters of a Public Schoolboy (killed in 1917). With memoir by his father. Cassell 1918. 6*s.*

Keeling's Letters and Recollections. Edited by E.T. with Introduction by H. G. Wells. Allen & Unwin 1918. 12*s.* 6*d.*

Krieg, Der deutsche, in Feldpostbriefen. Hrsg. v. J. Delbrück. Bd. I-X. 1915-17. 5 mk. 50 per vol.

Leigh, Dell. The Background of Battle (Letters from a Red Cross worker in France). Stoughton 1916. *2s. 6d.*

Le Roux, Hugues. Au champ d'honneur (Letters from an only son, with memoir by his father). Plon-Nourrit. 3 fr. 50.

Letters from a French Hospital. Constable 1917. *2s.*

Lettres d'un Soldat (1914-1915). Préface de André Chevrillon. Chapelot 1917. 3 fr.

—— Transl. under title Letters of a Soldier. With introduction by A. Clutton-Brock. Constable 1917. *4s. 6d.*

Love Letters under fire (written by an officer to his fiançée). By John Merton. Duckworth 1916. *5s.*

Letters, The, of Thomasina Atkins, Private (W.A.A.C.) on active service. With foreword by Mildred Aldrich. Hodder & Stoughton 1918. *6s.*

Manwaring, G. B. If we return (Letters of a Soldier of Kitchener's Army). John Lane 1918. *3s. 6d.*

Masson, P. M. Lettres de Guerre (M. Masson, a distinguished scholar, was killed in May, 1916). Hachette 1917. 3 fr. 50.

Mercier, Cardinal. A shepherd among wolves: war-time letters, selected by A. Boutwood. Faith Press 1920. *6s.*

Moine et soldat : Lettres de Frère Aimé, frère hospitalier de Saint-Jean de Dieu, sergent d'infanterie tué en Alsace. Lecoffre 1917.

Montvert, J. Lettres de soldats russes. Payot 1916. 2 fr.

Nielsen, Harold (edr.). Danske Soldaterbreve (Letters of Danish soldiers in the Allied Armies). Copenhagen: Gyldendalske Boghandel 1917.

Parr, Olive K. (edr.). The Soul of Two Knights (correspondence of two brothers). Longmans 1918. *1s.*

Private 7664 : A faithful soldier of the brave Worcesters. Letters from a soldier killed in France, Oct. 1914, edited by E. Smith, J.P. Religious Tract Society. *6d.*

R.A.L. Letters of a Canadian stretcher-bearer. Edited by Anna Chapin Ray. 1918. $1.35.

Rohden, G. v. Zwei Brüder. Feldpostbriefe u. Tagebuchblätter. I, Leutnant Gotthold v. Rohden. Mit 3 Abb. II, Leutnant d. Reserve Heinz v. Rohden. Mit 2 Abb. 1917. I, 2 mk. 20. II, 3 mk. 60; or I, II in 1 vol. 5 mk. 15.

Rosher, Lieut. Harold (the late). In the Royal Naval Service. War Letters, with introduction and memoir by Arnold Bennett. Chatto & Windus 1916. *3s. 6d.*

Roux, X. L'Ame de nos soldats. Extracts from letters and diaries written by French soldiers during the war. Le Soudier. 3 fr. 50

Seeger, Alan. Letters and Diary of Alan Seeger (An American who enlisted in the Foreign Legion and was killed in July 1916). Constable 1917. 5*s.*

Souchon, P., Les Mots héroïques de la Guerre. Extracts from letters, diaries, etc. Larousse 1915.

Sparr, H. Feldpostbriefe 1914-1915. Berichte u. Stimmungsbilder v. Mitkämpfern u. Miterlebern. 2nd edn. 1915. 3 mk. 85.

Steege, Klyda R. We of Italy. (Italian soldiers' letters). Dent 1917. 4*s.* 6*d.*

Student in Arms, A. [Donald Hankey.] Letters to the Spectator from the Front. Introduction by J. St. Loe Strachey. Melrose 1916. 5*s.*

Tisdall, A. W. St. C. Memoirs, letters and poems. (The author won the V.C. at Gallipoli; whence the letters are written). Sidgwick & Jackson 1916. 3*s.* 6*d.*

Townshend, Eric (late). The Happy Hero. Appreciation by James Douglas. (A letter written before battle to his parents). Nisbet 1917. 1*s.*

Uncensored Letters from the Dardanelles. Written by a French medical officer to his English wife. Heinemann 1916. 3*s.* 6*d.*

Valentini, Enzo, Conte di Laviano. Letters (by an Italian volunteer). Illustrated. Constable 1917. 4*s.* 6*d.*

Van Vorst, Marie. War letters of an American woman (from France, England and Italy, July 1914-Nov. 1915). Illustrated. Lane 1916. 5*s.*

Vernède, Lieut. R. E. Letters to his Wife. (From France and Flanders, Nov. 1915-April 1917). Collins 1917. 6*s.*

Walcott, Stuart. Above the French Lines. (Letters of an American Aviator, killed in Dec. 1917). Milford 1918. 4*s.* 6*d.*

War Stories of Private Thomas Atkins. A selection of the best things in his letters from the Front, &c. Newnes 1914. 1*s.*

(5) *Anecdotic.*

Adcock, A. St. John. In the Firing Line. Stories of the War by land and sea. Daily Telegraph War Books. Hodder & Stoughton. 1*s.*

Aspern, K. Kriegsanekdoten. Bd. I-X. 2 mk. 25 per vol.

Buffin, le Baron W. (edr.) Recits de combattants. Narratives of Belgian soldiers. Maps and illustrations. Plon-Nourrit 1916. 3 fr. 50.

Buley, E. C. Glorious Deeds of Australasians in the Great War. Melrose 1915. 3*s.* 6*d.*

Butts, M. Héros! Episodes de la grande Guerre. (Illustrations by F. Bovard, and portraits). Payot 1915. 3 fr. 50.

Cable, Boyd. Action Front. Smith, Elder 1916. 5*s*.

—— Between the Lines. Fourteen stories from the Western Front. Smith, Elder 1915. 5*s*.

Candler, Edmund. The Year of Chivalry. War sketches and stories. Simpkin, Marshall 1916. 5*s*.

Copping, Arthur E. Tommy's Triangle. Sketches and Tales of Y.M.C.A. work at the Front. Hodder & Stoughton 1917. 2*s*. 6*d*.

Courson, The Countess de. The Soldier-Priests of France. Their gallant conduct at the front. Dublin: Irish Messenger, 5, Gr. Denmark St. 1*d*.

Dawson, Capt. A. J. Back to Blighty. Illustrated by Capt. Bairnsfather. Hodder & Stoughton 1917. 2*s*. 6*d*.

—— The Great Advance. (Battle stories of wounded soldiers, recorded by A. J. D.). Cassell 1916. 1*s*.

Deeds that thrill the Empire. True stories of . . . acts of heroism of . . . soldiers and sailors during the Great War. By well-known authors. Vol II. With preface by Lord Derby. Hutchinson 1917. 12*s*.

Fielding-Hall, H. The Field of Honour. Constable 1915. 3*s*. 6*d*.

Foss, M. Der See- u. Kolonialkrieg 1914-16. Seeleute u. Schutztruppen im Weltkriege. I. Die beiden ersten Kriegsjahre. Mit ii Kart. u. Plän. 1919. 20 mk.

Franc-Nohain and Delay, Paul. Histoire anecdotique de la Guerre de 1914-15. In parts. Lethielleux. 60 c. each fasc.

Fraser, John Foster. Deeds that will never die: stories of Heroism in the Great War. Cassell. 1*s*.

Gaëll, René. Les Soutanes sous la mitraille: scènes de la guerre. French priests at the front. Gautier. 1 fr.

Grey, C. G. Tales of the Flying Services. The adventures and humours of aerial warfare. Newnes 1915. 5*s*.

Harper, C. G. Overheard at the Front. War conditions, military transport, and soldiers' conversations. Iliff. 1*s*.

Hermes. The Hornets. Tales of the air. Nash 1917. 3*s*. 6*d*.

Herries, James W. Tales from the Trenches. Hodge 1915. 1*s*.

Langlois, Gabriel. Anecdotes Pathétiques et Plaisantes. (War stories). Berger-Levrault 1917. 90 c.

Lauterbach, F. Deutche Heldentaten. Schilderungen aus dem Weltkriege. 2 Bde. 1916. 4 mk. 80.

Mackenzie, Donald A. Brave Deeds of the War. Blackie 1915. 1*s*. 6*d*.

Mackenzie, Donald A. Heroes and Heroic Deeds of the Great War. Blackie 1915. 1*s.*

Mariani, Maria. Colloqui con la morte (psychological stories of the war). Milan: Sonzogno 1918. 3.50 l.

Maurras, Charles. Tombeaux (Vies des héros, écrites à la mémoire des morts de la grande guerre). Nouv. Libr. Nationale 1921. 12 fr. 50.

Middleton, Edgar. Glorious exploits of the Air. Simpkin, Marshall 1917. 5*s.*

Mortane, J. Chasseurs de Boches (le livre d'or des aviateurs). L'Edition Française illustrée 1918. 3 fr. 50.

Newbolt, Sir Henry. Tales of the Great War. Illustrated. Longmans 1916. 6*s.*

O'Connor, T. P. (edr.). T. P.'s Journal of Great Deeds of the Great War. Daily Telegraph Office 1915. 4*s.* 6*d.* each vol.

Our gallant Guards. (Daring Deeds Series.) Gale & Polden 1916. 1*s.*

Our heroic Highlanders. (Daring Deeds Series). Gale & Polden 1916. 1*s.*

Peter (pseud). French Yarns for Subalterns and others. Cassell 1916. 1*s.*

Ross, Capt. Malcolm, and Ross, Noel. Light and Shade in War. (By a war correspondent with the New Zealand troops). Arnold 1916. 5*s.*

Rosen, E. Der grosse Krieg. Ein Anekdotenbuch. (Anekdoten-Bibliothek 14-16, 21). Bd. I-IV. 1916-18. 4 mk. per vol. Vols. bound up together 4 mk. 50.

Royal Artillery, The. (Daring Deeds Series). Gale & Polden 1916. 1*s.*

Sapper (pseud). Sergeant Michael Cassidy, R.E. Hodder & Stoughton 1915. 1*s.*

—— Lieutenant and Others. Tales from the Front. Hodder & Stoughton 1915. 1*s.*

—— Men, Women, and guns. (War stories). Hodder & Stoughton 1916. 5*s.*

Soldiers' Tales of the Great War. (A series of authentic experiences.) Heinemann 1916. 3*s.* 6*d.*

Tallents, Stephen G. The Starry Pool, and other tales (from the War). By an officer in the Guards. Constable 1918 3*s.* 6*d.*

Thirty Canadian V.C.'s. (An account of their exploits, April 23 1815 to March 30, 1918, compiled by the Canadian War Records Office). Skeffington 1918. 2*s.* 9*d.*

Thrilling Deeds of Valour: Stories of Heroism in the Great War. Blackie 1916. 1*s.* 6*d.*

Tiplady, Thomas. The Kitten in the crater, and other fragments from the front. (Mostly from the Methodist Recorder.) Kelly 1917. 3*s.* 6*d.*

Told in the Huts: The Y.M.C.A. Gift-book. Contributed by soldiers and war-workers. With Introd. by Arthur K. Yapp. Drawings by Sir R. Baden-Powell and others; oil-colours by the late Cyrus Cuneo. Jarrold 1916. 3*s.* 6*d.*

Victory Adventure Book, The. Edited by Herbert Haynes. Collins Press 1916. 2*s.* 6*d.*

Vidal, Gaston. Figures et Anecdotes de la Grande Guerre. 1918. 3 fr. 50.

Wallace, Edgar. Smithy. Newnes 1915. 7*d.*

—— Smithy and the Hun. Pearson 1915. 1*s.*

Watson, A. R. Golden Deeds on the Field of Honour. Macmillan 1914. 2*s.*

Winning the V.C. in the Great War. True stories of heroism, from official records and accounts of eye-witnesses). Illustrated. N. Y.: Dutton 1918. $2.50.

Wood, Eric. Thrilling Deeds of British Airmen. (For the Young.) Harrap 1917. 3*s.* 6*d.*

Wood, Walter (edr.). In the Line of Battle. Soldiers' stories of the War. Chapman & Hall 1916. 6*s.*

Wren, Captain P. C. Stepsons of France. True tales of the French Foreign Legion. Murray 1918. 5*s.*

E.—War Newspapers.

B.E.F. Times, The. (Trench Magazine: facsimile reprint.) Herbert Jenkins 1918. 7*s.* 6*d.*

Lead-Swinger, The. (The Bivouac Journal of the 1/3 W. Riding Field Ambulance.) Vol. I., Sept. to Dec., 1915. Sheffield: Northend 1916.

Maple Leaf, The. Magazine of the Overseas Military Forces of Canada. Vol. IV., December, 1918. Canadian Pay Office. 1916-1918.

Tenedos Times, The. A monthly journal of the Mediterranean Destroyer Flotilla in the early part of the War. Allen & Unwin 1917. 21*s.*

Tous les Journaux du Front. Préface par Pierre Albin. Selections from the journals published at the Front. Berger-Levrault 1915. 3 fr.

Whippet, The, No. 1 (December, 1918). The Tanks Corps Magazine. Winchester: Warren 1918.

Wipers Times, The. (Facsimile reprint of the paper written and printed by British soldiers at the front.) Jenkins 1917. 10*s.* 6*d.*

F.—Illustrations.

An der Somme. Hrsg. von einem deutschen Reservekorps. Mit 321 Lichtbildern. 1917. 4 mk.

Ashern, K. Illustrierte Geschichte d. europ. Krieges 1914-17. Bd. I-IX. 7 mk. per vol.

Blanche, Jacques. Cahiers d'un Artiste. 3me. Série. Paris: Emile-Paul 1917. 3 fr. 50.

Bone, Muirhead. The Western Front. Ten parts; 200 drawings, with descriptive text, and introduction by Gen. Sir Douglas Haig. 1916-17. 20*s.*

—— War Drawings. 5 Parts. (Published by authority of the War Office.) Country Life 1917-18. 10*s.* 6*d.*

—— With the Grand Fleet. (Drawings. Published by authority of the Admiralty.) Country Life 1917. 20*s.*

Britain Transformed. New energies. Illustrated. (Munitions, munition-making, etc., photographs.) Fisher Unwin 1916. 6*d.*

British Artists at the Front. By Nevinson, C. R. W. Part I (15 plates). Introduction by Campbell Dodgson and C. E. Montague. Country Life 1918. 5*s.*

—— Part II. By Sir John Lavery, A.R.A. With introductions by Robert Ross and C. E. Montague (15 drawings). Country Life 1918. 5*s.*

—— Part III. By Paul Nash and Eric Kennington. (War landscapes.) Country Life 1918. 5*s.*

Caunell, W. Otway. Fighting Types. Pictures by W.O.C.: verses by Hampden Gordan. John Lane 1918. 2*s.* 6*d.*

Dardanelles, The: An Epic told in pictures. A hundred photographs, many taken under fire, with descriptions from Sir Ian Hamilton's despatch. Alfieri Picture Service 1916. 2*s.* 6*d.*

Dide, Maurice. Ceux qui combattent et qui meurent. Série de portraits . . . du 24e chasseurs alpins. Payot 1917.

Dyson, Lieut. Will. Australia at War. Drawings at the Front (21 drawings). Palmer & Hayward 1918. 7*s.* 6*d.*

Foulon, l'Abbé E. Arras sous les obus. With 100 photographs. Preface by the Bishop of Arras. Bloud et Gay 1915. 3 fr. 50.

Galopin, Arnould. Sur la ligne de feu. Carnet de campagne d'un correspondant de guerre (une série de croquis). Fontemoing 1917. 3 fr. 50.

German War and Catholicism. Photographs illustrating the conduct of French and German armies respectively with regard to the Catholic Church. (Album No. 1.) Bloud et Gay. 1*s*

Guerre, La. Documents de la Section photographique de l'Armée (Ministère de la guerre.) Published in fortnightly parts Vols. I, II (20 parts, containing 480 plates). Colin 1916 30 fr.

Haig's, Sir Douglas, Great Push. The Battle of the Somme. (Illustrated by 700 official photographs.) Hutchinson 1917. 12*s*.

Harvey, Harold. A Soldier's Sketches under Fire. (Forty-two drawings in pencil and pen.) Sampson Low, 1916. 3*s*. 6*d*.

Holme, Charles (editor). The War Depicted by distinguished British Artists. The Studio 1918. 10*s*. 6*d*.

In the Trail of the German Army. Illustrated with special photographs. Daily Chronicle 1914. 1*s*.

Joy-Stick, The. An artistic and literary tribute to officers and men of the R.A.F. Illustrated. Blighty 1918. 3*s*. 6*d*.

Lüdersdorff, H. Die Maschinen des Weltkrieges. Mit 58 Bildertafeln. 1917. 5 mk. 50.

Made in the Trenches. Illustrated. (Composed from articles and sketches contributed by soldiers serving with the colours.) Edited by Treves, Sir F., and Goodchild, G. Allen & Unwin 1916. 3*s*. 6*d*. Edn. de Luxe 42*s*.

Montague, C. E. The Front Line. With illustrations by Muirhead Bone. Hodder & Stoughton 1917. 6*d*.

—— Notes from Calais Base, and pictures of its many activities (photographs and descriptions). Fisher Unwin 1918. 1*s*.

Nevinson, C. R. W. Modern War: Pictures by C. R. W. Nevinson (24 reproductions in black and white and 1 in colour): with criticism by P. G. Konody. Grant Richards 1916. 31*s*. 6*d*.

—— Modern War Paintings. Grant Richards 1917. 10*s*. 6*d*.

—— The Great War: Fourth Year. 24 reproductions of paintings by C. R. W. N. Introductory essay by J. E. Crawford Flitch. Grant Richards 1918. 15*s*.

Nevinson, Henry W. The Dardanelles Campaign. Nisbet 1918. 18*s*.

Pennell, J. Pictures of War Work with an Introduction by H. G. Wells. (Issued under the Auspices of the Ministry of Munitions.) Heinemann 1916. 6*s*.

—— Pictures of War Work in America. (Lithographs, with notes and introduction by the artist.) Lippincott 1918. 9*s*.

Reid, Frank. Foot Slogging in East Africa. 46 sketches of the East African campaign. Maskew Miller 1918.

Smart, H. C. Australia in the Great War. A collection of photographs. In 8 parts. Part I. Cassell 1918. 6*s*.

War Budget, The. A photographic record of the Great War. Daily Chronicle 1916. 5*s*. each vol.

War in Italy, The. Part I, On the High Mountains; Part II, The Carso; Part III, The Battle between the Brenta and the Adige. (Photographs published November, 1916.) Milan: Treves 1917. 3*s*. each.

Wilkins, Capt. G. H., M.C. Australian war photographs. A pictorial record from Nov., 1917, to the end of the war. Australia House 1919. 4*s.*

Wilkinson, Norman. The Dardanelles: Colour Sketches from Gallipoli. 30 plates reproduced from drawings made on the spot. Longmans 1915. 12*s.* 6*d.*

XI. BIOGRAPHIES.

(a) *Collective.*

Admirals of the British Navy. Portraits in Colours by F. Dodd, with Introduction and Biographical Notes. Parts I and II. Country Life 1917. 5*s.* each.

Barnett, Lieut. Gilbert, R.A.F. V.C.'s of the air. A national record of 18 men. With additional chapter on heroes of America. Illustrations by Dudley Tennant. Simpkin Marshall 1918. 5*s.*

Bennett, A. H. English Medical Women: glimpses of their work in peace and war. I. Pitman 1914. 3*s.* 6*d.*

Britain's Great Men: Roberts, Kitchener, French. Illustrated Newnes 1914. 2*s.* 6*d.*

Cambridge Review War List. (Members of the University on active service.) Latest edn. Cambridge Review, April 1917 3*s.* 6*d.*

Cambridge University War List, 1914-18. Ed. by G. V. Carey Camb. Univ. Press 1921. 20*s.*

Clutterbuck, Col. L. A., and others. The Bond of Sacrifice. A biographical record of all British Officers who fell in the Great War. Vol. I, Aug.-Dec. 1914. Anglo-African Publ. Contractors 1916. 31*s.* 6*d.*

Delvert, Capitaine. Quelques Héros (non-combatant as well as combatant). Illustrated. Berger-Levrault 1918. 3 fr. 50.

Destrée, Jules. Figures Italiennes d'aujourd'hui. (Character Sketches of ten Notable Italians.) Van Oest 1918.

Gardiner, A. G. War Lords. (Wayfarer's Library.) Dent 1915. 1*s.*

—— —— Also with 16 portraits by Clive Gardner. Enlarged and revised. Dent. 7*s.* 6*d.*

General French and Admiral Jellicoe. (Noble Lives series Collins 1915. 1*s.* 6*d.*

Generals of the British Army. By F. Dodd. Portraits in colours with introduction and biographical notes. Parts I and II Country Life 1917-18. 5*s.* each.

Gli uomini della guerra, 1914-16. (Diplomazia, Politica, Spionaggio, Milizia, Giornalismo.) By S. Bargellini. Milan 191[illegible] 4 l.

Harden, Maximilian. Word Portraits: character sketches of famous men and women (William I, the Empress Frederick, Bismarck, Holstein, etc.). Transl. by Julius Gabe. Blackwood 1911. 10*s*. 6*d*.

Howe, M. A. de Wolfe. Memoirs of the Harvard Dead in the war against Germany. Vol. II. Harvard Univ. Press 1921 17*s*.

Jouve, P. J. Men of Europe 1915. Translated by R. F. Omega Workshops 1915. 2*s*.

Leask, A. V.C. Heroes of the War. Illustrated. Harrap 1916. 3*s*. 6*d*.

Leslie, Lieut.-Col. J. H. An Historical Roll (with portraits) of the Women of the British Empire to whom the Military Medal has been awarded, 1914-1918. Sheffield: Leng 1919. 1*s*.

Lloyd's Who's Who in the Great War. Hodder & Stoughton 1914.

Oxford University Roll of Service. Edited by E. S. Craig and W. M. Gibson. Oxford Univ. Press 1920.

Radziwill, Princess Catherine. Sovereigns and Statesmen of Europe. Cassell 1915. 10*s*. 6*d*.

Royal Navy List, The; or Who's Who in the Navy. War Supplement. Witherby 1917. 10*s*.

Silhouettes allemandes. (Studies of notable Germans, Bethmann-Hollweg, Tirpitz, Harden, &c.) By P. L. Hervier. Paris: Nouv. Revue 1916. 3 fr. 50.

Translated under title, The Super-Huns. Eveleigh Nash 1917. 3*s*. 6*d*.

Soldier Poets. For remembrance. (Biographies of 44 poets who have fallen in the War.) By A. St. J. Adcock. Hodder & Stoughton 1918. 7*s*. 6*d*.

University of Dublin: Trinity College War List. Hodges Figgis 1916. 1*s*.

Who's Who in the War. With Maps of Europe and the Franco-German frontier. Edited by George L. Polsue. Gough House 1914. 1*s*.

Wile, Frederick William. Men around the Kaiser. Thirty-one biographical sketches. Heinemann. 2*s*.

Zimmern, Helen. Italian Leaders of To-Day. Portraits. Williams & Norgate 1915. 5*s*.

(b) *Individual.*

Abdul Hamid.

Life, by Sir Edwin Pears (Makers of the 19th Century Series). Constable 1917. 6*s*.

ALBERT, KING OF THE BELGIANS.

Albert et Elisabeth de Belgique. By M. Bierme. Préface de Emile Verhaeren. Payot 1917. 3 fr. 50.

Life of H.M. Albert, King of the Belgians. By John de C. MacDonnell. Long 1915. 1*s*.

BALL, CAPT., V.C.

A Biography, by W. A. Briscoe and H. R. Stannard. Illustrated. Herbert Jenkins 1918. 6*s*.

BOTHA, GENERAL.

Louis Botha: or, Through the Great Thirst Land. By K. Morris. Stevens 1915. 1*s*.

General Botha: the career and the man. By Harold Spender. Constable 1916. 7*s*. 6*d*.

BÜLOW, PRINCE.

Le Prince de Buelow. By André Tardieu. Paris 1909. 3 fr. 50.

CAVELL, EDITH.

Case of Miss Cavell. By James M. Beck. Central Committee. 1*d*.

The Martyr Nurse: the Death and Achievement of Edith Cavell. By Douglas Blackburn. Ridd Masson Co. 1915. 6*d*.

Martyrdom of Nurse Cavell: the Life Story of the victim of Germany's most barbarous crime. By W. T. Hill. Hutchinson 1915. 7*d*.

Edith Cavell: her Life Story: a Norfolk tribute. By Herbert Leeds. Jarrold 1915. 1*s*.

In Memoriam: Edith Cavell. By William S. Murphy. F. & E Stoneham 1916. 6*d*.

Nurse Cavell: the Story of Her Life and Martyrdom. Pearson 1915. 6*d*.

A Noble Woman: the Life Story of Edith Cavell. By Ernest Protheroe. Kelly 1916. 1*s*.

The Murder of Nurse Cavell. With Appendix giving the correspondence. By Charles Sarolea. Allen & Unwin 1916 1*s*.

Edith Cavell, la vie et la mort de: d'après des documents inédit récits de témoins [&c.]. Preface by M. Painlevé, membr de l'Institut. Portraits. Fontemoing 1915. 3 fr. 50.

CHAMBERLAIN, HOUSTON STEWART.

Houston Stewart Chamberlain. By Ernest Seillière. Renaissance du Livre 1917. 2 fr.

CLEMENCEAU, GEORGES.

Georges Clemenceau: the Tiger of France. By Georges Lecompte. Transl. from the French. New York: Dutton 1919.

Georges Clemenceau: the man and his times. By H. M. Hyndman. Grant Richards 1919. 12*s*. 6*d*.

CONSTANTINE, KING.

Constantin Ier, roi des Hellènes. By Léon Maccas. Bossard 1917. 1 fr. 50.

Constantine, King and Traitor. By Demetra Vaka. (Illustrated.) Lane 1918. 12*s*. 6*d*.

Ex-King Constantine and the War. By Major G. M. Melas (his former secretary). Hutchinson 1920. 12*s*. 6*d*.

CORNWELL, JOHN T

Jack Cornwell: The Story of J. T. C., V.C. Boy: 1st Class. By the author of Where's Master? Hodder & Stoughton 1917. 1*s*. 3*d*.

DON, ARCHIBALD.

A Memoir. Edited by Charles Sayle. Murray 1918. 10*s*. 6*d*.

FERDINAND OF BULGARIA.

Ferdinand of Bulgaria: the Amazing Career of a Shoddy Czar. By the author of The Real Kaiser. Melrose 1916. 2*s*.

Les Complices des auteurs de la guerre. I. Ferdinand 1er tsar de Bulgarie. By Ernest Daudet. Attinger 1917. 3 fr. 50.

FOCH, MARSHAL.

Marshal Foch: His Life and Theory of Modern War. By Capt. A. H. Atteridge. With introduction by Col. John Buchan. Skeffington 1918. 6*s*.

Marshal Foch: His life, his work, his faith. By René Puaux. Transl. from the French. Hodder & Stoughton 1918. 5*s*.

FORBES, J. K.

Student and Sniper-sergeant. A Memoir of J. K. Forbes, M.A., who died for his country on Sept. 25, 1915. By W. Taylor and P. Diack. Hodder & Stoughton 1916. 3*s*. 6*d*.

FRANCIS JOSEPH, EMPEROR.

The Life of the Emperor Francis Joseph. By Francis Gribble Nash 1914. 16*s*.

The Emperor Francis Joseph and his Times. By Lieut.-Gen. Baron von Margutti. Transl. from the German. Hutchinson 1921. 24*s*.

Behind the Scenes at the Court of Vienna. The private life of the Emperor of Austria. By H. de Weindel, and P. W. Sergeant. Long. 2*s*.

FRENCH, FIELD-MARSHAL LORD.

Sir John French: an authentic biography. By Cecil Chisholm. With introduction by Sir Evelyn Wood. Portrait. Jenkins. 1*s*.

Field-Marshal Sir John French: the Story of His Life and Battles. By Walter Jerrold. Hammond 1915. 1*s*.

GEORGE, DAVID LLOYD.

David Lloyd George. By Herbert Du Parcq. Newnes 1915. 2*s*. 6*d*.

The Life of David Lloyd George By J. Hugh Edwards. Illustrated. Waverley Book Co. 1914. 7*s*. 6*d*.

Lloyd George: the man and his story. By F. Dilnot. Fisher Unwin 1917. 3*s*. 6*d*.

Lloyd George and the War. By an independent Liberal. Hutchinson 1917. 2*s*.

GEORGE, KING OF GREECE.

King George of Greece. By Walter Christmas. Illustrated. Nash 1914. 15*s*.

GRENFELL, F. AND RIVERSDALE (BROTHERS).

A Memoir. By John Buchan (illustrated). 1920. 15*s*.

GRENFELL, JULIAN.

Julian Grenfell. By Viola Meynell. (Reprinted from the Dublin Review.) Burns & Oates 1917. 1*s*.

GREY, SIR EDWARD (VISCOUNT).

Sir Edward Grey: the Man and his Work. Newnes 1915. 2*s*. 6*d*.

GUYNEMER (AVIATOR).

Le Chevalier de l'air: vie héroïque de Guynemer. By Henri Bordeaux. Avec portrait. Plon-Nourrit 1918. 4 fr. 50.

—— Transl. under title Guynemer, Knight of the Air, with preface by Rudyard Kipling. Chatto & Windus 1918. 6*s*.

HEATH, ARTHUR GEORGE.

Letters of Arthur George Heath (of New College). With memoir by Gilbert Murray. Blackwell 1917. 3*s*. 6*d*.

HINDENBURG, FIELD-MARSHAL VON.

Generalfeldmarschall v. Hindenburg. Sein Leben u. seine Taten. By E. Ginschel. Mit 20 Vollbild. u. zahlr. Textabb. 1917. 15 mk.

HUGHES, WILLIAM MORRIS.

From Boundary Rider to Prime Minister: Hughes of Australia, the Man of the Hour. By Douglas Sladen. Hutchinson 1916. 1*s*.

INGLIS, DR. ELSIE.

A biography of the leader of the Scottish Women's Hospital. By Lady Frances Balfour. Hodder & Stoughton 1918 6*s*.

JELLICOE, ADMIRAL.

Admiral Jellicoe. By Arthur Applin. Pearson. 1*s*.

JOFFRE, GENERAL.

General Joffre. By French Gunner (pseud.). Simpkin 1915. 6*d*. & 1*s*.

Life of General Joffre: the Cooper's son who became Commander in-Chief. By Alexander Kahn. Heinemann 1915. 1*s*.

Notre Joffre, Maréchal de France. By E. Hinzelin. Lettre-Préface autographe du Maréchal. Delagrave 1918. 10 fr.

General Joffre and his battles. By Recouly, Raymond (Capt. X). Maps. Scribner 1916. $1.25.

K. S. P.

Records of a Rectory Garden (Memoir of one who fell in the War). Longmans 1917. 2*s.*

KITCHENER, LORD.

Life of Lord Kitchener. By Sir G. Arthur. 3 vols. Macmillan 1920. 52*s.* 6*d.*

The Story of Lord Kitchener (Little Stories of Great Lives). By A. O. Cook. Ed. by Herbert Strang. Frowde; Hodder & Stoughton 1916. 1*s.*

L'Œuvre et le prestige de Lord Kitchener. By Henry D. Davray. Plon-Nourrit 1917. 2 fr.

Lord Kitchener. By Henry D. Davray. Introductory letter by M. Paul Cambon. Fisher Unwin 1917. 2*s.* 6*d.*

The Tragedy of Lord Kitchener. By Viscount Esher. Murray 1921. 10*s.*

Field-Marshal Lord Kitchener. His Life and Work for the Empire. By E. S. Grew and others. Vol. I, II & III (to be completed in 3 vols.). Illustrated. Gresham Publ. Co. 1916. 8*s.* 6*d.*

Lord Kitchener: the Story of His Life. By Horace G. Groser. New edn., brought down to date. Pearson 1914. 1*s.*

Kitchener in his own words. By J. B. Rye and H. G. Groser. Fisher Unwin 1917. 10*s.* 6*d.*

Earl Kitchener of Khartoum: the Story of His Life. By Walter Jerrold. Hammond 1915. 1*s.*

Lord Kitchener: Memorial Sermon preached on Whit-Sunday, 1916, by a Country Parson. Bale, Danielssohn 1916. 1*s.*

Lord Kitchener of Khartoum: a Biography. By the author of King Edward the Seventh. Nisbet 1914. 1*s.*

Lord Kitchener (for young readers). By D. A. Mackenzie. Blackie 1917. 1*s.*

Lord Kitchener Memorial Book, The. (Published on behalf of the Lord Kitchener Memorial Fund.) With a collection of Lord Kitchener's speeches, and illustrations. Ed. by Sir Hedley le Bas. Hodder & Stoughton 1916. 3*s.* 6*d.*

Lord Kitchener. By Mortimer Menpes. (Portrait biographies.) Black 1915. 2*s.*

Lord Kitchener. By Ernest Protheroe. Kelly 1916. 1*s.*

Sécrets de Lord K. By C. D. Ventallo. Madrid 1914. 5*s.*

—— Transl. into German under title, Kitcheners Geheimnis Barcelona 1915. 2 mk.

KRAMARSCH, D.K.

Dr. K. K. der Anstifter des Weltkriegs. By F. Wichte. Munich 1918. 5 mk.

"LE CAPITAINE J.R." (P. Jérome).

Un Moine soldat. Xavier Thérésette, en religion. Fr. Marcel de Reims, des Frères mineurs capucins. Beauchesne 1917. 1 fr. 50.

LENIN, N.

Life. By M. A. Landau-Aldanov. Paris, Povolozky. n.d. 5 fr.

LISTER, CHARLES.

Letters and Recollections of Charles Lister; with a memoir by his father, Lord Ribblesdale. Fisher Unwin 1916. 12*s*. 6*d*.

LUDENDORFF, GENERAL.

Ludendorff. By Gen. Buat. (A criticism of his operations and an examination of the value of his military doctrines.) Payot 1921. 6 fr.

LUSK, JAMES.

Letters and Memories (of an officer in the Cameronian Highlanders, killed in Dec., 1915). Blackwell 1917. 2*s*.

MCGREGOR, A. W.

A memoir; by his father. Cape Times 1918. n.p.

MERCIER, CARDINAL.

Le Cardinal Mercier. Illustré. By G. Goyau. Perrin 1918. 2 fr. 40.

NICHOLAS II, TSAR.

Tsar Nicholas II. By Elchaninov, A. Illustrated. H. Rees 1914. 7*s*. 6*d*.

Le dernier Romanoff. By C. Rivet. Perrin 1917. 3 fr. 50.

The Last of the Romanoffs. By C. Rivet. Illustrated. Constable 1917. 6*s*.

Nichoļas II inconnu. By General A. A. Noskoff (Jarson). Plon-Nourrit 1919. 5 fr.

Treize années à la cour de Russie (1905-18). (By Pierre Gilliard, former tutor of the Tsarevitch.) Illustré. Payot 1921. 10 fr.

PÉGOUD (Aviator).

Le Premier As, Pégoud. By Paul Bonnefon. Berger-Levrault 1918. 4 fr. 55.

PÉGUY, CHARLES.

Avec Charles Péguy, de la Lorraine à la Marne, Août.-Sept., 1914. By Victor Boudon. Preface by Maurice Barrès. Portrait. Hachette 1916. 3 fr. 50.

Charles Péguy et les Cahiers de la Quinzaine. By Daniel Halévy. Paris: Payot 1918. 4 fr. 50.

PETER, KING OF SERBIA.

Pierre Ier, roi de Serbie. (Pages actuelles.) By René Chambry. Blond & Gay 1917. 60 ct.

POINCARÉ, RAYMOND.

Raymond, Poincaré: a Sketch. Duckworth 1914. 5*s.*

POLLARD (Brothers).

Two Brothers. (Letters, etc.) With introduction by Mr. A. W. Pollard, compiled from his sons' letters. Sedgwick & Jackson 1917. 1*s.* 6*d.*

RASPUTIN, GREGORY.

Autour de Raspoutine. By Jean Finot. (Extrait de La Revue.) La Revue 1917. 1 fr.

Rasputin: Prophet, Libertine, and Plotter. Translated from the Danish by W. F. Harvey. Fisher Unwin 1917. 3*s.* 6*d.*

Rasputin and Russia. The tragedy of a throne. By Victor E. Marsden. Bird 1919. 6*d.*

REDMOND, MAJOR WILLIAM.

From the Trenches: a Plea and a Claim Preceded by Memories of Major Redmond, by Mgr. Arthur Ryan, and followed by an In Memoriam signed W.M. Burns & Oates 1917. 1*s.* 6*d.*

Trench Pictures from France. With Biographical Introduction by E. M. Smith-Dampier. Melrose 1917. 3*s.* 6*d.*

ROBERTS, LORD.

Story of Lord Roberts. By Harold F. B. Wheeler. Harrap 1915. 3*s*. 6*d*.
Lord Roberts, K.G., V.C. By Owen Wheeler. Ward, Lock 1915. 3*s*. 6*d*.

ROBERTSON, SIR WILLIAM.

The Life Story of the Chief of the Imperial General Staff. By G. A. Leask. Cassell 1916. 1*s*.
From Private to Field-Marshal. (Autobiogr., illustrated.) Constable 1921. 21*s*.

SEDDING, GEORGE ELTON.

Life and Work of an Artist Soldier. Edited by his brother. Garden City Press 1918. 5*s*.

SMUTS, GENERAL.

Character Sketch of General, the Right Hon. J. C. Smuts. By N. Levi. Portraits and illustrations. Longmans 1917. 7*s*. 6*d*.

TIRPITZ.

Life. By E. Bassermann. Berlin 1916. 1 mk.

VENIZELOS.

Life. By H. A. Gibbons. Unwin 1921. 14*s*.
Eleftherios Venizelos: his Life and Work. By C. Kerofilas. With introduction by Take Jonescu. Murray 1915. 3*s*. 6*d*.
Venizelos and the War: A Sketch of Personalities and Politics. By Crawfurd Price. Simpkin Marshall.
Venizelos: a Study. By H. A. Gibbons. (Illustrated.) Fisher Unwin 1921. 14*s*.

WILLIAM II, GERMAN EMPEROR.

Guillaume II (1890-'99). By Madame Adam. Paris: Alcan 1917. 3 fr. 50.
The Last of the War Lords. By an anonymous author. Grant Richards 1918. 10*s*. 6*d*.
The Kaiser under the Searchlight. By A. H. Catling. Fisher Unwin. 2*s*.
The Kaiser I Know. My Fourteen Years with the Kaiser 1904-1918. By A. N. Davis, D.D.S. Hodder & Stoughton 1918. 10*s*. 6*d*.

Wilhelm Hohenzollern & Co. (The Kaiser and his chief associates.) By Edward Lyell Fox. New York: McBride 1917. $1.50.

Der Kaiser. Eine Betrachtung. By Walther Rathenau. Berlin: Fischer 1919. 1 mk.

The German Emperor and the Peace of the World. By Alfred Hermann Fried. (Nobel Peace Prize.) With a preface by Norman Angell. Hodder & Stoughton. 6*s.*

The German Emperor as shown in his public utterances. By Christian Gauss. (The author is Professor of Modern Languages at Princeton University.) Heinemann. 6*s.*

William II, judged on evidence of his own speeches and on writings of his contemporaries. By S. C. Hammer. Heinemann 1917. 5*s.*

The Two Williams. Studies of the Kaiser and the Crown Prince. By P. L. Hervier. Nash 1916. 7*s.* 6*d.*

Stories of the Kaiser and his Ancestors. By Clare Jerrold. Paul 1915. 2*s.* and 2*s.* 6*d.*

Impressions of the Kaiser. By David Jayne Hill, former U.S. Ambassador at Berlin. Chapman & Hall 1918. 12*s.* 6*d.*

The Gospel according to William II. By A. D. McLaren. An Australian in Germany. Constable. 6*s.*

L'Évolution Belliqueuse de Guilluame II. By M. Muret. Payot 1917. 3 fr. 50.

Germany and the German Emperor. By G. H. Perris. Melrose. 2*s.* 6*d.*

Caligula: a Study in Imperial Insanity. By Prof. Ludwig Quidde. A famous pamphlet published in 1894, now translated into English, by Claud Field, under the title, The Kaiser's Double. Rider. 1*d.*

Wilhelm II. By Adolf Stein. Leipzig: Dieterich 1909. 3 mk.

With the Kaiser in the East in 1898. By Sir William Treloar. Horace Marshall 1915. 6*d.*

Is the Kaiser Insane? A study of the Great Outlaw. By Arnold White. Pearson 1915. 1*s.*

The War Lord. By J. M. Kennedy. A character study of Kaiser William II, by means of his speeches, letters and telegrams. F. & C. Palmer. 7*d.*

The Public and Private Life of Kaiser William II. By E. Legge. Includes the author's experiences in France in 1870. Nash. 7*s.* 6*d.*

The Kaiser: his Personality and Career. By Joseph M'Cabe. Unwin 1915. 5*s.*

The Psychology of the Kaiser. By Morton Prince, LL.D., an American Physician. Fisher Unwin. 2*s*. 6*d*.

The Kaiser 1859-1914. By Stanley Shaw. Methuen. 1*s*.

William, Crown Prince.

Crosland, T. W. H. The Soul of a Crown Prince. W. Laurie 1916. 1*s*.

Kaiser's Heir, The: a Pen-Portrait. Illustrated. Mills & Boon 1914.

The Real Crown Prince. A record and an indictment. By the author of King Edward VII. Newnes. 2*s*. 6*d*.

Kronprinz Wilhelm. By Major Kurt Anker. Berlin: Mittler 1920. 5 mk.

Wilson, Capt. T. I. W.

Memoir and letters Sidgwick & Jackson 1917. 1*s*. 6*d*.

Wilson, President.

President Wilson. By Daniel Halévy. Étude sur la démocratie américaine. Payot 1918. 4 fr.

—— English transl., by Hugh Stokes. Lane 1920. 7*s*. 6*d*.

The Peace President: a brief appreciation. By William Archer. Hutchinson 1918. 2*s*.

President Wilson: his Problems and his Policy. By H. Wilson Harris. New edn., enlarged. Headley 1918. 2*s*. 6*d*.

President Wilson: the Man and his Message. By C. Sheridan Jones. Rider 1918. 1*s*. 6*d*.

Woodrow Wilson et son peuple. By A. G. de Lapradelle. Paris: Bossard 1918. 7 fr. 50.

Le Président Wilson, la guerre, la paix, recueil des déclarations du président des États-Unis d'Amérique sur la guerre et la paix 20 décembre 1916-6 avril 1918. By M. T. H. MacCarthy. Avec portrait. Berger-Levrault 1918. 2 fr.

President Wilson from an English Point of View. New York: Stokes 1917. $1.75.

Woodrow Wilson: an interpretation. Little, Brown & Co. 1918. $2.00.

Woodrow Wilson and his Work. By Prof. W. E. Dodd. Simpkin 1920. 15*s*.

XII.—BREACHES OF INTERNATIONAL LAW

A—*Official*.

Alleged German Outrages, Report of the Committee on. Appointed by H.M. Government, and presided over by Lord Bryce. [Cd. 7894.] H.M.S.O. 1915. With maps, fol. 6*d*.; no maps, 8vo, 1*d*.

Alleged German Outrages, Report of the Committee on. Evidence and Documents laid before the above Committee. Appendix to the Report (8vo). [Cd. 7895.] H.M.S.O. 1915. 6*d.*

Allemands, Les, destructeurs de Cathédrales et de trésors du passé. The destruction of Reims, Arras, Senlis and Louvain. Piéces Justificatives and photographs. Hachette. 1*s.* 8*d.*

Baralong, H.M. Auxiliary Cruiser. Memorandum of the German Government in regard to Incidents alleged to have attended the destruction of a German submarine and its crew by H.M. Auxiliary Cruiser Baralong on 19th August, 1915, and Reply of H.M. Government thereto. Miscellaneous No. 1 (1916). [Cd.. 8144.] H.M.S.O. 1916. 2½*d.*

—— Further Correspondence with the German Government in regard to the destruction of a German submarine and its crew by, 19th August 1915. Miscellaneous No. 7 (1916). [Cd. 8176.] H.M.S.O. 1916. 1*d.*

Belgian Commission of Enquiry on the violation of the Rights of Nations, and of the Laws and Customs of War in Belgium. Reports: Vol. II, 13th to 22nd Reports of the Commission. Containing Facsimiles of German Soldiers' Diaries; Correspondence between His Eminence Cardinal Mercier and the German Authorities; Solemn Protest of Mgr. Heylen, Bishop of Namur. H.M.S.O. 1916. 6*d.*

Belgischen Greuelthaten, die, gegen die Deutschen. Der Franktireurkrieg und die Verwendung von Dumdum-Geschossen im Kriege 1914. Aemtliche und glaubwürdige Berichte. 60 pf.

Belgium, Case of, in the Present War. An account of the violation of the Neutrality of Belgium and of the Laws of War on Belgian territory. Published for the Belgian delegates to the United States. N.Y.: Macmillan & Co. 1*s.*

Belgium, Violation of the Rights of Nations and of the Laws and Customs of War in. Reports of the Official Commission of the Belgian Government. With preface and plates. Wyman 1915. 6*d.*

—— Reports of the Commission of Enquiry into the Violation of International Law. H.M.S.O. 1915. 1*d.* each.

Black Book of the War. German Atrocities in France and Belgium. Full text of the Official Reports. Transl. Daily Chronicle Office. 2*d.*

British Hospital Ships, Alleged Misuse of. Correspondence with the German Government regarding the. Miscellaneous No. 16 (1917). [Cd. 8692.] H.M.S.O. 1917. 3*d.*

British Hospital Ships—Torpedoing by German Submarines of the British Hospital Ships Rewa, Glenart Castle, Guildford Castle, and Llandovery Castle—Circular Despatch addressed to H.M. Diplomatic Representatives in Allied and Neutral Countries respecting the. Miscellaneous No. 26 (1918). H.M.S.O. 1918. 3*d*.

Cavell, Miss, Correspondence with U.S. Ambassador respecting the Execution of, at Brussels. [Cd. 8013.] H.M.S.O. 1915. 1*d*.

Chuguet, Arthur. Prouesses allemandes. (Collective statement of German crimes, based on official reports). Fontemoing: Paris. 3 fr. 50.

Dampierre, J. de. L'Allemagne et le Droit des Gens, d'après les sources allemandes et les archives du gouvernement français. Berger-Levrault 1915. 6 fr.

—— Translated under title German Imperialism and International Law. Illustrations from facsimiles. Constable 1916. 10*s*. 6*d*.

Deportation of Belgians to Germany and the Forced Labour imposed upon them by the German Authorities—Correspondence with the Belgian Minister respecting the. Miscellaneous, No. 37 (1916). [Cd. 8404.] H.M.S.O. 1916. 1*d*.

Dresden, Sinking of the. Notes exchanged with the Chilean Minister respecting the Sinking of the German Cruiser Dresden in Chilean Territorial Waters. [Cd. 7859.] Miscellaneous, No. 9 (1915). H.M.S.O. 1915. ½*d*.

Falaba, s.s. Report of formal investigation into the circumstances attending the foundering on 28th March, 1915, of s.s. Falaba. [Cd. 8021.] H.M.S.O. 1915. 1½*d*.

—— Proceedings on a formal investigation into the loss of s.s. Falaba. 1st, 2nd, 3rd and 4th days. H.M.S.O. 1915. 1*s*. each.

Fifth Report of the Commission of Enquiry on the Violation of the Rules of International Law and of the Laws and Customs of Warfare. H.M.S.O. 1914. 1*d*.

Genower, J.P., Able Seaman. Correspondence with the German Government respecting the death by burning of, when prisoner of war at Brandenburg Camp. Miscellaneous, No. 6 (1918). [Cd. 8987.] H.M.S.O. 1918. 1½*d*.

German Atrocities and Breaches of the Rules of War in Africa, Papers relating to. [Cd. 8306.] H.M.S.O. 1916. 9½*d*.

German Atrocities in France. A translation of the Official Report of the French Commission. Published by authority. United Newspapers Ltd.

German Breaches of the Laws of War. Transl. from the French Official Report and evidence. Heinemann 1915. 5*s.*

German War Trials. Report of proceedings before the Supreme Court in Leipzig, with appendices. [Cmd. 1450.] H.M.S.O. 1921. 7½*d.*

L'Allemagne et le Droit des Gens. Faits criminels commis à l'égard des combattants et du personnel sanitaire. Reports III and IV of the French Commission of Inquiry. Imp. des Journ off. 1915. 5 c.

Lusitania, s.s. Report of a formal investigation into the circumstances attending the foundering on 7th May, 1915, of s.s. Lusitania. [Cd. 8022.] H.M.S.O. 1915. 1½*d.*

—— Proceedings on a formal investigation into the loss of s.s. Lusitania. H.M.S.O. 1915. 1st to 3rd days, 1*s.* each; 5th day, 1*s.*

—— Shipping Casualties (loss of s.s. Lusitania). Proceedings in camera on June 15th and 18th at the formal investigation into the circumstances attending the foundering on May 7, 1915, of the British steamship Lusitania. [Cmd. 381.] H.M.S.O. 1919. 3*d.*

Microbe Culture at Bukarest. Discoveries at the German Legation from Rumanian Official Documents. Hodder & Stoughton 1917. 1*d.*

Morgan, Prof. J. H. German Atrocities: an official investigation. By the late Home Office Commissioner with the British Expeditionary Force. Fisher Unwin 1916. 1*s.*

Official Book of the German Atrocities: told by victims and eye-witnesses. Complete verbatim report of the Belgian, French and Russian Commissions of Inquiry. Published by authority. Pearson. 1*s.*

Papers relating to German Atrocities and breaches of the Rules of War in Africa. [Cd. 8306.] Wyman, July 1916. 9½*d.*

Rapports et Procès-verbaux d'Enquête de la Commission instituée en vue de constater les actes commis par l'ennemi en violation du Droit des Gens. Documents relatifs à la Guerre, 1914-15. With photographs. Imp. Nat. 1915. 1 fr. 50.

—— (Décret du 23 septembre, 1914.) 3 vols. Imprimerie du Journal Officiel 1916. 3 fr. 50 each.

Rapports sur la violation du Droit des Gens en Belgique. Collective edition of the 12 Official Reports, with preface by M. J. Van den Heuvel, Ministre d'Etat, and other matter. (The Reports of the Commission d'Enquête were published separately in the Moniteur Belge, Aug. 1914-Jan. 1915.) Berger-Levrault. 1 fr. 25.

Rapports sur la violation du Droit des Gens en Belgique. English transl. (official) of the above. Published on behalf of the Belgian Legation. H.M.S.O. *6d.*

Rapports sur les violations du Droit des Gens en Belgique. Publication officielle du Gouvernement Belge. Rapports 13-22 de la Commission d'Enquête (with facsimiles, etc.). Berger-Levrault 1916. 1 fr. 50.

Report of the French Commission d'Enquête instituée en vue de constater les actes commis pas l'ennemi en violation du Droit des Gens. Journal Officiel, Jan. 8, 1915.

Sammlung von Nachweisen für die Verletzungen des Völkerrechts durch die mit Œsterreich-Ungarn kriegführenden Staaten. Abgeschlossen mit 31 Jan., 1915. Published by the Austro-Hungarian Foreign Office. Vienna: K. K. Hof- und Staatsdruckerei 1915. *2s. 6d.*

B.—*Personal.*

Andler, Charles. Les Usages de la Guerre et la Doctrine de l'état major allemand. Alcan 1915. 1 fr. 25.

—— —— Transl. under title, Frightfulness in theory and practice. Fisher Unwin. *2s. 6d.*

Andriulli, Giuseppe. Il libro della guerra: Tedeschi ed Austriaci contro il diritto della guerra. Florence 1917. 1 l. 90.

Anton, Reinhold. Der Lügenfeldzug uneerer Feinde. 2 vols. Leipzig 1914, 15.

Ballard, Frank. Plain Truths versus German Lies. Documents. Kelly. *1s.*

Bédier, Joseph. Les crimes allemands d'après des témoignages allemands. Paris 1915.

—— Comment l'Allemagne essaie de justifier ses crimes. Paris 1916.

Booth, J. B. The Gentle Cultured German. (Documents.) Grant Richards. *2s.*

Chambry, Réné. The truth about Louvain. Reprinted from the Echo Belge. Hodder & Stoughton 1915. *1s.*

Colin, L. Les Barbares à la Trouée des Vosges. Evidence as to German atrocities collected in the district concerned. Preface by Maurice Barrès. Bloud et Gay. 3 fr. 50.

Crimes of Germany, The. (Special Supplement to The Field, revised and brought up to date, with extra illustrations.) Preface by Sir T. A. Cook. The Field Office 1916. *1s.*

D. M. C. The Irish Nuns at Ypres: an Episode of the War. Ed. by G. R. Barry O'Brien. Smith, Elder. *2s. 6d.*

Dampierre, Jacques de. L'Allemagne et le Droit des Gens, d'après les sources allemandes et les archives du gouvernement français. Maps and illustrations. Berger-Levrault 1915. 6 fr.

Davignon, Henri. Les Procédés de Guerre des Allemands en Belgique. Extrait du Correspondant, Jan. 25, 1915. De Soye.

Gaultier, Paul. La Barbarie allemande : Les Faits. Les Origines. Les Causes. La Théorie. Plon-Nourrit 1917. 3 fr. 50.

German Atrocities on Record. With authentic illustrations. Supplement to The Field, Feb. 13, 1915. Field Office. *6d.*

Grondijs, L. H. Les Allemands en Belgique. (Series, Pages d'Histoire.) Berger-Levrault. 60 c.

Gruben, Hervé de. Les Allemands à Louvain : souvenirs d'un témoin. Plon. 2 fr.

Hale, Col. Sir Lonsdale. The Horrors of War in Great Britain. Love and Malcolmson. *2d.*

Horrors of Louvain, The. By an Eye-witness. Introduction by Lord Halifax. Sunday Times 1916. *3d.*

Kuttner, Max. Deutsche Verbrechen (reply to Bédier). Leipzig 1915.

Langenhove, F. van. Comment naît un cycle de légendes : Francs-tireurs et atrocités en Belgique. Payot 1916. 3 fr.

Le Queux, William. German Atrocities : a Record of Shameless Deeds. Newnes 1914. *1s.*

Lynden-Bell, Col. C. P. How Germany makes War. Guernsey : The Star Office. *2d.*

Maccas, Léon. La Guerre de 1914. Les cruautés allemandes : réquisitoire d'un neutre. By a Greek savant. Nouv. Libr. Nationale. 3 fr. 50.

Maeterlinck, Maurice. The Massacre of the Innocents. Translated by Alfred Allinson. Allen & Unwin. *1s.*

Marre, F. Les Armes déloyales des Allemands. (Pages actuelles, No. 94.) Bloud et Gay 1916. 60 c.

Mears, E. Grimwood. The Destruction of Belgium. A reply to the German White Book defending the conduct of the Germans in Belgium. Heinemann 1916. *3d.*

Müller, Ernst. Der Weltkrieg und das Völkerrecht (The World-War and International Law). Eine Anklage gegen die Kriegsführung des Dreiverbandes (Against the conduct of war by the Entente Powers). Berlin : Reimer 1915.

Mullins, Claud. The Leipzig Trials. An account of the war criminals' trial and a study of German mentality. With introduction by Sir Ernest Pollock. Witherby 1921. *8s. 6d.*

Prüm. La conduite allemande des hostilités en Belgique et les instructions de Benoît XV. Lettre ouverte à M. M. Erzbergen, deputé au Reichstag. Paris 1915.

Reiss, Prof. R. A. Comment les Austro-Hongrois ont fait la guerre en Serbie. (Essais et Documents sur la guerre.) Colin. 50 c.

—— Les infractions aux règles et lois de la guerre (especially in South-Eastern Europe). Payot 1917. 3 fr.

—— Report upon the Atrocities committed by the Austro-Hungarian army during the first invasion of Serbia. Transl. by F. S. Copeland. Simpkin, Marshall, 1916. 5*s*.

—— Réponses aux accusations austro-hongroises contenues dans les deux Recueils de Témoignages concernant les actes de violation de droit des gens commis par les États en guerre avec l'Autriche-Hongrie. Payot. 1 fr.

—— The Kingdom of Serbia. Infringements of the Rules and Laws of War committed by the Austro-Bulgaro-Germans. Allen and Unwin 1919. 3*s*. 6*d*.

Renault, Prof. Les premières violations du Droit des Gens par l'Allemagne. Paris 1917.

—— Transl. under title, First violations of International Law by Germany : Luxemburg and Belgium. Longmans 1917. 2*s*.

Rezanoff, A. S. Les Atrocités Allemandes du Côté Russe. Transl. into French by R. Marchand. Petrograd 1916.

Roberts, A. A. The Poison War: Facts and Revelations. (Reveals the fact that the Germans were preparing for asphyxiation long ago.) Heinemann. 5*s*.

Robida, A. Les villes martyres. Illustrations and text. Folio. Baudelot 1915. 20 f.

Sefton-Jones, H. German Crimes and our Civil Remedy. Lane 1916. 6*d*.

Terwagne, Dr. Pour le Défense du Pays (a collection of documents illustrating crimes committed by Germany against Belgium and Holland). Van Oest 1916. 3 fr. 50.

The Germans in Belgium. The experiences of a Neutral. Heinemann. 1*s*.

The Truth About German Atrocities. Founded on the Report of Lord Bryce's Committee. Parl. Recruiting Committee.

Their Crimes. Transl. from the French. (German crimes against the people of Belgium and Northern France.) Documentary. Cassell 1917. 6*d*.

Van Houtte, Paul. Le crime de Guillaume II et la Belgique : Récits d'un témoin oculaire. With appendices and 2 plates. Picard 1915. 3 fr. 50.

—— Transl., The Pan-Germanic Crime. Impressions and investigations in Belgium during the German occupation. By an Eye-witness. Hodder & Stoughton. 1*s*.

Wampach, Gaspard. Le Grand-Duché de Luxembourg et l'invasion allemande. Alcan 1915. 60 c.

Weiss, André. La violation de la neutralité belge et luxembourgeoise par l'Allemagne. (Etudes et Documents sur la Guerre.) Arm. Colin. 50 c.

XIII.—PRISONERS.

A—*Official.*

Agreement between the British and German Governments concerning combatants and civilian Prisoners of War. [Cd. 8590.] Miscellaneous, No. 12 (1917). H.M.S.O. 1917 (July). 2*d.*

—— Miscellaneous, No. 20 (1918). [Cd. 9147.] H.M.S.O. 1918 (Oct.). 3*d.*

Agreement between the British and Ottoman Governments respecting Prisoners of War and Civilians. Miscellaneous, No. 10 (1918). [Cd. 9024.] H.M.S.O. 1918. 3*d.*

British and German Prisoners of War in Poland and France, Correspondence respecting the Employment of. Miscellaneous, No. 19 (1916). [Cd. 8260.] H.M.S.O. 1916. 1*d.*

British and German Wounded and Sick Combatant Prisoners of War, Correspondence with the U.S. Ambassador respecting the transfer to Switzerland of. Miscellaneous, No. 17 (1916). [Cd. 8236.] H.M.S.O. 1916. 1*d.*

Cameroons. Correspondence relating to the alleged Ill-treatment of German subjects captured in the Cameroons. With Appendices. [Cd. 7974.] H.M.S.O. 1915. 5*d.*

Correspondence between H.M. Government and the U.S. Ambassador respecting the Treatment of German Prisoners of War and Interned Civilians in the U.K. Miscellaneous, No. 5 (1915). [Cd. 7815.] H.M.S.O. 1915. 1*d.*

—— Prisoners of War and Interned Civilians in the U.K. and Germany respectively. Miscellaneous, No. 7 (1915). [Cd. 7817.] H.M.S.O. 9½*d.*

Correspondence between H.M. Government and the U.S. Ambassador respecting the release of Interned Civilians, and the exchange of Diplomatic and Consular Officers, and of certain classes of Naval and Military Officers, prisoners of war in the U.K. and Germany respectively. Miscellaneous, No. 8 (1915). [Cd. 7857.] H.M.S.O. 7½*d.*

Correspondence between H.M. Government and the U.S. Ambassador respecting the Treatment of Prisoners of War and Interned Civilians in Germany; April 27-June 1, 1915. Miscellaneous, No. 14 (1915). [Cd. 7959.] H.M.S.O. 1915 6*d.*

Correspondence, Further, with the U.S. Ambassador respecting the treatment of British Prisoners of War and Interned Civilians in Germany. Miscellaneous, No. 15 (1915). [Cd. 7961]; in continuation of Miscellaneous, No. 14 (1915). [Cd. 7959.] H.M.S.O. 1915. 2½*d.*

Correspondence with the U.S. Ambassador respecting the Treatment of British Prisoners of War and Interned Civilians in Germany. Miscellaneous, No. 19 (1915), in continuation of No. 15 (1915). [Cd. 8108.] H.M.S.O. Dec. 1915. 7*d.*

Correspondence, Further, with the U.S. Ambassador respecting the treatment of British Prisoners of War [etc.]. Miscellaneous, No. 16 (1916). [Cd. 3235.] In continuation of Miscellaneous, No. 19 (1915). H.M.S.O. May 1916. 9*d.*

Correspondence respecting the employment of British and German Prisoners of War in Poland and France respectively. Miscellaneous, No. 19 (1916). [Cd. 8260.] H.M.S.O. 1*d.*

Correspondence, Further, on the Treatment of British Prisoners of War and Interned Civilians in Germany, with the U.S. Ambassador respecting the. Miscellaneous, No. 26 (1916). [Cd. 8297.] H.M.S.O. 1916. 6*d.*

—— Further Correspondence with the U.S. Ambassador respecting the. .Miscellaneous, No. 7 (1917). [Cd. 8477.] H.M.S.O. 1917. 3*d.*

Documents publiés à l'occasion de la Guerre de 1914-15. Rapports de MM. Ed. Naville, V. van Berghem, C. de Marval et Eugster sur leurs visites aux camps des Prisonniers en Angleterre, France et Allemagne. Series I. March 1915. Fischbacher. 1 f.

Gardelegen, Typhus Epidemic at, during the Spring and Summer of 1915. Report by the Government Committee on the Treatment by the Enemy of British Prisoners of War. Miscellaneous, No. 34 (1916). [Cd. 8351.] H.M.S.O. 1916. 1½*d.*

Genower, J. P., Death by Burning of Able Seaman, when Prisoner of War at Brandenburg Camp. Correspondence with the German Government respecting the. Miscellaneous, No. 6 (1918). [Cd. 8987.] H.M.S.O. 1918. 1*d.*

Internment Camps in the U.K. Report of Visits of Inspection made by Officials of the United States Embassy. Miscellaneous, No. 30 (1916). [Cd. 8324.] H.M.S.O. 1916. 4½*d.*

Kriegsgefangene, Deutsche in Feindesland. Amtl. Material. Frankreich 1919. 1 m.

Organisation and Methods of the Central Prisoners of War Committee. Report of the Joint Committee. [Cd. 8615.] H.M.S.O. 1917. 2*d.*

Prisoners' Camps in Germany, Use of Police Dogs in. Correspondence respecting the. Miscellaneous, No. 9 (1917). [Cd. 8480.] H.M.S.O. 1917. *2d.*

Proposed Release of Civilians Interned in the British and German Empires. Further Correspondence respecting the. Miscellaneous, No. 35 (1916). [Cd. 8352.] H.M.S.O. 1916. *1d.*

—— Miscellaneous, No. 1 (1917). [Cd. 8437.] H.M.S.O. 1917. *1d.*

Rapport des délégués du gouvernement espagnol sur les camps de prisonniers français en Allemagne 1914-1917. Hachette 1918. 4 f.

Report on the Treatment of Prisoners of War in England and Germany during the first eight months of the War. Miscellaneous, No. 12 (1915). [Cd. 7862.] H.M.S.O. *1d.*

Report on the Employment in Coal and Salt Mines of British Prisoners of War in Germany. Miscellaneous, No. 23 (1918). [Cd. 9150.] H.M.S.O. 1918. *1d.*

Report on the Treatment by the Enemy of British Prisoners of War behind the firing lines in France and Belgium. With two appendices. Miscellaneous, No. 7 (1918). [Cd. 8988.] H.M.S.O. 1918. *4d.*

Report on the Treatment by the Enemy of British Officers, Prisoners of War in Camps under the 10th (Hanover) Army Corps, up to March 1918. Miscellaneous, No. 28 (1918). H.M.S.O. 1918. *2d.*

Report on the Treatment by the Germans of Prisoners of War taken during the Spring offensives of 1918. Miscellaneous, No. 19 (1918). [Cd. 9106.] H.M.S.O. 1918. *2d.*

Report, Further, on the Treatment by the Germans of Prisoners of War taken during the spring offensives of 1918. Miscellaneous, No. 27 (1918). In continuation of Miscellaneous, No. 19 (1918). H.M.S.O. 1918. *2d.*

Reports by the United States officials on the Treatment of British Prisoners of War and Interned Civilians at certain places of detention in Germany. Miscellaneous, No. 11 (1915); in continuation of Miscellaneous, No. 7 (1915). [Cd. 7861.] H.M.S.O. *3d.*

Report on the Treatment of British Prisoners of War in Turkey. Miscellaneous No. 24, (1918). [Cd. 9208.] H.M.S.O. 1918. *3d.*

Reports on the Treatment by the Germans of British Prisoners. and Natives in German East Africa. Miscellaneous, No. 13 (1917). [Cd. 8689.] H.M.S.O. 1917. *4d.*

Reports on British Prison Camps in India and Burma, visited by the Internat. Red Cross Committee in 1917. Fisher Unwin 1917. *3d.*

Ruhleben. Note from the United States Ambassador transmitting a Report, dated June 8, 1915, on the conditions at present existing in the Internment Camp at Ruhleben. [Cd. 7863.] H.M.S.O. 1915. *1d.*

Ruhleben, Internment Camp at. Correspondence with the U.S. Ambassador respecting conditions in the. Miscellaneous, No. 3 (1916). [Cd. 8161.] H.M.S.O. 1916. *2½d.*

Ruhleben, Internment Camp at. Report by Dr. A. E. Taylor on the Conditions of Diet and Nutrition in the. Miscellaneous, No. 18 (1916). [Cd. 8259.] H.M.S.O. *1½d.*

Ruhleben. Correspondence, Further, respecting the conditions of diet and nutrition in the Internment Camp at Ruhleben. Miscellaneous, No. 21 (1916). [Cd. 8262.] In continuation of Miscellaneous, No. 18 (1916). H.M.S.O. 1916. *1½d.*

Ruhleben. Correspondence, Further, respecting the Conditions of Diet and Nutrition at the Internment Camp at Ruhleben and the proposed release of interned civilians. Miscellaneous, No. 25 (1916). [Cd. 8296.] In continuation of Miscellaneous, No. 21 (1916). H.M.S.O. Aug. 1916. *1d.*

Transport of British Prisoners of War to Germany, August-December 1914. Report on the. Miscellaneous, No. 3 (1918). [Cd. 8984.] H.M.S.O. 1918. *6d.*

Wittenberg. Report by the Government Committee on the Treatment by the enemy of British Prisoners of War, regarding conditions obtaining at Wittenberg Camp during the typhus epidemic of 1915. Miscellaneous, No. 10 (1916). [Cd. 8224.] H.M.S.O. *1½d.*

Wittenberg, Horrors of. Official report to the British Government by the Committee on the Treatment by the Enemy of British Prisoners of War. In pamphlet form. Pearson 1916. *1d.*

B.—*Personal.*

Arvengas, Gilbert. Entre les fils de fer : Carnet d'un prisonnier de Guerre entre 1914 et 1917 (au camp d'Ohrdruf). Jouve 1918. 3 fr. 50.

Aubry, l'Abbé Augustin. Ma captivité en Allemagne. (From Sept. 1914 to Feb. 1915.) Perrin 1916. 2 fr. 50.

Austin, L. J. My Experiences as a German Prisoner. Melrose. *2s.*

Batteler, J. F. Les étapes et l'évasion d'un prisonnier civil en Allemagne. Altinger 1916. 2 fr.

Baud-Bovy, D. L'Evasion. (Escape from the prison camp of Hammelburg.) Berger-Levrault 1917. 3 fr. 50.

Behind the Prison Bars in Germany. A detailed record of six months' experiences in German prisons and detention camps. Newnes 1915. 1*s.*

Blanchin, L. Chez eux. (Recollections of a prisoner lately repatriated.) Delagrave 1916. 2 fr.

Bury, Rt. Rev. Herbert. My visit to Ruhleben. Mowbray 1917. 2*s.* 6*d.*

Caunter, Capt. J. A. L. Thirteen Days. My escape from a German prison. (The author escaped in June, 1917.) Bell & Sons 1918. 4*s.* 6*d.*

Célarie, Henriette. En Esclavage, journal de deux déportées. Bloud et Gay 1918. 3 fr. 50.

Christmas, Dr. de. Le Traitement des prisonniers français en Allemagne, d'après l'interrogatoire des prisonniers ramenés d'Allemagne en Suisse pour raisons de santé. Préface de Maurice Letulle. Chapelot 1917. 3 fr.

Close, P. L. A Prisoner of the Germans in South-West Africa. Fisher Unwin 1916. 6*s.*

Cohen, Israel. The Ruhleben Prison Camp. A record of nineteen months' internment. Illustrations and plan. Methuen 1917. 7*s.* 6*d.*

D'Anthouard, Le Baron. Les Prisonniers de Guerre : Renseignements pratiques sur les moyens de retrouver les prisonniers, de correspondre avec eux [etc.]. Colin. 1 fr. 25.

Davies, Alfred. Student Captives. An account of the British Prisoners-of-War Book-scheme. Board of Education, Whitehall 1917. 6*d.*

Desson, G. Souvenirs d'un ôtage (during a year's detention in Germany). Bloud & Gay 1916. 2 fr. 50.

—— Transl. under title A Hostage in Germany. Illustrated. Constable 1917. 3*s.* 6*d.*

Doitsh, Corporal E. The First Springbok Prisoner in Germany. (Experiences in South-West Africa, France, and German prisons.) McBride 1917. 2*s.*

Doyle, Sir A. Conan (edr.). The Story of British Prisoners. Based on Government Reports and the public prints. Central Committee. 1*d.*

Dufour, Jean Jules. Dans les Camps de Réprésailles (témoignage des choses éprouvés et souffertes). Hachette 1918. 3 fr. 50.

Durnford, H. G., M.C. The Tunnellers of Holzminden. Illustrated. Camb. Univ. Press 1921. 14*s.*

Ellison, Wallace. Escaped! Adventures in German captivity. Blackwood 1918. 6*s.*

Evans, H. J. The Escaping Club. 4th edn. Lane 1921. 7*s.* 6*d.*

Gilliland, Captain H. G. My German Prisons. (The truth about the treatment of our prisoners in Germany.) Hodder & Stoughton 1918. 6*s.*

Green, Arthur. The Story of a Prisoner of War. Reprinted from The Morning Post. More light on Wittenberg. Chatto & Windus 1916. 1*s.*

Gwatkin-Williams, Mrs. In the Hands of the Senoussi. Compiled from the diary of Capt. R. Gwatkin-Williams. Pearson 1916. 2*s.*

Hennebois, Charles. Journal d'un Grand Blessé. Aux mains de l'Allemagne. (Wounded Oct. 12, 1914, he remained a prisoner till July 21, 1915.) With preface by E. Dandet. Plon-Nourrit 1916. 3 fr. 50.

—— Translated under title In German Hands. Heinemann 1916. 3*s.* 6*d.*

Hopford, W. Twice Interned: Transvaal 1901-2; Germany 1914-18. 1919. 5*s.*

Hopkins, Tighe. Prisoners of War. Illustrated. Simpkin 1914. 2*s.*

In the Hands of the Huns. An account of 15 months' imprisonment at Ruhleben. By a British civil prisoner of war. Simpkin, Marshall 1916. 1*s.*

Keith, Eric A. My Escape from Germany. Nisbet 1918. 6*s.*

Knowles, Christine. A Visit to Switzerland in War Time. (Condition of British prisoners interned in that country.) British Prisoners of War Fund 1917. 6*d.*

Knox, Marcus. The Silent Baltic: or, Detained near Kiel. Academy Architecture 1914. 6*d.*

Krebs, E. Die Behandlung der Kriegsgefangenen in Deutschland. Dargestellt auf Grund amtlichen Materials. 1917. 5 mk. 40.

Krey, A. In französischer Kriegsgefangenschaft 1914-15. 7 pf.

La Barre, G. Captive of the Kaiser in Belgium. With The Fall of Namur. Mills & Boon. 1*s.*

Larmandie, H. de. Blessé, Captif, Délivré. Bloud et Gay 1916. 3 fr. 50.

—— Les 100 Numéros du Petit Français, organe authentique des officiers français prisonniers à Brandebourg et Halle. Illustrations. Bloud et Gay 1917. 6 fr.

Lévêque, A. J. Erinnerungen aus meiner Kriegsgefangenschaft. 1918. 4 mk. 20.

McCarthy, Daniel J. The Prisoner of War in Germany. The care and treatment of the prisoner, with a history of the development . . . of neutral inspection and control. Skeffington 1918. 12*s.* 6*d.*

Mahoney, Henry C. Reminiscences of Ruhleben. Illustrated. Sampson Low 1917. 6*s.*

—— Sixteen Months in Four German Prisons: Wesel, Sennelager, Klingelputz, Ruhleben. Chronicled by Frederick A. Talbot. Sampson Low 1917. 6*s.*

Marshall, L. H. Experiences in German Gaols. Simpkin 1915. 6*d.*

Martin, Jean. Captivity and Escape. By a French sergeant-major. Illustrated. Murray 1917. 5*s.*

Montvert, J. En Captivité. La vie que nous y menons. Lettres et récits de soldats français, anglais et belges, prisonniers en Allemagne. Payot 1916. 2 fr.

O'Brien, Lieut. Pat. Outwitting the Hun. My escape from a German prison camp. Heinemann 1918. 6*s.*

Olivier, Capitaine. Onze Mois de Captivité dans les Hôpitaux Allemands. Chapelot 1916. 3 fr. 50.

O'Rorke, Rev. B. G. In the Hands of the Enemy. (The author was taken prisoner at Landrécies, and was a prisoner of war for ten months in Germany.) Longmans 1915. 1*s.*

Picot, Lieut.-Col. H. F. British Interned in Switzerland. Life and activities of British soldiers while interned. 1919.

Powell, J., and Gribble, F. History of Ruhleben: a record of British organisation in a prison camp in Germany. 1919. 10*s.* 6*d.*

Prisonniers Allemands, les, âu Maroc. (Defence of the French treatment of German prisoners in Morocco.) Illustrated. Hachette 1917. 2 fr.

Prisonnier des Allemands. Par un prêtre . . . infirmier militaire. Lethielleux 1916. 1 fr. 50.

Pult, Lieut. W. Siebzehn Monate in englischer Kriegsgefangenschaft. Siegen: Montraus 1917. 1 mk. 50.

Pyke, Geoffrey. To Ruhleben and Back. By an escaped prisoner. Constable 1915. 6*s.*

—— —— Experiences in prison, and escape. Constable 1916. 4*s.* 6*d.*

Roger, Mme. Noëlle. Le Cortège des Victimes; les Repatriés d'Allemagne 1914-16. Perrin 1916.

—— Soldats internés en Suisse. Genève: Atar, Corraterie, 12 1917. 2 fr.

Roscher, Maria. Zwei Jahre Kriegsgefangen in West und Nord-afrika. Erlebnisse einer deutschen Frau. 1918. 2 mk. 50.

Roxburgh, R. F. The Prisoners of War Information Bureau in London. With introduction by Prof. Oppenheim. Longmans 1915. 2*s.* 6*d.*

Schenk, R. Zwei Jahre in russischen Gefangenschaft. 2 mk. 50.
Schmidt-Reder, B. In England Kriegsgefangen. 2 mk.
—— Meine Erlebnisse im Gefangenlager Dorchester 1915. 2 mk.
Sladen, D. (edr.). In Ruhleben: Letters from a Prisoner to his Mother. Hurst & Blackett 1917. 6*s*.
Spanton, Rev. E. F. In German Gaols. A narrative of two years' imprisonment in German East Africa. With preface by Sir H. H. Johnston. Illustrated. S.P.C.K. 1917. 2*s*. 6*d*.
Stauck, H. Kriegsgefangene. Ein Beitrag z. Völkerkunde im Weltkriege. 100 Steinzeichn. Mit Einf.v.F.v. Luschan. 1917. 20 mk.
Trimbalet, l'Abbé A. De Soyécourt à Wittenberg, ou l'invasion et la captivité. Amiens: Yvest 1916.
Two Years' Captivity in German East Africa. Being the personal experiences of Surgeon E.C.H., R.N. Hutchinson 1918. 6*s*. 9*d*.
Waldstätter, R. S. Im französischer Gefangenschaft. 1918. 4 mk.
Warnod, André. Prisonnier de Guerre. An account, with illustrations, of nine months in a German camp. Fasquelle. 3 fr. 50.
—— Transl. under title Prisoner of War. Translated from the French. Heinemann 1916. 3*s*. 6*d*.
Williams, Albert Rhys. In the Claws of the German Eagle. (The author was tried as a spy at Brussels.) Dutton 1917. $1.50.
Wounded and a Prisoner of War. By an Exchange Officer. Illustrated. Blackwood 1916. 5*s*.
Zavie, E. Prisonniers en Allemagne. (By a prisoner, Sept. 1914—July 1915.) Chapelot 1917.

XIV—LEGAL WORKS.

A.—*Domestic Law.*

Behrens, W. H. (edn.). Excess Profits Duty at a Glance: being a complete chart of part 3 of the Finance Act (No. 2) 1915. Odhams 1916. 6*d*.
Campbell, H. The Law of War and Contract; including the present decisions at home and abroad. Milford 1918. 15*s*.
Carpenter, C. H. War Restrictions as they affect your Business. A Guide to the Emergency Legislation and Regulations. Effingham Wilson 1916. 6*d*.
Charles, John. The Munitions of War Acts 1915-16. An analysis, with notes, the texts of the Acts, &c. Stevens 1916. 5s.
Clements, A. F.; and Waterson, H. G. Commercial Law in War Time. Dawson 1914. 2*s*. 6*d*.

Coddington, F. J. O. Soldier's Guide to obtaining State Assistance under the Military Service (Civil Liabilities) Regulations. Gale & Polden 1916. 1*s.*

Defence of the Realm Acts and Regulations. Passed and made to July 31, 1915. With an Analytical Index and Introductory and other Notes. H.M.S.O. 1915. 1*s.*

Defence of the Realm Manual. 4th edn. Revised to May 31, 1917. Introductory Note; Defence of the Realm Act, with notes; Regulations, Orders of a general character, Index &c. Ed. by Alex. Pulling. Publd. by authority (Manuals of Emergency Legislation). H.M.S.O. May 1917. 5*s.*

D'Egville, Howard (edr.). Summary of Emergency Legislation passed by the Parliaments of the Empire in consequence of the War. Empire Parliaments Assn. 1916. 2*s.* 6*d.*

Emergency Legislation, Manuals of. Defence of the Realm Regulations. Consolidated and revised to Nov. 30, 1918. H.M.S.O. 1918. 6*d.*

Fyfe, Thomas Alexander. Employers and Workmen: a Handbook explanatory of their Duties and Responsibilities under the Munitions of War Acts 1915-16. W. Hodge. 2*s.* 6*d.*

Gore-Browne, F. The Effect of the War on Commercial Engagements. Jordan 1914. 2*s.* 6*d.*

Hanna, Henry. The War and Suspension of Legal Remedies. Sweet & Maxwell 1914. 2*s.* 6*d.*

Kitson, Eric. How to Conduct your Case before the Tribunal. Poke 1916. 1*s.*

Langdon, A. M., and Lawson, Robertson. The Excess Profits Duty and the Excess Mineral Rights Duty (Finance Acts 1915 and 1916). 2nd edn. Stevens & Haynes 1916. 5*s.*

Législation de la Guerre de 1914. Pichon. 5 fr.

Liquor Control. Defence of the Realm Regulations 1915. First Report of the Central Control Board (Liquor Traffic) appointed under the Defence of the Realm (Amendment) (No. 3) Act 1915. [Cd. 8117.] H.M.S.O. 1915. 1*d.*

Mackinnon, F. D. The Effect of the War on Contracts. With a resumé of the principal cases decided in English Courts during the War. Oxf. Univ. Press 1917. 2*s.* 6*d.*

Nathan, Manfred. The Influence of War on Contracts and other Liabilities. Sweet & Maxwell 1916. 10*s.* 6*d.*

National Registration Act 1915. With N. R. (Instr.) Board, and Local Government Board Circular. Introduction by R. A. Leach. Local Govt. Board Co. 1915. 3*d.*

Page, A. War and Alien Enemies: the Law affecting their Personal and Trading Rights. 2nd edn. Stevens 1915. 6*s.* 6*d.*

Pommereuil, R. La Guerre Economique 1914-17. (Collection of laws and regulations on enemy trading, contraband, prohibitions, &c.). Poitiers: Oudin 1917. 5 fr. 50.

Postponement of Payments Act 1914. Copies of the Postponement Act 1914, and of the Proclamations issued thereunder. [Cd. 7633.] H.M.S.O. 1914-15. 1½*d.*

Rivet, A. Législation provisoire des œuvres de guerre. Bonne Presse 1916. 2 fr.

Sanders, William. The Practice and Law of Excess Profits Duty. Gee 1916. 1*s.* 6*d.* and 2*s.*

Scott, Leslie. Trading with the Enemy: the Effect of War on Contracts. 2nd edn. 2*s.* 6*d.*

Snelling, W. E. Excess Profits and Excess Mineral Rights Duty. Pitman 1916. 7*s.* 6*d.*

Special Constable, The: His Duties and Privileges. Pearson 1914. 1*s.*

Spicer, Ernest Evan, and Pegler, Ernest C. The Excess Profits Duty and Profits of Controlled Establishments. Lynch 1916. 6*s.*

—— —— The same. 1918. 10*s.* 6*d.*

Trotter, W. Finlayson. Supplement to the Law of Contact during War. With recent cases, statutes and orders in Council. W. Hodge 1915. 12*s.* 6*d.*

B.—*Naval and Military Law.*

Anderson, Commissioner Maxwell H. The Navy and Prize. An essay (by a Naval Officer and Barrister in the Prize Court). Portsmouth: Gieve 1916. 1*s.* 3*d.*

Banning, Lieut.-Col. S. T. Military Law Made Easy. 8th edn. Gale & Polden 1915. 3*s.* 6*d.*

Barclay, Sir Thomas. Law and Usage of War. A practical handbook. Constable 1914. 5*s.*

Baty, T., and Morgan, J. H. War: its Conduct and Legal Results. Murray 1915. 10*s.* 6*d.*

British and Colonial Prize Cases Part I. Stevens 1915; Sweet & Maxwell. 7*s.* 6*d.*

Browne, G. W. Courts-martial for Presidents and Members. Harrison 1916. 5*s.*

Coddington, F. J. O. Young Officer's Guide to Military Law. Gale & Polden 1916. 2*s.* 6*d.*

Collins, Capt. G. R. N. Pocket Manual of Military Law and Procedure. Hugh Rees 1916. 1*s.*

Courts-Martial. By an Army Officer. Stevens & Haynes 1915. 1*s.* 6*d.*

Décisions du Conseil des Prises, et Décrets rendus en Conseil d'Etat en matière de Prises Maritimes. Publd. by the French Admiralty. Paris: Challernel 1917.

Dennistoun, Lieut.-Col. Notes on District Courts-Martial. 2nd edn. revised. Hugh Rees 1917. 1*s.*

German War Book, The. Being the Usages of War on Land, issued by the Great General Staff of the German Army. Transl., with a critical introduction, by Prof. J. H. Morgan. Murray 1914. 2*s.* 6*d.*

Grierson, Capt. F. D. The ABC of Military Law. A book for quick reference, alphabetically arranged. Fisher Unwin 1916. 1*s.* 6*d.*

Gruet, Paul Louis. Réquisitions militaires (armées de terre et de mer). On the law and practice of requisitioning. Alcan 1915. 3 fr. 50.

Hall, J. A. The Law of Naval Warfare. Chapman & Hall 1914. 6*s.*

Hannay, David. Naval Courts-Martial. Seven illustrations. Camb. Univ. Press 1914. 8*s.*

Hawtin, W. G. Law and Practice, The, of Military Conscription under the Military Service Acts, 1918. Part 2: The Military Service (No. 2) Act, 1918; Medical Grading, &c. Harrison 1918. 2*s.*

King, Major T. Guide to Courts-Martial Duty. Groom 1915. 1*s.* 6*d.*

—— Field General Courts-Martial. Forster, Groom 1916. 6*d.*

Lowry, James M. Martial Law within the Realm of England. Long. 1*s.*

Major, The. Guide to Court-Martial Procedure. Gale & Polden 1915. 1*s.*

Mayers, Edward C. Admiralty Law and Practice in Canada. Sweet & Maxwell 1916. 50*s.*

Military Law in Tables. With notes by a military lawyer. Hugh Rees 1917. 9*d.*

Peant, E. H. Practice of Courts-Martial at a Glance. Law Times 1915. 6*d.*

Pope, Major E. W. The Canadian Officer's Guide to the Study of Military Law. Methuen 1916. 2*s.*

Pratt, Sisson C. Military Law: its Procedure and Practice. 19th edn., revised and corrected to Sept. 1915. Kegan Paul 1915. 5*s.* Routledge 1916. 5*s.*

Rice, Joseph A. If Conscription Comes: the Present Position under the Militia Ballot Act Explained. Browne & Nolan 1914. 3*d.*

Rothery, H. C. Prize Droits. A Report to H.M. Treasury on Droits of the Crown and of Admiralty in times of War. Revised and annotated by E. S. Roscoe. Spottiswoode 1915. 5*s*.

Scanlan, Capt. A. A. Courts of Inquiry on Illegal Absence. By a Barrister. Forster, Groom 1916. 1*s*. 6*d*.

Spaight, J. M. War Rights on Land. MacMillan 1915. 12s.

Stoker, W. H., and Bentwich Herbert. The Military Services Acts Practice. (The Consolidated Acts, Proclamations, &c., with notes and decisions.) Stevens 1918. 7*s*. 6*d*.

Thomas, Capt. K. G. Courts of Inquiry. (A manual for officers sitting upon Courts of Inquiry.) Gale & Polden 1916. 2*s*.

Trehern, E. C. M. (edr.). British and Colonial Prize Cases. Part I. Stevens 1915. 7*s*. 6*d*.

C.—*International Law.*

(1) Official.

British Nationality and Status of Aliens Act 1914, as amended in accordance with the British Nationality [Etc.] Act 1918. H.M.S.O. 1918. 1*d*.

Claims preferred against H.M. Government for Damages sustained by the Netherlands Steamships Elve and Bernisse through the Action of German Submarines, Correspondence with the Netherlands Government respecting the. Miscellaneous No. 1 (1918). [Cd. 8909.] H.M.S.O. 1918. 2*d*.

Contraband of War, List of Articles declared to be. Miscellaneous No. 12 (1916). [Cd. 8226.] H.M.S.O. 1916. ½*d*.

Conventions et Déclarations entre les Puissances concernant l'arbitrage, la guerre, et la neutralité (1856-1909). In French, German and English. The Hague: Nijhoff. 5 fr.

Correspondence between H.M. Government and the U.S. Government respecting the Rights of Belligerents. White Paper Miscellaneous No. 6 (1915). [Cd. 7816.] H.M.S.O. 1915. 3*d*.

Correspondence, Further, between H.M. Government and the U.S. Government respecting the Rights of Belligerents (in continuation of Miscellaneous No. 6, 1915). Miscellaneous No. 14 (1916). [Cd. 8233.] H.M.S.O. 2½*d*.

Declaration of London, Correspondence respecting the. [Cd. 5418.] H.M.S.O. 1910. 3*d*.

Declaration of London Orders in Council, Withdrawal of the. Note addressed by H.M. Government to Neutral Representatives in London respecting the. Miscellaneous No. 22 (1916). [Cd. 8293.] H.M.S.O. 1916. ½*d*.

Defensively Armed British Merchant Vessels, Correspondence with the Netherlands Government respecting. Miscellaneous No. 14 (1917). [Cd. 8690.] H.M.S.O. 1917. 3*d.*

Dresden, The. Notes exchanged with the Chilean Minister respecting the sinking of the German cruiser Dresden in Chilean Territorial Waters. Miscellaneous No. 9 (1915). [Cd. 7859.] H.M.S.O. ½*d.*

International Law Documents. Neutrality; Breaking of Diplomatic Relations; War. With notes. (Naval War College.) Washington: Government Printing Office 1918.

Jurisprudence française en matière de Prises Maritimes. Recueil de Décisions, suivi des Textes intéressant le Droit International Maritime publiés par la France pendant la guerre de 1914. With introduction by P. Fauchille. Paris: Pedone 1916.

Prizes. Convention between the United Kingdom and France relating to prizes captured during the present European War; signed Nov. 9, 1914. Treaty Series 1915. No. 2. [Cd. 7739.] H.M.S.O. 1*d.*

Rights of Belligerents. Treatment of Mails on Neutral Vessels, Correspondence with the U.S. Ambassador respecting the. Miscellaneous No. 5 (1916). [Cd. 8173.] H.M.S.O. 1916. ½*d.*

—— Further Correspondence between H.M. Government and the U.S. Government respecting the. Miscellaneous No. 14 (1916). [Cd. 8233.] H.M.S.O. 1916. 2½*d.*

—— —— Miscellaneous. No. 15 (1916). [Cd. 8234.] H.M.S.O. 1916. 3*d.*

—— Examination of Parcels and Letter Mails, Note to the U.S. Ambassador regarding the. Miscellaneous No. 23 (1916). [Cd. 8294.] H.M.S.O. 1911. ½*d.*

Seaplanes, Internment of, etc., salved on the High Seas and brought into Netherlands Jurisdiction, Correspondence respecting the. Miscellaneous No. 4 (1918). [Cd. 8985.] H.M.S.O. 1918. 3*d.*

Submarines. Memorandum respecting the treatment of Belligerent Submarines in neutral waters, communicated by the Allied Governments to the Governments of certain Neutral Maritime States. Miscellaneous No. 33 (1916). [Cd. 8349.] H.M.S.O. 1916. ½*d.*

United States White Books, 1, 2, 3, 4. (Diplomatic Correspondence with Belligerent Governments relating to Neutral Rights and Duties.) Washington: Government Printing Office 1915-1918.

(2) Books.

Adams, William. The Declaration of London. King. 6*d*.

Angell, Norman. The World's Highway. On the so-called Freedom of the Seas. New York: Doran 1916. $1.50.

Balfour, Arthur J. Freedom of the Seas. An interview. Unwin 1916. 2*d*.

Armstrong, J. W. Scobell. War and Treaty Legislation affecting British Property in Germany and Austria and Enemy Property in the United Kingdom. Hutchinson 1921. 28*s*.

Baty, T. (edr.) Prize Law and Continuous Voyage. Stevens & Haynes 1915. 4*s*. 6*d*.

Bray, F. E. British Rights at Sea under the Declaration of London. King. 1*s*.

Brewer, D. C. Rights and Duties of Neutrals: a Discussion of Principles and Practices. By an American Lawyer. Putnam 1916. 5*s*.

Brown, Philip M. Foreigners in Turkey: their judicial status. Milford 1914. 5*s*. 6*d*.

Butler, G. G. International Law and Autocracy. (A lecture delivered before the University of Pennsylvania.) Hodder 1917. 1*d*.

Cababé, Michael. The Freedom of the Seas (from the legal, political and popular point of view). Murray 1918. 5*s*.

Corbett, Sir Julian. The League of Peace and a Free Sea. Hodder & Stoughton 1917. 1*d*.

—— The League of Nations and Freedom of the Seas. Milford 1918. 3*d*.

Dembski, N. Europe and the New Sea Law: a Manual of International Politics and Maritime Law. Cheaper edn. Simpkin 1914. 2*s*.

Egerton, W. A. Contraband of War. Portsmouth: Gieve 1915. 1s. 6d.

Frasca, Carlo. Espropriazione e requisitione in tempo di guerra. Rome 1917. 12 l.

Freedom of the Seas, The. A subtle German challenge. Beware! 1916. 6*d*.

Frobenius, W. Das Ende der englischen Gewaltherrschaft. Die Freiheit der Meere Deutschlands vornehmter Kriegsziel Berlin: Curtius 1917. 1 mk. 50.

Garner, Prof. Wilford. International Law and the World War. 2 vols. Longmans 1920. 72*s*.

Gregory, Charles Noble. Neutrality and Arms Shipments. Reprint of article by the Chairman of the Standing Committee of International Law of the American Bar Association, from the New York World, May 16, 1915. Darling.

Grotius, Hugo. The Freedom of the Seas. Translated by R. Van Deman Magoffin. Edited with an Introductory Note by J. B. Scott (Carnegie Endowment for International Peace). Milford 1916. 5*s.*

Grotius Society. Problems of the War. Papers read before the Society in 1915. Vol. I. Sweet & Maxwell 1916. 5*s.* ... ...

—— —— Papers read before the Society in 1916. 2 vols. Sweet & Maxwell 1917. 11*s.*

Hague Conventions of 1899 and 1907. A series of 18 pamphlets (Nos. 3-20), issued by the Carnegie Institution, giving the various Conventions in full. Washington: Carnegie Endowment 1915.

Hall, W. E. Treatise on International Law. 7th edn. Oxford Univ. Press 1918. 24*s.*

Halleck, H. W. International Law. 4th edn. Edited by G. S. Baker. 2 vols. Kegan Paul 1908.

Higgins, A. Pearce. Armed Merchant Ships. Stevens & Sons 1914. 1*s.* 6*d.*

—— The Law of Nations and the War. (O.P.) Oxford Univ. Press. 2*d.*

—— War and the Private Citizen. Studies in International Law. King 1912. 5*s.*

—— The Hague Peace Conference and other International Conferences concerning the Laws and Usages of War. Stevens 1904. 3*s.*

—— Defensively-armed Merchant Ships and Submarine Warfare. Stevens 1917. 1*s.*

—— Non-Combatants and the War. (O.P.) Oxford Univ. Press. 2*d.*

—— The Hague Peace Conferences. . . . Texts of Conventions. Cam. Univ. Press 1909. 15*s.*

Holland, T. E. Letters to The Times upon War and Neutrality 1881-1909. With some commentary. 2nd edn. Longmans 1914. 7*s.* 6*d.*

—— A Supplement to Letters to The Times upon War and Neutrality, containing letters from 1914 to 1916. Longmans 1916. 1*s.*

Holls, F. W. The Peace Conference at The Hague, and its bearing on International Law and Policy. By an American representative at the Conference. New York: Macmillan 1900. 17*s.*

Katz, E. Die Freiheit der Meere im Kriege. Berlin 1915. 80 pf.

Krauel, W. Neutralität, Neutralisation, und Befreiung im Völkerrecht. Munich: Duncker 1915.

Lammasch, Prof. Das Völkerrecht nach dem Kriege. Christiania 1917.

Lawrence, T. J. Documents illustrative of International Law. Macmillan 1914. 7*s*. 6*d*.

Mancunian. The Freedom of Commerce in War. King. 1*s*.

Montmorency, J. E. G. de. International Law after the War. (Reprint from Scientia.) Williams & Norgate 1917.

Moore, J. Bassett. International Arbitrations to which the United States have been a party. 6 vols. Washington Government Printing Office 1898.

Morris, R. C., D.C.L. International Arbitration and Procedure. New Haven: Yale Univ. Press 1916. $1.35.

Müller-Meiningen, Dr. Weltkrieg und Völkerrecht. Berlin 1915. 7 mk.

—— Der Weltkrieg 1914-17 und der Zusammenbruch des Völkerrechts. Eine Abwehr und Anklage. 2 vols. 4th edn. 1917. 25 mk. 90.

Muir, Prof. Ramsay. Mare Liberum. The Freedom of the Seas. Hodder & Stoughton 1917. 1*d*.

Nippold, Prof. Otfried. Die Gestaltung des Völkerrechts nach dem Weltkrieg. Zürich: Füssli 1917. 8 fr.

Omond, G. W. T. The Law of the Sea. A short history of some questions relating to neutral merchant shipping. Black 1917. 2*s*. 6*d*.

Oppenheim, Prof. L. International Law. Vol I, Peace; Vol. II, War and Neutrality. Edited by R. F. Roxburgh. 3rd edn. Longmans 1920-21. 60*s*.

Pchédécki, Elias. Le Droit international maritime et la Grande Guerre. Librairie générale de droit 1916. 7 fr. 50.

Pellet, Prof. A. La Guerre actuelle et le Droit des Gene. Paris: Pedone 1916.

Pflugk-Harttung, J. v. Der Kampf um die Freiheit d. Meere. Trafalgar, Skagerrak. Mit 1 Schiffsliste u. 1 Karterskigge im Text. 1917. 6 mk.

Phillimore, R. Commentaries upon International Law. 3rd edn. 4 vols. Butterworth 1879-89. 122*s*.

Phillipson, Coleman. International Law and the Great War. With introduction by Sir John Macdonell. Unwin 1915. 15*s*.

—— Termination of War and Treaties of Peace. Fisher Unwin 1916. 21*s*.

Picciotto, Cyril M. Relation of International Law to the Law of England and of the United States of America. McBride, Nash & Co. 1915. 6*s*.

Piggott, Sir Francis. The Neutral Merchant in Relation to the Law of Contraband of War and Blockade. London Univ. Press 1916. *2s. 6d.*

—— The Free Seas in War: a talk to the men and women of Britain. Together with extracts from the writings, etc., of David Urquhart, compiled and commented by M. S. Parry. King 1918. *1s. 6d.*

—— The Declaration of Paris 1856. Hodder & Stoughton 1919. *36s.*

Pyke, H. Reason. Contraband and the War. (O.P.) Milford 1915. *2d.*

—— Law of Contraband of War. Oxford Univ. Press 1915. *12s. 6d.*

Richards, Sir H. Erle. Does International Law still exist? (O.P.) Oxford Univ. Press. *2d.*

—— International Law: some Problems of the War. An Oxford Lecture. Oxford Univ. Press 1915. *1s.*

Rolland, Prof. L. Les Pratique de la guerre aérienne dans le conflit de 1914, et le Droit des Gens. Paris: Pedone 1916.

Schücking, W. Die völkerrechtl. Lehre d. Weltkrieges. 1918. 15 mk. 60.

Scott, Leslie, M.P., and Shaw, Hon. Alex, M.P. Great Britain and Neutral Commerce: (1) The Right of Search; (2) The Blockade of Germany. Darling 1915.

Smith, Sir Frederick E. [Lord Birkenhead]. The Destruction of Merchant Ships under International Law. Dent 1917. *4s. 6d.*

—— International Law. 5th edn. Revised and enlarged by Coleman Phillipson. 1918. *16s.*

Stockton, Charles H. Outlines of International Law. Allen & Unwin 1915. *10s. 6d.*

Verzije, Dr. J. H. W. Het Prijsrecht tegenover Neutralen in den Wereldoorlog van 1914 en volgende Jarendoor. (The Law of Prize as applied by the different belligerent States during the war, with full details.) The Hague: Nijhoff 1917.

Villeneuve-Trans, R. de. La Liberté des mers. Le Blocus de l'Allemagne, la guerre sous-marine (étude de droit international). Pedone 1817. 3 fr. 50.

Wehberg, H. Die internationale Beschränkung d. Rüstungen. (Polit. Bücherei.) 1919. 25 mk. 60.

Westlake, John. Collected Papers on Public International Law. Edited by L. Oppenheim. Camb. Univ. Press 1915. *18s.*

Wijnveldt, Dr. J. Neutraliteitsrecht te Land. (Laws of neutrality on land.) The Hague: Nijhoff 1918. 2 fr. 40.

XV.—ECONOMICS AND FINANCE.

A.—*Theoretical and Historical.*

Alberti, Mario. L'Economia del mondo, prima, durante e dopo la Guerra. A technical study of present and future conditions. Rome: Athenæum. 5 l.

Ancona, Ugo. L'Aspetto finanziario della Guerra. (Quaderni della Guerra.) Milan: Treves 1915. 1 l. 50 c.

Ashley, W. J. War in its Economic Aspects. (O.P.) Milford. 2*d*.

Bachi, Riccardo. L'Italia economica nel 1918. Le repercussioni della guerra mondiale ed italiana sull' economia nazionale. Città di Castello: Lapi 1919. 15 l.

Barker, J. Ellis. Economic Statesmanship. The great industrial and financial problems arising from the War. Murray 1918. 12*s*.

Bossière, René E. Towards Peace through Money. Abridged from Vers l'apaisement par l'argent. Simpkin 1915. 2*s*. 6*d*.

Bowley, A. L. Prices and Earnings in Time of War. (O.P.) Oxf. Univ. Press. 2*d*.

—— The War and Employment. (O.P.) Oxf. Univ. Press. 2*d*.

—— Prices and Wages in the United Kingdom 1914-20. (Economic and Social History of the World War, British series.) Publd. for the Carnegie Endowment. Oxf. Univ. Press 1921. 15*s*.

Brand, Hon. R. H. War and National Finance. Arnold 1921. 15*s*.

Brown, H. Gunnison. Foreign Exchange. Macmillan 1916. 4*s*.

Burrows, Roland. The New Income Tax in relation to the War and Business. Murray & E. 1915. 1*s*

Carli, Filippo. La Ricchezza e la Guerra. The Economic Position of the Great Powers. Milan: Treves 1916. 5 l.

Chapsal, F., and others. Intérêts économiques et rapports inter nationaux à la vieille de la Guerre (lectures). Alcan 1915.

Charriaut, H., and Hacault, R. La Liquidation financière de la Guerre.

Clapp, E. F. Economic Aspects of the War. New Haven: Yale Univ. Press 1915.

Cox, Harold. The Economic Strength of Great Britain. Macmillan. 1*d*.

Crammond, Edgar. Finance and the War. Hugh Rees. 6*d*.

Davies, E. F. The Finances of Great Britain and Germany. Fisher Unwin 1916. 2*d*.

Davis, H. Valentine. The Food Problem (Domestic and National): During and after the War. Manchester: Vegetarian Society 1916. 1*d.*

De Launay, M. L. France-Allemagne (études des problèmes économique nés de la guerre). Colin 1917. 3 fr. 50.

Dicksee, Prof. L. R. Business and the War. Camb. Univ. Press. 2*s.*

Economic and Social History of the World War. A short war Bibliography of German periodical literature on Economics. London School of Economics, Clare Market, for Carnegie Endowment for International Peace.

Economist. The Economics of War. (Arguments for better pay and security for those serving their country.) King. 3*d.*

Edgeworth, Prof. F. Y. The Cost of War: and Ways of Reducing it suggested by Economic Theory. A lecture. Oxf. Univ. Press 1915. 1*s.*

—— On the Relations of Political Economy to War. A lecture. Oxf. Univ. Press. 1*s.*

—— Currency and Finance in time of War. A lecture. Oxf. Univ. Press 1917. 1*s.*

Edsall, E. W. England Must Be Fed. (The reply to the U-boat menace.) Croydon: Waddon 1916. 6*d.*

Eltzbacher, Prof. Paul (edr.). Germany's Food: Can it Last? Essays by German experts. English version of Die deutsche Volksernährung, edited by S. R. Wells. Hodder & Stoughton 1915. 2*s.*

England's Financial Supremacy. Transl., with introduction and notes, from the Frankfürter Zeitung. Macmillan 1917. 3*s.*

Eulenberg, F. Das Geld im Kriege u. Deutschlands finanzielle Rüstung. 1915. 75 pf.

Farrow, T., and Crotch, W. W. How to Win the War: the Financial Solution. With Introduction by Lord Devonport. (Advocates National Thrift.) Werner Laurie 1916. 1*s.*

Fayolle. Les Forces économiques des puissances belligérantes. Berger-Levrault 1916. 60 c.

Final Report of Departmental Committee on Production of Food in England and Wales. H.M.S.O. 1915. 1½*d.*

Financial Mobilization for War. By various authors. Camb Univ. Press 1918. 2*s.* 6*d.*

First Report of Committee on Public Retrenchment. H.M.S.O. 1915. 1*d.*

Fisher, Irving. Why is the Dollar Shrinking? Macmillan 1914 5*s.* 6*d.*

Frewen, Moreton. A Memorandum on the Finance of the Great War. Spottiswoode 1915. 6*d.*

Gibson, A. H., and Kirkaldy, Prof. A. W. British Finance 1914-21. Pitmans 1921. 15*s.*

Guevara, L. Towards Reorganisation of International Finance. Simpkin 1916. 3*s.* 6*d.*

Gregory, T. E. The Foreign Exchanges and the War. A report to the Nottingham Chamber of Commerce. Nottingham: Saxton. 1*s.*

Guyot, Yves. La province rhénane et la Westphalie: étude économique. (The value of these provinces and their future.) Attinger 1915.

Hirst, F. W. The Political Economy of War. Dent 1915. 5*s.*

Hobson, J. A. The new Protectionism (discusses the proposals of the Paris Economic Conference). Fisher Unwin 1916. 2*s.* 6*d.*

Hoover, Herbert. Food in War. A speech delivered to the Pittsburg Press Club, April 11, 1918. Introduction by Rt. Hon. J. R. Clynes. W. H. Smith 1918. 3*d.*

Horniman, Roy. How to make the railways pay for the War; or the Transport Problem solved. With Introduction by Lord Headley. Routledge 1916. 10*s.* 6*d.*

Hubert, Lucien. L'Effort allemand: La France et l'Allemagne au point de vue économique. Alcan. 3 fr. 50.

Jansson, Wilhelm. Arbeiterinteressen und Kriegsergebniss (a Trade Union War-book; economic importance of the connexion between Germany and Turkey). Berlin: Baumeister 1915.

Jèze, Gaston. Les Finances de Guerre de l'Angleterre. Giard et Brière 1915. 5 fr.

—— La Réparation intégrale des dommages causés par les faits de guerre. Giard et Brière. 2 fr. 50.

—— Barthélemy, J., and others. Problèmes de politique et finances de la guerre. Lectures delivered at the Ecole des hautes études sociales. Paris: Alcan. 3 fr. 50.

Johnston, Joseph. Food Production in France in time of War. Maunsel 1917. 6*d.*

Jones, J. H. The Economics of War and Conquest. An examination of Mr. Norman Angell's economic doctrines. King 1916. 2*s.* 6*d.*

Kirkaldy, A. W. (edr.). Credit, Industry and the War. Papers read in the Economic Science Section of the British Association at Manchester 1915. Pitman. 2*s.* 6*d.*

—— Labour, Finance, and the War. Results of inquiries arranged by the Economic Section of the British Association during 1915 and 1916. Pitman 1916. 3*s.* 6*d.*

Kirkland, John. Three centuries of prices of Wheat, Flour, and Bread. War prices and their causes. Borough Polytechnic Institute, S.E.1. 1917. 3*s*.

Kirkpatrick, F. A. Imperial Defence and Trade. Royal Colonial Institute 1915. 2*s*.

Koch, W. Handelskrieg u. Wirtschaftsexpansion. Ueberblick üb. d. Massnahmen u. Bestrebungen d. feindl. Auslandes. 1917. 6 mk. 5.

Kolchin, Morris. War Taxation 1914-17. A list of references to material in the New York Public Library. New York Public Library 1917.

Lachapelle, Georges. Nos finances pendant la Guerre. On the financial position of France. Colin 1916. 3 fr. 50.

La Guerre et la vie économique. Addresses by D. Zolla, P. E. Flandin, and others. Alcan 1916. 3 fr. 50.

Landau, Fab. Wie die Kriegführenden Staaten das Geld beschatten. Deren Schulden bis zum Kriege. Wochenausweise der Staatsbanken von Deutschland, England, Frankreich und Russland, ende juli 1914 und 1917. Dresden: Globus 1920. 2 mk.

Lawson, W. R. British War Finance 1914-15. Constable 1915. 6*s*.

Lebon, André. Problèmes économiques nés de la Guerre. Payot 1918. 4 fr. 50.

Lehfeldt, R. A. Economies in the light of war. Wesley 1916. 1*s*.

Lowell, A. Lawrence, and others. The financial administration of Great Britain. Appleton 1917. $2.50.

Mallock, W. H. Capital, War and Wages. Blackie 1918. 2*s*. 6*d*.

Mappin, G. E. Can we compete? Germany's assets in Trade, Finance, &c. Skeffington 1918. 4*s*. 6*d*.

Maroi. Come si calcola e a quanto ammonta la richiezza d'Italia et delle altre principali nazioni. 1919.

Massé, A. Le troupeau français et la guerre. Sub-title: Home-grown and Imported Meat. Paris: Libr. Agric. de la Maison Rustique 1915. 3 fr. 50.

Martin, E. W. Food, Wages and Economy: To-day and To-morrow. Emphasises the value of land and its produce. Birmingham: Cornish 1916. 2*d*.

Médelsheim, G. Cerfbeer de. Le nerf de la guerre (an explanation of the technicalities of war finance). Berger-Levrault 1916. 1 fr. 50.

Murray, J. Alan. The Economy of Food. New edn. Constable 1916. 2*s*.

Nicholson, Prof. Shield. War Finance (including prices before the War, the quantity theory of money, &c.). King 1918. 10*s*. 6*d*.

Noyes, A. D. Financial Chapters of the War. By the author of Forty Years of American Finance. Macmillan 1916. 5*s*.

O'Farrell, H. H. The Franco-German War Indemnity and its Economic Results (Gaston Foundation). With introduction by Lord Esher. Harrison 1913. 1*s*.

Parliamentary Committee of the Trades Union Congress: Final Report on the Cost of Living. Allen & Unwin 1921. 4*s*. 6*d*.

Perez-Triana, Santiago. The Pan-American Financial Conference of 1915. Heinemann 1916. 1*s*. 6*d*.

Philip, Alex. J. Rations, Rationing, and Food Control. The Book World 1918. 12*s*. 6*d*.

Pigou, Prof. A. C. Economy and Finance of the War. Dent 1916. 1*s*.

—— The Political Economy of War. Macmillan 1921. 8*s*. 6*d*.

Powell, Ellis T. Evolution of the Money Market 1885-1915. Re-issue. Pitman 1916. 10*s*. 6*d*.

Pratt, E. H. British Railways and the Great War. 2 vols. Selwyn & Blount 1921. 42*s*.

Problèmes de politique et finances de guerre. On the emergency measures adopted in France, England and Germany. By four Professors of Law. Paris: Alcan 1916. 3 fr. 50.

Pupin, René. La Richesse de la France devant la Guerre. 1916.

Radclyffe, Raymond. The War and Finance: how to save the situation. W. Dawson & Sons 1914. 1*s*.

Records of Railway Interest in the War. Part 1: British. Railway News 1915. 1*s*.

Rew, R. H. Food Supplies in War-Time. (O.P.) Oxf. Univ. Press. 2*d*.

Riesser, Dr. J. The German Great Banks (Publications of the National Monetary Commission). Washington: Govt. Printing Office 1911.

—— Préparation et conduite financières de la guerre. Transl. from the 2nd edn. of the German work 1913; with preface by André Sayous. Payot 1916. 5 fr.

Robertson, Rt. Hon. J. M., M.P. Tariffist Imperialism (Cobden Club Pamphlets). Cassell 1917. 3*d*.

Russian Customs Tariff. Transl. of the new temporary customs tariff, showing the former and revised rates of import duty H.M.S.O. 1915. 7*d*.

Samuelson, J. Drink and the War (favouring local rather than total prohibition or purchase by the State). Liverpool: Philip Son & Nephew; Sidmouth: Day & Bath 1917. 1*s.*

Schumacher, Prof. Hermann. Meistbegunstigungen und Zollunterscheidung. 1915.

Schwabe, Walter S., and Guedalla, P. Effect of War on Stock Exchange Transactions. Effingham Wilson 1915. 3*s.* 6*d.*

Scurr, John. Casting the Silver Bullets: a Suggested Method of raising the necessary Taxation to pay for the War. Limit Printing & Publ. Co. 1915. 1*s.*

Smetham, Alfred. Present conditions in relation to food supplies. Preston, Lancs.: Agric. Society's Journal 1917. 1*s.*

Some of Germany's Troubles: her blockaded merchantmen and the stoppage of her cotton supply. King 1915. 6*d.*

Sonne, H. C. The City: its Finance, July 1914-July 1915, and Future. Effingham Wilson 1915. 5*s.*

Stamp, J. C. British Incomes and Property: the Application of Official Statistics to Economic Problems. King 1916. 12*s.* 6*d.*

Stokes, Wilfrid. How to Pay fór the War. British Engineers' Assn. 1915. 6*d.*

Sunampadu Arumugam. Golden Key to World-Power and the War. Longmans 1915. 1*s.*

Swain, A. H. The War and Life Assurance. Insurance Press 1915. 2*s.*

Tarde, Alfred de. L'Europe court-elle à sa ruine? (On the financial results of the War.) Colin 1916. 1 fr. 25.

Turnor, Christopher. Our Food Supply: Perils and Remedies. Country Life 1916. 2*s.* 6*d.*

Verrinder, Frederick. German Efficiency versus British Liberty. English League for the Taxation of Land Values 1915. 1*d.*

Wall, W. W. The War and our Financial Fabric. Chapman & Hall. 5*s.*

War and British Economic Policy. (Tariff Commission). T. C. Office 1915. 1s.

Webb, Sidney (edr.). How to Pay for the War; being ideas offered to the Chancellor of the Exchequer by the Fabian Research Department. Fabian Society 1916. 6*s.*

Willoughby, W. P., and others. The financial administration of Great Britain. With introduction, by A. Lawrence Lowell. Appleton 1917. $2.75.

Withers, Hartley. International Finance. Smith, Elder 1916. 3*s.* 6*d.*

—— War and Lombard Street. 2nd edn. (Lombard Street Library.) Smith, Elder 1916. 3*s.* 6*d.*

Wood, T. B. The National Food Supply in Peace and War. Camb. Univ. Press 1917. 6*d.*

World's Largest Loan, The. (An Account of the last British War Loan.) Fisher Unwin 1917. 1*d.*

Young, E. Hilton. System of National Finance. Smith, Elder 1915. 7*s.* 6*d.*

Zimmern, A. E. The economic weapon in the War against Germany. Allen & Unwin 1918. 2*d.*

B.—*Practical.*

Brett, W. War Time Gardening: How to Grow your own Food. Smallholder Office 1915. 6*d.*

Byron, May. How-to-Save Cookery: a War-time Cookery Book. Hodder & Stoughton 1915. 2*s.* 6*d.*

De Lissa, Nellie R. War-time Cookery. Simpkin 1915. 6*d.*

Economy in Food: Some Suggestions for Simple and Nourishing Meals for the Home. (Circular 917. Issued by the Board of Education.) H.M.S.O. 1915. 1*d.*

How to Economize. Simpkin 1915. 6*d.*

How to Save Money in War Time. The National Econ. League Handbook for Housewives. 11th edn. enlarged. 3, Woodstock Street, 1916. 2*d.*

Kennedy, Sidney S. Buy Consols and War Loan Mixed. Aldine Publishing Co. 1915. 6*d.*

—— Keep Your Consols. Aldine Publishing Co. 1915. 6*d.*

Manners, Clifford. Economics, Real and Practical: How to Spend, How Not to Spend. Newnes 1916. 1*s.*

Marden, Orison Swett, and Brown, Arthur. Economy: the Self-denying Depositor and Prudent Paymenter of the Bank of Thrift. Rider 1915. 1*s.*

Miles, Hallie Eustace. Economy in War Time: or, Health without Meat. Methuen 1915. 1*s.*

Oldmeadow, Ernest. Home Cookery in War Time. Richards 1914. 2*s.*

Praga, Mrs. Alfred. How Can I Save. Hodder & Stoughton 1916. 1*s.*

Senn, C. Herman. War-time Cooking Guide. Simpkin 1915. 3*d.*

Smith, H. H. The High Price of Sugar, and How to Reduce it. Bale, Danielssohn 1916. 1*s.*

Stevenson, Lieut. A. F. Income Tax for Service Men, their Wives and Next-of-kin. A handbook for officers and men [etc.] With foreword by Basil E. Peto, M.P. King 1918. 2*s.* 6*d.*

Urwick, E. J. Spending in War Time. Milford 1915. 2*d.*

War-time Gardening: How to Grow your own Food. The Smallholder Office 1915. *6d.*

Wood, T. B., and Hopkins, F. G. Food Economy in War Time. Camb. Univ. Press 1915. *6d.*

XVI.—TRADE, COMMERCE AND INDUSTRY.

A.—*Trade and Commerce.*

Bowley, Prof. A. L. The Effect of the War on the External Trade of the United Kingdom. Camb. Univ. Press. *2s.*

Brown, H. Gunnison. International Trade. Macmillan 1916. *4s.*

Chapman, S. J. The War and the Cotton Trade. Oxford Univ. Press. *2d.* o.p.

Distributing Trades in Scotland. First Report of the Government on War Organization. H.M.S.O. 1915. *1½d.*

Foreign Trade and Commerce. Accounts relating to, including figures received up to Dec. 24, 1919. H.C. Paper 17—x (Session 1919). H.M.S.O. 1920. *6d.*

Hauser, Henri. Germany's Commercial Grip on the World: Her Business Methods Explained. Translated by Manfred Emanuel. Nash 1916. *5s.*

—— —— 4th edn. 1918. *6s.*

Herzog, S. The Iron Circle. The future of German industrial exports. (German methods of commercial victory.) Translated from the German. Hodder & Stoughton 1918. *6s.*

Hooker, W. H. The Handicap of British Trade: with special regard to East Africa. With a foreword by Charles E. Musgrave. Murray 1916. *2s. 6d.*

How to Capture German Trade. Hodder & Stoughton 1914. *1d.*

Molesworth, Sir G. German Trade-War on England. Odhams 1916. *1d.*

Morgan, H. E. Munitions of Peace: our Preparations for the Trade War. Nisbet 1916. *2s. 6d.*

Musgrave, Charles E. (edr.). Trade and the War: Trade Maps, Charts, and Statistics. G. Gill 1914. *1s.*

Raffalovitch, Arthur (edr.). Russia: its Trade and Commerce. (A collection of articles, with statistical tables.) King 1918. *12s. 6d.*

Salter, J. A. Allied Shipping Control: an Experiment in International Administration. (Economic and Social History of the Great War, British Series.) Published for the Carnegie Endowment. Oxford Univ. Press 1921. *15s.*

Syren and Shipping: Mercantile War Loss Book. List of steamships destroyed 1914-18, with the losses of the world's principal steamship companies. Syren and Shipping 1918. *2s. 6d.*

Vallet, Maurice. Le Répertoire de l'avant-guerre. Les établissements industriels et commerciaux allemands et autrichiens mis sous séquestre en France pendant la guerre, d'après les publications du journal officiel. Introduction by M. de Roux. Nouv. Libr. nationale 1916. 5 fr.

War on German Trade: Hints for a Plan of Campaign. Heinemann 1914. 1*s.*

Whyte, Adam Gowans, and Elder, T. C. The Underwar. A reasoned statement of the true strategy involved in the War upon Germany's trade. Electrical Press 1914. 1*s.*

B.—*Industry.*

Carpenter, Edward. Towards Industrial Freedom. Allen & Unwin 1917. 2*s.* 6*d.*

Cole, G. D. H. The World of Labour. Discusses the problems involved, especially that of the Trade Union Army working on munitions. Revised edn. Bell 1915. 2*s.*

—— Labour in War Time. Bell 1915. 2*s.* 6*d.*

Connolly, James. Labour in Ireland. (On some of the causes of unrest which led to the insurrection, by one of its leaders.) Mannsel 1917. 4*s.*

Coulton, G. C. Workers and War. Bowes & Bowes. 1*d.*

Dawson, W. Harbutt. The German Danger and the Working Man. Central Committee. 1*d.*

Industrial Councils. The Whitley Report, with the letter of the Minister of Labour explaining the Government's view. Published by the Ministry of Labour. H.M.S.O. 1917. 1*d.*

Industrial Outlook, The. By several authors. Edited by H. S. Furniss. Chatto & Windus 1916. 3*s.* 6*d.*

Industry and Finance: War expedients and Reconstruction. Being results of enquiries arranged by the Brit. Association in 1916 and 1917. Edited by Prof. A. W. Kirkaldy. Pitman 1918. 4*s.* 6*d.*

Macara, Sir Charles W., Bart. The War: its Effect upon Industry. Republished from the Financial Review of Reviews for Sept. 1914. Financial Rev. of Reviews Office.

Memorandum on the Industrial Situation after the War. By members of the Garton Foundation. Harrison 1916. 1*s.*

Orwin, C. S. The Farmer in War Time. (O.P.) Oxford Univ. Press. 2*d.*

Peddie, J. Taylor. British Industry and the War. Longmans 1914. 1*s.*

Stewart, Andrew. British and German Industrial Conditions. A comparison. Rentell 1916. 6*d.*

Toogood, G. E. Labour Unrest: War-time Thoughts on a National Danger. Brown 1915 and 1916. 6*d.*
Webberley, T. War-time Farming. Pearson 1916. 6*d.*
Women in the Labour Market during the War. Manchester: Women's War Interests Committee 1916. 1*d.*

XVII.—EDUCATION.

Burnet, Prof. John. Higher Education and the War. By the Prof. of Greek at St. Andrew's. Macmillan 1917. 4*s.* 6*d.*
Hovre, Fr. de. German and English Education. By a former Lecturer in Louvain University. Constable 1917. 2*s.* 6*d.*
Leeson, Cecil. The Child and the War. Being notes on juvenile delinquency. King 1917. 1*s.*
Pellatt, T. Public School Education and the War. An answer to the attack upon Eton education. Duckworth 1917. 2*s.* 6*d.*
Sarraut, A. L'Instruction publique et la Guerre. Didier 1916. 3 f. 50.

XVIII.—SCIENCE AND PHILOSOPHY.

A.—*Science.*

Achalme, Dr. La Science des civilisés et la Science allemande. Avec préface de M. Edmond Perrier, et une réponse du Prof. Ostwald. Payot 1916. 3 fr. 50.
Arnold, J. O. British and German Steel Metallurgy. (O.P.). Oxford Univ. Press. 2*d.*
Barnwell, F. S. Aeroplane Design: and a Simple Explanation of Inherent Stability by W. H. Sayers. McBride 1916. 2*s.* 6*d.*
Burls, G. A. Aero-Engines: with a general introductory account of the theory of the Internal-Combustion Engine. 4th edn. C. Griffin 1916. 8*s.* 6*d.*
Haldane, J. S. Self-contained Rescue Apparatus for use in Irrespirable Atmospheres. Institute of Mining Engineers 1914. 2*s.* 6*d.*
Heald, William. Scientific Deductions respecting the European War. Colour Service Co. 1915. 1*s.*
Kempster, J. W. Presidential Address to the Belfast Association of Engineers on the War. Belfast: Baird.
Marre, Francis. La Chimie meurtrière des Allemands. Illustrated. (Pages actuelles.) Bloud et Gay 1916. 60 c.
Osler, Prof. Sir William. Science and War. An address. Oxford Univ. Press 1915. 1*s.* 6*d.*
Petit d'Alfort, Prof. G., and M. Leudet (edrs.). Les Allemands et la Science (Opinions of leading French scientists, scholars, etc.). With preface by Paul Deschanel. Alcan 1916. 3 fr. 50.

Poulton, E. B. Science and the Great War. (Romanes Lecture). Milford 1915. *2s.*

Riach, M. A. S. Air Screws. An introduction to the aerofoil theory of screw-propulsion. Crosby Lockwood 1916. 10*s.* 6*d.*

Thomson, J. Arthur. Biology and War. (Papers for War Time). Milford 1915. 2*d.*

B.—*Philosophy.*

Bergson, Henri. The Meaning of the War: Life and Matter in conflict. An address delivered by the author as President of the Académie des Sciences morales et politiques, Dec. 1914. Fisher Unwin. 1*s.*

Boutroux, Emile. Philosophy and War. Authorised transl. by Fred Rothwell. Constable 1915. 4*s.* 6*d.*

Carus, Paul. Nietzsche and other Exponents of Individualism. Open Court Publishing Co. 1914. 5*s.*

Cousins, James H. War: a Theosophical View. Theosoph. Publ. Society 1915. 6*d.*

Ethics of War. Ramsgate: S. R. Wilson 1915. 2*d.*

Guillet, Prof. C. Is War ever Right? By a Canadian Professor of Psychology. Toronto: E. Guillet 1916. 10 c.

Lambert, Henri. Ethics of International Trade. (Papers for War Time.) Milford 1915. 2*d.*

Le Bon, Gustave. Enseignements psychologiques de la guerre européenne. Flammarion 1916. 3 f. 50.

Matters, Muriel. The False Mysticism of War. An address, published by the Society of Friends. Headley. 2*d.*

Maxwell, J. La Philosophie sociale et la guerre. Alcan 1917. 3f. 50.

Mitchell, P. Chalmers. Evolution and the War. An examination of the theory that development is due to conflict. Murray. 2*s.* 6*d.*

Murray, Prof. Gilbert. Ethical Problems of the War. An address. Nelson 1915. 1*d.*

Perry, Prof. R. B. The Present Conflict of Ideals. A study of the philosophical background of the Great War. New York: Longmans 1918. $4.50.

Plater, Charles, *S.J.* (edr.). A Primer of Peace and War: the Principles of International Morality. Edited for the Catholic Social Guild. King. 2*s.*

Sinnett, Alfred P. Spiritual Powers and the War. Theosophical Publishing Society 1915. 6*d.*

—— Unseen Aspects of the War. Theosophical Publishing Co. 1915. 6*d.*

Taylor, G. R. S. The Psychology of the Great War. Secker. 2*s.*

Underhill, Evelyn. Mysticism and War. Watkins. 3*d.*

XIX.—MEDICINE AND SURGERY.

A.—*General.*

Abbott-Brown, Major C. How to do it. The A.S.C. Subaltern's and N.C.O.'s Vade Mecum. Forster Groom 1916. 1*s.*

Barker, Granville. The Red Cross in France. With preface by Sir F. Treves. Hodder & Stoughton 1916. 2*s.* 6*d.*

Barrett, James W., and Deane, Lieut. P. E. The Australian Army Medical Corps in Egypt. Lewis 1918. 12*s.* 6*d.*

Barrow, K. M., and Cunynghame, A. B. de M. How Women can Help the Wounded. Hodder & Stoughton 1914. 7*d.*

Beggs, S. T. Notes on Corps Dutes for Officers joining the Royal Army Medical Corps. Gale & Polden 1916. 6*d.*

—— Training in First Aid and Nursing: by Question and Answer. Scientific Press 1915. 1*s.* 6*d.*

Berry, James and F. M. D., and Blease, W. L. A Red Cross Unit in Serbia. (Illustrations and map.) Churchill 1916. 6*s.*

Bevaix, T. de. L'Été du silence. Préface par M. G. Lenôtre. (Médecins de France; Soldats de France; Infirmières françaises, etc.) L'Association nationale pour la protection des familles des morts pour la patrie, 5 rue du Pré-aux-clercs 1915. 4 fr.

Billington, Mary Frances. The Red Cross in War: Woman's Part in the Relief of Suffering. Hodder & Stoughton 1914. 1*s.*

Boardman, Mabel T. Under the Red Cross Flag: at Home and Abroad. Illustrated. Lippincott 1915. 6*s.*

British Medicine in the War 1914-1917. Essays on problems of Medicine, Surgery and Pathology arising among the British Forces. By various authors. Brit. Med. Association 1918. 2*s.* 6*d.*

British Red Cross Handbook. Milford 1914. 1*s.*

Camus, Dr. Physical and Occupational Re-education of the Maimed. Translated from the French by Surgeon W. F. Castle. Baillière Tindall & Co. 1918. 5*s.*

Cantlie, James M. B. British Red Cross Society Manuals. (First Aid—Nursing—Training.) Cassell. 1*s.* each.

Church, Col. J. R. The Doctor's Part. (The work of the American Medical Corps in the war.) Appleton 1918. $1.50.

Creswick, P., Pond, G. S., and Ashton, P. H. Kent's Care for the Wounded. Preface by Sir Gilbert Parker. Hodder & Stoughton 1915. 1*s.* and 2*s.*

Fox, R. F., M.D. Physical remedies for disabled soldiers. With chapters by Major R. T. McKenzie, R.A.M.C., and others. Baillière 1917. 7*s.* 6*d.*

Herringham, Major-Gen. Sir W. A Physician in France. Arnold 1919. 15*s.*

Huntley, Emily. The Watchers. (An account of hostels in France provided to Y.M.C.A. for relatives visiting soldiers in hospital.) Red Triangle Press 1917. 6*d.*

Hutchinson, Woods. A Doctor in War. Illustrated. Cassell 1919. 7*s.* 6*d.*

Lagarde, Dr. M., and Perraud, V. Pour les sourds de la guerre. Précis de lecture sur les lèvres. (Lip-reading for the deaf.) Illustrated. Boune Presse 1917. 1 fr. 20.

Livingston, St. Clair, and Steen-Hansen, Ingeborg. Under Three Flags. With the Red Cross in Belgium, France and Serbia. Macmillan 1916. 3*s.* 6*d.*

Macpherson, Major-Gen. Sir W. G. History of the Great War, based on official sources. Medical Services, General History. Vol. I. (To be completed in 12 vols.) H.M.S.O. 1921. 21*s.*

Matthews, Dr. Caroline. Experiences of a Woman Doctor in Serbia. Mills & Boon 1916. 5*s.*

Our Work. (On the work of the Red Cross, V.A.D., etc.) Red Cross, Head Office 1917. Gratis.

Power, Lieut.-Col. Sir D'Arcy. Oxford War Primers of Medicine and Surgery. Intended for the use of practitioners taking temporary commissions in the Navy and the R.A.M.C., or working in connection with Red Cross and Ambulance Societies. Frowde 1915. 2*s.* 6*d.* and 3*s.* 6*d.* each vol.

Roffidal, M. Guide pour les formations sanitaires des armées dans leurs relations avec le Bureau de comptabilité du service de santé des armées. Charles-Lavauzelle 1918. 4 fr.

Saint-Paul, G. Le Rôle mondial du médicin militaire, précédé d'une étude sur le Rôle du groupes de brancardiers (G.B.D.) pendant la guerre. Alcan. 3 fr. 50.

Sergeant-Major, R.A.M.C. (*pseud.*). With the R.A.M.C. in Egypt. Cassell 1918. 6*s.*

Spearing, Miss E. M., V.A.D. From Cambridge to Camiers under the Red Cross. Cambridge: Heffer 1917. 2*s.*

Vivian, C. C. With the Royal Army Medical Corps at the Front. (Daily Telegraph War Books.) Hodder & Stoughton 1914. 1*s.*

—— and Hodder Williams, J. E. The Way of the Red Cross. A survey of Red Cross work abroad and at home. Hodder & Stoughton 1915. 2*s.* 6*d.*

Vivian, C. C., and Hodder Williams, J. E. The Way of the Red Cross. With preface by Queen Alexandra. Cheap edn. Hodder & Stoughton 1915. 1*s*.

Westerdale, T. L. B. Under the Red Cross Flag. With the Medicals in action. Kelly 1915. 1*s*.

B.—*Medicine and Hygiene.*

Ash, Edwin L., M.D. Nerve in War Time. Causes and cure of nervous breakdown. Mills & Boon 1915. 1*s*.

—— Notes on the Nervous System. Scientific Press 1915. 1*s*.

Collie, Col. Sir John. The Management of Neurasthenia and Allied Disorders Contracted in the Army. Bale & Danielsson 1917.

Cummings, B. F. The Louse and its Relation to Disease: its life history . . . and how to deal with it. British Museum (Natural History). 1*d*.

Eder, M. D. War Shock. The Psycho-neuroses in War. Heinemann 1917. 5*s*.

Elkington, Lieut.-Col. H. P. G. Notes on Military Sanitation. St. John Ambulance 1914. 6*d*.

Ford, Joseph H. Elements of Field Hygiene and Sanitation. Illustrated. Heinemann 1918. 6*s*.

Galtier-Bossière, le Dr., and others. Larousse médical de guerre illustré (volume supplementaire). Larousse 1918. 16 fr.

Harris, Wilfred. Nerve Injuries and Shock. (Oxford War Primers.) Oxford Univ. Press 1915. 3*s*. 6*d*.

Havard, Valery. Manual of Military Hygiene: for the services of the United States. 2nd edn. Bale 1914. 25*s*.

Hindle, Edward. Flies in relation to Disease: Blood-sucking Flies. Illustrated. Cambridge Univ. Press 1914. 12*s*. 6*d*.

Hurst, Major A. F. Medical Diseases of the War. Arnold 1916. 6*s*.; 2nd edn. (1918), 12*s*. 6*d*.

Kenwood, Lieut.-Col. H. R., R.A.M.C. Health in the Camp: a Talk to Soldiers. H. K. Lewis, 136, Gower Street, W.C. 3*d*.

Lelean, Major P. S. Sanitation in War. Introduction by Surgeon-Gen. Sir Alfred Keogh. Churchill 1917. 6*s*.

Lépine, Jean. Troubles mentaux de la guerre. Masson 1917. 4 fr.

Lloyd, Lieut. Ll. Lice, and their Menace to Man. With a chapter on Trench Fever by Major W. Byam. Hodder & Stoughton 1918.

McMillan, J. F. Infectious Disease in Serbia. Baillière 1915. 6*d*.

Maxwell-Lefroy, H. Measures for Avoidance and Extermination of Flies, Mosquitoes, Lice and other Vermin. 2nd edn. Thacker 1916. 1*s.*

Moores, S. Guise. British Red Cross Society Hygiene and Sanitation Manual. No. 4. Illustrated. Cassell 1914. 1*s.*

Nankivell, Capt. Austin T. Health in Camp. (Chadwick Trust Lecture, amplified.) Constable 1917. 1*s.*

Plowman, C. F., and Dearden, W. F. Fighting the Fly Peril. A popular and practical handbook. With introduction by A. E. Shipley. Unwin 1915. 1*s.*

Prinzing, Friedrich. Epidemics resulting from wars. Edited by Prof. H. Westergaard, of Copenhagen. Clarendon Press 1916. 7*s.* 6*d.*

Roussy, Dr. G., and Lhermitte, J. Psychoneuroses of War (Shell Shock). Edited by Lieut.-Col. Aldren Turner. (Military Medical Manuals.) Univ. of London Press 1918. 7*s.* 6*d.*

Shipley, A. E. Minor Horrors of War. Illustrated. 3rd edn. (This book deals with various insect and other pests, and suggests remedies.) Smith, Elder 1916. 1*s.* 6*d.*

—— More Minor Horrors. Illustrated. Smith, Elder 1916. 1*s.* 6*d.* and 2*s.*

Smith, G. Elliot, and Pear, T. H. Shell Shock and its Lessons. By two Professors of Manchester University. Longmans 1917. 2*s.* 6*d.*; 2nd edn. (1918), 4*s.*

Squire, J. Edward. Medical Hints for the Use of Medical Officers temporarily employed with Troops. (Oxford War Primers.) Milford 1915. 2*s.* 6*d.*

Stewart, Purves, and Evans, Arthur. Nerve Injuries and their Treatment. (Oxford Medical Publications.) Frowde & Hodder 1916. 8*s.* 6*d.*

Strong, Richard P. Trench Fever. Report of Medical Research Committee; American Red Cross. Oxford Univ. Press 1918. 21*s.*

Sykes-Brown, Hy. E. How to take care of your Teeth. Specially written for Soldiers and Sailors. Foreword by J. Sim Wallace, M.D. Forster Groom 1917. 1*s.*

C.—*Surgery, First Aid, Bandaging, &c.*

Bowser, Thekla, F. J. J. The whole art of Bandaging. With introduction by J. Cantlie, F.R.C.S. Illustrated. Bale & Danielsson 1916. 1*s.*

Braun, H. Local Anæsthesia: its Scientific Basis and Practical Use. H. Kimpton 1914. 21*s.*

British Red Cross Anatomical Diagrams. Six linen charts. Milford 1914. 30*s.*

Broca, A., and Ducroquet, Dr. Artificial limbs. Ed. and transl. by Major R. C. Elmslie, M.S., F.R.C.S. Military Medical Manuals. Univ. of London Press 1918. 7*s.* 6*d.*

Bryan, M. Theresa. The Soldier's First-Aid Book. Macmillan. 2*d.*

Carrel, A., and Dehelly, G. The Treatment of Infected Wounds (transl. from the French). With introduction by Sir A. A. Bowlby. Baillière 1917. 5*s.*

Carvell, J. M. First Aid in Few Words. Bale & Danielssohn 1916. 2*d.*

—— Index of First Aid. A vade-mecum for the ambulance worker and all interested in the subject of first aid to the injured. Bale 1915. 1*s.*

Chalier, A., & Chalier J. La Gangrène gazeuse. Alcan 1918. 8 fr. 50.

Davies, H. Morriston. A Manual of Minor Surgery and Bandaging. Heath, Pollard, 15th edn. 1914; Churchill. 7*s.* 6*d.*

Delorme, Edmond. War Surgery. Transl. by H. de Méric. Illustrated. Lewis 1915. 5*s.*

Dolbey, Capt. R. V., R.A.M.C. A Regimental Surgeon in War and Prison (experiences during the earlier part of the War). Murray 1917. 5*s.*

Eliason, E. L. Practical Bandaging: including Adhesive and Plaster-of-Paris Dressings. Lippincott 1914. 6*s.*

Finny, W. E. St. L. Dr. Finny's First Aid. A notebook for ambulance students. T. Murby 1914. 6*d.*

Fitzwilliam, D. C. L., M.D. Practical Manual of Bandaging. Baillière 1915. 3*s.* 6*d.*

Fletcher, N. Corbet, M.R.C.S. Compendium of Aids to First Aid. Bale 1914. 6*d.*

—— Why and Wherefore in First Aid. Bale 1914. 6*d.*

—— Aids to First Aid. A compendium of aids to memory, invaluable to students. With introduction by J. Cantlie, F.R.C.S. Bale & Danielssohn 1916. 6*d.*

General Principles Guiding the Treatment of Wounds. H.M.S.O. 1918. 3*d.*

Grove, E. W. Hey. Gunshot Injuries of Bones. (Oxford War Primers.) Oxf. Univ. Press 1915. 3*s.* 6*d.*

Guermonprez, Fr. Gangrène gazeuse pendant la guerre de 1914-16. 4 vols. (By a physician in the military hospital at Calais.) Rousset 1916.

Hall, Col. Alfred J. Surgery in War. With a Preface by Lt.-Gen. Goodwin, Director-General A.M.S. 2nd edn. Churchill 1918. 25*s.*

Hastings, Somerville. First Aid for the trenches. Simple instructions for saving life. Murray 1916. 1*s.*

Hughes, Basil, and Banks, Stanley. War Surgery: from Firing Line to Base. With special chapters by Col. L. P. Smith and Miss C. Bilton, and introduction by Col. Sir T. Crisp English, K.C.M.G. Baillière 1918. 30*s.*

Injuries in War, Memorandum on the Treatment of, based on experience of the present campaign. (July 1915.) H.M.S.O. 1916. 4*d.*

Johnson, Francis H. Localisation of Bullets and Shell Fragments. A record of personal experience. Lewis 1915. 1*s.*

Jones, R. Injuries of the Joints. (Oxford War Primers.) Oxf. Univ. Press, 1915. 3*s.* 6*d.*

Lagarde, L. A. Gunshot Injuries. Bale 1914. 18*s.*

Lejars, Felix. Urgent Surgery. 3rd English impression. Transl. from the 7th French edn. by William S. Dickie and Ernest Ward. Wright 1915. 25s. each vol.

Makins, G. H. Gunshot Injuries of the Arteries. (Oxford Medical Publications.) Milford 1914. 2*s.* 6*d.*

Manual of Splints and Appliances for the treatment of bone and joint injuries (American Red Cross). Hodder & Stoughton 1917. 2*s.* 6*d.*

Military Medical Manuals (Treatment of fractures, nerve lesions, artificial limbs, &c.). Ed. by Sir A. Keogh. 7 vols. Transl. from the French. Univ. of London Press 1918. 6*s.* each.

Morison, Rutherford, and Richardson, W. G. Abdominal injuries. (Oxford War Primers.) Milford 1915. 2*s.* 6*d.*

—— Bipp Treatment of War Wounds. Frowde & Hodder 1918. 2*s.* 6*d.*

Murphy, J. K. Wounds of the Thorax in War. (Oxford War Primers.) Oxf. Univ. Press 1915. 2*s.* 6*d.*

Notes on First Aid for N.C.O.'s and Men. Gale & Polden. 6*d.*

Penhallow, Dunlop P. Military Surgery. 2nd edn. Henry Frowde; Hodder & Stoughton 1918. 21*s.*

Power, Lt.-Col. Sir d'Arcy. Wounds in War: Their Treatment and Results. (Oxford War Primers). Oxf. Univ. Press 1915. 2*s.* 6*d.*

Preston, Howard M. The Triangular Bandage. Introduction by James Cantlie. Illustrated with 116 figures. Bale & Danielssohn 1916. 1*s.*

Ramsay, A. M., and others. Injuries of the Eyes, Nose, Throat and Ears. (Oxford War Primers.) Milford 1915. 2*s.* 6*d.*

Rawling, L. B. Surgery of the Head. (Oxford War Primers.) Oxf. Univ. Press 1915. 3*s.* 6*d.*

Roth, Paul Bernard. Notes on Military Orthopædics. Kimpton 1916. 1*s.*

Sartory, A. Le Traitement des plaies de guerre. Illustré. Berger-Levrault 1917. 2 fr.

Short Cuts to First Aid. By a Metropolitan Police Surgeon attached to the R.A.M.C. S. Paul 1914. 7*d.*

Tommy's A.B.C. British Red Cross Society 1916. 1*s.*

Wallace, Cuthbert, C.M.G. War Surgery of the Abdomen. Churchill 1918. 10*s.* 6*d.*

—— and Fraser, John, M.C. Surgery at a Casualty Clearing Station. Black 1918. 10*s.* 6*d.*

Warwick, F. J., and Tunstall, A. C. First Aid to the Injured and Sick. An advanced Ambulance Handbook. Illustrated. 8th edn. Bristol: Wright 1915. 1*s.*

Watson, J. K. Wounds and their Treatment. (Pocket Guide series.) Scientific Press 1914. 1*s.*

Wilson, Andrew. Common Accidents in Peace and War, and how to treat them. 10th edn. Chatto & Windus 1915. 6*d.*

Wright, Sir Almroth E. Wound Infections and some New Methods for the study of the various factors which come into consideration in their treatment. Univ. of London Press 1915. 2*s.* 6*d.*

D.—*Hospitals, Ambulances, Nursing, etc.*

Abraham, J. J. My Balkan Log. (Hospital experiences in Serbia 1914-16.) Chapman & Hall 1921. 15*s.*

Alexinsky, Tatiana. Parmi les blessés. Carnet de route d'une aide-doctoresse russe. Colin 1916. 2 fr. 50.

Anglo-French-American Hospital, The. Work under homœopathic auspices during 1915-1916 in conjunction with the French Red Cross Society at Neuilly-sur-mer. 1918. 2*s.* 6*d.*

Antelme, Jeanne. Notes d'une infirmière à Moudros. Emile-Paul Frères 1916. 3 fr. 50.

Army General Hospital Administration, Memoranda on. By various authors. Edited by Lieut.-Col. P. Mitchell. Baillière 1917. 5*s.*

Ashdown, A. Millicent. A Complete System of Nursing. New York: Dutton 1918. $5.00

Bagnold, Enid. A Diary without Dates. Thoughts and impressions of a V.A.D. Heinemann 1918. 2*s.* 6*d.*

Barnes, Leonard S. Martin's Questions and Answers upon Ambulance Work. Revised and brought up to date. 18th edn. Baillière 1915. 1*s.*

Barton, E. C. Hints to V.A.D. Members in Hospital. Nursing Times. 6*d.*

Bessières, A. Le Train rouge. Deux ans en train sanitaire. Beauchesne 1917. 3 fr. 50.

Blighties. Ups and downs in a Home Hospital. By one of "those V.A.D.'s." Stockwell 1918. 2*s.*

Bourceret, J. M. Sur les Routes du Front de Meuse, souvenirs d'un infirmier-major. Perrin 1917. 3 fr. 50.

Bowser, Thekla. The Story of British V.A.D. Work in the Great War. Melrose 1917. 5*s.*

Burwell, Leslie. Ambulance No. 10. Personal letters from the front. (By a member of the American Ambulance Corps.) Illustrated. Boston: Houghton Mifflin 1916. $1.00.

Campbell, Phyllis. Back of the Front. Experiences of a nurse. With introduction by W. L. Courtney. Newnes 1915. 1*s.*

Casualty Clearing Station, The Tale of a. (Ends with the Battle of Festubert.) By a Royal Field Leech. Blackwood 1917. 5*s.*

Catchpool, T. Corder. On Two Fronts. (Experiences of a Quaker as (1) ambulance worker, and (2) conscientious objector.) Edited by his sister, with preface by J. Rendel Harris. Headley 1918. 2*s.*

Cator, Dorothy. In a French Military Hospital. Longmans 1915. 2*s.* 6*d.*

Chauveau, L. Derrière la bataille. (Experiences in an ambulance.) Payot 1917. 3 fr.

Childe, Charles P. Surgical Nursing and Technique. A book for nurses, dressers, house surgeons, etc. 2nd edn. Baillière 1916. 3*s.* 6*d.*

Chivers, Ellen. A Farmer in Serbia. (The experiences of a lady engaged in the British Farmers' Military Hospital Unit, June 1915-Feb. 1916.) Methuen 1916. 6*s.*

Clarke, E. M. The Nurse's Enquire Within. New edn., with much additional information. Scientific Press 1914. 2*s.*

Cook, Mrs. Thornton. General Service Hints for V.A.D. Members. Revised by Miss L. Dennler. With preface by [Dame] Katherine Furse. Scientific Press 1917. 1*s.* 3*d.*

Dearmer, Mabel. Letters from a Field Hospital. With memoir by Stephen Gwynn. Macmillan. 2*s.* 6*d.*

Démians, M. Notes d'une infirmière (1914). Plon-Nourrit. 3 fr.

Dent, Olive. A V.A.D. in France (Hospital life). Grant Richards 1917. 5*s.*

Duhamel, Georges. Vie des Martyrs (in the Military Hospitals). Mercure de France 1917. 3 fr. 50.

—— Transl. under title The New Book of Martyrs (*see also* Thévenin). Heinemann 1918. 5*s.*

Dupuy, Georges M., M.D. The Stretcher-Bearer. A companion to the R.A.M.C. Training Book. Oxford Univ. Press. 2*s.*

Eydoux-Demains, M. In a French Hospital. Translated from the French. Fisher Unwin 1915. 2*s.* 6*d.*

Fitzwilliam, D. C. L., M.D. A Nursing Manual for Nurses and Nursing Orderlies. Oxford Univ. Press. 6*s.*

Fitzroy, Yvonne. With the Scottish Nurses in Rumania. Illustrations and maps. Murray 1918. 5*s.*

Fox, E. Margaret. First Lines in Nursing. Scientific Press 1914. 2*s.* 6*d.*

Friends of France. (The Field Service of the American Ambulance described by its members.) Illustrated. Houghton Mifflin 1916. $2.00.

Grove, S. W. Textbook for Nurses. Oxford Univ. Press. 12*s.* 6*d.*

Hancock, Bernard M. Encouragement: a Word of Good Cheer to Nurses. (Manchester Books.) Society of SS. Peter and Paul 1916. 6*d.* and 1*s.*

Happy—though Wounded. The Book of the 3rd London Hospital. Country Life 1917. 2*s.* 6*d.*

Harrard, E. M., and Harrard, Mrs. A. R. Practical Nursing: for Male Nurses in the R.A.M.C. and other Forces. Oxford Univ. Press. 3*s.* 6*d.*

James, Henry. The American Volunteer Motor-Ambulance Corps in France. A letter to the Editor of an American Journal. Macmillan. 1*d.*

Kirkpatrick, T. Percy C. Nursing Ethics. Dublin Univ. Press 1915. 1*s.*

Laurie, Jessie M. A War Cookery Book for the Sick and Wounded. Werner Laurie. 6*d.*

Leng, William St. Q. La Section Sanitaire Anglaise. (A diary of ambulance work with the French, 1915-1917.) With many photographs. Sheffield: Leng & Co. 1918. £1 1*s.*

Lucas, E. V. Outposts of Mercy. (Record of a visit to British Red Cross stations in Italy, Nov.-Dec. 1916.) Methuen 1917. 1*s.* 3*d.*

McDougall, Grace. A Nurse at the War. By an English nurse New York: McBride 1917. $1.25.

McLaren, Eva S. (edr.). History of the Scottish Women's Hospitals. 1919. 6*s.*

Manual of Drill and Camping for the St. John Ambulance Brigade St. John Ambulance Association 1914. 5*d.*

Martin. Questions and Answers upon Ambulance Work. 18th edn., revised by Leonard S. Barnes. Baillière 1915. 1*s.*

Martin-Nicholson, Sister. My Experiences on Three Fronts (in Belgium, Russia, and France). Allen & Unwin 1916. 4*s.* 6*d.*

Mason, Charles F. A Complete Handbook for the Hospital Corps of the U.S. Army and Navy, and State Military Forces. New edn. Bale 1914. 20*s.*

Mengens, H. Hospital Handbook in English and French. Simpkin 1915. 1*s.*

Muir, Ward, Lance-Corp. Observations of an Orderly. Some glimpses of life and work in an English War Hospital. Simpkin, Marshall 1917. 3*s.* 6*d.*

Navarro, Antonio de. The Scottish Women's Hospital at the French Abbey at Royaumont. Illustrated. (The only hospital in France run entirely by women.) Allen & Unwin 1917. 7*s.* 6*d.*

Newsome, Edith. Home Nursing. Comprising lectures given to the detachments of the British Red Cross Society. Scientific Press 1916. 2*s.* 6*d.*

Nightingale, Florence. Notes on Nursing. New edn. Harrison. 1*s.* 6*d.*

—— To her Nurses. Selections from addresses. Macmillan 1914. 1*s.*

No. 31540, R.A.M.C. Fields and Battlefields. (Stories of life in hospital and ambulance work.) Constable 1918. 5*s.*

Norton, Félicie. Practical Hints to Would-be Nurses. Scientific Press 1916. 6*d.*

Nursing Adventures: a F.A.N.Y. (First Aid Nursing Yeomanry) in France and Belgium. Illustrated. Heinemann 1917. 2*s.* 6*d.*

Oxford, M. N. Nursing in War Time. Methuen. 1*s.*

Peek, Emily. Practical Instruction in Cutting-out and Making-up Hospital Garments for the Sick and Wounded. (Approved by the Red Cross Society.) Illustrated. Bale & Danielsohn 1916. 1*s.*

Platoon Commander (*pseud.*). Hospital Days. Unwin 1916. 2*s.* 6*d.*

Pope, Amy E. Medical Dictionary for Nurses. Putnam 1915. 3*s.* 6*d.*

—— Textbook of Anatomy and Physiology for Nurses. 2nd edn., revised and enlarged. Illustrated. Putnam 1915. 7*s.* 6*d.*

Rae, James. Medical Emergencies. A handbook for nurses. Scientific Press 1915. 1*s.*

Reckitt, H. J. A French Military Hospital. Illustrated. 1921. 21*s.*

Return as to Hospital Accommodation in England and Wales. H.M.S.O. 1915. 3*s.*

Roussel-Lépine, José. Une Ambulance de gare: croquis des premieres jours de guerre (août 1914). Plon-Nourrit 1916. 2 fr. 50.

Saundby, Prof. R. Open-Air Hospitals in War Time. (Reprinted from the Lancet, Sept. 19, 1914.) Bale & Danielssohn. 6*d.*

Senn, C. Herman. British Red Cross Society Cookery Manual. Cassell 1915. 1*s.*

Shipley, Sir A. E. The Open-Air Treatment of the Wounded. Description of the First Eastern General Hospital at Cambridge, its methods and results. Country Life Library. 1*s.*

Souttar, H. S. A Surgeon in Belgium. Account of the work of the Belgian Field Hospital, the nature of wounds, etc. Arnold. 2*s.* & 8*s.* 6*d.*

Stobart, Mrs. St. Clair. War and Women: from Experience in the Balkans and elsewhere. Women's work in hospitals, etc. With preface by Lord Esher. Bell. 3*s.* 6*d.*

Thévenin, Denis (Georges Duhamel). Civilisation. (Hospital experiences. Sequel to Vie des Martyrs, *see* Duhamel.) Mercure de France 1918. 3 fr. 50.

Thurston, Violetta. Field Hospital and Flying Column: being the Journal of an English Nursing Sister in Belgium and Russia. Putnam 1915.

—— A Textbook of War Nursing. Putnam 1917. 3*s.* 6*d.*

Toland, E. D. The Aftermath of Battle. With preface by Owen Wister. Experiences of an American in French hospitals. New York: Macmillan 1916. $1.00.

Twiss, George E. Manual for St. John Voluntary Aid Detachments. 2nd edn. St. John Ambulance Association 1914. 6*d.*

Wards, The, in War Time. By a Red Cross Pro. Blackwood 1916. 5*s.*

Welham, Sydney. Manual for Nurses. 2nd edn. Mills & Boon 1916. 1*s.* 6*d.*; cheaper edn., 1*s.*

XX. RELIGIOUS WORKS.

A.—*Prayers and Devotions.*

Benson, R. H. (edr.). Vexilla Regis. A book of devotions and intercessions on behalf of all our authorities, our soldiers and sailors, etc., arranged, translated and compiled by the Very Rev. Mgr. Benson. Longmans 1914. 1*s.* 6*d.*

Canterbury, Archbishop of, and others. Prayers in time of War. Jarrold 1915. *3d.* and *1s.*

Christ's Sentry. A manual of prayer for soldiers. S.P.C.K. 1916. *4d.*

Coles, V. S. S. A Litany for the War. Music by H. A. Branscombe. Blackwell 1914. *3s. 6d.* per 100.

Cuddesdon Manual of War Intercessions. Mowbray 1915. *3d.*

Forms of Prayer for Public and Private Use in Time of War. S.P.C.K. 1916. *6d.*

Healing Christ, The. Prayer for the wounded and the dying in time of war. Foulis 1619. *6d.*

Litany, A, for time of War and a Penitential Leaflet. Words and music. W. Heffer 1914. *2d.* net; words only, *1d.*

Per Christum Vinces: Prayers in Time of War. 2nd edn. Longmans 1914. *4d.*

Prayers and Thoughts for the Trenches. (Trench Booklets). 1915. *6d.*

Prayers for Britain's Warriors and others. Thynne 1915. *2d.*

Prayers in Time of War. Burns and Oates 1914. *6d.*

Simple Prayer Book for Soldiers. Catholic Truth Society. *2d.*

Trevelyan, Rev. W. B. A Nation at Prayer: a Manual for Use in War Time for those at Home. Longmans. *1s.* and *1s. 6d.*

—— Versicles, Responses, and Antiphons from War Prayers for a Week. Longmans 1916. *1d.*

—— War Prayers for a Week on Liturgical Lines. Longmans 1916. *6d.*

War Manual of Prayer, A. Longmans 1914. *6d.*

War Prayers of One Hundred Years Ago. Special forms of prayer issued in 1796, 1804, and 1811. With preface by the Bishop of London. S.P.C.K. *3d.*

B.—*Sermons and Addresses.*

Armitage, Rev. J. J. R. No Church, no Empire. (Addresses on the case against Germany, the Church, social evils, &c.). Rob. Scott 1916. *3s. 6d.*

Bernard, Most Rev. J. H., Archbishop of Dublin. In War Times. Addresses delivered during the War. Mowbray 1917. *1s. 6d.*

Brent, Rt. Rev. C. H., Bishop of the Philippines. The Commonwealth of Mankind. Sermon preached in St. Paul's Cathedral, April 20, 1917. Mowbray 1917.

Brown, Rev. Charles, D.D. The War and the Faith. Sermons by a Baptist divine. Morgan and Scott. *2s. 6d.*

Browne, Rev. G. R. National Service: a Plain Sermon. Gloucester: Acton. *6d.*

Bull, Rev. Paul B. Peace and War. Notes of Sermons and Addresses (addressed especially to conscientious objectors). Longmans 1918. *2s. 6d.*

Burroughs, E. A. Faith for the Firing Line. Addresses to officers of the Expeditionary Force. Nisbet 1914. *6d.*

Canterbury, The Archbishop of. Quit you like men. Six sermons. S.P.C.K. 1915. *1s.*

—— and others. Christ and the World at War (Sermons). J. Clarke 1917. *2s. 6d.*

Denison, Rev. H. P. The Lord in His Temple. The message of Habakkuk to a world at war. Scott 1916. *1s. 6d.*

—— Some Spiritual Lessons of the War. Five sermons. Scott 1915. *1s. 6d.*

Dudden, Rev. F. Homes. The Problem of Human Suffering and the War. Four sermons. Longmans 1916. *1s.*

—— The Heroic Dead, and other sermons. Longmans 1918. *3s. 6d.*

Evans, E. T. Vision of Victory. Sermons. Stockwell 1915. *2s.*

Faith and the War. Guidance and comfort for anxious times from great preachers. Smith's Publishing Co. 1915. *6d.*

G. The End is not Yet. Five War sermons. Hunter and Longhurst 1915. *6d.*

Gordon, Rev. Geoffrey.. An Interpreter of War: the Prophet Habakkuk. Addresses at St. Margaret's, Westminster. Longmans, 1916. *1s.*

Gore, Charles, Bishop. The War and the Church, and other addresses. Mowbray 1914. *1s. 6d.*

Henson, Dean. War-time Sermons. Macmillan. *4s. 6d.*

Hertslet, E. L. A. Cup and the Sacrifice, and other Sermons on the War. Simpkin 1915. *2s. 6d.*

Hicks, Edward Lee (Bishop of Lincoln). Church and the War. (O.P.). Milford 1915. *2d.*

Irvine, Dr. Alexander. God and Tommy Atkins (Addresses to soldiers and men of the Y.M.C.A.). Hutchinson 1918. *3s. 6d.*

London, the Bishop of. The Soul of a Nation. Address delivered at St. Paul's, July 25, 1915. Pearson 1915. *6d.*

Macewen, Rev. Prof. A. R. The War and Christianity. The Moderator's address before the U.F.C. Assembly, May 1915. Edinburgh: MacNiven. *6d.*

Mackarness, Charles Coleridge. Faith and Duty in time of War. Sermons preached in the Parish Church of St. Martin's, Scarborough. Mowbray 1916. *1s. 6d.*

Macnutt, Frederic B. The Reproach of War. Addresses given in St. Saviour's Cathedral, Southwark. R. Scott 1914. *1s. 6d.*

Martineau, James, D.D. Right of War. A sermon. Longmans. *2d.*

Mellor, Stanley A. Which Gospel do You Accept? Five addresses in time of war. Liverpool Booksellers Co. 1915. *6d.*

Mercier, Cardinal. Lettre Pastorale, sur le Patriotisme et l'Endurance. Mâlines, Christmas 1914. Official transl. into English. Burns and Oates. *2d.*

—— On the Papacy: a Pastoral Letter. Washbourne. *2d.*

—— Pastoral Letter, Christmas 1914. Official transl. Burns and Oates 1915. *2d.*

—— Per crucem ad lucem (principales lettres pastorales du Cardinal Mercier). Bloud 1917. 3 fr. 50.

Millard, F. L. H. Short War Sermons for Good Friday and Easter. Skeffington 1916. *2s.*

Mozley, J. B. War: a Sermon. Longmans 1915. *3d.*

Mursell, Walter A. Bruising of Belgium, and other Sermons during war time. Gardner 1915. *2s. 6d.*

Nurse, Euston J. Christmas Time and the War. Skeffington 1915. *2s.*

—— The Churches of the Allies. Six addresses by the Rector of Windermere. Skeffington 1916. *2s. 6d.*

—— Prophecy and the War. Sermons preached at the Parish Church, Windermere. Skeffington 1915. *2s.*

Paget, Francis, Bishop. The Redemption of War. Sermons preached in the Cathedral Church of Christ, Oxford. Longmans 1914. *1s.*

Paterson, W. P. In the Day of the Muster. (Sermons in Time of War). Hodder and Stoughton 1914. *2s.*

—— In the Day of the Ordeal (Sermons). T. & T. Clark 1917. *4s. 6d.*

Potter, J. Haslock. Discipline of War. Nine addresses on the lessons of the war in connection with Lent. Skeffington 1915. *2s.*

—— Judgment of War. Skeffington 1915. *2s.*

—— and Whitehouse, F. Cowley. Red Cross in Origin and Action. Two sermons. Skeffington 1915. *1s.*

—— Craigie, J. A., and Worsey, F. W. Harvest Thanksgiving in War Time. Plain sermons. Skeffington 1915. *2s.*

Prosser, D. L. Addresses at Church Parade Services. S.P.C.K 1915. *1s.*

Randolph, E. S. L. In the Time of War and Tumult. Three sermons. Selkirk: Scottish Chronicle Office 1915. *3d.*

Ryle, Right Rev. H. E. The Attitude of the Church towards War. The Liverpool lecture. Longmans 1915. *6d.*

Scott-Murray, Rev. A. The Good Fight of Faith. Addresses to children on war subjects. Stockwell 1916. 1*s.*

Sermons for the Times. (1) Four Sermons on War. (2) Sermons in Time of War. (3) Sermons on Citizenship. (4) Sermons on the Holy War. Griffiths 1914. 1*s.*

Sinker, Rev. John. The War: its deeds and lessons. (Ten sermons). With introduction by the Bishop of Manchester. Skeffington 1916. 2*s.* 6*d.*

Smith, George Adam. War and Peace. Two sermons in King's College Chapel, University of Aberdeen. Hodder & Stoughton 1915. 6*d.*

Stephen, Rev. W. L. The Re-building of Arras. (A sermon preached in the ruins of the Cathedral). Oliphant 1917. 2*d.*

Streeter, B. H. War: this War and the Sermon on the Mount. (Papers for War Time). Milford 1915. 2*d.*

Strong, T. B. Christmas and the War. (O.P.). Milford. 2*d.*

Studdert-Kennedy, Rev. G. A. Rough Talks by a Padre; delivered to officers and men. Hodder and Stoughton 1918. 5*s.*

Temple, Rev. W. Christianity and War: a Word to Teachers. S.P.C.K. 1d.

—— Holy War. (Missionary Tracts for the Times).

Thomas, Rev. J. M. Lloyd. The Immorality of Non-Resistance, and other Sermons of the War. Cornish 1915. 1*s.*

Tissier, Mgr. J. Pour la victoire. Nouvelles consignes de guerre. (Addresses by the Bishop of Châlons). Téqui 1916. 3 fr. 50.

Velimirovic, Rev. Nicholas. The Agony of the Church (Lectures delivered at St. Margaret's, Westminster). Preface by Rev. Alexander Whyte. Student Christian Movement 1917. 2*s.* 6*d.*

Viollet, l'abbé Jean. Le Catholicisme et la guerre. (Six conferences données par l'auteur à l'eglise Saint Louis d'Antin). Librairie Roblot 1917. 2 f.

Wace, Henry, D.D., Dean of Canterbury. The War and the Gospel. Sermons and addresses. Thynne 1917. 2*s.* 6*d.*

Ward, J. H. Belief and War: Addresses to Men. Howells 1916. 1*s.*

Webster, F. S. Enemies Reconciled: or, The Cross in the Light of the War. Sermons preached in St. Paul's Cathedral. Marshall Bros. 1915. 1*s.*

Williams, J. H. Lenten Thoughts in War Time. Nine addresses. Skeffington 1916. 2*s.* 6*d.*

Woods, F. T. War Watchwords from Bradford Parish Church. Jackson 1915. 1*s.*

Woods, Rev. H. G. Christianity and War. Sermons by the late Master of the Temple. With introduction by Margaret L. Woods. Scott 1916. 3*s.*

Worsey, F. W. Praying Always. Addresses from Ash Wednesday to Easter in War Time. With an introductory hymn of prayer by John Stanhope Arkwright. Skeffington 1916. *2s. 6d.*

—— Under the War Cloud. Being nine sermons on the war. Skeffington 1914. *2s.*

—— War and the Eastern Hope. Four addresses. Skeffington 1915. *1s. 6d.*

Wynn, Walter. The Bible and the War. Addresses. Garden City Press 1915. *6d.*

York, The Archbp. of. The Church and the Clergy at this Time of War. A charge delivered on Feb. 14 and 15, 1916. S.P.C.K. *1s.*

C.—*Other Religious Works.*

Adams, J. Esslemont. Chaplain and the War. T. & T. Clark 1915. *6d.*

—— Great Sacrifice: or the Altar-Fire of War. Clark 1915. *1s.*

Allan, Andrew. Armageddon: before and after. Potter-Sarvent Publishing Co. 1915. *1s.*

Allan, Charles. The Beautiful Thing that has happened to our Boys: Messages in War Time. Greenock: McKelvie 1915. *2s. 6d.*

Anderson, Sir Robert. The Higher Criticism and the War. Being a re-issue of Pseudo-Criticism. Nisbet 1915. *2s. 6d.*

Ballard, Frank. Christianity after the War. Kelly 1916. *2s. 6d.*

—— The Mistakes of Pacifism: or, Why a Christian can have anything to do with the War. Kelly 1915. *3d.*

Barry, F. R. Religion and the War. By an Oxford divine. Methuen. *1s.*

—— The War and Christian Ethics. B. H. Blackwell 1914. *6d.*

Bartlett, W. T. The World's Crisis in the Light of Prophecy. Fowler 1915. *1s.*

Bell, Rev. G. K. A. (edr.). The War and the Kingdom of God. Essays by Canon Scott Holland, Canon Goudge, &c. Longmans 1915. *2s. 6d.*

Berry, Digby M. European History foretold: or, St. John's Foreview of Christendom. Thynne 1916. *3s. 6d.*

Booth, Adjutant Mary. With the B.E.F. in France (describes Salvationist work with the Army). Salvation Army 1916. *6d.*

Braithwaite, G. H. The Society of Friends and War (To fight in defence of King and Country is not anti-Christian). Scott 1917. *6d.*

Brash, W. B. Peace in Time of War. C. H. Kelly 1914. *6d.*

Brown, E. V. Christianity and War. 3rd edn. Friends' Peace Comm. 1916. *1d.*

Bull, Paul B., *C.R.* God and our Soldiers. New edn. Mowbray 1914. *1s. 6d.*

Burroughs, E. A. Eternal Goal. Three letters to the Times on the spiritual issues of the present situation. Longmans 1915. *3d.*

—— The Fight for the Future. With preface by the Archbishop of Canterbury. Nisbet 1916. *1s.*

Byron, May (edr.). The Red Cross of Comfort for all those who are afflicted in mind, body, or estate. Hodder & Stoughton 1914. *3s. 6d.*

Campbell, R. J. War and the Soul. Chapman & Hall 1916. *6s.*

Canterbury, Archbishop of, and others. War and Christianity. Jarrold 1914. *6d.*

Can England's Church win England's Manhood? A study . . of the spiritual condition of English soldiers. By an Army chaplain. Macmillan 1917. *1s.*

Carnegy, Mildred (edr.). A little Book for those who mourn. Mills & Boon 1915. *1s. 6d.*

Carpenter, Dr. J. E. (edr.). Ethical and Religious Problems of the War. Lindsey Press 1916. *2s. 6d.*

Caudwell, Irene (edr.). In the Morning: Thoughts for the Sick and Wounded. Society of SS. Peter & Paul 1915. *2d.*

Christian Ideals in War Time. A series of essays by Members of the Churchmen's Union, and others. Macmillan. *5s.*

Clarke, Rev. F. J. The World, the War, and the Church (by a Wesleyan Methodist Minister). Allen & Unwin 1916. *2s.*

Comfort and Consolation: Thoughts for the Bereaved. Mowbray 1915. *4d.*

Comfort of the Cross. A little book for all who are afflicted or distressed. Hodder & Stoughton 1915. *1s.*

Cook, V. Our Brave Dead: What Becomes of Them? Kelly 1916. *4d.*

Cox, J. Bell. Remember Your Dead! Being words of comfort for the bereaved. Gardner 1915. *1s.*

Crafer, T. W. Prophets' Visions and the War. Skeffington 1916. *2s.*

—— Soldiers of Holy Writ: their Lessons for the present War of the Nations, and for the ever-present Warfare of the Soul. Skeffington 1915. *2s.*

Crosse, Rev. E. C., C.F., D.S.O. The God of Battles: a Soldier's Faith. Being an attempt to reveal the power of God in War. Preface by Gen. Sir H. de la P. Gough. Longmans 1917. 1*s.*

Cunningham, Archibald W. Christianity and Politics. (The Lowell Lectures.) Murray 1916. 6*s.*

Daily Musings for the Bereaved. Being words of comfort for those in sorrow. Grafton 1916. 1*s.* 6*d.*

Dawson, Joseph. Christ and the Sword. Words for the War-perplexed. With an introduction by F. J. C. Hearnshaw. Kelly 1916. 2*s.* 6*d.*

Denney, Rev. Principal J., D.D. War and the Fear of God. Hodder & Stoughton 1916. 2*s.* 6*d.*

Desgranges. l'Abbé Jean. La religion et la guerre (brochure). Bloud et Gay 1917.

Dobson, Rev. C. C. God, the War and Britain. Elliot Stock 1917. 1*s.*

Downes, Robert P. Our Fallen Heroes and Their Destiny. Horace Marshall 1915. 1*s.*

Drawbridge, Rev. C. L. Christianity and the War. St. Catherine Press, 34, Norfolk Street, W.C. 3*d.*

—— The War and Religious Ideals. Disputes the contention that Christianity is opposed to all forms of war. Longmans. 1*s.*

Duke, Rev. John A. The Religions of our Allies. Hodder & Stoughton 1917. 3*s.* 6*d.*

Eddy, Sherwood. Suffering and the War. Longmans 1916. 1*s.*

—— The Meaning of Suffering (Extracts from Suffering and the War, printed at request of the Y.M.C.A.). Longmans 1917. 3*d.*

Elphinstone, Rev. M. C. War and the Gospel of Christ. War only to be abolished by Christianity. Skeffington 1915. 2*s.* 6*d.*

Felce, Walter. War of Freedom and the Unity of Christ. Griffiths 1915. 2*s.* 6*d.*

Figgis, Rev. J. N., *C.R.* The Will to Freedom; or the Gospel of Nietzsche and the Gospel of Christ. Longmans 1917. 6*s.*

Five Articles on War. Reprinted from the New-Church Magazine. New-Church Press 1915. 6*d.*

Foakes-Jackson, F. J. (edr.). The Faith and the War. Essays by Members of the Churchmen's Union and others. Macmillan 1915. 5*s.*

For the healing of the nations. Report of the British and Foreign Bible Society 1915-16. B.F.B.S. 1916.

Forsyth, A. T., D.D. The Christian Ethic of War. Longmans 1916. 6*s*.

Franks, R. S. The Cross and the War. (Papers by Congregationalists.) Congregational Union of England and Wales 1916. 2*d*.

Gell, Hon. Mrs. Happy Warrior: Daily Thoughts 1916. Foreword by Field Marshal Earl Roberts. Mowbray 1915. 2*d*. & 6*d*.

Gibbon, J. Morgan. The Peacemaker and the Pacifist. (Papers by Congregationalists.) Congregational Union of England and Wales 1916. 2*d*.

God and the War, and other sketches. By J.M.S. Stockwell 1916. 1*s*.

Goldsack, S. J. C. Killed in Battle and After. Gardner 1915. 3*d*.

Goodman, H. God, the World and the War. Heffer 1915. 6*d*.

Gorham, Charles T. Religion and the War. Watts 1916. 1*d*.

Graham, J. W. War from a Quaker point of view. Headley. 1*s*. 6*d*.

Griffith-Jones, Principal E. The Challenge of Christianity to a World at War. Duckworth. 2*s*. 6*d*.

Handcock, John. God's Dealings with the British Empire. Bell 1916. 5*d*.

Henley, T. After the War. Christendom and the coming peace. The Christian Church's Opportunity. Hodder & Stoughton 1917 9*d*.

Hogg, A. G. Christianity and Force. Milford 1915. 2*d*.

Holland, Canon H. Scott. So as by Fire: Notes on the War. Reprinted from The Commonwealth. Wells Gardner. 1*s*.

—— —— 2nd series. 1*s*. & 2*s*.

Horton, R. F. The War and Humanity. (Papers by Congregationalists.) Congregational Union of England and Wales 1916. 2*d*.

Hunt, Rev. J. B. War, Religion and Science. Shows that war is not incompatible with Christianity, and pleads for national service. Melrose 1915. 2*s*.

International Relationships in the Light of Christianity. A series of lectures given at the Inter-Denominational Summer School, Swanwick. Simpkin 1916. 2*s*. 6*d*.

James, H. R. The Empire's Immortal Dead: Aug. 1914-Aug 1915. Longmans 1915. 6*d*.

Jeffs, Harry. When the Lads Come Home: What will the Churches do with them? Johnson 1915. 1*s*.

Jones, J. D. The Great Hereafter. Questions raised by the Great War, concerning the destiny of our dead. Clarke 1915. 1*s.*

Jowett, J. H. They that Wait. A message for war time. J. Clarke 1914. 6*d.*

Kent, Charles. New Guide to the Perfect Existence: or the way Home from the Battlefield. Forgiveness and Salvation possible beyond the grave. Stockwell 1915. 1*s.*

Klein, Félix (l'abbé). Dieu nous aime (entretiens avec les victimes de la guerre). Gabalda 1918. 3 fr. 60.

—— Les Douleurs qui espèrent. Perrin 1916. 3 fr. 50.

—— Transl. under title Hope in Suffering. Memories and Reflections of a French Army Chaplain. With introduction by Canon Scott-Holland. Melrose 1916. 4*s.* 6*d.*

Lenwood, Frank. Pharisaism, and War from a Pharisaic point of view. (Papers for War Time.) Milford 1915. 2*d.*

Letters from Another Battlefield. MacDonald 1916. 1*s.*

Lincoln, Bishop of. Church and the War. (O.P.) Milford 1915. 2*d.*

Linton, E. C. Notes on the Absolution of the Sick and Dying. Longmans 1915. 2*s.* 6*d.*

Loisy, Alfred. Réligion et Guerre. Paris: Nourry 1915.

—— —— Translated under title, Religion and War. Blackwell 1915.

London, The Bishop of. The Church in Time of War. Wells Gardner 1915. 2*s.* 6*d.*

—— and others. Kaiser or Christ? The War and its Issues. J. Clarke. 1*s.*

Lucas, Rev. E. Primitive Methodism and the War. 2*d.*

M'Cabe, Joseph. War and the Churches. Watts 1915. 6*d.* and 1*s.*

Maclennan, Kenneth. Price of Blood. (Papers for War Time.) Milford 1915. 2*d.*

Masson, F. Guerre de Religions (articles publiés dans l'Echo de Paris, Excelsior, et le Gaulois). Bloud et Gay 1917. 1 fr. 50.

Maud, Rev. J. P. Our Comradeship with the Blessed Dead. 7th edn. Longmans 1918. 1*s.* 3*d.* and 2*s.* 6*d.*

Mayhew, D. M. (edr.). Lift up your Hearts. A book for those whom the war has put in mourning. Hodder & Stoughton 1915. 1*s.*

Meanwhile. A packet of war letters. Comfort for non-combatants. By H. L. G. Murray 1916. 2*s.* 6*d.*

Moberly, W. H. Christian Conduct in War Time. 2*d.*

Morgan, G. Campbell. God, Humanity and the War. J. Clarke 1914. 1*s.*

Mott, John R. Present World Situation: with special referenc to the demands made upon the Christian Church in relation t non-Christian lands. Student Christian Movement 1915 2*s*. 6*d*.

Muir, John. War and Christian Duty. A. Gardner 1916 2*s*. 6*d*.

Murray, Marr. Bible Prophecies and the Plain Man, with speci reference to the present War. Hodder & Stoughton 1915. 6*s*

—— Bible Prophecies and the Present War. Hodder & Stoughton 1915. 1*s*.

—— (edr.). The Christian's War Book. Hodder & Stoughto 1914. 2*s*.

Nicoll, Sir W. Robertson. Prayer in War Time. (Collecte articles from the British Weekly.) Hodder & Stoughton 1916 2*s*. 6*d*.

Oakley, G. R. Under the Flag: Talks to Young Soldiers S.P.C.K. 1915. 4*d*.

Osborne, Charles E. Religion in Europe and the World Crisis Fisher Unwin 1917. 3*s*. 6*d*.

Padre, The. By Temporary Chaplain. Hodder 1916. 1*s*.

Paget, Rt. Rev. H. L., Bishop of Stepney. In the Day o Battle: under the guidance of the Lord's Prayer. With intro duction by the Bishop of London. Longmans. 2*s*. 6*d*.

Paravy, l'Abbé. Corpe blessés, coeurs meutris, âmes immortelles Allocutions aux blessés et discours de circonstance. Tégu 1916. 3 fr. 50.

Paterson-Smyth, J. The Men who Died in Battle. 2nd edn Hodder & Stoughton 1916. 1*s*.

—— God and the War. Some lessons of the present crisis Hodder & Stoughton 1915. 2*s*. 6*d*.

Proctor, Francis Bartlett. National Crisis and Why the Churche Fail. Stockwell 1915. 2*s*.

Rollings, W. Swift. The Great Assize. War studies in the ligh of Christian ideals. (By a New Zealander.) Allenson 1916 3*s*. 6*d*.

Romanes, Mrs. G. J. The Hallowing of Sorrow. Preface by Rev. H. S. Holland, D.D. (7th edn.). Longmans 1918. 2*s*

Roscoe, J. E. War Messages to the Nation. Skeffington 1915 2*s*.

—— War Saints and Subjects. Skeffington 1915. 2*s*.

Rouzie, l'Abbé L. Théologie de la guerre en dix-huit leçons (On the attitude of the Catholic Church towards war, &c.) Bloud et Gay 1916. 3 fr. 50.

Scott-Moncrieff, C. E. War Thoughts for the Christian Year Skeffington 1915. 2*s*. 6*d*.

Seaver, Richard W. What of our Dead in the Great War? With a foreword by Arthur Chambers. 2nd edn. Taylor 1915. 1*s.*

Selbie, W. B. The War and Theology. (O.P.) Oxford Univ. Press. 2*d.*

Sellers, William E. With our heroes in Khaki. (The story of Christian work with our Soldiers and Sailors.) R.T.S. 1918. 3*s.* 6*d.*

Service, W. J. Nichol. War and the Peace of God. Maclehose 1915. 2*s.* 6*d.*

Shillito, Edward. Through the War to the Kingdom. Morgan & Scott 1915. 2*s.*

Smith, A. L. Christian Attitude to War. (O.P.) Milford 1915. 2*d.*

Snell, Bernard J. How are we to Love our Enemies? Simpkin 1915. 2*d.*

—— Praying for the Dead. Simpkin 1915. 2*d.*

So Fight I! A soldier's daily thought. Bagster 1915. 3*d.* & 6*d.*

Soldier's Companion, The: Message of Hope, Comfort and Love. Oliphants 1916. 1*s.*

The Lord of Hosts is With Us. Baines and Scarsbrook 1915. 2*d.*

Soloviev, Vladimir. Trois Entretiens sur la guerre, la Morale et la religion. Traduit du russe par E. Tavernier. Plon-Nourrit 1916. 3 fr. 50.

—— Transl. under title War and Christianity from the Russian point of view. Three conversations. With introduction by Stephen Graham. Constable. 4*s.* 6*d.*

—— War, Progress and the End of History, including a short story of the Antichrist. Three discussions. Hodder & Stoughton 1915. 6*s.*

Sonnenschein, E. A. Idols of Peace and War. (O.P.) Oxford Univ. Press. 3*d.*

Stevenson, Lilian. Amor vincit omnia: thoughts on the war. With notes on what to read and helps to intercession. Student Christian Movement 1915. 3*d.*

Streeter, B. H. War: this War and the Sermon on the Mount. (Papers for War Time.) Milford 1915. 2*d.*

Strong, T. B. Christmas and the War. (O.P.) Milford. 2*d.*

Talbot, Rev. Neville S. Thoughts on Religion at the Front. By the Assistant Chaplain-General to the Forces. Macmillan 1917. 2*s.*

—— Religion Behind the Front and after the War. Macmillan 1918. 2*s.* 6*d.*

Taylor, Mrs. Howard. Though War should rise. Morgan & Scott 1914. 6*d*.

Temple, Rev. W. Christianity and War: a Word to Teachers. S.P.C.K. 1*d*.

—— Holy War. (Missionary Tracts for the Times.) S.P.C.K. 1915. 1*d*.

Thomas, Gilbert. Grapes and the Thorns: Thoughts in War Time. Headley 1915. 1*s*. & 2*s*.

Thompson, Miss Theodora. The Coming Dawn. Lane 1918. 3*s*. 6*d*.

Thurston, Herbert, *S. J*. The War and the Prophets. Notes on certain popular predictions current in this latter age. Burns & Oates. 2*s*. 6*d*.

Tiplady, Thomas, *C. F*. The Soul of the Soldier. (A Chaplain's account.) Methuen 1918. 6*s*.

Titterton, C. H. Armageddon, or the Last War. With foreword by the Rev. E. W. Moore. Thynne 1916. 1*s*. 6*d*.

Tudor-Pole, W. Great War: some Deeper Issues. Bell 1915. 1*s*. & 2*s*.

Vaughan, Bernard. What of To-day? Cassell 1914. 7*s*. 6*d*.

Wace, Very Rev. Henry, D.D. Religion and the War. (From The Record.) C. J. Thynne 1918. 3*d*.

Walker, Rev. W. L. The War, God and our Duty. Robt. Scott 1917. 2*s*.

Ward, Mgr. B. Thoughts in War Time. Catholic Truth Society 1915. 1*s*. & 1*s*. 6*d*.

Watkin, Edward Ingram. A Little Book of Comfort in Time of War. Catholic Truth Society 1914. 3*d*.

Watson, W. C. The War, the Church and the Adolescent. Bale & Danielssohn 1915. 6*d*.

Who Dies if England Live? Letters of comfort to the sorrowing from the One who looked on. Stock 1916. 1*s*.

Wilberforce, Basil. Why does not God stop the War? Stock 1915. 1*s*. 6*d*.

Wilson, William E. Christ and War: a Peace Study Textbook. F. Clarke 1914. 1*s*.

With the Colours: for God, King and Country. Psalms and Hymns for soldiers in the field, with a Welsh supplement. Constable 1915. 1*d*.

Woodroffe, C. A. A Call to the Nation on the Anniversary of its Declaration of War. Stock 1915. 6*d*.

Yoxall, Sir J. H. Marching Away. A book of consolation for war sorrow. Articles contributed to the Daily News. Marshall 1916. 6*d*.

XXI. ESSAYS, ADDRESSES, REFLECTIONS, &c.

A.—*English and American.*

Adler, Felix. The World Crisis and its meaning. A series of addresses. Appleton 1916. 4*s.* 6*d.*

Alderson, Albert W. Why the War cannot be final. P. S. King 1915. 1*s.*

Angell, Norman. War Aims. The need for a Parliament of the Allies. Headley 1917. 2*s.* 6*d.*

—— Foundations of International Polity. Heinemann 1914. 3*s.* 6*d.*

—— The political conditions of allied success. Putnam 1918. 7*s.* 6*d.*

Archer, William. Colour-blind neutrality. An open letter to Dr. George Brandes. Hodder & Stoughton 1916. 2*d.*

—— To neutral peace-lovers: a plea for patience. (Pamphlet.) Causton 1916.

Arnold, E. V. War-time Lectures (on Germany's strength and weakness, social organisation after the war, &c.). Allen & Unwin 1916.

Baldwin, Mark. The Super-State and the Eternal Values. Oxford Univ. Press 1916. 1*s.* 6*d.*

Balfour Browne, J. H. War Problems. Longmans. 1*s.*

Barker, Ernest. Mothers and Sons in War Time. Six essays reprinted from The Times. Humphreys. 1*s.*

—— —— New edn., with other pieces. Humphreys 1918. 3*s.* 6*d.*

Barre, J. M. Echoes of the War. Hodder & Stoughton 1918. 6*s.*

Beck, A. M. de. The Imperial War: Personalities and Issues. With an Introduction by Wm. Perkins Bull, K.C. Hurst & Blackett 1916. 6*s.*

Beckh, Robert Harold. Swallows in Storm and Sunlight. (The author fell in France, Aug. 1916.) Chapman & Hall 1917. 3*s.* 6*d.*

Beer, George Louis. The English-speaking peoples. (A plea for a closer political union.) New York: Macmillan 1917. $1.50.

Bell, E. P. The British Censorship. An address given Nov. 19, 1915, by the London Correspondent of the Chicago Daily News. Fisher Unwin 1915. 2*d.*

Besant, Annie. War Articles and Notes. Theosophical Publishing Society 1915. 1*s.*

Bevan, Edwyn. Brothers All: the War and the Race Question. Milford. 2*d.*

Bipin, Chandra Pal. Nationality and Empire. Thacker 1916. 6*s.*

Blakeslee, Prof. G. H. (edr.). The problems and lessons of the War. Clark University Addresses, Dec. 1915. (24 addresses by various authors.) Putnam 1916. $2.00.

Bodart, Gaston, and Kellogg, Vernon Lyman. Losses of Life in Modern Wars: Austria-Hungary, France. Military selection and race deterioration. Ed. by H. Westergaard. (Carnegie Endowment for International Peace.) Milford 1916. 6*s*.

Boden, J. F. W. Freedom's Battle. Being historical essays occasioned by the Great War. Studies of politics and strategy with historical parallels. Hugh Rees 1916. 2*s*. 6*d*.

Bosanquet, Bernard. Social and international ideals: being studies in Patriotism. Macmillan 1917.

Boyle, Mary E. Aftermath. Heffer 1916. 1*s*.

Brailsford, Henry Noel. The War of Steel and Gold. 3rd edn., with an additional chapter. Bell 1915. 2*s*.

Braut, Jules. La Réparation des dommages artistiques causés par l'invasion. (Criticism of the projet de loi voté le 23 janvier 1917). l'Emancipation 1917.

Bryce, James (Viscount Bryce). Neutral Nations and the War. Macmillan. 2*d*.

—— Race Sentiment as a Factor in History. A lecture. Hodder & Stoughton 1915. 1*s*.

—— Some historical reflections on war, past and present. (Addresses to the British Academy.) Oxford Univ. Press 1916. 1*s*.

—— Essay and addresses in war time. Macmillan 1918. 6*s*.

Buckell, A. C. The Greatest War. Six addresses. Skeffington 1915. 1*s*. 6*d*.

Burns, C. D. The Morality of Nations. Univ. of London Press 1916. 5*s*.

Butterfield, W. R. A National War Museum. Reprinted from The Museums Journal, vol. XVI., May 1917.

Cairns, Rev. Prof. D. S. An Answer to Bernhardi. (Papers for War Time, No. 12.) Milford 1915. 2*d*.

Carpenter, Edward. The Healing of Nations and the Hidden Sources of their Strife. Essays on various subjects connected with the War, with a useful appendix of documents and quotations. Allen & Unwin. 2*s*.

Carter, G. R. Co-operation and the Great War. King. 3*d*.

Cestre, Charles. France, England, and European Democracy, 1215-1915. (An historical survey of the principles underlying the Entente.) New York: Putnam 1918. $2.50.

Chapman, Rev. Hugh B. Home truths about the War. (On the necessity of patriotism and piety.) Allen & Unwin 1917 2*s*. 6*d*.

Charity Commission. War Charities List to March 31, 1917. H.M.S.O. 1917. 1*s*. 3*d*.

Clayton, I. M. Shadow on the Universe: or the Physical Results of War. Simpkin 1915. 2*s*. 6*d*.

Clutton-Brock, A. Are we to Punish Germany if we can? A discussion of the theory of revenge. Milford. 2*d*.

—— Bernhardism in England. (Papers for War Time.) Milford 1915. 2*d*.

—— Cure for War. (Papers for War Time.) Milford. 2*d*.

—— Thoughts on the War. Leading articles from the Literary Supplement of The Times. Two series. Methuen. 1*s*. each.

—— More Thoughts on the War. From The Times Literary Supplement. Methuen 1915. 1*s*.

—— The ultimate belief. Constable 1916. 2*s*. 6*d*.

Coar, J. F. Democracy and the War. New York: Putnam 1918. $1.25.

Collin, Prof. Christen. The war against war. Macmillan 1917.

Collings, Rt. Hon. Jesse, M.P. The Great War: Its Lessons and its Warnings. Rural World Publ. Co. 1915. 2*s*.

Corelli, Marie. Is all well with England? Jarrolds 1917. 6*d*.

Cowen, Hettie B. What is War? And two other Essays (supporting the war, conscription, and a League of Nations). Cursitor Pub. Co. 1918. 9*d*.

Crichton-Browne, James. Bernhardi and Creation: a New Theory of Evolution. Maclehose 1916. 1*s*.

Crile, G. W. A mechanistic view of war and peace. (By an American surgeon in charge of a hospital unit of the American ambulance in France.) Ed. by Amy F. Rowland. Werner Laurie 1916. 6*s*.

Dawbarn, C. Y. C. Some Considerations Suggested by the present War. An address read before the Liverpool Philomathic Society. Liverpool: Marples.

Dawson, Coningsby. Khaki Courage (on the spirit of our men at the front). Lane 1917. 3*s*. 6*d*.

Dawson, W. J. The father of a soldier (experiences and feelings of a father with sons fighting). Lane 1918. 4*s*.

Dearmer, Rev. Percy. Patriotism. (Papers for War Time.) Milford 1915. 2*d*.

—— Patriotism and Fellowship. (Six papers.) Smith, Elder, 1917. 2*s*.

D'Egville, Howard. The Invasion of England. With introduction by Lord Sydenham. Hodder & Stoughton. 6*d*.

De Wend-Fenton, West F. Realities. Being reprints of articles which have appeared in The World since the outbreak of war. Society Periodicals 1915. 1*s*.

Dickinson, G. Lowes. The European Anarchy. Allen & Unwin 1916. *2s. 6d.*

Dillon, E. J. Ourselves and Germany. With an introduction by the Rt. Hon. W. M. Hughes. (A plea for a general change of views.) Chapman & Hall 1916. *7s. 6d.*

Duchesne, A. E. Democracy and Empire (Royal Colonial Institute Monographs). Milford 1916. *2s. 6d.*

Dymond, Jonathan. War: its causes, consequences, lawfulness, etc. An essay. Newman West 1915. *6d.*

Empire Day Book of Patriotism. Evans Bros. 1916. *1s. 6d.*

Ellis, H. Essays in War Time. Constable 1916. *5s.*

Fayle, C. Ernest. The New Patriotism: a Study in Social Obligations. (The Garton Foundation.) Harrison. *1s.*

Fiennes, Gerard. Sea Power and Freedom. An historical study. Skeffington 1917. *10s. 6d.*

Finch, Daisy (edr.). Voice of Empire: a Patriotic Thought for every Day in the Year. Hill 1915. *2s. 6d.*

Fisher, H. A. L. The Value of Small States. (O.P.) Oxford Univ. Press. *2d.*

For the Right. Essays and Addresses by members of the Fight for Right movement. Fight for Right, Trafalgar House, 1916. *5s.*

Fortescue, Hon. J. W. Military History. Lectures delivered at Trinity College, Cambridge. Camb. Univ. Press. *1s.*

Future of Militarism, The. An examination of F. S. Oliver's Ordeal by Battle. By "Roland." Fisher Unwin 1916. *2s. 6d.*

Galsworthy, John. A Sheaf (essays on war-subjects, &c.). Heinemann 1916. *5s.*

Gardner, Alice. Our Outlook as changed by the War. A paper read in Newnham College. Heffer. *2d.*

Gell, Mrs. Lyttelton. The War and the objects of the Mothers' Union. A course of model addresses. Wells Gardner 1916. *4d.*

General's letters, A, to his Son on obtaining his commission. Cassell 1917. *1s.*

Gibbs, Philip. The Soul of the War. Heinemann 1916. *7s. 6d.*

—— —— Cheap edn. 1917. *2s.*

Gill, Conrad. National power and prosperity. With introduction by George Unwin. Fisher Unwin 1916. *4s. 6d.*

Gosse, Edmund. Inter Arma. (A collection of essays on war-subjects and others.) Heinemann 1916. *6s.*

Grant, Robert. Their spirit. Some impressions of the English and French during the summer of 1916. Houghton Mifflin 1916. 50c.

Gray, Herbert. The Only Alternative to War. (Papers for War Time.) Milford 1915. *2d.*

Gribble, Francis. Women in war. Sampson, Low, 1916. 7*s.* 6*d.*

Hallowes, Frances S. Women and War: an Appeal to the Women of all Nations. Headley 1914. *2d.*

Hammond, F. War—and the Average Man. F. Hammond, 30, Dane's Inn House, Strand, W.C. 1*d.*

[Hankey, Lieut. Donald W. A.] A student in arms. With introduction by J. St. Loe Strachey. (Articles mostly reprinted from The Spectator.) Melrose 1916. 5*s.*

—— Beloved Captain. Selected chapters from A Student in Arms. Melrose 1917. 1*s.*

—— A Student in Arms. Second Series. (With fragment of autobiography.) Melrose 1917. 5*s.*

Haward, Lawrence. Effect of War upon Art and Literature. Longmans 1916. 3*d.*

Hay, Ian [pseud. Captain I. H. Beith]. Getting together. (A discussion between an American and a Briton.) Hodder & Stoughton 1917. 1*s.*

Hayward, Charles W. War and Rational Politics. Watts 1915. 1*s.* and 1*s.* 6*d.*

Hobhouse, L. T. Questions of war and peace. (Three papers on nationality, internationalism, &c.) Fisher Unwin 1916. 3*s.* 6*d.*

Hodson, James. The Soul of a Soldier. Routledge 1918. 1*s.* 6*d.*

Holdich, Col. Sir Thomas. Political frontiers and boundary-making. (Throws light on present conditions and future problems.) Macmillan 1916. 10*s.*

Holland, W. Lancelot. Final call to arms, or Armageddon. Worthing: Jones 1915. 2*s.* 6*d.*

Holmes. Ven. E. E. The Message of the Soldiers. With illustrations by L. J. Pocock. Mowbray 1917. 1*s.* 6*d.*

Hope, Anthony (A. Hope Hawkins). Militarism: German and British. Darling.

Horton-Smith, L. G. H. The value of Sea-Power. Perthshire Courier 1916. 3*d.*

Humphrey, A. W. International Socialism and the War. King. 3*s.* 6*d.*

Hyndman, H. M. The Future of Democracy. Essays reprinted from the Fortnightly and the English Review, on the hope of permanent peace. Allen & Unwin 1915. 2*s.* 6*d.*

Irwin, Will. The Latin at War. Constable 1917. 6*s.*

Jordan, David Starr. War and Waste. A series of discussions on war and war accessories. Unwin 1914. 5*s.*

Kennedy, Sinclair. The Pan-Angles. A consideration of the federation of the seven English-speaking nations. (Publ. in the U.S. 1914.) Longmans 1918. 7*s.* 6*d.*

Kenyon, Sir F. G. Ideals and Characteristics of English Culture. The Rede Lecture 1915. Smith, Elder, 1916.

Kettle, Prof. T. M. The Ways of War. With Memoir and Portrait. Constable 1917. 7*s.* 6*d.*

Kirkpatrick, Prof. J. War Studies. Black. 3*d.*

Knowles, F. L. The Value of Courage. (Value of Friendship series.) L. B. Hill 1914. 3*s.* 6*d.*

Lafontaine, Henry Cart de. Dante and War. Constable 1916. 3*s.* 6*d.*

Lambert, Henri. International Morality and Exchange. (By a manufacturer of Charleroi.) With preface by Lord Courtney. Allen & Unwin 1916. 6*d.*

Lancaster, G. Harold. Prophecy, the War, and the Near East. Marshall Brothers 1916. 6*s.*

Lee, Sir Sidney. Shakespeare and the Red Cross. Address delivered at the opening of the Shakespeare Exhibition on Jan. 19, 1917. Chiswick Press 1917. 3*d.*

Leigh, Dell. The Vigil, and other studies in Khaki. Hodder 1916. 1*s.*

Lind-af-Hageby, L. Mountain Meditations, and some subjects of the day and the War. Allen & Unwin 1917. 4*s.* 6*d.*

Lindsay, A. D. War against War. (O.P.) Oxford Univ. Press. 2*d.*

Lippman, Walter. Drift and Mastery: an Attempt to Diagnose the Current Unrest. Unwin 1914. 5*s.*

Logan, Rev. James. On the King's Service. Inward Glimpses of Men at Arms. Hodder & Stoughton 1917. 2*s.* 6*d.*

Low, Sidney (edr.). The Spirit of the Allied Nations. A collection of Lectures by different authors dealing with each nation in turn. Black. 2*s.* 6*d.*

Lucas, Sir C. P. The Call of the War. (An address delivered on April 20, 1917.) S.P.C.K. 1917. 3*d.*

Lucas, Sir Charles. Patriotism (an address). S.P.C.K. 1918. 4*d.*

Lucas, E. V. Remember Louvain: a little book of Liberty and War. Selected by E. V. L. Methuen. 1*s.*

Lynd, Robert. If the Germans conquered England, and other Essays. Maunsel 1917. 3*s.* 6*d.*

McCabe, Joseph. The Soul of Europe: a Character-Study of the Militant Nations. Fisher Unwin. 10*s.* 6*d.*

McCall, S. W. Liberty of Citizenship. Milford 1915. 5*s.*

Macdonald, J. A. Democracy and the Nations: Canadian view. Milford 1915. 5*s.* 6*d.*

MacDonald, J. Ramsay, M.P. National Defence: a study in Militarism. Allen & Unwin 1917. 2*s*. 6*d*.

McNair, Wilson. Blood and iron. Dutton 1917. $2.00.

Magnus, Laurie. The Third Great War in relation to Modern History. Arrowsmith. 1*s*.

Mahan, Admiral A. T. The Problem of Asia, and its effect on International Policies. Maps. Sampson Low. 10*s*. 6*d*.

Mais, S. P. B. A Public School in War Time. On the effect the War has had and will have on Public Schools. Murray 1916. 3*s*. 6*d*.

Marriott, J. A. R. The European Commonwealth. Problems historical and diplomatic. Oxford Univ. Press 1919. 15*s*.

Martin, E. M. Dreams in Wartime: a faithful record. Shakespeare Head Press 1915. 2*s*. 6*d*.

Marvin, F. S. The Leadership of the World. (O.P.). Oxford Univ. Press. 2*d*.

—— (edr.). Unity of Western Civilisation. Milford 1915. 7*s*. 6*d*.

Matheson, P. E. National Ideals. (O.P.) Oxford Univ. Press. 3*d*.

Militarism versus Feminism. An inquiry and a policy demonstrating that militarism involves the subjection of women. Allen & Unwin 1915. 6*d*.

Mocran, J. W. W. Illustrations from the Great War. R. Scott 1915. 2*s*. 6*d*.

Morel, E. D. Truth and the War. (35 collected papers). With introduction by Philip Snowden. Nat. Labour Press 1916. 2*s*.

Moulton, James H. British and German Scholarship. (Papers for War Time). Milford 1915. 2*d*.

Muir, Prof. Ramsay. Nationalism and Internationalism. The culmination of Modern History. Constable 1916. 4*s*. 6*d*.

Mullins, Claud. The Patriotism of Ramsay Macdonald and others. Nash 1916. 6*d*.

Murray, Prof. Gilbert. How Can War ever be Right? (O.P.) Oxford Univ. Press. 2*d*.

—— Thoughts on the War. (O.P.) Oxford Univ. Press. 2*d*.

—— Faith, War, and Policy. Addresses and Essays on the European War. Houghton, Mifflin 1917. $1.25.

Murray, Marr. Drink and the War, from the Patriotic Point of View. For temperance, not total abstinence. Chapman & Hall. 1*s*.

Neilson, Francis. How Diplomats make war. (An indictment of the present system, on the lines of the U.D.C) New York: Huebsch 1917. $1.50.

Nurse, Rev. E. J. Prophecy and the War. 7th Edn. Skeffington 1918. 3*s*.

Oliver, F. S. Ordeal by Battle. In four parts: The Causes of War; the Spirit of German Policy; the Spirit of British Policy; Democracy and National Service. Macmillan 1915. 6*s*.

Oxford Pamphlets, 1914-15. Eighty-seven Pamphlets. Crown 8vo. Separately, in paper covers. Also in volumes as numbered (I-XIX), stiff covers, One Shilling net each volume, except XVIII, which is One Shilling and Sixpence. The historical pieces illustrated by sketch-maps:—

I

1. The Deeper Causes of the War. By W. Sanday. 3*d*.
2. To the Christian Scholars of Europe and America. A reply from Oxford to the German Address to Evangelical Christians, here reprinted. 2*d*.
3. The Responsibility for the War. By W. G. S. Adams. 2*d*.
4. Great Britain and Germany. By Spenser Wilkinson. 2*d*. Three letters to the Springfield Republican: By Prof. Spenser Wilkinson, stating Great Britain's case—By Prof. John W. Burgess, stating Germany's case—By Prof. Wilkinson, in reply to Prof. Burgess.
5. Just for a Scrap of Paper. By Arthur Hassall. 1*d*.

II

6. The Germans, their Empire, and how they have made it. By C. R. L. Fletcher. 2*d*.
7. The Germans, their Empire, and what they covet. By C. R. L. Fletcher. 2*d*.
8. Might is Right. By Sir Walter Raleigh. 2*d*.
9. Austrian Policy since 1867. By Murray Beaven. 3*d*.
10. Italian Policy since 1870. By Keith Feiling. 2*d*.

III

11. French Policy since 1871. By F. Morgan and H. W. C. Davis. 2*d*.
12. Russia: the Psychology of a Nation. By Paul Vinogradoff. 1*d*.
13. Serbia and the Serbs. By Sir Valentine Chirol. 2*d*.
14. Germany and The Fear of Russia. By Sir Valentine Chirol. 2*d*.
15. The Eastern Question. By F. F. Urquhart. 3*d*.

IV

16. War against War. By A. D. Lindsay. *2d.*
17. The Value of Small States. By H. A. L. Fisher. *2d.*
18. How can War ever be Right. By Gilbert Murray. *2d.*
19. The National Principle and the War. By Ramsay Muir. *3d.*
20. Nietzsche and Treitschke: the Worship of Power in Modern Germany. By E. Barker. *2d.*

V

21. The British Dominions and the War. By H. E. Egerton. *2d.*
22. India and the War. By Sir Ernest Trevelyan. *1d.*
23. Is the British Empire the result of wholesale robbery? By H. E. Egerton. *2d.*
24. The Law of Nations and the War. By A. P. Higgins. *2d.*
25. England's Mission. By W. Bennett. *2d.*

VI

26. August 1914: the Coming of the War. By Spenser Wilkinson. *1s.*

VII

27. The Retreat from Mons. By H. W. C. Davis. *3d.*
28. The Battles of the Marne and Aisne. By H. W. C. Davis. *4d.* The Dispatches, with commentary, maps, etc.
29. The Navy and the War. By J. R. Thursfield. *3d.*
30. Bacilli and Bullets. By Sir William Osler. *1d.*

VIII

31. The Double Alliance versus The Triple Entente. By James M. Beck. *3d.*
32. The Germans in Africa. By Evans Lewin. *3d.*
33. All for Germany: or the World's Respect Well Lost. By E. Barker. *2d.*
34. Germany, the Economic Problem. By C. Grant Robertson. *2d.*
35. German Sea-Power. By C. S. Terry. *3d.* With a Map of the North Sea.

IX

36. What Europe owes to Belgium. By H. W. C. Davis. *2d.*
37. Poland, Prussia, and Culture. By Ludwik Ehrlich. *3d.*
38. Turkey in Europe and Asia. *2d.* (Map).
39. Greek Policy since 1882. By A. J. Toynbee. *4d.* (Map.)
40. North Sleswick under Prussian Rule, 1864-1914. By W. R. Prior. *2d.* (Map.)

X

41. Thoughts on the War. By Gilbert Murray. *2d.*
42. The Leadership of the World. By F. S. Marvin. *2d.*
43. The Leading Ideas of British Policy. By the Hon. Gerard Collier. *2d.*
44. The War and its Economic Aspects. By W. J. Ashley. *2d.*
45. Food Supplies in War Time. By R. H. Rew, C.B. *2d.*

XI

46. The Battle of Ypres-Armentières. By H. W. C. Davis. *6d.* (Despatches and Maps.)
47. Troyon: an Engagement in the Battle of the Aisne. By A. N. Hilditch. *2d.*
48. The Action off Heligoland: August 1914. By L. Cecil Jane. *3d.* (Despatches, with charts.)
49. Non-Combatants and the War. By A. P. Higgins. *2d.*

XII

50. The Church and the War. By Dr. Hicks, Bishop of Lincoln. *2d.*
51. Christmas and the War. By T. B. Strong. *2d.* A Sermon preached in Christ Church Cathedral.
52. The Christian Attitude to War. By A. L. Smith. *2d.*
53. The War and Theology. By W. B. Selbie. *2d.*
54. Concerning True War. By Wilhelm Wundt. Transl. by Grace E. Hadow. *2d.*
55. How We Ought to Feel about the War. By A. V. Dicey. *2d.* An address to working men.

XIII

56. Scandinavia and the War. By E. Bjorkman. *2d.*
57. The War through Danish Eyes. By a Dane. *2d.*
58. The Southern Slavs. By N. Forbes. *4d.*

59. Asia and the War. By A. E. Duchesne. *2d.*
60. The War through Canadian Eyes. By W. Peterson. *2d.*

XIV

61. Through German Eyes. By E. A. Sonnenschein. *2d.*
61*a*. Idols of Peace and War. By E. A. Sonnenschein. *3d.*
62 German Philosophy and the War. By J. H. Muirhead. *2d.*
63. Outlines of Prussian History to 1871. By E. F. Row. *2d.*
64. The Man of Peace. By Roy Norton. *2d.* (By an American.)
65. Fighting a Philosophy. By William Archer. *2d.* (Opinions and temperament of Nietzsche.)

XV

66. Britain's War by Land. By John Buchan. *2d.*
67. Sea Power and the War. By J. R. Thursfield. *2d.*
68. The Stand of Liège. By A. N. Hilditch. *4d.*
69. Contraband and the War. By H. Reason Pyke. *2d.*
70. Does International Law still Exist? By Sir H. Erle Richards.. *2d.*

XVI

71. The Farmer in War Time. By C. Orwin. *2d.*
72. British and German Steel Metallurgy. By J. O. Arnold. *2d.*
73. The War and the Cotton Trade. By S. J. Chapman. *2d.*
74. The War and Employment. By A. L. Bowley. *2d.*
75. Prices and Earnings in Time of War. By A. L. Bowley. *2d.*

XVII

76. Alsace-Lorraine. By F. Y. Eccles. *2d.* (Conditions since 1870.)
77. The Evolution of Thought in Modern France. By Ernest Dimnet. *2d.*
78. Russia and Britain. By P. Dearmer. *2d.*
79. Rumania: her History and Politics. By D. Mitrany. *4d.*
80. Poetry and War. By Sir Herbert Warren. *3d.*

XVIII

81. Selected Treaties. By R. B. Mowat. 1*s.* 6*d.*

XIX

82. National Ideals. By P. E. Matheson. *3d.*
83. Bombastes in the Shades. By Laurence Binyon. *4d.* A Play in one Act.
84. Canada and the War. By A. B. Tucker. *2d.*
85. The Historical Precedent for the New Army. By Ivo D'O. Elliott, I.C.S. *3d.*
86. Coronel and the Falkland Islands. By A. N. Hilditch. *3d.*

Outhwaite, R. L. Ghosts of the Slain. Illustrated by J. E. Southall. National Labour Press 1915. *1s.*

Oxenham, John. Every Woman and War: a suggestion and its application. Headley 1915. *6d.*

Page, Frederick (edr.). An Anthology of Patriotic Prose. Oxford Univ. Press. *2s.*

Paget, Stephen. Essays for Boys and Girls: a First Guide towards the Study of the War. Macmillan 1915. *5s.*

Papers for War Time. Published under the auspices of a Committee drawn from various Christian bodies and political parties, and edited by the Rev. W. Temple. Oxford Univ. Press 1914-15. *2d.* each:—

FIRST SERIES.

1. Christianity and War. By W. Temple.
2. Are we worth fighting for? By Richard Roberts.
3. The Women's part. By Mrs. Luke Paget.
4. Brothers all: the War and the Race Question. By Edwyn Bevan.
5. The decisive hour: is it lost? By J. H. Oldham.
6. Active Service: the Share of the Non-Combatant. By W. R. Maltby.
7. The War Spirit in our National Life. By A. H. Gray.
8. Christian Conduct in War Time. By W. H. Moberly.
9. The Witness of the Church in the Present Crisis. By X.
10. The Real War. By W. E. Orchard.
11. Love Came Down at Christmas. By G. Hare Leonard.
12. An Answer to Bernhardi. By D. S. Cairns.

SECOND SERIES.

13. Patriotism. By Percy Dearmer.
14. Spending in War Time. By E. J. Urwick.
15. Christianity and Force. By A. G. Hogg.
16. Germany and Germans. By Eleanor McDougall
17. Pharisaism and War. By Frank Lenwood.

18. The Cure for War. By A. Clutton Brock
19. Our Need of a Catholic Church. By W. Temple.
20. War, this War, and the Sermon on the Mount. By B. H. Streeter.
21. The Removing of Mountains. By the Author of Pro Christo et Ecclesia.
22. International Control. By W. G. S. Adams.
23. The Price of Blood. By Kenneth Maclennon.
24. Biology and War. By J. Arthur Thomson.

THIRD SERIES.

25. The Visions of Youth. By the Bishop of Winchester.
26. Bernhardism in England. By A. Clutton Brock.
27. The Only Alternative to War. By A. Herbert Gray.
28. Chariots of Fire. By Frank Lenwood.
29. The Ethics of International Trade. By Henri Lambert.
30 India and the War. By John Matthai.
31. British and German Scholarship. By J. H. Moulton.
32. Are We to Punish Germany if We Can? By A. Clutton Brock.
33. Peace with Empire: the Problem. My Edwyn Bevan.
34. The Reasonable Direction of Force. By Louise Matthaei.
35. What is at Stake in the War? By R. W. Seton Watson.
36. The Church the Hope of the Future. By J. H. Oldham.

Petre, M. D. Reflections of a Non-Combatant. By the author of the Life of Father Tyrrell. Longmans. 2*s*. 6*d*.

Phayre, Ignatius. America's Day: Studies in light and shade. Constable 1918. 12*s*. 6*d*.

Phillips, L. March. Europe unbound (Ideals of national and international liberty). Duckworth 1916. 6*s*.

Plowden-Wardlaw, James. The Test of War. War addresses given at Cambridge. R. Scott 1916. 2*s*. 6*d*.

Ponsonby, Rev. Maurice. Visions and vignettes of War. (A series of Short Papers.) Longmans 1917. 2*s*. 6*d*.

Raleigh, Prof. Sir W. England and the War; sundry addresses delivered during the War. Oxford Univ. Press 1918. 4*s*. 6*d*.

Re-Bartlett (Mrs.) Lucy. Our nascent Europe (Conscription, &c.). Nat. Polit. League 1915. 1*s*.

Repplier, Agnes. Counter-currents. (Essays by an American writer, on the war and other things.) Boston: Houghton, Mifflin 1916. $1.25.

Roberts, W. Rhys. Patriotic Poetry: Greek and English. Address given on the 500th anniversary of Agincourt. With supplementary notes and references. Illustrated. Murray 1916. 3*s*. 6*d*.

Robertson, Rt. Hon. J. M., M.P. Neutrals and the War. An open letter to Herr L. Simons. Fisher Unwin 1917. *2d.*

—— War and Civilisation : an Open Letter to a Swedish Prof. Allen & Unwin 1916. *2s. 6d.*

Roosevelt, Theodore. The Foes of our own Household. N.Y. : Doran Co. 1917. $1.50.

Rose, J. Holland. Nationality as a factor in modern history. (Ten lectures, mainly historical.) Rivington 1916. *4s. 6d.*

Russell, Hon. Bertrand. Political ideals. Nat. Council for Civil Liberties 1916. *1d.*

—— Justice in War Time. Nat. Labour Press 1916. *1s.*

—— Why men fight. N.Y. : Century Co. 1917. $1.50.

Sanday, Prof. W. In view of the End : A Retrospect and A Prospect. Milford 1916. *1s.*

Schreiner, Olive. Women and War. Fisher Unwin. 6

Seton-Watson, R. W., and others. The War and Democracy. Macmillan 1915. *2s.*

Slater, Gilbert. Peace and War in Europe. Constable 1915. *7s. 6d.*

Smith, H., and Williams, E. H. Modern Warfare. A popular work by two American physicians. Illustrated. Grant Richards 1915. *6s.*

Smith, Prof. Munroe. Militarism and Statescraft. (The Mistakes of German Policy.) Putnam 1918. *7s. 6d.*

Stoddard, T. Lothrop. Present-day Europe : its national states of mind. New York : Century Co. 1917.

Sulley, Henry. Is it Armageddon? Being a reprint of Britain in Prophecy, with additions and appendix. Simpkin 1915. *6d.*

Swanwick, H. M. The war in its effect upon women. Women's International League 1917. *2d.*

Tagore, Sir Rabindranath. Nationalism (in the West, in Japan, and in India). Macmillan 1917. *4s. 6d.*

Touchstone (pseud.) and C. E. B. Fife and Drum. Simpkin 1915. *1s.*

Trotter, W. Instincts of the Herd in Peace and War. Unwin 1916. *3s. 6d.*

University of Chicago War Papers. (Tracts by various authors, on German World-Politics, Americans and the World-Crisis, The War and Industrial Readjustments, &c.). Chicago Univ. Press and Cambridge Univ. Press 1918. 5 c. each.

Vigilant (pseud.). Revolution and War : or Britain's Peril and Her Secret Foes. Revised edn. Stanley Paul. *1s.*

W. B. Freedom. (Patriotism, discipline, conscientious objection, &c.) Clarendon Press 1916. *6d.*

Waldstein [Walston], Sir Charles. Aristodemocracy: from the Great War back to Moses, Christ and Plato. Murray 1916 10*s.* 6*d.*

—— Patriotism, national and international. An Essay. Longmans 1917. 2*s.* 6*d.*

—— The next war. Wilsonism and Anti-Wilsonism. With an open letter to Col. Roosevelt. Camb. Univ. Press 1918. 1*s.*

Ward, Sir A. W. Founders' Day in War-time. (An address delivered before the University of Manchester, March 1917.) Longmans 1917. 1*s.* 6*d.*

Warde Fowler, W. Essays in brief for war-time. Blackwell 1916. 2*s.* 6*d.*

Warren, Sir Herbert. Poetry and War. (O.P.) Oxford Univ. Press. 3*d.*

Warwick, The Countess of. A woman and the war (on the problems of the hour). Chapman & Hall 1916. 7*s.* 6*d.*

Webb, Clement. In time of War. Addresses upon several occasions. Blackwell 1918. 2*s.* 6*d.*

Wells, H. G. An Englishman looks at the World. Being a series of unrestrained remarks upon contemporary matters. Cassell 1916. 1*s.*

—— The War and Socialism. Clarion Press 1915. 1*d.*

—— War that will End War. Palmer. 1*s.*

Wharton, Edith (edr.). The Book of the Homeless (Le Livre des Sans-Foyer). Contains articles by various distinguished writers: Henry James, T. Hardy, Conrad, etc. Published in aid of orphans of soldiers, Belgian refugees, etc. Macmillan 1916. 21*s.*

Whittingham, Rev. G. N. Who is to Blame? Thoughts on the attitude of Church and State to the present crisis. Four lectures. Grant Richards 1916. 1*s.*

Wilkinson, Prof. H. Spenser. Some neglected aspects of the war. An Oxford lecture. Oxford Univ. Press 1917. 1*s.*

—— The Way to Victory. A lecture delivered before the University of Oxford, Feb. 26, 1916. Constable. 1*s.*

—— War and Policy. Constable 1900. 7*s.* 6*d.*

—— Government and the War. Constable 1918. 6*s.*

Williams, C. The Coming End of the Age: its Imminent Nearness and What it Means for our Race. Jarrold 1916. 1*s.*

Withers, Hartley. War and Self-denial. A lecture. Dent. 2*d.*

Wood, General L. The Military Obligation of Citizenship. Three addresses given at Princeton, U.S.A. Milford. 3*s.* 6*d.*

Woods, Rev. E. S. Knights in armour. (By the Chaplain of the Royal Military College, Sandhurst.) With preface by Gen. Sir W. Robertson. Rob. Scott 1916. 1*s.*

Wordsworth, William. Tract on the Convention of Cintra (1809): with Two Letters written in 1811. With introduction by Prof. Dicey. Oxford Univ. Press 1915. 2*s*. 6*d*.

Zangwill, Israel. The Principle of Nationalities. (Conway Memorial Lecture.) Introduction by Percy Allden, M.P. Watts 1917. 9*d*.

—— The War for the World. Heinemann 1916. 6*s*.

B.—*French.*

Adam, Paul. La Litterature et la Guerre. Crès 1916. 1 fr. 75.

Arbouin, Gabriel. Les Nations d'après leurs journaux. (A study of contemporary journalism, especially in Germany and Italy.) Bouard 1917. 2 fr. 50.

Barthélemy, Prof. Joseph. Démocratie et politque étrangère. (Lectures given at the École des Hautes-Études Sociales.) Alcan 1918. 11 fr.

Barthou, L. l'Heure du droit (collection Bellum). Crès 1916. 1 fr. 75.

Bazin, René. Aujourd'hui et Demain. Pensées du temps de la guerre. Calmann-Lévy 1916. 3 fr. 50.

Bérard, Victor. Les Nations européennes et la Caserne germanique. (Pages d'histoire 1914-16). Berger-Levrault 1916. 60 c.

Blondel, G. La Guerre et le Problème da la population: conférence donnée le 9 mai 1916 en faveur de la plus grande Famille. Lethielleux 1916. 60 c.

Bonnet, Georges. L'Ame du Soldat. Payot 1917. 3 fr. 50.

Bordeaux, Henry. Trois tombes. (17th Edn.) Plon-Nourrit. 3 fr. 50.

Bourgeois, Emile; Renault, Louis, and others. La Guerre. Essays on the origin of the war, Germany and International Law, etc. Alcan 1915. 3 fr. 50.

Bouloc, E. Tu ne tueras pas. (A new conception of War and Peace.) Plon-Nourrit 1918. 3 fr. 50.

Boutroux, Emile. On Military Duty. Nutt 1914. 1*s*.

Cochin, H. Les deux Guerres. (Memories of L'année Terrible and of the present conflict). Plon-Nourrit 1917. 3 fr. 50.

Colin, L. Reliques sacrées: Lettres ouvertes sur des tombes. Bloud et Gay 1916. 3 fr.

Condé, Martin de. Sur l'impossibilité de supprimer la guerre, demain comme aujourd'hui. Librairie Littéraire. 3 fr.

De Morgan, J. Essai sur les Nationalités. (What nationality means). Berger-Levrault 1917. 3 fr.

Dessaint, J. Les enseignements de la guerre. Avant tout, un pouvoir central. Perrin 1916. 2 fr.

Destrée, J. Les Socialistes et la guerre européenne. Van Oest 1915.
Dide, A. Les Emotions et la Guerre. Alcan 1918. 5 fr. 50.
Donat, J., and Signorel, J. Les crimes inexpiables. Préface de A. Méringhac. Delagrave 1918. 3 fr. 50.
Finot, Jean. L'agonie et la naissance d'un monde. Flammarion 1918.
—— Civilisés contre Allemands. Rev. des Deux Mondes. 3 fr. 50.
Flat, Paul. Vers la victoire. Essays on various subjects connected with the war, by the Editor of the Revue Bleue. Two series. Plon-Nourrit 1916. 1 fr. 50 each.
Folliet, le Capitaine. Vouloir! La Volonté à la guerre. Chapelot 1915. 6 fr.
Fribourg, André. La Guerre et le Passé: les leçons de l'histoire. Alcan 1916. 3 fr. 50.
Gennep, A. van. Le Génie de l'organisation. La formule française et anglaise opposée à la formule allemande. Payot 1916. 1 fr. 50.
Gourmont, Rémy De. Pendant l'orage. Reflections on German psychology, young writers dead, "Tipperary," English biographies, etc. Paris: Champion. 5 fr.
Hamon, Prof. Augustin. Lessons on the World-war. Transl. by Bernard Miall. Fisher Unwin 1918. 16*s*.
Hanotaux, Gabriel. Pendant la Grande Guerre. Plon-Nourrit 1916.
Hauser, Prof. Henri. Le Principle des Nationalitiés: ses origines historiques. Alcan 1916. 60 c.
—— La Guerre et les Neutres. Étude sur le sentiment démocratique dans ses rapports avec le guerre européenne. (A lecture delivered on Jan. 16, 1917). Giard et Brière 1917.
Hennessy, Jean. Réalités de Guerre. Crès 1918. 2 fr.
Henry-Rosier, Marguerite (Mme.). Le Chagrin sous les vieux toits. (La vie et les souffrances des humbles). de Boccard 1918. 3 fr. 50.
Hersch, Dr. L. La mortalité chez les neutres en temps de guerre. Paris: Giard et Brière 1915. 1 fr.
Huot, Louis, and Voivenel, Paul, Drs. Le Courage. Alcan 1917. 3 fr. 50.
—— Le Cafard. (Un affaisement de l'énergie psychique). Grasset 1918. 3 fr. 50.
Imbart de la Tour, P. L'opinion catholique et la guerre. (Shows it to be generally favourable to Germany.) Bloud et Gay. 50 c.
Jullian, Camille. La Valeur éducative de la guerre. Alcan 1916. 2 fr. 50.

Lacroix, L. Le Clergé et la guerre de 1914 (a series of pamphlets: 10 pubd. by Dec. 1916). Bloud et Gay 1915-16.

Larronde, Carlos. Anthologie des écrivans morts pour la patrie. 4 vols. Larousse 1916. 1 fr. 50. each.

Lavedan, H. Dialogues de guerre. Fayard 1916.

Le Bon, Gustave. Les enseignements psychologiques de la guerre européenne. Flammarion 1915.

—— Transl. under title, The Psychology of the Great War. Fisher Unwin 1916. 10*s.* 6*d.*

—— Premières consequences de la guerre: Transformations mentales des peuples. Flammarion 1917. 3 fr. 50.

L'Hommage français. (A series of pamphlets by distinguished Frenchmen explaining the part played by the different allied nations in the War.) Bloud et Gay 1916.

Loisy, Alfred. The War and Religion. Transl. from the French by Arthur Galton. Blackwell 1916. 1*s.* 6*d.*

Lote, René. Le sens des réalités, sagesse des États: leçons politiques de la guerre. Berger-Levrault 1917. 3 fr. 50.

Loti, Pierre. Quelques aspects du vertige mondial. Flammarion 1917. 3 fr. 50.

—— L'horreur allemande. Calmann Lévy 1918. 4 fr. 75.

—— War. Transl. from the French. Werner Laurie 1917. 2*s.* 6*d.*

Maccas, Léon. La Grande Guerre, les nations et les hommes, réflexions d'un contemporain. Berger-Levrault 1918. 3 fr. 50.

Malleterre, Général. Études et impressions de guerre. Tallandier 1918. 3 fr. 50.

Margueritte, Paul. Contre les Barbares (1914-15). Flammarion 1915. 3 fr. 50.

Mayer, Lt.-Col. Autour de la guerre actuelle; essai de psychologie militaire (hors commerce). 1917.

Rédier, Lieut. Méditations dans la tranchée. Reflections, soldiers' talk, etc. Payot 1916. 3 fr. 50.

Retté, Adolphe. Ceux qui saignent. Notes de guerre. Bloud et Gay 1918. 3 fr. 50.

Reynes-Monlaur, M. Pages de deuil et d'héroisme. Les paroles secrètes. Plon, Nourrit 1915. 3 fr. 50.

Richepin, Jean. La Clique. (Essays, including Le Miracle Anglais and Verdun.) Flammarion 1917. 3 fr. 50.

Rolland, Romain. Au dessus de la mêlée. A collection of articles published during the war. Paris: Ollendorff 1915. 2 fr.

—— —— English transl. by C. K. Ogden, under title Above the Battle. Allen & Unwin 1916. 2*s.* 6*d.*

Sageret, J. La Guerre et le Progrès (aucun parallélieme ou antagonisme entre la guerre et le progrès). Payot 1917. 3 fr. 50.

Salmon, A. Le Chass' bi: Notes de Campagne (les types crées par la guerre). Perrin 1917. 3 fr. 50.

Spire, André. Les Juifs et la Guerre. Payot 1917. 3 fr. 50.

Valois, Charles. Le Cheval de Troie. Réflexions sur la philosophie et la conduite de la guerre. Nouv. Libr. Nationale 1918. 4 fr.

Wetterlé, l'Abbé. Propos de guerre. Têtes de boches. L'edition franç. illustrée. 1916. 3 fr. 50.

C.—*German.*

Berg, Leo. Der Uebermensch in der modernen Literatur. An attempt to trace the origin and development of the Superman idea in literature. Munich: Langen 1915.

—— —— Transl under title The Superman in Modern Literature. Jarrold 1916. 5*s*.

Fournier, Prof. A. Heute und vor hundert Jahren. Vienna 1914.

Frank, Leonhard. Der Mensch ist gut (anti-militarist; by a Bavarian author). Zürich: Rascher 1918. 4 mk. 50.

Freytag-Loringhoven, Gen. Frhr. von. Feldherrngrösse. Vom Denken und Handeln hervorragender Heerführer (sketches). Berlin: Mittler 1920. 32 mk.

Latzko, Andreas. Menschen in Krieg. (Sketches and stories descriptive of the horrors of war.) Rascher 1918. 4 mk. 50.

—— Transl. under title, Men in Battle. Cassell 1918. 6*s*.

Lensch, Paul. Three years of World-Revolution. Transl. from the German. Constable 1918. 5*s*.

Meyer, A. O. Deutsche Freiheit und Englischer Parliamentarismus. Munich 1915. 50 pf.

Nicolai, Prof. G. F. Die Biologie des Krieges. Betrachtungen eines deutschen Naturforschers. Zürich: Füssli 1917. 10 fr.

Nippold, Prof. O. Das Erwachen des Deutschen Volkes und die Rolle der Schweiz. Zürich: Orell Füssli 1917.

Novicow, J. Der Krieg und seine angebliche Wohlthaten: Uebersetzung von. Dr. A. H. Fried. Zürich: Füssli 1915. 1 fr. 50.

Reinke, J. Politische Lehren des grossen Krieges. 2nd edn. 1918. 3 mk. 80.

Renner, Karl. Marxismus, Krieg und Internationale. Kritische Studien über offene Probleme . . . in und nach dem Weltkrieg. Stuttgart: Dietz Nachf. 1917. 6 mk.

Rühlmann, P. Europa am Abgrunde. Die wichtigsten Bestimmungen des Versailles Friendensentwurfes in ihren Wirkungen. 1919. 2 mk. 50.

Wilke, F. Ist der Krieg sittlich berechtigt? Leipzig 1915. 2 mk.

Wundt, Wilhelm. Concerning True War. Transl. by Grace E. Hadow. (O.P.) Clarendon Press 1915. *2d.*

D.—*Other Nations.*

Brandes, Georg. The World at war. New York: Macmillan 1917. $1.50.

Briantchaninoff, A. N. Quo vadis, Europa? Copenhagen: Ursin's Efterf. 1918.

Carton de Wiart, H. The Way of Honour. (Articles published since the outbreak of the war, by the Belgian Minister of Justice.) Allen & Unwin 1918. 5*s.*

Ferrero, Guglielmo. Le Gènie latin et le monde moderne. (The ideals of France and Italy.) Grasset 1917. 3 fr. 50.

—— La Vecchia Europa e la nuova, saggi e discorsi. (Essays and addresses, 1907-1918.) Milano: Treves 1918. 4 fr.

Jespersen, Otto. Reflections d'un Danois sur la guerre. Bologna: Zanichelli 1918.

Kjellén, R. Studien zur Weltkrise. Uebersetzt von Fr. Stieve. 3rd edn. 1918. 3 mk. 60.

Maeterlinck, Maurice. The Wrack of the Storm. (Les Débris de la Guerre.) Transl. by A. Teixeira de Mattos. Methuen 1916. 5*s.*

Maeztu, Ramiro de. Authority, Liberty and Function in the light of the war. Allen & Unwin 1916. 4*s.* 6*d.*

Masaryk, Prof. T. G. The Problem of Small Nations in the European Crisis. Council for Study of Internat. Relations 1916. 3*d.*

Nyrop, Kr. Er Krig Kultur? (Un recueil d'articles.) Copenhagen: Gyldendalske 1916.

—— Transl. under title, Is war civilisation? Heinemann 1917. 2*s.* 6*d.*

Pérez-Triana S. Some Aspects of the War. By a Spanish-American once on the Court of Arbitration at The Hague. Anti-German. Fisher Unwin. 3*s.* 6*d.*

Stapfer, Paul. Les Leçons de la Guerre. Mostly articles published in the Bibliothèque Universelle of Lausanne, for one of which the Review was seized. Fischbacher 1915. 3 fr.

Zurlinden, von S. Der Weltkrieg. Vorläufige Orientirung von einem schweizischen Standpunkt aus. Zürich: Orell Füssli.

XXII. POETRY AND DRAMA.

A.—*Anthologies and Reprints.*

At the Front: a Pocket Book of Verse. Anthology. Warne. 1*s.*

Bell, Henry James. Camp Fire Recitations. W. Scott 1915. 1*s.*

Book, A, of verse of the Great War. Yale Univ. Press 1917. $2.00.

Camp Song Book for use by the Y.M.C.A. with H.M. Forces. Nat. Council Y.M.C.A. 1915. 1*s.* 6*d.*

Carter, H. Petit recueil de chants français. The accompaniments edited by G. Dyson. Milford 1914. 4*s.* 6*d.*; words only, 2*s.*

Colmer, Francis. Shakespeare in Time of War. Excerpts from the plays arranged with topical allusion. Smith, Elder, 1916. 3*s.* 6*d.*

Country's Call, The. A short selection of Patriotic Verse. Chosen by E. B. and Marie Sargant. Macmillan. 2*d.*

Crown of Amaranth. Being a collection of poems to the memory of the brave and gallant gentlemen who gave their lives for Great and Greater Britain. Macdonald 1915. 1*s.*

—— —— New edn., revised, with additions. Macdonald 1917. 2*s.* 6*d.*

Ditchfield, Rev. P. H. A little book of comfort for soldiers. (A religious anthology in prose and verse.) Robert Scott 1917. 2*s.*

Downes, John N. (edr.). The Soldier's and Sailor's Hymn Book. Dent 1914. 6*d.*

Elliott, H. B. (edr.). Lest we Forget. A war anthology. Preface by Baroness Orczy. Jarrold. 2*s.* 6*d.*

Evans, Charles Seddon (edr.). Our Glorious Heritage: a Book of Patriotic Verse for Boys and Girls. Heinemann 1914. 1*s.*

Garvin, J. W. (edr.). Canadian Poems of the Great War (selected from the works of 73 poets). Toronto: McClelland 1918. $1.50.

Goodchild, George. England, my England. A war anthology. 2*s.*

Halliday, W. J. Pro Patria. A book of patriotic verse. Compiled by W. J. H. Dent. 2*s.* 6*d.*

In hoc signo. Hymns of War and Peace, with tunes. A supplementary tune book for use with existing collections. S.P.C.K. 1915. 6*d.* and 1*s.*

Hymns in Time of National Crisis. Lindsey Press 1915. 1*d.*

Kitchener Army Song Book. Newnes 1915. 6*d.*

Kitchener March Album, The. J. Williams 1914. 1*s.*

Knight, Prof. W. (edr.). Pro Patria et Rege. Poems on war, its characteristics and results. Two series. Bennett. 2*s.* 6*d.* each.

L., M. A. A. (edr.). Patriotic War Songs and Poems for Fleet, Camp, and Country. Spottiswoode 1914. 4*d.*

Leonard, R. M. (edr.). Patriotic Poems. (Oxford Garlands.) Milford 1914. 7*d.*

Lloyd, Bertram (edr.). Poems written during the Great War, 1914-1918. Allen & Unwin 1918. 2*s.* 6*d.*

Locker-Lampson, Godfrey. A Soldier's book of Love-poems. An anthology, arranged by G. L.-L. Humphreys 1917. 2*s.* 6*d.*

Macklin, Alys Eyne (edr.). The Lyceum book of War Verse. Erskine Macdonald 1918. 1*s.* 6*d.*

Macnaught, W. G. (edr.). Pocket Sing-Song Book. Novello 1915. 1*s.*

Manning-Foster, A. E. (edr.). Lord God of Battles. A war anthology. Cope & Fenwick 1914. 1*s.*

Marching Songs : together with Tommy's tunes. S. Paul 1914. 6*d.*

Maxwell, Gordon S. War Songs of Britain. Brodie & Co. 1915. 6*d.*

Müller, E. (edr.). 1914. Das Kriegsliederbuch. Leipzig : Xenien-Verlag 1914. 2 mk.

National Anthems of the Allies, The. G. Schirmer 1914. 9*d.*

National Songs of the Allies, and others. Harmonized and arranged by Arthur Grenville. F. Williams 1914. 1*s.*

Nesbit, E. (edr.). Battle Songs. Goschen 1914. 1*s.*

Nettleinghame, Lieut. F. T., R.F.C. Tommy's Tunes (collection of soldiers' songs, &c.). Erskine Macdonald 1917. 2*s.* 6*d.*

—— More Tommy's Tunes. Erskine Macdonald 1918. 1*s.* 6*d.*

Osborn, E. B. (edr.). The Muse in Arms (a representative anthology). With introduction. Murray 1917. 6*s.*

Patriotic Airs of All Nations. Williams 1914. 1*s.*

Patriotic Songs and Poems. A selection. Macdonald 1914. 1*d.*

Poems of the Great War. Chatto 1914. 1*s.*

Poètes de la Guerre. A collection of French war poetry. Berger-Levrault. 75 c.

Rhymes of the R.N.D. Methuen 1917. 1*s.* 3*d.*

Royal Navy War-Song Album. Newnes 1914. 6*d.*

Salt, L. Godwin (edr.). English Patriotic Poety. (Pitt Press series.) Camb. Univ. Press 1914. 6*d.*

Soldier Poets. Songs of the Fighting Men. (Verses by 24 soldiers.) Macdonald 1916. 2*s.* 6*d.*

Soldier Poets (Second Series). More songs by the fighting men. Erskine Macdonald 1917. 2*s.* 6*d.*

Songs for the Army and Navy. (Music by Gowrie Ruthven.) Nisbet 1916. 1*s.* 6*d.*

Songs and Sonnets for England in War Time. Being a collection of lyrics by various authors inspired by the Great War. Lane 1914. 1*s*.

Tait, S. B. (edr.). Chambers's Patriotic Poems for the Young. Chambers 1915. 1*s*.

Taylor, Mary A. Famous National Songs and Their Story. Stockwell 1916. 1*s*.

Tennyson, Lord. Patriotic Poems. Macmillan. 1*d*.

Thompson, Theodora. The Coming Dawn. A war anthology in prose and verse. With introduction by Sir Oliver Lodge. Lane 1918. 5*s*.

Townsend, M. E., and Fosbery, Rev. T. V. Voices of Comfort (selections in prose and verse for the sick and suffering). Longmans 1918. 2*s*. 6*d*. and 3*s*. 6*d*.

Wehe dir, England! Collection of German war songs and poems. Leipzig: Xenien-Verlag. 1 mk.

Wheeler, Reginald, and Lewis, Charlton. A Book of Verse of the Great War. (Containing works by Gibson, Hewlett, C. Chesterton, Galsworthy, Amy Lowell, Masters, Noyes, and Tagore.) New Haven: Yate Press 1918. $2.

Wordsworth, William. The Patriotic Poetry of William Wordsworth. A selection, with notes, by A. H. D. Acland. Oxford Univ. Press. 1*s*.

B.—*Poems*.

(a) English.

Adamson, Margot R. A Year of War and other Poems. Simpkin Marshall 1917. 2*s*. 6*d*.

Adcock, A. St. John. Songs of the World-War. Palmer 1916. 1*s*. 6*d*.

Anderson, M. B. ("A Citizen of the United States.") The Great Refusal: a War Poem. French Wounded Emergency Fund 1916. 2*s*.

Asquith, Herbert. The Volunteer and other Poems. Sidgwick & Jackson 1916. 1*s*.

Ainger, A. C. Marching Songs for Soldiers, adapted to well-known tunes. Jarrold 1915. 1*s*.; pocket edn., 2*s*.

Baring, Maurice. In Memoriam Auberon Herbert, Captain Lord Lucas, R.F.C., killed Nov. 1916. (A Poem.) Blackwell 1917. 1*s*.

Beckett, Arthur. Sussex at War, and Poems of Peace. Sussex County Herald 1917. 6*d*.

Begbie, Harold. Fighting Lines. Patriotic Poems. Harrap. 3*s*.

Bendall, Colonel F. W. D. Front-line Lyrics. Elkin Mathews 1918. *2s.*

Bewsher, Capt. Paul. The Dawn Patrol (poems of aviation). Erskine Macdonald 1917. *1s.*

—— The Bombing of Bruges (Poems). Hodder & Stoughton 1918. *5s.*

Binyon, Laurence. The Anvil. Poems. Elkin Mathews 1916. *1s.*

—— Bombastes in the Shades: a Play in one Act. Characters—Bombastes, a German hero; Socrates, Heine, Bayard, Queen Elizabeth. (O.P.) Oxford Univ. Press. *4d.*

—— The Winnowing-Fan: Poems on the Great War. Elkin Mathews. *1s.*

—— For the Fallen, and other Poems. Hodder & Stoughton 1917. *5s.*

—— The Cause: Poems of the War. Elkin Mathews 1918. *2s.*

—— The New World: Poems. Elkin Mathews 1918. *2s.*

—— The Four Years. War Poems collected and newly augmented. With portrait by Strang. Elkin Mathews 1919. *7s. 6d.*

Blackall, C. W. Songs from the Trenches. Lane 1915. *1s.*

Blair, Wilfred. For Belgium: Poems on behalf of the Daily Telegraph Christmas Shilling Fund. Blackwell 1914. *1s.*

Blakeney, E. H. War Poems. (Privately printed, King's School, Ely.) Author 1915.

Blunden, E. C. Pastorals. A book of verses (by a young officer). Erskine Macdonald 1916. *1s.*

Booth, W. Gentlemen All! and other Poems of the War. Manchester: Fagan 1915. *6d.*

Bostock, Adelaide H. E. A. Guard our Soldiers and our Sailors. Intercessory hymn, with music. Simpkin 1914. *1d.*

Bourdillon, F. W. Christmas Roses for 1914. Poems arising out of the war. Humphreys. *1s.*

British War Poems. By an American. Harrison 1915. *6d.*

Brittain, Vera M. Verses of a V.A.D. Erskine Macdonald 1918. *2s. 6d.*

Brooke, Rupert. 1914, and other Poems. Sidgwick & Jackson 1915. *3s. 6d.*

—— Selected Poems. Sidgwick & Jackson 1917. *3s. 6d.*

Brown, F. S. Contingent Ditties, and other Soldier Songs of the Great War. Lowe 1915. *1s.*

Brown, J. L. Crommelin. Dies Heroica: War Poems 1914-18. Hodder & Stoughton 1918. *5s.*

Bruce, Sir M. W. S. Songs from the Saddle (fighting and colonial adventures). Hodges & Figgis 1917. 2*s*.

C.C. (pseud.). Triumph, and other Poems. Chapman & Hall 1916. 1*s*.

Callaghan, Stella. Battle Song of the Fleet at Sea. Set to music by Martin Shaw. Milford 1915. 6*d*.

Cameron, W. J. War and Life. Poems. Chapman & Hall 1916. 1*s*. 6*d*.

Campbell-Strickland, Amy. A Call to Arms and other Poems. Stockwell 1915. 6*d*.

Cannan, May W. In War Time. (Poems.) Blackwell 1917. 2*s*. 6*d*.

Carroll, John S. and Kathleen M. Heroes All. War and other Verses. R. Gibson 1915. 6*d*.

—— Or sing a Sang at least. War and other verses. R. Gibson 1915. 6*d*.

Cobber, Lance-Corporal. The Anzac Pilgrim's Progress. Ballads of Australia's Army. Edited by A. St. John Adcock. Simpkin, Marshall 1918. 3*s*. 6*d*.

Colcord, Lincoln. Vision of War. Macmillan 1915. 5*s*. 6*d*.

Commandant (pseud.). The Song of the V.A.D.: with Legends of Sussex and Surrey, old and new. St. Catherine Press 1914. 1*s*. 6*d*.

Cone, Helen Gray. Chant of Love for England and other poems. By an American. Dent 1915. 2*s*. 6*d*.

Cooper, E. T. Soliloquies of a Subaltern somewhere in France. Poems. Burns & Oates 1915. 1*s*.

Cooper, Major Eric. Tommies of the Line, and other Poems. Jenkin 1918. 3*s*. 6*d*.

Corbett, Lieut. N. M., R.N. A Naval Motley (Verses written at sea during and before the war). Methuen 1916. 1*s*.

Coulson, Sergt. Leslie. From an outpost, and other Poems. Erskine Macdonald 1917. 1*s*.

Crawshay-Williams, Major E. Songs on Service (By the late M.P. for Leicester). Blackwell 1917. 2*s*. 6*d*.

—— The Gutter and the Stars. Poems. Erskine Macdonald 1915. 5*s*.

Cross, H. H. V. A Young Soldier's De Profundis. (Poems.) Erskine Macdonald 1916. 6*d*.

Cramp, Major Geoffrey. Mattins. Poems. Erskine Macdonald 1918. 2*s*. 6*d*.

Curchod, Mme. Henri. Union Jack and other Battle Songs, and Poems on incidents connected with the War of Nations. Gardner 1915. 1*s*.

Curzon, Lord, of Kedleston. War Poems and other Translations. Includes seven translations from M. Cammaerts. Lane. 4*s.* 6*d.*

Dearmer, Geoffrey. Poems. Heinemann 1918. 2*s.* 6*d.*

Defaulter, The (pseud). Outpost and other verses. Illustrated. McBride, Nash 1916. 1*s.*

Dennys, Richard. There is no death. Poems. With introduction by Captain D. Coke, and portrait. Lane 1917. 2*s.* 6*d.*

Doak, H. L. Verdun and other Poems. Maunsel 1917. 1*s.*

Dodderidge, G. V. War Poems. Hereford: The Author. 1915.

Doyle, Lily. Bound in Khaki. Introduction by the Rt. Hon Sir Ignatius O'Brien. (Poems.) Elliott Stock 1916. 2*s.*

Drinkwater, John. Swords and Ploughshares. Poetry. Sidgwick & Jackson. 2*s.* 6*d.*

Du Cann, C. G L. Triolets from the Trenches. Erskine Macdonald 1917. 1*s.*

Edgar, Aimée E. Our Heroes. E. Macdonald 1916. 1*s.*

"Etienne" (Lieut. R.N.). Verses from the Grand Fleet Erskine Macdonald 1917. 1*s.*

Evans, W. Killed in Action. (Poems of Consolation.) Foreword by the Lord Bishop of Stepney. Macdonald 1916. 1*s.*

Fanshawe, R. By Yser Banks: an Elegy on a Young Officer. Blackwell. 1*s.*

Fawside, John (edr.). The Flag of England: Ballads of the Brave and Poems of Patriotism. Nash 1914. 3*s.* 6*d.*

Ferguson, John. On Vimy Ridge, and other Poems. Gowans & Gray 1917. 2*s.* 6*d.*

Ferrar, W. J. The Little Brothers, and other Poems. Erskine Macdonald 1918. 1*s.* 6*d.*

Ford, Gertrude S. Poems of War and Peace. E. Macdonald 1914. 1*s.*

—— A Fight to a Finish, and other Songs of Peace. Daniel 1917. 3*d.*

Forster, R. H. War Poems of a Northumbrian. 2nd series. Newcastle: Noble 1915. 1*s.*

Foulke, William Dudley. Lyrics of War and Peace. Milford 1916. 2*s.* 6*d.*

Fox Smith (Miss), C. Naval Crown-Ballads and Songs of the War. Mathews 1915. 1*s.*

—— Fighting Men (Verse, mostly Naval). Elkin Mathews 1916. 1*s.*

Frankau, Gilbert. The City of Fear, and other Poems. Chatto & Windus 1917. 3*s.* 6*d.*

Freston, H. Rex. The Quest of Truth, and other Poems. Blackwell 1916. 2*s*. 6*d*.

—— Collected Poems. Blackwell 1916. 5*s*.

Frith, J. Cartwright. The Verge of Victory, and other verses written during the War. Allen & Unwin 1916. 1*s*. 6*d*.

Gellert, Leon. Songs of a Campaign (by an Australian in the Dardanelles). Illustrated by Norman Lindsay. Sidney: Angus & Robertson 1918.

Gibson, William W. Battle. Poems 1915. 1*s*.

Gilbert, Bernard. Gone to the War, and other Poems in the Lincolnshire dialect. Loncoln: Ruddock 1915. 1*s*.

—— War Workers and other Verses. E. Macdonald 1916. 1*s*. 6*d*.

Girling, T. A. The Salient, and other Poems. Palmer & Hayward 1918. 2*s*. 6*d*.

Gorell-Barnes, Hon. R. Days of Destiny: War Poems at home and abroad. Longmans 1917. 3*s*. 6*d*.

Graves, Arnold T. Long Retreat and other doggerel. March 1915. 1*s*.

Graves, C. L. War's Surprises, and other verses. Sidgwick & Jackson 1917. 3*s*. 6*d*.

Graves, Robert. Fairies and Fusiliers. War Poems. Heinemann 1918. 3*s*. 6*d*.

Green, A. R. Peace and War. A verse pamphlet. Poetry Bookshop. 3*d*.

Gregory, Hugh. August, 1914. A poem. Fifield 1916. 1*s*.

Gretton, M. Sturge. Kalendar of the War. Gloucester: Bellows 1915. 1*s*.

Grindlay, I. Ripples from the Ranks of the Q.M.A.A.C. (First Verse Book of Women's Legion.) Erskine Macdonald 1918. 1*s*. 6*d*.

Gurner, Ronald. War's Echo (Poems). Fisher Unwin 1917. 1*s*.

Gwynn, Stephen. Clare's Brigade: Marching Song for the Irish Division. Music by Martin Shaw. Milford 1915. 1*s*.

—— and Kettle, T. M. (edrs.). Battle Songs for the Irish Brigades. Maunsel. 6*d*.

Hall, Arthur Vine. The Submarine and the Aeroplane. Poems. Blackwell 1917. 2*s*.

Hallett, C. Turner. Follow the Flag. Poems and Prose written and selected. Relfe 1915. 1*s*.

Hammond, Irene. War Verses and others. St. Catherine Press 1915. 1*s*.

Harvey, F. W. A Gloucestershire Lad at Home and Abroad. (Poems, mostly written at the Front.) Sidgwick & Jackson 1916. 1*s*. 6*d*.

—— Gloucestershire Friends. Poems from a prison camp. With introduction by Rev. Canon Frodsham. Sidgwick & Jackson 1917. 2*s*. 6*d*.

Haselden, Percy. In the Wake of the Sword. (Georgian Verse Series.) Macdonald 1917. 1*s*.

Henslow, T. G. W. War Poems. Bridge 1918. 1*s*. 6*d*.

Herbert, Lieut. A. P. The Bombed Gipsy, and other poems. Mostly from Punch. (The Officer's life and its incidents.) Metheun 1918. 3*s*. 6*d*.

Herschel-Clarke, May. Behind the Firing Line, and other poems. Erskine Macdonald 1917. 6*d*.

Hewlett, Maurice. Sing-Songs of the War. Poetry Bookshop, 35, Devonshire Street, W.C., 1914. 6*d*.

Heywood, Lieut. Raymond. Roses, Pearls and Tears. Poems. Macdonald 1918.

Hodgson, W. N. (Edward Melbourne). Verse and Prose in Peace and War. Smith, Elder 1916. 2*s*. 6*d*.

Holmes, W. Kersley. Ballads of Field and Billet. Gardner, 1915. 1*s*. 6*d*.

—— More Ballads of Field and Billet and other verses. Gardner 1915. 1*s*. 6*d*.

Hopwood, Capt. R. A., R.N. The Secret of the Ships (Poems). Murray 1918. 3*s*. 6*d*.

Hudson, William. Wilhelm and his god, and other War Sonnets. Drane 1916. 1*s*.

Hueffer, Ford Madox. On Heaven, and other Poems written on active service. Lane 1918. 3*s*. 6*d*.

In Time of War. A hymn; words only. Simpkin 1914. 1*s*. 6*d*. per 100.

James, G. de S. Wentworth. A Rubaiyat of the Trenches (Poem). Fawcett 1917. 3*s*. 6*d*.

Jerram, C. S. War. Patriotic Poems. Elkin Mathews. 2*s*. 6*d*.

Johnston-Smith, Fred J. Union Jack Lyrics, and a foreword concerning the Flag. Macdonald 1914. 6*d*.

Kaufman, Herbert. The Song of the Guns. Unwin 1914 1*s*.

Kenny, Muriel. Khaki Soldiers and other Poems for Children. Heffer 1916. 6*d*.

Klaxon (pseud). Songs of the Submarine. (Published for the funds of the Union Jack.) McBride, Nash 1917. 2*s*. 6*d*.

Kipling, Rudyard. Song of the English. Illustrated by W. Heath Robinson. Hodder & Stoughton 1915. 5*s*.

Kipling, Rudyard. Hymn Before Action. Methuen 1914. 1*d.*
—— If—. Macmillan 1916. 2*d.*
—— For all we Have and Are. Methuen 1916. 1*d.*

L., D. O. Songs of a Subaltern. Chapman & Hall 1915. 1*s.*

Lawson, Henry. My Army! O, my Army. (Australian War songs.) Sydney: Tyrrell 1915. 1*s.*

—— Song of the Dardanelles, and other verses. Harrap 1916. 2*s.* 6*d.*

Latymer, Lord. Ballad of the War. Reprinted from the English Review. Humphreys 1915. 1*s.*

Lea, Donald H. Stand Down. War Poems. Elkin Mathews 1917. 2*s.* 6*d.*

Leask, G. A. (edr.). Hymns in War Time. Jarrold 1915. 1*s.*

Lee, Corporal Joseph. Ballads of Battle. Illustrated by the Author. Murray 1916. 2*s.* 6*d.*

—— [now Lieut.] Work-a-day Warriors. War Poems. Illustrated. Murray 1917. 2*s.* 6*d.*

Le Gallienne, Richard. Silk-hat Soldier and other poems. Lane 1915. 1*s.*

Leslie, Shane. Verses in Peace and War. Burns & Oates 1916. 2*s.* 6*d.*

Letts. W. M. (Miss). Hallow-e'en, and Poems of the War. Smith, Elder 1916. 2*s.* 6*d.*

Looker, Samuel I. Slaves of the Sword and other verses. Daniel 1917. 3*d.*

Lyons, J. Sons of the Empire and other poems. Heywood 1916. 1*s.*

Lyon, Lieut. P. H. B. Songs of Youth and War. Erskine Macdonald 1918. 2*s.* 6*d.*

Lyon, W. S. S. Easter at Ypres, 1915; and other poems. (By a young Scotsman, killed near Ypres in May, 1915.) MacLehose 1916. 2*s.* 6*d.*

M. A. C. (pseud.). The Call. (Recollections of Y.M.C.A. tents.) Marshall Bros. 1916. 7*d.*

Macfie, Ronald Campbell. War: a Poem. Murray 1918. 3*s.* 6*d.*

Macgill, Patrick. Soldier Songs. Jenkins 1916. 3*s.* 6*d.*

Mackereth, James A. The Red, Red Dawn. (Poems.) Erskine Macdonald 1917. 3*s.* 6*d.*

Mackintosh, Lieut. E. A. M.C. A Highland Regiment (the Seaforths). Poems. Lane 1917. 3*s.* 6*d.*

—— War the Liberator, and other pieces. (Poems.) Lane 1918. 5*s.*

Mallet, John. Writing on the Wall: an indictment. A poem. Mallay 1915. 1*s.*

Mason, Captain John. The Valley of Dreams. Macdonald 1918. 2*s.* 6*d.*

Maynard, C. L. Watching the War. Allenson 1915. 6*d.* each part.

Meyer, Sebastian B., and Young, Geoffrey. Bolts from the Blues. (Sketches by S.B.M. and rhymes by G.Y., from the Italian front.) British Red Cross Society 1917. 3*s.* 6*d.*

Mitchell, A. Gordon. War Songs. Stirling: Scott 1916. 1*s*, 6*d.*

Moffatt, Warneford. An ode on the Canadian Soldiers who fell near Ypres, with other poems. Simpkin 1916. 1*s.*

Murray, Charles. A Sough of War. (Poems.) Constable 1917. 1*s.*

Nadja (pseud.). Love and War. 4th edn. Humphreys 1915. 1*s.*

Nesbitt, H. A. Neuve Chapelle and other poems. Kegan Paul 1916. 1*s.* 6*d.*

Newbolt, Sir Henry. St. George's Day, and other poems. Murray 1918. 3*s.* 6*d.*

Nichols, Robert. Invocation. War poems and others. Mathews 1915. 1*s.*

—— Ardours and Endurances. (Poems.) Chatto & Windus 1917. 3*s.* 6*d.*

Noyes, Alfred. A Salute from the Fleet, and other poems. Methuen. 5*s.*

Ord, Hubert. Poems of Peace and War. St. Catherine Press 1915. 1*s.*

Oxenham, John (pseud.) All's Well! Some helpful verses for these dark days of war. Methuen 1915. 1*s.* & 2*s.* 6*d.*

—— The Vision Splendid. (Verse.) Methuen 1917. 3*s.*

Oyler, Leslie Mary. Children's Entente Cordiale. Pictures by George Borrow. Jack 1915. 1*s.*

Pakenham-Walsh, W. S. Chants in War. Elliot Stock 1917. 1*s.* 6*d.*

Pope, Jessie. War Poems. Mostly reprinted from Punch and the Daily Mail. Grant Richards 1915. 1*s.*

—— War Poems, 2nd series. Grant Richards 1915. 1*s.*

Powell, Constance. War Poems. Maunsel 1915. 6*d.*

Prevost, C. M. Roll of Honour and other Verses. Warren 1915. 9*d.*

Pughe, A. O. Cypress and Amaranth. War poems. Heath, Cranton 1916. 1*s.*

Rawnsley, Rev. Canon. The European War, 1914-15. Poems. Bennett. 2*s.*

Rentoul, J. L. At the Sign of the Sword. By Four in a Family. Poems by the Chaplain-General of the Australian Forces, and others. Melbourne: Melville 1916.

Roberts, Cecil. War Poems. Clarke 1916. *2s. 6d.*

Roberts, Morley. War Lyrics. (Scenes and episodes of the War.) Selwyn & Blount 1918. *2s. 6d.*

Robertson, Alexander. Comrades. (Memories of Oxford, of military training, of scenes of the campaign.) Elkin Mathews 1916. *1s.*

Robertson, J. Logie. Petition to the Deil, and other War Verses. Gardner 1917. *1s. 6d.*

Ross-Lewin, the Brothers. In Britain's Need (verses). Hodges & Figgis 1917.

Rowlands, Victor. Particles of War (poems). Stockwell 1918. *2s.*

Sackville, Lady Margaret. The Pageant of War. Simpkin 1916. *1s.*

Samways, G. R., R.F.C. War Lyrics. Stockwell 1916. *1s.*

—— Ballads of the Flying Corps. McBride, Nast 1917. *2s. 6d.*

Sarson, H. S. From a Field Hospital. Poems by a Canadian. Erskine Macdonald 1916. *1s.*

Sassoon, Siegfried. Counter-attack and other poems. Heinemann 1918. *2s. 6d.*

—— The War Poems of: (collected). Heinemann 1919. *3s. 6d.*

Scott, Rev. F. G. In the Battle Silences. Poems written at the Front. By the Senior Chaplain to the Canadian Expeditionary Force. Constable 1916. *1s.*

Seaman, Sir Owen. War-Time Verses from Punch. Constable. *1s.*

—— War-Time Verses. 2nd impression, with some additions. Constable 1915. *1s.*

—— Made in England. Verses reprinted from Punch. Constable 1916. *1s.*

—— From the Home Front. Verses reprinted from Punch. Constable 1918. *1s. 6d.*

Seeger, Alan. Poems. With introduction by William Archer. By a young American, a soldier in the Foreign Legion, killed in action. Constable 1917. *5s.*

Service, Robert W. The Rhymes of a Red Cross Man. Experiences with the Red Cross in France. Fisher Unwin 1916. *3s. 6d.*

Shakspeare, William G. Ypres and other Poems. Sidgwick & Jackson 1916. *2s.*

Shillito, Edward. The Omega and other Poems. Oxford: Blackwell 1916. *2s.*

Short, W. A., Lieut.-Col. Poems. Humphreys 1918. *2s.*

Skeyhill, Signaller Tom. Soldier Songs from Anzac. With introduction by Major-Gen. J. W. McCay, C.B. Fisher Unwin 1916. 1*s*.

Smith, Frederick J. J. The Union Jack: What it is and what it means. With 12 lyrics. Simpkin 1915. 6*d*.

Smith, Lieut. F. W. The Great Sacrifice. Poems. Erskine Macdonald 1918. 1*s*.

Smith, Lieut. G. Bache. A Spring Harvest. Poems. Erskine Macdonald 1918. 2*s*. 6*d*.

Song of War, A, and other Poems. By Feathered Heels. Elliot Stock 1917. 1*s*.

T. B. D. (pseud.). Songs of the Sailor Men. Hodder & Stoughton 1916. 1*s*.

Sorley, C. H. Marlborough and other Poems. 3rd edn. With illustrations in prose. Camb. Univ. Press 1916. 5*s*.

Spender, Emily, and Constance (edrs.). Briton's Calendar: a Guide for Patriots. Palmer & Hayward 1915. 2*s*. 6*d*.

Squire, J. C. Survival of the Fittest and other Poems. Allen & Unwin 1916. 1*s*.

Stead, Robert J. C. Kitchener and other Poems. With introduction by Prof. Allison. Toronto: Masson 1918. n.p.

Steele, Howard. Cleared for Action. Unwin 1914. 1*s*.

Stephens, W. H. Fightings and Fears of 1915. Poems. Cairo: Nile Mission Press 1916.

—— On the All-Red Trail. Poems. Cairo: Nile Mission Press 1916.

Stewart, Capt. T. E., M.C. Grapes of Thorns. Poems. Erskine Macdonald 1917.

Streets, J. W. The Undying Splendour. Poems by a Derbyshire miner and Wesleyan worker, who died in action, July 1916. Erskine Macdonald 1917. 2*s*. 6*d*.

Stodart, Walker A. Verses of Consolation and other lines written in war time. Maclehose 1915. 1*s*. 6*d*.

Studdert-Kennedy, G. A., M.C. More Rough Rhymes of a Padre. Hodder & Stoughton 1918. 1*s*. 6*d*.

Strong, A. T. Sonnets of the Empire before and during the War. By an Australian poet. Macmillan. 3*s*.

Swinglehurst, H. E. Patriotic Poems. Unwin Brothers 1915. 1*s*.

Tatham, C. M. The Airman. Poem. Milford 1917. 8*d*.

Templeton, Capt. W. F. Songs of the Ayrshire Regiment and other Verses. Alex. Gardner 1917. 2*s*. 6*d*.

Terry, E. Blanche. Broken Promise and other war poems. Stockwell 1915. 6*d*.

Terry, E. Blanche. Roll of Honour and other war poems. Stockwell 1915. 6*d*.

Thomas, C. E. Patriot's Calendar, The. T. Murby 1914. 6*d*.

Thomas, Gilbert. Towards the Dawn and other poems. Headley 1918. 1*s*. 3*d*.

Todd, Nicholas H. Poems and Plays. (The author fell in France on Oct. 7, 1916.) Jackson 1918. 5*s*.

Tommy, A. (pseud.). If I goes West. Verses. Harrap 1918. 2*s*. 6*d*.

Tovey, Duncan. Grey Kilts. A collection of war verses, etc. (By a former sergeant of the London Scottish.) London Scottish Regimental Gazette 1918.

Thorpe, Elphinstone. Nursery Rhymes for Fighting Times. Illustrated by G. A. Stevens. Everett 1914. 1*s*.

Thrush, Arthur. Day of Battle: an Epic of War. (20th Century Poetry Series.) Macdonald 1915. 1*s*.

Trench, Herbert. Ode from Italy in time of war: Night on Mottarone. (The ode was written in April, 1915. The book was printed in Florence.) Methuen. 1*s*. 6*d*.

Trevelyan, W. B. A Nation at Prayer. Longmans 1914. 1*s*. 6*d*.

Tynan, Katharine. Flower of Youth: Poems in War Time. Sidgwick & Jackson. 3*s*. 6*d*.

—— Holy War. Sidgwick & Jackson 1916. 3*s*. 6*d*.

Unexpected Tidings of the War and of the Future. With a Preface by the Countess of Portsmouth. Kegan Paul 1915. 1*s*.

Van Dyke, Henry. The Red Flower. Poems written in war time. Hodder & Stoughton 1918. 2*s*. 6*d*.

Vernède, R. E. War Poems and other Verses. With introductory note by Edmund Gosse. Heinemann 1917. 3*s*. 6*d*.

Vincent, Charles. Coronel and other war poems. Dent 1917. 4*s*. 6*d*.

Walkerdine, W. E. Poems of the Great War. Simpkin 1916. 1*s*.

Watching the War: Thoughts for the People. Parts 1 and 2. Allenson 1914. 6*d*. each.

Waterhouse, G. Railhead and other poems. Erskine Macdonald 1916. 2*s*. 6*d*.

Watson, William. The Man who Saw, and other poems arising out of the war. Murray 1917. 3*s*. 6*d*.

Watt, L. M. Britannia's Answer and other war poems. Low 1915. 1*s*. and 2*s*. 6*d*.

Weatherby, Fred E. Bravo! Bristol. Arrowsmith 1914. 1*s*.

Weddell, George. Battle of the World. Verse. R. Scott 1915. 6*d*.

Weeks, Raymond. Ode to France. Oxford Univ. Press 1917. *2s.*

Wells, F. Barber. Roll of the Drum and other war verses. Harrap 1916. *1s.*

Westbrook, Frank. Anzac and after: in verse and song. By a Gunner of the Australian Artillery. Duckworth 1916. *1s.*

White, Bernard C. de B. Remembrance and other verses. Edited, with a memoir, by De V. Payen-Payne. Selwyn & Blount 1917. *3s. 6d.*

Wilkinson, E. F. Sunrise Dreams and other poems. 1916.

Williams, Alfred. War Sonnets and Songs. E. Macdonald 1916. *2s. 6d.*

Wodehouse, E. Armine. On Leave. (Poems.) With preface by Sir A. Quiller-Couch. Elkin Mathews 1917. *1s.*

Wood, Lieut. E. H. Rhodes. Splinters. Poems, descriptive of private soldiers' feelings. Erskine Macdonald 1918. *2s. 6d.*

Wood, Frank N. Songs amid Strife. Hull: Johnston 1917. *1s.*

X. (pseud.). War Poems. Martin Secker 1916. *2s.*

Young, F. B. Poems 1916-18. Collins 1919. *5s.*

(*b*) French.

Baerlein, Henry. Rimes of the Diables Bleus (*i.e.*, the Chasseurs Alpins). Selwyn & Blount 1917. *2s. 6d.*

Botrel, Théodore. Les Chants de Bivouac. (Réfrains de guerre, 1e série.) Preface by Maurice Barrés. Illustrated. Payot 1915. 3 fr. 50.

—— Chansons de route (Jan. 1-Aug. 31, 1915). (Réfrains de guerre, 2e série.) Illustrated. Payot 1916. 3 fr. 50.

—— Songs (by the French soldier-poet). Translated in verse by Winfred Byers. Duckworth 1916. *2s. 6d.* & *10s. 6d.*

Bourgoin, Alphonse. Bleuets de France: Chansons et Poèmes de guerre. Lettre-Préface par M. Theodore Botrel. Bloud et Gay 1916. 2 fr.

Claudel, Paul. Trois Poèmes de la Guerre. Nouv. Rev. française 1916. 1 fr.

D'Arcangues, Pierre. Les Lauriers sur les tombes Poèmes Illustré par P. de Montaut. Paris 1916.

Dérieux, Henry. En ces Jours Dèchirants. (Poems by a French soldier.) Payot 1917. 3 fr. 50.

Fort, Paul. Poèmes de France. Bulletin lyrique de la guerre (1914-15). 1e série. Avec une préface de M. Anatole France. Payot 1916. 3 fr. 50.

Leclerc, M. La Passion de Notre Frère le Poilu. (Poem.) Crès 1916. 1 fr. 25.

Leclerc, M. Souvenirs de tranchées d'un Poilu. Poèmes. Crès 1917. 1 fr. 50.

Normand, Gilles. Les Voix de la fournaise : Poèmes d'un Poilu. Perrin 1916. 3 fr. 50.

Régnier, Henri de. 1914-1916 (War Poems). Mercure de France 1918. 3 fr.

Roudie, Emile. La Légende des Poilus : poèmes à dire. Berger-Levrault 1916, 2 fr.

(*c*) Other Nations.

Cammaerts, Emile. Belgian Poems. Chants patriotiques et autres Poèmes. In the original French, with translation by Tita Brand-Cammaerts. Lane. 4*s*. 6*d*.

—— New Belgian Poems. With translations by Tita Brand-Cammaerts. Portrait. Lane 1916. 3*s*. 6*d*.

—— Messines and other Poems. Translated by Tita Brand-Cammaerts. John Lane 1918. 3*s*. 6*d*.

Lanzalone, Giovanni. Epigrammi di Guerra. Preface by Prof. Manzoni. Salerno: Fratelli Jovane 1917. 60 c.

Verhaeren, Emile. Les Ailes rouges de la Guerre (Poems). Paris 1916.

Visiak, E. H. The Battle Fiends. E. Mathews 1916. 1*s*.

Wolzogen, H. von. Vom Kriege zum Frieden. 1 mk.

Wyseur, Marcel. La Flandre Rouge (Poems by a Belgian officer). With preface by Emile Verhaeren. Perrin 1916. 3 fr. 50.

C.—*Drama*.

Andreyev, Leonid. The Sorrows of Belgium : a Play in six scenes. Translated from the Russian by Herman Bernstein. New York : Macmillan. 5*s*. 6*d*.

Lee, Vernon. Ballet of the Nations : a Present-day Morality. With pictorial commentary by Maxwell Armfield. Chatto & Windus 1915. 3*s*. 6*d*.

Lepsius, J. John Bull. Eine politische Komödie. 1919. 3 mk.

Monkhouse, Allan. War Plays. Constable 1916. 2*s*.

Phillips, Stephen. Armageddon : a Modern Epic Drama in a prologue, series of scenes and an epilogue written partly in prose and partly in verse. Lane 1915. 2*s*. 6*d*.

Wentworth, Marion Craig. War Brides. A Play in one act. Heinemann 1915. 1*s*. 6*d*.

XXIII.—HUMOUR AND SATIRE.

A.—*Literary*.

Adams, Lieut. Bernard. Nothing of Importance. (Pictures of life at the front.) New York : McBride 1918. $1.50.

All for Germany: or, The World's Respect well lost. Being a Dialogue, in the satyrick manner, between Dr. Pangloss and M. Candide. (O.P.) Oxford Univ. Press. *2d.*

Alphabet of the War. Reprinted from Punch Almanack. Jarrold 1915. *6d.*

Ballad of Kaiser Wilhelm, The: or, The Invasion of Belgium. By an Anglo-American. St. Catherine Press 1915. *1s.*

Bairnsfather, Capt. Bruce. Bullets and Billets. (Illustrated.) Grant Richards 1916. *5s.*

Burton, H. B. Der Kaiser von Potsdam. Hodges, F. 1915. *6d.*

Cammell, Charles Richard. Casus Belli: a Satire, with other Poems. Humphreys 1915. *2s. 6d.*

D. S. M. Another Neutral. A satire on the Vatican. Maclehose. *6d.*

Eassie, R. M. Odes to Trifles, and other rhymes (humorous). By a member of the Canadian Force. Lane 1917. *2s. 6d.*

Emanuel, Walter, and Hassall, John. Keep Smiling: More News by Liarless for German Homes. Illustrated. Nash 1914. *6d.*

Fay, Stanley J. The Allies' Alphabet. By Norman Morrow. Daily Chronicle 1914. *1s.*

Garstin, Crosbie. The Mud-Larks (sketches of army life in France from Punch). Methuen 1918. *3s. 6d.*

Hamund, St. John. The Rubáiyát of William the War Lord. (Illustrated.) Richards 1914. *1s.*

—— War Men-agerie. Illustrated by Walter H. Cobb. Richards 1915. *1s.*

Herbert, A. P. Half-hours at Helles. (Humorous verses, most of which have appeared in Punch.) Blackwell 1916. *1s.*

Hun Hunters, The. Cautionary tales from the Trenches (in verse). Grant Richards 1916. *2s. 6d.*

Johnston, Lieut. A. L. (the late). At the Front. (Papers contributed to Punch.) Introduction by Sir Owen Seaman. Constable 1917. *3s. 6d.*

Lucas, E. V., and Morrow, George. In Gentlest Germany. By Hun Svedend. A parody on Dr. Sven Hedin's With the German Armies in the West. Lane. *1s.*

—— Swollen-headed William (after the German). Verses adapted by E. V. L.; drawings adapted by G. M. Methuen 1914. *1s.*

Norton, Frederic. The Mad Dog of Potsdam. Adapted by Frederic Norton, pictured by Lewis Baumer, after R. Caldecott. Warne 1914. *1s.*

Diary of the Great War, A. Pepys, Samuel, junior. (Humorous.) Lane 1916. 5*s*.

—— A Second Diary of the Great War. Illustrated by John Kettelwell. Hodder & Stoughton 1917. 5*s*.

—— A Last Diary of the Great War. With effigies by John Kettlewell. Lane 1919. 6*s*.

Powell, George H. The Crown Prince's First Lesson-Book. Decorations by Scott Calder. Richards 1914. 1*s*.

Rawlins, Margaret A. Wicked Willie. Illustrated by Gwen Forwood and Florence Holms. Longmans 1914. 2*s*. 6*d*.

Shell Shocks. By the New Zealanders in France. Introductory contributions by Lt.-Gen. Sir A. Godley, K.C.B., and D. C. Calthrop. (Illustrated.) Jarrold 1917. 1*s*. 6*d*.

Stone, Eric. The Raving: a Ballad of Berlin. Sidgwick and Jackson 1915. 6*d*.

Studd, C. T. Quaint Rhymes for the Battlefield. J. Clarke 1914. 1*s*.

Ten Kultured Germans, and What Happened. Southward & Co. 1916. 6*d*.

Ward, W. J. Bosch: a Collection of altogether Hun-necessary matter. Cardiff: Ward Maritime Pubs. 1915. 5*s*.

Wideawake, Captain (pseud.). Jovial Jottings from the Trenches. Harrap 1915. 1*s*.

Wussow, O. E. von. Humor im Felde. 1 mk. 20.

Wyatt, Horace. Malice in Kulturland. Illustrated by W. Tell. Car Illustrated Office 1915. 1*s*.

B.—*Pictorial*.

Adam, H. Pearl. International Cartoons of the War. Chatto and Windus 1916. 1*s*. and 3*s*. 6*d*.

Avenarius, F. Das Bild als Narr. Die Karikatur in der Völkerverhetzung. Was sie aussagt—und was sie verrät. Mit 350 Bildern. 2nd edn. 1919. 5 mk.

Bairnsfather, Bruce. Fragments from France. Bystander Office 1916. 1*s*.

—— —— Edition de luxe. Bystander Office 1916. 5*s*.

—— More Fragments from France. Vol. II. Bystander Office 1916. 1*s*.

Dowd, J. H. The Doings of Donovan in and out of Hospital. Caricatures. Country Life 1918. 3*s*. 6*d*.

Catalogue of War Literature issued by H.M. Government 1914-19. (Pages 1-77 contain pictorial posters and art reproductions, with some illustrations.) H.M.S.O. 1921. 6*d*.

Dyson, Will. Kultur Cartoons. With foreword by H. G. Wells. Stanley Paul. 2*s*.

Dyson, Will. War Cartoons. With descriptive letterpress. Hodder and Stoughton 1916. 1*s.*

England-Album des Kladderadatsch. Von der Zeit des Burenkrieges bis zur Gegenwart. Many Illustrations. Berlin: Kladderadatsch-Verlag. 1 mk. 50.

Fuchs, E. Der Weltkrieg in der Karikatur. Bd. I. Bis zum Vorabend d. Weltkrieges mit 333 Textillustr. u. 47 Beilagen. 1916. 22 mk. 50.

Germania. Allemands, Les, peints par eux-mêmes: Illustré (reproductions from various satirical German papers). L'Edition française 1917. 3 fr. 50.

Gott strafe England! eine Kampfschrift in Bild und Wort. 130 drawings from the comic paper Simplicissimus. Munich: Simplicissimus-Verlag. 1 mk.

Grand-Carteret, M. J. Verdun: Images de guerre (collection de caricatures, avec une introduction). Chapelot 1917. 6 fr.

Grane, C. Hun's Handbook for the Invasion of England. Humorous cartoons. Echo and Evening Chronicle 1915. 3*d.*

Hadjich, T. D. (edr.). The World's War Cartoons: the Balkans in caricature. Palmer & Hayward 1916. 1*s.*

Haselden, W. K. Daily Mirror Reflections of War and Peace. Pictorial Newspaper Co. 1914. 6*d.*

—— Sad Experiences of Big and Little Willie during the first six months of the war. Caricatures from the Daily Mirror. Daily Mirror Office. 1*s.*

Herscher, Lieut. E. Quelques images de la guerre (55 drawings by the author). Berger-Levrault 1917. 3 fr. 50.

Hohenzollerns, The, Through German Eyes. (Cartoons from Simplicissimus, 1903-14, attacking the German Government.) Hutchinson 1917. 1*s.*

Kato, Satori (edr.). A History of the War in 61 Cartoons. Hitherto unpublished in Europe. Shimpo 1914. 6*d.*

Lane, Mrs. John. War Phases according to Maria. Illustrations by Fish. Lane 1917. 2*s.* 6*d.*

Leete, Alfred. The Bosch Book (80 drawings). Dudeworth 1917.

L'Esprit français. Les Caricaturistes. Préface d'Arsène Alexandre. Illustré. Berger-Levrault 1915. 2 fr.

L'Imposture par l'image: recueil de gravures falsifiées et calomnieuses publiées par la presse austro-allemande pendant la guerre. Payot 1918. 3 fr.

McIntosh, Dorothy M. Our Allies' A.B.C. War Book. Drawings by Chris. Heaps. Harrison 1915. 1*s.*

Moreland, Arthur. The History of the Hun (caricatures). New edn. with 20 additional drawings. Palmer & Hayward 1917. 2*s.* 6*d.*

Owen, Will. Alleged Humour. (Cartoons about the War from the Sketch.) Duckworth 1917. 1*s.*

Poy (pseud.). War Cartoons. (From the Evening News.) With introduction by W. McCartney. Simpkin 1915. 7*d.*

Raemaekers, Louis. Het toppunt der Beschaving. Cartoons of the war. Six parts. Amsterdam: Elsevier 1915. 1*s.* 6*d.* each.

—— Cartoons, No. 1-5. Fine Art Society 1915. 10*s.*

—— Cartoons. Hodder & Stoughton 1916. 2*d.* (This cheap edition was also produced with text in almost all languages, including German, Chinese, Japanese, Catalan and Basque.)

—— Great War: a Neutral's Indictment. 100 cartoons. With an appreciation by H. Perry Robinson, and descriptive notes by E. Garnett. Fine Art Society 1916. £10 10*s.*

—— —— In 26 parts. Land and Water. 1*s.* each.

—— Cartoons; with descriptive letterpress. In 24 quarto parts, each containing 8 cartoons. Land and Water 1916-17. 1*s.* each.

—— The Great War in 1916. A Neutral's Indictment. 60 cartoons and descriptive notes. Fine Art Society 1917. £6 6*s.*

—— Cartoons. Edition de luxe. Vol. I. Folio, in colours, £10 10*s.* Vol. II., black and white, £5 5*s.* Fine Art Society 1917.

—— America in the War (cartoons). Century Co. 1918. $5.00.

Régamey, F. (edr.). La caricature allemande pendant la guerre. (Illustré). Berger-Levrault 1921. 10 fr.

Robinson, Boardman. Cartoons on the War. Dent 1915. 3*s.* 6*d.*

Robinson, W. Heath. Some "Frightful" War Pictures. Duckworth 1915. 2*s.* 6*d.*

—— —— Cheap edn. Duckworth 1916. 1*s.*

—— The Saintly Hun: a Book of German Virtues (cartoons, grotesques and silhouettes). Duckworth 1916. 1*s.*

Sacre (pseud.). Sidelights: an official series of caricature portraits. Military. First series. Constable 1918. £3 3*s.*

Schulz-Besser, E. (edr.). Die Karikatur im Weltkriege. 115 drawings from various countries.) Leipzig: Seemann.

Stieve, Fr. Unsere Feinde: wie sie die Deutschen passen. 80 Karikaturen. 4 mk.

Soutar, D. H. War Cartoons. Reprinted from The Stock Journal. W. Brooks 1915. 1*s.*

Sullivan, E. G. The Kaiser's Garland. Cartoons. Heinemann 1915. 5*s.*

Têtes de Boches. Les Allemands peints par eux-mêmes. Texte de M. Henriot. Dessins de Simplicissimus. 3 Fascicules. Vermot 1917. 1 fr. 50 each.

Thomas, Bert, and Williams, Wilton. 100 War Cartoons from London Opinion. London Opinion 1918. 2*s.* 6*d.*

You! The amazing unheard-of and utterly incredible Adventures of a Scrap of Paper. Pictured on a film by Mr. and Mrs. Bannister Merwin and transcribed by Harold Begbie. Mills and Boon 1916. 1*d.*

XXIV.—LINGUISTIC WORKS.

A.—*Grammars.*

Bisschop, E. V. English Grammar for Flemings (Engelsche Spraakkunst voor Scholen en Beginners). L. B. Hill 1915. 6*d.*

—— Grammaire anglaise (English grammar for French people): les règles fondamentales de la grammaire anglaise et leur application. L. B. Hill 1915. 6*d.*

Forbes, Nevill. First Russian Book (chiefly on case-endings). Oxford Univ. Press 1917. 3*s.* 6*d.*

—— Second Russian Book (chiefly on the Russian verb). Oxford Univ. Press 1917. 4*s.* 6*d.*

—— Russian Grammar. 2nd edn. revised (practical). Oxford Univ. Press 1917. 7*s.* 6*d.*

Hopfen, B. Nelson's Simplified Russian Grammar. Nelson 1917. 1*s.* 6*d.*

Ivanoff, A. Russian Grammar. Translated, enlarged and arranged for the use of English students of the Russian language by W. E. Gowan. New edn. Kegan Paul 1915. 3*s.* 6*d.*

Magnus, L. A. A concise Grammar of the Russian Language. Murray 1916. 5*s.*

Panagulli, A. C. Key to Italian Grammar Self-taught. Marlborough 1916. 6*d.*

Russian Grammar Simplified: Russian Reading Made Easy. (Hugo's Simplified System series.) Hugo's Institute 1916. 1*s.* 6*d.* each.

B.—*Dictionaries.*

Active Service Pocket Dictionary and Letter Wallet. Gale & Polden. 1*s.*

Atkinson, C. F. Dictionary of English and German Military Terms, and of other words useful to officers. 2 vols. Rees 1916. 2*s.* 6*d.* each vol.

Barrère, Albert. Dictionnaire des Termes Militaires: I, Anglais-Français; II, Français-Anglais. 2 vols. Paris: Hachette. 5 fr.

Beckwith, E. G. A. Military Expressions in English, French and German. Hachette. 1*s.* 6*d.*

Bellows, John. Dictionary for the Pocket: French and English, English and French. 3rd edn. Revised by Wm. Bellows. Longmans & Kegan Paul 1916. 9*s.*

Bisschop, E. V. Flemish-English and English-Flemish Dictionary: with conversations and idioms. (Hill's Vest-pocket Dictionaries.) L. B. Hill 1914. 1*s.*

Bruce, Aline. Military Terms: English, German, French. Larby 1915. 6*d.*

Cahen, Louis. Serbian-English and English-Serbian Pocket Dictionary. Kegan Paul 1916. 2*s.* 6*d.*

Coutanseau, Léon. Pocket Dictionary for the French and English Languages. Revised by Ludovic Coutanseau. Longmans 1915 1*s.* 6*d.*

Czarnowski, F. B. Hill's Polish-English and English-Polish Vest-pocket Dictionary. L. B. Hill 1916. 1*s.*

Dauzat, Albert. L'Argot de la guerre, d'après une enquête des officiers et soldats. Colin 1918. 3 fr. 50.

Delbos, Léon. Nautical Terms in English and French, and French and English. New and cheaper edn. Williams & Norgate 1914. 5*s.*

Dictionnaire des Termes et de l'Argot du Poilu. Larousse 1916. 2 fr. 50.

Dictionary of English and French military terms, and of other words useful to officers. Part I, French-English. Hugh Rees 1916. 2*s.* 6*d.*

Esnault, Gaston. Le Poilu tel qu'il se parle (Dictionnaire des termes populaires . . . employés aux Armées en 1914-18). Paris: Bossard 1919. 7 fr. 50.

Farrow, Edward S. Dictionary, A, of Military Terms. Library Press 1918. 12*s.* 6*d.*

Fursdon, F. R. M. How to Speak French: an Active Service French and English Word-book. Simpkin 1914. 4*d.*

Freese, J. H. Pocket Dictionary of the English and Russian Languages. Kegan Paul 1916. 5*s.*

Goldingham, C. S. Dictionary of Modern Naval Technical Terms: German-English and English-German. H. Rees 1914. 3*s.* 6*d.*

Hodgson, E. S. Tri-lingual Artillery Dictionary. Vol. I: English, French, Italian. Vol. II: Français, Italien, Anglais. Griffin 1918. 5*s.* each.

Hossfeld's Technical Dictionary: English-German and German English. Compiled by C. N. Caspar. Hirschfeld 1914. 4*s.*

Latham, E. French-English and English-French Military Vocabulary. Kegan Paul. 3*d.*

Lockhart, J. H. B. A French Picture Vocabulary, together with a German Vocabulary. Illustrated by George Morrow. Bell 1914. 1*s.*

Luboff, S. J. Hill's English-Russian Vest-pocket Dictionary and Self-instructor, with conversations and idioms. Hill 1915. 1*s.*

Lucas, Frederick. English-French and French-English Dictionary of the Motor-car, Cycle and Boat. New impression. Spon 1915. 2*s.*

Lysle, A. de R. Modern rational-practical English-Italian Dictionary, for the use of Englishmen and Italians. Nutt 1914. 12*s.* 6*d.*

Pagé, Lieut. V. W., and Montariol, Lieut. P. Glossary of Aviation Terms. Termes d'Aviation. Crosby Lockwood 1918. 5*s.*

Sainéan, L. L'Argot des Tranchées d'après les lettres des Poilus et les Journaux du Front. Boccard 1916. 2 fr.

Soldier's Word and Phrase Book. Compiled by a Committee of well-known teachers from actual experience of soldiers' needs. English, French, German, with pronunciation. Harrap. 6*d.*

Spiers, Victor B. French Vocabularies for Repetition, containing 3,000 most important words and phrases. 5th edn. Simpkin 1915. 1*s.* 6*d.*

Weekly Telegraph French-English and English-French Pronouncing Dictionary. Sir C. W. Leng 1915. 1*s.* 6*d.*

Wisdom, J. M., and Murray, Marr. Practical Pocket Dictionary of the French and English Languages. Melrose 1914. 1*s.*; swd., 6*d.*

—— Practical Pocket Dictionary, Russian-English and English-Russian. Melrose 1916. 6*d.* and 1*s.*

Zimmerman, Prof. F. G. Military Vocabulary: German-English and English-German. Hugh Rees 1915. 2*s.*

C.—*Manuals, Conversation Books, etc.*

Ackerley, F. G. A Rumanian Manual for Self-tuition, containing a concise grammar with exercises, etc. Kegan Paul 1917. 2*s.*

Ajax (pseud.). Soldier's Language Manual: English-French. Marlborough 1915. 6*d.*

Ajax (pseud.). and Harris, E. F. The Active Service French Book. With Phonetic pronunciation. Marlborough 1916. 7*d.*

Anastassiou, N. Greek (Modern) Self-taught: with phonetic pronunciation. Marlborough. 2*s.* 6*d.*

Bisschop, E. V. Shops and Shopping Phrase-book in English, French, and Flemish. L. B. Hill 1914. 6*d.*

Bithell, J. Easy Lessons in German. Pitman 1915. 1*s.*

Buller, Henry. The Soldier's English-German Conversation Book. Werner, Laurie 1918. 7*d.*

Cahen, L., and Forbes, Nevill. English-Serbian Phrase-book: with easy Grammar. Blackwell 1915. 1*s.*

Cross, Hélène. Soldiers' Spoken French: with correct phonetic pronunciation, and vocabulary of military and general terms. Christchurch, N.Z. Whitcombe 1917. 2*s.* 6*d.*

Davies, E. Chivers. A Little Serbian Phrase Book. Kegan Paul 1916. 6*d.*

Dearmer, Percy, and Tananevich, V. A. A First Russian Reader. Oxford Univ. Press 1917. 2*s.*

Desgenettes, Clifton, and Dufriche. Manual of Conversation: English-French and Français-Anglais. (Polyglot Guides.) L. B. Hill 1916. 2*s.* 6*d.*

Easy Roumanian for Our Men Abroad, and How to Pronounce It. Kegan Paul 1916. 6*d.*

First Lessons in Russian without a Master. Hugo's Language Institute 1915. 2*s.*

Foakes, G. M. Soldier's English-Russian Conversation Book. Laurie 1915. 7*d.*

Forbes, N., and Keyworth, Captain. Easy Serbian for our Men Abroad, and How to Pronounce It. Kegan Paul 1915. 6*d.*

Forbes, Nevill. First Russian Book. A Russian Reader for Beginners. Milford 1915. 2*s.* 6*d.*

Freese, J. H. Polish Manuel for Self-tuition. Kegan Paul 1918. 3*s.*

French Lessons for Soldiers: the Adventures of Corporal Atkins With vocabulary. Country Life 1914. 3*d.*

French Self-taught (for learning by the natural method; phonetic pronunciation). Marlborough 1916. Paper, 1*s.*; cloth, 1*s.* 6*d.*

Gallichan, W. M. The Soldier's English-French Conversation Book. Werner Laurie. 7*d.*

Gardiner, W. H. T., and Sheikh Kurayyim Saltam. Egyptian Colloquial Arabic. A conversation grammar and reader. Heffer 1917.

H[arnden]. G. F. French Conversation Guide. Harnden 1915. 6*d.*

H[arnden], G. F. French Conversation: Words and Phrases in alphabetical order for instant reference. Ealing: Harnden 1915. 6*d*.

Hernan, W. J. What you want to say, and how to say it in French. War edn. Hernan 1915. 6*d*.

How to Say it in French: with a Guide to Pronunciation. For the use of our soldiers and sailors. Arrowsmith 1914. 6*d*.

Hugo's Russian Reading Made Easy. (Hugo's Simplified System.) Hugo 1916. 1*s*. 6*d*.

Italian Self-taught: by the Natural Method with Phonetic Pronunciation. Revised and enlarged by G. Dalla Vecctua. 5th edn. (Marlborough's Self-taught series.) Marlborough 1914. 1*s*.

Jeffrey, Shaw. German Words and Phrases for Red Cross Workers. Hachette. 6*d*. each.

Karrachy-Smitt, M. B. Lessons in Russian: regular verb, its conjugations and aspects. 2nd course. S. Low 1916. 2*s*.

—— Lessons in Russian: the alphabet, sounds and letters, orthography. S. Low 1915. 1*s*. 6*d*.

Keyworth, Captain. Easy French for our Men Abroad, and How to Pronounce it. Hove: Combridge. 6*d*.

—— Easy German for our Men Abroad. Combridge 1915. 3*d*.

—— Easy Italian, and How to Pronounce it. Combridge 1915. 3*d*.

Lombardo, G. M. Commercial French. Nutt 1914. 3*s*. 6*d*.

Manual of the Russian Language: with Vocabulary and List of Phrases. Unwin 1914. 1*s*. 6*d*.

Marriott, Major, D.S.O. Egyptian (Arabic) Self-taught. A handbook of colloquial Arabic for soldiers and others. 2*s*. & 2*s*. 6*d*.

Marshall, J. Russian Self-taught, with Phonetic Pronunciation. 5th edn., revised. Marlborough 1915. 2*s*. & 2*s*. 6*d*.

Maude, Col. F. N., and Scudamore, Frank. Sprechen Sie Deutsch and Parley Voo. Practical French and German phrases, and how to pronounce them. Forster Groom 1916. 4*d*.

Nutt's Soldier's Manual: English-French-German. Nutt 1915. 3*d*.

Phillips, E. G. French for British Soldiers. Revised edn., with rules for pronunciation and dictionary of military terms. Phillips. 1*d*.

Pitt, George E. Manual of Military French. (Daily Telegraph War Books.) Hodder & Stoughton 1915. 1*s*.

Plumon, Eugène. English-Flemish Military Guide for the present Campaign. Harrison 1915. 10*d*.

—— Vade-mecum for the use of Officers and Interpreters in the present Campaign: French and English technical and military terms. New and revised edn. Hachette 1915. 2*s*.

Raffi, A. Easy Turkish for our Men Abroad: and How to Pronounce it. Kegan Paul. 6*d.*

Rees, D. J. The Briton in France. A pocket interpreter and guide. 6th edn. L. B. Hill 1914. 1*s.*

Russian Manual for Self-tuition. (Trübner's Language Manuals.) Kegan Paul 1915. 2*s.*

Scudamore, Frank. Arabic for our Armies. Groom 1915. 3*d.*

—— Parley Voo. Practical French Phrases, and How to Pronounce Them. Groom 1915. 3*d.*

—— Turkish for Tommy and Tar. Words and phrases with their equivalent in colloquial Turkish (phonetic). Groom. 3*d.*

Segal, Louis. The Self-educator in Russian. Hodder & Stoughton 1916. 3*s.* 6*d.*

Smirnoff, P. M. A Progressive Russian Course (thirty lessons in conversation). Blackie 1917. 3*s.* 6*d.*

Soldier's English and French Conversation Book. T. W. Laurie 1914. 7*d.*

Soldier's English-French Friend for our Soldiers in France and Belgium. Church Army Book Room 1915. 2*d.*

Soldier's First Aid to German. Y.M.C.A. 1914. 1*d.*

Soldier's Language Manuals, The. 1. English - French. 2. English-German. 3. French for the Front. Marlborough 1916. 3*d.* each.

Soldier's Word and Phrase Book: French and German. Harrap 1915. 1*s.*

Solomonoff, J. First Steps in Russian. Kegan Paul 1917. 2*s.* 6*d.*

Taylor, Susette M., and Keyworth, Captain. Easy Russian for our Men Abroad, and How to Pronounce it. Kegan Paul 1915. 6*d.*

Thimm, C. A. Turkish Self-taught: with English Phonetic Pronunciation. 4th edn. Revised by G. Hagopian. Marlborough 1915. 2*s.* 6*d.*

Trofimov, Michael V., and Scott, James P. Handbook of Russian. Vol. I. Constable 1918. 3*s.* 6*d.*

Van Ess, Rev. John. The Spoken Arabic of Mesopotamia. By a member of the American Mission in Basra. (Official.) Oxford Univ. Press 1917. 4*s.* 6*d.*

What a British Soldier wants to say in French, and the Way to Say it. An English-French booklet for the use of the Expeditionary Forces. War Unity Booklets, 19, North Road, Hythe. 3*d.*

Whittem, A. F., and Long, P. W. French for Soldiers. (Prepared for the Dept. of Univ. Extension, Massachusetts Board of Education.) Oxford Univ. Press 1918. 3*s.* 6*d.*

Wilkins, Ernest H., and Coleman, Algernon. Army French. An introduction to spoken French for men on military service. Camb. Univ. Press 1918. n.p.

Wisdom, J. H. Briton in Russia: a Pocket Interpreter and Guide to Russia and its Language. Hill 1915. 1*s.*

Witteryck, A. J. L'anglais usuel sans professeur en 15 jours. For French people to learn English. Simpkin 1914. 6*d.*

—— Esperanto Conversation Book in Four Languages: English, Français, Nederlandsch, Esperanto. Simpkin 1916. 1*s.* 6*d.*

—— Flemish for Home Study in Ten Lessons. Simpkin 1914. 6*d.*

—— Het Engelsch voor het dagelijksch verkeer in 15 lessen. For Flemish people to learn English. Simpkin 1914. 6*d.*

Zimmermann, Prof. F. G. An easy Handbook of German for Soldiers. Hugh Rees. 3*s.* 6*d.*

XXV.—PEACE AND RECONSTRUCTION.

A.—*The Peace.*

(1) Anticipations.

Armstrong, G. A. Peace with Security. Blackfriars Press, 1916. 3*d.*

Ashton, Henry Allen. The Price of Peace. Suggestions regarding terms. British American Overseas Field Hospital. 175, Piccadilly, 1917. 1*s.*

Aulard, A. La paix future, d'après la Revolution Française et Kant. Colin 1916. 50 c.

Baie, Eugène. La Belgique de demain. Perrin 1916. 60 c.

Beck, James M. The Reckoning (including a discussion of the 14 points). Hodder & Stoughton 1918. 6*s.*

Bevan, Edwyn. Peace with Empire: the Problem. (Papers for War Time.) Milford. 2*d.*

Biottot, le Colonel. L'Europe qu'il nous faut faire: la Guerre: la Paix: l'Organisation du droit-force. Fournier 1915. 1 fr.

Boulanger, Omer. La Grande Belgique après la Paix. Avec 1 portrait et 1 dessin. Editions et Librairie 1917. 1 fr. 25.

Buxton, C. Roden (edr.). Towards a lasting settlement (Essays by various writers, G. L. Dickinson, Philip Snowden, &c.) Allen & Unwin 1916. 2*s.* 6*d.*

Chéradame, André. The Essentials of an Enduring Victory. Scribner 1918. $1.50.

Castéran, J. Pent en supprimer la guerre? (In favour of an entente or an alliance between Great Britain, France and the United States.) Written in 1912. Sansot 1916. 3 fr. 50.

Chauveau, Franck. La Paix et la Frontière du Rhin. Perrin. 50 c.

Conditions de paix, les, de l'Entente. Nice: Petit Niçois 1917. 1 fr.

Cressaty, le Comte. La Syrie française. The claims of France in the liquidation of the Ottoman Empire. Floury 1915. 60 c.

Davis, R. J. America's View of the Sequel. (Views expressed in America on the terms of peace, economic consequences, &c.) Headley 1916. *2s.*

Des Ombiaux, Maurice. Les revendications territoriales de la Belgique. Blond et Gay 1916. 60 c.

Dickinson, G. Lowes (edr.). Documents and Statements relating to Peace Proposals and War Aims, Dec. 1916-1918. With introduction. Allen & Unwin 1919. *8s. 6d.*

Driault, Edouard. La France et la guerre: les solutions françaises. Cerf 1915. 1 fr.

—— La République et le Rhin (a demand for the Rhine Frontier). Paris: Tépin 1916.

—— Les traditions politiques de la France et les conditions de la paix. Alcan 1916. 3 fr. 50.

—— Le fer de Lorraine et la paix. Tenin 1917.

Dudon, Paul. La Syrie à la France. (Demande occupation de ce pays par la France.) Lethielleux 1916. 50 c.

Durand, Luc. La paix définitive. Comment la conquérir? Comment l'organiser? (qu'on impose à l'Allemagne une paix implacable). Giard et Brière 1917. 3 fr. 50.

Fayle, C. E. The Great Settlement. A discussion of the rearrangement of Europe after the War. With introduction by Lord Esher. Murray. *1s.*

Fels, le Comte de. L'Entente et le Problème autrichien. (The Allies should not destroy Austria but re-establish her as a counterpoise to Germany.) Grasset 1918. 3 fr. 50.

Férasson, Louis. La Question du fer: le problème franco-allemande du fer. Payot 1918. 3 fr.

For a Lasting Peace. Discusses especially the future of Poland. Soc. Générale d'Imprimerie. *6d.*

Goetz, W. and Hoffman, O. (edrs.). Deutschland und der Friede. Notwendigkeiten u. Möglichkeiten deutscher Zukunft. 1918. 19 mk. 60.

Grailly, F. de. La Vérité territoriale et la Rive gauche du Rhin. Berger-Levrault 1916. 3 fr. 50.

Gümpel, C. Godfrey. The Solution of the Alsace-Lorraine Question and the Maintenance of Peace. Allen 1914. *6d.*

Guyot, Yves. Les Garanties de la Paix. I. Les Leçons du passé. Alcan 1918. 4 fr. 55.

Hanotaux, Gabriel. Le Problème de la Paix. Revue de deux Mondes 1917.

Hauser, Prof. Henri (of Dijon). Essai sur l'Allemagne future. On the nature of the peace to be made with Germany. Revue politique, 36 rue Vaneau.

Headlam, J. W. The Issue. (German utterances on the Terms of Peace.) Constable 1916. 2*s*. 6*d*.

—— The Peace Terms of the Allies. Clay 1917.

Hugins, Roland. The possible peace. New York: Century Co. 1917. $1.25.

Jastrow, Prof. Morris. The War and the Coming Peace. The Moral Issue. Lippincott 1918. 5*s*.

Jullian, Camille. Le Rhin français: le Rhin gaulois. Attinger 1915. 60 c.

Kluck, von, Wilamowitz, und andere. Das deutsche Volk und der Friede. Berlin 1918. 1 mk.

Lange, Chr. L. Les Conditions d'une paix durable. (Exposé des travaux de l'Union.) Kristiania: Bureau interparlementaire 1917.

Larnaude, Barthélemy and others. La Réparation des dommages de guerre. (Conferences faites à l'École des Hautes études sociales sous l'aspect juridique.) Alcan 1917. 3 fr. 50.

Laskine, Edmond. La Démocratie française et le Rhin (la question de la rive gauche du Rhin). Fleury 1918. 1 fr.

L'Enquête, l'sur les conditions d'une paix durable. By various writers. Les Temps Nouveaux 1917.

Lorin, Prof. H. La Paix que nous voudrons. Alcan 1916. 60 c.

Lyde, Prof. L. W. Some Frontiers of To-morrow: an Aspiration for Europe. Maps. Black 1915 and 1917. 2*s*. 6*d*.

Macfall, Major Haldane. Beware the German's Peace. Cassell 1918. 2*s*.

Madelin, Louis. L'Expansion Française: de la Syrie au Rhin. Plon-Nourrit 1918. 4 fr. 50.

Monteyer, G. de (edr.). Austria's Peace Offer, 1916-17, with introductory letter from Prince Sixte de Bourbon. 1921. 25*s*.

Masaryk, T. G. The New Europe. (Privately printed.) 1918.

Moutran, Natra. La Syrie de Demain. Avec 2 cartes et 1 graphique. (Un pays autonome, sous la direction d'un résident français.) Plon-Nourrit 1915. 6 fr.

Müller-Meiningen, Dr. Der Reichstag und der Friedenschluss. Munich 1918. 60 pf.

Münsterberg, Prof. Hugo. To-morrow: letters to a German Friend. New York: Appleton 1917. $1·10.

Peace Conference, The, and After. (Two articles reprinted from The Round Table), with introduction by Viscount Grey. Macmillan 1918. 1*s.*

Peace Made in Germany. Hodder & Stoughton 1917. 6*d.*

Pouvourville, A. de. Jusqu'au Rhin : les terres meurtries et les terres promises. (The boundary between France and Germany must be the Rhine.) Paris : Berger-Levrault 1916. 3 fr. 50.

Powers, H. H. The Great Peace. (A discussion of nationality and the general principles of the new order.) New York : Macmillan 1918. $2.25.

Preston, Sir Jacob. Peace and Victory (a plea for " thorough "). Nisbet 1917. 4*d.*

Privat, Maurice. Pour en finir avec l'Allemagne. (The future settlement.) Editions et Librairie 1916. 2 fr. 50.

—— Qu'entendez-vous par détruire le militarisme allemand? ou de la nécessité de la rive gauche du Rhin. Floury 1917. 60 c.

Problems of the International Settlement (a series of papers by European and American jurists and publicists). With introduction by G. Lowes Dickinson. Allen & Unwin 1918. 6*s.*

Raestad, Arnold. Problèmes de la guerre et de la paix. Kristiania : Cappelen 1918.

Puaux, René. La Question des colonies allemandes. Attinger 1918. 1 fr. 50. Transl. under title The German Colonies : What is to Become of Them? Wightman 1918.

Rawnsley, Canon. Against a Premature and Inconclusive Peace. An address delivered Aug. 4, 1917. Carlisle : Thurnam 1917. 6*d.*

Recueil de Rapports sur les différents points du programme minimum. 3 parts. (By Starr Jordan, C. R. Buxton, A. Forel, Henri Lambert, and others.) The Hague : Nijhoff 1916-17. 10 fr.

Reparation, La, des dommages de guerre. (Bibl. Générale des Sciences Sociales.) Addresses by various authorities. Alcan 1917. 3 fr. 50.

Replies, The, of the Socialist Parties of the Central Powers to the Inter-Allied Memorandum on War Aims, . . . with draft of a peace programme, and an open letter . . . from S. J. Troelstra to Arthur Henderson. Labour Party 1918. 6*d.*

Rey, Barthélemy. Quatre cents milliards : étude sur le coût de la guerre et les indemnités que les puissances ennemies pourront payer. Berger-Levrault 1916. 1 fr. 50.

Rignano, E. Les facteurs de la Guerre et le problème de la Paix. Reprint from Scientia, Vol. XIII. Milan · Zanichelli 1915.

Rignano, E. Translated under title, The War and the Settlement. Introduction by Prof. Ramsay Muir. Council for Study of Internat. Relations 1916. 6*d.*

Robertson, Rt. Hon. J. W. The German Idea of Peace Terms. Hodder 1917. 1*d.*

Raederer, le Dr. Paul. La Syrie et la France. Avec une carte (veut le régime du protectorat libéral). Berger-Levrault 1917. 4 fr.

Rotheit, Rudolf. Die Friedensbedingungen der deutschen Presse. Berlin: 1915.

Ruelens-Marlier, V. H. S. Le Rhin Libre: (1) The neutralizing of the navigation of the Rhine; (2) The neutralizing of the whole Rhine basin. Attwyer 1916. 3 fr. 50.

Sageret, Jules. Impossibilité de la Paix indécise. Pochy 1916. 50 c.

Salvemini, Gaetano. Delenda Austria! Il faut détruire l'Autriche. Bossard 1918. 1 fr.

Savarit, C. M. La frontière du Rhin. Floury 1914. 50 c

Savić, Vladislav R. The Reconstruction of South-Eastern Europe. With preface by Sir J. G. Frazer. Chapman & Hall 1917. 7*s.* 6*d.*

Stoddard, Lothrop, and Frank, Glenn. Stakes of the War. (Summary of facts of race, trade, &c., concerning countries to be considered in the Peace Congress.) With 17 racial and territorial maps. Century Co. 1918. $2.50.

Taylor, C. F. A Conclusive Peace (neutral). Philadelphia: Winston Co. 1917. $0.50.

Veblen, Thorstein. The Nature of Peace. An inquiry . . . showing the necessity of the destruction of the German Imperial State. New York: Macmillan 1917. $2.00.

Wallace, Edgar. 1925: the Story of a Fatal Peace. Newnes 1915. 1*s.*

Wells, H. G. In the Fourth Year: Anticipation of a World Peace. Chatto & Windus 1918. 3*s.* 6*d.*

Wilson, A. J. No Deluding Peace. Essays on the main lines on which alone peace can be granted. The Investor's Review. 1*s.*

Wilson Peace Terms, The. National Peace Council 1918. 3*d.*

Wilson, President, The Policy of. Speeches &c. including the Fourteen Points. (Peace handbooks, published under direction of the Foreign Office, No. 161.) H.M.S.O. 1920. 2*s.* 6*d.*

X., Général. La Paix française. Préface de Junius (de l'Echo de Paris.) (L'Annexion pure et simple de la rive gauche du Rhin.) Echo de Paris 1917. 2 fr.

(2) The Conference of Paris.

Baruch. The making of the Reparation and Economic Sections of the Treaty. New York: Harper 1920. 12*s*. 6*d*.

Dillon, E. J. The Inside Story of the Peace Conference. Hutchinson 1919. 21*s*.

House, E. M., and Seymour, C. (edrs.) What really happened at Paris. By American delegates to the Conference. Hodder & Stoughton 1921. 25*s*.

Haskins, C. H., and Lord, R. H. Some Problems of the Peace Conference. Harvard Univ. Press 1920. 12*s*. 6*d*.

Huddleston, Sisley. Peace-making at Paris. Unwin 1919. 7*s*. 6*d*.

Lansing, Robert. The Peace Negotiations: a personal narrative. Constable 1921. 16*s*.

Tardieu, André. La Paix. Preface by G. Clemenceau. Payot 1921. 12 fr.

Temperley, H. W. V. (Edr.) A History of the Peace Conference. Published under the auspices of the Institute of International Affairs. 5 vols. Frowde and Hodder & Stoughton 1920-21. 42*s*. each.

(3) The Treaties.

Congrès de la Paix: Traités et Conventions. 2 vols. (Collection). Paris: Imprimerie Nationale 1919-20.

Reply of the Allied and Associated Powers to the Observations of the German Delegation on the Conditions of Peace. Miscellaneous No. 4 (1919). [Cmd. 258.] H.M.S.O. 1919. 9*d*.

Treaty of Peace between the Allied and Associated Powers with Germany. Signed at Versailles, June 28, 1919. (With maps.) (Treaty Series 1919, No. 4.) [Cmd. 153.] H.M.S.O. 1919. 4*s*.

Treaty of Peace between the Allied and Associated Powers and Germany . . . and the Treaty between France and Great Britain respecting assistance to France. . . . Signed at Versailles, June 28, 1919. With maps and facsimiles. H.M.S.O. 1919. 21*s*.

Treaty of Peace between the Allied and Associated Powers and Germany, signed at Versailles, June 28, 1919, Index to the. (Treaty Series 1920, No. 1.) [Cmd. 516.] H.M.S.O. 1920. 6*d*.

Treaty of Peace between the Allied and Associated Powers and Germany together with other Treaties, Agreements, etc., signed at Versailles, June 28, 1919, and the reply of the Allied and Associated Powers to the German observations on the Treaty. (Collection.) H.M.S.O. 1920. 2*s*. 6*d*.

Protocol Supplementary to the Treaty of Peace. Signed at Versailles, June 28, 1919. (Treaty Series 1919, No. 5.) [Cmd. 220.] H.M.S.O. 1919. 1*d*.

German Treaty Text, The. Introduction by Lord R. Cecil. Preface by H. W. Temperley. Hodder & Stoughton 1920. 5*s*.

Agreement between the U.S.A., Belgium, the British Empire and France and Germany with regard to the Military Occupation of the territories of the Rhine. Signed at Versailles, June 28, 1919. (Treaty Series, No. 7, 1919.) [Cmd. 222.] H.M.S.O. 1919 1*d*.

Treaty respecting Assistance to France in the event of Unprovoked Aggression by Germany. Signed at Versailles, June 28, 1919. (Treaty Series, 1919, No. 6.) [Cmd. 221.] H.M.S.O. 1919. 1*d*.

Treaty of Versailles (Deliveries in kind). Papers relating to an agreement between the French and German Governments, signed at Wiesbaden, concerning the application of Part VIII of the Treaty. [Cmd. 1547.] H.M.S.O. 1921. 6*d*.

Convention between the United Kingdom and France relative to Art. 296 of the Treaty of Versailles of June 28, 1919 (Enemy Debts). (Treaty Series, No. 18.) [Cmd. 1542.] H.M.S.O. 1921. 2*d*.

Convention between the United Kingdom and Belgium relative to Art. 296 of the Treaty of Versailles of June 28, 1919 (Enemy Debts). [Cmd. 1543.] H.M.S.O. 1921. 2*d*.

Treaty of Peace between the U.S.A., the British Empire, France, Italy and Japan, and Poland. Signed at Versailles, June 28, 1919. (Treaty Series, No. 8, 1919.) [Cmd. 223.] H.M.S.O. 1919. 3*d*.

Treaty between the Principal Allied and Associated Powers and Poland, Roumania, the Serb-Croat-Slovene State and the Czecho-Slovak State, relative to certain frontiers of those States. Signed at Sèvres, Aug. 10, 1920. British Ratification deposited July 26, 1921. [Cmd. 1548.] H.M.S.O. 1921. 4*d*.

Treaty of Peace between the Allied and Associated Powers and Austria, together with the Protocol and Declarations annexed thereto. Signed at St. Germain-en-Laye, Sept. 10, 1919. (With Appendix.) (Treaty Series, No. 11, 1919.) [Cmd. 400.] H.M.S.O. 1919. 1*s*. 6*d*.

Treaty between the principal Allied and Associated Powers and the Serb-Croat-Slovene State. Signed at St. Germain-en-Laye, Sept. 10, 1919. (Treaty Series, No. 17, 1919.) [Cmd. 461.] H.M.S.O. 1919. 1*d*.

Treaty between the principal Allied and Associated Powers and Czecho-Slovakia. Signed at St. Germain-en-Laye, Sept. 10, 1919. (Treaty Series, 1919, No. 30.) [Cmd. 479.] H.M.S.O. 1919. 1*d*.

Italian Reparation Payments, Agreement between the Allied and Associated Powers with regard to the. Signed at St. Germain-en-Laye, Sept. 10, 1919. (Treaty Series, 1919, No. 15.) [Cmd. 459.] H.M.S.O. 1919. 1*d*.

Contributions to the cost of Liberation of the Territories of the former Austro-Hungarian Monarchy. Agreement between the Allied and Associated Powers with regard to the. Signed at St. Germain-en-Laye, Sept. 10, 1919. (Treaty Series, 1919, No. 14.) [Cmd. 458.] H.M.S.O. 1919. 1*d*.

Convention revising the General Act of Berlin, Feb. 26, 1885, and the General Act and Declaration of Brussels, July 2, 1890. Signed at St. Germain-en-Laye, Sept. 10, 1919. (Treaty Series, 1919, No. 18.) [Cmd. 477.] H.M.S.O. 1919. 1*d*.

Treaty of Peace between the Allied and Associated Powers and Austria together with other Treaties, Agreements, etc., signed at St.-Germain-en-Laye, September 10th, 1919. (Collection.) H.M.S.O. 1921. 1*s*. 6*d*.

Treaty of Peace between the Allied and Associated Powers and Bulgaria, and Protocol. Signed at Neuilly-sur-Seine, Nov. 27, 1919. With map. (Treaty Series, 1920, No. 5.) [Cmd. 522.] H.M.S.O. 1920. 1*s*. 3*d*.

Convention between Greece and Bulgaria. Signed at Neuilly-sur-Seine, Nov. 27, 1919. Miscellaneous No. 3, 1920. [Cmd. 589.] H.M.S.O. 1920. 1*d*.

Declaration of accession by the Serb-Croat-Slovene State to the Treaty of Peace with Austria; the Treaty between the principal Allied and Associated Powers and the Serb-Croat-Slovene State [etc.]. Signed at Paris, Dec. 5, 1919. [Cmd. 638.] H.M.S.O. 1920. 1*d*.

Treaty between the principal Allied and Associated Powers and Rumania. Signed at Paris, Dec. 9, 1919. (Treaty Series, 1920, No. 6.) [Cmd. 588.] H.M.S.O. 1920. 1*d*.

Treaty of Peace between the Allied and Associated Powers and Hungary, with Protocol and Declaration. Signed at Trianon, June 4, 1920. With map. [Cmd. 896.] H.M.S.O. 1920. 2*s*.

Treaty of Peace with Turkey. Signed at Sèvres, August 10, 1920. With maps. [Cmd. 964.] H.M.S.O. 1920. 3*s*.

Treaty between the principal Allied and Associated Powers and Greece. Signed at Sèvres, Aug. 10, 1920. [Cmd. 960.] H.M.S.O. 1920. 1½*d*.

Treaty between the Allied Powers and Greece relative to Thrace. Signed at Sèvres, Aug. 10, 1920. [Cmd. 1390.] H.M.S.O. 1921. 2*d*.

Tripartite Agreement between the British Empire, France and Italy respecting Anatolia. Signed at Sèvres, Aug. 10, 1920 With map. [Cmd. 963.] H.M.S.O. 1920. 9*d*.

(4) Reflections on the Peace.

Gérard, A. (Ambassadeur de France). L'Extrême Orient et la Paix. (Future relations of the West with Japan and China.) Payot 1919. 4 fr. 50.

Hanotaux, Gabriel. Le Traité de Versailles du 28 Juin 1919. L'Allemagne et l'Europe. Plon-Nourrit 1919. 12 fr.

Hobson, J. A. The Economics of Reparation. Allen & Unwin 1921. 1*s*.

Keynes, J. Maynard. The Economic Consequences of the Peace. Macmillan 1920. 8*s*. 6*d*.

—— A Revision of the Treaty; being a sequel to The Economic Consequences of the Peace. Macmillan 1921. 7*s*. 6*d*.

Lansing, Robert. The Big Four, and others [Venizelos, Botha, Feisal and Paderewski] of the Peace Conference. Hutchinson 1921. 8*s*. 6*d*.

Lévy, Raphael Georges. La juste paix, ou la vérité sur le Traité de Versailles. (A reply to J. M. Keynes.) Plon-Nourrit 1920. 7 fr.

Nitti, F. S. L'Europa senza pace. English transl. under title, Peaceless Europe. Cassell 1921. 12*s*.

Scott, Prof. A. P. An Introduction to the Peace Treaties. Chicago Univ. Press 1920. 12*s*.

B.—*The League of Nations and other schemes.*

Ashbee, C. R. The American League to enforce Peace. With introduction by G. Lowes Dickinson. Allen and Unwin 1916. 2*s*. 6*d*.

Atkins, Gaius G. The Maze of the Nations and the Way Out. Revell 1915. 2*s*. 6*d*.

Barclay, Sir Thomas. New Methods of Adjusting International Disputes and the Future. Constable 1918. 6*s*. 6*d*.

Barker, Ernest. A Confederation of the Nations: Its Powers and Constitution. Milford 1918. 1*s*.

Brailsford, H. N. A League of Nations (for the maintenance of peace, on the lines of the American League to enforce peace). Headley 1917. 5*s*.

Brailsford, H. N. The Covenant of Peace: an Essay on the League of Nations. Headley 1918. 7*d.*

Bryce, Viscount, and others. Proposals for the prevention of future Wars. Allen & Unwin 1917. 1*s.*

Butler, Sir Geoffrey. A Handbook to the League of Nations. With introduction by Lord R. Cecil. Longmans 1919.

Capel, Arthur. Reflections on Victory; and a Project for the Federation of Governments. Werner Laurie 1917. 2*s.*

Cecil, Lord Robert. A League of Nations. Address delivered at Birmingham, Nov. 12, 1918. Cornish 1918. 3*d.*

Darby, W. Evans. International Tribunals. A collection of various schemes which have been propounded, and of instances in the 19th century. 4th edn. Dent 1904.

De Bary, Richard. The International King. A War appeal for federal union. Longmans 1918. 2*s.*

Dickinson, G. Lowes. The Choice before us. (A sketch of the reorganisation necessary to prevent war in future.) Allen and Unwin 1917. 6*s.*

Eliot, Dr. C. W. (ex-President of Harvard). The Road to Peace. (A collection of papers contributed to various magazines.) London: Constable. 4*s.* 6*d.*

Enforced Peace. Proceedings of the First Annual National Assembly of the League to enforce peace. New York: League to Enforce Peace 1916.

Erzberger, Mathias. A League of Nations (transl. from the German). Hodder & Stoughton 1918. 7*s.* 6*d.*

Forel, Auguste. Les États-Unis de la Terre. Lausanne: Peytrequin 1915. 60 c.

Forsyth, Principal P. T. The roots of a World Commonwealth. Hodder & Stoughton 1918. 4*d.*

Goldsmith, Robert. A League to enforce peace. New York: Macmillan 1917.

Gore, Right Rev. Charles. The League of Nations: the opportunity of the Churches. Hodder & Stoughton 1918. 1*s.*

Grey, Viscount. The League of Nations. Oxford Univ. Press 1918. 3*d.*

Handbook for Speakers on a League of Nations. Compiled by the L. of N. Society. Allen & Unwin 1918. 1*s.* 6*d.*

Hart, Heber, L, LL.D The Bulwarks of Peace. (Criticism of the proposed League of Nations). Methuen 1918. 3*s.* 6*d.*

Heath, C. The Pacific Settlement of International Disputes. 1917.

Hecht, J. S. Economic War and a League of Nations; or why Germany must pay. King 1918. 6*d.*

Henderson, Rt. Hon. Arthur, The League of Nations and Labour. Milford 1918. 3*d.*

Hennessy, Jean. L'Organisation fédérale de la Société des nations. Les Principes d'une constitution internationale et un projet de constitution. (Divers articles publiés en 1917 dans L'Œuvre). Wellhoff et Roche. 1918.

Hobson, J. A. Towards International Government. Allen and Unwin 1915. 2*s.* 6*d.*

Hooper, C. E. The wider outlook beyond the World War. An essay on permanent peace by means of an International Council. Watts. 6*d.*

Hyde, H. E. The Two Roads: International Government or Militarism. King 1916. 1*s.* 3*d.*

—— The International Solution. Will Great Britain lead the way? (Scheme for an International Parliament, Law Court, and Army). Grellier 1917. 6*d.*

—— The International Solution. Allen & Unwin 1918. 3*s.* 6*d.*

Jacobs, A. T. Neutrality *versus* Justice. An essay on International Relations. Fisher Unwin 1917. 2*s.*

Kant, Immanuel. Perpetual Peace: a Philosophical Essay, 1795. Transl. with introduction and notes by M. Campbell Smith. Cheap edn. Allen & Unwin 1915. 2*s.*

Keen, Frank Noel. World in Alliance: a Plan for Preventing Future Wars. Southwood 1915. 1*s.*

—— A League of Nations with large Powers. With Preface by Sir W. H. Dickinson. Allen & Unwin 1918. 1*s.*

Kirby, Augusta. The Way of Peace. Methuen 1916. 3*s.* 6*d.*

League of Nations, A. Draft Agreement for, presented to the Plenary Inter-Allied Conference of Feb. 14, 1919. Miscellaneous, No. 1 (1919). [Cmd. 2.] H.M.S.O. 1919. 1*d.*

League of Nations: Covenant of the. With a Commentary thereon. Miscellaneous, No. 3 (1919). [Cmd. 151.] H.M.S.O. 1919. 2*d.*

League of Nations, A. Scheme of Organisation prepared by a sub-committee of the L. of N. Society. With a foreword by Sir W. H. Dickinson, M.P. League of Nations Society 1918. 3*d.*

Lepert, H. Projet de constitution pour la Société des Nations. 5, Cité Cardinal-Lemoine 1917. 1 fr.

Leroy, Maxime. L'Ère Wilson: la Société des nations. Giard et Brière 1917. 3 fr. 50.

Lippmann, Walter. The Stakes of Diplomacy. On the means of rendering wars less frequent. New York: Holt 1915. $1.25.

Mackaye, Percy. Substitute for War. With Introduction by Irving Fisher. Prefatory letters by Viscount Bryce and Norman Angell. Macmillan 1915. *2s.*

Maclagan, O. F. Britain's Opportunity: or, How to Make Victory Permanent. Maclagan, 35, Monsell Road, N. *6d.*

—— How Britain can Abolish War. E. R. Duke, 35, Monsell Road, N. 6d.

—— International Prohibition of War. 5th edn., enlarged. Duke 1015. *3d.*

—— Mutual Defence of Nations. Suggestions of an international scheme for the maintenance of a world-peace. 6th edn. Published for the International Defence League. Letchworth: Garden City Press 1916. *2s. 6d.*

—— Proposals for an Immediate Council of the Nations, as submitted to the British, Allied and Neutral Governments. Letchworth: Garden City Press 1916. *6d.*

—— The Way to Victory. A scheme for an immediate League of Nations. With an introduction by C. A. McCurdy, M.P. Duke 1918.

Marburg, Theodore. Draft convention for League of Nations. Description and comment. Macmillan 1918. 25 c.

—— League of Nations, A. A chapter in the history of the movement. New York: Macmillan 1918. 50 c.

—— A League of Nations: Its principles examined. New York: Macmillan 1918. 60 c.

Mater, André. La Société des Nations. Didier 1918. 1 fr. 25.

Matthaei, Louise. Reasonable Direction of Force. A plea for investigation before war. (Papers for War Time). Milford 1915. *2d.*

Memorial. By the Swiss Committee for the Study of the Principles of a durable Treaty of Peace. Published also in French and German. Olten: Trösch 1915. 1 fr. 25.

Milhaud, Prof. Edgar. Du Droit de la Force à la Force du Droit. In favour of an international force to compel regard for treaties. Geneva: Atar 1916. 1 f.

—— La Société des Nations. Grasset 1918. 4 fr.

Minor, Prof. Raleigh C. A Republic of Nations. A study of the organization of a Federal League of Nations (by an American Professor). Oxf. Univ. Press 1918. *12s. 6d.*

Moch, Gaston. La Garantie de la Société des Nations (conditions de la paix future). Rivière 1917. 40 c.

Mügge, Max A. The Parliament of Man (Bibliography, and Appendix of Peace Conventions, etc.) Daniel 1916. *6s.*

Murray, Prof. Gilbert. The League of Nations and the Democratic Idea. (A practical discussion). Milford 1918. *6d.*

O.B.I.T. Great War: a Plan for Peace: a World State. Salmond 1915. 6*d.*

Olivier, Sir Sydney. The League of Nations and Primitive Peoples. Milford 1918. 3*d.*

Oppenheim, Prof. L. The League of Nations and its problems. Three lectures. Longmans 1919. 6*s.*

Organisation centrale pour une paix durable. Recueil de Rapport sur les différents points du Programme-minimum. The Hague: Nijhoff 1916.

Otlet, P. Constitution mondiale de la Société des Nations. Crès 1918. 3 fr. 50.

Paish, Sir George. A permanent League of Nations. Fisher Unwin 1918. 6*s.*

Pares, Prof. Bernard. The League of Nations, and other questions of Peace. Hodder & Stoughton 1918. 3*s.* 6*d.*

Penn, William. An essay towards the Present and Future Peace of Europe. First published in 1693-4. Bellows 1915. 2*d.*

—— The Peace of Europe: the Fruits or Solitude and other Writings. With introduction by Joseph Besse. Everyman's Library. Dent 1915. 1*s.*

Phillimore, Lord. Schemes for promoting and maintaining a general peace. (Peace Handbooks, published under direction of the Foreign Office, No. 160.) H.M.S.O. 1920. 2*s.*

Pollard, Prof. A. F. The League of Nations in History. Milford 1918. 3*d.*

—— The League of Nations. An historical argument. Milford 1918. 1*s.*

Pollock, Sir Frederick. The League of Nations and the coming Rule of Laws (mainly a study of the scheme proposed by Lord Parker). Milford 1918. 3*d.*

Pollock, Rt. Hon. Sir F. The League of Nations. Stevens 1820. 10s.

Ponsonby, Arthur, M.P. The basis of International Authority. (Peace and Freedom pamphlets). League of Peace and Freedom 1916. 1*d.*

Ponti, Ettore. La Guerre dei Popoli, e la futura Confederazione Europea, secondo un metodo anologico storico. Milan: Hoepli. 4 l.

—— La Guerre des peuples et la future confédération européenne. Traduit de l'Italien. Preface par M. Stéphen Pichon. Alcan 1917. 3 fr. 50.

Project of a League of Nations. Contributions by G. P. Gooch, L. S. Woolf, T. J. Lawrence, Rt. Hon. W. H. Dickinson, and others. League of Nations Society 1917. 6*d.*

Redmond-Howard, L. G. Ireland, the Peace Conference, and the League of Nations. Dublin: Kiersey 1918. 3*s*. 6*d*.

Reinsch, Paul S. Public International Unions. Boston: World Peace Bureau. $1.65.

Rousseau, Jean Jacques. A Lasting Peace through the Federation of Europe, and the The State of War. Transl., edited by Prof. C. E. Vaughan. Constable 1917. 2*s*.

Schwan, A. Les bases d'une paix durable. Alcan 1917. Transl under title The Foundations of Permanent Peace. Grant Richards 1918. 5*s*.

Scott, J. Brown. The Status of the International Court of Justice. With appendix of addresses and official documents (Carnegie Endowment). Oxf. Univ. Press 1918. 6*s*. 6*d*.

Séché, A. Les guerres d'enfers. On the problem of ensuring permanent peace. Sansot. 3 f. 50.

Shumaker, E. Ellsworth. World Crisis and the Way to Peace. Putnam 1915. 2*s*. 6*d*.

Smutz, Rt. Hon. General J. C. The League of Nations: a practical suggestion. Hodder & Stoughton 1918. 6*d*.

Speeches on a League of Nations (includes speeches by Lord Bryce, Lord Hugh Cecil, Gen. Smuts, and others). League of Nations Society 1917. 2*d*.

Spire, E. De quelques garanties d'une paix durable. Rue Vaneau 36 1916. 3 f.

Stallybrass, W. T. S. A Society of States; or Sovereignty, Independence and Equality in a League of Nations. Kegan Paul 1918. 1*s*. 9*d*.

Trygaeus (pseud.). United States of the World: an Utopian essay towards a better ordering of the affairs of men. Routledge 1916. 6*d*.

Waechter, Sir Max. After the War: The United States of Europe. Longmans 1916. 1*d*.

War obviated by an International Police. A series of essays, written in various countries. The Hague: Nijhoff 1916. fl. 1.25.

Weeks, H. T. How to assure future Peace. (Aims and methods of a League of Nations.) Murby & Co. 1917. 2*d*.

Wehberg, Dr. Hans. The problem of an International Court of Justice. Transl. from the German (Carnegie Endowment). Oxf. Univ. Press 1918. 7*s*. 6*d*.

Weiss, José. The Alternative: Armed Peace or Federation. Chancery Lane Printing Works. 1*d*.

Wells, H. G. The Peace of the World. On the prospects of permanent international peace. Daily Chronicle Office. 6*d*.

Wells, H. G. What is Coming? A forecast of things after the war. Cassell 1916. 6*s*.

Win the War for Permanent Peace. 46 addresses at the National Convention of the League to enforce Peace, May 16 and 17, 1918. New York: The League 1918. n.p.

Withers, Hartley. The League of Nations: Its Economic Aspect. Milford 1918. 3*d*.

Woolf, L. S. International Government. Two Reports prepared for the Fabian Research Department. Allen & Unwin 1916. 6*s*.

—— (edr.). The Framework of a lasting Peace. (A summary of seven schemes for a League of Nations, with introduction by Editor.) Allen & Unwin 1917. 4*s*. 6*d*.

Wrangel, F. von. Internationale Anarchie oder Verfassung? Zürich: Füssli 1915. 60 c.

C.—*Reconstruction and after-war Problems.*

After Victory. By an Amateur Officer. Melrose 1917. 5*s*.

After War: a Future Policy. (Concordat between Capital and Labour.) St. Catherine Press 1918. 3*d*.

Angell, Norman. The Political Conditions of Allied Success. A plea for the protective Union of the Democracies. Putnams 1918. 7*s*. 6*d*.

Bankes, C. Nugent. National Regeneration, and a way thereto. Some reflections and a suggestion. Reprinted from the Nineteenth Century. Allen & Donaldson 1917.

Betts, C. H., and Watts, Mathias. The Next War. (The Economic War by which Britain is to establish her commercial supremacy.) Simpkin Marshall 1916. 1*s*.

Bodley, J. H. Education after the War. By the Headmaster of Bedale's School. Blackwell 1917. 3*s*. 6*d*.

Butler, President N. Murray. A World in Ferment. Interpretations of the War for a New World. Scribner 1917. $1.25.

Buxton, C. R. and D. E. The World after the War. Allen & Unwin 1919. 7*s*. 6*d*.

Cambon, Victor. Notre Avenir. Payot 1916. 3 fr. 50.

Carey, Alfred E. War's Aftermath. On the division of territory after the war. McBride. 6*d*.

Carter, Huntly (edr.) Industrial Reconstruction. A Symposium on the Industrial Situation after the war and how to meet it. Fisher Unwin 1917. 6*s*.

Chapman, S. J. (edr.) Labour and Capital after the War. Essays by Bishop of Birmingham, Sir Hugh Bell, J. R. Clynes, and others. Introduction by Rt. Hon. J. H. Whitley. Murray 1918. 6*s*.

Clifford, W. G. The Ex-Soldier, by himself. (A study of the ex-soldier problem.) Black 1916. *2s. 6d.*

Coal Trade after the War, Report of the Departmental Committee appointed by the Board of Trade to consider the Position of the. With Appendix. [Cd. 9093.] H.M.S.O. 1918. *4d.*

Commercial and Industrial Policy, Committee on. Interim Report on certain Essential Industries. [Cd. 9032.] H.M.S.O. 1918. *2d.*

—— Interim Report on the Importation of Goods from the present Enemy Countries after the War. [Cd. 9033.] H.M.S.O. 1918. *1d.*

—— Interim Report on the Treatment of Exports from the U.K. and British Overseas Possessions and the Conservation of the Resources of the Empire during the Transitional Period after the War. [Cd. 9034.] H.M.S.O. 1918. *2d.*

Courtney, W. L. Armageddon—and after. Chapman & Hall. *1s.*

D'Acosta, Uriel. Peace Problems in Economics and Finance. (An anticipation of after-war conditions.) Kegan Paul 1917. *2s. 6d.*

Daudet, Léon. Hors du joug allemand. On the conduct of international relations after the war. Nouv. Libr. Nationale. 3 fr. 50.

D'Aunet, B. Après la Guerre : pour remettre de l'ordre dans la maison. Préface de M. Etienne Lamy. Payot 1917. 3 fr. 50.

Dawson, W. Harbutt (edr.) After-war Problems. (Essays by Lord Cromer, Lord Haldane, Mrs. Fawcett, Prof. Alfred Marshall and others.) Allen & Unwin 1916. *7s. 6d.*

Denman, Thomas. The Discharged Consumptive Soldier. Bale & Danielssohn 1918. *1s.*

Dickinson, G. Lowes. After the War. Fifield 1916. *6d.*

Dontenville, J. Après la guerre : les Allemagnes, la France, la Belgique, et la Hollande. Floury 1915. 60 c.

Edsall, E. W. The Coming Scraps of Paper. (An essay on the finance of the future.) Allen & Unwin 1916. *2s. 6d.*

Electrical Trades after the War, Report of the Departmental Committee appointed by the Board of Trade to consider the Position of the. [Cd. 9072.] With Appendices. H.M.S.O. 1918. *2d.*

Elements, The, of Reconstruction. Reprinted from The Times, with an introduction by Viscount Milner. Nisbet 1916. *1s.*

Emard, Paul. Dans la nuit laborieuse : essai sur la ré-éducation des soldats aveugles. Avec 44 illustrations. Préface de M. Brieux. (À l'établissement de Reuilly, à Paris.) Victorion 1917. 5 fr.

Empire, The, and the Future. (A reprint of six lectures delivered in the autumn of 1915 at King's College, London.) Macmillan 1916. 2*s*.

Empire Settlement. Report of the Committee appointed to consider the Measures to be taken for settling within the Empire Ex-service Men who may desire to Emigrate after the War. [Cd. 8672.] H.M.S.O. 1917. 9*d*.

Engineering Trades after the War, Report of the Departmental Committee appointed by the Board of Trade to consider the Position of the. [Cd. 9073.] H.M.S.O. 1918. 6*d*.

Esher, Viscount. After the War. (Essays dealing with the Crown, the Cabinet, War Aims, etc.) Murray 1918.

Fernau, Hermann. Durch . . zur Demokratie. Berne: Benteli 1917.

—— —— Transl. under title, The Coming Democracy. Constable 1917. 6*s*.

Fried, Alfred H. Europäische Wiederherstellung. Zürich: Füssli 1915. 2 fr. 50.

—— Transl. under title, The Restoration of Europe. New York: Macmillan Co. 1916. 4*s*. 6*d*.

Gardner, Lucy (edr.). The Hope for Society. Essays on Social Reconstruction after the War. By various writers. Bell 1917. 3*s*.

Geddes, Patrick, and Branford, Victor. The Coming Polity: a study in Reconstruction. Williams and Norgate 1917. 5*s*.

Gide, Ch. La Politique commerciale après la guerre. (Faudra-t-il après la paix boycotter l'Allemagne? Non!) Ligue des droits de l'homme 1917. 40 c.

—— Transl. under title, Commercial Policy after the War. Preface by Rt. Hon. J. M. Robertson. Cobden Club 1917. 3*d*.

Gray, H. B., and Turner, S. Eclipse or Empire. (On the necessity of an educational revolution.) Nisbet 1916. 2*s*.

Hall, A. D. Agriculture after the War. (Based on the Supplementary Report of the Departmental Committee on Food Supplies, 1915.) Murray 1916. 3*s*. 6*d*.

Hamilton, General Sir Ian. The Millennium? Arnold 1918. 2*s*. 6*d*.

Hatt, C. W. The Future of the Disabled Soldier. Fisher Unwin 1917. 6*s*.

Hobson, J. A. Democracy after the War. Allen & Unwin 1917. 4*s*. 6*d*.

Hodge, Harold. In the Wake of the War. Parliament or Imperial Government? Lane 1917. 5*s*.

Hopkinson, Sir Alfred. Rebuilding Britain. (A general view of Reconstruction Problems.) Cassell 1918. 5*s*.

Hurd, Percy and Archibald. New Empire Partnership: Defence, Commerce, Policy. Murray 1915. 6*s*.

Industrial Councils and Trade Boards. Memorandum by the Minister of Reconstruction and the Minister of Labour. [Cd. 9085.] H.M.S.O. 1918. 1*d*.

Iron and Steel Trades after the War, Report of the Departmental Committee appointed by the Board of Trade to consider the Position of the. With Appendix. [Cd. 9071.] H.M.S.O. 1918. 6*d*.

Jane, L. C. The Nations at War; the Birth of a New Era. A forecast of political and moral results. Dent. 2*s*. 6*d*.

Knight, Alfred E. World-War and After: an Inquiry and a Forecast. Morgan & Scott 1915. 2*s*.

Lagàrdère, le Chanoine. France . . . demain! Aux ouvriers et ouvrières de reconstruction après guerre. Téqui 1917. 3 fr. 50.

L'Avenir de la France. (Plans of 23 experts.) Introduction by Maurice Herbette. Alcan 1918. 11 fr.

Lavergne, B. L'Union commerciale des alliés après la guerre. (Faudra-t-il après la paix boycotter l'Allemagne? Oui!) Alcan 1917. 1 fr. 50.

Le Bon, Dr. Gustave. Premières Conséquences de la Guerre. (After-war mental conditions.) Flammarion 1917. 3 fr. 50.

Lodge, Prof. Sir Oliver. The War and After. Methuen.

Louis, Paul. L'Europe nouvelle. Alcan 1915.

Lynch, Frederick. Last War: a Study of things present and to come. Revell 1915. 2*s*. 6*d*.

Macdonald, J. Ramsay, M.P. Socialism after the War. Nat. Labour Press 1918. 1*s*.

Meyer, H. R. After the War: the Changes and Chances that will come with Peace. Simpkin, Marshall. 2*s*.

M'Ewan, Col. R. D., and Dallas, John. Demobilization. A Glasgow scheme. Menzies 1917. 2*d*.

Maillard, C. Le Socialisme et la reconstitution intégrale de la France. (Addressed by a Socialist to Socialists, and advocating the dismemberment of Germany.) Attinger Frères 1916. 1 fr.

Marcosson, Isaac F. The War after the War. (On the future of trade.) John Lane 1917. 5*s*.

Mawson, Thomas H. An Imperial Obligation: Industrial Villages for partially disabled sailors and soldiers. Introduction by Sir Douglas Haig. Grant Richards 1917. 4*s*. 6*d*.

Mazel, Henri. La nouvelle cité de France. Réorganisation nationale d'après guerre. Alcan 1918. 5 fr. 50.

Ministry of Labour. Openings in Industry suitable for Disabled Sailors and Soldiers. Reports upon:—I, Attendants at Electricity Sub-stations; II, Employment in Picture Theatres; III, Tailoring (Retail Bespoke); IV, Agricultural Motor Tractor Work; V, Furniture Trade; VI, Leather Goods Trade; VII, Boot and Shoe Making and Repairing; VIII, Gold, Silver, Jewellery, and Watch and Clock Jobbing; IX, Dental Mechanics; X, Aircraft Manufacture. H.M.S.O. 1917. 1*d*. each.

—— —— Reports (Nos. XI-XXIV) upon:—Wholesale Tailoring, Boot and Shoe Manufacture, Basket Making Trade, Engineering, Printing, etc., Picture Frame Making, Brush Making, Lettering, Pharmacists, etc. H.M.S.O. 1918. 1*d*. each (1 at 2*d*.).

—— Demobilisation and Resettlement. Regulations made by the Military Service (Civil Liabilities) Committee, with the concurrence of the Lords Commissioners of H.M. Treasury. [Cmd. 88.] H.M.S.O. 1919. 1*d*.

Ministry of Pensions. Professional Re-education and other questions of interest to Soldiers and Sailors disabled by the War, Inter-Allied Conference, held at Paris, May 8 to 12, 1917, for the Study of, Report on. H.M.S.O. 1917. 3*d*.

—— Treatment and Training of Disabled Men, Instructions and Notes on the. H.M.S.O. 1917. 3*d*.

Ministry of Reconstruction. Sub-Committee on Relations between Employers and Employed. Interim Report on Joint Standing Industrial Councils. [Cd. 8606.] H.M.S.O. 1917. 1*d*.

—— Reconstruction Committee. Final Report of the Foresry Sub-Committee. With Appendices. [Cd. 8881.] H.M.S.O. 1918. 1*s*.

—— Commissions and Committees set up to deal with questions which will arise at the close of the war, A List of. [Cd. 8916.] H.M.S.O. 1918. 4*d*.

—— Committee on Relations between Employers and Employed:—(1) Supplementary Report on Works Committees. [Cd. 9001.] (2) Second Report on Joint Standing Industrial Councils. [Cd. 9002.] H.M.S.O. 1918. 1*d*. *each*.

—— Agricultural Policy Sub-Committee. Home-grown Food Supplies, Report on the Methods of effecting an increase in. . . . With Reports by Sir Matthew G. Wallace, and Appendices. [Cd. 9079.] H.M.S.O. 1918. 1*s*. 3*d*.

—— —— Summaries of Evidence taken. With Index. [Cd. 9080.] H.M.S.O. 1918. 1*s*. 3*d*.

Ministry of Reconstruction. Committee on Relations between Employers and Employed. Report on Conciliation and Arbitration. [Cd. 9081.] [Superseded by Cd. 9099.] H.M.S.O. 1918. 1*d*.

—— Coal Conservation Committee. Final Report. With Appendices and Maps. [Cd. 9084.] H.M.S.O. 1918. 1*s*.

—— Housing in England and Wales. Memorandum by the Advisory Housing Panel on the Emergency Problem. With Appendix. [Cd. 9087.] H.M.S.O. 1918. 2*d*.

—— Committee on Relations between Employers and Employed. Report on Conciliation and Arbitration. [Cd. 9099.] [In substitution of Cd. 9081.] H.M.S.O. 1918. 1*d*.

—— Reports of the Committee appointed by the Attorney-General to consider the Legal Interpretation of the term Period of the War. [Cd. 9100.] H.M.S.O. 1918. 6*d*.

—— Adult Education Committee. Interim Report. Industrial and Social Conditions in relation to Adult Education. [Cd. 9107.] H.M.S.O. 1918. 3*d*.

—— Civil War Workers' Committee. 1st (Interim) Report. [Cd. 9117.] H.M.S.O. 1918. 2*d*.

—— Committee on Relations between Employers and Employed. Final Report. [Cd. 9153.] H.M.S.O. 1918. 1*d*.

—— Civil War Workers' Committee. 2nd, 3rd, 4th and 5th (Interim) Reports. [Cd. 9192.] H.M.S.O. 1918. 3*d*.

—— Building Industry, Position of the, after the War. Report of the Committee. With Appendix. [Cd. 9197.] H.M.S.O. 1918. 3d.

—— Substitute Labour. Final Report of the Civil War Workers' Committee. [Cd. 9228.] H.M.S.O. 1918. 1*d*.

—— Women's Advisory Committee. Report on the Domestic Service Problems; with Reports by Sub-Committees on Training, Machinery of Distribution, Organisation, and Conditions. [Cmd. 67.] H.M.S.O. 1919. 3*d*.

—— Local Reconstruction Organisations. Report of Advisory Committee. With Appendix. [Cmd. 136.] H.M.S.O. 1919. 1*d*.

—— Women's Advisory Committee. Report of the Sub-Committee appointed to consider the Position after the War of Women holding Temporary Appointments in Government Departments. [Cmd. 199.] H.M.S.O. 1919. 1*d*.

—— Returned Sailors and Soldiers, Employment on the Land of. Report of the Committee of Section IV of the Advisory Council; with a Report by Mr. R. V. Lennard. H.M.S.O. 1919. 1*s*.

Ministry of Reconstruction. Reconstruction Problems. Monographs dealing with Labour Conditions, Land Settlement, Public Health, Business Management, Aerial Transport, Industrial Research, etc., etc. Nos. 10-38. H.M.S.O. 1919. *2d.* each.

P., G. C. Land after the War: a Business Proposition. St. Catherine Press 1915. *1s.*

P. D. Sur l'Après Guerre. (L'état moral de la société avant et depuis la guerre.) Giard & Brière 1917. 1 fr. 50.

Poynter, Ambrose. The Coming War. (The Industrial Conflict of the future.) Murray 1916. *3s. 6d.*

Problems of Reconstruction. Lectures and Addresses delivered at the Hampstead Garden Suburb, August, 1917. With introduction by the Marquess of Crewe. (Manch. Univ. Publications.) Longmans 1918. *5s.*

Ramsay, Alex. Terms of Industrial Peace. Constable 1917. *3s.*

Rawson, F. L. The War and the great World-change to follow. Lecture. Crystal Press 1915. *1s. 6d.*

Recalled to Life. (A journal, edited by Lord Charnwood, dealing with the return to civil life of disabled soldiers and sailors.) Bale & Danielssohn 1918. *2s.*

Religious Reconstruction after the War. A Cambridge Programme, by James Plowden-Wardlaw and others. (St. Edward's Cambridge Series.) Scott 1916. *2s. 6d.*

Ritchie, D. L. The Church After the War. Papers by Congregationalists. Congregational Union of England and Wales 1916. *2d.*

Ritzeman, T. P. Temperance, Taxation and Housing Reform: the Lesson of the War. 2nd edn. Blackburn: Northern Telegraph Office 1915. *2d.*

Robinson, J. J. National Reconstruction. A study in practical politics and statesmanship. Hurst & Blackett 1918. *2s. 6d.*

Russell, Bertrand. Principles of Social Reconstruction. Allen and Unwin 1916. *6s.*

Rutherford, V. H. Commonwealth or Empire. Headley 1917. *1s. 3d.*

Scott, W. R. Economic problems of Peace after War. (The Jevons Lectures, delivered at Univ. College 1917.) Camb. Univ. Press 1917. *4s. 6d.*

—— —— (Second series.) The Stanley Jevons lectures at Univ. College in 1918. Camb. Univ. Press 1918. *6s.*

Seignobos, Prof. C., and others. La Réorganisation de la France: Conférences faites à l'École des hautes études sociales (novembre 1915 à janvier 1916). Alcan 1917. 3 fr. 50.

Settlement and Employment on the Land in England and Wales of Discharged Sailors and Soldiers. Part II of the Final Report of the Departmental Committee appointed to consider the. [Cd. 8277.] H.M.S.O. 1916. 4*d*.

—— Departmental Committee on Minutes of Evidence. [Cd. 8347.] H.M.S.O. 1916. 3*s*. 3*d*.

Springer, Leonard. Some Aspects of Financial and Commercial After-war Conditions. King 1918. 2*s*. 6*d*.

Storey, Harold. The Paris Conference and Trade after the War. Fisher Unwin 1916. 2*d*.

Textile Trades after the War. Report of the Departmental Committee appointed by the Board of Trade to consider the position of the. [Cd. 9070.] H.M.S.O. 1918. 1*s*. 3*d*.

Toynbee, Arnold J. Nationality and the War. An essay on the Reconstruction of Europe after the War. Dent. 7*s*. 6*d*.

—— The New Europe. Some essays in reconstruction. Dent 1915. 1*s*. 6*d*.

Unwin, Raymond. The War: and What After? Letchworth: Garden City Press. 1*s*. 6*d*. & 6*d*.

Urban, Henri. L'Effort de demain. Les grands problèmes économiques. Perrin 1917. 3 fr. 50.

Village Life after the War. Reports of conferences on the development of Rural Life (1917). Headley 1918. 1*s*.

Villiers, Brougham. Britain after the Peace. Revolution or Reconstruction? Fisher Unwin 1918. 8*s*. 6*d*.

Vinogradoff, Prof. S. P. (edr.). The Reconstruction of Russia. (Essays by various authors.) Oxford Univ. Press 1919. 1*s*. 6*d*.

Warburg, F. S. Reconstruction during the War. (A guide to the literature on reconstruction.) Charity Organisation Society 1917. ½*d*. postage.

Warman, W. H. The Soldier Colonists (a plan for post-bellum emigration). With a preface by Lord Selborne. Chatto & Windus 1918. 5*s*.

Webb, Sidney, and Freeman, Arthur. Great Britain after the War. Being facts and figures, quotations and queries [etc.] designed to help inquiries . . . with regard to trade, employment, wages, prices [etc.]. Allen & Unwin 1916. 1*s*.

Weber, M. Parliament und Regierung im neugeordneten Deutschland. 1918. 5 mk.

Wells, H. G. What is Coming? A forecast of things after the War. Cassell 1916. 6*s*.

When Peace Comes. The Way of Industrial Reconstruction. Fabian Society 1916. 2*d*.

Whetham, W. C. D. The War and the Nation. A study in Constructive Politics Murray 1917. 6*s*.

Wingate, Sir Andrew. Before and after the War: History and Prophecy. Holmes 1915. *6d.*

Women in Industry. Report of the War Cabinet Committee on. [Cd. 135.] H.M.S.O. 1919. *1s. 6d.*

D.—*Pacificism and Anti-pacificism: Conscientious objectors: Union of Democratic Control.*

Addams, Jane. Newer Ideals of Peace. New edn. Macmillan 1916. *2s.*

Allen, J. W. The Danger of Peace. A lecture, showing the evils of a premature pacification. Bell 1915. *1s.*

Aulard, A. La Paix future d'après la Révolution Français et Kant. A lecture. Colin. 50 c.

Bell, Clive. Peace at Once. (National Honour is all rubbish. Better have allowed Germany to conquer France, Russia and ourselves.) National Labour Press. *6d.*

Browne, Porter Emerson. Peace at Any Price. Appleton 1916. *2s.*

Carpenter, Edward. Never Again! A protest and a warning addressed to the Peoples of Europe. Allen & Unwin 1916. *6d.*

Chesterton, Cecil. The Perils of Peace. With introduction by Hilaire Belloc. Werner Laurie 1916. *2s.*

Commentitus (pseud.). Great War for the Greater Peace: a Conversation in the Year 2020. Murby 1915. *1s.*

Cosby, D. S. A. Towards Universal Peace. Bedford: Beds. Times. *7d.*

Conscientious Objectors, Employment of. Rules made by the Committee on. [Cd. 8627.] H.M.S.O. 1917. *1d.*

Conscientious Objectors, Committee on Employment of. Rules. [Cd. 8550.] H.M.S.O. 1917. *1d.*

Conscientious Objectors. Additional Rules of the Committee on Employment of. [Cd. 8884.] H.M.S.O. 1917. *1d.*

Cosmos (pseud.). The Basis of a Durable Peace. (Articles contributed to the New York Times, Nov.-Dec. 1916.) Scribners 1917.

Coulton, G. G. The Main Illusions of Pacifism. A criticism of Mr. Norman Angell and of the Union of Democratic Control. Cambridge: Bowes 1916. *5s.*

—— Pacifist Illusions: a Criticism of the Union of Democratic Control. Cambridge: Bowes 1915. *6d.*

Dickinson, G. Lowes. After the War. How to avoid war in future. Fifield. *6d.*

—— The War and the Way Out. False theory of the State the chief cause of war. Bonner.

Dickinson, G. Lowes. Snowden, P., and others. Towards a Lasting Settlement. Allen & Unwin 1915. 2*s.* 6*d.*

Duckers, J. Scott. Handed Over. Prison experiences of the author, a conscientious objector, under the Military Service Act. Foreword by T. Harvey, M.P. Daniel 1917. 1*s.* 6*d.*

Dunlop, H. The Supreme Will: or The Danger of a Premature Peace. (The author is Dutch by birth, but Scottish by descent.) The Hague: Nijhoff 1916.

Faguet, Emile. Le Pacifisme. Soc. Franç. d'Imprimerie 1908. 3 fr. 50.

Fielding-Hall, H. The Way of Peace. Hurst & Blackett. 10*s.* 6*d.*

Fortescue, Rev. Adrian. A Word with Conscientious Objectors. Catholic Truth Society 1916. 1*d.*

Fry, Isabel. To Them that Say: Peace, peace, When there is no Peace. Miss Fry, 31, Gayton Road, Hampstead.

George, Samuel. Woman's World-Wide Work with War: or, Preparing for the Great International Peace. Power Book Co. 1915. 7*d.*

Goblet D'Alviella. Le vrai et le faux pacifisme. Avec une carte. Alcan 1917. 1 fr. 20.

—— Transl. under title The True and the False Pacifism. (By the Vice-President of the Belgian Senate.) Fisher Unwin 1917. 6*d.*

Grane, William Leighton. The Passing of War: a Study in Things that Make for Peace. 4th edn. Macmillan 1914. 2*s.* 6*d.*

Greenwood, George A. Civilization in the Melting-pot. With preface by Arthur Ponsonby. Headley 1915. 1*s.*

Guy-Grand, Georges. Les Sophismes de Paix. Grasset 1918. 75 c.

Hallowes, Mrs. J. S. Mothers of Men and Militarism. An appeal against war, with suggestions for a League of Women to oppose it. Headley. 1*s.*

Harrison, Jane E. Peace with Patriotism. 2nd edn. Deighton Bell 1915. 2*d.*

Hayward, C. W. What is Diplomacy? Written on democratic and pacifist lines. Grant Richards 1916. 2*s.* 6*d.*

Heath, Carl. Pacifism in Time of War. The work of a thorough-going pacifist. Headley. 1*s.*

Heitland, W. E. If We Win: a Search for a Path to Stable Peace. With some remarks on the so-called Union of Democratic Control. Cambridge: Heffer. 3*d.*

Herron, G. D. The Menace of Peace (against a compromise). Allen & Unwin 1916. 2*s.* 6*d.*

Hobhouse, Mrs. Henry. I Appeal unto Cæsar. (On the wrongs of the conscientious objector.) With an introduction by Prof. Gilbert Murray. Allen & Unwin 1917. 1*s.*

Independent Labour Party's Report of the Norwich Conference, April 1915. St. Bride's House, Salisbury Square. 3*d.*

Innes, Charles E. Britain's Great Opportunity to Kill Militarism and to Secure Permanent Peace. Birmingham Printers. 1*d.*

James, Stanley B. The Man who Dared. (Story and defence of the Conscientious Objectors.) Daniel 1917. 1*s.*

Key, Ellen. War, Peace, and the Future. A consideration of Nationalism and Internationalism, and of the relation of women to war. New York: Putnam 1916. $1.50.

Kitson, Arthur. The Great Pacifist Conspiracy. Stamford: Dolby Bros. 1918. 3*d.*

Krehbirl, Prof. E. Nationalism, War, and Society: a Study of Nationalism and its Concomitant, War, in their Relation to Civilisation [etc.]. With introduction by Norman Angell. New York: Macmillan 1916. 6*s.* 6*d.*

Looking Towards Peace (discusses a possible settlement). Friend's Peace Comm. 1916. 1*d.*

McClure, S. S. Obstacles to Peace. Houghton, Mifflin 1917. $2.00.

McCormick, Harold F. Via Pacis. How terms of peace can be automatically prepared while the war is still going on. A suggestion offered by an American. Allen & Unwin 1916. 1*s.*

Marshall, Henry Rutgers. War and the Ideal of Peace. A study of those characteristics of man that result in war, and of the means by which they may be controlled. Unwin 1916. 4*s.* 6*d.*

Mason, E. Williamson. Made Free in Prison. (By a C.O.) With introductory note by Edward Carpenter. Allen & Unwin 1918. 2*s.* 6*d.*

Moody, R. A. Ending the War. A plea for an understanding, viz., of the real mind of Germany. Glasgow: Smith. 2*d.*

Morel, E. D. The Union of Democratic Control. A defence, reprinted from the Contemporary Review, July 1915. Contemporary Review Co.

—— Africa and the Peace of Europe (on neutralisation, internationalisation, etc.). Nat. Labour Press 1917. 2*s.*

Nordentoft, Dr. Severin. Practical Pacifism and its Adversaries. With an introduction by G. K. Chesterton. Allen & Unwin 1917. 4*s.* 6*d.*

P.-D. De l'Or, de la Gloire et du Sang (quel profit matériel vienne en compensation du préjudice causé par la guerre). Giard et Brière 1918. 2 fr.

Peake, Prof. A. S. Prisoners of Hope (conscientious objectors). Allen & Unwin 1918. 1*s.* 6*d.*

Phillips, E. A. W. Democratic Constitutional Reform: or, After the War. Griffiths 1915. 1*s.*

Picton, Harold. Is it to be Hate? An essay in war time. Allen & Unwin 1915. 3*d.*

Ponsonby, Arthur, M.P. Democracy and Diplomacy. A plea for popular control of foreign policy. Methuen. 2*s.* 6*d.*

Potter, B. Open Letter to the Union of Democratic Control. Godalming: Lindsey.

Price, Theodore. Crucifiers and Crucified. An account of his experiences, by a Conscientious Objector. The Bungalow, Alvechurch, Worc. 1917. 1*s.* 6*d.*

Quin, Malcolm. The Problem of Human Peace: Studied from the Point of View of Scientific Catholicism. Fisher Unwin 1916. 7*s.* 6*d.*

Rimington, A. W. The Conscience of Europe. The War and the Future. Allen & Unwin 1918. 3*s.* 6*d.*

Roux, M. de. Le Défaitisme et les Manœuvres pro-allemandes (1914-1917) (les affaires Bolo, Almereyda, Caillaux, Malvy et autres). Librairie nationale 1918. 1 fr. 80.

Royden, A. Maude. The Great Adventure: the Way to Peace. Headley Brothers. 2*d.*

Russell, Bertrand. Justice in War Time. Mostly a reprint of pacifist articles. Chicago: Open Court Publishing Co. 1916. $1.00.

Ryder, C. F. The Price of Victory. King 1916. 3*d.*

Solano, Capt. E. J. Pacifist Lie, The. A book for sailors and soldiers. Murray 1918. 1*s.* 6*d.*

Stilwell, A. E. To all the World (except Germany). An indictment of war, with proposals for universal peace, by an American business man. Allen & Unwin. 3*s.* 6*d.*

Thomas, Gilbert. The Voice of Peace. Chapman & Hall 1914. 2*s.* 6*d.*

Towards Ultimate Harmony. Report of Conference on Pacifist Philosophy of Life, Caxton Hall, July 1915. Headley. 1*s.*

Trotsky, Leon. The Bolsheviki and World Peace. With introduction by Lincoln Steffens. New York: Boni & Liveright 1918.

Whence come Wars? Papers prepared by members of the Yearly Meetings Committee on War and the Social Order, for their Second Conference, held at Jordans, April 7-10, 1916. Headley Brothers. 1*s.*

Wilson, W. E. The Foundations of Peace. A discussion on Pacifism and the prevention of wars. Headley 1918. 2*s.* 6*d.*

ADDENDA.

I.—BIBLIOGRAPHIES.

Catalogue de publications sur la Guerre 1914 . . . (tom. 2, 1916). Paris : Cercle de la Librairie, 1916-17.

Grand-Carteret, John. La Museé et l'encyclopédie de la guerre. Recueil mensuel : Nos. 1-12, etc. Paris, 1917-18.

Les livres de la Guerre, août 1914-août 1916. Preface by E. Rostand. Paris 1916.

Mestrblätter zur Schuldfrage I . . . (in progress) 1921 . . . Zentralstelle für Erforschung der Kriegsursachen. Berlin : Luisenstrasse 31*a*, N.W.6.

Sawyer, Rollin A. Diplomatic History of the European War. A list of references in the New York Public Library. New York 1917.

XXII. B.—POETRY.

Housman, A. E. Last Poems. [Contains Epitaph on an Army of Mercenaries, first published in *The Times* October 31, 1917.*] Grant Richards, 1922. 5*s*.

* Reprinted by The Times in a leading article, 31st Oct., 1919 ; also in Jacqueline T. Trotter's Anthology of War Poems, Valour and Vision, 1920 ; also (very incorrectly) in Cambridge Readings in Literature, Book V, 1918. There have been versions of it—with which the original was reprinted—in Greek, Latin, and Hebrew in certain classical journals.

INDEX.

Names of authors, periodicals, societies, committees and institutions are combined in a single alphabet. No attempt has been made to index anonymous official publications of countries. Pseudonyms and initials serving as pseudonyms are in italics.

Aall 194
Aaronsohn 236
Abbot 106, 113
Abbott 3, 20
Abbott-Brown ... 314
Abensour 155
Ablay 141
Abraham 320
Acandia, d' (*see* D'Acandia).
Achalme 312
Ackerley 378
Ackerman ... 161, 165
Adam, G. 212
Adam, H. P. ... 373
Adam, Mme. J. 132, 156, 277
Adam, P. ... 200, 352
Adams, B. ... 212, 371
Adams, J. E. ... 329
Adams, M. 101
Adams, W. 299
Adams, W. G. S. 124, 344, 349
Adamson 359
Adcock 147, 200, 262, 269, 359
Addams 404
Adkins 124
Adler 337
Africanus 34
Agate 90, 205
Aghion 205
Agnel, d' (*see* D'Agnel).
Agresti 37
Aguilar 200
Aicard 156
Aimé, Frère 261
Ainger 359
Aitchison 7
Aitken 212
Ajalbert 176
Ajax 378, 379
Akiyama 179
Alaux 175
Alazard 176
Alberti 303
Albert-Petit 156
Albin 3, 7
Aldanov, Landau- (*see* Landau-Aldanov).
Alderson 337
Aldrich 212
Aldridge 232
Alexander, H, M. ... 212
Alexandre ... 156, 222
Alexinsky, G. 46, 183
Alexinsky, T. ... 320
Alfort, Petit d' (*see* Petit d'Alfort).
Allan, A. 329
Allan, C. 329
Allatini 230
Allen, G. H. 200
Allen, H. W. ... 212
Allen, J. W. ... 23, 404
Allen, W. 231
Allier 219
Almeida, d' (*see* D'Almeida).
Alphaud ... 156, 190
Altham 81
Altrock 205
Altsheler 228
Alype, Pierre- (*see* Pierre-Alype).
Amendola 176
American Ambulance 322
American Red Cross 319
Anastassion 379
Ancona 303
Anderson, C. C. ... 81
Anderson, M. B. ... 359
Anderson, M. H. ... 295
Anderson, R. 329
Anderson, R. C. ... 88
Andler 26, 31, 165, 166
Andrassy ... 136, 140
André 14
André, d' (*see* D'André).
Andreas, M. S. ... 19
Andréieff 183, 185, 371
Andrews, C. M. ... 3
Andrews, L. C. ... 81
Andreyev (*see* Andréieff).
Andrillon 23
Andriulli ... 123, 283
Anet 185, 186
Angell 110, 124, 191, 299, 337, 396
Angle 219
Anglo-French-American Hospital ... 320
Anker 279
Annual Register ... 3
Annunzio, d' (*see* D'Annunzio).
Ansac 256
Antelme 320
Anthonis 141
Anthouard, d' (*see* D'Anthouard).
Anton, R. 283
Applin, A. 273
Applin, R. K. V. ... 100
Aramais 180
Arbouin 352
Arc, d' (*see* D'Arc).
Arcangues, d' (*see* D'Arcangues).
Archer, W. 31, 106, 124, 161, 279, 337, 347
Ardant 156
Arguilbert, d' (*see* D'Arguilbert).
Arman, d' (*see* D'Arman).
Armitage, J. J. R. ... 325
Armstrong, G. A. ... 382
Armstrong, G. G. ... 124
Armstrong, J. W. S. 299
Army and Navy Gazette 209
Arnauld, Duval- (*see* Duval-Arnauld).
Arnold, E. V. ... 337
Arnold, J. O. 312, 347
Arnold, W. T. ... 26
Arthur, G. 274
Arumugam, Sunampadu (*see* Sunampadu Arumugam).
Arvengas 289
Ash 316
Ashbee 390
Ashdown 320
Ashern 266
Ashley, W. J. 161, 303, 346
Ashmead Bartlett 213, 234, 247
Ashton, H. 213
Ashton, H. A. 124, 382
Ashton, P. H. ... 314
Askenazy 43
Askew 232
Aspern 262
Asquith, H. 359
Asquith, H. H. 76, 77, 79
Associations Slesvicoises 26
Aston, G. ... 81, 213
Athenæum, Index to periodicals 1
Atkins, G. G. ... 390
Atkins, Thomasina ... 261
Atkinson, C. F ... 377

Atteridge ... 81, 100, 110, 200, 271
Attwood ... 88, 106
Aubrey, J. ... 160
Aubry ... 289
Audebert ... 90
Auerbach ... 11
Aulard ... 200, 382, 404
Aulneau ... 180
Aunet, d' (*see* D'Aunet).
Aureli ... 36
Austin, L. J. ... 289
Avenarius ... 373
Ayres ... 200
Ayscough ... 213
Axe ... 101
Azan ... 81, 90

B., W. ... 350
B.E.F. Times ... 265
Babin ... 219
Bachi ... 303
Backhouse ... 19
Bacon, publishers 114, 115
Bacon, E. V. ... 90
Baden-Powell 86, 88
Baer ... 197
Baerlein ... 370
Baggs ... 247
Bagnold ... 320
Bagot ... 36
Bahr ... 26, 169
Baie ... 382
Bailey, L. H. ... 81
Bailey, W. F. 14, 50
Baillod ... 133
Bainville 21, 133, 176, 186
Bairnsfather 372, 373
Balaam, Jr. ... 127
Baldacci ... 9
Baldwin, E. F. ... 6
Baldwin, J. M. 31, 191
Baldwin, M. ... 337
Balfour, A. J. 77, 245, 299
Balfour, F. ... 273
Balfour Browne ... 337
Balincourt ... 106
Balkanicus ... 19
Ballard, F. 124, 283, 329
Ballard, G. A. ... 38
Ballesteros ... 195
Ballin ... 174
Balmer ... 166
Banbury ... 90
Bang ... 174
Bankes ... 396
Banks ... 319
Banning ... 90, 295
Barber, C. ... 237
Barber, H. ... 113
Barbosa ... 197
Barbour ... 85
Barbusse ... 219
Barby ... 180, 232
Barclay, T. ... 295, 390
Bareilles ... 39
Bargellini ... 268
Baring ... 46, 359
Barker, E. 27, 31, 124, 259, 337, 345, 390
Barker, G. ... 314
Barker, J. E. 27, 33, 147, 303
Barlow ... 86
Barnard ... 156
Barnes, Gorell- (*see* Gorell-Barnes).
Barnes, L. S. ... 321
Barnett ... 268
Barnwell ... 312
Barrault ... 11
Barre ... 337
Barrère ... 377
Barrès ... 110, 156, 230
Barrett, C. ... 236
Barrett, J. W. ... 314
Barroetavena ... 174
Barron ... 124
Barrow ... 314
Barry, F. R. ... 329
Barry, W. ... 124
Barthélemy ... 27, 352
Bartholomew ... 7, 115
Barthou ... 156, 352
Bartimeus ... 106, 241
Bartlett, Ashmead- (*see* Ashmead-Bartlett).
Bartlett, Re- (*see* Re-Bartlett).
Bartlett, V. ... 213
Bartlett, W. T. ... 329
Barton, A. ... 124
Barton, E. C. ... 321
Baruch ... 387
Barzilai ... 80, 176
Barzini 82, 200, 219, 230
Basly ... 156, 219
Bassermann ... 277
Basset ... 176
Bassompierre ... 141
Basu ... 147
Bates, J. V. ... 14
Bates, Montague- (*see* Montague-Bates).
Batiffol ... 9, 133
Batteler ... 289
Battine ... 201
Battisti ... 36, 231
Baty ... 295, 299
Baud-Bovy ... 289
Baudin ... 21
Baudrillart ... 156
Baudry ... 88
Baulu ... 219
Baumgarten-Crusius 226
Bazin ... 156, 352
Beadnell ... 213
Bean ... 259
Beatson ... 86
Beaufort ... 161
Beaulieu, Leroy (*see* Leroy-Beaulieu).
Beaume ... 256
Beaumont ... 86
Beauregard ... 156
Beaven ... 344
Beaverbrook (*see* Aitkin).
Beazley ... 45
Beca ... 90
Bechhofer ... 183
Beck, A. M. de 154, 337
Beck, G. ... 133
Beck, J. M. 124, 125, 191, 270, 345, 382
Becker ... 169
Beckett, A. ... 359
Beckh ... 337
Beckwith ... 377
Beddington ... 86
Bédier ... 166, 283
Beer, G. L. ... 337
Beer, M. ... 119
Begbie 17, 206, 228, 359, 376
Beggs ... 86, 314
Behrens ... 293
Beith, I. H. (*see* *Hay, I.*)
Belevsky ... 183
Bell, C. ... 404
Bell, E. P. ... 337
Bell, G. K. A. ... 329
Bell, H. J. ... 357
Bell, J. J. ... 106
Bell, Lynden- ... 284
Bell, R. W. ... 152
Bellasis ... 258
Bellegarde ... 110
Bellet ... 82, 133
Belloc ... 82, 117, 125, 201
Bellows ... 377
Belmont ... 259
Below ... 136
Bendall ... 360
Benedetti ... 231
Beneš ... 11
Benians ... 147
Benjamin, R. ... 110, 219
Bennett, A. ... 125, 213
Bennett, A. H. ... 268
Bennett, W. ... 147, 345
Benoist ... 206
Benson, B. G. ... 125
Benson, E. F. 39, 180, 182
Benson, R H. ... 324
Bent ... 90
Bentinck ... 259
Bentwich ... 42
Bérard ... 27, 48, 352
Berden ... 142
Berg ... 355
Bergelvasser ... 136
Berger, M. ... 219, 253
Berget ... 103
Berggrav-Jensen ... 194
Bergson ... 313
Bermejo de la Rica 156
Bernard, A. ... 39
Bernard, J ... 201
Bernard, J. H. ... 325
Bernhardi 27, 28, 82, 99, 169.
Bernstorff ... 191
Berriman ... 103
Berry, D. M. ... 329
Berry, F. M. D ... 314
Berry, J. ... 314
Berry, W. H. ... 113
Berry, W. T. ... 2
Bertha, de ... 11
Bertrand, A. ... 11, 219
Bertrand, G. ... 90
Bertrand, P. ... 133
Besant ... 337

Besser, Schulz- (*see* Schulz-Besser).
Bessières 321
Betham-Edwards ... 21
Bethmann Hollweg 79, 206, 246
Betts 396
Bevaix 314
Bevan, E. 31, 42, 125, 161, 337, 348, 349, 382
Bevan, T. 213
Bewsher 360
Beyens 9, 27
Bibikoff 110
Bidon 219
Bierme 270
Bigwood 234
Bikanir 77
Billing, Pemberton- (*see* Pemberton-Billing).
Billington ... 154, 314
Billy 259
Bilse 110
Binet 253
Binyon ... 147, 348, 360
Biottot 382
Bipin 337
Birkenhead (*see* Smith, F. E.).
Birkett 45
Birmingham, Bp. of 247
Birmingham Free Libraries 1
Bishop, G. B. H. ... 46
Bishop, J. B. ... 50
Bishop, W. A. ... 247
Bismarck 23
Bisschop 376, 377, 379
Bissing 136
Bithell 379
Bitterauf 136
Bjorkman ... 194, 346
Black 247
Black Tab 237
Blackall 360
Blackburn 270
Blair 360
Blakeney 360
Blakeslee 338
Blanche 156, 256, 266
Blanchin 290
Blanchon ... 82, 88, 206
Bland 19
Blatchford 161
Blease 314
Bleibtreu 27
Bley 27, 136
Blinkhorn 113
Bloeher 142
Bloem 256
Blondel ... 31, 34, 352
Blücher, Princess ... 161
Blumenthal 10
Blunden 360
Boardman 314
Bocquet 219
Bodart 338
Boden 338
Bodin, Soulange- (*see* Soulange-Bodin).
Bodley, J. E. C. ... 21
Bodley, J. H. ... 396
Bolwell 213
Bone 266, 267
Bonhard 31
Bonn 161
Bonnal 82
Bonnefon 276
Bonnet 352
Bonnett 86
Booth, J. B. 283
Booth, M. 329
Booth, W. 360
Boppé 190, 232
Bordeaux 219, 273, 352
Borden 77, 206
Borgese 27, 176
Bosanquet ... 127, 338
Bossière, Galtier- (*see* Galtier-Bossière).
Bossière, R. E. ... 303
Bostock, A. H. E. A. 360
Bostock, J. ... 91, 100
Boswell 43
Botrel 370
Boubée 142, 219
Boucher 253
Boudon 276
Bouillier 247
Boulanger 382
Boulger 19
Bouloc 352
Bourceret 321
Bourdaire 82
Bourdillon 360
Bourdon 27
Bourgeois 21, 119, 133, 352
Bourgin 166
Bourgoin 370
Bourguet 259
Bourne 148
Boutroux 166, 313, 352
Bovy, Baud- (*see* Baud-Bovy).
Bowley 303, 310, 347
Bowman 7
Bowser 317, 321
Boyle, J. F. 154
Boyle, M. E. 338
Bracht 228
Bracq 21
Bradley, A. C. ... 127
Bradley, S. 247
Brailsford 42, 186, 338, 390, 391.
Braithwaite 330
Brand 303
Brandes 31, 43, 206, 356
Brandstaedter ... 201
Brandt, R. 228
Branford 398
Brangwyn 16
Branialti 176
Brash 330
Brassey 106
Braun, von 169
Braun, H. 317
Braut 338
Bray 299
Bréant 253
Brennan, A. 196
Brennan, H. 183
Brent, C. H. 325
Brereton 125
Breton, J. 253
Breton, W. 219
Brett 309
Brewer, D. C. ... 299
Brewer, R. W. A. ... 103
Briantchaninoff 46, 356
Bridge 88
Bridges, R. 234
Bridges, T. C. ... 234
Brilla 206
Brinkley 38
Brinon 220
Brinville 27
Briscoe, W. A. ... 270
British and Foreign Bible Society ... 331
British Medical Association 314
British Museum ... 2
British Red Cross Society 210, 318, 320
Brittain, H. E. ... 213
Brittain, V. M. ... 360
Broad, W. J. 91
Broca 318
Brock, Clutton- (*see* Clutton-Brock).
Brockington 86
Broman 91
Brooke 360
Brooks 42
Broughton 148
Brown, A. 309
Brown, Abbott- (*see* Abbott-Brown).
Brown, C. 325
Brown, E. V. 330
Brown, F. S. 360
Brown, H. 213
Brown, H. G. 303, 310
Brown, Haigh- (*see* Haigh-Brown).
Brown, J. 86, 101
Brown, J. L. 360
Brown, P. M. ... 299
Brown, R. N. R. ... 48
Brown, Sykes- (*see* Sykes-Brown).
Browne, Balfour (*see* Balfour Browne).
Browne, Crichton- (*see* Crichton-Browne).
Browne, Gore- (*see* Gore-Browne).
Browne, G. R. ... 325
Browne, G. W. ... 295
Browne, P. E. ... 404
Brownlow 213
Brownrigg ... 148, 206
Bruccoleri 177
Bruce, A. 377
Bruce, E. S. 103
Bruce, M. W. S. ... 361
Bruchmüller 206
Bruhl, Lévy- (*see* Lévy-Bruhl).
Brunel 21
Bryan 318
Bryce 148, 279, 338, 391, 395
Buat 275
Bucaille ... 177, 259

Buchan, J. 201, 213, 241, 272, 347
Buchan, W. 241
Buchanan, A. ... 239
Buchanan, M. ... 186
Bucher, Steinmann- (*see* Steinmann-Bucher).
Buchner, E. 198
Buckell 338
Buckrose 148
Bülow ... 27, 169, 174
Buffin 220, 262
Buist 103
Buisson 186
Bujac 182
Buley 235, 262
Bull ... 148, 326, 330
Bullard ... 3, 125, 191
Buller 379
Bulletin des Armées 199
Bullitt 161
Burgess ... 125, 127, 191
Burgoyne 106
Burke 213
Burls 312
Burne 162
Burnell 238
Burnet 312
Burns, C. D. 338
Burns, J. 86
Burroughs, E. A. 125, 326, 330
Burrows 303
Burton 372
Burwell 321
Bury, G. W. 41
Bury, H. ... 183, 247, 290
Bury, J. B. 162
Busson 21
Buteau 253
Butler, G. 391
Butler, G. G. ... 299
Butler, N. M. ... 396
Butler, T. 162
Butterfield 338
Butts, M. 263
Buxton, C R. 141, 382 385, 396
Buxton, D. E. ... 396
Buxton, H. 41
Buxton, N. ... 40, 41
Buyse 48
Byford 46
Byron 309, 330
Bywater 243

C., D. M. 283
C., M. A. (*see M. A. C.*).
C.C. 361
C.M. 148
Cababé 299
Cable ... 148, 206, 263
Caburi 36, 177
Cadenhead 248
Cadorna 231
Cadoux 166
Cafandaris 80
Cahen 377, 379
Cahuet 20
Caillet 91
Caine, H. ... 154, 206
Cairns 338, 348
Caix de Saint-Aymour 220
Calippe 220
Callaghan 361
Calthrop 157
Calvert 34
Calvo 206
Cambo 27
Cambon 396
Cambridge Modern History 3
Cambridge Review ... 268
Cambridge University 105, 268
Cameron, L. C. ... 101
Cameron, W. J. ... 361
Cammaerts 80, 142, 206, 371
Cammell 372
Campbell, G. 213
Campbell, G. L. ... 113
Campbell, H. ... 142
Campbell, H. ... 293
Campbell, P. ... 321
Campbell, R. W. 206, 248, 330
Campbell-Strickland 361
Camus 314
Cana 34, 201
Candler 238, 263
Canelini 196
Cannan 361
Canonge ... 201, 220
Cantacuzene 186
Canterbury, Archbp. of ... 325, 326, 330
Cantlie 314
Canudo 235
Capek 1, 11
Capel 391
Capello 231
Cappuyns 248
Caprin 177
Captain 91
"*Captain*" 237
Carey, A. E. 396
Carey, G. V. 268
Carli 303
Carnbee 248
Carnegie Endowment 300
Carnegy 330
Carnovale 177
Carpenter, A. F. B. 241
Carpenter, C. H. ... 293
Carpenter, E. 311, 338, 404
Carpenter, J. E. ... 330
Carrel 318
Carrère 3
Carrière 136
Carrillo 207, 220
Carroll 361
Carson 77
Carter, G. R. ... 338
Carter, H. ... 357, 396
Carter, L. B. ... 101
Carteret, Grand- (*see* Grand-Carteret)
Carton de Wiart 147, 356
Cartwright, J. C. ... 91
Carus 313
Carvell 318
Casalis 259
Casement 125
Caspar 378
Cassavetti 35
Casserly 91
Cassi 36
Castellini ... 36, 177
Castéran 382
Casualty 213
Catchpool 321
Catellani 177
Catholic Truth Society 325
Catling 277
Cato 241
Cator 321
Caudel 6, 204
Caudwell 330
Caunell 266
Caunter 290
Cawston 91
Cazalet 45
Cazamian 148
Cecil, H. 395
Cecil, R. ... 78, 391
Célarie 166, 290
Central Association V.T. Corps ... 98
Central Prisoners of War Committee ... 287
Centurion 248
Cerfberr 166
Cesarò, Colonna di (*see* Colonna di Cesarò).
Cestre 148, 338
Chalier, A. 318
Chalier, J. 318
Chamberlain, B. H. 38
Chamberlain, H. S. 31, 136, 169
Chambrun ... 110, 220
Chambry ... 276, 283
Channing 50
Chapin 259
Chapman, H. B. ... 338
Chapman, J. J. ... 162
Chapman, S. J. 310, 347, 396
Chapsal 303
Charity Commission 339
Charles 293
Charmatz 11
Charmes 201
Charnwood 402
Charriant ... 177, 303
Charteris, N. K. ... 100
Chasles 186
Chauveau ... 321, 383
Checchia 190
Chenu 201
Chéradame 3, 11, 20, 21, 32, 35, 133, 166, 191, 382
Chervin 11
Chesterton, C. 162, 404
Chesterton, G. K. 142, 162
Chevrillon ... 148, 166
Chicago University 350
Child 183
Childe 321
Childs 39
Chirol 19, 42, 48, 153, 162, 344
Chisholm 272
Chitwood 125

Chivers 321
Chlumecky 12
Chopin, J ... 12, 133
Choublier 20
Christian-Frogé ... 220
Christmas ... 272 290
Chuquet ... 28, 281
Church Army ... 381
Church, J. R. ... 314
Church, L. F. ... 10
Church, S. H. ... 125
Churchill, Lady R.... 85
Churchill, W.... 77, 78, 79
Churchmen's Union... 330
Ciobanian 41
Civis Italicus 36, 177
Civray 256
Civrieux, de 201
Claes 34
Clairens 141
Clapham 142
Clapp 303
Clark 238
Clarke, B. 248
Clarke, E. B. ... 142
Clarke, E. M. ... 321
Clarke, F. J. ... 330
Clarke, G. H. ... 191
Clarke, G. S. ... 88
Clarke, Herschel- (*see* Herschel-Clarke).
Clarke, H. B. ... 49
Clarke, M. E. ... 157
Class 136, 169
Claudel 370
Clausewitz 82
Clauss 115
Claxton 103
Clayton, I. M. ... 339
Clemenceau 133
Clements 293
Clercq, de 7
Clermont 157
Clifford, H. 35
Clifford, J. 125
Clifford, W. G. 100, 397
Clockener 170
Close 290
Clouard 166
Clowes 106
Clutterbuck 268
Clutton-Brock 150, 339, 349
Coar 191, 339
Cobb 201
Cobber 361
Coblenz, Mehrmann- (*see* Mehrmann-Coblenz).
Cochin, D. 166
Cochin, H. 352
Cochin, J. 259
Coddington ... 293, 295
Coffey 91
Cohen 290
Cohn 148
Colajanni 139
Colcord 361
Cole 311
Coleman, A. 382
Coleman, F. ... 213, 214
Colin, A. 220
Colin, L. ... 283, 352
Collie 316
Collier, G. ... 17, 346
Collier, P. 28
Collin 339
Collings 339
Collins 91, 295
Colmer 357
Colonna di Cesarò 141, 177
Colquhoun 127
Combarieu 157
Comité catholique de propagande française 134
Commandant 361
Commander 91
Commentitus 404
Committee of Imperial Defence ... 198
Committee on the Treatment of British Prisoners 289
Comnène ... 44, 232
Company Commander 91
Condé 352
Cone 361
Coney 95
Connaught Rangers 210
Connolly 311
Conrad 12
Contact 248
"*Contour*" 99
Conway 14
Conybeare ... 125, 126
Cook, A. O. 274
Cook, E. 125, 126, 148, 150
Cook, Mrs. T. ... 321
Cook, T. A. 162
Cook V. 330
Cooke, F. G. 101
Coolidge 3, 39
Cooper, B. 235
Cooper, E. 361
Cooper, E. T. ... 361
Copping 263
Copplestone 241
Coppola 177
Corbett, J. 148, 241, 299
Corbett, N. M. ... 361
Corbett-Smith ... 214
Corbin 103
Cordier 19, 20
Corelli 106, 339
Cornet, L. 201
Cornford ... 106, 241
Cornish 7, 17
Cosby 404
Cosmos 404
Costa 126
Coubertin 21
Coulson 361
Coulton ... 82, 311, 404
Country Life ... 268, 322
Courrière 220
Courson 263
Courson 157
Courtney 397
Courtney of Penwith 21
Cousins 313
Coust 195
Coutanseau 377
Coutras 253
Cowan 126
Cowen 339
Cox, H. 303
Cox, J. B. 330
Coxhead 110
Coxon 241
Coxwell 183
Crafer, T. W. ... 330
Craig 269
Craigen 101
Cramb 17
Crammond 303
Cramon 140
Cramp 361
Cravath 148
Crawshay-Williams 248, 361
Crazannes 148
Creed, Mrs. (*see* Mack).
Creighton, O. 235, 248
Cressaty 383
Creswick 314
Crichton-Browne ... 339
Crile 339
Crispi, Palamenghi- (*see* Palamenghi-Crispi).
Crispolti 36
Croft, Page- (*see* Page-Croft).
Crokaert 227
Cromer 41, 162
Crosland ... 228, 279
Cross, H. 379
Cross, H H. V. ... 361
Crosse 331
Crotch 304
Crouvezier 103
Crowe 239
Crusius, Baumgarten- (*see* Baumgarten-Crusius).
Cuddesdon 325
Cuinet 39
Cummings 316
Cunningham, A. W. 331
Cunynghame 314
Curchod 361
Currey 88, 242
Curry 214
Curtin 162
Curzon 42, 362
Custance 88
Cuttriss 248
Cviéticha 194
Cvijić 12, 14
Czaplicka ... 39, 180
Czarnowski 377
Czernin 246

D., P. (*see* P.D.).
D.S.M. 372
D'Acandia 43
D'Acosta 397
Dacquois 256
D'Agnel 196
Daily Chronicle 115, 267
Daily Express 115, 165
Daily Mail 115
Daily Telegraph ... 116
D'Almeida 111

Dalton 231
Damé 44
Dammert 232
Dampier, Smith- (*see* Smith-Dampier).
Dampierre 256, 281, 284
Danby, P. 111
D'André 92
Dane, E. 92, 214, 232
Daniélou 133
D'Annunzio 80
D'Anthouard 290
Darbishire ... 116, 118
Darby 391
D'Arc 166
D'Arcangues 370
Dardanelles Commission 234
Darde 207, 242
Dareste 6
D'Arguilbert ... 257
Dark 126, 157
D'Arman 55
Darvillé 82
Darwin 162
Dascovici 39
Daudet, E. 133, 201, 260, 271
Daudet, L. ... 23, 397
D'Aunet 397
Dauriac 26
Dauzat 253, 377
Dauzet 157, 220
Davenport 126, 149, 201
Davies, A. 290
Davies, E. C. ... 379
Davies, E. F. ... 303
Davies, H. M. ... 318
Davies, O. St. L. ... 92
Davignon ... 142, 284
Davis, A. N. ... 277
Davis, H. 304
Davis, H. W. C. 21, 32, 142, 214, 344, 345, 346
Davis, M. O. ... 126
Davis, R. H. 160, 214, 248
Davis, R. J. ... 383
Davis, W. S. ... 126
Davray 149, 274
Davson 92
Dawbarn 111, 157, 339
Dawson, A. J. 86, 214, 263
Dawson, C. 191, 207, 260, 339
Dawson, J. 331
Dawson, L. H. ... 129
Dawson, W. H. 23, 28, 34, 126, 311, 397
Dawson W. J. ... 339
Day 214
Daye 239
Deane 314
Dearden 317
Dearmer, G. ... 362
Dearmer, M. ... 321
Dearmer, P. 183, 339, 347, 348, 379
De Bary 391
Debidour 3
Debrit 133, 201
De Civrieux 201
Defaulter (*The*) ... 362
De Filippi 177
De Flemalle ... 142, 214
Degouy 242
Deguise 220
D'Egville 78, 294, 339
Dehelly 318
Dekobra 111
Delay 263
Delbos 377
Delbrück, H. 28, 170, 183
Delbrück, J. 260
Delécraz 157
De Lissa 309
Delorme 318
Deloy 202
Delstanche 16
Del Vecchio 177
Delvert ... 220, 257, 268
Demains, Eydoux- (*see* Eydoux-Demains).
De Marès 142
Demblin 140
Demblon 220
Dembski 299
Démians 321
Demombynes ... 6
De Morgan, J. ... 352
Denikin 186
Denis 12, 49, 133, 134, 159, 166
Denison 326
Denman 397
Denney 331
Dennistoun 296
Dennys 362
Dent 321
Deploige 195
De Pratz (*see* Pratz).
Derby 110
Deribespray 166
Dérieux 370
Dernburg ... 136, 137
Descamps, E. 16
Descamps, P. 166
Desgenettes 379
Desgranges 331
Desjardins 149
Des Ombiaux 142, 221, 383
Dessaint 352
Desson 290
Des Touches 221
D'Estre, C. H. ... 221
D'Estre, H. 253
Destrée 16, 142, 149, 177, 231, 268, 353
Des Vignes-Rouges (*see* Vignes-Rouges).
Devenish 260
Deville 257
Devine 39
De Viti de Marco ... 177
Dewar, G. A. B. ... 149
De Wend-Fenton ... 339
Dewey 32
De Windt (*see* Windt).
D'Hartoy 221
Diack 272
Diaz-Retg 227
Dicey, A. V. 346
Dicey, E. 19
Dick 242
Dickinson, G. L. 340, 383, 391, 397, 404, 405
Dickinson, W. H. ... 394
Dicksee 304
Dide 266, 353
Dieterich, K. ... 39
Dieterlen 221
Dillon, E. J. ... 126, 186, 340, 387
Dilnot 272
Dimier 134
Dimnet 22, 347
Diplomaticus ... 196
Ditchfield 357
Dix 170
Dixhuit ... 92, 99
Dixie, A. E. 103
Dixon, A. M. 207
Dixon, G. M. 106
Dmowski 6, 43
Doak 362
Dobson 331
Doc 260
Dodd, F. 268
Dodd, W. E. 279
Dodderidge 362
Doerkes 177
Doitsh 290
Dolbey 239, 318
Dollé 253
Domelier 170
Domerque 186
Dominian 6, 7
Dommett 88, 103, 113
Domville-Fife ... 88
Donat 353
Donohoe 238
Dontenville 16, 134, 397
Dorling 105
Doroshevitch 184
Dorr 186
Doty 174
Doughty 41
Douglas, H. 92
Douglas, R. K. 20, 38
Douin 237
Doumic 190
Dowd 373
Downes, J. N. ... 357
Downes, R. P. ... 331
Doyle, A. C. 126, 149, 201, 207, 214, 290
Doyle, L. 362
Drage 12, 47
Draper 149
Drawbridge 331
Drew, A. N. 184
Drew, T. 101
Driault 3, 20, 383
Driggs 113
Drinkwater 362
Driver 85
Drogoslav ... 43, 182
Droysen 7
Drumont 257
Dubail 221
Dubarle 260
Dublin University ... 269
Dubois, Paul- (*see* Paul-Dubois).
Duboscq ... 20, 180
Dubrelle 221

Du Cann 362
Duchene 103
Duchesne 126, 149, 340, 347
Duckers 405
Ducroquet 318
Dudden 326
Dudon 383
Dufour 290
Dufriche 379
Dugard, H. 221
Dugard, M. 157
Duhamel ... 322, 324
Duhem 10
Duke 331
Dumont-Wilden ... 16
Dumur 195
Duncan, J. 214
Duncan, M. 155
Dunkmann 170
Dunlop 405
Dunn 248
Dunsterville 238
Du Parcq 272
Dupierreux 231
Dupont 221, 253, 254, 257
Dupuy 322
Durand 383
Durell 214
Durham 14
Durkheim 134, 159, 166
Durnford 290
Duval-Arnauld ... 92
Duwez 221
Dwight 40
Dymond 340
Dyson ... 266, 373, 374
Dyssord 167

Earll 196
Eassie 372
Eastman, M. 174
Eberlein 256
Eccles 10, 347
Eckhardstein 23, 137, 246
Economist 304
Eddy 331
Edelsheim 88
Eder 316
Edgar 362
Edgeworth, E. ... 162
Edgeworth, F. Y. ... 304
Edleston 177
Edmondson 36
Edsall 304, 397
Edwards, Betham- (*see* Betham-Edwards).
Edwards, E. 180
Edwards, J. H. ... 272
Egan 238
Egelhaaf 3
Egerton, H. E. 17, 153, 345
Egerton, W. A. ... 299
Eggar 101
Egli 202
Ehrhardt 170
Ehrlich ... 43, 346
Einstein 180
Eisenmann 12
Elchanninov ... 47, 275
Elder 311
Eley 88
Eliason 318
Eliot, C. (*see* *Odysseus*).
Eliot, C. W. ... 191, 391
Elkington 316
Elliott, H. B. ... 357
Elliott, I. d'O. 111, 348
Ellis, H. 340
Ellis, T. M. 85
Ellison 290
Elphinstone 331
Eltzbacher 304
Elwell-Sutton ... 162
Emanuel 372
Emard 397
Empey 248
Engelbrecht 170
Engelhardt 179
Engerand ... 34, 221
Ensor 16
Eppstein 23
Erichsen 248
Erlande 207
Erzberger ... 246, 391
Escouflaire 154
Esher 274, 398
Esnault 377
Essen, Van der (*see* Van der Essen).
Esson 92
Estre, d' (*see* D'Estre).
Etienne ... 242, 362
Eucken 32
Eulenberg 304
Evans, A. 317
Evans, Sir A. ... 50
Evans, C. S. 357
Evans, E. T. 326
Evans, H. J. 290
Evans, W. 362
Eveleigh 35
Everitt 207
Eversley ... 40, 43
Ewing 238
Ex-Intelligence Officer 162
Export World ... 34
Ex-Royal Navy ... 106
Ex-Trooper 111
Eydoux-Demains ... 322
Eye-Witness 215

F., G. 242
F., H. 242
F., J. I. 92
Fabian Society ... 403
Fabrequettes 221
Fage, A. 103
Fage, André ... 157, 221
Faguet 405
Faiz El-Ghusein ... 180
Falconer 78
Falkenhayn 202, 207, 228
Fallon 235
Fanshawe 362
Farbman 186
Farnol 248
Farrer 260
Farrow, E. S. ... 377
Farrow, T. 304
Fatio, Morel- (*see* Morel-Fatio).
Faure 207, 231
Favre 106
Fawcett, H. W. ... 242
Fawside 362
Fay 372
Fayle ... 242, 340, 383
Fayolle 304
"*Feathered Heels*" 368
Fedele 177
Federn 137
Fehr 226
Feiling 36, 344
Felce 331
Feldman 43
Fels 140, 383
Felstead 207
Fendall 239
Férasson ... 134, 383
Ferguson, A. 104
Ferguson, J. 362
Fernau 137, 398
Ferraby 88
Ferrar 362
Ferrero ... 139, 207, 356
Ferri-Pisani ... 191, 232
Festing 86
Fetterless 248
Feyler ... 196, 207, 227
Field (The) ... 283, 284
Field Central Committee 28
Field, C. ... 88, 106
Fielding-Hall 263, 405
Fiennes 106, 340
Fierre 242
Fife, Domville- ... 88
Fife, R. H. 23
Figgis 331
Fight for Right Movement 340
Filippi, de (*see* De Filippi).
Finch, D. 340
Finnemore 229
Finny 318
Finot ... 157, 276, 353
Finzi 248
Fiolle 221
Fischer, W. 82
Fish 191
Fisher, H. A. L. 126, 149, 340, 345
Fisher, H. W. ... 23
Fisher, I. 304
Fitzpatrick 126
Fitzroy 322
Fitzwilliam ... 318, 322
Flandin ... 28, 306
Flat 353
Flemalle, de (*see* De Flemalle).
Fleming 242
Fletcher, C. B. ... 149
Fletcher, C. R. L. 28, 344
Fletcher, N. G. ... 318
Fletcher-Vane ... 82
Fleury-Lamure ... 221
Flight Lieutenant ... 103
Floericke 229

Florent-Matter ... 10
Foakes 379
Foakes-Jackson ... 331
Foch 82
Foerster 207
Foley, C. 260
Foley, F. W. ... 92
Folliet 353
Fonsegrive 167
Foot, P. B. 101
Forbes 14, 45, 50, 346, 376, 379
Ford, G. S. 362
Ford, H. E. 196
Ford, J. H. 316
Foreign Opinion ... 126
Forel 385, 391
Forestier 16
Forge 254
Formby 149
Forster, R. H. ... 362
Forsyth, A. T. ... 332
Forsyth, P. T. ... 391
Forsyth-Major ... 92
Fort 370
Fortescue, A. ... 405
Fortescue, G. 157, 235, 249
Fortescue, J. W. ... 340
Fosbery 359
Foss 170, 263
Foster, H. 82
Foster, H. C. 249
Foster, Manning- (*see* Manning-Foster).
Foulke 362
Foulon 266
Fournier ... 12, 355
Fournol 12
Fowle 40
Fowler, G. H. ... 89
Fowler, Warde (*see* Warde Fowler).
Fox, E. L. ... 162, 278
Fox, E. M. 322
Fox, F. 14, 19, 142, 215
Fox, R. F. 315
Fox Smith 362
Foxwell 155
Fraccaroli 231
Fraknoi ... 3, 120
France, A. 157
Francke 174
Franc-Nohain 202, 244, 263
François 167
François-Poncet ... 28
Frank, G. 386
Frank, L. 355
Frank, R. 143
Frankau 362
Frankfürter Zeitung 304
Franklin 82
Franks 332
Frasca 299
Fraser 184, 263
Fredenheim 139
Freeman, A. 403
Freeman, E. A. ... 7
Freeman, L. R. ... 207
Freese 377, 379
French, J. 78, 212, 215
French Gunner ... 273
Frennsen 239
Freston 363
Frewen 304
Freytag-Loringhoven 82, 83, 186, 202, 207, 355
Fribourg ... 222, 353
Fried, A. H. ... 278, 398
Friedjung 3
Friedlaender 184
Friend 92
Friends' Peace Comm. 406
Frith, J. C. 363
Frobenius 28, 170, 202, 299
Froelich ... 32, 167
Frogé, Christian- (*see* Christian-Frogé).
Frost, J. A. 86
Frost, W. 242
Früs-Môller 16
Fry 128, 405
Fryer 249
Fuchs 374
Fuehr 143
Fulda 191
Fuller 92
Fullerton ... 4, 192
Furniss 311
Fursdon 377
Furse 149
Fusilier 93
Fyfe, H. C. 89
Fyfe, T. A. 294
G. 326
G., H.L. 333
Gaëll ... 111, 254, 263
Gävernitz, Schultze- (*see* Schultze-Gävernitz).
Gaffarel 22
Gagneur 254
Gaillard 195
Galiano 139, 195, 227
Gallichan 379
Galliéni 246
Gallishaw 235
Gallwey, Payne- (*see* Payne-Gallwey).
Galopin 222, 254, 266
Galsworthy 340
Galtier-Bossière ... 316
Galtrey 99
Gandeau 167
Gardiner, A. G. ... 268
Gardiner, J. B. W. 162
Gardiner, W. H. T. 379
Gardner, A. 340
Gardner, L. 398
Gardner, M. M. ... 43
Gargas 12
Garner 299
Garnett 14
Garnier 228
Garofalo 37
Garstin 184, 372
Garton Foundation 311
Garvin 357
Gasztowit 182
Gatti 207
Gattier-Boissière ... 222
Gaucher 93
Gaultier ... 167, 284
Gaunt, F. 257
Gauss 192, 278
Gautier 28
Gauvain 4, 134, 176, 202
Gayda 12, 36
Gayer 242
Geare 260
Geddes 127, 398
Geiger 170
Geijerstam 256
Gell 332, 340
Gellert 363
Gemelli 111
Genevoix 222
Genisty 222
Gennep 353
Gentili 178
Genty 257
Geoffrey 157
George V. 121
George, E. 83
George, L. 78
George, S. 405
Georgevitch 180
Gérard, A. 20, 38, 179, 390
Gerard, J. W. 174, 246
Gerlache de Gomery 143
Gettlich 47
Gezelle 227
Ghelli 12
Giachetti 157
Gibbins 236
Gibbon 332
Gibbons ... 6, 9, 180, 277
Gibbs 215, 340
Gibson, A. H. ... 305
Gibson, H. 143
Gibson, R. H. ... 242
Gibson, W. M. ... 269
Gibson, W. W. ... 363
Gide 398
Gilbert 363
Gilbreath 186
Gill, C. 340
Gill, C. C. 242
Gill, N. J. 103
Gillam 235
Gillespie 260
Gilliard ... 45, 276
Gilliland 291
Ginisty 254
Ginsburg 79
Ginschel 273
Giordani 35
Giran 143
Giraud 134
Giraudoux 222
Girling 363
Gizycki 83
Gleason 149
Gleichen ... 198, 208
Gobart 222
Gobineau 32
Goblet d'Alviella ... 405
Goetz 383
Gohier 157
Golding 107
Goldingham 377
Goldsack 332
Goldsmith 391
Goltz 83, 170

Gomery, Gerlache de (*see* Gerlache de Gomery).
Gompert 93
Gooch 4, 394
Goodchild 242, 267, 357
Goode 186
Goodman 332
Goodwin 93
Gooss 120
Gopčevič ... 9, 39, 149
Gordon, G. .. 217, 326
Gordon, G. S. ... 215
Gordon, J. ... 49, 232
Gordon, Mrs. W. 14, 45, 141
Gordon-Smith ... 232
Gore 326, 391
Gore-Browne 294
Gorell-Barnes ... 363
Gorham 127, 332
Gorky 185
Gorse 167
Gosse 157, 340
Gottberg 243
Gould 192
Gourko 184
Gourmont 353
Gourraigne 210
Gouvieux 222
Gowans 171
Goyau 275
Gozdawa - Turczynowicz 229
Graevenitz 187
Graham, J. W. ... 332
Graham, S. 111, 184, 208
Grahame-White 103, 104, 113
Grailly 383
Grand, Guy- (*see* Guy-Grand).
Grand-Carteret 199, 374, 408
Grande 83, 111
Grandmaison 254
Grandvilliers ... 28
Grane 374, 405
Grant, A. J. 4
Grant, H. 83
Grant, M. 158
Grant, N. F. 23
Grant, R. 340
Grant, W. L. ... 127
Graphic (The) ... 240
Grasshoff 143
Graux 208
Graves, A. T. ... 215, 363
Graves, C. L. 363
Graves, R. 363
Gray, A. 163
Gray, A. H. 341, 348, 349
Gray, E. 36
Gray, E. M. ... 34, 143
Gray, H. B. 398
Green, A. 291
Green, A. O. 41
Green, A. R. 363
Green, J. 235
Greene 192
Greener 93
Greenwood, A. ... 4
Greenwood, G. A. ... 405
Gregory, C. N. ... 299
Gregory, H. 363
Gregory, T. E. ... 305
Grell 32
Grelling 16, 136, 137, 170
Grenadier ... 93, 99
Grenville 358
Gretton, M. S. 198, 363
Grew 274
Grey, C. G. ... 113, 263
Grey, W. E. 215
Grey of Fallodon 78, 121, 391
Gribble ... 143, 272, 292, 341
Grice 17
Grierson 296
Griffith 101
Griffith-Jones 332
Grigg 127
Grimautz 254
Grindlay 363
Grinling 101
Griselle 180
Grondijs 284
Groser 274
Gross 116
Grothe 28, 180
Grotius 300
Grotius Society 130, 300
Grove, E. W. H. ... 318
Grove, S. W. ... 322
Gruben 284
Gruet 296
Grumbach ... 137, 171
Gruner 177
Guéchoff 15
Guedalla 308
Gümpel 383
Guermonprez ... 318
Guevara 305
Guezoni 127
Guihéneuc 243
Guilland 32
Guillaume 32
Guillet 313
Guirand 119
Gullett 236
"*Gunlayer*" 99
Gurlitt 28
Gurner 363
Gurney 43
Gutmann, K. 132
Guttenbrunn, Müller- (*see* Müller-Guttenbrunn).
Guy-Grand 405
Guyot ... 134, 305, 383
Gwatkin 127
Gwatkin-Williams 237, 291
Gwinner 174
Gwynn 363

H., E.C. 293
H., G.F. (*see* Harnden).
Hacault 303
Hachette 209
Hacobian 180
Hadjich 374
Hänsch 171
Hagemann 256
Haigh 212
Haigh-Brown ... 111
Halasi 143
Haldane, Viscount 4, 18, 23
Haldane, J. S. ... 312
Hale, L. 86, 149, 284
Hales 231
Halévy 276, 279
Hall, A. D. 398
Hall, A. J. 319
Hall, A. V. 363
Hall, B. 249
Hall, C. ... 85, 86
Hall, Fielding- (*see* Fielding-Hall).
Hall, J. A. 296
Hall, J. N. 249
Hall, M. 93
Hall, O. S. 163
Hall, R. 249
Hall, W. E. 300
Hallays 167
Halleck 300
Hallett 363
Halliday 357
Hallowes ... 341, 405
Hamel 104
Hamelius ... 16, 215
Hamley 83
Hamilton, A. 42
Hamilton, C. 215
Hamilton, E. 215
Hamilton, E. W. ... 154
Hamilton, Mrs. G. W. 178
Hamilton, I. 234, 257, 398
Hamilton, W. H. ... 93
Hammann 24
Hammer 278
Hammerton 215
Hammond, F. ... 341
Hammond, I. ... 363
Hamon 208, 353
Hampe 143
Hampstead Garden Suburb 402
Hamund 372
Hanbury 93
Hancock 322
Handcock 332
Hankey ... 262, 341
Hanna 235, 294
Hannah 6
Hannay ... 89, 296
Hanotaux 4, 15, 22, 192, 202, 222, 353, 384, 390
Hansen, M. H. P. ... 48
Hansen, Steen- (*see* Steen-Hansen).
Harbou 171
Harcourt 78
Hard 149
Harden ... 171, 222, 269
Hardie 231
Hardwicke 87
Hardy 111
Hargrave 235
Harley 43
Harnack ... 171, 174
Harnden ... 379, 380
Harper, C. G. ... 263

Harper, E. H. ... 104
Harper, H. ... 103, 113
Harrard, A. R. ... 322
Harrard, E. M. ... 322
Harris, H. W. ... 279
Harris, J. H. ... 163
Harris, W. 316
Harrison, A. ... 32, 127
Harrison, E. J. ... 38
Harrison, F. ... 29, 149
Harrison, J. E. ... 405
Harrison, M. ... 10
Hart, A. B. ... 50, 127
Hart, H. 391
Hartl 24
Hartmann 83
Hartoy, d' (*see* D'Hartoy).
Harttung, Pflugk- (*see* Pflugk-Harttung).
Harvey, F. W. ... 364
Harvey, H. 267
Harvey, W. F. ... 276
Haselden ... 364, 374
Haskins 387
Hassall, A. ... 127, 344
Hassall, J. 372
Hasse 29
Hassler 254
Hastings 319
Hatt 398
Hauser 29, 34, 35, 134, 190, 310, 353, 384
Hauvette 178
Havard 316
Havard de la Montagne 143
Haward 341
Hawkin 143
Hawkins, A. H. (*see* *Hope, A*).
Hawley 40
Hawtin 296
Hay, A. W. 93
Hay, I. ... 208, 215, 341
Hay, M. F. 89
Hayashi 246
Hayden 18
Haydon 153
Hayens 127, 215
Haynes, H. 265
Hayward ... 341, 405
Hazen 10
Headlam, C. 22
Headlam, J. W. 6, 35, 119, 127, 143, 149, 150, 384
Heald 312
Hearn 38
Hearne 104
Hearnshaw ... 83, 127
Heath, A. G. ... 260, 273
Heath, C. ... 391, 405
Hecht 391
Hedin 171, 227
Heilgers 249
Heitland 405
Helfferich 80, 137, 202
Helmer 10
Helmolt 122, 199, 202
Hélys 158
Hemberger 202
Henches 260
Henderson, A. 147, 392
Henderson, D. ... 101
Henderson, E. F. ... 24
Henderson, K. ... 260
Henley, T. 332
Hennebois 291
Hennessy, J. ... 353, 392
Hennessy, Pope- (*see* Pope-Hennessy).
Hennig 239
Henriot ... 222, 257, 376
Henrique 22
Henriques 101
Henry 29
Henry-Rosier ... 353
Henslow 364
Henson 326
Herbert 372
Herford 23
Hermes 263
Hernan 380
Herries 263
Herringham ... 249, 315
Herriot 184
Herron 405
Hersch 353
Herschel-Clarke ... 364
Herscher ... 223, 374
Hertslet, E. 7, 8
Hertslet, E. L. A. ... 326
Herval 187
Hervé 158, 208
Hervier ... 192, 208, 278
Herzog 310
Hessen 187
Hettner 150, 171
Heubner 226
Heuled 256
Heuvel, van der (*see* Van der Heuvel).
Hewett 260
Hewlett 364
Heyking ... 47, 187
Heylen 280
Heywood 364
Hicks, E. L. 326, 333, 346
Hicks, P. M. 100
Higgins, A. P. 300, 345, 346
Hildebrand ... 140
Hilditch 208, 215, 243, 346, 347, 348
Hill, D. J. ... 4, 278
Hill, G. F. 163
Hill, H. W. 99
Hill, N. 43
Hill, W. T. 270
Hillis 127
Hindenburg ... 171, 246
Hindle 316
Hinkovitch ... 12, 50
Hinzelin ... 10, 273
Hippius 188
Hirschberg 187
Hirst 305
Hislam 107
Hoar 107
Hobhouse, Mrs. H.... 406
Hobhouse, L. T. 127, 341
Hobohm 171
Hobson ... 305, 390, 392, 398
Hodder 111
Hodder Williams ... 316
Hodge 398
Hodgson, E. S. ... 378
Hodgson, W. N. ... 364
Hodson 341
Höffner 171
Hölscher 203
Hœniger ... 122, 184
Hœtzsch ... 203, 208
Hofer 137
Hoffman 383
Hogg 332
Hogge 87
Hogue 235
Hohenlohe-Schillingfürst 24
Holbrook 93
Holdich ... 40, 341
Holewinski 43
Holland, A. W. 10, 29, 35
Holland, H. S. ... 332
Holland, T. E. 8, 300
Holland, W. L. ... 341
Hollebecque 158
Hollister 24
Holls 300
Hollweg, Bethmann (*see* Bethmann Hollweg).
Holm, Müller- (*see* Müller-Holm).
Holme 267
Holmes, E. 29
Holmes, E. E. ... 341
Holmes, R. 111
Holmes, R. D. ... 249
Holmes, W. K. ... 364
Hood 93
Hoog 158
Hooker 310
Hooper 392
Hoover 305
Hope, A. ... 163, 341
Hopfen 376
Hopford 291
Hopkins, F. G. ... 310
Hopkins, T. 291
Hopkinson 399
Hopwood 364
Hornbeck 20
Hornby 93
Horniman 305
Horton 332
Horton-Smith ... 341
Hossfeld 378
Hosten 219
Houghton 163
Hourticq ... 223, 254
House 387
Housman 408
Houtte, van (*see* Van Houtte).
Hovelaque 134
Hovgaard 89
Hovre 312
Howard, B. E. ... 29
Howard, C. 93
Howard, K. 243
Howard, Redmond- (*see* Redmond-Howard).
Howe, F. C. 29

Howe, M. A. de W. 208, 269
Howe, S. E. 47
Howell 85
Hrebelelianovich, Lazarovich- (*see* Lazarovich-Hrebelelianovich).
Huard 158, 216
Hubback 184
Huberich 170
Hubert 4, 167, 305
Huddleston 387
Hudson, S. 208
Hudson, W. 364
Hueffer ... 158, 163, 364
Hügel 32
Hünerwadel 137
Hugessen, Knatchbull- (*see* Knatchbull-Hugessen).
Hughes, B. 319
Hughes, J. D. ... 4
Hughes, W. M. ... 79
Hugins 384
Hugo ... 376, 379, 380
Huillard 167
Hume 49
Humphrey, A. W. ... 341
Humphrey, F. ... 249
Hunfalvy 45
Hunt, A. L. ... 99
Hunt, J. B. 332
Huntley 315
Huot 353
Hurd, A. 89, 107, 243, 399
Hurd, P. ... 216, 399
Hurgronje, Snouck- (*see* Snouck-Hurgronje).
Hurst, A. F. 316
Hurst, A. H. 45
Hurst, G. B. 235
Hutchinson, W. ... 16
Hutchinson, Woods... 315
Hutter 107, 243
Huysmans 80
Hyamson 42
Hyde 392
Hyndman ... 271, 341

Ibañez 203
Ibero 20
Ilitsch 20
Illyricus ... 36, 50
Imbart de la Tour 32, 353
Imelmann 150
Immanuel ... 203, 233
Independent Labour Party 406
Ingpen 216
Innes, A. D. ... 18, 24
Innes, C. E. 406
Instructor ... 96, 101
Inter-Denominational Summer School, Swanwick 332
International Red Cross Committee ... 289
International Union of Ethical Societies 131
Invicta 94
Iredell 85
Ironside 100
Irvine 326
Irwin ... 208, 249, 341
Iswolsky 46
Ivanoff 376

J.T. 178
Jabotinsky 181
Jacks 127
Jackson, Foakes (*see* Foakes-Jackson).
Jackson, L. E. S. ... 99
Jacobs 392
Jacques 150
Jäckh 29, 171
Jagow 137
Jairazbhoy ... 153, 181
James, D. McG. ... 100
James, G. de S. W. 364
James, H. ... 150, 322
James, H. R. 332
James, S. B. 406
James, W. H. 83
Jane 107, 108, 109, 346, 399
Jannasch 35
Jannaway 42
Jansson 305
Jarintzoff 47
Jastrow 127, 128, 384
Jaulmes 134
Jaurès 83
Jefferey 108
Jeffrey 380
Jeffs 332
Jellicoe 243
Jensen, Berggrav- (*see* Berggrav-Jensen).
Jephson 163
Jerram 364
Jerrold, C. 278
Jerrold, L. 158
Jerrold, W. ... 272, 274
Jersey 150
Jespersen 356
Jessen 48
Jèze 305
Jörgensen 139, 158, 227
Joffre 77
Johnson, D. W. 83, 174, 192, 208
Johnson, F. H. ... 319
Johnson, O. 158
Johnson, S. C. ... 105
Johnson, W. 192
Johnson, Webb- (*see* Webb-Johnson).
Johnston, A. 260
Johnston, A. L. ... 372
Johnston, H. H. ... 208
Johnston, H. J. ... 100
Johnston, J. 305
Johnston, W. & A. K. 117
Johnstone, H. M. ... 83
Johnston-Smith ... 364
Jollivet ... 198, 203, 223
Jolly 89
Jones, B. E. 87
Jones, C. S. 24, 150, 279
Jones, D. 257
Jones, E. R. 19
Jones, F. 233
Jones, Griffith- (*see* Griffith-Jones).
Jones, J. 238
Jones, J. D. 333
Jones, J. H. 305
Jones, J. P. ... 24, 163
Jones, P. 260
Jones, R. 319
Jones, S. 187
Jones, Sefton- (*see* Sefton-Jones).
Jonesco 80, 139
Jonquière 40
Jordan, D. S.... 341, 385
Jorga 12, 15, 45
Joubaire 257
Jourdan 158
Jouve 269
Jowett 333
Joynson-Hicks ... 11
Jubert 223
Julia 254
Jullian 353, 384
Junker 199
Juvenis 235

Kadontzeff 187
Kadoré 223
Kahn, A. 273
Kahn, O. H. 128
Kalau vom Hofe ... 243
Kammerer 137
Kanner 140
Kant 392
Karageorgevitch ... 190
Karrachy-Smitt ... 380
Kassner 9
Kato 374
Katz 300
Kaufman 364
Kautsky ... 122, 171
Kawakami 38
Keating 208
Keeling 260
Keen, E. 24
Keen, F. N. 392
Keith, A. B. 153
Keith, E. A. 291
Kellner 12
Kellogg, P. V. ... 143
Kellogg, V. L. ... 338
Keltie 6
Kemal 9
Kempster 312
Kennard, D. 183
Kennard, H. P. ... 47
Kennedy J. 239
Kennedy, J. M. 32, 128, 209, 216, 278
Kennedy, L J. ... 216
Kennedy, S. 342
Kennedy, Studdert- (*see* Studdert-Kennedy).
Kennedy, S. S. ... 309
Kennington 266
Kenny 364
Kent, C. 333
Kent, J. 83

Kenwood 316
Kenyon 342
Keogh 319
Kerensky 187
Kerlen 172
Kerner 1
Kernshaw 83
Kerofilas 277
Kerr, P. H. 4
Kerr, S. P. 209
Kervyn de Lettenhove 143
Kettle 249, 342
Key 406
Keynes 390
Keyworth ... 380, 381
Kiersch 32
Kikuchi 38
Kilpatrick 111
King, B. 36
King, T. 296
King's College, London 398
Kinsman 94
Kipling 89, 108, 111, 158, 364, 365
Kirby 392
Kirchner 243
Kirkaldy 85, 305, 311
Kirke 45
Kirkland 306
Kirkpatrick, F. A. 195, 306
Kirkpatrick, J. 128, 342
Kirkpatrick, T. P. C. 322
Kitson, A. 406
Kitson, E. 294
Kjellén 139, 356
Kladderadatsch ... 374
Klaxon ... 108, 243, 364
Klein 254, 333
Kluchevsky 46
Kluck ... 172, 226, 384
Knatchbull-Hugessen 12
Knight, A. E. ... 399
Knight, W. 357
Knight, W. S. M. 150, 203
Knott 154
Knowles, C. 291
Knowles, F. L. ... 342
Knox, A. 229
Knox, M. 291
Knyvett 208
Koch 306
König 243
Köster 229, 333
Kolchin 306
Koppe 85
Kotschubey 183
Kowalczyk 43
Kozicki 43
Krauel 300
Krebs 291
Krehbirl 406
Krek 12, 50
Kressenstein 237
Krey 291
Krunsky 13
Kucharski, R. ... 43
Kucharzewski, J. ... 184
Kühn 257
Kuhl ... 203, 209, 226
Kuhne 155
Kutscher 257
Kuttner 284
Kylie 128

L., D.O. 365
L., M.A.A. 358
L., R.A. 261
La Barre 291
Labbé 158
Labberton 172
La Brière 197
Labry 233
Lachapelle 306
La Chesnais 46, 167, 187
Lacroix, Gén. ... 183
Lacroix, F. 254
Lacroix, L. 354
Laffan 49
Laffargne 94
Laflotte 223
Lafont 223
Lafontaine 342
La Frégeolière ... 257
Lagarde, L. A. ... 319
Lagarde, M. 315
Lagardère ... 158, 399
Lair 29
Lake, B. C. 94
Lake, C. S. 101
Lake, H. 233
Lake, S. 108
Laloz 24
Lamb, C. 111
Lambert, H. 313, 342, 349, 385
Lambert, R. C. ... 150
Lammasch ... 137, 301
La Montagne, Havard de (*see* Havard de la Montagne).
Lamprecht 24
Lampson, Locker- (*see* Locker-Lampson).
Lamure, Fleury- (*see* Fleury-Lamure).
Lancaster 342
Lanchester 104
Land and Water ... 117
Landau 306
Landau-Aldanov ... 275
Lane 374
Lane-Poole, R. ... 7
Lane-Poole, S. ... 40
Lanessan 18, 24, 29, 135
Langdon 294
Lange, C. L. ... 187, 384
Lange, F. W. T. ... 2
Langenhove 120, 144, 284
Langevin 209
Langlois ... 167, 263
Lanino 178
Lanoir 167
Lanrézac 223
Lansbury 187
Lansing 387, 390
Lanux 50
Lanzalone 371
Lanzel 170
Lapradelle 279
La Revelière 39
Larguier 254
La Rica, Bermejo de (*see* Bermejo de la Rica).
Larmandie 291
Larmeroux 13
Larnaude ... 135, 384
Larousse 114
Larronde 354
Lash 150
Laskine ... 32, 384
Lasserre ... 32, 167
Latham 378
La Tour, Imbart de (*see* Imbart de la Tour).
Latymer ... 108, 365
Latzko 355
Lauder 158
Laughton 108
Launay 158, 304
Laurie 322
Lauterbach 263
Lauzanne 254
Lavedan 158, 209, 354
Lavergne 399
Lavery 208, 266
Lavine 159
Lavisse ... 4, 10, 24, 135, 167
Lavressan 167
Law, A. B. ... 77, 79
Law, H. A. 128
Lawley 238
Lawrence, T. J. 301, 394
Lawson, H. 365
Lawson, R. 294
Lawson, W. R. ... 306
Lawton 22
Lazarovich-Hrebelelianovich ... 49
Lea 365
Lead-Swinger (The) ... 265
League of Nations Society 391, 392, 394, 395
League to enforce peace 391, 396
Learned 29
Leary 238
Leask ... 269, 277, 365
Le Bail 223
Le Berquier 167
Leblanc 1
Lebon, A. 306
Le Bon, G. 313, 354, 399
Lebrun 45
Le Bruyère 243
Lechartier 192
Lecky 108
Leclerc 370, 371
Lecompte 271
Lecomte 144
Ledochowska 44
Lee, A. 79
Lee, J. 365
Lee, S. 342
Lee, V. 371
Leeds 270
Leeper 183
Leese 141
Leeson 312
Leete 374
Lefroy, Maxwell- (*see* Maxwell-Lefroy).

Le Gallienne 365
Léger 13, 47, 50, 140, 158
Legge, E. ... 128, 278
Legge, J. G. 163
Legge, R. F. 94
Légionnaire 17889 ... 249
Le Goffic ... 158, 223
Lehautcourt, P. (*see* Palat).
Lehfeldt 306
Leigh 261, 342
Lejars 319
Lelean 316
Leleux 257
Le Loghe 235
Lémonon ... 18, 36, 197
Leng 322
Lenin 187
Lenotre 167
Lensch ... 172, 209, 355
Lenwood 333, 348, 349
Leonard, G. H. ... 348
Leonard, R. M. ... 358
Lepert 392
Lépine, J. 316
Lépine, Roussel- (*see* Roussel-Lépine).
Lepsius 371
Le Queux 150, 203, 284
Lerch, Suter- (*see* Suter-Lerch).
Leroux, E. 159
Le Roux, H. ... 159, 261
Leroy 392
Leroy-Beaulieu 47, 203
Léry 223
Leslie, J. H. 269
Leslie, S. 365
Le Strange 40
Le Sueur 35
Lethbridge, A. ... 47
Lethbridge, M. ... 47
Lethbridge, M. C. ... 111
Lettenhove, Kervyn de (*see* Kervyn de Lettenhove).
Lettow-Vorbeck ... 246
Letts 365
Leudet 312
Leutrum-Okoricsamzi 13, 140
Leutwein 172
Lévêque 291
Levey, J. H. ... 83, 94
Lévi, C. 144
Levi, N. 277
Levine 187
Levison 236
Lévy, A. 159
Lévy, M. 22
Lévy, R. G. 390
Lévy-Bruhl ... 135, 159
Lewin, P. E. 29, 35, 163, 345
Lewin, Ross- (*see* Ross-Lewin).
Lewis 359
Lewisohn 174
Leyland 108, 243
Libermann 223, 233, 254
"Librarian" 1
Librarie française ... 1
Lichnowsky 246
Lichtenberger 10, 24, 34, 135, 168, 192
Lichtervelde 144
Liddell, K. 108
Liddell, R. S. 184, 216, 229
Liebig 172
Liebknecht 172
Liesse 168
Liman von Sanders ... 181
Limosin 254
Lincoln, Bishop of (*see* Hicks).
Lind-af-Hageby ... 342
Lindbaek 4
Lindenberg ... 229, 231
Lindsay 345
Lindsay, A. D. ... 342
Lings 94
Lintier 254
Linton 333
Lipkowski 44
Lippmann ... 342, 392
Lipton 233
Lister 275
Little 44
Little nun 144
Litvinoff 187
Litwinski 44
Liveing 249
Liverpool Women's War Service Bureau 155
Livingston ... 250, 315
Lloyd, B. 358
Lloyd, G. 250
Lloyd, Ll. 316
Lobbedey 222
Locker-Lampson ... 358
Lockhart 378
Lodge, H. C. 80
Lodge, O. 399
Loebnitz, Müller- (*see* Müller-Loebnitz).
Logan 342
Loisy 333, 354
Lombardo 380
London, Bishop of 326, 333
London District School of Instruction 96
London Gazette 199, 211, 238
London School of Economics 304
Long 229
Longstaff 100
Looker 365
Lord 387
Loreburn 128
Lorin 384
Losch 172
Lote 29, 354
Loti ... 38, 144, 209, 354
Louis ... 135, 168, 399
Lourié, Ossip- (*see* Ossip-Lourié).
Lovett 18
Low ... 18, 178, 342
Lowe 111
Lowell 6, 306
Lowndes 205
Lowry 296
Loyson 135, 159
Luboff 378
Lucas, C. P. 18, 153, 342
Lucas, E. 333
Lucas, E. V. 322, 342, 372
Lucas, F. 378
Lucatelli 159
Ludendorff 199, 209, 246
Ludlow 83
Ludwig 233
Lüdersdorff 267
Lugaro 174
Luke 150
Lumet 199
Lupold 227
Lusk 275
Lux Animæ 163
Lyde 384
Lynch, A. 154
Lynch, F. 399
Lynch, G. 94
Lynd 342
Lynden-Bell 284
Lyon, P. H. B. ... 365
Lyon, W. S. S. ... 365
Lyons, Library ... 1
Lyons, A. N. 112
Lyons, J. 365
Lysle 378
Lytton 209
Lyttleton ... 128, 150

M., D.R. 218
M.A.C. 365
MacAlister 99
Macara 311
Macartney 87
McAuley 164
M'Cabe ... 32, 278, 333, 342
McCall 342
McCarthy, D. J. ... 291
McCarthy, J. 18
MacCarthy, M. T. H. 279
McCartney 235
Maccas 175, 176, 271, 284, 354
McClean 94
McClure, E. 32
McClure, S. S. 128, 406
McConnell 250
McCormick, F. ... 179
McCormick, H. F. ... 406
McCormick, R. ... 229
McCudden ... 114, 250
McCurdy ... 128, 164
McCustra 235
McDermaid 108
MacDonagh ... 209, 216
Macdonald, J. A. ... 342
Macdonald, J. N. ... 178
Macdonald, J. R. 343, 399
MacDonald, M. ... 216
Macdonald, Mina ... 140
Macdonald, R. ... 126
MacDonell, J. de C. 17, 270
McDougall, E. ... 348
McDougall, G. ... 322
M'Ewan 399
Macewen 326
Macfall ... 84, 164, 258, 384
Macfie, R. C. 365
MacGill ... 216, 365

McGovern 38
McGregor 275
MacGuarrie 94
Mach 119, 128
Machen 228
McIntosh, D. M. ... 374
Macintosh, J. C. ... 216
Mack, L. 144
Mackail 47
Mackarness 326
Mackaye 393
Mackenna 168
MacKenzie, D. A. 205, 263, 264, 274
MacKenzie, F. A. 154, 216
Mackereth 365
Mackinnon 294
Mackintosh, E. A. ... 365
Macklin 358
Maclagan 393
McLaglen 94
McLaren, A. D. 164, 278
McLaren, Mrs. B. ... 154
McLaren, E. S. ... 322
McLaren, W. W. ... 38
Maclean, A. M. ... 216
Maclean, F. 35
Maclean, J. K. ... 209
Maclear 101
McLennan, J. S. ... 153
Maclennan, K. 333, 349
MacLeod 164
McMaster 192
McMillan 316
McMinnies 104
MacMurray 20
McNair ... 216, 343
Macnaught 358
Macnaughtan ... 258
Macnutt 326
MacOrlan 223
Macpherson 315
Madariaga 150
Madelin 168, 224, 384
Maeterlinck 182, 284, 356
Maeztu 356
Magne 254
Magnus, L. 343
Magnus, L. A. 45, 128, 376
Maguire 150
Mahan 89, 343
Mahoney 292
Maillard 399
Mais 343
Major, The ... 98, 296
Major, Forsyth- (*see* Forsyth-Major).
Makins 319
Malcolm 216
Malherbe 159
Malleson 24
Mallet, C. ... 255, 258
Mallet, J. 365
Malleterre 209, 224, 354
Mallock 306
Mallory 87
Malo 144, 224
Maltby 87, 348
Manchester Guardian 202
Mancunian 301
Mandelstam 181
Manen 24, 168
Mann, A. J. 233
Mann, T. 172
Mann, W. M.... ... 94
Manners 309
Manning-Foster ... 358
Mantegazza 36
Mantel 137
Mantey 244
Manwaring 261
Maple Leaf (The) ... 265
Mappin 306
Marabini 224
Marbeau 224
Marburg 393
Marc 258
Marcosson 84, 187, 216, 399
Marden 309
Marès, de (*see* De Marès).
Margerie 135
Margerison ... 89, 108
Margueritte 354
Margutti 272
Mariani 139, 175, 264
Marie, *Queen of Roumania* 45
Marini 178
Mario 178
Markham 164
Markland 144
Markovitch 187
Marlier, Ruelens- (*see* Ruelens-Marlier).
Marlowe 154
Maroi 306
Marre ... 99, 284, 312
Marriott, Major ... 380
Marriott, J. A. R. 18, 20, 25, 343
Marsden 276
Marshall, A. 85
Marshall, H. R. ... 406
Marshall, J. 380
Marshall, L. H. ... 292
Marten 128
Martens 8
Marti 128
Martian 95
Martin, A. A. ... 250
Martin, E. 343
Martin, E. W. ... 306
Martin, G. 85
Martin, H. ... 155, 250
Martin, J. 292
Martin, W. 29, 159, 168
Martineau 327
Martin-Nicholson ... 323
Martyn 196
Marvin 343, 346
Masaoka, Naoichi- (*see* Naoichi-Masaoka).
Masaryk 13, 47, 356, 384
Masefield ... 216, 235
Mason, C. F. 323
Mason, E. W. ... 406
Mason, F. H. 89
Mason, J. 366
Mason, R. C. 100
Massart 144
Massé 306
Massey 237
Massingham 128
Masson, A. 224
Masson, F. ... 224, 333
Masson, P. M. ... 261
Massow 198
Masterman 237
Matarollo 183
Mater 393
Matheson ... 343, 348
Matter 168
Matter, Florent (*see* Florent-Matter).
Matters 313
Matthaei ... 349, 393
Matthai 153, 349
Matthews, C. 315
Matthews, R. B. ... 104
Maud 333
Maude 84, 380
Maugain 178
Maunder 102
Maurel 178
Maurice, F. 217
Maurice, L. 39
Maurie 255
Maurras 4, 22, 159, 196, 264
Maury 195
Mausset 2
Mauveaux 225
Mavor 46
Mavrodin ... 45, 183
Mawson 399
Maxe 187
Maxwell, G. S. ... 358
Maxwell, J. 313
Maxwell-Lefroy ... 317
Mayer, A. 178
Mayer, E. 354
Mayers 296
Mayhew 333
Maynard 366
Mazé 224
Mazel 399
Meakin 84
Mears 284
Meath 95
Médelsheim 306
Medley 129
Mehrmann-Coblenz ... 181
Meinecke 137, 171, 172
Meiningen, Müller- (*see* Müller-Meiningen).
Melas 271
Melbourne, E. (*see* Hodgson, W. N.).
Mellor 327
Mélot 168
Mendonça 139
Mengens 323
Menke, Spruner- (*see* Spruner-Menke).
Menpes 274
Mercier, Cardinal 80, 144, 246, 261, 279, 327
Mercier, R. ... 224, 258
Merewether 217
Mermeix 199
Merriman 95
Merry 184
Merton 261
Merwin 376

Mesopotamia Commission 237
Metchim 203
Meunier 255
Mévil 4
Meyer, A. O. 138, 172, 355
Meyer, E. 150
Meyer, H. H. B. ... 2
Meyer, H. R. ... 399
Meyer, S. B. ... 366
Meynell 272
Michael 150
Michaelis 25
Michaux, J. ... 159, 258
Michelin Guides ... 222
Middleton 104, 217, 264
Mieille 224
Miessner 229
Mijatovitch ... 15, 49
Milan 244
Miles 309
Milhaud 393
Milioukov (*see* Milyukov).
Millard, F. L. H. ... 327
Millard, T. F. ... 238
Mille 112
Miller, F. 151
Miller, W. ... 15, 40
Millerand 210
Millet 210
Millioud 135
Mills 18, 153
Milne, A. B. 244
Milne, J. ... 112, 210
Milner 41
Milton, Major ... 95
Milyukov 46, 184, 188
Minor 393
Mirecourt 22
Mitchell, A. G. ... 366
Mitchell, P. 320
Mitchell, P. C. ... 313
Mitrany ... 45, 183, 347
Mitrosanoff 183
Mittler, Tœche- (*see* Tœche-Mittler).
Mitton 13, 250
Moberly ... 333, 348
Moch 393
Mocran 343
Möller, Früs- (*see* Früs-Möller).
Mœller, J. C. ... 48
Moffatt 366
Moffitt 95
Mohr 181
Mokveld ... 144, 224
Molesworth 310
Moltke 25
Monash 217
Monk 95
Monkévitz 229
Monkhouse 371
Monlaur, Reynes- (*see* Reynes-Monlaur).
Monod 3
Monroe 19
Monsenergue 99
Montagu 79
Montague 267
Montague-Bates ... 102
Montariol 378
Montesquiou 45
Monteyer 384
Montgelas 122
Montier 40
Montmorency 301
Montran 42
Montvert ... 261, 292
Moody 406
Moonan 18
Moore, H. C. 244
Moore, J. B. 301
Moores 317
Moraht 203, 210
Morant 159
Morejkowsky 188
Morel ... 39, 126, 343, 406
Moreland 375
Morel-Fatio 138
Morfill 47
Morgan, F. ... 21, 344
Morgan, G. C. ... 333
Morgan, H. E. ... 310
Morgan, J. H. 250, 282, 296
Morgan, J. V. ... 151
Morgenthau 181
Morison 319
Morning Post ... 207
Morretta 231
Morse, H. B. 20
Morse, J. 229
Morris, A. 95
Morris, C. 129
Morris, K. ... 239, 270
Morris, R. C. ... 301
Morrow 372
Mortane 264
Moseley 235
Moser 210
Mott 334
Moulin 197
Moulton ... 343, 349
Mourey 224
Moutran 384
Mowat 8, 347
Moysset 29
Mozley 327
Mügge 393
Mühlon 138, 172
Müller, E. ... 284, 358
Müller, K. 226
Müller, K. H. ... 40
Müller, M. 159
Müller - Guttenbrunn 141
Müller-Holm ... 172
Müller-Loebnitz ... 226
Müller-Meiningen 138, 172, 301, 384
Münsterberg 129, 192, 384
Mugerditchian ... 181
Mugnier 224
Muir, J. 334
Muir, R. 4, 18, 129, 301, 343, 345
Muir, W. 323
Muirhead ... 164, 347
Mullins 284, 343
Mumby 203
Munin 141
Munro 129
Munthe 251
Murat 188
Muret 168, 278
Murphy, J. K. ... 319
Murphy, W. S. ... 270
Murray, A. 237
Murray, A. M. ... 203
Murray, C. 366
Murray, D. 38
Murray, G. 18, 127, 151, 195, 313, 343, 345, 346, 393
Murray, H. R. ... 129
Murray, J. A. ... 306
Murray, M. 229, 334, 343, 378
Murray, Scott- (*see* Scott-Murray).
Murray, S. L. ... 84
Murray, W. S. ... 15
Mursell 327
Musgrave ... 250, 310
Myers 8

N., C. 94
Nabokoff 247
Nadaud 255
Nadja 366
Nagpur, Bishop of ... 250
Namier 13, 129
Nankivell 317
Naoichi Masaoka ... 38
Narsy 144
Nash, publishers ... 84
Nash, P. 266
Nasmith 210
Nathan 294
National Committee for Relief in Belgium 143
National Economy League 309
National Peace Council 386
Natkowski 44
Naumann 29, 155, 172, 182
Navarro 323
Naville 287
Navy League 109
Naylor 95
Neilson 343
Nekludoff ... 46, 246
Nelson 117
Nesbit 358
Nesbitt 366
Nettleinghame ... 358
Neumann 114
Nevinson, C. R. W. 266, 267
Nevinson, H. W. ... 267
Newbigin 15
Newbold 87
Newbolt, H. 89, 112, 244, 264, 366
New Church Magazine 331
Newsome 323
Newton, A. P. ... 18
Newton, W. G. 102, 217
New York Times ... 201
New Zealand Division 210
Nichols 366
Nicholson, J. S. ... 192

Nicholson, Martin- (*see* Martin-Nicholson).
Nicholson, S.... ... 307
Nicolai, G. F. ... 355
Nicolai, W. 172
Nicolas 258
Nicoll 334
Nicol-Speyer 170
Nicot 135, 224
Nielsen 138, 261
Niemann 138, 172, 229
Nietzsche 33
Nightingale 323
Niox 15
Nippold 172, 173, 301, 355
Nitti 390
No. 31540, *R.A.M.C.* 323
Nobbs 250
Noble 109, 244
Nohain, Franc- (*see* Franc-Nohain).
Nolde 188
Noradounghian ... 8
Norcock 102
Norden 144
Nordentoft 406
Nordmann 255
Normand 371
North 205
North American ... 211
North Britain ... 151
Northcliffe 210
Norton, F. ... 323, 372
Norton, H. T. J. ... 131
Norton, R. 347
Norway, Mrs. H. ... 154
Nosek 141
Noskoff 276
Nothomb 17, 145, 159, 224
Novakovitch 190
Novicow 355
Novikoff ... 47, 185
Nowak 138
Noyes, A. 89, 244, 366
Noyes, A. D. ... 307
Nurse 327, 344
Nutt 380
Nyrop ... 22, 145, 356
Nyström 25

O., F. O. ... 99, 250
O.B.I.T. 394
Oakes 8
Oakley 334
O'Brien, G. R. B. ... 283
O'Brien, P. 292
Observer 250
O'Connor, J. K. ... 151
O'Connor, T. P. ... 264
Odavitch 2
O'Donnell ... 95, 100
Odysseus ... 40, 250
Oechsli 49
O'Farrell 307
Ogg 4
Ogston 250
Ohlinger 192
Ohnet 159
Ojetti 178
Okakura 38
Okey 36
Okie 129, 192
Okoricsamzi, Leutrum (*see* Leutrum-Okoricsamzi).
Oldberg 229
Oldham, J. H. 348, 349
Oldmeadow 309
Olgin 188
Olijff 145
Oliphant 25
Oliver 84, 344
Olivier, Captain ... 292
Olivier, S. 394
Olozwski 182
Olszewski 175
O'Mahoney ... 19, 155
Oman 129
Omessa 188
Ommundsen 96
Omond 16, 301
Oncken 173, 192
One of the Jocks ... 251
O'Neill, E. 205
O'Neill, H. C. ... 239
Oppenheim ... 301, 394
Orchard 348
Ord 366
O'Regan ... 8, 198
Organisation centrale pour une paix durable 394
Orlando 80
Orlet 135
O'Rorke 292
Orr 42
Orsi 5
Orwin 311, 347
Osborn, E. B. ... 358
Osborn, M. 229
Osborne, C. E. ... 334
Osborne, S. 164
Osler 312, 345
Ossianilsson ... 140, 145
Ossip-Lourié ... 185, 188
Osten - Sacken - Rhein 173
Ostrorog 181
Osuzky 12
Otlet 394
Otto 244
Ouroussow 8
Outhwaite 348
Outis 244
Ouy-Vernazobres ... 258
Overseas Club ... 114
Owen 375
Oxenham, J. 217, 348, 366
Oxford, M. N. ... 323
Oxford Pamphlets 344-348
Oxford Scholars ... 129
Oxford University ... 269
Oyler 366

P., G. C. 402
P., R. 89
P. D. 402, 406
Pace 178
Packer 175
Page, A. 294
Page, E. J. 151
Page, F. 348
Pagé, V. W. 378
Page-Croft 251
Pagès 119, 133
Paget, F. 327
Paget, H. L. 151, 334
Paget, Mrs. L. 86, 348
Paget, S. 348
Paish 394
Pakenham-Walsh ... 366
Palacio-Valdés ... 140
Paladini 18
Palamenghi-Crispi ... 37
Palat 224
Paléoloque 188
Palmer, F. 192, 217, 251
Palmer, Mrs. J. P. 151
Palmer, L. S. ... 102
Panagulli 376
Pan-German League 28
Pangloss, Dr. ... 372
Pankhurst 79
Pantaleoni 178
Panzini 37
Paravy 334
Pares 229, 394
Parfit 40, 42, 238
Paribeni 37
Paris, J. L. 255
Pariset 135
Parker, E. H. ... 20
Parker, G. 129
Parliamentary Recruiting Committee 127, 285
Parr 261
Parrott 205
Parry 87
Pasley 18
Pasquier 33
Passaris 176
Passelecq ... 145, 175
Pastre 224, 255
Paterson, W. P. 28, 327
Paterson-Smyth ... 334
Pathfinder 102
Patterson, J. E. ... 109
Patterson, J. H. ... 236
Pattini 37
Paul 18
Paul-Dubois 151
Payne-Gallwey ... 129
Pchédécki 301
Peacock, N. 47
Peacock, W. 9
Peake 407
Peant 296
Pear 317
Pearce 84
Pears 40, 269
Pearson 228
Péchenard 225
Peckelsheim 258
Peddie 311
Peek 323
Peez 19
Pegler 295
Péladan 168
Pelissier ... 30, 135
Pellatt 312
Pellet 301
Pemberton-Billing ... 104

Penhallow 319
Penn 394
Pennell 267
Pepys, Samuel, jr. ... 373
Percy, Earl 204
Péret 22
Perez-Triana ... 307, 356
Péricard ... 225, 255
Perkins 217
Pernice 15
Perraud 315
Perrier, E. ... 22, 190
Perrin 159, 255
Perris 217, 278
Perry 313
Peshall 245
Pétain 135
Peter 264
Petermann 7
Peterson ... 153, 347
Petit, Albert- (*see* Albert-Petit).
Petit, P. ... 34, 168
Petit d'Alfort ... 312
Petre 129, 349
Petrovitch 49
Pfister 10
Pflugk-Harttung 5, 226, 230, 301
Phayre 349
Phillimore, R. ... 301
Phillimore, W. G. F. 5, 394
Philip, publisher ... 118
Philip, A. J. 307
Phillips, E. A. W. 407
Phillips, E. G. ... 380
Phillips, L. M. ... 349
Phillips, S. 371
Phillips, W. A. 5, 35, 44
Phillipson, C. 5, 10, 40, 301
Philosophoff 188
Piazza 139
Pic 225
Picciotto 301
Piccoli 178
Pichon, J. E. (*see* *Chopin, J.*).
Pickard, Sutton- (*see* Sutton-Pickard).
Picot 292
Picton 407
Piérard ... 145, 194
Piermarini 164
Pierre-Alype 168
Pierrefeu 225
Piggott 302
Pigou 307
Pilon 255
Pim 154
Pinchard 196
Pingaud 37, 168, 256
Pinon ... 5, 22, 40, 181
Piper 1
Piquet 39
Pirenne 225
Pisani, Ferri- (*see* Ferri-Pisani).
Pitt 380
Pittard 45
Plant 96
Plater 313
Platoon - Commander 90, 251, 323
Plehn 25
Plowden - Wardlow 349, 402
Plowman 317
Plumer 251
Plumon 380
Plunkett 154
Pochhammer 244
Pohl 244
Poincaré 22, 80, 121, 135
Poirier 225
Pokrowski 47
Pole, Tudor- (*see* Tudor-Pole).
Polish Information Comm. ... 34, 44
Politis 80
Pollard, A. F. 129, 153, 204, 394
Pollard, A. W. ... 276
Pollard, H. ... 96, 217
Pollen 89, 244
Pollock, F. ... 129, 394
Pollock, H. W. A. ... 96
Pollock, J. 188
Polsue 269
Polybius 35
Pommereuil 295
Poncet, François- (*see* François-Poncet).
Pond 314
Pons 160
Ponsonby, A. 5, 394, 407
Ponsonby, M. 349, 351
Ponti 394
Poole, E. 188
Poole, Lane- (*see* Lane-Poole).
Pooley 38, 179
Pope, A. E. 323
Pope, E. W. 296
Pope, J. 366
Pope-Hennessy ... 118
Popovici 13
Popovitch 180
Porcelli 196
Porter 38
Poseck 227
Posner 44, 182
Postgate 188
Potez 160
Potter, B. 407
Potter, J. H. 327
Poulton 313
Pourtalès 247
Pouvourville 385
Powell, Baden- (*see* Baden-Powell).
Powell, C. 366
Powell, E. A. 217, 231
Powell, E. T. ... 307
Powell, G. H. ... 373
Powell, J. 292
Power 315, 319
Powers 130, 385
Powys 30
Poy 375
Poynter 402
Praga 309
Pratt, E. A. ... 87, 307
Pratt, S. C. 296
Pratz ... 157, 160, 255
Preston, H. M. ... 319
Preston, J. 385
Prevost, C. M. ... 366
Prévost, M. 225
Preziozi ... 37, 179
Prezzolini ... 13, 231
Pribram 8, 13
Price, C. 15, 49, 141, 155, 233, 277
Price, J. M. 231
Price, M. P. ... 188, 204
Price, T. 407
Price, W. H. 244
Priestman 236
Prigge 236
Prignet 10
Primorác, Vouk 50, 194
Prince 130, 279
Princetown Univ. ... 193
Prinzing 317
Prior 25, 346
Privat 182, 385
Private No. 940 ... 251
Private 7664 261
"*Probus*" 160
Probyn 37
Prochazka 13
Proctor 334
Prosser 327
Prothero 25, 130, 151
Protheroe 109, 270, 274
Prüm 130, 284
Prussian 33
Prussian Officer ... 30
Puaux 135, 175, 210, 271, 385
Pughe 366
Pulitzer 251
Pull 87
Pulling 294
Pult 292
Punch 372
Pupin 307
Purlitz 204
Putnam 10, 17
Pyke, E. L. 164
Pyke, G. 292
Pyke, H. R. ... 302, 347
Pym 217

Quadrotta 196
Quercy 258
Quidde 278
Quin 407

R., Lieut. E. (*see* Tuffrau).
R., S. 193
R., S. (*see also* Raffalovitch, S.).
R., S. R. 131
Rachfahl 25
Radclyffe 307
Radelet 145
Radiquet 84
Radziwill 13, 25, 188, 269

Rae, E. 217
Rae, J. 323
Raemaekers 375
Raestad 385
Raffalovitch 185, 189, 310
Raffi 381
Raffin 112
Railway News ... 307
Raineri 37, 194
Rait 130
Raker 96
Raleigh, W. 130, 151, 344, 349
Rambaud 4, 46
Ramsay, A. 402
Ramsay, A. M. ... 320
Ramsay, W. M. 40, 41
Ramsey 85
Randolph, C. F. ... 130
Randolph, E. S. L. 327
Randolph, J. A. ... 145
Randolph, W. ... 160
Rankin 15
Ransome 188
Raphaël 168
Rappoport 189
Rathenau 278
Ratti 9
Rawes 100
Rawling 320
Rawlins 373
Rawnsley 130, 366, 385
Rawson 402
Raymond 30
Rayner 239
Réau 189
Re-Bartlett ... 179, 349
Recalled to life ... 402
Reckitt 323
Recouly ... 176, 273
Reddle 209
Reder, Schmidt- (*see* Schmidt-Reder).
Rédier 354
Redmond, J. E. ... 79
Redmond, W. ... 276
Redmond-Howard 154, 395
Reed 230
Rees, D. T. 381
Rees, J. A. 130
Reeve 109
Régamey ... 30, 375
Regiment (The) 90, 91, 92, 102
Régnier 371
Reich 30
Reiche 2
Reid 267
Reinach, J. 10, 122, 190, 210, 225
Reinke 355
Reinsch 395
Reiss 233, 285
Renard 160
Renaud 255
Renault 285
René 225
Renner 355
Rentoul 366
Renwick 251
Repington 258
Repoulis 80
Repplier ... 130, 349
Retg, Diaz- (*see* Diaz-Retg).
Retté 354
Reuter 244
Révai 138
Rivelli 37
Reventlow 5, 19, 25, 151, 173, 246
Revol 225
Revue Franco-Macédoine 232
Revue Polonia ... 182
Rew 307, 346
Rey, A. ... 21, 160, 189
Rey, B. 385
Reynes-Monlaur ... 354
Rezanoff 285
Rhys 217
Riach 313
Ribot 135
Rice 296
Richard, E. 25
Richard, H. 181
Richards, H. E. 302, 347
Richardson, A. R. ... 96
Richardson, W. G. 319
Richepin 354
Richet 182
Rickard 217
Riesser 307
Rifat 151
Riggs 96
Rignano 139, 385, 386
Rimbaud 255
Rimbault 258
Rimington 407
Rineheart 251
Rion 258
Ritchie, D. L. ... 402
Ritchie, M. 239
Ritter 138
Ritzeman 402
Rivet, A. 295
Rivet, C. ... 189, 275
Rivista di Roma ... 1
Rizoff 155
Roberts, Lord ... 151
Roberts, A. A. ... 285
Roberts, C. 367
Roberts, C. G. D. ... 218
Roberts, M. 367
Roberts, R. ... 152, 348
Roberts, W. R. ... 349
Robertson, A. ... 367
Robertson, C. G. 7, 164, 345
Robertson, J. L. ... 367
Robertson, J. M. 130, 164, 307, 350
Robertson, J. W. ... 386
Robertson, W. ... 277
Robertson-Scott ... 179
Robida 285
Robinson, B. 375
Robinson, E. E. ... 193
Robinson, E. H. ... 96
Robinson, H. P. ... 218
Robinson, J. J. ... 402
Robinson, J. P. K. ... 239
Robinson, W. H. ... 375
Robinson, W. J. ... 251
Robson 104
Rocheblave 194
Rockhill 8
Roederer 42, 181, 386
Röhl 239
Rösemeier 173
Roffidal 315
Roger 258, 292
Rogers 130
Rohden 261
Rohrbach, P. 21, 30, 35, 138, 173, 185, 189, 230
"*Roland*" 340
Rolin 255
Rolland, L. 302
Rolland, R. ... 33, 354
Rollings 334
Roloff 25
Romanes 334
Ronze 9
Roosevelt 50, 193, 350
Root 50, 80
Roscher, M. 292
Roscher, W. 35
Roscoe 84, 334
Rose, J. H. 5, 131, 164, 350
Rosebery 79
Rosen 264
Rosendal 48
Rosher 114, 261
Rosier, Henry- (*see* Henry-Rosier).
Ross, E. A. 189
Ross, J. N. MacB. ... 204
Ross, M. 264
Ross, N. 264
Ross, R. B. 218
Ross-Lewin 367
Rosso 179
Roth, P. 182
Roth, P. B. 320
Rotheit 386
Rothery 297
Rothschild 210
Roudie 371
Roudil 96
Roujon 258, 259
Round Table 41, 124, 129, 132, 163, 385
Rouquette 193
Rouse 100
Rousseau, A. 89, 109, 244
Rousseau, J. J. ... 395
Rousselet 7
Roussel-Lépine ... 324
Roussy 317
Roux, M. ... 160, 407
Roux, X. 261
Rouzie 334
Rovito 232
Row 347
Rowlands 367
Roxburgh 292
Royal Colonial Institute 129
Royal field Leech ... 321
Royce 193
Royden 407
Royer 164
Rudwitsky 47
Rühlmann 356
Ruelens-Marlier ... 386

Ruffin ... 210, 218, 225
Ruhl 251
Rumeau 197
Ruplinger 168
Ruppin 42
Rural League ... 130
Russell, B. 189, 350, 402, 407
Russell, C. E. ... 189
Russell, G. W. ... 154
Russell, G. W. E. ... 152
Russian Union of Zemstvos 185
Rutherford 402
Ruyssen 136
Ryan, A. 276
Ryan, N. 13
Ryder 407
Rye 274
Ryle, A. L. 102
Ryle, H. E. 327

S., J. M. 332
S.P.C.K. 325
Sabatier 160
Sacerdote 179
Sackville 367
Sacre 375
Sänger 138
Sageret ... 355, 386
Saillens 160
Sainéan 378
Saint-Cyr 179
St. John Ambulance Association ... 322
St. Martin 7
Saint-Paul 315
Saint Pierre 245
Saintyves 136
Saison 233
Salandra 80
Salmon 355
Salomon 138
Salt 358
Salter 310
Salvemini 37, 139, 179, 386
Salvioni 7
Sampson 239
Samuel 131
Samuelson 308
Samways 367
Sanborn 127
Sanday ... 131, 344, 350
Sanders, Liman von (*see* Liman von Sanders).
Sanders, L. C. ... 18
Sanders, W. 295
Sandes 233, 238
Sanger 131
Santayana 164
Santo 169
Sapper 218, 264
Sargant 357
Sarolea 5, 47, 146, 160, 164, 185, 189, 218, 270
Sarrail 233
Sarraut 312
Sarson 367
Sartiaux 236
Sartory 320
Sassoon 367
Sauerbeck 122
Saundby ... 104, 324
Savarit 386
Savic 21, 386
Savodjian 155
Savtchenko 185
Sawyer 408
Sayle, C. 271
Sayous 169
Scanlan 297
Schäfer, D. ... 138, 204
Schaffstein 204
Schanz 173
Scheer 245, 247
Schefer 5
Schenk 293
Schewaebel 225
Schian 210
Schiemann ... 26, 138
Schillingfürst, Hohenlohe- (*see* Hohenlohe - Schillingfürst).
Schlicht 112
Schlieben 30
Schmidt 189
Schmidtbonn ... 233
Schmidt-Reder ... 293
Schmitt 19
Schmitz 255
Schmoller 34
Schnee 240
Schneider 30
Schoen 247
Schönborn 146
Schopfer, I. (*see* Anet.
Schopin 85
Schreiner, G. A. ... 165
Schreiner, O. 350
Schuchardt 173
Schücking ... 122, 302
Schuler 153
Schulte 138
Schulthess ... 5, 198
Schultze-Gävernitz ... 19
Schulz-Besser ... 375
Schumacher 308
Schurman 15
Schwabe 308
Schwan 395
Schwarte ... 210, 211
Schweder 181
Schwering 26
Scialoja 179
Scott, A. P. 390
Scott, F. G. 367
Scott, J. B. ... 193, 395
Scott, J. C. 251
Scott, L. ... 295, 302
Scott, M. J. 30
Scott, Robertson- (*see* Robertson-Scott).
Scott, T. W. R. ... 194
Scott, W. R. 402
Scott-Moncrieff ... 334
Scott-Murray 328
Scudamore 381
Scurr 308
Séailles 160
Seaman 367
Searchlight 96
Seaver 335
Séché 395
Second in Command 96
Secrétan 196
Sedding 277
Seeger 262, 367
Sefton-Jones ... 165, 285
Segal 381
Seignobos ... 5, 402
Seillière ... 30, 271
Selbie 335, 346
Seldes 193
Seligman 233
Sellers 105, 335
Sembat 22
Senior Major ... 97
Senn 309, 324
Serao 179
Serbesco 183
Sergeant, L. 36
Sergeant, P. W. ... 272
Sergeant - Major, R.A.M.C. 315
Sering 185
Séris 160
Service, R. W. ... 367
Service, W. J. N. ... 335
Seton-Watson 13, 15, 33, 50, 131, 183, 190, 349, 350
Sette 228
"*Severus*" 179
Seymour ... 131, 387
Shakespeare 367
Shaw, F. G. 97
Shaw, K. E. 251
Shaw, S. 279
Sheahan 251
Shearwood 46
Sheehan 160
Sheppard 251
Sherwell 47
Shillito ... 335, 367
Shipley ... 317, 324
Shirley, R. 228
Shirley, W. 84
Short 367
Shumaker 395
Sibille 225
Sidgwick ... 30, 127
Sidler 152
Siebert 5
Siebold 152
Siefert 47
Silas 236
Silva-Vildósola ... 195
Sime 26
Simmonds, R. ... 104
Simms, J. J. 131
Simonds, F. H. ... 204
Simonin 255
Simplex ... 97, 100
Simplicissimus 374, 376
Simpson, G. 89
Simpson, J. U. ... 185
Sims 245
Sinclair 251
Singer 5
Singh 112, 153
Singleton 100
Sinker 328
Sinnett 313

Sirianu 45
Skaggs 193
Skeyhill 368
Skrine 46, 84
Sladen ... 131, 273, 293
Slater 127, 350
Sleeman 97
Sloane 127
Slocombe 44
Sloss 152, 153
Smart 267
Smetham 308
Smirnoff 381
Smith, A. L. ... 335, 346
Smith, Corbett- (*see* Corbett-Smith).
Smith, Fox (*see* Fox Smith).
Smith, F. E. 302
Smith, F. J. J. ... 368
Smith, F. W. ... 368
Smith, Gordon- (*see* Gordon-Smith).
Smith, G. A. ... 42, 328
Smith, G. B. 368
Smith, G. E. 317
Smith, G. V. 251
Smith, H. 350
Smith, Horton- (*see* Horton-Smith).
Smith, H. D. 152
Smith, H. H. ... 309
Smith, Johnston- (*see* Johnston-Smith).
Smith, J. S. 97
Smith, M. ... 175, 350
Smith, S. 165
Smith, T. F. A. 30, 165
Smith-Dampier ... 276
Smitt, Karrachy- (*see* Karrachy-Smitt).
Smuts 79, 395
Smyth, E. J. 97
Smyth, Paterson- (*see* Paterson-Smyth).
Snell 335
Snelling 295
Snouck-Hurgronje 140, 181
Snowden 126
Socialist Parties of the Central Powers 385
Société de Geógraphie 165
Solano ... 94, 97, 100, 407
Solbert 90
Solegub 185
Solf 173
Solomonoff 381
Soloviev 335
Somlo, Stier- (*see* Stier-Somlo).
Sommerfeld 173
Sommers 112
Somville ... 146, 225
Sonne 308
Sonnenschein ... 335, 347
Sonnino 80
Sorgnes 195
Sorley 368
Sosnosky 14
Souchon 262
Soulange-Bodin 26, 169
Soutar 376
Souttar 324
Souza 204
Spagnolo 179
Spahn 197
Spaight 104, 297
Spalajkovic 15
Spanton 293
Sparr 262
Sparrow ... 204, 218
Spearing 315
Spender, C. 368
Spender, E. 368
Spender, H. 270
Speyer, Nicol- (*see* Nicol-Speyer).
Spicer 295
Spiers 378
Spin 251, 252
Spire 355, 395
Spitsbergen, Conference 48
Spivey 97
Sprague 175
Springer 403
Spruner-Menke ... 7
Spurgeon 87
Spurr 105
Squire, J. C. 368
Squire, J. E. 317
Stallybrass 395
Stamp 308
Standaert 146
Standing 330
Stanford 118
Stanley 233
Stannard 270
Stapfer 356
Star (The) 118
Stauck 293
Stead, F. H. 152
Stead, R. J. C. ... 368
Stebbing ... 189, 234
Steed 14
Steege 262
Steele 368
Steen-Hansen ... 250, 315
Steers 87
Stein, General von ... 247
Stein, A. 278
Stein, H. 22
Steinmann-Bucher ... 152
Steinwäger 245
Stephen 328
Stephens, J. 154
Stephens, W. 185
Stephens, Miss W. ... 156
Stephens, W. H. ... 368
Steveni 47, 112
Stevenson, A. F. ... 309
Stevenson, F. S. ... 39
Stevenson, L. 335
Stewart, A. 311
Stewart, A. T. ... 245
Stewart, B. 97
Stewart, H. 218
Stewart, H. A. ... 259
Stewart, H. L. ... 33
Stewart, P. 317
Stewart, R. 105
Stewart, T. E. ... 368
Stiénon ... 230, 236, 240
Stier-Somlo 173
Stieve 195, 375
Stillman 37
Stilwell 407
Stirling, J. 112
Stirling, Y. 89
Stobart 234, 324
Stockton 302
Stodart 368
Stoddard ... 6, 350, 386
Stoianovitch 15
Stoker 297
Stokes, H. 16
Stokes, W. 308
Stone, E. 373
Stone, E. H. 97
Stone, G. 155
Storey 403
Story 9
Stout 127
Stowell 119
Streeter ... 328, 335, 349
Streets 368
Strickland, Campbell- (*see* Campbell-Strickland).
Strong, A. T. 153, 368
Strong, R. ... 160, 259
Strong, R. P. ... 317
Strong, T. B. 328, 335, 346
Strupp 146
Stuart, C. 152
Studd 373
Studdert-Kennedy 328, 368
Stuermer 181
Sturdza 230
Sturzenegger ... 234
Suarès 160
Suchier 240
Suchomlinov 185
Sugden 211
Sulley 350
Sullivan 376
Sumichrast 193
Sunampadu Arumugam 308
Sunday Times ... 284
Sunderland 180
Suter 137
Suter-Lerch 173
Sutherland 252
Sutton, Elwell- (*see* Elwell-Sutton).
Sutton-Pickard ... 160
Swain 308
Swaine 182
Swanwick 350
Swayne 238
Sweeter 252
Swinglehurst 368
Swinton 204
Swiss Committee for the study of the principles of a durable peace ... 393
Swope 175
Sydenham 153
Sykes, M. 41
Sykes, P. M. 43
Sykes-Brown 317
Synton 211
Syren and Shipping 310
Szillassy 141

T.B.D. 368
Tactician 97
Taffrail 109, 241, 245
Taft 193
Tagore 350
Tait 359
Talbot, F. A. 89, 104
Talbot, N. S. ... 335
Tallents 264
Talmeyr 160
Tamaro 37
Tananevich 379
Tannenberg 30
Tappen 227
Tarde 308
Tardieu 5, 23, 26, 259, 270, 387
Tariff Commission ... 308
Taslauanu 230
Tatham 368
Taylor, A. E. ... 289
Taylor, A. H. E. 51, 194
Taylor, A. W. 97, 98
Taylor, C. F. ... 386
Taylor, G. R. S. ... 314
Taylor, Mrs. H. ... 335
Taylor, I. E. ... 228
Taylor, M. A. ... 359
Taylor, R. O. P. ... 165
Taylor, S. M. ... 381
Taylor, W. 272
Tchobanian (*see* Ciobanian).
Temperley ... 49, 387
Temple 328, 336, 348, 349
Templeton 368
Temporary Chaplain 334
Tenedos Times (The) 265
Tennant 238
Tennyson 359
Terrell 102
Terry 38
Terry, C. S. 33, 109, 241, 345
Terry, E. B. ... 368, 369
Terwagne 285
Tesson 225
Testis 236
Tétot 8
Thamin 160
Thande 160
Thayer 131
Thévenin, D. (*see* Duhamel, G.).
Thimm 381
Thomas, B. 376
Thomas, C. E. ... 369
Thomas, G. 336, 369, 407
Thomas, J. M. L. ... 328
Thomas, K. G. ... 297
Thomas, L. 255
Thomas, W. B. ... 218
Thommessen 195
Thompson, G. ... 252
Thompson, T. 336, 359
Thomson, J. A. 313, 349
Thomson, L. L. ... 234
Thorburn 165
Thornton 237
Thorpe 369
Thrush 369
Thursfield 88, 90, 345, 347
Thurstan ... 185, 324
Thurston 336
Thyssen 162
Tillett 131
Tilney 102
Times (The) 48, 109, 112, 118, 155, 174, 198, 204, 209, 397
Tiplady ... 265, 336
Tirpitz 247
Tisdall 262
Tissier 222, 328
Tissot 169
Titterton 336
Tittoni 37, 80, 139
Todd, C. 98
Todd, N. H. 369
Toeche-Mittler ... 245
Toland 252, 324
Tolstoi 230
Tonelli 161
Toogood 312
Torn 146
Touchet 197
Touchstone 350
Toutey 136
Tovey 369
Tower 30
Townsend 359
Townshend 262
Toynbee 36, 41, 146, 182, 218, 346, 403
Tracy 98
Trades Union Congress 307
Trans, Villeneuve- (*see* Villeneuve-Trans).
Trapman 98
Trefusis 211
Trehern 297
Treitschke ... 33, 84
Treloar 278
Trench 369
Treub 194
Trevelyan, E. J. 153, 345
Trevelyan, W. B. 325, 369
Treves 267
Triana, Pérez- (*see* Pérez-Triana).
Trimbalet 293
Trœltsch 90
Trofimov 381
Trotsky 189, 407
Trotter, W. 350
Trotter, W. F. ... 295
Trübner 381
Trydell 98
Tucić 15
Tucker, A. B. 153, 218, 348
Tudesq 30, 112, 218, 225, 236
Tudor-Pole 336
Tuffrau 257
Tunstall 320
Tuohy 211
Turczynowicz, Gozdawa- (*see* Gozdawa-Turczynowicz).
Turmann 196
Turner, C. C. 104, 114, 211
Turner, S. 398
Turnor 308
Turquan 26
Turr 232
Tweney 87
Twiss 324
Tyan 42
Tygæus 395
Tymms 35
Tynan 369
Tyrrell 197

Ubique 84
Underhill 314
Universal Service League 84
Union Hellénique de Suisse 176
Unus 152
Unwin 403
Urban 403
Urquhart ... 4, 21, 344
Urwick 309, 348
Usborne 155
Usher 33, 193

Vachon 161, 225
Vaillat 161
Vaka 271
Valdés, Palacio- (*see* Palacio-Valdés).
Valentini 262
Vallet 311
Valloton 10, 161, 218
Valois, C. 355
Van der Essen 17, 228
Van der Heuvel ... 146
Van der Linden 16, 17
Vandervelde ... 146, 189
Van Dyck, E. A. ... 41
Van Dyke, H. 194, 369
Vane, Fletcher- (*see* Fletcher-Vane).
Van Ess 381
Van Houtte 285
Vanneufville 197
Van Vorst, B. ... 204
Van Vorst, M. ... 262
Variot 225
Varlez 146
Vassal 236
Vaucher ... 176, 232
Vaughan 336
Vaux 109, 245
Veblen 165, 386
Vecchio, Del (*see* Del Vecchio).
Vecctua 380
Vedel 245
Vedette 131, 252
Velimirovic ... 190, 328
Vellay 37
Venizelos 80
Ventallo 274
Vergnet 33
Verhaeren ... 146, 371
Vernazobres, Ouy- (*see* Ouy-Vernazobres).
Vernède ... 262, 369
Verner 100
Verow 189
Verrier 30
Verrinder 308
Verzije 302

Vesnitch 190
Vial 112
Viallate... ... 6, 193, 204
Vic 2
Vidal 265
Vidal de la Blache 10, 23
Vigilant 350
Vignes-Rouges ... 226
Vildósola, Silva- (*see* Silva-Vildósola).
Villard 31, 131
Villeneuve-Trans 193, 302
Villetti 232
Villiers 403
Vincent 369
Vinogradoff 48, 185, 344, 403
Viollet 328
Visiak 371
Visscher ... 146, 169
Vivante 37
Vivian, C. C. 315, 316
Vivian, E. C. 112, 252
Vivian, H. 179
Viviani 77, 80
Vizetelly 6, 11
Voivenel 353
Volksrecht 165
Voluntary Service Committee 84
Vorbeck, Lettow- (*see* Lettow-Vorbeck).
Vorst 169
Vosnjak 14, 141, 194
Vossaert 146

Wace ... 15, 328, 336
Waddington 259
Wade 105
Waechter 395
Waële 17
Wagger 252
Wagner, E. R. 169, 195
Wagner, K. 33
Waite 87
Wakefield 98
Walcott 262
Waldstätter 293
Waldstein ... 165, 351
Waliszewski 44
Walker, F. 114
Walker, H. F.. B. ... 240
Walker, S. F. ... 90
Walker, W. L. ... 336
Walkerdine 369
Wall 308
Wallace, C. 320
Wallace, D. M. ... 48
Wallace, E. 113, 204, 265, 386
Wallace, W. K. ... 179
Wallez 146
Walpole 19
Walsh, H. P. 102
Walsh, Pakenham- (*see* Pakenham-Walsh).
Walston (*see* Waldstein).
Walter, H. A. ... 31
Walter, R. 238
Walzogen 371
Wampach 17, 136, 286
Warburg 403
Ward, A. W. 26, 351
Ward, B. 336
Ward, H. 113
Ward, Mrs. H. ... 152
Ward, J. H. 328
Ward, W. 132
Ward, W. J. 373
Warde Fowler ... 351
Wardlaw, Plowden- (*see* Plowden-Wardlaw).
Warfield 41
Waring 49
Warman 403
Warnod 293
Warr ... 147, 218, 228
Warren 347, 351
Warwick, Countess of 351
Warwick, F. J. ... 320
Washburn 230
Wastelier du Parc ... 256
Watchman ... 132, 197
Waterhouse 369
Waterson 293
Watkin 336
Watkins... 252
Watson, A. R. ... 265
Watson, H. W. ... 205
Watson, J. K. ... 320
Watson, Seton- (*see* Seton-Watson).
Watson, W. 369
Watson, W. C. ... 336
Watson, W. H. L. ... 252
Watt 252, 369
Watts, C. N. 98
Watts, M. 396
Waxweiler 147
Weale 155
Weatherby 369
Weatherhead 102
Weaver 98
Webb, C. 351
Webb, S. ... 308, 403
Webberley 312
Webb-Johnson ... 98
Weber, G. 6
Weber, M. 403
Webster, C. K. ... 6
Webster, F. A. M. 98, 113
Webster, F. S. ... 328
Webster, N. H. ... 86
Webster, R. G. ... 152
Weddell 369
Weekly Dispatch ... 109
Weekly Telegraph ... 378
Weeks, H. T. ... 395
Weeks, R. 370
Weerdt 165
Wehberg, H. 197, 302, 395
Weigall 42
Weindel 272
Weiss, A. 286
Weiss, J. 395
Welham 324
Wellman 175
Wells, F. B. 370
Wells, H. G. 189, 211, 351, 386, 395, 396, 403
Wells, W. B. 154
Welschinger 6, 11, 197, 221
Wentworth 371
Wertheimer, E. ... 14
Wertheimer, F. 174, 230
Wesselitsky ... 48, 140
West, A. G. 259
West, V. J. 193
Westbrook 370
Westerdale 316
Westlake 302
Weston, F. 35
Weston, G. R. Hunter- 211
Weston, H. C. ... 85
Weston, J. L. ... 132
Weston, W. M. ... 193
Wetterlé 11, 26, 169, 355
Wetzell 227
Wharton 226, 252, 351
Wheeler, H. F. B. 245, 277
Wheeler, O. 277
Wheeler, R. 359
Whetham 403
Whippet (The) ... 265
Whitaker 147
Whitbridge 132
White, A. ... 109, 278
White, B. C. de. B. ... 370
White, C. 113
White, Grahame- (*see* Grahame-White).
White, J. W. 130, 132
Whitehouse 147
Whitlock 147
Whittall 240
Whittem 381
Whittingham ... 351
Whitton ... 44, 218
Whittuck 9
Whitworth 205
Whyte 311
Wiart, Carton de (*see* Carton de Wiart).
Wichte 275
Wichter 34
Wichtl 139
Wideawake, Captain 373
Widner 102
Wiener 48
Wierzlicki 175
Wieting 245
Wigforss 140
Wijnveldt 302
Wilberforce 336
Wilde 259
Wilden, Dumont- (*see* Dumont-Wilden).
Wildgrube 81
Wile ... 31, 132, 152, 269
Wiliamowitz 384
Wilke 356
Wilkins, E. H. ... 382
Wilkins, G. H. ... 268
Wilkinson, E. F. ... 370
Wilkinson, H. S. 84, 152, 211, 344, 345, 351
Wilkinson, N. ... 268
William II, *German Emperor* 23, 28, 29, 81
Williams, A 370

Williams, A. R. ... 293
Williams, B. 98
Williams, C. 351
Williams, Crawshay- (*see* Crawshay-Williams).
Williams, E. H. ... 350
Williams, G. 86
Williams, G. V. ... 252
Williams, Gwatkin- (*see* Gwatkin-Williams).
Williams, Mrs. H. ... 189
Williams, Hodder (*see* Hodder Williams).
Williams, J. H. ... 328
Williams, Wilton ... 376
Williams, Wythe ... 252
Williams, W. L. ... 41
Williamson, J. A. ... 19
Willich 240
Willmore 132, 176, 182
Willoughby, W. P. ... 308
Willoughby, W. W. 175
Wilson, A. 320
Wilson, A. J. ... 386
Wilson, B. 218
Wilson, F. S. ... 102
Wilson, H. W. ... 205
Wilson, P. W. ... 205
Wilson, R. 205
Wilson, T. I. W. ... 279
Wilson, W. ... 81, 386
Wilson, W. E. 336, 407
Wilton, R. 189
Winans 99
Winchester, Bishop of 349
Windischgraetz ... 247
Windt 48
Wing Adjutant 114, 252
Wingate 404
Wingfield 99
Wings 253
Winnifrith 253
Winslow 253
Winterstein 31
Winterstetten ... 174
Wipers Times ... 265
Wirth 33
Wisdom 378, 382
Wister 175
Withers ... 308, 351, 396
Witteryck 382
Wodehouse 370
Wolf, A. 33
Wolf, L. 132
Wolff, J. 174
Wolff, J. S. 161
Woltmann 33
Women's War Interests Committee 312
Wood, Eric 265
Wood, Evelyn ... 106
Wood, E. F. 253
Wood, E. H. R. ... 370
Wood, F. N. 370
Wood, L. 351
Wood, T. B. ... 309, 310
Wood, T. McK. ... 147
Wood, W. 109, 245, 265
Woodhouse 105
Woodroffe 336
Woods, E. S. 351
Woods, F. T. 328
Woods, H. C. 132, 141, 328
Woolf, L. 9
Woolf, L. S. 182, 394, 396
Wordsworth ... 352, 359
Workers' Educational Association 2
Woroniecki 44
Worsey 329
Wram 161
Wrangel 396
Wray 161
Wren, P. C. ... 245, 265
Wright, A. E. ... 320
Wright, P. 211
Wrong, G. M. 152, 165
Wundt 346, 356
Wussow 373
Wyatt, G. N. ... 102
Wyatt, H. ... 85, 373
Wylie 113
Wyllie 245
Wyndham ... 99, 113
Wynn 329
Wynne 234
Wyrall 205
Wyseur 371
Wyzewa 169
X. 370
X., avocat ... 141, 145
X., le commandant ... 226
X., général 386
X.Y.Z. 99

"*Y*" 245
Y.M.C.A. 265, 357, 381
Yachting monthly ... 241
Yakchitch ... 14, 49
Yapp 211
Yarmolinsky 46
Yates 155
Year (The) 211
Yearly Meetings Committee on War 407
Yeo 253
Yexley 110
Yolland 14
York, Archbp. of ... 329
Young, A. 17
Young, E. H. ... 309
Young, F. 245
Young, F. B. 240, 370
Young, G. ... 21, 44
Young, G. W. W. 218, 366
Young, H. 245
Yovanowitch 21
Yoxall 132, 336
Ysiad 31

Z. 113
Zagorsky ... 189, 190
Zaleski 44
Zangwill 352
Żavie 293
Zerta 218
Zévort 23
Zimmermann, A. ... 35
Zimmermann, E. 26, 174
Zimmermann, F. G. 378, 382
Zimmermann, K. ... 147
Zimmern, A. E. ... 309
Zimmern, H. ... 37, 269
Zolla 306
Zupanić ... 49, 118
Zurlinden 139, 196, 211, 356
Zwehl 227

(38317) Wt. 7703—351 500 2/23 H. St. G. 36